Presidential Documents

In this lively, authoritative collection, Thomas J. McInerney presents famous and lesser-known speeches, letters, and other important documents from every U.S. president from George Washington to Barack Obama.

Whether printed in full or excerpted, these history-making documents are an invaluable resource as well as a fascinating browse. Including familiar documents such as the Emancipation Proclamation, to personal correspondence such as a letter from George H. W. Bush to his children, this collection brings together the famous statements that came to represent each administration with intimate glimpses into the thought processes of various presidential leaders.

Now in its second edition, *Presidential Documents* has been re-designed to increase its usefulness in the classroom. Section openers introduce each era of the American presidency with a concise political and historical overview, highlighting the challenges each leader faced, and placing the documents in context. Whether used as a complement to an American history survey text or as a collection of primary documents for courses on the American presidency, *Presidential Documents* provides an engrossing look at the work of the leaders of the United States, in all their complexity.

Thomas J. McInerney is Professor of History at Metropolitan State University in Denver, Colorado.

Fred L. Israel is Professor Emeritus of American History at the City College of New York. His previous works include the five-volume *History of Presidential Elections 1789–1988* (1988), which he co-edited with Arthur M. Schlesinger, Jr., and *Running for President* (1995).

Presidential Documents

Words that Shaped a Nation from Washington to Obama

Second Edition

Edited by

Thomas J. McInerney
with Fred L. Israel

NEW YORK AND LONDON

This edition published 2013
by Routledge
711 Third Avenue, New York, NY 10017

Simultaneously published in the UK
by Routledge
2 Park Square, Milton Park, Abingdon, Oxon OX14 4RN

Routledge is an imprint of the Taylor & Francis Group, an informa business

First edition published by Routledge 1999

Library of Congress Cataloging-in-Publication Data
Presidential documents : words that shaped a nation from Washington
to Obama / edited by Thomas J. McInerney, Fred L. Israel.
p. cm.
Rev. ed. of: Presidential documents, edited by J.F. Watts, Fred l. Israel, 2000.
1. Presidents–United States–History–Sources. 2. United States–Politics
and government–Sources. 3. United States–History–Sources. 4. Speeches,
addresses, etc., American. I. Israel, Fred L. II. McInerney, Thomas J.,
1940– III. Israel, Fred L.
E176.1.P889 2012
973.09'9--dc23
2012012015

ISBN: 978-0-415-89574-3 (hbk)
ISBN: 978-0-415-89575-0 (pbk)

Typeset in Minion
by Keystroke, Station Road, Codsall, Wolverhampton

Printed and bound in the United States of America
by Edwards Brothers, Inc.

Contents

Acknowledgments

This second edition of *Presidential Documents* is successor and stands on the shoulders of the first. Consequently, it is fitting and proper to offer a salute to Fred L. Israel and the late J. F. Watts for their collaboration in formulating the original work while colleagues at the City College of New York.

This edition represents a complete and total overhaul and reconstruction of the first. As indicated in the Preface and witnessed in the Contents listing, this edition, entitled *Presidential Documents: Words that Shaped a Nation from Washington to Obama*, has been reorganized and reconfigured with three parts, twelve sections and forty-four chapters. Each president has been allocated a chapter which contains important original word documents marking their administrations. Most are formal documents, even state papers such as inaugural addresses, annual messages, and farewells to the nation, but some are rather intimate and personal. In any event, the documents attached to their tenure in office have been selected as meaningful markers of American history on their presidential watch. They serve as windows on their administrations or pages in the American presidential pageant and often testify to their service to the Republic.

In constructing this work, many people have contributed their time, skills, or wisdom which is here acknowledged and celebrated with gratitude. A leading contributor was Stephen J. Leonard, Chairman of the History Department at Metropolitan State University of Denver, who agreed to read two sample narratives and review the proposed selection of documents. Dr. Leonard gave excellent advice and guidance. Another department contributor in the preliminary stages of the project was Donna Potempa, who typed the original proposal and performed other early preparatory tasks.

In addition, I wish to thank Jeffrey Flannery, Head: Manuscript Division at the Library of Congress for many useful suggestions now and over many years. His staff also merits mention. Ellen Metter, Chief Librarian at Auraria Library, contributed much and was willing to give more. Others deserving notes of thanks go to: Bill Francis, Research Center, Baseball Hall of Fame; Ray Wilson, Archivist, Reagan Presidential Library; Herbert L. Pankratz, Archivist, Eisenhower Presidential Library; Matthew Benz, Research Director, Ohio State Historical Society; and Tammy Kelly, Archivist, Truman Presidential Library. There were many others along the way too numerous to mention, yet deserving of commendation.

Special acknowledgement is due to Kimberly Guinta, Senior Editor at Routledge, who wisely perceived the need for a second edition. Her able assistant editor Rebecca Novack helped us negotiate a few late bumps in the road. Production editor Margaret Lindsey-Jones and copy editor Graham Bradbury are likewise much appreciated members of the team.

Singular thanks are due to my son Michael E. McInerney who saved the project more than once with his special skills and superior knowledge. He sacrificed time from his own work at Colorado

School of Mines in Golden, Colorado in order to keep this work breathing. His multi-faceted gifts and his dedication to this endeavor can in no way be overstated. Among his many contributions to this effort is the Index, which he crafted with great care.

Finally, a word of appreciation is due to my daughters, Monica and Jennifer, for their inspiration and support. Special mention is in order for my daughter Kathleen E. McInerney who resides in Washington, DC for making arrangements for a number of the illustrations included in this work. The very talented professional photographer who provided with generous courtesy his time and work product is Ian Wagreich. His art and symbolic images have enhanced the presentation in several particulars. Alissa Ogen likewise played a part in the artwork department.

Note on the Sources: It should be emphasized that every document is from the public domain. Documents in Parts One and Two are almost exclusively from *A Compilation of Messages and Papers of the Presidents* by James D. Richardson with a few presidential words extracted from elsewhere, such as newspapers. From 1900 to the present, documents have been selected from the MPOPUS, presidential collections at the Library of Congress, Manuscript Division; individual Presidential Libraries; the National Archives; the Federal Register and newspaper clippings housed in such places as the Baseball Hall of Fame. Readers may wish to note the dates on documents as a helpful route to trace the original documents.

Preface to the Second Edition

The American presidency now spans four distinct centuries. Born in the Age of Enlightenment in the eighteenth century, it lives on in the Nuclear World of the twenty-first century. It has entered upon a New Millennium. The Constitution gave birth to the presidency and the Republic. Both are framed by the Constitution and to that founding document owe their existence and identity. The enduring quality of the institution is in part explained by the fact that it was a collaborative work of reason, an intelligent construction embedded in Article II of the Constitution of the United States of America. Section I of Article II explains: "The executive Power shall be vested in a President of the United States of America. He shall hold his Office during the Term of four Years."

The establishment of an elected chief executive with a specific term of office was a novel experiment in free government fashioned by the Founding Fathers. The United States was the first nation to have an elected president— and with a stated term of office. The presidency is the centerpiece of the Republic. Every four years since the adoption of the Constitution in 1789, the nation has held a presidential election. This quadrennial act of renewal by the citizens of the United States underpins long-lasting sinews of the system. The clockwork regularity of renewal provides an essential leg of stability to American governance.

The first edition of *Presidential Documents* traced a selected documentary base from the initial administration of George Washington in the eighteenth century to the edge of presidential closure in the twentieth century under William Jefferson Clinton. It was the work of J. F. Watts and Fred Israel, historical colleagues at the City College of New York. That first edition was published in 2000 by Routledge.

This second edition stands on the shoulders of the first. It is, however, more than a simple update and revision of the earlier work. It is that and more. The work now extends from Washington to Obama. Beyond the deletion of certain documents or the addition of new ones, this edition involves a basic overhaul and reconstruction of the original manuscript. The body of the work has been fundamentally transformed. An entirely new structure and fresh reorganization is here applied. The table of contents has been shifted from a bare listing of the presidential documents to a parade of presidents over the march of time. This new frame chronicles all forty-four presidents by chapter, with words that marked their administrations and should be remembered.

Thus the work is organized into three parts, twelve sections, and forty-four chapters. The parts and the sections organize the history of the presidency according to important benchmarks of time, mood, and national challenge. Each section begins with a narrative introduction. The sections contain appropriate presidential photographs or illustrations. The chapters provide for the assemblage of documents for each individual president. The first forty-two chapters contain new entries. Chapters 43 and 44 obviously contain completely new document additions. Mapping out the passage of presidential time in this format is intended to make it a smoother transit for the reader to navigate.

Naturally, the documents selected vary in nature, topic, scope, and significance. Some documents obviously have higher priority than others. High priority examples include Washington's Farewell Address, the Monroe Doctrine, the Gettysburg Address, John F. Kennedy's Inaugural Address and Ronald Reagan's admonishment to the Soviets to tear down the Berlin Wall. Yet other documents deserve public attention and include presidential diary entries, a letter from a president to his children, a directive to staff, a telephone conversation or an address to a university commencement class. This edition attends to the ceremonial role of the President in his role as Head of State. Each document reveals a hidden piece of an otherwise lost world. Presidential words provide a window into the world of those men chosen by their fellow Americans to lead the nation.

Largely in keeping with the editing precepts of the first edition, select documents passed through the process with little residue on the cutting-room floor. Others needed more work. Care was taken to remember the importance of presidential words which shaped the growth of the American republic and the destiny of the American people.

This second edition, now entitled *Presidential Documents: Words that Shaped a Nation from Washington to Obama*, was the brainchild of Fred Israel, who wanted his work to remain a useful tool for students and interested readers. This new configuration is intended to realize his vision and to fill a scholarly and public need for a second updated and revised offering for prospective students, inquiring faculty, and a more fully informed American electorate and the reading public, wherever they might reside.

PART ONE

THE CONSTITUTIONAL PRESIDENCY IS LAUNCHED

I

THE NEW NATION

THE FIRST PRESIDENT OF THE UNITED STATES answered his country's call to command the birth of a new nation in the spring of 1789. George Washington methodically made his way from his Mount Vernon home in Virginia to New York City, the Republic's first Capitol of the United States of America. The journey north was unhurried as the President-elect passed through many villages and towns and cheering throngs of joyous and proud citizens. Americans along the route pressed the crowds eager to get a glimpse of the revolutionary hero and champion of the new Republic. The General had defeated Cornwallis and ended the British tyranny at Yorktown, thereby bringing the American Revolution to a successful conclusion. In the aftermath of that victory, the now independent American people faced a new crisis of government under the flawed Articles of Confederation. The Father of Our Country once again came forth to provide leadership and inspiration in forging a new instrument of governance in Philadelphia at the Convention which produced the Constitution of the United States.

At a time when the fate of the American Revolution was very much in doubt, Benjamin Franklin was representing the patriot cause at the Court of St. James in London. His Majesty George III inquired of Franklin as to what George Washington would do in the unlikely event that the ragtag Continental Army defeated the veteran forces of the British Empire. Franklin replied without hesitation that the Commander of the Continentals would put away his sword and quietly retire to his beloved Mount Vernon estate. King George was much impressed and said that if General Washington followed that path, he would be "the most admired man in the world." Indeed he did and was. In fact, he would be celebrated by leaders in Europe such as the gallant Marquis de Lafayette, and by revolutionary leaders throughout the world and in generations to come. The South American revolutionary icon Simon Bolivar modeled his own path to glory on the first President of the United States. Unfortunately, Bolivar did not seem to take notice that George Washington abandoned his sword and military uniform upon re-entering civilian life.

Now this "most admired man" was wending his way to New York and towards a rendezvous with presidential history. There was no rush. The first Congress displayed something of a harbinger of things to come. It had not yet arrived with a quorum at the Capitol. The delay in fact was welcomed by the people who lined the route. There were ceremonies and festivities all along the way, including firework displays. The tardy Congress would just have to wait for the Chief Executive Officer of the nation.

Washington faced the tremendous task of launching the new government. Enormously moved by the warm confidence placed in him by the people, the modest President wrote that he foresaw "an ocean of difficulties. . . . Integrity and firmness are all I can promise." This humility was central to his leadership style. Benjamin Franklin and Thomas Jefferson were hailed as American heroes by the people of France when they arrived in Paris. Washington's reception in that capital city would have been an even more spectacular triumph. Since he did not speak French he simply sent skilled diplomats who could, so as not to embarrass his newborn Republic. George Washington had character and integrity. He was the representative man of his time and he carried that inner virtue with him to the presidency. The Constitution vested him with the executive power, but he vested the office with dignity.

The man from Mt. Vernon had commanded the military fortunes of the American patriots and led them to victory. In the same fashion he presided over the deliberations at the Constitutional Convention which brought the new nation to life. In creating the Constitutional Presidency the delegates at Philadelphia would daily gaze on the face of Washington seated in the presiding officer's chair. Their deep respect had prompted them to elect Washington unanimously. The delegates then proceeded to create an office which all knew he would occupy. Therefore, they endowed the office with special powers, such as Commander-in-Chief. This likewise influenced the constitutional eligibility requirement that the president be a "natural born" citizen as a protective mechanism against a future Manchurian candidate in command of the army. Washington's presence had given shape to the office even before he was called upon to occupy it. The call to presidential duty was again unanimous and he was re-elected with 100 percent of the electoral vote. Having been a participant at the conception of the Republic, this indispensable leader was now at the helm, launching the first new nation from the moment of birth. Although the constitutional structure was already in place the administrative architecture was not. It was his mission to erect the first Administration on a solid foundation.

Figure SI.1 The Executive Mansion, later known as The White House, served as the Chief Executive's residence from John Adams to Barack Obama. George Washington never lived here. Courtesy of White House Photographs/John F. Kennedy Presidential Library and Museum, Boston/Robert Knudsen.

The administrative architecture of the presidency was given a permanent base upon which to rest a new nation in the two successive terms of the gentleman from Virginia. President Washington proved to be a master builder. The principal building material was his persona. The Administration emanated from his very being. He intended to provide a foundation that would endure for ages to come.

At the conclusion of the delegates' work at Philadelphia, Franklin commented that now you had a Republic, if you could keep it. Washington meant to keep it and make it last.

Reminiscent of the boy-scout motto, Washington was always prepared. Like a true Virginian he would think ahead and whenever he moved, he did so with a plan. Yet there was no blueprint available for conduct in the presidency. He was the first. It was he who set the mold and established first actions of sundry sorts. Thus he would be fastidious and meticulous in actions that he well realized would be precedents for the future. His words would live on and move a nation. They must be crafted with judicious care and prudence. The same care and caution was required with the formulation of administration of the federal government. He would take great pains to select his ministers, secretaries and judicial appointments.

It is often forgotten that the entire government, all three branches, had made their first home in the same building in downtown Manhattan, appropriately named Federal Hall. The Office of the President was just steps away from both Congressional chambers and the Supreme Court. It was President Washington's responsibility to appoint all the original members of the high court and in fact all the judges throughout the Federal Judiciary, in one fell swoop. Not only did he launch the Executive function but the Judiciary as well. Under the Constitution, the President of the United States is likewise installed as Chief Magistrate of the United States.

In his capacity as Chief Magistrate, the first President performed those duties more completely than any of his forty-three successors. Inescapably, Washington was intensely preoccupied with the administration of justice. He not only appointed the full slate of federal justices and judges, he established the Department of Justice and appointed the first Attorney General of the United States. For the job, he selected his fellow Virginian Edmund Randolph and wrote him a letter with the poignant advice or instruction: "The due Administration of Justice is the Pillar of Good Government." In a century to come, a courthouse built in Foley Square, just blocks away from Federal Hall, would bear the inscription: "The True Administration of Justice is the Pillar of Good Government." In any event, Washington's concerns about providing the proper cornerstone and foundation for justice and good government remain transparent.

The Chief Magistrate is not only responsible for the workings of the Justice Department and appointments (with the advice and consent of the U.S. Senate), he is also expected to preside over the administration of Justice and to correct judicial error and abuse. The corrective is the grant in Article II with respect to Amnesty and Pardons. Here again the first President set an example that his heirs to the office could find instructive. Treason is the highest crime known to man. In a just society, "the quality of mercy is not strained." Exercising great judicial leadership, President Washington found good cause to grant amnesty and pardon, even in favor of those who took up arms against the infant Republic.

Launching the new nation was an awesome burden. The nation needed to be nurtured from within and protected from foreign intrigue and aggression. The Chief Executive needed to promote prosperity and sound fiscal policy. The United States of America had to confront a debt problem, establish credit, provide a sound currency, and ensure a trusted banking operation. To accomplish this agenda, he turned to his trusted aide-de-camp from his military days. Alexander Hamilton was the man of the hour and Washington's choice for the post of Secretary of the Treasury

Department. It was a wise choice and a model for future administrations. The agenda was successfully implemented. It became commonplace for later administrations to claim that their Secretary of the Treasury was the best since Alexander Hamilton.

The first President fully comprehended the need for the young nation to abstain from being drawn into the European appetite for war. Neutrality with respect to belligerent nations and a policy of amity and friendship was the path Washington would pursue. This prudent policy decision required an able diplomat to execute the plan. Here again George Washington displayed his good judgment. For this neutral and independent foreign policy path Washington turned to the principal author of the Declaration of Independence, Thomas Jefferson, as his choice for Secretary of State.

"Integrity and firmness" was Washington's promise. He delivered that and more. Parsons Weems told the famous story of the young boy George and the cherry tree. The more than likely apocryphal tale has the father question the boy as to who chopped down the cherry tree. The well-known reply from little George is simply: "Father, I cannot tell a lie. It was I." The interesting thing about the story is that so many people believed the story, and retold it over generations, because it fits. In the New York Capitol, Washington ironically lived in lower Manhattan's East Side on Cherry Street. From that vantage point he could look across the East River to Brooklyn. It made him melancholy because it brought to mind the brave and fallen soldiers who gave their lives in battle there to give life to the new nation. It was a short walk from his Cherry Street home to the Executive Office at Federal Hall where the new nation under the Constitution was officially launched. It was Washington's veracity that floated the ship of state.

In his classic "Farewell Address" Washington cautioned and counseled his fellow citizens about lurking dangers and pitfalls. His caveats included how fragile the entire edifice of justice and good government was in fact. It rested on a foundation of words. Truth and the well-being of the nation went hand in hand. Oaths were the glue that sustained the structure of government. That of course included the Constitutional Oath of Office prescribed for the President in Article II. In bidding farewell he reminded the good people of America that "honesty is always the best policy."

The "pillar of good government" rested upon the foundation of due and true administration of justice. The seat of government would move in just a year and the building work of administrative architecture would continue in Philadelphia and beyond. For more than two hundred years now, the nation would seek renewal by touching base with those first principles of the nation and the virtues of that first generation of Americans. One feature of constant renewal is to return to the words and documents that, to paraphrase a fictional king, feelingly persuade us who we are. That first year of the Republic in New York City was a formative year, for that was where the master builder and his fellow Americans launched the new government.

The work would go on from New York, to Philadelphia, and ultimately to the permanent capital, Washington City. The Vice President, John Adams, after eight years of being underboss was now, as of 1797, the President of the United States. Adams was a man of many parts and a true and distinguished American patriot. It was his unfortunate fate to be sandwiched between the cherished figures of Washington and Jefferson. Clearly Washington was just about an impossible act to follow. Still Adams persevered and provided a presidential bridge between the Father of Our Country and the Chief Founder of the American Way of Life. It turned out to be, despite many trials and problems, an important and successful transition. It was during his watch that the country gained a permanent capital.

George Washington did not live to see the new century arrive. Had Washington lived, Adams might have weathered the political storm. Everything considered, President Adams deserves credit for stepping aside in 1801. He did not utilize his authority as Commander-in-Chief and call out the army to subdue his political rival, Vice President Thomas Jefferson, who bested him in the election of 1800. Adams had the better of the bargain in the 1796 contest but neither was the incumbent president at that time. For the first time in history a peaceful transition of power took place, and the people's will prevailed. Adams could have marked that event by attending the inauguration of Jefferson, but for whatever reason opted to simply leave town. An era had ended and a new century was about to begin. The first new nation had been successfully launched.

1

George Washington

1. THE FIRST INAUGURAL ADDRESS APRIL 30, 1789

Among the vicissitudes incident to life no event could have filled me with greater anxieties than that of which the notification was transmitted by your order, and received on the 14th day of the present month. On the one hand, I was summoned by my country, whose voice I can never hear but with veneration and love, from a retreat which I had chosen with the fondest predilection, and, in my flattering hopes, with an immutable decision, as the asylum of my declining years—a retreat which was rendered every day more necessary as well as more dear to me by the addition of habit to inclination, and of frequent interruptions in my health to the gradual waste committed on it by time.

On the other hand, the magnitude and difficulty of the trust to which the voice of my country called me, being sufficient to awaken in the wisest and most experienced of her citizens a distrustful scrutiny into his qualifications, could not but overwhelm with despondence one who (inheriting inferior endowments from nature and unpracticed in the duties of civil administration) ought to be peculiarly conscious of his own deficiencies. In this conflict of emotions all I dare aver is that it has been my faithful study to collect my duty from a just appreciation of every circumstance by which it might be affected. All I dare hope is that if, in executing this task, I have been too much swayed by a grateful remembrance of former instances, or by an affectionate sensibility to this transcendent proof of the confidence of my fellow-citizens, and have thence too little consulted my incapacity as well as disinclination for the weighty and untried cares before me, my error will be palliated by the motives which mislead me, and its consequences be judged by my country with some share of the partiality in which they originated.

Such being the impressions under which I have, in obedience to the public summons, repaired to the present station, it would be peculiarly improper to omit in this first official act my fervent supplications to that Almighty Being who rules over the universe, who presides in the councils of nations, and whose providential aids can supply every human defect, that His benediction may consecrate to the liberties and happiness of the people of the United States a Government instituted by themselves for these essential purposes, and may enable every instrument employed in its administration to execute with success the functions allotted to His charge. In tendering this homage to the Great Author of every public and private good, I assure myself that it expresses your sentiments not less than my own, nor those of my fellow-citizens at large less than either. No people can be bound to acknowledge and adore the Invisible Hand which conducts the affairs of men more than those of the United States. Every step by which they have advanced to the character of an independent nation seems to have been distinguished by some token of providential agency;

and in the important revolution just accomplished in the system of their united government the tranquil deliberations and voluntary consent of so many distinct communities from which the event has resulted cannot be compared with the means by which most governments have been established without some return of pious gratitude, along with an humble anticipation of the future blessings which the past seem to presage. These reflections, arising out of the present crisis, have forced themselves too strongly on my mind to be suppressed. You will join with me, I trust, in thinking that there are none under the influence of which the proceedings of a new and free government can more auspiciously commence.

By the article establishing the executive department it is made the duty of the President "to recommend to your consideration such measures as he shall judge necessary and expedient." The circumstances under which I now meet you will acquit me from entering into that subject further than to refer to the great constitutional charter under which you are assembled, and which, in defining your powers, designates the objects to which your attention is to be given. It will be more consistent with those circumstances and far more congenial with the feelings which actuate me, to substitute, in place of a recommendation of particular measures, the tribute that is due to the talents, the rectitude, and the patriotism which adorn the characters selected to devise and adopt them. In these honorable qualifications I behold the surest pledges that as on one side no local prejudices or attachments, no separate views nor party animosities, will misdirect the comprehensive and equal eye which ought to watch over this great assemblage of communities and interests, so, on another, that the foundation of our national policy will be laid in the pure and immutable principles of private morality, and the preeminence of free government be exemplified by all the attributes which can win the affections of its citizens and command the respect of the world. I dwell on this prospect with every satisfaction which an ardent love for my country can inspire, since there is no truth more thoroughly established than that there exists in the economy and course of nature an indissoluble union between virtue and happiness; between duty and advantage; between the genuine maxims of an honest and magnanimous policy and the solid rewards of public prosperity and felicity; since we ought to be no less persuaded that the propitious smiles of Heaven can never be expected on a nation that disregards the eternal rules of order and right which Heaven itself has ordained; and since the preservation of the sacred fire of liberty and the destiny of the republican model of government are justly considered, perhaps, as *deeply*, as *finally*, staked on the experiment entrusted to the hands of the American people. . . .

To the foregoing observations I have one to add, which will be most properly addressed to the House of Representatives. It concerns myself, and will therefore be as brief as possible. When I was first honored with a call into the service of my country, then on the eve of an arduous struggle for its liberties, the light in which I contemplated my duty required that I should renounce every pecuniary compensation. From this resolution I have in no instance departed; and being still under the impressions which produced it, I must decline as inapplicable to myself any share in the personal emoluments which may be indispensably included in a permanent provision for the executive department, and must accordingly pray that the pecuniary estimates for the station in which I am placed may during my continuance in it be limited to such actual expenditures as the public good may be thought to require.

Having thus imparted to you my sentiments as they have been awakened by the occasion which brings us together, I shall take my present leave; but not without resorting once more to the benign Parent of the Human Race in humble supplication that, since He has been pleased to favor the American people with opportunities for deliberating in perfect tranquility, and dispositions for deciding with unparalleled unanimity on a form of government for the security of their union and

Figure 1.1 George Washington statue, courtesy of Ian Wagreich.

the advancement of their happiness, so His divine blessing may be equally *conspicuous* in the enlarged views, the temperate consultations, and the wise measures on which the success of this Government must depend.

2. PROCLAMATION ON THE RESISTANCE TO THE EXCISE TAX   SEPTEMBER 13, 1792

Whereas certain violent and unwarrantable proceedings have lately taken place tending to obstruct the operation of the laws of the United States for raising a revenue upon spirits distilled within the same, enacted pursuant to express authority delegated in the Constitution of the United States, which proceedings are subversive of good order, contrary to the duty that every citizen owes to his country and to the laws, and of a nature dangerous to the very being of a government; and

Whereas such proceedings are the more unwarrantable by reason of the moderation which has been heretofore shown on the part of the Government and of the disposition which has been manifested by the Legislature (who alone have authority to suspend the operation of laws) to obviate causes of objection and to render the laws as acceptable as possible; and

Whereas it is the particular duty of the Executive "to take care that the laws be faithfully executed," and not only that duty but the permanent interests and happiness of the people require that every legal and necessary step should be pursued as well to prevent such violent and unwarrantable proceedings as to bring to justice the infractors of the laws and secure obedience thereto:

Now, therefore, I, George Washington, President of the United States, do by these presents most earnestly admonish and exhort all persons whom it may concern to refrain and desist from all unlawful combinations and proceedings whatsoever having for object or tending to obstruct the operation of the laws aforesaid, inasmuch as all lawful ways and means will be strictly put in execution for bringing to justice the infractors thereof and securing obedience thereto.

And I do moreover charge and require all courts, magistrates, and officers whom it may concern, according to the duties of their several offices, to exert the powers in them respectively vested by law for the purposes aforesaid, hereby also enjoining and requiring all persons whomsoever, as they tender the welfare of their country, the just and due authority of Government, and the preservation of the public peace, to be aiding and assisting therein according to law. . . .

3. NEUTRALITY   APRIL 22, 1793

Whereas it appears that a state of war exists between Austria, Prussia, Sardinia, Great Britain, and the United Netherlands of the one part and France on the other, and the duty and interest of the United States require that they should with sincerity and good faith adopt and pursue a conduct friendly and impartial toward the belligerent powers:

I have therefore thought fit by these presents to declare the disposition of the United States to observe the conduct aforesaid toward those powers respectively, and to exhort and warn the citizens of the United States carefully to avoid all acts and proceedings whatsoever which may in any manner tend to contravene such disposition.

And I do hereby also make known that whosoever of the citizens of the United States shall render himself liable to punishment or forfeiture under the law of nations by committing, aiding, or abetting hostilities against any of the said powers, or by carrying to any of them those articles which are deemed contraband by the modern usage of nations, will not receive the protection of the United States against such punishment or forfeiture; and further, that I have given instructions to those officers to whom it belongs to cause prosecutions to be instituted against all persons who shall, within the cognizance of the courts of the United States, violate the law of nations with respect to the powers at war, or any of them. . . .

4. SECOND PROCLAMATION ON THE WHISKEY INSURRECTION   SEPTEMBER 24, 1794

Whereas combinations to defeat the execution of the laws laying duties upon spirits distilled within the United States and upon stills have from the time of the commencement of those laws existed in some of the western parts of Pennsylvania; and Whereas the said combinations, proceeding in a manner subversive equally of the just authority of government and of the rights of individuals, have hitherto effected their dangerous and criminal purpose by the influence of certain irregular meetings whose proceedings have tended to encourage and uphold the spirit of opposition by misrepresentations of the laws calculated to render them odious; by endeavors to deter those who might be so disposed from accepting offices under them through fear of public resentment and of injury to person and property, and to compel those who had accepted such offices by actual violence to surrender or forbear the execution of them; by circulating vindictive menaces against all those who should otherwise, directly or indirectly, aid in the execution of the said laws, or who, yielding to the dictates of conscience and to a sense of obligation, should themselves comply therewith; by actually injuring and destroying the property of persons who were understood to have so complied; by inflicting cruel and humiliating punishments upon private citizens for no other cause than that of appearing to be the friends of the laws; by intercepting the public officers on the highways, abusing, assaulting, and otherwise ill treating them; by going to their houses in the night, gaining admittance by force, taking away their papers, and committing other outrages, employing for these unwarrantable purposes the agency of armed banditti disguised in such manner as for the most part to escape discovery; and Whereas the endeavors of the Legislature to obviate objections to the said laws by lowering the duties and by other alterations conducive to the convenience of those whom they immediately affect (though they have given satisfaction in other quarters), and the endeavors of the executive officers to conciliate a compliance with the laws by explanations, by forbearance, and even by particular accommodations founded on the suggestion of local considerations, have been disappointed of their effect by the machinations of persons whose industry to excite resistance has increased with every appearance of a disposition among the people to relax in their opposition and to acquiesce in the laws, insomuch that many persons in the said western parts of Pennsylvania have at length been hardy enough to perpetrate acts which I am advised amount to treason, being overt acts of levying war against the United States, the said persons having on the 16th and 17th July last past proceeded in arms (on the second day amounting to several hundreds) to the house of John Neville, inspector of the revenue for the fourth survey of the district of Pennsylvania; having repeatedly attacked the said house with the persons therein, wounding some of them; having seized David Lenox, marshal of the district of Pennsylvania, who previous thereto had been fired upon while in the execution of his duty by a party of armed men, detaining him for some time prisoner, till for the preservation of his life and the obtaining of his liberty he found it necessary to enter into stipulations to forbear the execution of certain official duties touching processes issuing out of a court of the United States; and having finally obliged the said inspector of the said revenue and the said marshal from considerations of personal safety to fly from that part of the country, in order, by a circuitous route, to proceed to the seat of Government, avowing as the motives of these outrageous proceedings an intention to prevent by force of arms the execution of the said laws, to oblige the said inspector of the revenue to renounce his said office, to withstand by open violence the lawful authority of the Government of the United States, and to compel thereby an alteration in the measures of the Legislature and a repeal of the laws aforesaid; and

Whereas by a law of the United States entitled "An act to provide for calling forth the militia to execute the laws of the Union, suppress insurrections, and repel invasions," it is enacted "that whenever the laws of the United States shall be opposed or the execution thereof obstructed in any State by combinations too powerful to be suppressed by the ordinary course of judicial proceedings or by the powers vested in the marshals by that act, the same being notified by an associate justice or the district judge, it shall be lawful for the President of the United States to call forth the militia of such State to suppress such combinations and to cause the laws to be duly executed. And if the militia of a State where such combinations may happen shall refuse or be insufficient to suppress the same, it shall be lawful for the President, if the Legislature of the United States shall not be in session, to call forth and employ such numbers of the militia of any other State or States most convenient thereto as may be necessary; and the use of the militia so to be called forth may be continued, if necessary, until the expiration of thirty days after the commencement of the ensuing session: *Provided always*, That whenever it may be necessary in the judgment of the President to use the military force hereby directed to be called forth, the President shall forthwith, and previous thereto, by proclamation, command such insurgents to disperse and retire peaceably to their respective abodes within a limited time;" and

Whereas James Wilson, an associate justice, on the 4th instant, by writing under his hand, did from evidence which had been laid before him notify to me that "in the counties of Washington and Allegany, in Pennsylvania, laws of the United States are opposed and the execution thereof obstructed by combinations too powerful to be suppressed by the ordinary course of judicial proceedings or by the powers vested in the marshal of that district;" and

Whereas it is in my judgment necessary under the circumstances of the case to take measures for calling forth the militia in order to suppress the combinations aforesaid, and to cause the laws to be duly executed; and I have accordingly determined so to do, feeling the deepest regret for the occasion, but withal the most solemn conviction that the essential interests of the Union demand it, that the very existence of Government and the fundamental principles of social order are materially involved in the issue, and that the patriotism and firmness of all good citizens are seriously called upon, as occasions may require, to aid in the effectual suppression of so fatal a spirit:

Wherefore, and in pursuance of the proviso above recited, I, George Washington, President of the United States, do hereby command all persons being insurgents as aforesaid, and all others whom it may concern, on or before the 1st day of September next to disperse and retire peaceably to their respective abodes. And I do moreover warn all persons whomsoever against aiding, abetting, or comforting the perpetrators of the aforesaid treasonable acts, and do require all officers and other citizens, according to their respective duties and the laws of the land, to exert their utmost endeavors to prevent and suppress such dangerous proceedings. . . .

Whereas from a hope that the combinations against the Constitution and laws of the United States in certain of the western counties of Pennsylvania would yield to time and reflection I thought it sufficient in the first instance rather to take measures for calling forth the militia than immediately to embody them, but the moment is now come when the overtures of forgiveness, with no other condition than a submission to law, have been only partially accepted; when every form of conciliation not inconsistent with the being of Government has been adopted without effect; when the well-disposed in those counties are unable by their influence and example to reclaim the wicked from their fury, and are compelled to associate in their own defense; when the proffered lenity has been perversely misinterpreted into an apprehension that the citizens will march with reluctance; when the opportunity of examining the serious consequences of a treasonable opposition has been employed in propagating principles of anarchy, endeavoring through emissaries to alienate the friends of order from its support, and inviting its enemies to perpetrate similar acts of insurrection; when it is manifest that violence would continue to be exercised upon every attempt to enforce the laws; when, therefore, Government is set at defiance, the contest being whether a small portion of the United States shall dictate to the whole Union, and, at the expense of those who desire peace, indulge a desperate ambition:

Now, therefore, I, George Washington, President of the United States, in obedience to that high and irresistible duty consigned to me by the Constitution "to take care that the laws be faithfully executed," deploring that the American name should be sullied by the outrages of citizens on their own Government, commiserating such as remain obstinate from delusion, but resolved, in perfect reliance on that gracious Providence which so signally displays its goodness towards this country, to reduce the refractory to a due subordination to the law, do hereby declare and make known that, with a satisfaction which can be equaled only by the merits of the militia summoned into service from the States of New Jersey, Pennsylvania, Maryland, and Virginia, I have received intelligence of their patriotic alacrity in obeying the call of the present, though painful, yet commanding necessity; that a force which, according to every reasonable expectation, is adequate to the exigency is already in motion to the scene of disaffection; that those who have confided or shall confide in the protection of Government shall meet full succor under the standard and from the arms of the United States; that those who, having offended against the laws, have since entitled themselves to indemnity will be treated with the most liberal good faith if they shall not have forfeited their claim by any subsequent conduct, and that instructions are given accordingly.

And I do moreover exhort all individuals, officers, and bodies of men to contemplate with abhorrence the measures leading directly or indirectly to those crimes which produce this resort to military coercion; to check in their respective spheres the efforts of misguided or designing men to substitute their misrepresentation in the place of truth and their discontents in the place of stable government, and to call to mind that, as the people of the United States have been permitted, under the Divine favor, in perfect freedom, after solemn deliberation, and in an enlightened age, to elect their own government, so will their gratitude for this inestimable blessing be best distinguished by firm exertions to maintain the Constitution and the laws.

And, lastly, I again warn all persons whomsoever and wheresoever not to abet, aid, or comfort the insurgents aforesaid, as they will answer the contrary at their peril; and I do also require all officers and other citizens, according to their several duties, as far as may be in their power, to bring under the cognizance of the laws all offenders in the premises. . . .

5. THE ADMINISTRATION OF JUSTICE: A LETTER FROM GEORGE WASHINGTON TO NEW ATTORNEY GENERAL EDMUND RANDOLPH   SEPTEMBER 28, 1789

. . . Impressed with a conviction that the due administration of justice is the firmest pillar of good Government, I have considered the first arrangement of the Judicial department as essential to the happiness of our Country, and to the stability of its political system; hence the selection of the fittest characters to expound the laws, and dispense justice, has been an invariable object of my anxious concern.

I mean not to flatter when I say, that considerations like these have ruled in the nomination of the Attorney General of the United States, and, that my private wishes would be highly gratified by your acceptance of the Office. I regarded the office as requiring those talents to conduct its important duties, and that disposition to sacrifice to the public good, which I believe you to possess and entertain; in both instances, I doubt not, the event will justify the conclusion; The appointment I hope, will be accepted, and its functions, I am assured, will be well performed. . . .

6. THE FAREWELL ADDRESS   SEPTEMBER 17, 1796

The period for a new election of a citizen to administer the executive government of the United States being not far distant, and the time actually arrived when your thoughts must be employed in designating the person who is to be clothed with that important trust, it appears to me proper, especially as it may conduce to a more distinct expression of the public voice, that I should now apprise you of the resolution I have formed to decline being considered among the number of those out of whom a choice is to be made. . . .

The acceptance of and continuance hitherto in the office to which your suffrages have twice called me have been a uniform sacrifice of inclination to the opinion of duty and to a deference for what appeared to be your desire. I constantly hoped that it would have been much earlier in my power, consistently with motives which I was not at liberty to disregard, to return to that retirement from which I had been reluctantly drawn. The strength of my inclination to do this previous to the last election had even led to the preparation of an address to declare it to you; but mature reflection on the then perplexed and critical posture of our affairs with foreign nations and the unanimous advice of persons entitled to my confidence impelled me to abandon the idea. . . .

In contemplating the causes which may disturb our Union it occurs as matter of serious concern that any ground should have been furnished for characterizing parties by geographical discriminations—Northern and Southern, Atlantic and Western—whence designing men may endeavor to excite a belief that there is a real difference of local interest and views. One of the expedients of party to acquire influence within particular districts is to misrepresent the opinions and aims of other districts. You cannot shield yourselves too much against the jealousies and heartburnings which spring from these misrepresentations; they tend to render alien to each other those who ought to be bound together by fraternal affection. The inhabitants of our Western country have lately had a useful lesson on this head. They have seen in the negotiation by the executive and in the unanimous ratification by the Senate of the treaty with Spain, and in the universal satisfaction at that event throughout the United States, a decisive proof how unfounded were the suspicions propagated among them of a policy in the general government and in the Atlantic states unfriendly to their interests in regard to the Mississippi. They have been witnesses to the formation of two treaties—that with Great Britain and that with Spain—which secure to them everything they could desire in respect to our foreign relations toward confirming their prosperity. Will it not be their wisdom to rely for the preservation of these advantages on the union by which they were procured? Will they not henceforth be deaf to those advisers, if such there are who would sever them from their brethren and connect them with aliens?

To the efficacy and permanency of your union a government for the whole is indispensable. No alliances, however strict, between the parts can be an adequate substitute. They must inevitably experience the infractions and interruptions which all alliances in all times have experienced. Sensible of this momentous truth, you have improved upon your first essay by the adoption of a Constitution of government better calculated than your former for an intimate union and for the efficacious management of your common concerns. This government, the offspring of our own choice, uninfluenced and unawed, adopted upon full investigation and mature deliberation, completely free in its principles, in the distribution of its powers, uniting security with energy, and containing within itself a provision for its own amendment, has a just claim to your confidence and your support. Respect for its authority, compliance with its laws, acquiescence in its measures, are duties enjoined by the fundamental maxims of true liberty. The basis of our political systems is the right of the people to make and to alter their constitutions of government. But the constitution which at any time exists till changed by an explicit and authentic act of the whole people is sacredly obligatory upon all. The very idea of the power and the right of the people to establish government presupposes the duty of every individual to obey the established government. . . .

However combinations or associations of the above description may now and then answer popular ends, they are likely in the course of time and things to become potent engines by which cunning, ambitious, and unprincipled men will be enabled to subvert the power of the people, and to usurp for themselves the reins of government, destroying afterwards the very engines which have lifted them to unjust dominion.

Toward the preservation of your government and the permanency of your present happy state, it is requisite not only that you steadily discountenance irregular oppositions to its acknowledged authority, but also that you resist with care the spirit of innovation upon its principles, however specious the pretexts. One method of assault may be to effect in the forms of the Constitution alterations which will impair the energy of the system, and thus to undermine what cannot be directly overthrown. In all the changes to which you may be invited remember that time and habit are at least as necessary to fix the true character of governments as of other human institutions; that experience is the surest standard by which to test the real tendency of the existing constitution of a country; the facility in changes upon the credit of mere hypothesis and opinion exposes to perpetual change, from the endless variety of hypothesis and opinion; and remember especially that for the efficient management of your common interests in a country so extensive as ours a government of as much vigor as is consistent with the perfect security of liberty is indispensable. Liberty itself will find in such a government, with powers properly distributed and adjusted, its surest guardian. It is, indeed, little else than a name where the government is too feeble to withstand the enterprises of faction, to confine each member of the society within the limits prescribed by the laws, and to maintain all in the secure and tranquil enjoyment of the rights of person and property.

I have already intimated to you the danger of parties in the state, with particular reference to the founding of them on geographical discriminations. Let me now take a more comprehensive view, and warn you in the most solemn manner against the baneful effects of the spirit of party generally.

This spirit, unfortunately, is inseparable from our nature, having its root in the strongest passions of the human mind. It exists under different shapes in all governments, more or less stifled, controlled, or repressed; but in those of the popular form it is seen in its greatest rankness and is truly their worst enemy.

The alternate domination of one faction over another, sharpened by the spirit of revenge natural to party dissension, which in different ages and countries has perpetrated the most horrid enormities, is itself a frightful despotism. But this leads at length to a more formal and permanent despotism. The disorders and miseries which result gradually incline the minds of men to seek security and repose in the absolute power of an individual, and sooner or later the chief of some prevailing faction, more able or more fortunate than his competitors, turns this disposition to the purposes of his own elevation on the ruins of public liberty.

Without looking forward to an extremity of this kind (which nevertheless ought not to be entirely out of sight), the common and continual mischiefs of the spirit of party are sufficient to make it the interest and duty of a wise people to discourage and restrain it.

It serves always to distract the public councils and enfeeble the public administration. It agitates the community with ill-founded jealousies and false alarms; kindles the animosity of one part against another; foments occasionally riot and insurrection. It opens the door to foreign influence and corruption, which find a facilitated access to the government itself through the channels of party passion. Thus the policy and the will of one country are subjected to the policy and will of another.

There is an opinion that parties in free countries are useful checks upon the administration of the government, and serve to keep alive the spirit of liberty. This within certain limits is probably true; and in governments of a monarchical cast patriotism may look with indulgence, if not with favor, upon the spirit of party. But in those of the popular character, in governments purely elective, it is a spirit not to be encouraged. From their natural tendency it is certain there will always be enough of that spirit for every salutary purpose; and there being constant danger of excess, the effort ought to be by force of public opinion to mitigate and assuage it. A fire not to be quenched, it demands a uniform vigilance to prevent its bursting into a flame, lest, instead of warming, it should consume.

It is important, likewise, that the habits of thinking in a free country should inspire caution in those entrusted with its administration to confine themselves within their respective constitutional spheres, avoiding in the exercise of the powers of one department to encroach upon another. The spirit of encroachment tends to consolidate the powers of all the departments in one, and thus to create, whatever the form of government, a real despotism. A just estimate of that love of power and proneness to abuse it which predominates in the human heart is sufficient to satisfy us of the truth of this position. The necessity of reciprocal checks in the exercise of political power, by dividing and distributing it into different depositories, and constituting each the guardian of the public weal against invasions by the others, has been evinced by experiments ancient and modern, some of them in our country and under our own eyes. To preserve them must be as necessary as to institute them. If in the opinion of the people the distribution or modification of the constitutional powers be in any particular wrong, let it be corrected by an amendment in the way which the Constitution designates. But let there be no change by usurpation; for though this in one instance may be the instrument of good, it is the customary weapon by which free governments are destroyed. The precedent must always greatly overbalance in permanent evil any partial or transient benefit which the use can at any time yield.

Of all the dispositions and habits which lead to political prosperity, religion and morality are indispensable supports. In vain would that man claim the tribute of patriotism who should labor to subvert these great pillars of human happiness—these firmest props of the duties of men and citizens. The mere politician, equally with the pious man, ought to respect and to cherish them. A volume could not trace all their connections with private and public felicity. Let it simply be asked, where is the security for property, for reputation, for life, if the sense of religious obligation desert the oaths which are the instruments of investigation in courts of justice? And let us with caution indulge the supposition that morality can be maintained without religion. Whatever may be conceded to the influence of refined education on minds of peculiar structure, reason and experience both forbid us to expect that national morality can prevail in exclusion of religious principle.

It is substantially true that virtue or morality is a necessary spring of popular government. The rule indeed extends with more or less force to every species of free government. Who that is a sincere friend to it can look with indifference upon attempts to shake the foundation of the fabric? Promote, then, as an object of primary importance, institutions for the general diffusion of knowledge. In proportion as the structure of a government gives force to public opinion, it is essential that public opinion should be enlightened. . . .

Observe good faith and justice toward all nations. Cultivate peace and harmony with all. Religion and morality enjoin this conduct. And can it be that good policy does not equally enjoin it? It will be worthy of a free, enlightened, and at no distant period a great nation to give to mankind the magnanimous and too novel example of a people always guided by an exalted justice and benevolence. Who can doubt that in the course of time and things the fruits of such a plan would richly repay any temporary advantages which might be lost by a steady adherence to it? Can it be that Providence has not connected the permanent felicity of a nation with its virtue? The experiment, at least, is recommended by every sentiment which ennobles human nature. Alas! Is it rendered impossible by its vices?

In the execution of such a plan nothing is more essential than that permanent, inveterate antipathies against particular nations and passionate attachments for others should be excluded, and that in place of them just and amicable feelings toward all should be cultivated. The nation which indulges toward another a habitual hatred or an habitual fondness is in some degree a slave. It is a slave to its animosity or to its affection, either of which is sufficient to lead it astray from its duty and its interest. Antipathy in one nation against another disposes each more readily to offer insult and injury, to lay hold of slight causes of umbrage, and to be haughty and intractable when accidental or trifling occasions of dispute occur.

Hence, frequent collisions, obstinate, envenomed, and bloody contests. The nation prompted by ill will and resentment sometimes impels to war the government contrary to the best calculations of policy. The government sometimes participates in the national propensity, and adopts through passion what reason would reject. At other times it makes the animosity of the nation subservient to projects of hostility, instigated by pride, ambition, and other sinister and pernicious motives. The peace often, sometimes perhaps the liberty, of nations has been the victim.

. . . a passionate attachment of one nation for another produces a variety of evils. Sympathy for the favorite nation, facilitating the illusion of an imaginary common interest in cases where no real common interest exists, and infusing into one the enmities of the other, betrays the former into a participation in the quarrels and wars of the latter without adequate inducement or justification. It leads also to concessions to the favorite nation of privileges denied to others, which is apt doubly to injure the nation making the concessions by unnecessarily parting with what ought to have been retained, and by exciting jealousy, ill will, and a disposition to retaliate in the parties from whom equal privileges are withheld; and it gives to ambitious, corrupted, or deluded citizens (who devote themselves to the favorite nation) facility to betray or sacrifice the interests of their own country without odium, sometimes even with popularity, gilding with the appearances of a virtuous sense of obligation, a commendable deference for public opinion, or a laudable zeal for public good, the base or foolish compliances of ambition, corruption, or infatuation. . . .

Europe has a set of primary interests which to us have none or a very remote relation. Hence she must be engaged in frequent controversies, the causes of which are essentially foreign to our concerns. Hence, therefore, it must be unwise in us to implicate ourselves by artificial ties in the ordinary vicissitudes of her politics or the ordinary combinations and collisions of her friendships or enmities.

Our detached and distant situation invites and enables us to pursue a different course. If we remain one people, under an efficient government, the period is not far off when we may defy material injury from external annoyance; when we may take such an attitude as will cause the neutrality we may at any time resolve upon to be scrupulously respected; when belligerent nations, under the impossibility of making acquisitions upon us, will not lightly hazard the giving us provocation; when we may choose peace or war, as our interest, guided by justice, shall counsel.

Why forego the advantages of so peculiar a situation? Why quit our own to stand upon foreign ground? Why, by interweaving our destiny with that of any part of Europe, entangle our peace and prosperity in the toils of European ambition, rivalship, interest, humor, or caprice?

It is our true policy to steer clear of permanent alliances with any portion of the foreign world, so far, I mean, as we are now at liberty to do it; for let me not be understood as capable of patronizing infidelity to existing engagements. I hold the maxim no less applicable to public than to private affairs that honesty is always the best policy. I repeat, therefore, let those engagements be observed in their genuine sense. But in my opinion it is unnecessary and would be unwise to extend them.

Taking care always to keep ourselves by suitable establishments on a respectable defensive posture, we may safely trust to temporary alliances for extraordinary emergencies.

Harmony, liberal intercourse with all nations is recommended by policy, humanity, and interest. But even our commercial policy should hold an equal and impartial hand, neither seeking nor granting exclusive favors or preferences; consulting the natural course of things; diffusing and diversifying by gentle means the screams of commerce, but forcing nothing; establishing with powers so disposed, in order to give trade a stable course, to define the rights of our merchants, and to enable the government to support them, conventional rules of intercourse, the best that present circumstances and mutual opinion will permit, but temporary and liable to be from time to time abandoned or varied as experience and circumstances shall dictate; constantly keeping in view that it is folly in one nation to look for disinterested favors from another; that it must pay with a portion of its independence for whatever it may accept under that character; that by such acceptance it may place itself in the condition of having given equivalents for nominal favors, and yet of being reproached with ingratitude for not giving more. There can be no greater error than to expect or calculate upon real favors from nation to nation. It is an illusion which experience must cure, which a just pride ought to discard. . . .

Relying on its kindness in this as in other things, and actuated by that fervent love toward it which is so natural to a man who views in it the native soil of himself and his progenitors for several generations, I anticipate with pleasing expectation that retreat in which I promise myself to realize without alloy the sweet enjoyment of partaking in the midst of my fellow citizens the benign influence of good laws under a free government—the ever—favorite object of my heart, and the happy reward, as I trust, of our mutual cares, labors, and dangers.

7. GEORGE WASHINGTON TO MARYLAND LEGISLATURE   DECEMBER 23, 1796

As George Washington concluded the final year of his second term as President, just days before Christmas, he wrote a letter commenting upon the friendly reception of the Maryland Legislature to his Farewell Address to the people of the United States.

. . . The manner in which the two branches of the legislature of Maryland have expressed their sense of my services is too honourable, and too affectionate ever to be forgotten. Without assigning to my exertions the extensive influence they are pleased to ascribe to them, I may with great truth say that, the exercise of every faculty I possessed was joined to the efforts of the virtue, talents and valour of my fellow-citizens to effect our Independence and I concur with the Legislature in repeating, with pride and joy, what will be an everlasting honor to our country, that our revolution was so distinguished for moderation, virtue and humanity, as to merit the eulogium they have pronounced of being unsullied with a crime.

With the same entire devotion to my country, every act of my civil Administration has been aimed to secure to it those advantages which result from a stable and free government, and with gratitude to Heaven, I unite with the Legislature of Maryland in the pleasing reflections, that our country has continued to feel the blessings of peace, liberty and prosperity, whilst Europe and the Indies have been convulsed with the horrors of a dreadful and desolating war. My ardent prayers are offered that those afflicted regions may now speedily see their calamities terminated, and also feel the blessings of returning peace.

I cannot omit my acknowledgements to the Senate and House of Delegates for the manner in which they have noticed my late Address to my fellow citizens. This notice, with similar acts in other States leads me to hope that the advice which therein I took the liberty to offer as the result of much experience and reflection, produce some good.

Their kind wishes for my domestic happiness, in my contemplated retirement, are entitled to my cordial thanks.

If it shall please God to prolong a life already far advanced into the vale of years, no attending felicity can equal that which I shall feel in seeing the administration of our government operating to preserve the Independence, prosperity and welfare of the American People. . . .

2

John Adams

1. REPORT TO CONGRESS ON THE XYZ AFFAIR   **MARCH 19, 1798**

The dispatches from the envoys extraordinary of the United States to the French Republic, which were mentioned in my message to both Houses of Congress of the 5th instant, have been examined and maturely considered.

While I feel a satisfaction in informing you that their exertions for the adjustment of the differences between the two nations have been sincere and unremitted, it is incumbent on me to declare that I perceive no ground of expectation that the objects of their mission can be accomplished on terms compatible with the safety, the honor, or the essential interests of the nation.

This result cannot with justice be attributed to any want of moderation on the part of this Government, or to any indisposition to forego secondary interests for the preservation of peace. Knowing it to be my duty, and believing it to be your wish, as well as that of the great body of the people, to avoid by all reasonable concessions any participation in the contentions of Europe, the powers vested in our envoys were commensurate with a liberal and pacific policy and that high confidence which might justly be reposed in the abilities, patriotism, and integrity of the characters to whom the negotiation was committed. After a careful review of the whole subject, with the aid of all the information I have received, I can discern nothing which could have insured or contributed to success that has been omitted on my part, and nothing further which can be attempted consistently with maxims for which our country has contended at every hazard, and which constitute the basis of our national sovereignty.

Under these circumstances I cannot forbear to reiterate the recommendations which have been formerly made, and to exhort you to adopt with promptitude, decision, and unanimity such measures as the ample resources of the country afford for the protection of our seafaring and commercial citizens, for the defense of any exposed portions of our territory, for replenishing our arsenals, establishing foundries and military manufactures, and to provide such efficient revenue as will be necessary to defray extraordinary expenses and supply the deficiencies which may be occasioned by depredations on our commerce.

The present state of things is so essentially different from that, in which instructions were given to the collectors to restrain vessels of the United States from sailing in an armed condition that the principle on which those orders were issued has ceased to exist. I therefore deem it proper to inform Congress that I no longer conceive myself justifiable in continuing them, unless in particular cases where there may be reasonable ground of suspicion that such vessels are intended to be employed contrary to law. In all your proceedings it will be important to manifest a zeal, vigor, and concert in defense of the national rights proportioned to the danger with which they are threatened.

2. ESTABLISHMENT OF A PERMANENT CAPITAL IN WASHINGTON CITY

NOVEMBER 22, 1800

Immediately after the adjournment of Congress at their last session in Philadelphia I gave directions, in compliance with the laws, for the removal of the public offices, records and property. These directions have been executed and the public officers have since resided and conducted the ordinary business of the Government in this place.

I congratulate the people of the United States on the assembling of Congress at the permanent seat of their Government, and I congratulate you gentlemen, on the prospect of a residence not to be changed. Although there is cause to apprehend that accommodations are not now so complete as might be wished, yet there is great reason to believe that this inconvenience will cease with the present session.

It would be unbecoming the representatives of this nation to assemble for the first time in this solemn temple without looking up to the Supreme Ruler of the Universe and imploring His Blessing.

II

THE EARLY REPUBLIC

ONCE THE FOUNDATION WAS PUT IN PLACE and the new nation launched, the next challenge was to build upon those firm underpinnings and grow the Republic. The new century came with a new Chief Executive who did just that. The presidential election of 1800 was a major turning point in American history. The torch was passed peacefully from the Federalist party of John Adams to the Republican party of Thomas Jefferson. This transfer of power as a consequence of a free election was truly novel on this Earth and a significant moment for the new nation.

Congressional party caucuses selected candidates for President and Vice President. The Republicans chose Thomas Jefferson and Aaron Burr. The Federalists remained true to form and endorsed the incumbent, President John Adams and also selected C. C. Pinckney from South Carolina. Both national party tickets retained a geographical or sectional balance that had begun with George Washington and John Adams.

The gloves came off in this classic election. The patriot idea of consensus was abandoned. The Farewell Address caveat of Washington against evil factions and parties was ignored. The first American party system was now fully evident. The bitter campaign was waged through letter writing and biting newspaper articles. The Republicans championed limited, frugal government and individual liberty as the core issues of the election. The Federalists warned that the Republic was threatened by radical Jacobins who threatened American political stability and the social order. The Republicans, so it was claimed, would bring on class war and a reign of terror. There were also personal attacks levied against the candidates. Adams was portrayed as an aristocrat and a monarchist, while Jefferson was presented as an American Robespierre and a madman. Each side postured with pride and pointed with alarm. Fear moved people, and politicians put that fear to work. Robespierre and the French deadly turn to the Reign of Terror remained fresh and repugnant in the American mind.

Jefferson was no Robespierre. He wanted less government and more liberty whereas Robespierre wanted intense government control. In any event each side in the presidential contest masterfully mobilized its forces, marking the beginning of modern political elections.

The American public was politically polarized. The electorate tilted towards the Republicans. Republican electors dutifully cast their votes for Jefferson and Burr. They tied. Each candidate received 73 votes. Adams obtained 65 votes and Pinckney 64.

The Constitution mandated that the House of Representatives, with each state delegation casting one vote, had to choose between Jefferson and Burr for the presidency. On the 36th ballot, Jefferson won a majority of the states and became the third President of the United States. Clearly this result conformed to the wishes of the American electorate. Ironically the dilemma was resolved via a clever stratagem devised by another of Jefferson's Federalist rivals, Alexander Hamilton. It was the retiring House of Representatives members who voted and that body was controlled by Federalists. The wily and wise Hamilton persuaded enough Federalists to abstain from voting. Those votes might well have been cast in favor of Burr simply to spite Jefferson. The stratagem worked. Jefferson triumphed.

Hamilton trusted Jefferson over his fellow New Yorker, the treacherous Burr. He had many reasons for this action, but in the end it is not too much to say that the great nation builder put the interests of his country over partisan considerations. Within the space of just over three years, Alexander Hamilton would be put to rest in the graveyard of Trinity Church appropriately located above Wall Street and the Stock Exchange. Hamilton had made the fatal mistake of crossing the Hudson to New Jersey to meet Burr on the field of honor. There Burr shot Hamilton dead. The brilliant leader of the Federalists was gone, as Thomas Jefferson led the nation from the presidential chair in Washington City.

It had long been popularly believed that at noon, 4 March 1801, Jefferson, unattended by a living soul, rode up the Capitol Hill, tied his horse to the picket fence, entered the Senate chamber, and took the oath of office as President. Although this story is not true, it served for many generations to illustrate the inauguration of the "Man of the People." In reality, Jefferson, surrounded by a crowd and some militiamen, left his boarding-house and walked across the open space between it and the new city of Washington. The ceremony was held in the small Senate chamber. Afterward, the President read his address in a low, almost inaudible voice. The soft-spoken master of the written word would soon cease to give live addresses to Congress. With his first Annual Address to Congress on December 8, 1801 he began the practice of presenting annual addresses in writing, a pattern that lived on for more than a hundred years. Woodrow Wilson, accustomed to lectures, returned to more dramatic live action.

The problem attached to the 1800 election originated with an oversight by the constitutional delegates in Philadelphia, who simply did not anticipate a tie vote. The structural defect in the frame of government was rectified prior to Jefferson's re-election. The Twelfth Amendment to the Constitution adopted in 1804 resolved that irksome problem by requiring electors to vote separately for the offices of President and Vice President. Thus the constitutional building blocks continued to be put in place in the young Republic. American ingenuity and a special genius for politics and problem solving were in play.

The Sage of Monticello summoned Americans in soft tones to surmount their differences and come together in the new century. In the aftermath of a fierce election contest a bitter aftertaste remained. The new leader expressed confidence that all would "unite in common efforts for the common good." His words to achieve this harmony were as usual chosen with great care. Jefferson reminded his fellow citizens that "every difference of opinion is not a difference of principle" and that "we are all Republicans, we are all Federalists."

During his administration important and lasting steps were taken to weld the new nation and solve problems. There was the Constitution repair work already mentioned and the call for Americans to come together to accomplish great things. The new President set about the task to grow the Republic and secure the tender edges for the future.

Before his first year at the helm had been completed, Jefferson confronted a challenge to America at sea. The Barbary Pirates of Tripoli threatened American commercial interests with attack. Their reach stretched from the Atlantic to Gibraltar and their home base in the Mediterranean and North Africa. The President swiftly responded to this affront to the nation's honor and its commerce by commanding a squadron of frigates to engage the Pirates. The encounter demonstrated the new nation's mettle. The Commander-in-Chief reported to Congress: "The bravery exhibited . . . will be a testimony to the world that it is not want of that virtue which makes us seek their peace."

An even more impressive success came without any show of force. The President wished to secure the national borders of the young Republic and protect the interior trade routes. In this connection he fully understood the importance of New Orleans. "There is on the globe one single spot, the possessor of which is our natural and habitual enemy," wrote Jefferson to Robert Livingston, the American minister to France. "It is New Orleans, through which the produce of three-eighths of our territory must pass to market."

Jefferson's concern about access to the port were confirmed when the Spanish in 1802, still the rightful authority, suspended the "right of deposit." Shortly thereafter an opportunity presented itself when the area was transferred to French ownership. The President now sent James Monroe to Paris. Together with Livingston he had instructions to purchase the city of New Orleans. When these ministers made the overture to the Emperor Napoleon Bonaparte they were astonished at his response. Napoleon offered the entire Louisiana Territory to the Americans at a discount bargain basement price of $15,000,000. The deal was done and the United States acquired some 828,000 square miles lying between the Mississippi River and the Rocky Mountains. An exuberant Livingston exclaimed: "We have lived long, but this is the noblest work of our whole lives . . . From this day the United States take their place among the powers of the first rank."

One difficulty remained. The purchase challenged Jefferson's philosophical principles. An anchor of his constitutional belief system was strict construction of the founding document. The news of the great purchase came as a shock to the perplexed President. Since Livingston and Monroe had exceeded their instructions the President wondered how he could justify the purchase, given his constitutional scruples. Yet here was an opportunity to truly grow the Republic and double the size of the nation. Did the President under the Constitution have the authority to purchase foreign territory? The dilemma was resolved when Jefferson decided to bow to the good sense of the American people who favored expansion. Ultimately the resourceful Chief Diplomat found the justification in the treaty-making power and approved the sale: "If our friends think differently, certainly I shall acquiesce with satisfaction." On 20 December 1803, the United States formally took possession of the Louisiana Territory.

Thus was the greatest real estate deal in history transacted. It was Thomas Jefferson's greatest triumph. Not only was it a tremendous moment for the young Republic, it placed the nation forever after amongst the first rank of nations. It set a marker for future presidents and for further growth in the future. At the same time, the great deal also secured the re-election of Jefferson as President of the United States of America.

During his second term as President, Jefferson once again turned his attention to the troublesome question of restricting the African slave trade from American shores. By the outbreak of the American Revolution, most of the colonies had taken steps to restrict the importation of slaves from Africa. Virginia had done so in 1768 and other colonies in short order followed Virginia's lead. Jefferson had condemned the slave trade in the original draft of the Declaration of Independence, but the New England traders joined the planters of Georgia and South Carolina to strike out the clause. The Articles of Confederation made no mention of the slave trade.

The Constitution of the United States (Article I, Section 9) forbade congressional interference with the foreign slave trade until 1808. In keeping with Jefferson's recommendation offered on December 2, 1806, Congress officially stopped the foreign traffic of slaves on March 2, 1807 so that slave importation into the United States would cease, effective January 1, 1808. The law provided a penalty of forfeiture of vessel and cargo, with the disposal of the seized slaves to be left to the state in which the ship was condemned.

The importation of slaves did not stop. Both New England traders and southern planters opposed the action of Congress, and smuggling soon became a profitable enterprise. It is estimated that between 1808 and 1816, more than 15,000 slaves were annually smuggled into the United States. Congress at first made little attempt to push for the law's enforcement. However, after 1820, when the slave trade was made piracy, an agency was set up to end the practice.

President Jefferson faced tremendous difficulties during his second administration as the leader of a neutral nation at a time of a ruthless general European war. He decided to rely on economic pressure to bring the belligerent powers to terms.

The underlying cause for the embargo was a series of restrictions upon American commerce imposed by the warring factions. In the early years of the Napoleonic wars, the United States had grown wealthy as the chief neutral carrier trading with both England and France. Roughly speaking, this period of prosperity lasted from 1793 to 1805. Restrictions then cut these profits. Subsequently, the British Orders in Council (1807) and the French Berlin and Milan Decrees (1806, 1807) threatened direct penalties to any neutral ship entering a port of their enemy.

Jefferson never considered taking sides with either of the European rivals. He relied on diplomacy supplemented by the threat of economic pressure. When diplomacy failed, he fell back on economic instruments. One such instrument was the embargo. It was perhaps Jefferson's most original and daring measure of statesmanship. It also proved to be his greatest failure. The aim was to suspend foreign commerce for an indefinite period. Attempts to enforce this arbitrary power by the federal government led to an infringement on individual rights, which was contrary to Jefferson's most cherished ideals. But Jefferson was determined to bring the proud belligerents to their knees by withholding from them the raw materials and finished products that they normally received from the United States. The President opposed war but he did not realize that his peaceful substitute posed a galling dilemma.

Jefferson's embargo failed to achieve its objective. The President had calculated that war-causing incidents would stop. In addition, he believed that hundreds of thousands of British laborers would be deprived of work as foreign importations halted. Under these economic circumstances, England would reconsider provocative policies such as seizing American ships and the impressment of American seamen.

Within one year, this unilateral attempt to secure a peaceful redress of grievances created an economic depression in the United States. Jefferson received bitter letters from all parts of the country expressing hostile attitudes toward the President and his embargo. In New England there was serious talk of secession. Annual exports fell from $108,000,000 to $22,000,000. Businesses failed. Shipbuilding stopped. Tobacco glutted idle wharves. On March 1, 1809 as his presidential tenure was about to expire, Jefferson signed a congressional resolution repealing his futile attempt at economic coercion. "The Embargo Act," admitted the President, "is certainly the most embarrassing we ever had to execute."

As his presidency was coming to awkward closure, Jefferson wrote his friend Pierre Samuel DuPont de Nemours venting his anxieties about the economic situation and his relief on his departure from "the boisterous ocean of political passions." "Never did a prisoner, released from his chains," lamented Jefferson on his exodus from the executive office, "feel such relief as I shall on shaking off the shackles of power."

The executive shackles now passed to his Secretary of State, James Madison who would come to know the burden of leading the nation through tumultuous times. During President Madison's administration, East and West Florida belonged to Spain. Madison was eager to acquire both territories while Spain resisted entreaties from Washington to obtain physical possession. Great Britain opposed annexation.

The Louisiana Treaty of 1803 made no reference to the status of East and West Florida, but the American posture maintained that the Louisiana Purchase included that portion of Spanish Florida between the Mississippi River to the west and the Perdido River to the east. In 1810, Southern expansionists led a revolt in the Spanish dominion. On September 26th, they proclaimed the independent state of the Republic of West Florida. Madison acted on the American claim and authorized military occupation as part of the Orleans Territory and promised the residents of the territory the protection of the United States "in the enjoyment of their liberty, property and religion."

The United States was treated as a pawn, during the Madison administration as it had been under his predecessor, in the wars between Great Britain and France. Both nations attempted to control American oceanic trade through a series of orders and decrees. These acts subjected neutral American shipping to illegal searches and seizures. Back-to-back presidencies believed that economic policy would deter such impudence. By withholding American products, the belligerents would be forced to acknowledge America's maritime rights as a neutral nation. They were sadly mistaken. The Embargo Act of 1807–1809 and the Non-Intercourse Act of 1809 misfired and hurt American economic interests.

In May 1810, the United States made another attempt at economic coercion. Macon's Bill No. 2 authorized the President to reopen trade with Great Britain and France. If either nation ceased its violation of American shipping, the President could prohibit trade with the other. Napoleon gladly seized the opportunity to gain an advantage against his English adversary. The French foreign minister wrote his American counterpart that the Berlin and Milan Decrees were now revoked. Madison quickly accepted the statement as a genuine change in French policy. On November 2, 1810, the President instituted a trade blockade against Great Britain.

The British continued to display a pattern of disrespect towards the United States. The litany of abuse heaped upon the young Republic included a series of violations of American rights on the high seas, trespasses against neutral prerogatives and jurisdiction, along with episodes of pillage and plunder disturbing the peace along the coasts. Even more at issue were the hostile assaults on the "sacred rights of persons."

On June 1, 1812, President Madison recommended a declaration of war against Great Britain. In his message to Congress, Madison cited the impressment of seamen and the repeated violation of America's neutral rights as major causes for war. In addition, spokesmen for the West held England responsible for encouraging Indian attacks by supplying them with powder and rifles. Canadian lands were coveted by Westerners and others. Even Jefferson believed that the taking of Canada was simply a matter of marching. In the South, hostile tribes and runaway slaves took refuge in Spanish Florida. The frontiersmen of Georgia and Louisiana said they would fight for the annexation of Canada if the North and West reciprocated in a military campaign in Florida against England's ally. Ironically, the greatest opposition to the war came from the maritime sections of New England that suffered the most from impressment and seizures.

Congress declared war on Great Britain on June 18, 1812. Madison knew that the war carried serious risks and that the young nation was not prepared for the conflict. Years later, he told the historian George Bancroft he decided upon war by throwing "forward the flag of the country, sure that the people would press forward and defend it."

The War of 1812 created financial havoc and emphasized anew the need for a national bank. This became even more evident as the British high command reconsidered the overall situation and objectives. The fact remained that the British possessed an imperial frame of mind. American Independence had not been accepted on the other side of the pond. Neither did they hold any respect for the idea that their "colonies" were now a sovereign nation. The war from their vantage point would restore the Empire on the battlefield. From the American perspective the conflict constituted a second war for Independence. Ultimately, the British decided to shift battlefields from military to economic. They prided themselves as a nation of shopkeepers who understood how to maintain economic dominance. Even before the fighting ceased the British prepared for economic war.

Madison did not receive high marks from historians in his constitutional role of Commander-in-Chief. Critics mocked his conduct of the war which was sometimes sarcastically called "Little Jimmy's War." The truth is that Americans had thwarted British military designs, from the Great Lakes and high seas to the spectacular military triumph of General Andrew Jackson at the famous battle of New Orleans. American military performance convinced the British to shift the fight to economic war.

Given this game change, President Madison had to alter his economic-political philosophy to counter the new British offensive. Two generations of Americans had debated the constitutionality of the Bank of the United States. Secretary of the Treasury Alexander Hamilton in 1790 had argued that a national bank was essential for the nation's prosperity and the Bank became a major part of his economic program. The Bank Charter had expired and was not renewed by the Republican-dominated Congress in 1811 on the grounds that there was no Constitutional authority for the institution. In 1791, Madison had argued that the framers of the Constitution never envisioned such sweeping national powers. A quarter-century later, on January 30, 1815 President Madison remained of the same mind as he vetoed a re-charter bill because he felt it failed three essential tests. First, he contended it was inadequate for "reviving the public credit." Second, the Bank did not provide "a national medium of circulation." Finally, it did not aid the Treasury in the tax collection department.

Suddenly, in the face of the new economic challenge from the British Empire, the "Father of the Constitution" appeared to have discovered that the nation's frame of government was a "living" instrument. The President experienced an epiphany and conceded the legal authority of Congress to enact such legislation, not only with respect to the Bank but with an entire list of economic initiatives, conveniently borrowed from the Federalist philosophy of government.

The early presidents took care to do what was necessary to protect the infant Republic. They were students of human nature and were vigilant as to what destructive course a prospective enemy might pursue. It was America's good fortune that James Madison occupied the presidential chair at that perilous hour. Like Jefferson's change of heart in bowing to the good sense of the American people in his negotiations for the purchase of Louisiana, Madison also moved deftly to a contrary philosophical posture in the nation's best interest. Madison's Annual Message of December 5, 1815 noted that if state banks could not restore a uniform national currency, "the probable operation of a national bank will merit consideration." At the same time Jefferson retreated from an earlier position in opposition to a national bank and endorsed Madison's recommendation. Congress witnessed a similar reversal and followed the leadership from the Executive Branch.

The Second Bank of the United States began operations on January 1, 1817. It was authorized to act as a depository for government funds without paying interest for their use. In most other respects, the provisions followed the First Bank charter. The central office remained in Philadelphia, and in time had twenty-five branches throughout the country.

The second war for Independence had inspired a widespread surge of American nationalism and could be discerned in every corner of the life of the Republic. Not only economic nationalism, but diplomatic, judicial, and cultural expressions were everywhere evident. President Madison could be found at the center of this mood and movement. In this vein he proposed the establishment of a National Seminary which would serve as a "central resort of youth and genius." As a promoter of intellectual or spiritual nationalism, Madison contended that a National Seminary would "contribute cement to our Union. . . ."

A notable feature of the constitutional and economic growth of the nation was the orderly admission of new states into the Union. The steady and stable procession of admission to statehood was suddenly interrupted by a controversy over Missouri. The problem pertained to the issue of the extension of slavery.

Prior to 1819, new states had entered the Union without much debate over slavery. Now, there were eleven slave and eleven free states. The admission of Missouri threatened to upset this delicate balance. At the core of the argument was the growing conviction that human bondage violated the very ethos of the Revolution and of the Republic.

On the issue of slavery, President James Monroe's sympathies were with the South. His concept of presidential duties, however, led him to abstain from all interference with the struggle over the Missouri bill until it came to him for his signature. The measure which Congress submitted provided for the admission of Missouri as a slave state but prohibited slavery north of the 36°30' parallel in the future. Monroe was by no means certain that Congress had the constitutional power to exclude slavery from states to be formed at some distant date. He submitted the question to the Cabinet. Most shared his apprehension. Monroe finally decided to permit this issue to remain unsettled. He signed the several measures, no doubt the most momentous of his administration.

Additional problems of governance accompanied the rapid growth of the United States. National growth and development stimulated the demand for better internal transportation facilities. Roads, for the most part, were rutted dirt ones which followed older Indian trails. By 1800, however, stone or macadam—spread 10 inches deep— was being used to make a nearly flat and stronger road. No state could afford the construction and repair of any extensive road system.

In 1806 Congress authorized the President to appoint three commissioners to survey a road from the Potomac to the Ohio Rivers. By 1816, a road linked Cumberland, Maryland with Wheeling in the western part of Virginia. By the 1820s, the road was crowded with emigrants pushing westward, their wagons laden with household goods. It was especially crowded with wagons bringing the produce of western farms to eastern markets.

Federal expenditures for roads and other internal improvements became a major domestic issue. Did the Constitution authorize such projects? Both Presidents Jefferson and Madison thought not and supported a constitutional amendment granting such power. President Monroe in his first annual message to Congress declared that he likewise was concerned that the national government did not have the right to spend monies for internal improvements.

President Monroe vetoed every bill which came before him involving federal construction projects. On May 4, 1822, in vetoing a bill for repairs on the Cumberland Road, he sent Congress a detailed explanation of his thoughts on internal improvements. He again recommended an amendment authorizing the government to make such expenditures. The debate underscored the sharp differences between a strict interpretation of the Constitution—that is, the federal government could do only what the document literally stated—and those who supported implied powers or a broader interpretation of its clauses.

An event in President Monroe's second administration has made his name immortal. In his Annual Message to Congress in December 1823, the President enunciated the so-called Monroe Doctrine, which has become a sacrosanct part of American foreign policy. The Chief Diplomat declared that Europe would henceforth be forbidden to establish any new dependencies in the Western Hemisphere. Nor could the Old World any longer interfere in the affairs of New World nations in any way as to threaten their independence. In future years, corollaries and interpretations would be added to Monroe's declaration comprising a cornerstone of America's international posture.

At the time this doctrine was promulgated, there existed few independent nations in the Americas. In 1815 there were only two, the United States and Haiti. The next seven years saw rebellious Spanish colonies establish new republics throughout Latin America. During the fall of 1823, Richard Rush, minister to England, advised Monroe that the European powers contemplated destroying these republics by reconquering Spain's former colonies. Russia's Tsar Alexander, in an October 1823 memorandum to the American government, further encouraged such speculation.

Long cabinet discussions followed in which Secretary of State John Quincy Adams played an undeniably influential part. But it was President Monroe who thought of dealing with the Spanish colonial question in his forthcoming Annual Message to Congress.

The President drafted the now famous paragraphs of his 1823 message. Both the initiative and the responsibility of the Doctrine belong to him. But, the principle that the American continents are no longer subject to European colonization had been enunciated by Secretary Adams in his negotiations with Russia over claims their explorers had made along the Pacific coast. It also should be noted that Monroe carefully avoided making any definite commitments when invited by the Colombian government to implement the language of the Doctrine into a treaty of alliance.

Americans cheered the President's message. Editorial comments were overwhelmingly favorable. But the President's words had little practical influence upon Europe's diplomacy. For the next twenty years, Great Britain and France violated the Doctrine with impunity. Not until the late nineteenth century, when the United States had become a major power, did the Old World finally respect the American manifesto.

During the height of the Cold War, when Soviet Premier Nikita Khrushchev embarked upon his risky adventure with his attempt to install nuclear weapons 90 miles from Florida, he openly declared that the Monroe Doctrine was "dead." The missiles would be strategically deployed on the Caribbean island nation that Khrushchev would refer disrespectfully to in his memoirs as "a little sausage." This Soviet challenge to the Monroe Doctrine aimed to install missiles with a range that would enable strikes on New York, Washington, Chicago and many other U.S. and Canadian cities like Montreal, plus they would be capable of hitting Mexico City, Lima, Caracas and other Central and South American targets. President Kennedy insisted that the Monroe Doctrine was a live instrument in this hemisphere and obtained a unanimous vote in the Organization of American States in support of this vital diplomatic peg upholding hemispheric hegemony. In the eyeball-to-eyeball confrontation, the Soviet Premier relented and withdrew his threat to the Western Hemisphere.

Returning to another President from Massachusetts, John Quincy Adams presented his vision of America and his broad plan of internal improvements in his Inaugural Address: "The great object of the institution of civil government is the improvement of those who are parties social to the compact." Towards the end of the year the President specifically described his ideas to promote the arts and the sciences. He did so in his first Annual Message to Congress on December 6, 1825. Here he offered a full program of American nationalism including in his proposal a national university, an astronomical observatory—a "lighthouse in the sky," and national roads and canals. The sixth American President announced plans to send out scientific expeditions to map the country. In short, the President stood ready to do whatever would improve the lives of the people. Adams expected to finance these programs from the sale of public lands.

Adams was proposing a Hamiltonian nationalism on steroids. Northern strict constructionists were alarmed. Southerners likewise dreaded the thought that such extensive executive powers could pose a lethal threat to slavery. Consequently, many sound recommendations from the Chief Executive were rudely rejected by Congress. Years later, under different circumstances, these same suggestions would receive more favorable treatment. The failure of Adams's domestic programs probably had profound consequences for the nation. His ideas could have strengthened American nationality and help stem the tide against the rising forces of sectionalism. A vast system of roads and canals might have tied the Union together. Instead, as Adams predicted, "the clanking chain of the slave" was riveted "into perpetuity."

Adams recommended a national naval academy following the outline John Paul Jones constructed during the Revolution. A small appropriation towards that end was placed in the 1827 naval appropriations bill only to be struck out after a raucous debate. Senator William Smith of South Carolina even pointed out that neither Julius Caesar nor Lord Nelson had attended a naval academy. He predicted that such a school would produce "effeminate leaders." It was not until 1845, on the eve of the Mexican War, that Secretary of the Navy George Bancroft obtained funds to establish "the Naval School."

John Quincy Adams was President of the United States "at the precise interval" that America celebrated fifty years of independence. Later that year he indulged in a reflection on that historic moment in his address to Congress, on December 5, 1826. The President turned the clock back to the summer and the 4th of July. "While every heart was bounding with joy . . . amid the blessings of freedom and independence" said Adams "which the sires of a former age had handed down to their children . . ." two patriots were summoned ". . . to the bosom of their God!" In this moving eulogy to men who had preceded him as President, John Quincy Adams paid homage to Thomas Jefferson and to his father, John Adams: ". . . the hand that penned the ever-memorable Declaration and the voice that sustained it in debate—were by one summons, at the distance of 700 miles from each other, called before the Judge of All to account for their deeds done upon earth."

3

Thomas Jefferson

1. FIRST INAUGURAL ADDRESS   MARCH 4, 1801

Called upon to undertake the duties of the first executive office of our country, I avail myself of the presence of that portion of my fellow-citizens which is here assembled to express my grateful thanks for the favor with which they have been pleased to look toward me, to declare a sincere consciousness that the task is above my talents, and that I approach it with those anxious and awful presentiments which the greatness of the charge and the weakness of my powers so justly inspire. A rising nation, spread over a wide and fruitful land, traversing all the seas with the rich productions of their industry, engaged in commerce with nations who feel power and forget right, advancing rapidly to destinies beyond the reach of mortal eye—when I contemplate these transcendent objects, and see the honor, the happiness, and the hopes of this beloved country committed to the issue, and the auspices of this day, I shrink from the contemplation, and humble myself before the magnitude of the undertaking. Utterly, indeed, should I despair did not the presence of many whom I here see remind me that in the other high authorities provided by our Constitution I shall find resources of wisdom, of virtue, and of zeal on which to rely under all difficulties. To you, then, gentlemen, who are charged with the sovereign functions of legislation, and to those associated with you, I look with encouragement for that guidance and support which may enable us to steer with safety the vessel in which we are all embarked amidst the conflicting elements of a troubled world.

During the contest of opinion through which we have passed the animation of discussions and of exertions has sometimes worn an aspect which might impose on strangers unused to think freely and to speak and to write what they think; but this being now decided by the voice of the nation, announced according to the rules of the Constitution, all will, of course, arrange themselves under the will of the law, and unite in common efforts for the common good. All, too, will bear in mind this sacred principle, that though the will of the majority is in all cases to prevail, that will to be rightful must be reasonable; that the minority possesses their equal rights, which equal law must protect, and to violate would be oppression. Let us, then, fellow-citizens, unite with one heart and one mind. Let us restore to social intercourse that harmony and affection without which liberty and even life itself are but dreary things. And let us reflect that, having banished from our land that religious intolerance under which mankind so long bled and suffered, we have yet gained little if we countenance a political intolerance as despotic, as wicked, and capable of as bitter and bloody persecutions. During the throes and convulsions of the ancient world, during the agonizing spasms of infuriated man, seeking through blood and slaughter his long lost liberty, it was not wonderful that the agitation of the billows should reach even this distant and peaceful shore; that this should be more felt and feared by some and less by others, and should divide opinions as to measures of safety. But every difference of opinion is not a difference of principle. We have called by different names brethren of the same principle. We are all Republicans, we are all Federalists. If there be any among us who would wish to dissolve this Union or to change its republican form, let them stand undisturbed as monuments of the safety with which error of opinion may be tolerated where reason is left free to combat it. I know, indeed, that some honest men fear that a republican government cannot be strong, that this Government is not strong enough; but would the honest patriot, in the full tide of successful experiment, abandon a government which has so far kept us free and firm on the theoretic and visionary fear that this Government, the world's best hope, may by possibility want energy to preserve itself? I trust not. I believe this, on the contrary, the strongest Government on earth. I believe it the only one where every man, at the call of the law, would fly to the standard of the law, and would meet invasions of the public order as his own personal concern. Sometimes it is said that man cannot be trusted with the government of himself. Can he, then, be trusted with the government of others? Or have we found angels in the forms of kings to govern him? Let history answer this question. . . .

About to enter, fellow-citizens, on the exercise of duties which comprehend everything dear and valuable to you, it is proper you should understand what I deem the essential principles of our Government, and consequently those which ought to shape its Administration. I will compress them within the narrowest compass they will bear, stating the general principle, but not all its limitations. Equal and exact justice to all men, of whatever state or persuasion, religious or political; peace, commerce, and honest friendship with all nations, entangling alliances with none; the support of the State governments in all their rights, as the most competent administrations for our domestic concerns and the surest bulwarks against anti-republican tendencies; the preservation of the General Government in its whole constitutional vigor, as the sheet anchor of our peace at home and safety abroad; a jealous care of the right of election by the people—a mild and safe corrective of abuses which are lopped by the sword of revolution where peaceable remedies are unprovided; absolute acquiescence in the decisions of the majority, the vital principle of republics, from which is no appeal but to force, the vital principle and immediate parent of despotism; a well-disciplined militia, our best reliance in peace and for the first moments of war, till regulars may relieve them; the supremacy of the civil over the military authority; economy in the public expense, that labor may be lightly burthened; the honest payment of our debts and sacred preservation of the public faith; encouragement of agriculture, and of commerce as its handmaid; the diffusion of information and arraignment of all abuses at the bar of the public reason; freedom of religion; freedom of the press, and freedom of person under the protection of the habeas corpus, and trial by juries impartially selected. These principles form the bright constellation which has gone before us and guided our steps through an age of revolution and reformation. The wisdom of our sages and blood of our heroes have been devoted to their attainment. They should be the creed of our political faith, the text of civic instruction, the touchstone by which to try the services of those we trust; and should we wander from them in moments of error or of alarm, let us hasten to retrace our steps and to regain the road which alone leads to peace, liberty, and safety. . . .

Relying, then, on the patronage of your good will, I advance with obedience to the work, ready to retire from it whenever you become sensible how much better choice it is in your power to make. And may that Infinite Power which rules the destinies of the universe lead our councils to what is best, and give them a favorable issue for your peace and prosperity.

Figure 3.1 Jefferson Memorial: View of an Architect, November 26, 2009, courtesy of Michael E. McInerney and Alissa Ogen.

2. TRIPOLI   DECEMBER 8, 1801

". . . Tripoli, the least . . . of the Barbary States, had come forward with demands unfounded either in right or in compact, and had permitted itself to denounce war on our failure to comply before a given day. The style of the demand admitted but one answer. I sent a small squadron of frigates into the Mediterranean, with assurances to that power of our sincere desire to remain in peace, but with orders to protect our commerce against the threatened attack. The measure was seasonable and salutary. The Bey had already declared war. His cruisers were out. Two had arrived at Gibraltar. Our commerce in the Mediterranean was blockaded and that of the Atlantic in peril. The arrival of our squadron dispelled the danger. One of the Tripolitan cruisers having fallen in with and engaged the small schooner *Enterprise,* commanded by Lieutenant Sterret . . . without the loss of a single one on our part. The bravery exhibited by our citizens on that element will . . . be a testimony to the world that it is not the want of that virtue which makes us seek their peace, but a conscientious desire to direct the energies of our nation to the multiplication of the human race and not to its destruction. . . ."

3. IMPORTANCE OF NEW ORLEANS   APRIL 18, 1802

. . . The cession of Louisiana and the Floridas by Spain to France, works most sorely on the United States. On this subject the Secretary of State has written to you fully, yet I cannot forbear recurring to it personally, so deep is the impression it makes on my mind. It completely reverses all the political relations of the United States, and will form a new epoch in our political course. Of all nations of any consideration, France is the one which, hitherto, has offered the fewest points on which we could have any conflict of right, and the most points of a communion of interest. From these causes, we have ever looked to her as our natural friend, as one with which we could never have an occasion of difference. Her growth, therefore, we viewed as our own, her misfortunes ours. There is on the globe one single spot, the possessor of which is our natural and habitual enemy. It is New Orleans, through which the produce of three-eighths of our territory must pass to market, and from its fertility it will ere long yield more than half of our whole produce and contain more than half of our inhabitants. France, placing herself in that door, assumes to us the attitude of defiance. Spain might have retained it quietly for years. Her pacific dispositions, her feeble state, would induce her to increase our facilities there so that her possession of the place would hardly be felt by us, and it would not, perhaps, be very long before some circumstance might arise, which might make the cession of it to us the price of something of more worth to her. Not so can it ever be in the hands of France: the impetuosity of her temper, the energy and restlessness of her character, placed in a point of eternal friction with us, and our character, which, though quiet and loving peace and the pursuit of wealth, is high-minded, despising wealth in competition with insult or injury, enterprising and energetic as any nation on earth; these circumstances render it impossible that France and the United States can continue long friends, when they meet in so irritable a position. They, as well as we, must be blind if they do not see this; and we must be very improvident if we do not begin to make arrangements on that hypothesis. The day that France takes possession of New Orleans fixes the sentence which is to restrain her forever within her low-water mark. It seals the union of two nations, who, in conjunction, can maintain exclusive possession of the ocean. From that moment, we must marry ourselves to the British fleet and nation. We must turn all our attention to a maritime force, for which our resources place us on very high ground; and having formed and connected together a power which may render reinforcement of her settlements here impossible to France, make the first cannon which shall be fired in Europe the Signal for the tearing up of any settlement she may have made, and for holding the two continents of America in sequestration for the common purposes of the United British and American nations. This is not a state of things we seek or desire. . . .

4. RECOMMENDATION TO END THE AFRICAN SLAVE TRADE   DECEMBER 2, 1806

. . . I congratulate you, fellow-citizens, on the approach of the period at which you may interpose your authority constitutionally to withdraw the citizens of the United States from all further participation in those violations of human rights which have been so long continued on the unoffending inhabitants of Africa, and which the morality, the reputation, and the best interests of our country have long been eager to proscribe. Although no law you may pass can take pro-hibitory effect till the first day of the year 1808, yet the intervening period is not too long to prevent by timely notice expeditions which can not be completed before that day. . . .

5. THE EMBARGO MESSAGE   DECEMBER 18, 1807

The communications now made, showing the great and increasing dangers with which our vessels, our seamen, and merchandise are threatened on the high seas and elsewhere from the belligerent powers of Europe, and it being of the greatest importance to keep in safety these essential resources, I deem it my duty to recommend the subject to the consideration of Congress, who will doubtless perceive all the advantages which may be expected from an inhibition of the departure of our vessels from the ports of the United States. Their wisdom will also see the necessity of making every preparation for whatever events may grow out of the present crisis.

6. THE NON-INTERCOURSE ACT   MARCH 1, 1809

. . . After using every effort which could prevent or delay our being entangled in the war of Europe, that seems now our only resource. The edicts of the two belligerents, forbidding us to be seen on the ocean, we met by an embargo. This gave us time to call home our seamen, ships and property, to levy men and put our seaports into a certain state of defense. We have now taken off the embargo, except as to France & England & their territories, because 50 millions of exports, annually sacrificed, are the treble of what war would cost us. Besides that by war we shall take something, & lose less than at present. But to give you a true description of the state of things here, I must refer you to Mr. Coles, the bearer of this, my Secretary, a most worthy, intelligent & well informed young man, whom I recommend to your notice, and conversation on our affairs. His discretion and fidelity may be relied on. I expect he will find you with Spain at your feet, but England still afloat, & a barrier to the Spanish colonies. But all these concerns I am now leaving to be settled by my friend Mr. Madison. Within a few days I retire to my family, my books, and farms & having gained the harbor myself, shall look on my friends still buffeting the storm, with anxiety indeed, but not with envy. Never did a prisoner, released from his chains, feel such relief as I shall on shaking off the shackles of power. Nature intended me for the tranquil pursuits of science, by rendering them my supreme delight. But the enormities of the times in which I have lived, have forced me to take a part in resisting them, and to commit myself on the boisterous ocean of political passions. I thank God for the opportunity of retiring from them without censure and carrying with me the most consoling proofs of public approbation. I leave everything in the hands of men so able to take care of them, that if we are destined to meet misfortunes, it will be because no human wisdom could avert them. Should you return to the U.S. perhaps your curiosity may lead you to visit the hermit of Monticello. . . .

4

James Madison

1. PROCLAMATION RESUMING TRADE WITH FRANCE   NOVEMBER 2, 1810

Whereas by the fourth section of the act of Congress passed on the 1st day of May 1810, entitled "An act concerning the commercial intercourse between the United States and Great Britain and France and their dependencies, and for other purposes," it is provided "that in case either Great Britain or France shall before the 3d day of March next so revoke or modify her edicts as that they shall cease to violate the neutral commerce of the United States, which fact the President of the United States shall declare by proclamation and if the other nation shall not within three months thereafter so revoke or modify her edicts in like manner, then the third, fourth, fifth, sixth, seventh, eighth, ninth, tenth, and eighteenth sections of the act entitled 'An act to interdict the commercial intercourse between the United States and Great Britain and France and their dependencies, and for other purposes,' shall from and after the expiration of three months from the date of the proclamation aforesaid be revived and have full force and effect so far as relates to the dominions, colonies, and dependencies, and to the articles, the growth, produce, or manufacture of the dominions, colonies, and dependencies, of the nation thus refusing or neglecting to revoke or modify her edicts in the manner aforesaid. And the restrictions imposed by this act shall, from the date of such proclamation cease and be discontinued in relation to the nation revoking or modifying her decrees in the manner aforesaid;" and

Whereas it has been officially made known to this Government that the edicts of France violating the neutral commerce of the United States have been so revoked as to cease to have effect on the 1st of the present month:

Now, therefore, I, James Madison, President of the United States, do hereby proclaim that the said edicts of France have been so revoked as that they ceased on the said 1st day of the present month to violate the neutral commerce of the United States, and that from the date of these presents all the restrictions imposed by the aforesaid act shall cease and be discontinued in relation to France and their dependencies. . . .

2. WAR MESSAGE TO CONGRESS   JUNE 1, 1812

I communicate to Congress certain documents, being a continuation of those heretofore laid before them on the subject of our affairs with Great Britain.

Without going back beyond the renewal in 1803 of the war in which Great Britain is engaged, and omitting unrepaired wrongs of inferior magnitude, the conduct of her Government presents a series of acts hostile to the United States as an independent and neutral nation.

British cruisers have been in the continued practice of violating the American flag on the great highway of nations, and of seizing and carrying off persons sailing under it, not in the exercise of a belligerent right founded on the law of nations against an enemy, but of a municipal prerogative over British subjects. British jurisdiction is thus extended to neutral vessels in a situation where no laws can operate but the law of nations and the laws of the country to which the vessels belong, and a self-redress is assumed which, if British subjects were wrongfully detained and alone concerned, is that substitution of force for a resort to the responsible sovereign which falls within the definition of war. Could the seizure of British subjects in such cases be regarded as within the exercise of a belligerent right, the acknowledged laws of war, which forbid an article of captured property to be adjudged without a regular investigation before a competent tribunal, would imperiously demand the fairest trial where the sacred rights of persons were at issue. In place of such a trial these rights are subjected to the will of every petty commander.

The practice, hence, is so far from affecting British subjects alone that, under the pretext of searching for these, thousands of American citizens, under the safeguard of public law and of their national flag, have been torn from their country and from everything dear to them; have been dragged on board ships of war of a foreign nation and exposed, under the severities of their discipline, to be exiled to the most distant and deadly climes, to risk their lives in the battles of their oppressors, and to be the melancholy instruments of taking away those of their own brethren.

Against this crying enormity, which Great Britain would be so prompt to avenge if committed against herself, the United States have in vain exhausted remonstrances and expostulations, and that no proof might be wanting of their conciliatory dispositions, and no pretext left for a continuance of the practice, the British Government was formally assured of the readiness of the United States to enter into arrangements such as could not be rejected if the recovery of British subjects were the real and the sole object. The communication passed without effect.

British cruisers have been in the practice also of violating the rights and the peace of our coasts. They hover over and harass our entering and departing commerce. To the most insulting pretensions they have added the most lawless proceedings in our very harbors, and have wantonly spilt American blood within the sanctuary of our territorial jurisdiction. The principles and rules enforced by that nation . . . and disturbing her commerce, are well known. When called on, nevertheless, by the United States to punish the greater offenses committed by her own vessels, her Government has bestowed on their commanders additional marks of honor and confidence. . . .

Not content with these occasional expedients for laying waste our neutral trade, the cabinet of Britain resorted at length to the sweeping system of blockades, under the name of orders in council, which has been molded and managed as might best suit its political views, its commercial jealousies, or the avidity of British cruisers. . . .

When deprived of this flimsy veil for a prohibition of our trade with her enemy by the repeal of his prohibition of our trade with Great Britain, her cabinet, instead of a corresponding repeal or a practical discontinuance of its orders, formally avowed a determination to persist in them against the United States until the markets of her enemy should be laid open to British products, thus asserting an obligation on a neutral power to require one belligerent to encourage by its internal regulations the trade of another belligerent, contradicting her own practice toward all nations, in peace as well as in war, and betraying the insincerity of those professions which inculcated a belief that, having resorted to her orders with regret, she was anxious to find an occasion for putting an end to them.

Abandoning still more all respect for the neutral rights of the United States and for its own consistency, the British Government now demands as prerequisites to a repeal of its orders as they relate to the United States that a formality should be observed in the repeal of the French decrees nowise necessary to their termination nor exemplified by British usage, and that the French repeal, besides including that portion of the decrees which operates within a territorial jurisdiction, as well as that which operates on the high seas, against the commerce of the United States should not be a single and special repeal in relation to the United States, but should be extended to whatever other neutral nations unconnected with them may be affected by those decrees. And as an additional insult, they are called on for a formal disavowal of conditions and pretensions advanced by the French Government for which the United States are so far from having made themselves responsible that, in official explanations which have been published to the world, and in a correspondence of the American minister at London with the British minister for foreign affairs such a responsibility was explicitly and emphatically disclaimed.

It has become, indeed, sufficiently certain that the commerce of the United States is to be sacrificed, not as interfering with the belligerent rights of Great Britain; not as supplying the wants of her enemies, which she herself supplies; but as interfering with the monopoly which she covets for her own commerce and navigation. She carries on a war against the lawful commerce of a friend that she may the better carry on a commerce with an enemy—a commerce polluted by the forgeries and perjuries which are for the most part the only passports by which it can succeed. . . .

In reviewing the conduct of Great Britain toward the United States our attention is necessarily drawn to the warfare just renewed by the savages on one of our extensive frontiers—a warfare which is known to spare neither age nor sex and to be distinguished by feature peculiarly shocking to humanity. It is difficult to account for the activity and combinations . . . among tribes in constant intercourse with British traders and garrisons without connecting their hostility with that influence and without recollecting the authenticated examples of such interpositions heretofore furnished by the officers and agents of that Government. . . .

Whether the United States shall continue passive under these progressive usurpations and these accumulating wrongs, or, opposing force to force in defense of their national rights, shall commit a just cause into the hands of the Almighty Disposer of Events, avoiding all connections which might entangle it in the contest or views of other powers, and preserving a constant readiness to concur in an honorable reestablishment of peace and friendship, is a solemn question which the Constitution wisely confides to the legislative department of the Government. In recommending it to their early deliberations I am happy in the assurance that the decision will be worthy of the enlightened and patriotic councils of a virtuous, a free, and a powerful nation. . . .

3. A NATIONAL BANK RECONSIDERED   DECEMBER 5, 1815

. . . The arrangements of the finances with a view to the receipts and expenditures of a permanent peace establishment will necessarily enter into the deliberations of Congress during the present session. It is true that the improved condition of the public revenue will not only afford the means of maintaining the faith of the Government with its creditors inviolate, and of prosecuting successfully the measures of the most liberal policy, but will also justify an immediate alleviation of the burdens imposed by the necessities of the war. It is, however, essential to every modification of the finances that the benefits of an uniform national currency should be restored to the community. The absence of the precious metals will, it is believed, be a temporary evil, but until they can again be rendered the general medium of exchange, it devolves on the wisdom of Congress to provide a substitute which shall equally engage the confidence and accommodate the wants of the citizens throughout the Union. If the operation of the State banks cannot produce this result, the probable operation of a national bank will merit consideration; and if neither of these expedients be deemed effectual it may become necessary to ascertain the terms upon which the notes of the Government (no longer required as an instrument of credit) shall be issued upon motives of general policy as a common medium of circulation. . . .

4. NATIONAL SEMINARY PROPOSED   DECEMBER 5, 1815

. . . The present is a favorable season . . . for bringing again into view the establishment of a national seminary of learning within the District of Columbia . . . subject to the authority of the General Government. Such an institution claims the patronage of Congress as a monument of their solicitude for the advancement of knowledge, without which the blessings of liberty cannot be fully enjoyed or long preserved; as a model instructive in the formation of other seminaries; as a nursery of enlightened preceptors, and as a central resort of youth and genius from every part of their country, diffusing on their return examples of those national feelings, those liberal sentiments, and those congenial manners which contribute cement to our Union and strength to the great political fabric of which that is the foundation. . . .

5

James Monroe

1. STATEHOOD FOR ILLINOIS   NOVEMBER 16, 1818

. . . I communicate with great satisfaction the accession of another State [Illinois] to our Union, because I perceive from the proof afforded by the additions already made the regular progress and sure consummation of a policy of which history affords no example, and of which the good effect cannot be too highly estimated. By extending our Government by the principles of the Constitution over the vast territory within our limits, on the Lakes and the Mississippi and its numerous streams, new life and vigor are infused into every part of our system. By increasing the number of States the confidence of the State governments in their own security is increased and their jealousy of the National Government proportionately diminished. The impracticality of one consolidated government for this great and growing nation will be more apparent and will be universally admitted. Incapable of exercising local authority except for general purposes, the General Government will no longer be dreaded. In those cases of a local nature and for all the great purposes for which it was instituted its authority will be cherished. Each government will acquire new force and a greater freedom of action within its proper sphere. Other inestimable advantages will follow. . . .

2. COMMENTS ON THE MISSOURI COMPROMISE   FEBRUARY 19, 1820

. . . The Intelligencer will communicate to you some account of the proceedings of Congress on the Missouri Question, & particularly of the late votes taken on different propositions in the Senate. It seems, that a resolution was adopted on the 17th , which establishes a line, to commence, from the western boundary of Missouri, in Lat: 36. 30. & run westward indefinitely, north of which slavery should be prohibited; but permitted South of it. Missouri & Arkansas, as is presumed, to be admitted, without restraint. By the terms applied to the restriction "forever" it inferre'd . . . that the restraint should apply to territories, after they become States, as well as before. This will increase the difficulty incident to an arrangement of this subject, otherwise sufficiently great, in any form, in which it can be presented. Many think that the right exists in one instance & not in the other. I have never known a question so menacing to the tranquility and even the continuance of our Union as the present one. All other subjects have given way to it, & appear to be almost forgotten. As however there is a vast portion of intelligence & virtue in the body of the people, & the bond of Union has heretofore prov'd sufficiently strong to triumph over all attempts against it, I have great confidence that this effort will not be less unavailing.

3. VETO OF THE CUMBERLAND ROAD BILL   MAY 4, 1822

Having duly considered the bill entitled "An act for the preservation and repair of the Cumberland road," it is with deep regret, approving as I do the policy, that I am compelled to object to its passage and to return the bill to the House of Representatives, in which it originated, under a conviction that Congress do not possess the power under the Constitution to pass such a law.

A power to establish turnpikes with gates and tolls, and to enforce the collection of tolls by penalties, implies a power to adopt and execute a complete system of internal improvement. A right to impose duties to be paid by all persons passing a certain road, and on horses and carriages, as is done by this bill, involves the right to take the land from the proprietor on a valuation and to pass laws for the protection of the road from injuries, and if it exist as to one road it exists as to any other, and to as many roads as Congress may think proper to establish. A right to legislate for one of these purposes is a right to legislate for the others. It is a complete right of jurisdiction and sovereignty for all the purposes of internal improvement, and not merely the right of applying money under the power vested in Congress to make appropriations, under which power, with the consent of the States through which this road passes, the work was originally commenced, and has been so far executed. I am of opinion that Congress do not possess this power; that the States individually cannot grant it, for although they may assent to the appropriation of money within their limits for such purposes, they can grant no power of jurisdiction or sovereignty by special compacts with the United States. This power can be granted only by an amendment to the Constitution and in the mode prescribed by it.

If the power exist, it must be either because it has been specifically granted to the United States or that it is incidental to some power which has been specifically granted. If we examine the specific grants of power we do not find it among them, nor is it incidental to any power which has been specifically granted.

It has never been contended that the power was specifically granted. It is claimed only as being incidental to some one or more of the powers which are specifically granted. The following are the powers from which it is said to be derived:

First, from the right to establish post-offices and post-roads; second, from the right to declare war; third, to regulate commerce; fourth, to pay the debts and provide for the common defense and general welfare; fifth, from the power to make all laws necessary and proper for carrying into execution all the powers vested by the Constitution in the Government of the United States or in any department or officer thereof; sixth and lastly, from the power to dispose of and make all needful rules and regulations respecting the territory and other property of the United States.

According to my judgment it cannot be derived from either of those powers, nor from all of them united, and in consequence it does not exist.

Having stated my objections to the bill, I should now cheerfully communicate at large the reasons on which they are founded if I had time to reduce them to such form as to include them in this paper. The advanced stage of the session renders that impossible. Having at the commencement of my service in this high trust considered it a duty to express the opinion that the United States do not possess the power in question, and to suggest for the consideration of Congress the propriety of recommending to the States an amendment to the Constitution to vest the power in the United States, my attention has been often drawn to the subject since, in consequence whereof I have occasionally committed my sentiments to paper respecting it. The form which this exposition has assumed is not such as I should have given it, had it been intended for Congress, nor is it concluded. Nevertheless, as it contains my views on this subject, being one which I deem of very high importance, and which in many of its bearings has now become peculiarly urgent, I will communicate it to Congress, if in my power, in the course of the day, or certainly on Monday next.

4. MONROE DOCTRINE   DECEMBER 2, 1823

. . . It was stated at the commencement of the last session that a great effort was then making in Spain and Portugal to improve the condition of the people of those countries, and that it appeared to be conducted with extraordinary moderation. It need scarcely be remarked that the result has been so far very different from what was then anticipated. Of events in that quarter of the globe, with which we have so much intercourse and from which we derive our origin, we have always been anxious and interested spectators. The citizens of the United States cherish sentiments the most friendly in favor of the liberty and happiness of their fellow-men on that side of the Atlantic. In the wars of the European powers in matters relating to themselves we have never taken any part, nor does it comport with our policy so to do. It is only when our rights are invaded or seriously menaced that we resent injuries or make preparation for our defense. With the movements in this hemisphere we are of necessity more immediately connected, and by causes which must be obvious to all enlightened and impartial observers. The political system of the allied powers is essentially different in this respect from that of America. This difference proceeds from that which exists in their respective Governments; and to the defense of our own, which has been achieved by the loss of so much blood and treasure, and matured by the wisdom of their most enlightened citizens, and under which we have enjoyed unexampled felicity, this whole nation is devoted. We owe it, therefore, to candor and to the amicable relations existing between the United States and those powers to declare that we should consider any attempt on their part to extend their system to any portion of this hemisphere as dangerous to our peace and safety. With the existing colonies or dependencies of any European power we have not interfered and shall not interfere. But with the Governments who have declared their independence and maintained it, and whose independence we have, on great consideration and on just principles, acknowledged, we could not view any interposition for the purpose of oppressing them, or controlling in any other manner their destiny, by any European power in any other light than as the manifestation of an unfriendly disposition toward the United States. In the war between those new Governments and Spain we declared our neutrality at the time of their recognition, and to this we have adhered, and shall continue to adhere, provided no change shall occur which, in the judgment of the competent authorities of this Government, shall make a corresponding change on the part of the United States indispensable to their security.

The late events in Spain and Portugal show that Europe is still unsettled. Of this important fact no stronger proof can be adduced than that the allied powers should have thought it proper . . . to have interposed by force in the internal concerns of Spain. To what extent such interposition may be carried, on the same principle, is a question in which all independent powers whose governments differ from theirs are interested, even those most remote, and surely none more so than the United States. Our policy in regard to Europe, which was adopted at an early stage of the wars which have so long agitated that quarter of the globe, nevertheless remains the same, which is, not to interfere in the internal concerns of any of its powers; to consider the government de facto as the legitimate government for us; to cultivate friendly relations with it, and to preserve those relations by a frank, firm, and manly policy, meeting in all instances the just claims of every power, submitting to injuries from none. But in regard to those continents circumstances are eminently and conspicuously different. It is impossible that the allied powers should extend their political system to any portion of either continent without endangering our peace and happiness; nor can anyone believe that our southern brethren . . . would adopt it of their own accord. It is equally impossible, therefore, that we should behold such interposition in any form with indifference. If we look to the comparative strength and resources of Spain and those new Governments, and their distance from each other, it must be obvious that she can never subdue them. It is still the true policy of the United States to leave the parties to themselves, in the hope that other powers will pursue the same course. . . .

6

John Quincy Adams

1. PLAN OF INTERNAL IMPROVEMENTS   DECEMBER 6, 1825

. . . Upon this first occasion of addressing the Legislature of the Union, with which I have been honored, in presenting to their view the execution so far as it has been effected of the measures sanctioned by them for promoting the internal improvement of our country, I cannot close the communication without recommending to their calm and persevering consideration the general principle in a more enlarged extent. The great object of the institution of civil government is the improvement of the condition of those who are parties to the social compact, and no government, in whatever form constituted, can accomplish the lawful ends of its institution but in proportion as it improves the condition of those over whom it is established. Roads and canals, by multiplying and facilitating the communications and intercourse between distant regions and multitudes of men, are among the most important means of improvement. But moral, political, intellectual improvement are duties assigned by the Author of Our Existence to social no less than to individual man. For the fulfillment of those duties governments are invested with power, and to the attainment of the end—the progressive improvement of the condition of the governed—the exercise of delegated powers is a duty as sacred and indispensable as the usurpation of powers not granted is criminal and odious. Among the first, perhaps the very first, instrument for the improvement of the condition of men is knowledge, and to the acquisition of much of the knowledge adapted to the wants, the comforts, and enjoyments of human life, public institutions and seminaries of learning are essential. So convinced of this was the first of my predecessors in this office, now first in the memory, as, living, he was first in the hearts, of our countrymen, that once and again in his addresses to the Congresses with whom he cooperated in the public service he earnestly recommended the establishment of seminaries of learning, to prepare for all the emergencies of peace and war—a national university and a military academy. With respect to the latter, had he lived to the present day, in turning his eyes to the institution at West Point he would have enjoyed the gratification of his most earnest wishes; but in surveying the city which has been honored with his name he would have seen the spot of earth which he had destined and bequeathed to the use and benefit of his country as the site for an university still bare and barren.

In assuming her station among the civilized nations of the earth it would seem that our country had contracted the engagement to contribute her share of mind, of labor, and of expense to the improvement of those parts of knowledge which lie beyond the reach of individual acquisition, and particularly to geographical and astronomical science. Looking back to the history only of the half century since the declaration of our independence, and observing the generous emulation with which the Governments of France, Great Britain, and Russia have devoted the genius, the intelligence, the treasures of their respective nations to the common improvement of the species in these branches of science, is it not incumbent upon us to inquire whether we are not bound by obligations of a high and honorable character to contribute our portion of energy and exertion to the common stock? The voyages of discovery prosecuted in the course of that time at the expense of those nations have not only redounded to their glory, but to the improvement of human knowledge. We have been partakers of that improvement and owe for it a sacred debt, not only of gratitude, but of equal or proportional exertion in the same common cause. Of the cost of these undertakings, if the mere expenditures of outfit, equipment, and completion of the expeditions were to be considered the only charges, it would be unworthy of a great and generous nation to take a second thought. One hundred expeditions of circumnavigation like those of Cook and La Perouse would not burden the exchequer of the nation fitting them out so much as the ways and means of defraying a single campaign in war. But if we take into the account the lives of those benefactors of mankind of which their services in the cause of their species were the purchase, how shall the cost of those heroic enterprises be estimated, and what compensation can be made to them or to their countries for them? Is it not by bearing them in affectionate remembrance? Is it not still more by imitating their example—by enabling countrymen of our own to pursue the same career and to hazard their lives in the same cause?

In inviting the attention of Congress to the subject of internal improvements upon a view thus enlarged it is not my design to recommend the equipment of an expedition for circumnavigating the globe for purposes of scientific research and inquiry. We have objects of useful investigation nearer home, and to which our cares may be more beneficially applied. The interior of our own territories has yet been very imperfectly explored. Our coasts along many degrees of latitude upon the shores of the Pacific Ocean, though much frequented by our spirited commercial navigators, have been barely visited by our public ships. The River of the West, first fully discovered and navigated by a countryman of our own, still bears the name of the ship in which he ascended its waters, and claims the protection of our armed national flag at its mouth. With the establishment of a military post there or at some other point of that coast, recommended by my predecessor and already matured in the deliberations of the last Congress, I would suggest the expediency of connecting the equipment of a public ship for the exploration of the whole northwest coast of this continent. . . .

Connected with the establishment of an university, or separate from it, might be undertaken the erection of an astronomical observatory, with provision for the support of an astronomer, to be in constant attendance of observation upon the phenomena of the heavens, and for the periodical publication of his observations. It is with no feeling of pride as an American that the remark may be made that on the comparatively small territorial surface of Europe there are existing upward of 130 of these light-houses of the skies, while throughout the whole American hemisphere there is not one. If we reflect a moment upon the discoveries which in the last four centuries have been made in the physical constitution of the universe by the means of these buildings and of observers stationed in them, shall we doubt of their usefulness to every nation? And while scarcely a year passes over our heads without bringing some new astronomical discovery to light, which we must fain receive at second hand from Europe, are we not cutting ourselves off from the means of returning light for light while we have neither observatory nor observer upon our half of the globe and the earth revolves in perpetual darkness to our unsearching eyes?. . . .

2. FIFTY YEARS OF INDEPENDENCE   DECEMBER 6, 1826

. . . I trust that it will not be deemed inappropriate to the occasion and purposes upon which we are here assembled to indulge a momentary retrospect, combining in a single glance the period of our origin as a national confederation with that of our present existence, at the precise interval of half a century from each other. Since your last meeting at this place the fiftieth anniversary of the day when our independence was declared has been celebrated throughout our land, and on that day, while every heart was bounding with joy and every voice was tuned to gratulation, amid the blessings of freedom and independence which the sires of a former age had handed down to their children, two of the principal actors in that solemn scene—the hand that penned the ever-memorable Declaration and the voice that sustained it in debate—were by one summons, at the distance of 700 miles from each other, called before the Judge of All to account for their deeds done upon earth. They departed cheered by the benedictions of their country, to whom they left the inheritance of their fame and the memory of their bright example. If we turn our thoughts to the condition of their country, in the contrast of the first and last day of that half century, how resplendent and sublime is the transition from gloom to glory! . . . we see the first day marked with the fullness and vigor of youth, in the pledge of their lives, their fortunes, and their sacred honor to the cause of freedom and of mankind; and on the last, extended on the bed of death, with but sense and sensibility left to breathe a last aspiration to Heaven of blessing upon their country, may we not humbly hope that to them too it was a pledge of gloom to glory, and that while their mortal vestments were sinking into the clod of the valley their emancipated spirits were ascending to the bosom of their God!

III

NATIONAL SECURITY AND GROWING PAINS

ANDREW JACKSON'S ADMINISTRATION ranks as one of the most important in American history. In the public view he was admired as a decisive man of action. This public estimate prompted a popular democratic movement which brought him to the Executive Mansion. In 1828, all but two states sanctioned popular voting for the electors, forcing politics to take on a new tone as the campaign was fought in newspapers, journals, and before mass meetings. The term "campaign" was a military term now carried over to the political arena. The mass meetings and the associated emergence of the professional politician indicated a new politics was taking shape.

Caucuses of state legislatures put forth two candidates—John Quincy Adams and Andrew Jackson. Little mention was made of the problems of the day. The tariff, internal improvements, and foreign policy, were shunted aside. Advocates concentrated instead on slanderous statements to arouse partisan hate.

An alliance of the West, the South, and the working classes of the Middle Atlantic States, won the election for Jackson. The indomitable Indian fighter and military hero received 171 ballots to 83 for Adams. It was a landslide electoral victory. There were coattails attached to this presidential mandate. The Democrats now controlled both houses of Congress. For the first time since the founding of the Republic, a president hailed from an inland state.

On March 4, 1829 the President-elect arrived at Capitol Hill. Surrounded by a throng of supporters and well-wishers of every description, the man of the hour stepped forward at noon, on the East Portico of the Capitol Building, and took the oath of office.

The following spring the President offered a memorable "Toast". The Jefferson Day Dinner, April 13, 1830, held at Brown's Indian Queen Hotel in Washington, was planned to align the Democratic Party with Jeffersonian principles and to celebrate the new alliance between the West and the South. Delivered in a most dramatic setting and with Vice President John C. Calhoun, the chief exponent of nullification seated at the table, the representative of the Union measured his words of tribute. The toast he proffered was later described as ringing through the banquet hall like one of the General's strident battlefield commands. The toast clarified Jackson's position on nullification.

The words of the President served to strengthen the hearts of unionists throughout the nation. The Jackson toast was reminiscent of the celebrated Webster-Hayne debate. Senator Robert Y. Hayne of South Carolina had urged the formation of a coalition of Southern and Western interests. He also promoted the right of a state to nullify a federal law. Webster did not dispute the right of a state or states to go to court or attempt to amend the constitution but he adamantly objected to the idea that a state could simply nullify federal laws. The renowned legal master from Massachusetts reasoned that the doctrine of nullification would produce anarchy and civil war. His answer to Hayne was: "Liberty and Union, now and forever, one and inseparable."

In the same spirit, Jackson raised his glass and directed his eyes at Vice President Calhoun. The Toast was simple. The salutation was "Our Union: It Must Be Preserved." Calhoun responded: "The Union, next to our liberty, most dear. May we always remember that it can only be preserved by distributing equally the benefits and burdens of the Union."

General Jackson was a man of action. He lived in a time of heroes. Historians have seen him as the embodiment of his time. The "Age of Jackson" bore his brand. He symbolized America for many of his fellow citizens. The victory he garnered over the British in the famous battle of New Orleans at the conclusion of the "Second War for Independence" was legendary. He was an American patriot who walked in the footsteps of the principal hero of the first struggle for Independence.

As a youth, Jackson was prone to violent behavior. Lacking fatherly direction and guidance, Jackson was in fact a juvenile delinquent engaged in street fighting and gang activity. He remained a fighter all his life. When the American people elevated him as their Commander-in-Chief, Jackson fought for his political principles. As President he used the veto as a weapon and waged war against the "monster" bank.

The second Bank of the United States had been granted a 20-year federal charter in 1816. A private corporation with immense financial powers, the Bank served as the depository for United States funds without paying interest. Its notes were exempt from taxation. The Bank established a reliable and more uniform currency.

As the Bank grew, its branches vigorously competed with local banks for business. When several states taxed the branch offices, the Supreme Court intervened. In McCulloch vs. Maryland (1819), the Court ruled that a state could not tax a corporation chartered by the United States. Chief Justice John Marshall explained: "the power to tax involves the power to destroy."

In his first Annual Message to Congress in 1829, Jackson attacked the Bank as monopolistic and unconstitutional. The President served notice to the directors and shareholders that he would not recommend renewal. Jackson vetoed the re-charter bill on July 10, 1832. In a stinging message, the President repudiated Marshall and Hamilton and lashed out at the rich men who "have besought us to make them richer by act of Congress. By attempting to gratify their desires we have in the results of our legislation arrayed section against section . . . in a fearful commotion which threatens to shake the foundations of our Union."

Nicholas Biddle, the director of the Bank, described the message as "a manifesto of anarchy." The Bank now became the major issue in the 1832 campaign. Jackson would ride it all the way for a return trip to the Executive Mansion.

Upon re-election Jackson responded to a challenge from another quarter. Nullification was an act by which a state suspended a federal law. The right of nullification was first asserted by Virginia and Kentucky in the Resolutions of 1798–1799. These resolutions stated that the Union was a compact between sovereign states. Therefore, the states could nullify federal legislation within its borders. The most noted example of nullification occurred in South Carolina. Opposition to the protective tariff developed in the South during the 1820s. Hostility grew to such proportions that the South Carolina legislature carried the issue to the voters. After Congress passed the Tariff Act of 1832, the legislature called a state convention (November 19, 1832). This body adopted an Ordinance of Nullification declaring the Tariff Acts of 1828 and 1832 oppressive, unconstitutional, null and void, and not binding. Appeals to the federal courts were forbidden and state officials were required to take an oath to support the Ordinance.

A furious President issued a proclamation which denounced nullification as rebellion and treason. He warned the people of South Carolina that he would use every power at his command to enforce the laws. Before the date for the Ordinance to take effect (February 1, 1833), measures for reducing the tariff were introduced by Congress. On March 11, 1833 another convention called by the South Carolina legislature rescinded the Ordinance of Nullification. A crisis between South Carolina and the national government had been averted.

Jackson took his duty and oath of office to the utmost level of gravity. There would be no breach of decorum on his watch. Protocol would be rigidly adhered to with military precision. Towards this end the President issued careful instructions to officers of the government underlining the Constitutional prohibition with regard to accepting gifts "under any circumstances" from foreign powers. Greatly disturbed at the news that the Consul of the United States at Tangiers had accepted a gift from the Emperor of Morocco of two horses and a lion, he moved with great dispatch to see those articles surrendered to the Government. It was to this end that Jackson communicated his thoughts to the Congress on January 6, 1834. The Constitution of the United States would be adhered to in every particular. Members of his administration were not to accept any award or gift from any foreign source.

In a related document, dated April 15, 1834, Jackson cited Article II of the Constitution. He pointed to two of the most central themes of the Constitutional Presidency. The first pertains to the vesting power. The Constitution grants executive power to the President in simple, unmistakable language: "the executive power is vested in a President of the United States." Second, Jackson clearly understood his sworn duty to take "care that the laws be faithfully executed." This duty applies, Jackson explained to "the entire action of the executive department." The faithful execution of the laws required that power "should remain in his hands."

On the first day of summer, President Jackson put his hands to work on an executive order to honor a friend of the United States. The idea of liberty is a theme that runs through the history of the American presidency. In announcing the death of the Marquis de Lafayette, the executive order paid solemn tribute to a friend of liberty and the rights of man. Jackson respected Lafayette for his courage and character and as a soldier of freedom. All patriotic Americans appreciated the enormous contribution of the distinguished Frenchman to the success of the American Revolution. As the tribute and remembrance noted: "In early life he embarked in that contest which secured freedom and independence to our country . . . his memory will be second only to that of Washington in the hearts of the American people. . . ." It was a well-deserved tribute to a loyal friend of liberty.

With respect to policy matters in the Jackson Administration which live on in American memory, nothing has quite the nasty aftertaste or odor of the President's Indian removal policy. Andrew Jackson relentlessly pursued the complete removal of Indians living east of the Mississippi. In 1830, at his insistence, Congress authorized the President to exchange lands held by tribes within the states for land in the Great Plains, an area then thought to be unsuited for Anglo-Saxon habitation. Forceful Indian cessions now accelerated as American settlers migrated from east to west.

It was in the South, however, that the removal policy encountered its most stubborn resistance. The policy and the resistance led to truly tragic results. Here the tribes, especially the Cherokee and the Creeks, had built permanent homes. On these lands they maintained cattle herds, raised varied crops, built grist mills, sent their children to missionary schools, and had representative governments. They opposed the arguments, threats and bribes offered by agents sent to induce them to remove to the Great Plains.

In 1828, Georgia declared the laws of the Cherokee Nation void after June 1, 1830. White residents living within the Nation had to obtain a license from the Governor of Georgia and vow allegiance to the state. Chief Justice John Marshall held for the Supreme Court in 1832 that the

Cherokee Nation had exclusive jurisdiction within its own territory and Georgia law "can have no force." Georgia defied the Court and was supported by Jackson who is reported to have said: "John Marshall has made his decision, now let him enforce it." Under the Treaty of December 29, the Cherokees surrendered all their lands east of the Mississippi in return for transportation costs and land in the new Indian Territory.

Jackson explained his removal policy of the southern Indians in his Seventh Annual Message to Congress on December 7, 1835. From the perspective of the Creeks and the Cherokee this was a date which could be said to live in infamy. Thus began the tragic journey along the famous "trail of tears."

Historians and students of the American presidency will benefit from a close inspection of Jackson's tenure in office. He met issues as they arose, sometimes acting on his own, but more often on suggestions of his advisors. He had little understanding of the democratic movement that bears his name. He supported it primarily because it supported him.

On the morning he left office, Jackson published his Farewell Address. He reviewed his two terms. Obviously writing about slavery, Jackson warned of the dangers emanating from sectional differences that based party divergence solely on geographical distinctions. He appealed for loyalty to the Union. On this vital subject, he never equivocated.

President Van Buren had big shoes to fill. As the successor to Jackson it was only natural that he would come under scrutiny. It was hardly a fair test. He tended to be perceived as something like the tail on the donkey. The truth is Martin Van Buren was a seasoned master of politics. In fact, he had earned a reputation for political ability and shrewdness. Hailing from Kinderhook in Columbia County in New York State, he became known as the "sly fox from Kinderhook." Van Buren was the brains behind the machine at the statehouse known as the "Albany Regency." There was a certain political genius attached to the man and by all rights he and Jackson deserve to be considered twin architects of the second American party system.

Van Buren planned to follow Jackson's lead by endorsing programs to help both southern and western farmers and the growing working class of the North. Within two months of his inauguration, a general financial and business collapse partially caused by over-speculative investments in land and industry confronted the President. The war on the Bank of the United States had also contributed to economic instability. In any event Van Buren was left with a serious financial panic. It was a ditch from which the President failed to extricate himself. In the "Panic of 1837" stock prices tumbled. Imports fell and customs revenue dwindled. In May 1837, banks had suspended specie payments so that no one could redeem paper money in gold or silver. In New York City, unemployed workers demonstrated against high rents and inflated food prices. In the South, cotton prices tumbled.

Van Buren blamed the situation on the banks and stock speculation. On September 4, 1837, he asked Congress to enact an independent treasury system. This would enable the federal government to keep its funds in its own depositories entirely separate from the banking system. The goal was to sharply reduce speculation since bankers would be deprived of government funds as reserves for issuing loans and making investments. Advisors believed that an independent treasury system would stabilize the economy and reduce financial panics. In January 1840, after more than two years of debate, the Independent Treasury Act finally passed.

Not only did the United States face a serious economic crisis but, as so often happens in history, internal domestic and economic weakness provoked internal and external actions which imperiled national security. So the economic correction cycle under the Van Buren watch tended to undermine American diplomatic policy and invited foreign foes to flirt with American border security.

Problems erupted on northern and southern borders. At such moments American citizens tend to view timid action or inaction of the national government as impotence with regard to protecting the national interest. Given that perception, citizens feel the need to take action into their own hands. Such was the general predicament of the Van Buren administration in 1837. Events trended beyond the resources available and both borders were precarious.

In November 1837, William Lyon Mackenzie began a rebellion in Upper Canada. Defeated by British forces, Mackenzie took refuge on Navy Island on the Canadian side of the Niagara River. American sympathizers supplied them with arms, food, and recruits. A small steamboat, the *Caroline,* was used to ferry supplies to the rebels. Canadian militia crossed to the American side of the border on December 29, 1837 and seized the ship. The steamer was towed to midstream and set afire.

Van Buren ordered the State Department to protest vigorously to the British Minister in Washington. The protest was ignored. Patriotic indignation flared up along the US–Canadian perimeter. The President called out the New York militia to prevent violence. On January 5, 1838, in order to avoid a third war with Britain, Van Buren issued a neutrality proclamation warning Americans to desist from hostile actions. Emotions raged at a feverish pitch. The border disorder persisted throughout the Van Buren years.

Border insecurity likewise prevailed on the southern boundary. Here again Van Buren displayed an inability to cope with the problem. Incidents transpired on a daily basis on the northern frontier and were reflected as well on the southern boundary, prompting the President to state on January 8, 1838 that "existing laws are insufficient to guard against hostile invasion." Under the circumstances he acknowledged the futility of any prosecution of illegal actions and lamented that "the Executive is powerless in many cases to prevent the commission of them, even when in possession of ample evidence of an intention on the part of evil-disposed persons to violate our laws." National solutions would have to await improved economic conditions and new leadership.

President William Henry Harrison was not the answer. His campaign for the presidency aped in many respects that of his fellow general Andrew Jackson. Both men brought their military backgrounds to the political arena, even changing the political vocabulary to reflect the language of war, combat, and the battlefield. Henceforth, prospective presidents would be organized in "campaigns" for the post of Commander-in-Chief. Harrison did not endure. His presidency ended shortly after his inauguration. Harrison presented the longest Inaugural Address and the briefest presidency on record. In that brief interim Harrison addressed the "great dread."

"The great dread," said Harrison, "seems to have been that the reserved powers of the States would be absorbed by those of the Federal Government and a consolidated power established, leaving to the States the shadow only of that independent action for which they had so zealously contended and on the preservation of which they relied as the last hope of liberty."

Upon the death of Harrison the torch was passed to Vice President John Tyler. This was a first for the nation. Would he be a full-fledged president? The answer was affirmative. "For the first time in our history the person elected to the Vice-Presidency of the United States, by the happening of a contingency provided for in the Constitution," wrote Tyler "has had devolved upon him the Presidential office." Tyler emphatically communicated to the nation that he was not "acting" president or "interim" president, but in fact President of the United States. Tyler passed the test with high marks. His posture was well received by the American people and the passage of the presidency was cemented in the public mind.

Meeting the first test head on, he laid claim to the constitutional powers of the presidency. The mess he inherited was addressed. A notable achievement of the Tyler administration was the

Webster–Ashburton Treaty. The various Canadian boundary disputes were settled by negotiation and ratification of this treaty in 1842. Secretary of State Daniel Webster usually has been given the credit for the settlement of the nation's boundary disputes with Great Britain. Many provisions were proposed, however, by Tyler. One treaty section included joint naval squadrons to operate off the coast of West Africa to suppress the slave trade. Both the President and the Secretary successfully concluded the complicated negotiations with skill, tact, and dignity.

The policy of the United States during the Texas War for Independence (1835–1836) was decidedly not neutral. The sentiments of Texans and many Americans favored immediate annexation by the United States. Mexico adamantly refused to recognize Texas independence. Annexation, under such circumstances, might provoke war. Another complication involved prospective incorporation of slave territory into the Union. Obviously, a development along those lines would accelerate the growing antislavery attitude in the North. The timing of events proved crucial. Jackson waited until his last day in office, March 4, 1837, before recognizing the new Texas Republic.

Tyler enthusiastically supported the admission of Texas into the Union. He believed that the expansion of slavery was vital to the southern economy. He ordered his Secretary of State to draft the necessary treaty with Texas. The treaty was submitted to the Senate on April 22, 1844 accompanied by a message from Tyler urging annexation. Tyler cited national interest, the security of the southern states, and the danger posed by Great Britain.

The Senate rejected the treaty, on June 8, 1844, by 35 votes to 16. Abolitionists contended President Tyler and Secretary Calhoun conspired with slaveholders to promote their interests. Tyler tried an end run. He submitted the Texas question in the form of a joint resolution of Congress. The proposal failed. After the 1844 presidential election but prior to the inauguration of the expansionist James K. Polk, Tyler again appealed for a joint resolution of annexation. This time he succeeded as Congress viewed Polk's election as a plebiscite. The joint resolution action of February 1845 marked the first time such a procedure was used to approve a treaty or acquire territory.

James K. Polk won the presidential election of 1844 by a slim margin. Polk had been a "dark horse" for his party's nomination. Coming from the back of the pack, his triumph presaged the birth of a race horse metaphor in American politics. Henceforth presidential candidates would be handicapped by political pundits. In the general election, Polk gained a clear majority of the electoral vote despite falling short of a popular majority. The narrow victory implied a public endorsement of continued territorial growth of the Republic.

On March 4, 1845 Polk was inaugurated. The crowd gathered before the Capitol stood in the pouring rain. The inaugural message reaffirmed the Democratic platform declaration on Texas. Polk slowly read statements accenting each word: "I regard the question of annexation as belonging exclusively to the United States and Texas as the prerogative of two independent powers."

Two days later, Mexico formally protested against the annexation of Texas, calling it the "most unjust act of aggression in the annals of modern history." At the end of March, the Mexican government broke diplomatic relations with the United States and took steps to augment its armed forces. Mexico mobilized and moved closer to war. From a vantage point south of the border, Texas was a province in rebellion. In response, the Commander-in-Chief deployed troops to the new state to protect it against a possible Mexican attack. He also had his eye on the Mexican province of California and the superb ports of San Francisco, Monterey, and San Diego. Given the prospects for war, Polk weighed the chances that military conflict with Mexico might whet colonial appetites in Europe. England, France, or even Russia conceivably could see an opportunity to seize California. The American consulate at Liverpool reported to Polk that "all Europe" coveted California.

Mexico ignored Polk's offer to buy California. Attempts to foster a local revolution aborted. War with Mexico came in 1846. California's annexation would follow war. In anticipation of that event, Polk expanded the Monroe Doctrine. In his first Annual Message on December 2, 1845, the President declared: "the people of this continent alone have the right to decide their own destiny." Pointedly the President gave due notice that "no future European colony or dominion" could be established in North America without United States approval. These corollaries enunciated by Polk became an integral part of American foreign policy.

President Polk fully embraced the concept of "Manifest Destiny." This was the belief that the United States was destined to expand its territory to the Pacific Ocean. In keeping with this destiny and the mission to absorb Texas and California, Polk's Inaugural Address also asserted the American title to Oregon to be "clear and unquestionable."

In September 1845, Polk appointed former Congressman John Slidell of Louisiana as envoy-minister on a secret mission to Mexico. His instructions were to secure Upper California and the territory of New Mexico. Slidell also was authorized to settle the southern boundary of Texas at the Rio Grande. In addition, the United States would assume the claims of its nationals against Mexico. The Mexican government refused to receive Slidell. They considered the American offer both an insult to their national honor and a threat to their territorial integrity.

When Slidell's report reached Washington, on January 12, 1846, President Polk immediately ordered General Zachary Taylor to move his army across the Nueces River and occupy the area up to the left bank of the Rio Grande. Taylor executed his orders by the end of March. American guns had the Mexican town of Matamoros in their sites. America's show of force might encourage the Mexicans to reconsider their refusal to negotiate a purchase.

The Mexican government, under new leadership, offered to negotiate the single issue of Texas. Polk dismissed this offer as insincere. The President informed the Cabinet on May 9, 1846, that he had begun to draft a war message to Congress. All nodded approval except Secretary of the Navy, George Bancroft, who thought that war should not be declared until Mexico initiated a hostile act. That day news reached Washington that Mexican cavalry had crossed the Rio Grande and had engaged in a skirmish with American soldiers. The Secretary's conscience had been placated. On Sunday, May 10th, Polk prepared his war message to Congress and confided to his diary: "I regretted the necessity . . . to spend the Sabbath in the manner I have."

On the northern border, Polk preferred diplomatic resolution. Towards that peaceful resolution of the U.S. and Canadian boundary dispute and the "state of doubt and uncertainty" attached to the territories northwest of the Rocky Mountains, plenipotentiaries were appointed to represent the two interested parties. The Oregon question held high priority for the President. Polk appointed his Secretary of State James Buchanan, while her Majesty the Queen of the United Kingdom selected Privy Council member Lord Richard Pakenham. The two were instructed to resolve the dispute via an "amicable compromise." The ministers did arrive at an amicable settlement and secured the western boundary for the future peace and welfare of their people. That proposed settlement was submitted to the Senate on June 10, 1848 for its consideration. The Senate concurred, and six days later the Treaty was formalized.

No sooner had the territory of California been scheduled to pass to American hands, when an event of world-shaking significance occurred in the Sierra Nevada mountain range. James W. Marshall discovered gold about 40 miles from present day Sacramento on January 24, 1848.

Marshall and his partner, John A. Sutter tried to keep the discovery secret. Their attempt to do so proved futile. Polk confirmed the discovery in his annual message to Congress, on December 5,

1848. The sensational announcement sparked the great California gold rush. Adventurers came from all parts of the United States and faraway places. The celebrated "forty-niners" grew the population of California by more than 100,000, all seeking the luck of the roaring camp. California, just as the United States, acutely felt growing pains.

7

Andrew Jackson

1. INAUGURAL ADDRESS   MARCH 4, 1829

About to undertake the arduous duties that I have been appointed to perform by the choice of a free people, I avail myself of this customary and solemn occasion to express the gratitude which their confidence inspires and to acknowledge the accountability which my situation enjoins. While the magnitude of their interests convinces me that no thanks can be adequate to the honor they have conferred, it admonishes me that the best return I can make is the zealous dedication of my humble abilities to their service and their good.

As the instrument of the Federal Constitution it will devolve on me for a stated period to execute the laws of the United States, to superintend their foreign and their confederate relations, to manage their revenue, to command their forces, and, by communications to the Legislature, to watch over and to promote their interests generally. And the principles of action by which I shall endeavor to accomplish this circle of duties it is now proper for me briefly to explain.

In administering the laws of Congress I shall keep steadily in view the limitations as well as the extent of the Executive power, trusting thereby to discharge the functions of my office without transcending its authority. With foreign nations it will be my study to preserve peace and to cultivate friendship on fair and honorable terms, and in the adjustment of any differences that may exist or arise to exhibit the forbearance becoming a powerful nation rather than the sensibility belonging to a gallant people.

. . . Considering standing armies as dangerous to free governments in time of peace, I shall not seek to enlarge our present establishment nor disregard that salutary lesson of political experience which teaches that the military should be held subordinate to the civil power. The gradual increase of our Navy, whose flag has displayed in distant climes our skill in navigation and our fame in arms; the preservation of our forts, arsenals, and dockyards, and the introduction of progressive improvements in the discipline and science of both branches of our military service are so plainly prescribed by prudence that I should be excused for omitting their mention sooner than for enlarging on their importance. But the bulwark of our defense is the national militia, which in the present state of our intelligence and population must render us invincible. As long as our Government is administered for the good of the people, and is regulated by their will; as long as it secures to us the rights of person and of property, liberty of conscience and of the press, it will be worth defending; and so long as it is worth defending a patriotic militia will cover it with an impenetrable aegis. Partial injuries and occasional mortifications we may be subjected to, but a million of armed freemen, possessed of the means of war, can never be conquered by a foreign foe. To any just system, therefore, calculated to strengthen this natural safeguard of the country I shall cheerfully lend all the aid in my power. . . .

Figure 7.1 Andrew Jackson statue, courtesy of Ian Wagreich.

2. VETO OF THE BANK BILL   JULY 10, 1832

The bill "to modify and continue" the act entitled "An act to incorporate the subscribers to the Bank of the United States" was presented to me on the 4th July instant. Having considered it with that solemn regard to the principles of the Constitution which the day was calculated to inspire, and come to the conclusion that it ought not to become a law, I herewith return it to the Senate, in which it originated, with my objections.

A bank of the United States is in many respects convenient for the Government and useful to the people. Entertaining this opinion, and deeply impressed with the belief that some of the powers and privileges possessed by the existing bank are unauthorized by the Constitution, subversive of the rights of the States, and dangerous to the liberties of the people, I felt it my duty at an early period of my Administration to call the attention of Congress to the practicability of organizing an institution combining all its advantages and obviating these objections. I sincerely regret that in the act before me I can perceive none of those modifications of the bank charter which are necessary, in my opinion, to make it compatible with justice, with sound policy, or with the Constitution of our country.

The present corporate body, denominated the president, directors, and company of the Bank of the United States, will have existed at the time this act is intended to take effect twenty years. It enjoys an exclusive privilege of banking under the authority of the General Government, a monopoly of its favor and support, and, as a necessary consequence, almost a monopoly of the foreign and domestic exchange. The powers, privileges, and favors bestowed upon it in the original charter, by increasing the value of the stock far above its par value, operated as a gratuity of many millions to the stockholders.

An apology may be found for the failure to guard against this result in the consideration that the effect of the original act of incorporation could not be certainly foreseen at the time of its passage. The act before me proposes another gratuity to the holders of the same stock, and in many cases to the same men, of at least seven millions more. This donation finds no apology in any uncertainty as to the effect of the act. On all hands it is conceded that its passage will increase at least 20 or 30 per cent more the market price of the stock, subject to the payment of the annuity of $200,000 per year secured by the act, thus adding in a moment one-fourth to its par value. It is not our own citizens only who are to receive the bounty of our Government. More than eight millions of the stock of this bank are held by foreigners. By this act the American Republic proposes virtually to make them a present of some millions of dollars. For these gratuities to foreigners and to some of our own opulent citizens the act secures no equivalent whatever. They are the certain gains of the present stockholders under the operation of this act, after making full allowance for the payment of the bonus.

Every monopoly and all exclusive privileges are granted at the expense of the public, which ought to receive a fair equivalent. The many millions which this act proposes to bestow on the stockholders of the existing bank must come directly or indirectly out of the earnings of the American people. It is due to them, therefore, if their Government sells monopolies and exclusive privileges, that they should at least exact for them as much as they are worth in open market. The value of the monopoly in this case may be correctly ascertained. The twenty-eight millions of stock would probably be at an advance of 50 per cent, and command in market at least $42,000,000, subject to the payment of the present bonus. The present value of the monopoly, therefore, is $17,000,000, and this act proposes to sell for three millions, payable in fifteen annual installments of $200,000 each.

It is not conceivable how the present stockholders can have any claim to the special favor of the Government. The present corporation has enjoyed its monopoly during the period stipulated in the original contract. If we must have such a corporation, why should not the Government sell out the whole stock and thus secure to the people the full market value of the privileges granted? Why should not Congress create and sell twenty-eight millions of stock, incorporating the purchasers with all the powers and privileges secured in this act and putting the premium upon the sales into the Treasury?

But this act does not permit competition in the purchase of this monopoly. It seems to be predicated on the erroneous idea that the present stockholders have a prescriptive right not only to the favor but to the bounty of Government. It appears that more than a fourth part of the stock is held by foreigners and the residue is held by a few hundred of our own citizens, chiefly of the richest class. For their benefit does this act exclude the whole American people from competition in the purchase of this monopoly and dispose of it for many millions less than it is worth. This seems the less excusable because some of our citizens not now stockholders petitioned that the door of competition might be opened, and offered to take a charter on terms much more favorable to the Government and country.

But this proposition, although made by men whose aggregate wealth is believed to be equal to all the private stock in the existing bank, has been set aside, and the bounty of our Government is proposed to be again bestowed on the few who have been fortunate enough to secure the stock and at this moment wield the power of the existing institution. I cannot perceive the justice or policy of this course. If our Government must sell monopolies, it would seem to be its duty to take nothing less than their full value, and if gratuities must be made once in fifteen or twenty years let them not be bestowed on the subjects of a foreign government nor upon a designated and favored class of men in our own country. It is but justice and good policy, as far as the nature of the case will admit, to confine our favors to our own fellow citizens, and let each in his turn enjoy an opportunity to profit by our bounty. In the bearings of the act before me upon these points I find ample reasons why it should not become a law.

It has been urged as an argument in favor of re-chartering the present bank that the calling in of its loans will produce great embarrassment and distress. The time allowed to close its concerns is ample, and if it has been well managed its pressure will be light, and heavy only in case its management has been bad. If, therefore, it shall produce distress, the fault will be its own, and it would furnish a reason against renewing a power which has been so obviously abused. But will there ever be a time when this reason will be less powerful? To acknowledge its force is to admit that the bank ought to be perpetual, and as a consequence the present stockholders and those inheriting their rights as successors be established a privileged order, clothed both with great political power and enjoying immense pecuniary advantages from their connection with the Government. . . .

On two subjects only does the Constitution recognize in Congress the power to grant exclusive privileges or monopolies. It declares that "Congress shall have power to promote the progress of science and useful arts by securing for limited times to authors and inventors the exclusive right to their respective writings and discoveries." Out of this express delegation of power have grown our laws of patents and copyrights. As the Constitution expressly delegates to Congress the power to grant exclusive privileges in these cases as the means of executing the substantive power "to promote the progress of science and useful arts," it is consistent with the fair rules of construction to conclude that such a power was not intended to be granted as a means of accomplishing any other end. On every other subject which comes within the scope of Congressional power there is an ever-living discretion in the use of proper means, which cannot be restricted or abolished without an amendment of the Constitution. Every act of Congress, therefore, which attempts by grants of monopolies or sale of exclusive privileges for a limited time, or a time without limit, to restrict or extinguish its own discretion in the choice of means to execute its delegated powers is equivalent to a legislative amendment of the Constitution, and palpably unconstitutional.

This act authorizes and encourages transfers of its stock to foreigners and grants them an exemption from all State and national taxation. So far from being "necessary and proper" that the bank should possess this power to make it a safe and efficient agent of the Government in its fiscal operations, it is calculated to convert the Bank of the United States into a foreign bank, to impoverish our people in time of peace, to disseminate a foreign influence through every section of the Republic, and in war to endanger our independence. . . .

Experience should teach us wisdom. Most of the difficulties our Government now encounters and most of the dangers which impend over our Union have sprung from an abandonment of the legitimate objects of Government by our national legislation, and the adoption of such principles as are embodied in this act. Many of our rich men have not been content with equal protection and equal benefits, but have besought us to make them richer by act of Congress. By attempting to gratify their desires we have in the results of our legislation arrayed section against section, interest against interest, and man against man, in a fearful commotion which threatens to shake the foundation of our Union. It is time to pause in our career to review our principles, and if possible revive that devoted patriotism and spirit of compromise which distinguished the sages of the Revolution and the fathers of our Union. If we cannot at once, in justice to interests vested under improvident legislation, make our Government what it ought to be, we can at least take a stand against all new grants of monopolies and exclusive privileges, against any prostitution of our Government to the advancement of the few at the expense of the many, and in favor of compromise and gradual reform in our code of laws and system of political economy. . . .

3. PROCLAMATION TO THE PEOPLE OF SOUTH CAROLINA   DECEMBER 10, 1832

Whereas a convention assembled in the State of South Carolina have passed an ordinance by which they declare "that the several acts and parts of acts of the Congress of the United States purporting to be laws for the imposing of duties and imposts on the importation of foreign commodities, and now having actual operation and effect within the United States, and more especially" two acts for the same purposes passed on the 29th of May 1828, and on the 14th of July 1832, "are unauthorized by the Constitution of the United States, and violate the true meaning and intent thereof, and are null and void and no law," nor binding on the citizens of that State or its officers; and by the said ordinance it is further declared to be unlawful for any of the constituted authorities of the State or of the United States to enforce the payment of the duties imposed by the said acts within the same State, and that it is the duty of the legislature to pass such laws as may be necessary to give full effect to the said ordinance; and

Whereas by the said ordinance it is further ordained that in no case of law or equity decided in the courts of said State wherein shall be drawn in question the validity of the said ordinance, or of the acts of the legislature that may be passed to give it effect, or of the said laws of the United States, no appeal shall be allowed to the Supreme Court of the United States, nor shall any copy of the record be permitted or allowed for that purpose, and that any person attempting to take such appeal shall be punished as for contempt of court; and, finally, the said ordinance declares that the people of South Carolina will maintain the said ordinance at every hazard, and that they will consider the passage of any act by Congress abolishing or closing the ports of the said State or otherwise obstructing the free ingress or egress of vessels to and from the said ports, or any other act of the Federal Government to coerce the State, shut up her ports, destroy or harass her commerce, or to enforce the said acts otherwise than through the civil tribunals of the country, as inconsistent with the longer continuance of South Carolina in the Union, and that the people of the said State will thenceforth hold themselves absolved from all further obligation to maintain or preserve their political connection with the people of the other States, and will forthwith proceed to organize a separate government and do all other acts and things which sovereign and independent states may of right do; and

Whereas the said ordinance prescribes to the people of South Carolina a course of conduct in direct violation of their duty as citizens of the United States, contrary to the laws of their country, subversive of its Constitution and having for its object the destruction of the Union—that Union which, coeval with our political existence, led our fathers, without any other ties to unite them than those of patriotism and a common cause, through a sanguinary struggle to a glorious independence; that sacred Union, hitherto inviolate, which, perfected by our happy Constitution, has brought us, by the favor of Heaven, to a state of prosperity at home and high consideration abroad rarely, if ever, equaled in the history of nations:

To preserve this bond of our political existence from destruction, to maintain inviolate this state of national honor and prosperity, and to justify the confidence my fellow-citizens have reposed in me, I, Andrew Jackson, President of the United States, have thought proper to issue this my proclamation, stating my views of the Constitution and laws applicable to the measures adopted by the convention of South Carolina and to the reasons they have put forth to sustain them, declaring the course which duty will require me to pursue, and, appealing to the understanding and patriotism of the people, warn them of the consequences that must inevitably result from an observance of the dictates of the convention. . . .

The ordinance is founded, not on the indefeasible right of resisting acts which are plainly unconstitutional and too oppressive to be endured, but on the strange position that any one State may not only declare an act of Congress void, but prohibit its execution; that they may do this consistently with the Constitution; that the true construction of that instrument permits a State to retain its place in the Union and yet be bound by no other of its laws than those it may choose to consider as constitutional. It is true, they add, that to justify this abrogation of a law it must be palpably contrary to the Constitution; but it is evident that to give the right of resisting laws of that description, coupled with the uncontrolled right to decide what laws deserve that character, is to give the power of resisting all laws; for as by the theory there is no appeal, the reasons alleged by the State, good or bad, must prevail. If it should be said that public opinion is a sufficient check against the abuse of this power, it may be asked why it is not deemed a sufficient guard against the passage of an unconstitutional act by Congress? There is, however, a restraint in this last case which makes the assumed power of a State more indefensible, and which does not exist in the other. There are two appeals from an unconstitutional act passed by Congress—one to the judiciary, the other to the people and the States. There is no appeal from the State decision in theory, and the practical illustration shows that the courts are closed against an application to review it, both judges and jurors being sworn to decide in its favor. But reasoning on this subject is superfluous when our social compact, in express terms, declares that the laws of the United States, its Constitution, and treaties made under it are the supreme law of the land, and, for greater caution, adds "that the judges in every State shall be bound thereby, anything in the constitution or laws of any State to the contrary notwithstanding." And it may be asserted without fear of refutation that no federative government could exist without a similar provision. Look for a moment to the consequence. If South Carolina considers the revenue laws unconstitutional and has a right to prevent their execution in the port of Charleston, there would be a clear constitutional objection to their collection in every other port; and no revenue could be collected anywhere, for all imposts must be equal. It is no answer to repeat that an unconstitutional law is no law so long as the question of its legality is to be decided by the State itself, for every law operating injuriously upon any local interest will be perhaps thought, and certainly represented, as unconstitutional, and, as has been shown, there is no appeal. . . .

The Constitution has given, expressly, to Congress the right of raising revenue and of determining the sum the public exigencies will require. The States have no control over the exercise of this right other than that which results from the power of changing the representatives who abuse it, and thus procure redress. Congress may undoubtedly abuse this discretionary power; but the same may be said of others with which they are vested. Yet the discretion must exist somewhere. The Constitution has given it to the representatives of all the people, checked by the representatives of the States and by the Executive power. The South Carolina construction gives it to the legislature or the convention of a single State, where neither the people of the different States, nor the States in their separate capacity, nor the Chief Magistrate elected by the people have any representation. Which is the most discreet disposition of the power? I do not ask you, fellow-citizens, which is the constitutional disposition; that instrument speaks a language not to be misunderstood. But if you were assembled in general convention, which would you think the safest depository of this discretionary power in the last resort? Would you add a clause giving it to each of the States, or would you sanction the wise provisions already made by your Constitution? If this should be the result of your deliberations when providing for the future, are you, can you, be ready to risk all that we hold dear, to establish, for a temporary and a local purpose, that which you must acknowledge to be destructive, and even absurd, as a general provision? Carry out the consequences of this right vested in the different States, and you must perceive that the crisis your conduct presents at this day would recur whenever any law of the United States displeased any of the States, and that we should soon cease to be a nation. . . .

These are the allegations contained in the ordinance. Examine them seriously, my fellow-citizens; judge for yourselves. I appeal to you to determine whether they are so clear, so convincing, as to leave no doubt of their correctness; and even if you should come to this conclusion, how far they justify the reckless, destructive course which you are directed to pursue. Review these objections and the conclusions drawn from them once more. What are they? Every law, then, for raising revenue, according to the South Carolina ordinance, may be rightfully annulled, unless it be so framed as no law ever will or can be framed. Congress have a right to pass laws for raising revenue and each State have a right to oppose their execution—two rights directly opposed to each other; and yet is this absurdity supposed to be contained in an instrument drawn for the express purpose of avoiding collisions between the States and the General Government by an assembly of the most enlightened statesmen and purest patriots ever embodied for a similar purpose. . . .

This right to secede is deduced from the nature of the Constitution, which, they say, is a compact between sovereign States who have preserved their whole sovereignty and therefore are subject to no superior; that because they made the compact they can break it when in their opinion it has been departed from by the other States. Fallacious as this course of reasoning is, it enlists State pride and finds advocates in the honest prejudices of those who have not studied the nature of our Government sufficiently to see the radical error on which it rests.

The people of the United States formed the Constitution, acting through the State legislatures in making the compact, to meet and discuss its provisions, and acting in separate conventions when they ratified those provisions; but the terms used in its construction show it to be a Government in which the people of all the States, collectively, are represented. We are one people in the choice of President and Vice-President. Here the States have no other agency than to direct the mode in which the votes shall be given. The candidates having the majority of all the votes are chosen. The electors of a majority of States may have given their votes for one candidate, and yet another may be chosen. The people, then, and not the States, are represented in the executive branch. . . .

The Constitution of the United States, then, forms a government, not a league; and whether it be formed by compact between the States or in any other manner, its character is the same. It is a Government in which all the people are presented, which operates directly on the people individually, not upon the States; they retained all the power they did not grant. But each State, having expressly parted with so many powers as to constitute, jointly with the other States, a single nation, cannot, from that period, possess any right to secede, because such secession does not break a league, but destroys the unity of a nation; and any injury to that unity is not only a breach which would result from the contravention of a compact, but it is an offense against the whole Union. To say that any State may at pleasure secede from the Union is to say that the United States are not a nation, because it would be a solecism to contend that any part of a nation might dissolve its connection with the other parts, to their injury or ruin, without committing any offense. Secession, like any other revolutionary act, may be morally justified by the extremity of oppression; but to call it a constitutional right is confounding the meaning of terms, and can only be done through gross error or to deceive those who are willing to assert a right, but would pause before they made a revolution or incur the penalties consequent on a failure.

Because the Union was formed by a compact, it is said the parties to that compact may, when they feel themselves aggrieved, depart from it; but it is precisely because it is a compact that they cannot. A compact is an agreement or binding obligation. . . .

Fellow-citizens of my native State, let me not only admonish you, as the First Magistrate of our common country, not to incur the penalty of its laws, but use the influence that a father would over his children whom he saw rushing to certain ruin. In that paternal language, with that paternal feeling, let me tell you, my countrymen, that you are deluded by men who are either deceived themselves or wish to deceive you. Mark under what pretenses you have been led on to the brink of insurrection and treason on which you stand. First, a diminution of the value of your staple commodity, lowered by overproduction in other quarters, and the consequent diminution in the value of your lands were the sole effect of the tariff laws. The effect of those laws was confessedly injurious, but the evil was greatly exaggerated by the unfounded theory you were taught to believe—that its burthens were in proportion to your exports, not to your consumption of imported articles. Your pride was roused by the assertion that a submission to those laws was a state of vassalage and that resistance to them was equal in patriotic merit to the opposition our fathers offered to the oppressive laws of Great Britain. You were told that this opposition might be peaceably, might be constitutionally, made; that you might enjoy all the advantages of the Union and bear none of its burthens. Eloquent appeals to your passions, to your State pride, to your native courage, to your sense of real injury, were used to prepare you for the period when the mask which concealed the hideous features of disunion should be taken off. It fell, and you were made to look with complacency on objects which not long since you would have regarded with horror. Look back to the arts which have brought you to this state; look forward to the consequences to which it must inevitably lead! Look back to what was first told you as an inducement to enter into this dangerous course. The great political truth was repeated to you that you had the revolutionary right of resisting all laws that were palpably unconstitutional and intolerably oppressive. It was added that the right to nullify a law rested on the same principle, but that it was a peaceable remedy. This character which was given to it made you receive with too much confidence the assertions that were made of the unconstitutionality of the law and its oppressive effects. Mark, my fellow-citizens, that by the admission of your leaders the unconstitutionality must be palpable, or it will not justify either resistance or nullification. What is the meaning of the word palpable in the sense in which it is here used? That which is apparent to everyone; that which no man of ordinary intellect will fail to perceive. Is the unconstitutionality of these laws of that description? Let those among your leaders who once approved and advocated the principle of protective duties answer the question; and let them choose whether they will be considered as incapable then of perceiving that which must have been apparent to every man of common understanding, or as imposing upon your confidence and endeavoring to mislead you now. In either case they are unsafe guides in the perilous path they urge you to tread. Ponder well on this circumstance, and you will know how to appreciate the exaggerated language they address to you. They are not champions of liberty, emulating the fame of our Revolutionary fathers, nor are you an oppressed people, contending, as they repeat to you, against worse than colonial vassalage. You are free members of a flourishing and happy Union. There is no settled design to oppress you. . . .

. . . Snatch from the archives of your State the disorganizing edict of its convention; bid its members to reassemble and promulgate the decided expressions of your will to remain in the path which alone can conduct you to safety, prosperity, and honor. Tell them that compared to disunion all other evils are light, because that brings with it an accumulation of all. Declare that you will never take the field unless the star-spangled banner of your country shall float over you; that you will not be stigmatized when dead, and dishonored and scorned while you live, as the authors of the first attack on the Constitution of your country. Its destroyers you cannot be. You may disturb its peace, you may interrupt the course of its prosperity, you may cloud its reputation for stability; but its tranquility will be restored, its prosperity will return, and the stain upon its national character will be transferred and remain an eternal blot on the memory of those who caused the disorder. . . .

4. MESSAGE ON THE REMOVAL OF SOUTHERN INDIANS   DECEMBER 7, 1835

. . . States to the country west of the Mississippi River approaches its consummation. It was adopted on the most mature consideration of the condition of this race, and ought to be persisted in till the object is accomplished, and prosecuted with as much vigor as a just regard to their circumstances will permit, and as fast as their consent can be obtained. All preceding experiments for the improvement of the Indians have failed. It seems now to be an established fact that they cannot live in contact with a civilized community and prosper. Ages of fruitless endeavors have at length brought us to knowledge of this principle of intercommunication with them. The past we cannot recall, but the future we can provide for. Independently of the treaty stipulations into which we have entered with the various tribes for the usufructuary rights they have ceded to us, no one can doubt the moral duty of the Government of the United States to protect and if possible to preserve and perpetuate the scattered remnants of this race which are left within our borders. In the discharge of this duty an extensive region in the West has been assigned for their permanent residence. It has been divided into districts and allotted among them. Many have already removed and others are preparing to go, and with the exception of two small bands living in Ohio and Indiana, not exceeding 1,500 persons, and of the Cherokees, all the tribes on the east side of the Mississippi, and extending from Lake Michigan to Florida, have entered into engagements which will lead to their transplantation.

The plan for their removal and reestablishment is founded upon the knowledge we have gained of their character and habits, and has been dictated by a spirit of enlarged liberality. A territory exceeding in extent that relinquished has been granted to each tribe. Of its climate, fertility, and capacity to support an Indian population the representations are highly favorable. To these districts the Indians are removed at the expense of the United States, and with certain supplies of clothing, arms, ammunition, and other indispensable articles; they are also furnished gratuitously with provisions for the period of a year after their arrival at their new homes. In that time, from the nature of the country and of the products raised by them, they can subsist themselves by agricultural labor, if they choose to resort to that mode of life; if they do not they are upon the skirts of the great prairies, where countless herds of buffalo roam, and a short time suffices to adapt their own habits to the changes which a change of the animals destined for their food may require. Ample arrangements have also been made for the support of schools; in some instances council houses and churches are to be erected, dwellings constructed for the chiefs, and mills for common use. Funds have been set apart for the maintenance of the poor; the most necessary mechanical arts have been introduced, and blacksmiths, gunsmiths, wheelwrights, millwrights, etc., are supported among them. Steel and iron, and sometimes salt, are purchased for them, and plows and other farming utensils, domestic animals, looms, spinning wheels, cards, etc., are presented to them. And besides these beneficial arrangements, annuities are in all cases paid, amounting in some instances to more than $30 for each individual of the tribe, and in all cases sufficiently great, if justly divided and prudently expended, to enable them, in addition to their own exertions, to live comfortably. And as a stimulus for exertion, it is now provided by law that "in all cases of the appointment of interpreters or other persons employed for the benefit of the Indians a preference shall be given to persons of Indian descent, if such can be found who are properly qualified for the discharge of the duties."

Such are the arrangements for the physical comfort and for the moral improvement of the Indians. The necessary measures for their political advancement and for their separation from our citizens have not been neglected. The pledge of the United States has been given by Congress that the country destined for the residence of this people shall be forever "secured and guaranteed to them." A country west of Missouri and Arkansas has been assigned to them, into which the white settlements are not to be pushed. No political communities can be formed in that extensive region, except those which are established by the Indians themselves or by the United States for them and with their concurrence. A barrier has thus been raised for their protection against the encroachment of our citizens, and guarding the Indians as far as possible from those evils which have brought them to their present condition. . . .

Some general legislation seems necessary for the regulation of the relations which will exist in this new state of things between the Government and people of the United States and these transplanted Indian tribes, and for the establishment among the latter, and with their own consent, of some principles of intercommunication which their juxtaposition will call for; that moral may be substituted for physical force, the authority of a few and simple laws for the tomahawk, and that an end may be put to those bloody wars whose prosecution seems to have made part of their social system. . . .

5. CONSTITUTIONAL PROHIBITION OF FOREIGN GIFTS   JANUARY 6, 1834

I communicate to Congress an extract of a letter recently received from a R. J. Lieb, Consul of the United States at Tangiers, by which it appears that that officer has been induced to receive from the Emperor of Morocco a present of a lion and two horses. . . .

I have directed instructions . . . to all our ministers and agents abroad requiring that in future, unless previously authorized by Congress, they will not under any circumstances accept presents of any description from any foreign state. . . .

The provision of the Constitution which forbids any officer without the consent of Congress, to accept any present from any foreign power may be considered as having been satisfied by the surrender of the articles to the Government and they might now be disposed of by Congress. . . .

As under the positive order now given similar presents cannot hereafter be received, even for the purpose of being placed at the disposal of the Government. . . .

6. EXECUTIVE POWER VESTED IN A PRESIDENT   APRIL 15, 1834

By the Constitution "the executive power is vested in a President of the United States." Among the duties imposed upon him and which he is sworn to perform is that of "taking care that the laws be faithfully executed." Being thus made responsible for the entire action of the executive department, it was but reasonable that the power of appointing, overseeing, and controlling those who execute the laws—a power in its nature executive—should remain in his hands.

7. A TRIBUTE TO A FRIEND OF LIBERTY AND THE RIGHTS OF MAN   JUNE 21, 1834

From Executive Orders, General Order 46: On the Death of the Marquis de Lafayette. President Andrew Jackson commanded the following tribute and remembrance.

. . . he was the distinguished friend of the United States. In early life he embarked in that contest which secured freedom and independence to our country. . . . his memory will be second only to that of Washington in the hearts of the American people. . . . Living at a period of great excitement and of moral and political revolutions, engaged in many of the important events which fixed the attention of the world. . . . He has been taken from the theater of action with faculties unimpaired . . . and an object of veneration wherever civilization and the rights of man have extended; and mourning . . . his departure, let us rejoice that this associate of Washington has gone . . . to rejoin his illustrious commander in the fullness of days and of honor. . . .

One melancholy duty remains . . . the President feels called on . . . to direct that appropriate honors be paid to the memory of this distinguished patriot and soldier [and] . . . orders that the same honors be rendered . . . as were observed upon the decease of Washington, the Father of his Country, and his contemporary in arms. . . .

8. FAREWELL   MARCH 4, 1837

Being about to retire finally from public life, I beg leave to offer you my grateful thanks for the many proofs of kindness and confidence which I have received at your hands. It has been my fortune in the discharge of public duties, civil and military, frequently to have found myself in difficult and trying situations, where prompt decision and energetic action were necessary, and where the interest of the country required that high responsibilities should be fearlessly encountered; and it is with the deepest emotions of gratitude that I acknowledge the continued and unbroken confidence with which you have sustained me in every trial. . . .

We have now lived almost fifty years under the Constitution framed by the sages and patriots of the Revolution. The conflicts in which the nations of Europe were engaged during a great part of this period, the spirit in which they waged war against each other, and our intimate commercial connections with every part of the civilized world rendered a time of much difficulty for the Government of the United States. We have had our seasons of peace and of war, with all the evils which precede or follow a state of hostility with powerful nations. We encountered these trials with our Constitution yet in its infancy, and under the disadvantages which a new and untried government must always feel when it is called upon to put forth its whole strength without the lights of experience to guide it or the weight of precedents to justify its measures. But we have passed triumphantly through all these difficulties. Our Constitution is no longer a doubtful experiment, and at the end of nearly half a century we find that it has preserved unimpaired the liberties of the people, secured the rights of property, and that our country has improved and is flourishing beyond any former example in the history of nations. . . .

We behold systematic efforts publicly made to sow the seeds of discord between different parts of the United States and to place party divisions directly upon geographical distinctions; to excite the South against the North and the North against the South, and to force into the controversy the most delicate and exciting topics—topics upon which it is impossible that a large portion of the Union can ever speak without strong emotion. Appeals, too, are constantly made to sectional interests in order to influence the election of the Chief Magistrate, as if it were desired that he should favor a particular quarter of the country instead of fulfilling the duties of his station with impartial justice to all; and the possible dissolution of the Union has at length become an ordinary and familiar subject of discussion. Has the warning voice of Washington been forgotten, or have designs already been formed to sever the Union? Let it not be supposed that I impute to all of those who have taken an active part in these unwise and unprofitable discussions a want of patriotism or of public virtue. The honorable feeling of State pride and local attachments finds a place in the bosoms of the most enlightened and pure. But while such men are conscious of their own integrity and honesty of purpose, they ought never to forget that the citizens of other States are their political brethren, and that however mistaken they may be in their views, the great body of them are equally honest and upright with themselves. Mutual suspicions and reproaches may in time create mutual hostility, and artful and designing men will always be found who are ready to foment these fatal divisions and to inflame the natural jealousies of different sections of the country. The history of the world is full of such examples, and especially the history of republics.

What have you to gain by division and dissension? Delude not yourselves with the belief that a breach once made may be afterwards repaired. If the Union is once severed, the line of separation will grow wider and wider, and the controversies which are now debated and settled in the halls of legislation will then be tried in fields of battle and determined by the sword. Neither should you deceive yourselves with the hope that the first line of separation would be the permanent one, and that nothing but harmony and concord would be found in the new associations formed upon the dissolution of this Union. . . . It is impossible to look on the consequences that would inevitably follow the destruction of this Government and not feel indignant when we hear cold calculations about the value of the Union and have so constantly before us a line of conduct so well calculated to weaken its ties.

There is too much at stake to allow pride or passion to influence your decision. . . . But in order to maintain the Union unimpaired it is absolutely necessary that the laws passed by the constituted authorities should be faithfully executed in every part of the country, and that every good citizen should at all times stand ready to put down, with the combined force of the nation, every attempt at unlawful resistance, under whatever pretext it may be made or whatever shape it may assume. Unconstitutional or oppressive laws may no doubt be passed by Congress, either from erroneous views or the want of due consideration; if they are within the reach of judicial authority, the remedy is easy and peaceful; and if, from the character of the law, it is an abuse of power not within the control of the judiciary, then free discussion and calm appeals to reason and to the justice of the people will not fail to redress the wrong. But until the law shall be declared void by the courts or repealed by Congress no individual or combination of individuals can be justified in forcibly resisting its execution. It is impossible that any government can continue to exist upon any other principles. It would cease to be a government and be unworthy of the name if it had not the power to enforce the execution of its own laws within its own sphere of action. . . .

There is, perhaps, no one of the powers conferred on the Federal Government so liable to abuse as the taxing power. The most productive and convenient sources of revenue were necessarily given to it, that it might be able to perform the important duties imposed upon it; and the taxes which it lays upon commerce being concealed from the real payer in the price of the article, they do not so readily attract the attention of the people as smaller sums demanded from them directly by the tax gatherer. But the tax imposed on goods enhances by so much the price of the commodity to the consumer, and as many of these duties are imposed on articles of necessity which are daily used by the great body of the people, the money raised by these imposts is drawn from their pockets. Congress has no right under the Constitution to take money from the people unless it is required to execute some one of the specific powers entrusted to the Government; and if they raise more than is necessary for such purposes, it is an abuse of the power of taxation, and unjust and oppressive. . . .

In reviewing the conflicts which have taken place between different interests in the United States and the policy pursued since the adoption of our present form of Government, we find nothing that has produced such deep-seated evil as the course of legislation in relation to the currency. The Constitution of the United States unquestionably intended to secure to the people a circulating medium of gold and silver. But the establishment of a national bank by Congress, with the privilege of issuing paper money receivable in the payment of the public dues, and the unfortunate course of legislation in the several States upon the same subject, drove from general circulation the constitutional currency and substituted one of paper in its place.

It was not easy for men engaged in the ordinary pursuits of business, whose attention had not been particularly drawn to the subject, to foresee all the consequences of a currency exclusively of paper, and we ought not on that account to be surprised at the facility with which laws were obtained to carry into effect the paper system. Honest and even enlightened men are sometimes misled by the specious and plausible statements of the designing. But experience has now proved the mischiefs and dangers of a paper currency, and it rests with you to determine whether the proper remedy shall be applied.

The paper system being founded on public confidence and having of itself no intrinsic value, it is liable to great and sudden fluctuations, thereby rendering property insecure and the wages of labor unsteady and uncertain. The corporations which create the paper money cannot be relied upon to keep the circulating medium uniform in amount. In times of prosperity, when confidence is high, they are tempted by the prospect of gain or by the influence of those who hope to profit by it to extend their issues of paper beyond the bounds of discretion and the reasonable demands of business; and when these issues have been pushed on from day to day, until public confidence is at length shaken, then a reaction takes place, and they immediately withdraw the credits they have given, suddenly curtail their issues, and produce an unexpected and ruinous contraction of the circulating medium, which is felt by the whole community. The banks by this means save themselves, and the mischievous consequences of their imprudence or cupidity are visited upon the public. Nor does the evil stop here. These ebbs and flows in the currency and these indiscreet extensions of credit naturally engender a spirit of speculation injurious to the habits and character of the people. . . .

Recent events have proved that the paper-money system of this country may be used as an engine to undermine your free institutions, and that those who desire to engross all power in the hands of the few and to govern by corruption or force are aware of its power and prepared to employ it. Your banks now furnish your only circulating medium, and money is plenty or scarce according to the quantity of notes issued by them. While they have capitals not greatly disproportioned to each other, they are competitors in business, and no one of them can exercise dominion over the rest; and although in the present state of the currency these banks may and do operate injuriously upon the habits of business, the pecuniary concerns, and the moral tone of society, yet, from their number and dispersed situation, they cannot combine for the purposes of political influence, and whatever may be the dispositions of some of them their power of mischief must necessarily be confined to a narrow space and felt only in their immediate neighborhoods.

But when the charter for the Bank of the United States was obtained from Congress it perfected the schemes of the paper system and gave to its advocates the position they have struggled to obtain from the commencement of the Federal Government to the present hour. The immense capital and peculiar privileges bestowed upon it enabled it to exercise despotic sway over the other banks in every part of the country. From its superior strength it could seriously injure, if not destroy, the business of any one of them which might incur its resentment; and it openly claimed for itself the power of regulating the currency throughout the United States. In other words, it asserted (and it undoubtedly possessed) the power to make money plenty or scarce at its pleasure, at any time and in any quarter of the Union, by controlling the issues of other banks and permitting an expansion or compelling a general contraction of the circulating medium, according to its own will. The other banking institutions were sensible of its strength, and they soon generally became its obedient instruments, ready at all times to execute its mandates; and with the banks necessarily went also that numerous class of persons in our commercial cities who depend altogether on bank credits for their solvency and means of business, and who are therefore obliged, for their own safety, to propitiate the favor of the money power by distinguished zeal and devotion in its service. The result of the ill-advised legislation which established this great monopoly was to concentrate the whole moneyed power of the Union, with its boundless means of corruption and its numerous dependents, under the direction and command of one acknowledged head, thus organizing this particular interest as one body and securing to it unity and concert of action throughout the United States, and enabling it to bring forward upon any occasion its entire and undivided strength to support or defeat any measure of the Government. In the hands of his formidable power, thus perfectly organized, was also placed unlimited dominion over the amount of the circulating medium, giving it the power to regulate the value of property and the fruits of labor in every quarter of the Union, and to bestow prosperity or bring ruin upon any city or section of the country as might best comport with its own interest or policy.

We are not left to conjecture how the moneyed power thus organized and with such a weapon in its hands, would be likely to use it. The distress and alarm which pervaded and agitated the whole country when the Bank of the United States waged war upon the people in order to compel them to submit to its demands cannot yet be forgotten. The ruthless and unsparing temper with which whole cities and communities were oppressed, individuals impoverished and ruined, and a scene of cheerful prosperity suddenly changed into one of gloom and despondency ought to be indelibly impressed on the memory of the people of the United States. If such was its power in a time of peace, what would it not have been in a season of war, with an enemy at your doors? . . .

It is one of the serious evils of our present system of banking that it enables one class of society— and that by no means a numerous one—by its control over the currency, to act injuriously upon the interests of all the others and to exercise more than its just proportion of influence in political affairs. The agricultural, the mechanical, and the laboring classes have little or no share in the direction of the great moneyed corporations, and from their habits and the nature of their pursuits they are incapable of forming extensive combinations to act together with united force. Such concert of action may sometimes be produced in a single city or in a small district of country by means of personal communications with each other, but they have no regular or active correspondence with those who are engaged in similar pursuits in distant places; they have but little patronage to give to the press, and exercise but a small share of influence over it; they have no crowd of dependents about them who hope to grow rich without labor by their countenance and favor, and who are therefore always ready to execute their wishes. The planter, the farmer, the mechanic, and the laborer all know that their success depends upon their own industry and economy, and that they must not expect to become suddenly rich by the fruits of their toil. Yet these classes of society form the great body of the people of the United States; they are the bone and sinew of the country—men who love liberty and desire nothing but equal rights and equal laws, and who, moreover, hold the great mass of our national wealth, although it is distributed in moderate amounts among the millions of freemen who possess it. But with overwhelming numbers and wealth on their side they are in constant danger of losing their fair influence in the Government, and with difficulty maintain their just rights against the incessant efforts daily made to encroach upon them. The mischief springs from the power which the moneyed interest derives from a paper currency which they are able to control, from the multitude of corporations with exclusive privileges which they have succeeded in obtaining in the different States, and which are employed altogether for their benefit; and unless you become more watchful in your States and check this spirit of monopoly and thirst for exclusive privileges you will in the end find that the most important powers of Government have been given or bartered away, and the control over your dearest interests has passed into the hands of these corporations. . . .

In presenting to you, my fellow-citizens, these parting counsels, I have brought before you the leading principles upon which I endeavored to administer the Government in the high office with which you twice honored me. Knowing that the path of freedom is continually beset by enemies who often assume the disguise of friends, I have devoted the last hours of my public life to warn you of the dangers. The progress of the United States under our free and happy institutions has surpassed the most sanguine hopes of the founders of the Republic. Our growth has been rapid beyond all former example in numbers, in wealth, in knowledge, and all the useful arts which contribute to the comforts and convenience of man, and from the earliest ages of history to the present day there never have been thirteen millions of people associated in one political body who enjoyed so much freedom and happiness as the people of these United States. You have no longer any cause to fear danger from abroad; your strength and power are well known throughout the civilized world, as well as the high and gallant bearing of your sons. It is from within, among yourselves from cupidity, from corruption, from disappointed ambition and inordinate thirst for power—that factions will be formed and liberty endangered. It is against such designs, whatever disguise the actors may assume, that you have especially to guard yourselves. You have the highest of human trusts committed to your care. Providence has showered on this favored land blessings without number, and has chosen you as the guardians of freedom, to preserve it for the benefit of the human race. May He who holds in His hands the destinies of nations make you worthy of the favors He has bestowed and enable you, with pure hearts and pure hands and sleepless vigilance, to guard and defend to the end of time the great charge He has committed to your keeping.

My own race is nearly run; advanced age and failing health warn me that before long I must pass beyond the reach of human events and cease to feel the vicissitudes of human affairs. I thank God that my life has been spent in a land of liberty and that He has given me a heart to love my country with the affection of a son. And filled with gratitude for your constant and unwavering kindness, I bid you a last and affectionate farewell.

8

Martin Van Buren

1. INDEPENDENT TREASURY MESSAGE   **SEPTEMBER 4, 1837**

The act of the 23d of June 1836, regulating the deposits of the public money and directing the employment of State, District, and Territorial banks for that purpose, made it the duty of the Secretary of the Treasury to discontinue the use of such of them as should at any time refuse to redeem their notes in specie, and to substitute other banks, provided a sufficient number could be obtained to receive the public deposits upon the terms and conditions therein prescribed. The general and almost simultaneous suspension of specie payments by the banks in May last rendered the performance of this duty imperative in respect to those which had been selected under the act, and made it at the same time impracticable to employ the requisite number of others upon the prescribed conditions. The specific regulations established by Congress for the deposit and safe-keeping of the public moneys having thus unexpectedly become inoperative, I felt it to be my duty to afford you an early opportunity for the exercise of your supervisory powers over the subject.

I was also led to apprehend that the suspension of specie payments, increasing the embarrassments before existing in the pecuniary affairs of the country, would so far diminish the public revenue that the accruing receipts into the Treasury would not, with the reserved five millions, be sufficient to defray the unavoidable expenses of the Government until the usual period for the meeting of Congress, whilst the authority to call upon the States for a portion of the sums deposited with them was too restricted to enable the Department to realize a sufficient amount from that source. These apprehensions have been justified by subsequent results, which render it certain that this deficiency will occur if additional means be not provided by Congress.

The difficulties experienced by the mercantile interest in meeting their engagements induced them to apply to me previously to the actual suspension of specie payments for indulgence upon their bonds for duties, and all the relief authorized by law was promptly and cheerfully granted. The dependence of the Treasury upon the avails of these bonds to enable it to make the deposits with the States required by law led me in the outset to limit this indulgence to the 1st of September, but it has since been extended to the 1st of October, that the matter might be submitted to your further direction. . . .

During the earlier stages of the revulsion through which we have just passed much acrimonious discussion arose and great diversity of opinion existed as to its real causes. This was not surprising. The operations of credit are so diversified and the influences which affect them so numerous, and often so subtle, that even impartial and well-informed persons are seldom found to agree in respect to them. . . . I proceed to state my views, so far as may be necessary to a clear understanding of the remedies I feel it my duty to propose and of the reasons by which I have been led to recommend them. . . .

They are, to regulate by law the safe-keeping, transfer, and disbursement of the public moneys; to designate the funds to be received and paid by the Government; to enable the Treasury to meet promptly every demand upon it; to prescribe the terms of indulgence and the mode of settlement to be adopted, as well in collecting from individuals the revenue that has accrued as in withdrawing it from former depositories; and to devise and adopt such further measures, within the constitutional competency of Congress, as will be best calculated to revive the enterprise and to promote the prosperity of the country.

For the deposit, transfer, and disbursement of the revenue, national and State banks have always, with temporary and limited exceptions, been heretofore employed; but although advocates of each system are still to be found, it is apparent that the events of the last few months have greatly augmented the desire, long existing among the people of the United States, to separate the fiscal operations of the Government from those of individuals or corporations.

Again to create a national bank as a fiscal agent would be to disregard the popular will, twice solemnly and unequivocally expressed. On no question of domestic policy is there stronger evidence that the sentiments of a large majority are deliberately fixed, and I cannot concur with those who think they see in recent events a proof that these sentiments are, or a reason that they should be, changed. . . .

A danger difficult, if not impossible, to be avoided in such an arrangement is made strikingly evident in the very event by which it has now been defeated. A sudden act of the banks intrusted with the funds of the people deprives the Treasury, without fault or agency of the Government, of the ability to pay its creditors in the currency they have by law a right to demand. This circumstance no fluctuation of commerce could have produced if the public revenue had been collected in the legal currency and kept in that form by the officers of the Treasury. The citizen whose money was in bank receives it back since the suspension at a sacrifice in its amount, whilst he who kept it in the legal currency of the country and in his own possession pursues without loss the current of his business. The Government, placed in the situation of the former, is involved in embarrassments it could not have suffered had it pursued the course of the latter. These embarrassments are, moreover, augmented by those salutary and just laws which forbid it to use a depreciated currency, and by so doing take from the Government the ability which individuals have of accommodating their transactions to such a catastrophe.

A system which can in a time of profound peace, when there is a large revenue laid by, thus suddenly prevent the application and the use of the money of the people in the manner and for the objects they have directed cannot be wise; but who can think without painful reflection that under it the same unforeseen events might have befallen us in the midst of a war and taken from us at the moment when most wanted the use of those very means which were treasured up to promote the national welfare and guard our national rights? To such embarrassments and to such dangers will this Government be always exposed whilst it takes the moneys raised for and necessary to the public service out of the hands of its own officers and converts them into a mere right of action against corporations intrusted with the possession of them. Nor can such results be effectually guarded against in such a system without investing the Executive with a control over the banks themselves, whether State or national, that might with reason be objected to. Ours is probably the only Government in the world that is liable in the management of its fiscal concerns to occurrences like these. . . .

The foregoing views, it seems to me, do but fairly carry out the provisions of the Federal Constitution in relation to the currency, as far as relates to the public revenue. At the time that instrument was framed there were but three or four banks in the United States, and had the extension of the banking system and the evils growing out of it been foreseen they would probably have been specially guarded against. The same policy which led to the prohibition of bills of credit by the States would doubtless in that event have also interdicted their issue as a currency in any other form. The Constitution, however, contains no such prohibition; and since the States have exercised for nearly half a century the power to regulate the business of banking, it is not to be expected that it will be abandoned. The whole matter is now under discussion before the proper tribunal—the people of the States. Never before has the public mind been so thoroughly awakened to a proper sense of its importance; never has the subject in all its bearings been submitted to so searching an inquiry. It would be distrusting the intelligence and virtue of the people to doubt the speedy and efficient adoption of such measures of reform as the public good demands. All that can rightfully be done by the Federal Government to promote the accomplishment of that important object will without doubt be performed. . . .

The plan proposed will be adequate to all our fiscal operations during the remainder of the year. Should it be adopted, the Treasury, aided by the ample resources of the country, will be able to discharge punctually every pecuniary obligation. For the future all that is needed will be that caution and forbearance in appropriations which the diminution of the revenue requires and which the complete accomplishment or great forwardness of many expensive national undertakings renders equally consistent with prudence and patriotic liberality. . . .

2. BORDER INSECURITY   JANUARY 5, 1838

Recent experience on the southern boundary of the United States and the events now daily occurring on our northern frontier have abundantly shown that the existing laws are insufficient to guard against hostile invasion. . . .

The laws in force provide sufficient penalties for the punishment of such offenses after they have been committed, and provided the parties can be found, but the Executive is powerless in many cases to prevent the commission of them, even when in possession of ample evidence of an intention on the part of evil-disposed persons to violate our laws.

Your attention is called to this defect in our legislation. It is apparent that the Executive ought to be clothed with adequate power effectually to restrain all persons within our jurisdiction from the commission of acts of this character. They tend to disturb the peace of the country and inevitably involve the Government in perplexing controversies with foreign powers. I recommend a careful revision of all the laws now in force and such additional enactments as may be necessary to vest in the Executive full power to prevent injuries being inflicted upon neighboring nations by the unauthorized and unlawful acts of citizens of the United States or of other persons who may be within our jurisdiction and subject to our control. . . .

9

William Henry Harrison

1. THE GREAT DREAD   MARCH 4, 1841

. . . Upward of half a century has elapsed since the adoption of the present form of government. It would be an object more highly desirable than the gratification of the curiosity of speculative statesmen if its precise situation could be ascertained . . . of the powers which they respectively claim and exercise, of the collisions which have occurred between them or between the whole Government and those of the States. . . . We could then compare our actual condition after fifty years trial of our system with what it was in the commencement of its operation and ascertain whether the predictions of the patriots who opposed its adoption or the confident hopes of its advocates have been best realized. The great dread of the former seems to have been that the reserved powers of the States would be absorbed by those of the Federal Government and a consolidated power established, leaving to the States the shadow only of that independent action for which they had so zealously contended and on the preservation of which they relied as the last hope of liberty. Without denying that the result to which they looked with so much apprehension is in the way of being realized, it is obvious that they did not clearly see the mode of its accomplishment. . . . To a casual observer our system presents no appearance of discord between the different members which compose it. Even the addition of many new ones has produced no jarring. They move in their respective orbits in perfect harmony with the central head and with each other. But there still is an undercurrent at work by which, if not seasonably checked, the worst apprehensions of our anti-federal patriots will be realized, and not only will the State authorities be overshadowed by the great increase of power in the executive department of the General Government, but the character of that Government, if not its designation, be essentially and radically changed. . . .

10

John Tyler

1. A NEW TEST FOR THE CHIEF EXECUTIVE   APRIL 9, 1841

. . . For the first time in our history the person elected to the Vice-Presidency of the United States, by the happening of a contingency provided for in the Constitution, has had devolved upon him the Presidential office. The spirit of faction, which is directly opposed to the spirit of a lofty patriotism, may find in this occasion for assaults upon my Administration; and in succeeding, under circumstances so sudden and unexpected and to responsibilities so greatly augmented, to the administration of public affairs I shall place in the intelligence and patriotism of the people my only sure reliance. My earnest prayer shall be constantly addressed to the all-wise and all-powerful Being who made me, and by whose dispensation I am called to the high office of President of this Confederacy, understanding to carry out the principles of that Constitution which I have sworn "to protect, preserve, and defend." . . .

In view of the fact, well avouched by history, that the tendency of all human institutions is to concentrate power in the hands of a single man, and that their ultimate downfall has proceeded from this cause, I deem it of the most essential importance that a complete separation should take place between the sword and the purse. . . .

The spectacle is exhibited to the world of a government deriving its powers from the consent of the governed and having imparted to it only so much power as is necessary for its successful operation. Those who are charged with its administration should carefully abstain from all attempts to enlarge the range of powers thus granted to the several departments of the Government other than by an appeal to the people for additional grants, lest by so doing they disturb that balance which the patriots and statesmen who framed the Constitution designed to establish between the Federal Government and the States composing this Union. The observance of these rules is enjoined upon us . . . for the good of our children and our children's children through countless generations. An opposite course could not fail to generate factions intent upon the gratification of their selfish ends, to give birth to local and sectional jealousies and to ultimate either in breaking asunder the bonds of union or in building up a central system which would inevitably end in a bloody scepter and an iron crown. . . .

2. REQUEST FOR RATIFICATION OF THE WEBSTER–   AUGUST 11, 1842
ASHBURTON TREATY

I have received your Excellency's communication of the 25th instant, informing me of efforts making Mr. Dorr and others to embody a force in the contiguous States for the invasion of the State of Rhode Island, and calling upon the Executive of the United States for military's aid.

In answer I have to inform your Excellency that means have been taken to ascertain the extent of the dangers of any armed invasion by the citizens of other States of the State of Rhode Island, either to put down her government or to disturb her peace. The apparent improbability of a violation so flagrant and unprecedented of all our laws and institutions makes me, I confess, allow to believe that any serious attempts will be made to execute the designs which some evil-minded persons may have formed.

But should the necessity of the case require the interposition of the authority of the United States it will be rendered in the manner prescribed by the laws.

In the meantime I indulge a confident expectation, founded upon the recent manifestations of public opinion in your State in favor of law and order, that your own resources and means will be abundantly adequate to preserve the public peace, and that the difficulties which have arisen will be soon amicably and permanently adjusted by the exercise of a spirit of liberality and forbearance.

3. MESSAGE URGING ANNEXATION OF TEXAS   APRIL 22, 1844

I transmit herewith, for your approval and ratification, a treaty which I have caused to be negotiated between the United States and Texas, whereby the latter, on the conditions therein set forth, has transferred and conveyed all its right of separate and independent sovereignty and jurisdiction to the United States. In taking so important a step I have been influenced by what appeared to me to be the most controlling considerations of public policy and the general good, and in having accomplished it, should it meet with your approval, the Government will have succeeded in reclaiming a territory which formerly constituted a portion, as it is confidently believed, of its domain under the treaty of cession of 1803 by France to the United States.

The country thus proposed to be annexed has been settled principally by persons from the United States, who emigrated on the invitation of both Spain and Mexico, and who carried with them into the wilderness which they have partially reclaimed the laws, customs, and political and domestic institutions of their native land. They are deeply indoctrinated in all the principles of civil liberty, and will bring along with them in the act of reassociation devotion to our Union and a firm and inflexible resolution to assist in maintaining the public liberty unimpaired—a consideration which, as it appears to me, is to be regarded as of no small moment. The country itself thus obtained is of incalculable value in an agricultural and commercial point of view. To a soil of inexhaustible fertility it unites a genial and healthy climate, and is destined at a day not distant to make large contributions to the commerce of the world. . . .

To Mexico the Executive is disposed to pursue a course conciliatory in its character and at the same time to render her the most ample justice by conventions and stipulations not inconsistent with the rights and dignity of the Government. It is actuated by no spirit of unjust aggrandizement, but looks only to its own security. It has made known to Mexico at several periods its extreme anxiety to witness the termination of hostilities between that country and Texas. Its wishes however have been entirely disregarded. It has ever been ready to urge an adjustment of the dispute upon terms mutually advantageous to both. It will be ready at all times to hear and discuss any claims Mexico may think she has on the justice of the United States and to adjust any that may be deemed to be so on the most liberal terms. There is no desire on the part of the Executive to wound her pride or affect injuriously her interest, but at the same time it cannot compromit by any delay in its action the essential interests of the United States. Mexico has no right to ask or expect this of us; we deal rightfully with Texas as an independent power. The war which has been waged for eight years has resulted only in the conviction with all others than herself that Texas cannot be reconquered. I cannot but repeat the opinion expressed in my message at the opening of Congress that it is time it had ceased. The Executive, while it could not look upon its longer continuance without the greatest uneasiness, has, nevertheless, for all past time preserved a course of strict neutrality. It could not be ignorant of the fact of the exhaustion which a war of so long a duration had produced. Least of all was it ignorant of the anxiety of other powers to induce Mexico to enter into terms of reconciliation with Texas, which, affecting the domestic institutions of Texas, would operate most injuriously upon the United States and might most seriously threaten the existence of this happy Union. . . .

In full view, then, of the highest public duty, and as a measure of security against evils incalculably great, the Executive has entered into the negotiation, the fruits of which are now submitted to the Senate. Independent of the urgent reasons which existed for the step it has taken, it might safely invoke the fact (which it confidently believes) that there exists no civilized government on earth having a voluntary tender made it of a domain so rich and fertile, so replete with all that can add to national greatness and wealth, and so necessary to its peace and safety that would reject the offer. Nor are other powers, Mexico inclusive, likely in any degree to be injuriously affected by the ratification of the treaty. The prosperity of Texas will be equally interesting to all: in the increase of the general commerce of the world that prosperity will be secured by annexation.

But one view of the subject remains to be presented. It grows out of the proposed enlargement of our territory. From this, I am free to confess, I see no danger. The federative system is susceptible of the greatest extension compatible with the ability of the representation of the most distant State or Territory to reach the seat of Government in time to participate in the functions of legislation and to make known the wants of the constituent body. Our confederated Republic consisted originally of thirteen members. It now consists of twice that number, while applications are before Congress to permit other additions. This addition of new States has served to strengthen rather than to weaken the Union. New interests have sprung up, which require the united power of all, through the action of the common Government, to protect and defend upon the high seas and in foreign parts. Each State commits with perfect security to that common Government those great interests growing out of our relations with other nations of the world, and which equally involve the good of all the States. Its domestic concerns are left to its own exclusive management. But if there were any force in the objection it would seem to require an immediate abandonment of territorial possessions which lie in the distance and stretch to a far-off sea, and yet no one would be found, it is believed, ready to recommend such an abandonment. Texas lies at our very doors and in our immediate vicinity.

Under every view which I have been able to take of the subject, I think that the interests of our common constituents, the people of all the States, and a love of the Union left the Executive no other alternative than to negotiate the treaty. The high and solemn duty of ratifying or rejecting it is wisely devolved on the Senate by the Constitution of the United States.

11

James K. Polk

1. INAUGURAL ADDRESS   **MARCH 4, 1845**

The Republic of Texas has made known her desire to come into our Union, to form a part of our Confederacy and enjoy with us the blessings of liberty secured and guaranteed by our Constitution. Texas was once a part of our country, was unwisely ceded away to a foreign power, is now independent, and possesses an undoubted right to dispose of a part or the whole of her territory and to merge her sovereignty as a separate and independent state in ours. I congratulate my country that by an act of the late Congress of the United States the assent of this Government has been given to the reunion, and it only remains for the two countries to agree upon the terms to consummate an object so important to both.

I regard the question of annexation as belonging exclusively to the United States and Texas. They are independent powers competent to contract, and foreign nations have no right to interfere with them or to take exceptions to their reunion. Foreign powers do not seem to appreciate the true character of our Government. Our Union is a confederation of independent States, whose policy is peace with each other and all the world. To enlarge its limits is to extend the dominions of peace over additional territories and increasing millions. The world has nothing to fear from military ambition in our Government. While the Chief Magistrate and the popular branch of Congress are elected for short terms by the suffrages of those millions who must in their own persons bear all the burdens and miseries of war, our Government cannot be otherwise than pacific. Foreign powers should therefore look on the annexation of Texas to the United States not as the conquest of a nation seeking to extend her dominions by arms and violence, but as the peaceful acquisition of a territory once her own, by adding another member to our confederation, with the consent of that member, thereby diminishing the chances of war and opening to them new and ever increasing markets for their products.

To Texas the reunion is important, because the strong protecting arm of our Government would be extended over her, and the vast resources of her fertile soil and genial climate would be speedily developed, while the safety of New Orleans and of our whole southwestern frontier against hostile aggression, as well as the interests of the whole Union, would be promoted by it. . . .

None can fail to see the danger to our safety and future peace if Texas remains an independent state or becomes an ally or dependency of some foreign nation more powerful than herself. Is there one among our citizens who would not prefer perpetual peace with Texas to occasional wars, which so often occur between bordering independent nations? Is there one who would not prefer free intercourse with her to high duties on all our products and manufactures which enter her ports or cross her frontiers? Is there one who would not prefer an unrestricted communication with her citizens to the frontier obstructions which must occur if she remains out of the Union? Whatever is good or evil in the local institutions of Texas will remain her own whether annexed to the United States or not. None of the present States will be responsible for them any more than they are for the local institutions of each other. They have confederated together for certain specified objects. Upon the same principle that they would refuse to form a perpetual Union with Texas because of her local institutions our forefathers would have been prevented from forming our present Union. Perceiving no valid objection to the measure and many reasons for its adoption vitally affecting the peace, the safety, and the prosperity of both countries, I shall on the broad principle which formed the basis and produced the adoption of our Constitution, and not in any narrow spirit of sectional policy, endeavor by all constitutional, honorable, and appropriate means to consummate the expressed will of the people and Government of the United States by the re-annexation of Texas to our Union at the earliest practicable period.

Nor will it become in a less degree my duty to assert and maintain by all constitutional means the right of the United States to that portion of our territory which lies beyond the Rocky Mountains. Our title to the country of the Oregon is "clear and unquestionable," and already are our people preparing to perfect that title by occupying it with their wives and children. But eighty years ago our population was confined on the west by the ridge of the Alleghenies. Within that period—within the lifetime, I might say, of some of my hearers—our people, increasing too many millions, have filled the eastern valley of the Mississippi, adventurously ascended the Missouri to its headsprings, and are already engaged in establishing the blessings of self-government in valleys of which the rivers flow to the Pacific. The world beholds the peaceful triumphs of the industry of our emigrants. To us belongs the duty of protecting them adequately wherever they may be upon our soil. The jurisdiction of our laws and the benefits of our republican institutions should be extended over them in the distant regions which they have selected for their homes. The increasing facilities of intercourse will easily bring the States, of which the formation in that part of our territory cannot be long delayed, within the sphere of our federative Union. In the meantime every obligation imposed by treaty or conventional stipulations should be sacredly respected.

2. FIRST ANNUAL MESSAGE   DECEMBER 2, 1845

. . . The rapid extension of our settlements over our territories heretofore unoccupied, the addition of new States to our Confederacy, the expansion of free principles, and our rising greatness as a nation are attracting the attention of the powers of Europe, and lately the doctrine has been broached in some of them of a "balance of power" on this continent to check our advancement. The United States, sincerely desirous of preserving relations of good understanding with all nations, cannot in silence permit any European interference on the North American continent, and should any such interference be attempted will be ready to resist it at any and all hazards.

It is well known to the American people and to all nations that this Government has never interfered with the relations subsisting between other governments. We have never made ourselves parties to their wars or their alliances; we have not sought their territories by conquest; we have not mingled with parties in their domestic struggles; and believing our own form of government to be the best, we have never attempted to propagate it by intrigues, by diplomacy, or by force. We may claim on this continent a like exemption from European interference. The nations of America are equally sovereign and independent with those of Europe. They possess the same rights, independent of all foreign interposition, to make war, to conclude peace, and to regulate their internal affairs. The people of the United States cannot, therefore, view with indifference attempts of

European powers to interfere with the independent action of the nations on this continent. The American system of government is entirely different from that of Europe. Jealousy among the different sovereigns of Europe, lest any one of them might become too powerful for the rest, has caused them anxiously to desire the establishment of what they term the "balance of power." It cannot be permitted to have any application on the North American continent, and especially to the United States. We must ever maintain the principle that the people of this continent alone have the right to decide their own destiny. Should any portion of them, constituting an independent state, propose to unite themselves with our Confederacy, this will be a question for them and us to determine without any foreign interposition. We can never consent that European powers shall interfere to prevent such a union because it might disturb the "balance of power" which they may desire to maintain upon this continent. Near a quarter of a century ago the principle was distinctly announced to the world, in the annual message of one of my predecessors, that: The American continents, by the free and independent condition which they have assumed and maintain, are henceforth not to be considered as subjects for future colonization by any European powers.

This principle will apply with greatly increased force should any European power attempt to establish any new colony in North America. In the existing circumstances of the world the present is deemed a proper occasion to reiterate and reaffirm the principle avowed by Mr. Monroe and to state my cordial concurrence in its wisdom and sound policy. The reassertion of this principle, especially in reference to North America, is at this day but the promulgation of a policy which no European power should cherish the disposition to resist. Existing rights of every European nation should be respected, but it is due alike to our safety and our interests that the efficient protection of our laws should be extended over our whole territorial limits, and that it should be distinctly announced to the world as our settled policy that no future European colony or dominion shall with our consent be planted or established on any part of the North American continent. . . .

3. WAR MESSAGE   MAY 11, 1846

The existing state of the relations between the United States and Mexico renders it proper that I should bring the subject to the consideration of Congress. . . .

In my message at the commencement of the present session I informed you that upon the earnest appeal both of the Congress and convention of Texas I had ordered an efficient military force to take a position "between the Nueces and the Del Norte." This had become necessary to meet a threatened invasion of Texas by the Mexican forces, for which extensive military preparations had been made. The invasion was threatened solely because Texas had determined in accordance with a solemn resolution of the Congress of the United States, to annex herself to our Union, and under these circumstances it was plainly our duty to extend our protection over her citizens and soil.

This force was concentrated at Corpus Christi, and remained there until after I had received such information from Mexico as rendered it probable, if not certain, that the Mexican Government would refuse to receive our envoy.

Meantime Texas, by the final action of our Congress, had become an integral part of our Union. The Congress of Texas, by its act of 19 December 1836, had declared the Rio del Norte to be the boundary of that Republic. Its jurisdiction had been extended and exercised beyond the Nueces. The country between that river and the Del Norte had been represented in the Congress and in the convention of Texas, had thus taken part in the act of annexation itself, and is now included within one of our Congressional districts. Our own Congress had, moreover, with great unanimity, by the act approved 31 December 1845, recognized the country beyond the Nueces as a part of our territory by including it within our own revenue system, and a revenue officer to reside within that district has been appointed by and with the advice and consent of the Senate. It became, therefore, of urgent necessity to provide for the defense of that portion of our country. Accordingly, on the 13th of January last instructions were issued to the general in command of these troops to occupy the left bank of the Del Norte. This river, which is the southwestern boundary of the State of Texas, is an exposed frontier. . . .

The movement of the troops to the Del Norte was made by the commanding general under positive instructions to abstain from all aggressive acts toward Mexico or Mexican citizens and to regard the relations between that Republic and the United States as peaceful unless she should declare war or commit acts of hostility indicative of a state of war. . . .

The Mexican forces at Matamoras assumed a belligerent attitude, and on the 12th of April General Ampudia, then in command, notified General Taylor to break up his camp within twenty-four hours and to retire beyond the Nueces River, and in the event of his failure to comply with these demands announced that arms, and arms alone, must decide the question. But no open act of hostility was committed until the 24th of April. On that day General Arista, who had succeeded to the command of the Mexican forces, communicated to General Taylor that "he considered hostilities commenced and should prosecute them." A party of dragoons of 63 men and officers were on the same day dispatched from the American camp up the Rio del Norte on, its left bank, to ascertain whether the Mexican troops had crossed or were preparing to cross the river, "became engaged with a large body of these troops, and after a short affair, in which some 16 were killed and wounded, appear to have been surrounded and compelled to surrender." . . .

Our commerce with Mexico has been almost annihilated. It was formerly highly beneficial to both nations, but our merchants have been deterred from prosecuting it by the system of outrage and extortion which the Mexican authorities have pursued against them, whilst their appeals through their own Government for indemnity have been made in vain. . . .

In the meantime we have tried every effort at reconciliation. The cup of forbearance had been exhausted even before the recent information from the frontier of the Del Norte. But now, after reiterated menaces, Mexico has passed the boundary of the United States, has invaded our territory and shed American blood upon the American soil. She has proclaimed that hostilities have commenced, and that the two nations are now at war.

As war exists, and, notwithstanding all our efforts to avoid it, exists by the act of Mexico herself, we are called upon by every consideration of duty and patriotism to vindicate with decision the honor, the rights, and the interests of our country. . . .

In further vindication of our rights and defense of our territory, I invoke the prompt action of Congress to recognize the existence of the war, and to place at the disposition of the Executive the means of prosecuting the war with vigor, and thus hastening the restoration of peace. . . .

4. THE OREGON QUESTION   JUNE 10, 1846

I lay before the Senate a proposal . . . presented to the Secretary of State on the 6th instant by the envoy extraordinary and minister plenipotentiary of Her Britannic Majesty, for the adjustment of the Oregon question. . . . I submit this proposal to the consideration of the Senate, and request their advice, as to the action which in their judgment it may be proper to take in reference to it.

In the early periods of the Government the opinion and advice of the Senate were often taken in advance upon important questions of our foreign policy. General Washington repeatedly consulted the Senate and asked their previous advice upon pending negotiations with foreign powers, and the Senate in every instance responded to his call by giving their advice, to which he always conformed his action. This practice, though rarely resorted to in later times, was, in my judgment, eminently wise, and may on occasions of great importance be properly revived. The Senate are a branch of the treaty-making power, and by consulting them in advance of his own action upon important measures of foreign policy which may ultimately come before them for their consideration the President secures harmony of action between that body and himself. The Senate are, moreover, a branch of the war-making power, and may be eminently proper for the Executive to take the opinion and advice of that body in advance upon any great question which may involve in its decision the issue of peace or war. On the present occasion the magnitude of the subject would induce me under any circumstances to desire the debates and proceedings in Congress, which render it, in my judgment, not only respectful to the Senate, but necessary and proper, if not indispensable to insure harmonious action between that body and the Executive. In conferring on the Executive the authority to give the notice for the abrogation of the convention of 1827 the Senate acted publicly so large a part that a decision on the proposal now made by the British Government, without a definite knowledge of the views of that body in reference to it, might render the question still more complicated and difficult of adjustment. For these reasons I invite the consideration of the Senate to the proposal of the British Government for the settlement of the Oregon question, and ask their advice on the subject.

. . . Should the Senate, by the constitutional majority required for the ratification of treaties, advise the acceptance of this proposition, or advise it with such modifications as they may upon full deliberation deem proper, I shall conform my action to their advice. Should the Senate, however, decline by such constitutional majority to give such advice or to express an opinion on the subject, I shall consider it my duty to reject the offer. . . .

5. DISCOVERY OF GOLD IN CALIFORNIA   DECEMBER 5, 1848

. . . It was known that mines of the precious metals existed to a considerable extent in California at the time of its acquisition. Recent discoveries render it probable that these mines are more extensive and valuable than was anticipated. The accounts of the abundance of gold in that territory are of such an extraordinary character as would scarcely command belief were they not corroborated by the authentic reports of officers in the public service who have visited the mineral district and derived the facts which they detail from personal observation. Reluctant to credit the reports in general circulation as to the quantity of gold, the officer commanding our forces in California visited the mineral district in July last for the purpose of obtaining accurate information on the subject. His report to the War Department of the result of his examination and the facts obtained on the spot is herewith laid before Congress. When he visited the country there were about 4,000 persons engaged in collecting gold. There is every reason to believe that the number of persons so employed has since been augmented. The explorations already made warrant the belief that the supply is very large and that gold is found at various places in an extensive district of country.

Information received from officers of the Navy and other sources, though not so full and minute, confirms the accounts of the commander of our military force in California. It appears also from these reports that mines of quicksilver are found in the vicinity of the gold region. One of them is now being worked, and is believed to be among the most productive in the world.

The effects produced by the discovery of these rich mineral deposits and the success which has attended the labors of those who have resorted to them have produced a surprising change in the state of affairs in California. Labor commands a most exorbitant price, and all other pursuits but that of searching for the precious metals are abandoned. Nearly the whole of the male population of the country have gone to the gold districts. Ships arriving on the coast are deserted by their crews and their voyages suspended for want of sailors. Our commanding officer there entertains apprehensions that soldiers cannot be kept in the public service without a large increase of pay. Desertions in his command have become frequent, and he recommends that those who shall withstand the strong temptation and remain faithful should be rewarded.

This abundance of gold and the all-engrossing pursuit of it have already caused in California an unprecedented rise in the price of all the necessaries of life. . . .

IV

COMPROMISE AND CONFLICT

THE NATION STOOD EQUALLY DIVIDED IN 1850 with a balance of fifteen slave and fifteen free states. When California petitioned for admission as a free state, the mounting sectional antagonisms threatened to disrupt the Union. Once more an adjustment resulted—the Compromise of 1850. The spirit of moderation now became manifest as the temperate forces rallied to avoid secession. The plan proposed the admission of California as a free state. New Mexico and Utah would be organized into territories without mention of slavery. It provided for the establishment of more efficient procedures for the return of fugitive slaves to their masters. Slavery would continue in the District of Columbia (unless Maryland thought otherwise), but the slave trade would be abolished in the nation's capital. The Compromise called for federal compensation to Texas for territory ceded to New Mexico. North and South were compelled to sacrifice so that the Union could be preserved.

Vice President Fillmore had presided over the Senate debate for months. The Compromise package had been pieced together with care to prevent Civil War and save the Union. President Zachary Taylor, although a slaveholder, was a firm nationalist. Given his forty years of military service he was prepared to use force rather than compromise to preserve the Union. The President attended Independence Day ceremonies in the summer heat at the Washington Monument. Five days later, he was dead. Millard Fillmore, now President, supported the final passage of the Compromise bill. In the end, the forces of moderation triumphed and the nation endured for another decade.

The Compromise of 1850 was the outstanding achievement of Fillmore's administration. He explained his position on December 2, 1850. The preservation of the Union was above any specific settlement of the slavery question. His support for the Fugitive Slave Act, which ensured the return of runaway slaves, enraged abolitionists. His commitment to this portion of the Compromise package ended his political career. He did attempt a comeback as an anti-Catholic, anti-immigrant Know-Nothing candidate.

As Fillmore's tenure in office neared closure, it became his painful duty to announce, on October 25, 1852, the death of Daniel Webster on the previous day in Marshfield, Massachusetts. The demise of the Secretary of State brought a "mournful respect" and an "irreparable loss" to the President and his administration. The passing of this great mind, scholar, and statesman was felt throughout the nation as a "natural sorrow to every American heart."

Within days of the death of Webster, the American people went to the polls and elected Franklin Pierce President of the United States. The slogan boosting his election was: "We Polked them in 44, we'll Pierce them in 52." In a sense there was continuity from Polk to Pierce. The Gadsden Purchase concluded by President Pierce, Secretary of State W. L. Marcy and special envoy James Gadsden provided the final slice of Mexican land to be added to the Mexican Cession obtained by the Treaty of Guadeloupe Hidalgo. President Pierce issued a Proclamation in the City of Washington, on June 30, 1854. The President promulgated the Treaty which had been signed in Mexico City at the end of December 1853 and afterwards amended by the Senate of the United States. He proclaimed "In the Name of Almighty God," that the two nations "desiring to remove every cause of disagreement . . . and to strengthen and more firmly maintain the peace which happily prevails between the two republics" concluded the treaty and agreement. The purchase would "maintain the peace" between the two neighbors. It would add, however, a cause for internal discontent and conflict at home. Pierce supported the Compromise of 1850 and promised in his Inaugural Address a period of domestic tranquility. It was towards this end and to provide greater security for the United States that he embarked on his diplomatic mission with Mexico. It was his Secretary of War, Jefferson Davis who had convinced Pierce to appoint Gadsden. The idea was to purchase land in order to justify a transcontinental railroad along a southern route to the Pacific. Another leading Democrat, Stephen A. Douglas favored a northern route through Chicago. To realize his purpose, Douglas promoted the Kansas–Nebraska Act. Old wounds were reopened and new bleeding commenced. The peace promised by Pierce proved elusive.

On Inauguration Day, 1857 James Buchanan rode to the Capitol with the outgoing Pierce. From the East Portico, he read his long address. The new President had something to say on most great issues of the day. He recommended the construction of a national railroad to the Pacific for military purposes. He stood for economy. The public debt needed payment. Buchanan favored a small increase in the navy. Above all, he affirmed his decision to uphold the Kansas–Nebraska Act. For he ardently believed the people should be free to regulate slavery as they saw fit.

In an oblique reference Buchanan predicted the Supreme Court would shortly settle the issue of slavery in the territories once and for all. Omitted from his prediction and intentionally so, was the fact that he had advance information of the fateful Dred Scott decision which the high tribunal rendered two days after his Inauguration. Given his advance knowledge with respect to the forthcoming verdict in the Dred Scott case, he was worse than devious in addressing his fellow Americans after swearing the oath of office. In a piece of deceitful trickery, he urged all citizens to support the final judicial verdict on slavery. His first presidential words deserve special attention and close examination: "To their decision, in common with all good citizens, I shall cheerfully submit, whatever this may be . . ."

The Buchanan Inaugural Address stunned Americans for Buchanan launched his Presidency with a surprise announcement: "Having determined not to become a candidate for reelection, I shall have no motive to influence my conduct in administering the Government except the desire ably and faithfully to serve my country." In effect this declaration made Buchanan a lame-duck president from his very first day on the job. From that day forward there began a search for his successor. Buchanan was the only President of the United States who remained a bachelor throughout his tenure in office. Perhaps the job best suits the wedded.

In his Second Annual Message to Congress, on December 6, 1858 Buchanan boasted that the country had come a long way towards the attainment of domestic peace and tranquility. Comparing that moment with conditions of the prior year he professed his relief at averting dissention. "We have much reason for gratitude to that Almighty Providence which has never failed . . . One year ago the sectional strife . . . on the dangerous subject of slavery had again become so intense as to threaten the peace and perpetuity of the Confederacy." Much had transpired since then "to remove the excitement from the States and confine it to the Territory where it legitimately belonged." The "unhappy agitation" of the prior year had thankfully, he maintained, been forestalled. After patting Congress and his own administration on the back for deflecting that agitation, he went on to once again celebrate the role of the Supreme Court in the peaceful progress accomplished. The President took great pains to put the prestige and power of the Executive and Legislative Branches of the government squarely in support of the Supreme Court's judicial decision to nationalize slavery. Once again the words of the President remain instructive: "The Supreme Court of the United States had previously decided that all American citizens have an equal right to take into the Territories whatever is held as property under the laws of any of the States." Buchanan underscored his contention that the ruling of the court with respect to slavery was now "a well-established position." His conclusion to the Congress was that the Court and the Congress had been "vindicated." Consequently, "a fruitful source of dangerous dissension among them has been removed."

The presidential election of 1860 qualifies as a critical election. For the first time in the history of the Republic, a large segment of the American people simply refused to acquiesce in the result. A presidential election ignited a Civil War. Lincoln's electoral victory came November 6, 1860. He would not be inaugurated until March 4, 1861. In that interim period President Buchanan lingered as "lame-duck." The moment called for leadership that the lame-duck did not provide as he lacked the will to make commitments involving the impending crisis between the states.

In his final Annual Message to Congress, on December 3, 1861, Buchanan placed the blame for the crisis at the feet of the northern antislavery agitators. Opening his message with positive expressions about the peace, wealth, and health of the land, he then followed with this question: "Why is it, then, that discontent now so extensively prevails, and the Union of the States, which is the source of all these blessings, is threatened with destruction?" The answer, according to the President, was that there existed an "intemperate interference" emanating from the North with respect to slavery. "The immediate peril arises," said Buchanan ". . . from the fact that the incessant and violent agitation of the slavery question throughout the North for the last quarter of a century has at length produced its malign influence on the slaves and inspired them with vague notions of freedom." This is one instance where the President of the United States could be identified as being on the wrong side of freedom.

The President of all the people took sides against those intemperate northern agitators who disturbed the peace and security that had previously prevailed at the "family altar." In doing so he was also giving the back of his hand to the President-elect who had gained election from those same quarters. The easy solution was not war. The issue could be settled forever by simply allowing the slave States "to be let alone and permitted to manage their domestic institutions in their own way." President Buchanan deprecated the pending breakup of the Union. At the same time he insisted that the federal government could not use force to prevent secession.

Buchanan's message got a mixed and partisan reception. Voices of unqualified approval were scarce. Republicans found it outrageous in placing the blame for the crisis on their party while failing to meet head-on the threat of disunion. As the crisis deepened, President Buchanan delivered a special message on the State of the Union, on January 8, 1861. Here he acknowledged the obvious that "a great calamity" was at hand and the consequences would be "deplorable." His message expressed regret that he was unable to communicate a "more satisfactory" picture. The truth was the situation had gotten "worse" and hope was fleeting. The alarm assumed proportions "beyond Executive control." His message embodied a reckless abandonment of executive responsibility. He shamelessly kicked the can to the Congress as the only power able to meet the emergency saying that "On them and them alone, rests the responsibility. . . ." Overall, Buchanan made it patently clear that he had washed his hands of executive action to save the union. The President no longer commanded public respect nor did he exercise control of his party or the nation. We are left with the words of Lincoln: "And the War Came."

12

Zachary Taylor

1. STATEHOOD FOR CALIFORNIA

DECEMBER 4, 1849

. . . No civil government having been provided by Congress for California, the people of that Territory, impelled by the necessities of their political condition, recently met in convention for the purpose of forming a constitution and State government, which the latest advices give me reason to suppose has been accomplished; and it is believed they will shortly apply for the admission of California into the Union as a sovereign State. Should such be the case, and should their constitution be comfortable to the requisitions of the Constitution of the United States, I recommend their application to the favorable consideration of Congress. The people of New Mexico will also, it is believed, at no very distant period present themselves for admission into the Union. Preparatory to the admission of California and New Mexico the people of each will have instituted for themselves a republican form of government, "laying its foundation in such principles and organizing its powers in such form as to them shall seem most likely to effect their safety and happiness." By awaiting their action all causes of uneasiness may be avoided and confidence and kind feeling preserved. With a view of maintaining the harmony and tranquility so dear to all, we should abstain from the introduction of those exciting topics of a sectional character which have hitherto produced painful apprehensions in the public mind; and I repeat the solemn warning of the first and most illustrious of my predecessors against furnishing "any ground for characterizing parties by geographical discriminations." . . .

2. CLAYTON–BULWER TREATY

APRIL 22, 1850

I herewith transmit to the Senate, for their advice with regard to its ratification, a convention between the United States and Great Britain, concluded at Washington on the 19th instant by John M. Clayton, Secretary of State, on the part of the United States, and by the Right Hon. Sir Henry Lytton Bulwer, on the part of Great Britain.

This treaty has been negotiated in accordance with the general views expressed in my message to Congress in December last. Its object is to establish a commercial alliance with all great maritime states for the protection of a contemplated ship canal through the territory of Nicaragua to connect the Atlantic and Pacific oceans, and at the same time to insure the same protection to the contemplated railways or canals by the Tehuantepec and Panama routes, as well as to every other inter-oceanic communication which may be adopted to shorten the transit to or from our territories on the Pacific.

It will be seen that this treaty does not propose to take money from the public Treasury to effect any object contemplated by it. It yields protection to the capitalists who may undertake to construct any canal or railway across the isthmus, commencing in the southern part of Mexico and terminating in the territory of New Granada. It gives no preference to any one route over another, but proposes the same measure of protection for all which ingenuity and enterprise can construct. Should this treaty by ratified, it will secure in future the liberation of all Central America from any kind of foreign aggression. . . .

If thereby any who would desire to seize or annex any portion of the territories of these weak sister republics to the American Union, or to extend our dominion over them, I do not concur in their policy; and I wish it to be understood in reference to that subject that I adopt the views entertained, so far as I know, by all my predecessors. The principles by which I have been regulated in the negotiation of this treaty are in accordance with the sentiments well expressed by my immediate predecessor on the 10th of February 1847, when he communicated to the Senate the treaty with New Granada for the protection of the railroad at Panama. It is in accordance with the whole spirit of the resolution of the Senate of the 3rd of March 1835, referred to by President Polk, and with the policy adopted by President Jackson immediately after the passage of that resolution, who dispatched an agent to Central America and New Granada "to open negotiations with those Governments for the purpose of effectually protecting, by suitable treaty stipulations with them, such individuals or companies as might undertake to open a communication between the Atlantic and Pacific oceans by the construction of a ship canal across the isthmus which connects North and South America, and of securing forever by such stipulations the free and equal right of navigating such canal to all such nations on the payment of such reasonable tolls as might be established to compensate the capitalists who should engage in such undertaking and complete the work." . . .

Should the Senate in its wisdom see fit to confirm this treaty, and the treaty heretofore submitted by me for their advice in regard to its ratification, negotiated with the State of Nicaragua on the 3rd day of September last, it will be necessary to amend one or both of them, so that both treaties may stand in conformity with each other in their spirit and intention. The Senate will discover by examining them both that this is a task of no great difficulty.

I have good reason to believe that France and Russia stand ready to accede to this treaty, and that no other great maritime state will refuse its accession to an arrangement so well calculated to diffuse the blessings of peace, commerce, and civilization, and so honorable to all nations which may enter into the engagement.

3. PROCLAMATION OF PEACE   AUGUST 11, 1849

There is reason to believe that an armed expedition is about to be fitted out in the United States with an intention to invade the island of Cuba or some of the Provinces of Mexico. The best information, which the Executive has been able to obtain, points to the island of Cuba as the object of this expedition. It is the duty of this Government to observe the faith of treaties and to prevent any aggression by our citizens upon the territories of friendly nations. I have therefore thought it necessary and proper to issue this my proclamation to warn all citizens of the United States who shall connect themselves with such an enterprise so grossly in violation of our laws and our treaty obligations that they will thereby subject themselves to the heavy penalties denounced against them by our acts of Congress and will forfeit their claim to the protection of their country. No such persons must expect the interference of this Government in any form on their behalf. . . . An enterprise to invade the territories of a friendly nation, set foot and prosecuted within the limits of the United States, is in the highest degree criminal, as tending to endanger the peace and compromise the honor of this nation; and therefore I exhort all good citizens . . . to discountenance and prevent by all lawful means any such enterprise. . . .

13

Millard Fillmore

1. COMPROMISE OF 1850   **DECEMBER 2, 1850**

. . . The act, passed at your last session, making certain propositions to Texas for settling the disputed boundary between that State and the Territory of New Mexico was, immediately on its passage, transmitted by express to the governor of Texas, to be laid by him before the general assembly for its agreement thereto. Its receipt was duly acknowledged, but no official information has yet been received of the action of the general assembly thereon. It may, however, be very soon expected, as, by the terms of the propositions submitted they were to have been acted upon on or before the first day of the present month.

It was hardly to have been expected that the series of measures passed at your last session with the view of healing the sectional differences which had sprung from the slavery and territorial questions should at once have realized their beneficent purpose. All mutual concession in the nature of a compromise must necessarily be unwelcome to men of extreme opinions. And though without such concessions our Constitution could not have been formed, and cannot be permanently sustained, yet we have seen them made the subject of bitter controversy in both sections of the Republic. It required many months of discussion and deliberation to secure the concurrence of a majority of Congress in their favor. It would be strange if they had been received with immediate approbation by people and States prejudiced and heated by the exciting controversies of their representatives. I believe those measures to have been required by the circumstances and condition of the country. I believe they were necessary to allay asperities and animosities that were rapidly alienating one section of the country from another and destroying those fraternal sentiments which are the strongest supports of the Constitution. They were adopted in the spirit of conciliation and for the purpose of conciliation. I believe that a great majority of our fellow-citizens sympathize in that spirit and that purpose, and in the main approve and are prepared in all respects to sustain these enactments. I cannot doubt that the American people, bound together by kindred blood and common traditions, still cherish a paramount regard for the Union of their fathers, and that they are ready to rebuke any attempt to violate its integrity, to disturb the compromises on which it is based, or to resist the laws which have been enacted under its authority.

The series of measures to which I have alluded are regarded by me as a settlement in principle and substance—a final settlement of the dangerous and exciting subjects which they embraced. Most of these subjects, indeed, are beyond your reach, as the legislation which disposed of them was in its character final and irrevocable. It may be presumed from the opposition which they all encountered that none of those measures was free from imperfections, but in their mutual dependence and connection they formed a system of compromise the most conciliatory and best for the entire country that could be obtained from conflicting sectional interests and opinions.

For this reason I recommend your adherence to the adjustment established by those measures until time and experience shall demonstrate the necessity of further legislation to guard against evasion or abuse.

By that adjustment we have been rescued from the wide and boundless agitation that surrounded us, and have a firm, distinct, and legal ground to rest upon. And the occasion, I trust, will justify me in exhorting my countrymen to rally upon and maintain that ground as the best, if not the only, means of restoring peace and quiet to the country and maintaining inviolate the integrity of the Union. . . .

2. DEATH OF DANIEL WEBSTER   OCTOBER 25, 1852

The painful intelligence received yesterday enforces upon me the sad duty of announcing to the Executive Departments the death of the Secretary of State. Daniel Webster died at Marshfield, in Massachusetts, on Sunday, the 24th of October, between 2 and 3 o'clock in the morning.

Whilst this irreparable loss brings its natural sorrow to every American heart and will be heard far beyond our borders with mournful respect wherever civilization has nurtured men who find in transcendent intellect and faithful, patriotic service a theme for praise, it will visit with still more poignant emotion his colleagues in the Administration, with whom his relations have been so intimate and so cordial.

The fame of our illustrious statesman belongs to his country, the administration of it to the world. The record of his wisdom will inform future generations not less than its utterance has enlightened the present. He has bequeathed to posterity the richest fruits of the experience and judgment of a great mind conversant with the greatest national concerns. In these his memory will endure as long as our country shall continue to be the home and guardian of freemen.

The people will share with the Executive Departments in the common grief which bewails his departure from us. . . .

14

Franklin Pierce

1. THE SUPREME GOOD OF THESE UNITED STATES   DECEMBER 4, 1854

. . . Our forefathers of the thirteen united colonies, in acquiring their independence and in founding this Republic of the United States of America have devolved upon us, their descendants, the greatest and most noble trust ever committed to the hands of man, imposing upon all, and especially such as the public will may have invested for the time being with political functions, the most sacred obligations. We have to maintain inviolate the great doctrine of the inherent right of popular self-government; to reconcile the largest liberty of the individual citizen with complete security of the public order; to render cheerful obedience to the laws of the land, to unite in enforcing their execution, and to frown indignantly on all combinations to resist them; to harmonize a sincere and ardent devotion to the institutions of religious faith with the most universal religious toleration; to preserve the rights of all by causing each to respect those of the other; to carry forward every social improvement to the uttermost limit of human perfectibility, by the free action of mind upon mind, not by the obtrusive intervention of misapplied force; to uphold the integrity and guard the limitations of our organic law; to preserve sacred from all touch of usurpation, as the very palladium of our political salvation, the reserved rights and powers of the several States and of the people to cherish with loyal fealty and devoted affection this Union, as the only sure foundation on which the hopes of civil liberty rest; to administer government with vigilant integrity and rigid economy; to cultivate peace and friendship with foreign nations, and to demand and exact justice from all, but to do wrong to none; to eschew intermeddling with the national policy and the domestic repose of other governments, and to repel it from our own; never to shrink from war when the rights and honor of the country call us to arms, but to cultivate in preference the arts of peace, seek enlargement of the rights of neutrals, and elevate and liberalize the intercourse of nations, and by such just and honorable means . . . whilst exalting the condition of the Republic, to assure to it the legitimate influence and the benign authority of a great example amongst all the powers of Christendom.

Under the solemnity of these convictions the blessing of Almighty God is earnestly invoked to attend upon your deliberations and upon all the counsels and acts of the Government, to the end that, with common zeal and common efforts we may, in humble submission to the divine will, cooperate for the promotion of the supreme good of these United States.

15

James Buchanan

1. INAUGURAL ADDRESS   MARCH 4, 1857

I appear before you this day to take the solemn oath "that I will faithfully execute the office of President of the United States and will to the best of my ability preserve, protect, and defend the Constitution of the United States." . . .

Convinced that I owe my election to the inherent love for the Constitution and the Union which still animates the hearts of the American people, let me earnestly ask their powerful support in sustaining all just measures calculated to perpetuate these, the richest political blessings which Heaven has ever bestowed upon any nation. Having determined not to become a candidate for reelection, I shall have no motive to influence my conduct in administering the Government except the desire ably and faithfully to serve my country and to live in grateful memory of my countrymen.
. . .

What a happy conception, then, was it for Congress to apply this simple rule that the will of the majority shall govern, to the settlement of the question of domestic slavery in the Territories! Congress is neither "to legislate slavery into any Territory or State nor to exclude it therefrom, but to leave the people thereof perfectly free to form and regain their domestic institutions in their own way, subject only to the Constitution of the United States."

As a natural consequence, Congress has also prescribed that when the Territory of Kansas shall be admitted as a State it "shall be received into the Union with or without slavery, as their constitution may prescribe at the time of their admission."

A difference of opinion has arisen in regard to the point of time when the people of a Territory shall decide this question for themselves.

This is, happily, a matter of but little practical importance. Besides, it is a judicial question, which legitimately belongs to the Supreme Court of the United States, before whom it is now pending, and will, it is understood, be speedily and finally settled. To their decision, in common with all good citizens, I shall cheerfully submit, whatever this may be, though it has ever been my individual opinion that under the Nebraska–Kansas act the appropriate period will be when the number of actual residents in the Territory shall justify the formation of a constitution with a view to its admission as a State into the Union. But be this as it may, it is the imperative and indispensable duty of the Government of the United States to secure to every resident inhabitant the free and independent expression of his opinion by his vote. This sacred right of each individual must be preserved. That being accomplished, nothing can be fairer than to leave the people of a Territory free from all foreign interference to decide their own destiny for themselves, subject only to the Constitution of the United States.

The whole Territorial question being thus settled upon the principle of popular sovereignty—a principle as ancient as free government itself—everything of a practical nature has been decided. No other question remains for adjustment, because all agree that under the Constitution slavery in the States is beyond the reach of any human power except that of the respective States themselves wherein it exists. . . .

The Federal Constitution is a grant from the States to Congress of certain specific powers, and the question whether this grant should be liberally or strictly construed has more or less divided political parties from the beginning. Without entering into the argument, I desire to state at the commencement of my Administration that long experience and observation have convinced me that a strict construction of the powers of the Government is the only true, as well as the only safe, theory of the Constitution. Whenever in our past history doubtful powers have been exercised by Congress, these have never failed to produce injurious and unhappy consequences. Many such instances might be adduced if this were the proper occasion. Neither is it necessary for the public service to strain the language of the Constitution, because all the great and useful powers required for a successful administration of the Government, both in peace and in war, have been granted, either in express terms or by the plainest implication. . . .

HON. JAMES BUCHANAN,
Democratic Candidate for the Presidency, 1856.

Figure 15.1 James Buchanan, courtesy of the Library of Congress Prints and Photographs Division, Washington, DC.

Whilst deeply convinced of these truths, I yet consider it clear that under the war-making power Congress may appropriate money toward the construction of a military road when this is absolutely necessary for the defense of any State or Territory of the Union against foreign invasion. Under the Constitution Congress has power "to declare war," "to raise and support armies," "to provide and maintain a navy," and to call forth the militia to "repel invasions." Thus endowed, in an ample manner, with the war-making power, the corresponding duty is required that "the United States shall protect each of them [the States] against invasion." Now, how is it possible to afford this protection to California and our Pacific possessions except by means of a military road through the Territories of the United States, over which men and munitions of war may be speedily transported from the Atlantic States to meet and to repel the invader? In the event of a war with a naval power much stronger than our own we should then have no other available access to the Pacific Coast, because such a power would instantly close the route across the isthmus of Central America. It is impossible to conceive that whilst the Constitution has expressly required Congress to defend all the States it should yet deny to them, by any fair construction, the only possible means by which one of these States can be defended. Besides, the Government, ever since its origin, has been in the constant practice of constructing military roads. It might also be wise to consider whether the love for the Union which now animates our fellow-citizens on the Pacific Coast may not be impaired by our neglect or refusal to provide for them, in their remote and isolated condition, the only means by which the power of the States on this side of the Rocky Mountains can reach them in sufficient time to "protect" them "against invasion." I forbear for the present from expressing an opinion as to the wisest and most economical mode in which the Government can lend its aid in accomplishing this great and necessary work. I believe that many of the difficulties in the way, which now appear formidable, will in a great degree vanish as soon as the nearest and best route shall have been satisfactorily ascertained. . . .

2. DISUNION AVERTED   DECEMBER 6, 1858

When we compare the condition of the country at the present day with what it was one year ago at the meeting of Congress, we have much reason for gratitude to that Almighty Providence which has never failed to interpose for our relief at the most critical periods of our history. One year ago the sectional strife between the North and the South on the dangerous subject of slavery had again become so intense as to threaten the peace and perpetuity of the Confederacy. The application for the admission of Kansas as a State into the Union fostered this unhappy agitation and brought the whole subject once more before Congress. It was the desire of every patriot that such measures of legislation might be adopted as would remove the excitement from the States and confine it to the Territory where it legitimately belonged. Much has been done, I am happy to say, toward the accomplishment of this object during the last session of Congress.

The Supreme Court of the United States had previously decided that all American citizens have an equal right to take into the Territories whatever is held as property under the laws of any of the States, and to hold such property there under the guardianship of the Federal Constitution so long as the Territorial condition shall remain. . . .

This is now a well-established position, and the proceedings of the last session were alone wanting to give it practical effect. The principle has been recognized in some form or other by an almost unanimous vote of both Houses of Congress that a Territory has a right to come into the Union either as a free or a slave State, according to the will of a majority of its people. The just equality of all the States has thus been vindicated and a fruitful source of dangerous dissension among them has been removed.

3. INTEMPERATE INTERFERENCE   DECEMBER 3, 1860

Throughout the year since our last meeting the country has been eminently prosperous in all its material interests. The general health has been excellent, our harvests have been abundant, and plenty smiles throughout the land . . . no nation in the tide of time has ever presented a spectacle of greater material prosperity than we have done. . . .

Why is it, then, that discontent now so extensively prevails, and the Union of the States, which is the source of all these blessings, is threatened with destruction?

The long-continued and intemperate interference of the Northern people with the question of slavery in the Southern States has at length produced its natural effects. The different sections of the Union are now arrayed against each other. . . .

The immediate peril arises . . . from the fact that the incessant and violent agitation of the slavery question throughout the North for the last quarter of a century has at length produced its malign influence on the slaves and inspired them with vague notions of freedom. Hence a sense of security no longer exists around the family altar. . . .

How easy would it be for the American people to settle the slavery question forever. . . . All that is necessary to accomplish this object, and all that the slave States have ever contended is to be let alone and permitted to manage their domestic institutions in their own way. . . . For this the people of the North are not more responsible and have no more right to interfere with similar institutions in Russia or in Brazil.

4. STATE OF THE UNION IS BEYOND EXECUTIVE CONTROL   JANUARY 8, 1861

At the opening of your present session I called your attention to the dangers which threatened the existence of the Union. . . .

The fact that a great calamity was impending over the nation was even at that time acknowledged by every intelligent citizen. It had already made itself felt throughout the length and breadth of the land.

The necessary consequences of the alarm thus produced were most deplorable. . . .

I deeply regret that I am not able to give you any information upon the State of the Union which is more satisfactory than what I was then obliged to communicate. On the contrary, matters are still worse at the present than they then were. When Congress met, a strong hope pervaded the whole public mind that some amicable adjustment of the subject would speedily be made . . . which might restore peace between the conflicting sections. . . . That hope has been diminished by every hour of delay, and as the prospect of a bloodless settlement fades away the public becomes more and more aggravated.

. . . the dangerous and hostile attitude of the States toward each other has already far transcended and cast in the shade the ordinary executive duties already provided for by law, and has assumed vast and alarming proportions as to place the subject entirely above and beyond Executive control. The fact cannot be disguised that we are in the midst of a great revolution. I commend the question to Congress as the only human tribunal under Providence possessing the power to meet the existing emergency. . . . On them and them alone, rests the responsibility. . . .

V

WAR AND PEACE

PRESIDENTIAL ELECTIONS ARE FUNDAMENTAL to the American system of politics and government. These quadrennial events construct a chain of democracy across the timeline of the Republic. Each election constitutes a significant step in the continued mapping of the destiny of the United States. Even so, some elections are more important than others. The election of 1860 remains the most important election in American history. Even prior to the announcement of the result, threats of all sorts were sounded amongst the several states. It was said that the South would never countenance the election of Abraham Lincoln. Indeed his election marked the dissolution of the Republic as Americans knew it. The Union began to shatter.

During Buchanan's administration, sectional disputes had become more acrimonious. Passions grew more excited. Propagandists in both sections increased tensions. Violence surfaced everywhere. Blood began to spill in Kansas. Beecher Bibles and gun-running was now the order of the day. Border Ruffians and night riders joined the action. John Brown led his own private war and murderous raids. Eventually captured, his terror was rewarded with the gallows, which Emerson claimed was now made glorious like the Cross. Lawmakers reported for congressional debate with their side-arms. There was a prominent caning in the Congress of the United States. National churches seceded into sectional splinters such as Northern Methodists and Southern Methodists; Northern Baptists and Southern Baptists. Family unity gave way to segmentation and dissention. The infamous Dred Scott decision at the outset of the Buchanan administration in 1857 and John Brown's raid at Harper's Ferry in 1859 inflamed passions on all sides of the burning slavery issue.

The presidential election of 1860 was the watershed. When the Democratic Party met at Charleston in April 1860, southern delegates refused to accept any platform that did not guarantee federal protection of slavery in the territories. Stephen Douglas, the little giant from Illinois, controlled a majority of the delegates and would not agree—but his support did not muster the two-thirds necessary to gain the nomination. After ten days of futile balloting, the convention adjourned to meet again in Baltimore on June 18, 1860. Upon reassembling, the party remained divided into northern and southern wings. Most of the southern delegates now withdrew. That exit permitted the Northern rump of the party to nominate Douglas. The bolters gathered and named John C. Breckinridge of Kentucky for president on a platform supporting slavery in the territories. With this crucial Democratic split, another bond holding the Union together dissolved. Republican chances for victory now brightened.

The Republican Party nominated Abraham Lincoln. Now 53 years old, he had served as a Whig representative for one term (1847–49) and then resumed his law practice in Springfield, Illinois. In 1858, the year following the Dred Scott decision, Lincoln contended against the Democratic incumbent U.S. Senator from Illinois for that seat in the upper Chamber. The contest witnessed the historic Lincoln–Douglas debates which took place at select locations in each of the seven Illinois congressional districts. The Illinois State Legislature remained in Democratic hands when the state canvass was complete, so Douglas was able to retain his seat. Lincoln emerged with an enhanced and a national reputation for the mark that he had made in the debates with the brilliant Douglas. Lincoln had the political savvy to tie Douglas in knots in a series of questions that placed the seasoned incumbent and aspirant for the Executive Mansion in a virtual buzz saw. He adroitly placed Douglas between the sitting Democratic President Buchanan (in tandem with the activist Democrat-friendly Supreme Court) and the Douglas-adopted strategy of popular sovereignty with regard to the slavery issue. In so doing he split the Democratic Party into irreconcilable factions. The cornered Douglas lost his privileged standing in both North and South. The ingenious Democratic leader and pretender to the throne had been placed in a whipsaw by the skillful thrusts and parries of the upstart Republican lawyer. At one moment Douglas would seem to be with the Democratic solid South and slavery and the next he would appeal to the North and West on the side of freedom. Douglas had preserved his Senate seat but his Potomac bubble had been pricked.

Lincoln's rise to win the Republican nomination had begun. His abilities had been noticed but his greatness was not yet apparent to many observers. Few who voted for Lincoln at the 1860 Republican convention comprehended the historic proportions and character of their nominee. It is fair to say that his backers simply calculated that he had the best chance of winning the presidency.

In addition to Lincoln, Douglas, and Breckinridge, the former Whig-American party, renamed the Constitutional Union party, nominated John Bell of Tennessee. There would not be another four-way presidential contest for more than a half century with the epic election of 1912. When the results of 1860 were tabulated, Lincoln received 180 of the 303 electoral votes—all from free states. Breckinridge carried eleven slave states and 72 votes. Bell ran third with 39, winning three border slave states. Douglas captured only Missouri and three New Jersey votes for a total of 12. Lincoln received only 39.9% of the popular vote. The results clearly show the sectional pattern, almost as if two elections were being held: Lincoln vs. Douglas in the North and West, Breckinridge vs. Bell in the South. Although Lincoln pledged to uphold the Union, its future remained in southern hands.

Secession followed the election returns. South Carolina departed first, on December 20, 1860. The South Carolina Governor expounded on Lincoln's election predicting that it would "inevitably destroy our equality in the Union, and ultimately reduce the southern states to mere provinces of a consolidated despotism to be governed by a fixed majority in Congress hostile to our institutions and fatally bent upon our ruin." The Deep South followed suit, and during January 1861 Mississippi, Florida, Alabama, Georgia, Louisiana, and Texas passed secession ordinances. With the exception of South Carolina, this movement certainly was not unanimous. In Alabama, for example, 34 of the 95 delegates to the special convention voted against immediate secession. In Georgia, 133 out of 297 were unwilling to dissolve the Union. Nonetheless, the zealots triumphed. The South had been long attached to the idea of states' rights. Ironically, they now established a national government, the Confederate States of America.

Lincoln left Springfield on February 11, 1861. As he traveled toward Washington, he calmly explained to excited crowds the necessity of preserving the Union. His journey became one continuous ovation. "We mean to treat you as near as we possibly can, as Washington, Jefferson, and Madison treated you," he told a group of Kentuckians present in the Cincinnati crowd. "We mean to leave you alone, and in no way to interfere with your institutions, to abide by all and every compromise of the Constitution." At Pittsburgh he insisted "no crisis existed." He further advised:

"If the American people will only keep their temper . . . the troubles will come to an end and they will prosper as heretofore."

The president-elect arrived in Washington on February 23rd. Nine days later, before the stark unfinished Capitol, Lincoln took the oath of office. In a masterly Inaugural Address he invoked "the mystic chords of memory" in making a direct appeal to Southerners: "In your hands, my dissatisfied fellow countrymen, and not in mine, is the momentous issue of civil war. The government will not assail you. You can have no conflict without being yourselves the aggressors."

The Civil War began on April 12, 1861 with the firing on Fort Sumter in Charleston harbor by South Carolinians. Lincoln declared that an "insurrection" existed on April 15th and called for 75,000 three-month volunteers. At the same time, he called Congress to meet in special session on July 4, 1861.

Between April and July, Lincoln had summoned his militia into active duty, proclaimed a blockade, expanded the regular army beyond the legal limit, suspended habeas corpus privilege, directed governmental expenditures in advance of congressional appropriations and, in cooperation with his cabinet and the state governments, had launched a series of military measures to suppress the rebellion.

When Congress answered the President's call to assemble on Independence Day, Lincoln explained his policies since the firing on Fort Sumter. He recounted the steps that had led to war. The message also contained his concept of, and the necessity for, preserving the Union. He concluded with an appeal for ratification of his acts as well as for future cooperation. Congress ratified the President's actions—and the Supreme Court likewise sanctioned his leadership by declaring in the Prize Cases (1863), that executive proclamations were adequate to blockade Confederate ports. The Court ruled that the President could not initiate war but he was fulfilling his lawful duties in resisting insurrection, and that an insurrection was, in fact, war.

From the moment he took office, Lincoln struggled with the issue of freeing the slaves. Europeans and Africans had inflicted this enormous curse on the continent. Americans had largely been affected by the contagion of liberty even prior to Independence Day and grappled with this fundamental moral issue. The moment of decision had arrived. President Lincoln finally reached his decision during the summer of 1862.

President Lincoln declared, on September 22, 1862, that "persons held as slaves" within areas "in rebellion against the United States" would be free on January 1, 1863. When that day arrived, the final proclamation specifically designated those areas "wherein the people . . . are this day in rebellion" and ordered "that all persons held as slaves . . . [within those areas] are, and henceforward shall be, free."

The Proclamation was far from an abolition document as it did not apply to Tennessee, nor to specifically excepted portions of Virginia and Louisiana, nor to Border States within the Union. Since liberation took place in areas not under Union military control, the Proclamation had negligible effect on the immediate freeing of any individuals. Nevertheless, abolitionists hailed the Proclamation. Through his action, Lincoln ensured the death of slavery when the war was won. In fact, many slaves had already seized their own freedom in parts of the South, occupied by Federal troops.

It is worthy of note that as the Civil War proceeded in 1862 and 1863 and as Lincoln prepared and executed his Emancipation Proclamation, diplomatic negotiations between the United States of America and her Britannic Majesty continued with respect to the suppression of the African slave trade. The President, in cooperation with the British, was engaged in tightening the noose at sea upon slave traders. The two nations had agreed to this policy in a Treaty on April 7, 1862. An additional and even more severe Article was added to the Treaty on February 17, 1863, a little more than a month following the famous Emancipation Proclamation. This Article was ratified by the United States on March 5, 1863 and proclaimed by President Lincoln on April 22, 1863. The President reported to the Congress in his Third Annual Address, on December 8, 1863, on the favorable suppression of the slave trade.

The national cemetery at the Gettysburg battlefield was dedicated on November 19, 1863. The principal oration was delivered by Edward Everett, but Lincoln's brief remarks, in the course of which he referred to "a new birth of freedom," remains the most memorable of all American addresses.

Lincoln, as President, made very few public addresses, the chief examples being his inaugurals, his Gettysburg Address, and his last speech on April 11, 1865. Rather than addresses, Lincoln used the art of correspondence. When answering criticism or appealing to the people, he would prepare a letter which, while addressed to an individual delegation, would be intended for the nation.

In the fashion of the first President, Lincoln wisely employed the pardon power given to the President under the Constitution. On December 8, 1863 he issued a proclamation which offered amnesty, with certain exceptions, to those who would take an oath to support the Constitution and abide by federal laws and proclamations involving the freedmen. When oath takers equaled one-tenth of the state's voters in the 1860 election, they could proceed to "re-establish" a lawful government in a seceded state. Lincoln promised executive recognition to such governments.

Radical Republicans denounced both the plan and Lincoln's whole Southern policy as far too lenient to the Confederates. They accurately reflected the widespread feeling that, as the war became more bitter, southerners should be punished for secession. Since the Radicals controlled Congress, they prevented any settlement of the reconstruction issue during Lincoln's life. The deadlock between the President and Congress can be seen in the Wade–Davis bill that Lincoln killed by pocket veto on July 4, 1864. Lincoln issued a proclamation on July 8th explaining that he could not accept the radical plan as the only method of reconstructing the nation. Radical Republicans now excoriated Lincoln for his forbearance towards those who had caused the war.

No state was actually restored to the Union in accordance with Lincoln's plan, though he considered his terms fulfilled in Tennessee, Arkansas, and Louisiana. In his last public speech, on April 11, 1865, he advised leniency to the defeated South.

Lincoln delivered his short but brilliant Second Inaugural Address on March 4, 1865. For four years, the crusade to save the Union had raged. Now it neared a successful conclusion. Years of death and destruction had created an atmosphere of vindictiveness. Lincoln's memorable address stands above the hate associated with this horrible war. The nation should go forth "with malice toward none, with charity for all." This theme defined his policy and with it he soared above momentary passions. In so doing, the nation's leader captured something of the larger tragedy involved, embracing that feeling of renewed confidence so necessary in facing the future problems of reconstruction. There was one new and striking feature in the simple inaugural ceremony—the presence of a battalion of African-American troops in the escort party.

President Andrew Johnson generally followed Lincoln's plan of peace and reconciliation toward the defeated South, much to the chagrin of the Radical Republicans. By December 1865, every former Confederate state, except Texas, had conformed to Johnson's requirements for reestablishing civil government. Thus, the President informed Congress on December 4th, that the Union was restored.

The Union was not only restored. It was enlarged. The Johnson Administration had conducted highly successful negotiations with the Tsar of Russia through which a Treaty was concluded and the territory of Alaska purchased. The President and his Secretary of State, William H. Seward had managed to grow the Republic and extend the area of freedom to the far northern corner of the continent. Detractors called it "Seward's Folly" and "Icebox." In fact it was a brilliant stroke of diplomacy by President Johnson and his Secretary. In the City of Washington, the President issued a Proclamation on June 20, 1867 announcing the triumph and containing the particulars of the Treaty, word for word.

Congress was in no mood to rejoice or give credit to the visionary diplomacy of the President in obtaining Alaska. Throughout 1867, impeachment resolutions were introduced in Congress. By the end of the year, a collision between the President and Congress seemed inevitable. In his third Annual Message, on December 3, 1867, Johnson defended his views on Reconstruction as being constitutionally sound. The President explained his interpretation of the Tenure of Office Act (1867). Accused of violating this Act, Johnson was impeached on February 24, 1868. In a trial before the Senate (March 30–May 26) the President was acquitted of the charges against him by one vote short of the two-thirds necessary to remove him from office. Johnson proclaimed his final universal pardon to all parties in any way associated with the treason of the insurrection, on Christmas Day 1868.

In 1868 Ulysses S. Grant was elected President. Upon taking office in 1869, President Grant faced the same intractable political and social issues of Reconstruction that had brought his predecessor to impeachment. Unlike Andrew Johnson, Grant did not favor an unreconstructed South able to reform itself as if the Civil War never happened. Yet the new President also refused to employ full federal power to force fundamental change on a reconstructed South, as Radical Republicans demanded. In fact, beyond an occasional dispatch of force to support embattled Old South Republican governments, Grant did nothing. Deeply conservative and suspicious of executive power, the President hoped that circumstances would produce general social equity. Restoration of the Union topped the presidential agenda. "[T]here is one subject" Grant informed Congress "which concerns so deeply the welfare of the country that I deem it my duty to bring it before you." Grant proposed to the Congress, on April 7, 1869 that such restoration held high priority. He concluded "it is certainly desirable that all causes of irritation should be removed as promptly as possible, that a more perfect union may be established and the country be restored to peace and prosperity."

In his earliest days in the Executive Mansion, he unequivocally and successfully defended passage of the 15th Amendment, with the declaration that voting rights could not be denied "on account of race, color, or previous condition of servitude." Even so, President Grant more generally practiced a policy of accommodation with the South. As with the majority of his countrymen, Grant grew weary of solving the national problem of race, which continued unresolved even after the bloodiest fratricidal war in American history.

Dramatic new forces in the life of the nation called upon the Chief Executive for attention. The America over which Grant presided had been hurled full tilt into a new age of technology and industrial capitalism. Trade and enterprise radiated out across the continent. Oil and steel industries and their subsidiaries absorbed increasing thousands of workers, while altering the environment and producing material improvements, along with unprecedented capital and a rising Corporate America. The construction of a transcontinental railroad created a national market. The financial centers of the big cities resonated with busy markets, secret deals, and fortunes won and lost. In the midst of unprecedented social and economic change, the executive center of the nation withdrew its attention from old controversies attached to sectionalism and the South and turned its eyes to new battlefields. This new age needed a new order. In keeping with the emerging

Industrial Age, President Grant issued, on May 19, 1869, a Proclamation for an eight-hour day "for all laborers, workmen, and mechanics employed by or on behalf of the Government of the United States."

President Grant submitted his eighth and final Annual Message to Congress, on December 5, 1876. To the end of his presidency Grant, the stolid war hero and national icon, had retained popular adulation. Yet even as the crowds cheered, incompetence and corruption marred his presidency. The Civil War had preserved the Union but the federal government shorted the cause of racial justice. The Grant administration enabled the South to revert to racial separation, stripping from freedmen their constitutional protections through legal sophistry and the brutality of the Ku Klux Klan. Out on the high plains, the Government waged war against other peoples of color. Fighting with Indian tribes raged across the badlands. General Philip Sheridan said, "The only good Indian is a dead Indian."

Grant's extraordinary capacity for loyalty boomeranged to besmirch his administration. He trusted too widely and not too well. Before the 8-year Grant administration had passed, scandal would touch two Vice Presidents, a Secretary of the Interior, an Attorney General, the Speaker of the House and the President's personal secretary. Nor did the Grant Administration bestir itself as northern industrialists and financiers created powerful and lucrative monopolies. It was a material age attached to money and the mundane. Ornate and superficial, "Gilded Age" corruption predominated in both the public and private sectors. At the very end of his public life, President Grant took the unprecedented step of alluding to his own deficiencies. "Failures have been errors of judgment" acknowledged Grant, "not of intent."

Grant exited the presidency as Ruther B. Hayes entered. Hayes had gained the office in the most controversial election in American history. Only the exemplary character of this man—honest, pious, a war hero—shielded him from the venal circumstances of his ascendancy. Hayes's Democratic opponent, Samuel J. Tilden of New York, won the popular vote, but both parties charged fraud with respect to the returns from South Carolina, Louisiana and Florida. In each of those states, savage political battles over race separated the parties, with the Republicans clinging to office via the bayonet. The military occupation of the Federal forts constituted the last vestiges of protection for people of color.

The Democratic Party represented the values of the Old South. It was their mission to realize the indefinite postponement of racial justice. In counting the election returns, Republicans controlled the machinery and disqualified enough Democratic votes to retain the electoral edge for Hayes. Democrats raised objection, calling the presence of Federal troops a Republican army of occupation. Just days before the scheduled inauguration in Washington, on March 2, 1877, the Congressional special electoral commission appointed to resolve the dangerous situation decided all questions on the contested votes on the basis of an 8 to 7 straight party line vote, and gave all the electoral votes to Hayes.

Hayes supporters made the commission decision palatable to Democrats by pledges to withdraw the last of the Federal troops from the South. This action ended Reconstruction and restored the Democrats to their longstanding dominion of the region. Hayes, an optimist but not a hypocrite, clung to the belief that he could work with fair-minded Democrats and simultaneously build a Republican party in the South. In this endeavor, his conviction grew that protection for the freedmen would flower without Federal bayonets. In April, a month after the inauguration, the Commander-in-Chief ordered Federal troops to leave the South. Reconstruction finally ended, and with it—for the next 75 years—the national commitment to racial equality.

16

Abraham Lincoln

1. FIRST INAUGURAL ADDRESS **MARCH 4, 1861**

. . . Apprehension seems to exist among the people of the Southern States that by the accession of a Republican Administration their property and their peace and personal security are to be endangered. There has never been any reasonable cause for such apprehension. Indeed, the most ample evidence to the contrary has all the while existed and been open to their inspection. It is found in nearly all the published speeches of him who now addresses you. I do but quote from one of those speeches when I declare that—

I have no purpose, directly or indirectly, to interfere with the institution of slavery in the States where it exists. I believe I have no lawful right to do so, and I have no inclination to do so. . . .

I now reiterate these sentiments, and in doing so I only press upon the public attention the most conclusive evidence of which the case is susceptible that the property, peace, and security of no section are to be in any wise endangered by the now incoming Administration. I add, too, that all the protection which, consistently with the Constitution and the laws, can be given will be cheerfully given to all the States when lawfully demanded, for whatever cause—as cheerfully to one section as to another. . . .

I take the official oath today with no mental reservations and with no purpose to construe the Constitution or laws by any hypercritical rules; and while I do not choose now to specify particular acts of Congress as proper to be enforced, I do suggest that it will be much safer for all, both in official and private stations, to conform to and abide by all those acts which stand un-repealed than to violate any of them trusting to find impunity in having them held to be unconstitutional.

It is seventy-two years since the first inauguration of a President under our National Constitution. During that period fifteen different and greatly distinguished citizens have in succession administered the executive branch of the Government. They have conducted it through many perils, and generally with great success. Yet, with all this scope of precedent, I now enter upon the same task for the brief constitutional term of four years under great and peculiar difficulty. A disruption of the Federal Union, heretofore only menaced, is now formidably attempted.

I hold that in contemplation of universal law and of the Constitution the Union of these States is perpetual. Perpetuity is implied, if not expressed, in the fundamental law of all national governments. It is safe to assert that no government proper ever had a provision in its organic law for its own termination. Continue to execute all the express provisions of our National Constitution, and the Union will endure forever, as being impossible to destroy it except by some action not provided for in the instrument itself.

Again: If the United States be not a government proper, but an association of States in the nature of contract merely, can it, as a contract, be peaceably unmade by less than all the parties who made it? One party to a contract may violate it—break it, so to speak—but does it not require all to lawfully rescind it?

Descending from these general principles, we find the proposition that in legal contemplation the Union is perpetual, confirmed by the history of the Union itself. The Union is much older than the Constitution. It was formed, in fact, by the Articles of Association in 1774. It was matured and continued by the Declaration of Independence in 1776. It was further matured, and the faith of all the then thirteen States expressly plighted and engaged that it should be perpetual, by the Articles of Confederation in 1778. And finally, in 1787, one of the declared objects for ordaining and establishing the Constitution was "*to form a more perfect Union.*"

But if destruction of the Union by one or by a part only of the States be lawfully possible, the Union is less perfect than before the Constitution, having lost the vital element of perpetuity.

It follows from these views that no State upon its own mere motion can lawfully get out of the Union; that resolves and ordinances to that effect are legally void, and that acts of violence within any State or States against the authority of the United States are insurrectionary or revolutionary, according to circumstances.

I therefore consider that in view of the Constitution and the laws the Union is unbroken, and to the extent of my ability, I shall take care, as the Constitution itself expressly enjoins upon me, that the laws of the Union be faithfully executed in all the States. Doing this I deem to be only a simple duty on my part, and I shall perform it so far as practicable unless my rightful masters, the American people, shall withhold the requisite means or in some authoritative manner direct the contrary. I trust this will not be regarded as a menace, but only as the declared purpose of the Union that it will constitutionally defend and maintain itself.

In doing this there needs to be no bloodshed or violence and there shall be none unless it be forced upon the national authority. The power confided to me will be used to hold, occupy, and possess the property and places belonging to the Government and to collect the duties and imposts; but beyond what may be necessary for these objects, there will be no invasion, no using of force against or among the people anywhere. Where hostility to the United States in any interior locality shall be so great and universal as to prevent competent resident citizens from holding the Federal offices, there will be no attempt to force obnoxious strangers among the people for that object. While the strict legal right may exist in the Government to enforce the exercise of these offices, the attempt to do so would be so irritating and so nearly impracticable withal that I deem it better to forego for the time the uses of such offices.

The mails, unless repelled, will continue to be furnished in all parts of the Union. So far as possible the people everywhere shall have that sense of perfect security which is most favorable to calm thought and reflection. The course here indicated will be followed unless current events and experience shall show a modification or change to be proper, and in every case and exigency my best discretion will be exercised, according to circumstances actually existing and with a view and a hope of a peaceful solution of the national troubles and the restoration of fraternal sympathies and affections.

That there are persons in one section or another who seek to destroy the Union at all events and are glad of any pretext to do it I will neither affirm nor deny; but if there be such, I need address no word to them. To those, however, who really love the Union may I not speak?

Before entering upon so grave a matter as the destruction of our national fabric, with all its benefits, its memories, and its hopes, would it not be wise to ascertain precisely why we do it? Will you hazard so desperate a step while there is any possibility that any portion of the ills you fly from have no real existence? Will you, while the certain ills you fly to are greater than all the real ones you fly from, will you risk the commission of so fearful a mistake?

All profess to be content in the Union if all constitutional rights can be maintained. Is it true, then, that any right plainly written in the Constitution has been denied? I think not. Happily, the human mind is so constituted that no party can reach to the audacity of doing this. Think, if you can, of a single instance in which a plainly written provision of the Constitution has ever been denied. If by the mere force of numbers a majority should deprive a minority of any clearly written constitutional right, it might in a moral point of view justify revolution; certainly would if such right were a vital one. But such is not our case. All the vital rights of minorities and of individuals are so plainly assured to them by affirmations and negations, guaranties and prohibitions in the Constitution, that controversies never arise concerning them. But no organic law can ever be framed with a provision specifically applicable to every question which may occur in practical admin-istration. No foresight can anticipate nor does any document of reasonable length contain express provisions for all possible questions. Shall fugitives from labor be surrendered by national or by State authority? The Constitution does not expressly say. *May* Congress prohibit slavery in the Territories? The Constitution does not expressly say. *Must* Congress protect slavery in the Territories? The Constitution does not expressly say.

From questions of this class spring all our constitutional controversies and we divide upon them into majorities and minorities. If the minority will not acquiesce, the majority must, or the Government must cease. There is no other alternative, for continuing the Government is acqui-escence on one side or the other. If a minority in such case will secede rather than acquiesce, they make a precedent which in turn will divide and ruin them, for a minority of their own will secede from them whenever a majority refuses to be controlled by such minority. For instance, why may not any portion of a new confederacy a year or two hence arbitrarily secede again, precisely as portions of the present Union now claim to secede from it? All who cherish disunion sentiments are now being educated to the exact temper of doing this.

Is there such perfect identity of interests among the States to compose a new union as to produce harmony only and prevent renewed secession?

Plainly the central idea of secession is the essence of anarchy. A majority held in restraint by constitutional checks and limitations, and always changing easily with deliberate changes of popular opinions and sentiments, is the only true sovereign of a free people. Whoever rejects it does of necessity fly to anarchy or to despotism. Unanimity is impossible. The rule of a minority, as a permanent arrangement, is wholly inadmissible; so that, rejecting the majority principle, anarchy or despotism in some form is all that is left.

I do not forget the position assumed by some that constitutional questions are to be decided by the Supreme Court, nor do I deny that such decisions must be binding in any case upon the parties to a suit as to the object of that suit, while they are also entitled to very high respect and con-sideration in all parallel cases by all other departments of the Government. And while it is obviously possible that such decision may be erroneous in any given case, still the evil effect following it, being limited to that particular case, with the chance that it may be overruled and never become a precedent for other cases can better be borne than could the evils of a different practice. At the same time the candid citizen must confess that if the policy of the Government upon vital questions affecting the whole people is to be irrevocably fixed by decisions of the Supreme Court, the instant they are made in ordinary litigation between parties in personal actions the people will have ceased to be their own rulers, having to that extent practically resigned their Government into the hands of that eminent tribunal. Nor is there in this view any assault upon the court or the judges. It is a duty from which they may not shrink to decide cases properly brought before them, and it is no fault of theirs if others seek to turn their decisions to political purposes.

One section of our country believes slavery is right and ought to be extended, while the other believes it is wrong and ought not to be extended. This is the only substantial dispute. The fugitive-slave clause of the Constitution and the law for the suppression of the foreign slave trade are each as well enforced, perhaps, as any law can ever be in a community where the moral sense of the people imperfectly supports the law itself. The great body of the people abides by the dry legal obligation in both cases, and a few break over in each. This, I think, cannot be perfectly cured, and it would be worse in both cases after the separation of the sections than before. The foreign slave trade, now imperfectly suppressed, would be ultimately revived without restriction in one section, while fugitive slaves, now only partially surrendered, would not be surrendered at all by the other.

Physically speaking, we cannot separate. We cannot remove our respective sections from each other nor build an impassable wall between them. A husband and wife may be divorced and go out of the presence and beyond the reach of each other, but the different parts of our country cannot do this. They cannot but remain face to face, and intercourse, either amicable or hostile, must continue between them. Is it possible, then, to make that intercourse more advantageous or more satisfactory after separation than before? Can aliens make treaties easier than friends can make laws? Can treaties be more faithfully enforced between aliens than laws can among friends? Suppose you go to war, you cannot fight always; and when, after much loss on both sides and no gain on either, you cease fighting, the identical old questions, as to terms of intercourse, are again upon you.

This country, with its institutions, belongs to the people who inhabit it. Whenever they shall grow weary of the existing Government, they can exercise their constitutional right of amending it or their revolutionary right to dismember or overthrow it. I cannot be ignorant of the fact that many worthy and patriotic citizens are desirous of having the National Constitution amended. While I make no recommendation of amendments, I fully recognize the rightful authority of the people over the whole subject, to be exercised in either of the modes prescribed in the instrument itself; and I should, under existing circumstances, favor rather than oppose a fair opportunity being afforded the people to act upon it. I will venture to add that to me the convention mode seems preferable, in that it allows amendments to originate with the people themselves, instead of only permitting them to take or reject propositions originated by others, not especially chosen for the purpose, and which might not be precisely such as they would wish to either accept or refuse. I understand a proposed amendment to the Constitution—which amendment, however, I have not seen—has passed Congress, to the effect that the Federal Government shall never interfere with the domestic institutions of the States, including that of persons held to service. To avoid miscon-struction of what I have said, I depart from my purpose not to speak of particular amendments so far as to say that, holding such a provision to now be implied constitutional law, I have no objection to its being made express and irrevocable.

The Chief Magistrate derives all his authority from the people, and they have referred none upon him to fix terms for the separation of the States. The people themselves can do this if also they choose but the Executive as such has nothing to do with it. His duty is to administer the present Government as it came to his hands and to transmit it unimpaired by him to his successor.

Why should there not be a patient confidence in the ultimate justice of the people? Is there any better or equal hope in the world? In our present differences, is either party without faith of being in the right? If the Almighty Ruler of Nations, with His eternal truth and justice, be on your side of the North, or on yours of the South, that truth and that justice will surely prevail by the judgment of this great tribunal of the American people.

By the frame of the Government under which we live this same people have wisely given their public servants but little power for mischief, and have with equal wisdom provided for the return of that little to their own hands at very short intervals. While the people retain their virtue and vigilance no Administration by any extreme of wickedness or folly can very seriously injure the Government in the short space of four years.

My countrymen, one and all, think calmly and well upon this whole subject. Nothing valuable can be lost by taking time. If there be an object to hurry any of you in hot haste to a step which you would never take deliberately, that object will be frustrated by taking time; but no good object can be frustrated by it. Such of you as are now dissatisfied still have the old Constitution unimpaired, and, on the sensitive point, the laws of your own framing under it; while the new Administration will have no immediate power, if it would, to change either. If it were admitted that you who are dissatisfied hold the right side in the dispute, there still is no single good reason for precipitate action. Intelligence, patriotism, Christianity, and a firm reliance on Him who has never yet forsaken this favored land are still competent to adjust in the best way all our present difficulty.

Figure 16.1 Abraham Lincoln statue, courtesy of Ian Wagreich.

In your hands, my dissatisfied fellow-countrymen, and not in mine, is the momentous issue of civil war. The Government will not assail you. You can have no conflict without being yourselves the aggressors. You have no oath registered in heaven to destroy the Government, while I shall have the most solemn one to "preserve, protect, and defend it."

I am loath to close. We are not enemies, but friends. We must not be enemies. Though passion may have strained it must not break our bonds of affection. The mystic chords of memory, stretching from every battlefield and patriot grave to every living heart and hearthstone all over this broad land, will yet swell the chorus of the Union, when again touched, as surely they will be, by the better angels of our nature.

2. THE WAR MESSAGE   JULY 4, 1861

Having been convened on an extraordinary occasion, as authorized by the Constitution, your attention is not called to any ordinary subject of legislation.

At the beginning of the present presidential term, four months ago, the functions of the Federal Government were found to be generally suspended within the several States of South Carolina, Georgia, Alabama, Mississippi, Louisiana, and Florida, excepting only those of the Post-office Department.

Within these States all the forts, arsenals, dockyards, custom-houses, and the like, including the movable and stationary property in and about them, had been seized, and were held in open hostility to this government, excepting only Forts Pickens, Taylor, and Jefferson, on and near the Florida coast, and Fort Sumter, in Charleston Harbor, South Carolina. The forts thus seized had been put in improved condition, new ones had been built, and armed forces had been organized and were organizing, all avowedly with the same hostile purpose.

The forts remaining in the possession of the Federal Government in and near these States were either besieged or menaced by warlike preparations, and especially Fort Sumter was nearly surrounded by well-protected hostile batteries, with guns equal in quality to the best of its own, and outnumbering the latter as perhaps ten to one. A disproportionate share of the Federal muskets and rifles had somehow found their way into these States, and had been seized to be used against the government. Accumulations of the public revenue lying within them had been seized for the same object. The navy was scattered in distant seas, leaving but a very small part of it within the immediate reach of the government. Officers of the Federal army and navy had resigned in great numbers; and of those resigning a large proportion had taken up arms against the government. Simultaneously, and in connection with all this, the purpose to sever the Federal Union was openly avowed. In accordance with this purpose, an ordinance had been adopted in each of these States, declaring the States respectively to be separated from the National Union. A formula for instituting a combined government of these States had been promulgated; and this illegal organization, in the character of confederate States, was already invoking recognition, aid, and intervention from foreign powers.

Finding this condition of things, and believing it to be an imperative duty upon the incoming executive to prevent, if possible, the consummation of such attempt to destroy the Federal Union, a choice of means to that end became indispensable. This choice was made and was declared in the inaugural address. The policy chosen looked to the exhaustion of all peaceful measures before a resort to any stronger ones. It sought only to hold the public places and property not already wrested from the government, and to collect the revenue, relying for the rest on time, discussion, and the ballot-box. It promised a continuance of the mails at government expense, to the very people who were resisting the government; and it gave repeated pledges against any disturbance to any of the people, or any of their rights. Of all that, which a President might constitutionally and justifiably do in such a case, everything was forborne without which it was believed possible to keep the government on foot. . . .

It was believed, however, that to so abandon that position, under the circumstances, would be utterly ruinous; that the necessity under which it was to be done would not be fully understood; that by many it would be construed as a part of a voluntary policy; that at home it would discourage the friends of the Union, embolden its adversaries, and go far to insure to the latter a recognition abroad; that, in fact, it would be our national destruction consummated. This could not be allowed. Starvation was not yet upon the garrison, and ere it would be reached Fort Pickens might be reinforced. This last would be a clear indication of policy, and would better enable the country to accept the evacuation of Fort Sumter as a military necessity. An order was at once directed to be sent for the landing of the troops from the steamship *Brooklyn* into Fort Pickens. This order could not go by land, but must take the longer and slower route by sea. The first return news from the order was received just one week before the fall of Fort Sumter. The news itself was that the officer commanding the Sabine, to which vessel the troops had been transferred from the *Brooklyn*, acting upon some quasi armistice of the late administration (and of the existence of which the present administration, up to the time the order was dispatched, had only too vague and uncertain rumors to fix attention), had refused to land the troops. To now reinforce Fort Pickens before a crisis would be reached at Fort Sumter was impossible—rendered so by the near exhaustion of provisions in the latter-named fort. In precaution against such a conjuncture, the government had, a few days before, commenced preparing an expedition as well adapted as might be to relieve Fort Sumter, which expedition was intended to be ultimately used, or not, according to circumstances. The strongest anticipated case for using it was now presented, and it was resolved to send it forward. As had been intended in this contingency, it was also resolved to notify the governor of South Carolina that he might expect an attempt would be made to provision the fort; and that, if the attempt should not be resisted, there would be no effort to throw in men, arms, or ammunition, without further notice, or in case of an attack upon the fort. This notice was accordingly given; whereupon the fort was attacked and bombarded to its fall, without even awaiting the arrival of the provisioning expedition.

It is thus seen that the assault upon and reduction of Fort Sumter was in no sense a matter of self-defense on the part of the assailants. They well knew that the garrison in the fort could by no possibility commit aggression upon them. They knew—they were expressly notified—that the giving of bread to the few brave and hungry men of the garrison was all which would on that occasion be attempted, unless themselves, by resisting so much, should provoke more. They knew that this government desired to keep the garrison in the fort, not to assail them, but merely to maintain visible possession and thus to preserve the Union from actual and immediate dissolution—trusting, as hereinbefore stated, to time discussion, and the ballot-box for final adjustment; and they assailed and reduced the fort for precisely the reverse object—to drive out the visible authority of the Federal Union, and thus force it to immediate dissolution. . . .

Unquestionably the States have the powers and rights reserved to them in and by the National Constitution; but among these surely are not included all conceivable powers, however mischievous or destructive, but, at most, such only as were known in the world at the time as governmental powers; and certainly a power to destroy the government itself had never been known as a governmental, as a merely administrative power. This relative matter of national power and State rights, as a principle, is no other than the principle of generality and locality. Whatever concerns the whole should be confided to the whole—to the General Government; while whatever concerns only the State should be left exclusively to the State. This is all there is of original principle about it. Whether the National Constitution in defining boundaries between the two has applied the principle with exact accuracy, is not to be questioned. We are all bound by that defining, without question.

What is now combated is the position that secession is consistent with the Constitution—is lawful and peaceful. It is not contended that there is any express law for it; and nothing should ever be implied as law which leads to unjust or absurd consequences. The nation purchased with money the countries out of which several of these States were formed. Is it just that they shall go off without leave and without refunding? The nation paid very large sums (in the aggregate, I believe, nearly a hundred millions) to relieve Florida of the aboriginal tribes. Is it just that she shall now be off without consent or without making any return? The nation is now in debt for money applied to the benefit of these so-called seceding States in common with the rest. Is it just either that creditors shall go unpaid or the remaining States pay the whole? A part of the present national debt was contracted to pay the old debts of Texas. Is it just that she shall leave and pay no part of this herself?

Again, if one State may secede, so may another; and when all shall have seceded, none is left to pay the debts. Is this quite just to creditors? Did we notify them of this sage view of ours when we borrowed their money?

If we now recognize this doctrine by allowing the seceders to go in peace, it is difficult to see what we can do if others choose to go or to extort terms upon which they will promise to remain.

The seceders insist that our Constitution admits of secession. They have assumed to make a national constitution of their own, in which of necessity they have either discarded or retained the right of secession as they insist it exists in ours. If they have discarded it, they thereby admit that on principle it ought not to be in ours. If they have retained it by their own construction of ours, they show that to be consistent they must secede from one another whenever they shall find it the easiest way of settling their debts, or effecting any other selfish or unjust object. The principle itself is one of disintegration, and upon which no government can possibly endure.

If all the States save one should assert the power to drive that one out of the Union, it is presumed the whole class of seceder politicians would at once deny the power and denounce the act as the greatest outrage upon State rights. But suppose that precisely the same act, instead of being called "driving the one out," should be called "the seceding of the others from that one," it would be exactly what the seceders claim to do, unless, indeed, they make the point that the one, because it is a minority, may rightfully do what the others, because they are a majority, may not rightfully do. These politicians are subtle and profound on the rights of minorities. They are not partial to that power which made the Constitution and speaks from the preamble called itself "We, the People."

It may well be questioned whether there is today a majority of the legally qualified voters of any State, except perhaps South Carolina, in favor of disunion. There is much reason to believe that the Union men are the majority in many, if not in every other one, of the so-called seceded States. . . .

This is essentially a people's contest. On the side of the Union it is a struggle for maintaining in the world that form and substance of government whose leading object is to elevate the condition of men—to lift artificial weights from all shoulders; to clear the paths of laudable pursuit for all; to afford all an unfettered start, and a fair chance in the race of life. Yielding to partial and temporary departures, from necessity, this is the leading object of the government for whose existence we contend. . . .

It was with the deepest regret that the executive found the duty of employing the war power in defense of the government forced upon him. He could but perform this duty or surrender the existence of the government. No compromise by public servants could, in this case, be a cure; not that compromises are not often proper, but that no popular government can long survive a marked precedent that those who carry an election can only save the government from immediate destruction by giving up the main point upon which the people gave the election. The people themselves, and not their servants, can safely reverse their own deliberate decisions. . . .

3. EMANCIPATION PROCLAMATION   JANUARY 1, 1863

Whereas on the 22d day of September A.D. 1862, a proclamation was issued by the President of the United States, containing among other things, the following, to wit:

"That on the 1st day of January, A.D. 1863, all persons held as slaves within any State or designated part of a State the people whereof shall then be in rebellion against the United States shall be then, thenceforward, and forever free; and the executive government of the United States including the military and naval authority thereof, will recognize and maintain the freedom of such persons and will do no act or acts to repress such persons, or any of them, in any efforts they may make for their actual freedom."

"That the executive will on the 1st day of January aforesaid, by proclamation, designate the States and parts of States, if any, in which the people thereof, respectively, shall then be in rebellion against the United States; and the fact that any State or the people thereof shall on that day be in good faith represented in the Congress of the United States by members chosen thereto at elections wherein a majority of the qualified voters of such States shall have participated shall, in the absence of strong countervailing testimony, be deemed conclusive evidence that such State and the people thereof are not then in rebellion against the United States."

Now, therefore, I, Abraham Lincoln, President of the United States, by virtue of the power in me vested as Commander-in-Chief of the Army and Navy of the United States in time of actual armed rebellion against the authority and government of the United States, and as a fit and necessary war measure for suppressing said rebellion, do, on this 1st day of January, A.D. 1863, and in accordance with my purpose so to do, publicly proclaimed for the full period of one hundred days from the first day above mentioned, order and designate as the States and parts of States wherein the people thereof, respectively, are this day in rebellion against the United States the following, to wit:

Arkansas, Texas, Louisiana (except the parishes of St. Bernard, Plaquemines, Jefferson, St. John, St. Charles, St. James, Ascension, Assumption, Terrebonne, Lafourche, St. Mary, St. Martin, and Orleans, including the city of New Orleans), Mississippi, Alabama, Florida, Georgia, South Carolina, North Carolina, and Virginia (except the forty-eight counties designated as West Virginia, and also the counties of Berkeley, Accomac, Northhampton, Elizabeth City, York, Princess Anne, and Norfolk, including the cities of Norfolk and Portsmouth), and which excepted parts are for the present left precisely as if this proclamation were not issued.

And by virtue of the power and for the purpose aforesaid, I do order and declare that all persons held as slaves within said designated States and parts of States are, and henceforward shall be, free; and that the Executive Government of the United States, including the military and naval authorities thereof, will recognize and maintain the freedom of said persons.

And I hereby enjoin upon the people so declared to be free to abstain from all violence, unless in necessary self-defense; and I recommend to them that, in all cases when allowed, they labor faithfully for reasonable wages.

And I further declare and make known that such persons of suitable condition will be received into the armed service of the United States to garrison forts, positions, stations, and other places, and to man vessels of all sorts in said service.

And upon this act, sincerely believed to be an act of justice, warranted by the Constitution upon military necessity, I invoke the considerate judgment of mankind and the gracious favor of Almighty God.

4. GETTYSBURG ADDRESS   NOVEMBER 19, 1863

Four score and seven years ago our fathers brought forth on this continent, a new nation, conceived in Liberty, and dedicated to the proposition that all men are created equal.

Now we are engaged in a great civil war testing whether that nation or any nation so conceived and so dedicated, can long endure. We are met on a great battle-field of that war. We have come to dedicate a portion of that field, as a final resting place for those who here gave their lives that that nation might live. It is altogether fitting and proper that we should do this.

But, in a larger sense, we cannot dedicate—we cannot consecrate—we cannot hallow—this ground. The brave men, living and dead, who struggled here, have consecrated it, far above our poor power to add or detract. The world will little note, nor long remember what we say here, but it can never forget what they did here. It is for us the living, rather, to be dedicated here to the unfinished work which they who fought here have thus far so nobly advanced. It is rather for us to be here dedicated to the great task remaining before us—that from these honored dead we take increased devotion to that cause for which they gave the last full measure of devotion—that we here highly resolve that these dead shall not have died in vain—that this nation, under God, shall have a new birth of freedom—and that government of the people, by the people, for the people, shall not perish from the earth.

5. PLAN FOR RECONSTRUCTION: PARDON AND AMNESTY   DECEMBER 8, 1863

Whereas in and by the Constitution of the United States it is provided that the President "shall have power to grant reprieves and pardons for offenses against the United States, except in cases of impeachment;" and

Whereas a rebellion now exists whereby the loyal State governments of several States have for a long time been subverted, and many persons have committed and are now guilty of treason against the United States; and

Whereas, with reference to said rebellion and treason, laws have been enacted by Congress declaring forfeitures and confiscation of property and liberation of slaves, all upon terms and conditions therein stated, and also declaring that the President was thereby authorized at any time thereafter, by proclamation, to extend to persons who may have participated in the existing rebellion in any State or part thereof pardon and amnesty, with such exceptions and at such times and on such conditions as he may deem expedient for the public welfare; and

Whereas the Congressional declaration for limited and conditional pardon accords with well-established judicial exposition of the pardoning power; and

Whereas, with reference to said rebellion, the President of the United States has issued several proclamations with provisions in regard to the liberation of slaves; and

Whereas it is now desired by some persons heretofore engaged in said rebellion to resume their allegiance to the United States and to reinaugurate loyal State governments within and for their respective States:

Therefore, I, Abraham Lincoln, President of the United States, do proclaim . . . to all persons who have, directly or by implication, participated in the existing rebellion, except as hereinafter excepted, that a full pardon is hereby granted to them and each of them, with restoration of all rights of property, except as to slaves and in property cases where rights of third parties shall have intervened, and upon the condition that every such person shall take and subscribe an oath and thenceforward keep and maintain said oath inviolate, and which oath shall be registered for permanent preservation and shall be of the tenor and effect following, to wit:

I, ———, do solemnly swear, in presence of Almighty God, that I will henceforth faithfully support, protect, and defend the Constitution of the United States and the Union of the States thereunder; and that I will in like manner abide by and faithfully support all acts of Congress passed during the existing rebellion with reference to slaves, so long and so far as not repealed, modified, or held void by Congress or by decision of the Supreme Court; and that I will in like manner abide by and faithfully support all proclamations of the President made during the existing rebellion having reference to slaves, so long and so far as not modified or declared void by decision of the Supreme Court. So help me God.

The persons excepted from the benefits of the foregoing provisions are all who are or shall have been civil or diplomatic officers or agents of the so-called Confederate Government; all who have left judicial stations under the United States to aid the rebellion; all who are or shall have been military or naval officers of said so-called Confederate Government above the rank of colonel in the army or of lieutenant in the navy; all who left seats in the United States Congress to aid the rebellion; all who resigned commissions in the Army or Navy of the United States and afterwards aided the rebellion; and all who have engaged in any way in treating colored persons, or white persons in charge of such, otherwise than lawfully as prisoners of war, and which persons may have been found in the United States service as soldiers, seamen, or in any other capacity.

And I do further proclaim, declare, and make known that whenever in any of the States of Arkansas, Texas, Louisiana, Mississippi, Tennessee, Alabama, Georgia, Florida, South Carolina, and North Carolina a number of persons, not less than one-tenth in number of the votes cast in such State at the Presidential election of the year A.D. 1860, each having taken oath aforesaid, and not having since violated it, and being a qualified voter by the election law of the State existing immediately before the so-called act of secession, and excluding all others, shall re-establish a State government which shall be republican and in nowise contravening said oath, such shall be recognized as the true government of the State, and the State shall receive thereunder the benefits of the constitutional provision which declares that "the United States shall guarantee to every State in this Union a republican form of government and shall protect each of them against invasion, and, on application of the legislature, or the executive (when the legislature cannot be convened), against domestic violence."

And I do further proclaim, declare, and make known that any provision which may be adopted by such State government in relation to the freed people of such State which shall recognize and declare their permanent freedom, provide for their education, and which may yet be consistent as a temporary arrangement with their present condition as a laboring, landless, and homeless class, will not be objected to by the National Executive.

And it is suggested as not improper that in constructing a loyal State government in any State the name of the State, the boundary, the subdivisions, the constitution, and the general code of laws as before the rebellion be maintained, subject only to the modifications made necessary by the conditions hereinbefore stated, and such others, if any, not contravening said conditions and which may be deemed expedient by those framing the new State government.

To avoid misunderstanding, it may be proper to say that this proclamation, so far as it relates to State governments, has no reference to States wherein loyal State governments have all the while been maintained. And for the same reason it may be proper to further say that whether members sent to Congress from any State shall be admitted to seats constitutionally rests exclusively with the respective Houses, and not to any extent with the Executive. And still further, that this proclamation is intended to present the people of the States wherein the national authority has been suspended and loyal State governments have been subverted a mode in and by which the national authority and loyal State governments may be re-established within said States or in any of them; and while the mode presented is the best the Executive can suggest, with his present impressions, it must not be understood that no other possible mode would be acceptable. . . .

6. SUPPRESSION OF THE AFRICAN SLAVE TRADE   DECEMBER 8, 1863

. . . The efforts of disloyal citizens of the United States to involve us in foreign wars to aid an inexcusable insurrection have been unavailing. Her Britannic Majesty's Government . . . have exercised their authority to prevent the departure of new hostile expeditions from British ports. The Emperor of France has by a like proceeding promptly vindicated the neutrality which he proclaimed at the beginning of the contest. Questions of great intricacy and importance have arisen out of the blockade and other belligerent operations between the Government and several of the maritime powers, but they have been discussed in a spirit of frankness, justice, and mutual good will. It is especially gratifying that our prize courts, by the impartiality of their adjudications, have commanded the respect and confidence of maritime powers.

The supplemental treaty between the United States and Great Britain for the suppression of the African slave trade, made on the 17th day of February last, has been duly ratified and carried into execution. It is believed that so far as American ports and American citizens are concerned that inhuman and odious traffic has been brought to an end.

7. SECOND INAUGURAL ADDRESS   MARCH 4, 1865

At this second appearing to take the oath of the Presidential office there is less occasion for an extended address than there was at the first. Then a statement somewhat in detail of a course to be pursued seemed fitting and proper. Now, at the expiration of four years, during which public declarations have been constantly called forth on every point and phase of the great contest which still absorbs the attention and engrosses the energies of the nation, little that is new could be presented. The progress of our arms, upon which all else chiefly depends, is as well known to the public as to myself, and it is, I trust, reasonably satisfactory and encouraging to all. With high hope for the future, no prediction in regard to it is ventured.

On the occasion corresponding to this four years ago all thoughts were anxiously directed to an impending civil war. All dreaded it, all sought to avert it. While the inaugural address was being delivered from this place, devoted altogether to saving the Union without war, insurgent agents were in the city seeking to destroy it without war—seeking to dissolve the Union and divide effects by negotiation. Both parties deprecated war, but one of them would make war rather than let the nation survive, and the other would accept war rather than let it perish, and the war came.

17

Andrew Johnson

1. AMNESTY AND PARDON   MAY 29, 1865

Whereas the President of the United States, on the 8th day of December, A.D. eighteen hundred and sixty-three, and on the 26th Day of March, A.D. eighteen hundred and sixty-four, did with the object to suppress the existing rebellion, to induce all persons to return to their loyalty, and to restore the authority of the United States, issue proclamations offering amnesty and pardon to certain persons who had directly or by implication participated in the said rebellion; and whereas many persons who had so engaged in said rebellion have, since the issuance of said proclamations, failed or neglected to take the benefits offered thereby; and whereas many persons who have been justly deprived of all claim to amnesty and pardon thereunder, by reason of their participation directly or by implication in said rebellion, and continued hostility to the government of the United States since the date of said proclamation now desire to apply for and obtain amnesty and pardon:

To the end, therefore, that the authority of the government of the United States may be restored, and that peace, order, and freedom may be established, I, ANDREW JOHNSON, President of the United States, do proclaim and declare that I hereby grant to all persons who have, directly or indirectly, participated in the existing rebellion, except as hereinafter excepted, amnesty and pardon, with restoration of all rights of property, except as to slaves, and except in cases where legal proceedings, under the laws of the United States providing for the confiscation of property of persons engaged in rebellion, have been instituted; but upon the condition, nevertheless, that every such person shall take and subscribe the following oath, (or affirmation,) and thenceforward keep and maintain said oath inviolate; and which oath shall be registered for permanent preservation, and shall be of the tenor and effect following, to wit:

I, ———, do solemnly swear, (or affirm) in presence of Almighty God, that I will henceforth faithfully support, protect, and defend the Constitution of the United States, and the union of the States thereunder; and that I will, in like manner abide by, and faithfully support all laws and proclamations which have been made during the existing rebellion with reference to the emancipation of slaves. So help me God.

2. THE UNION RESTORED   DECEMBER 4, 1865

. . . I have sought to solve the momentous questions and overcome the appalling difficulties that met me at the very commencement of my Administration. It has been my stead-fast object to escape from the sway of momentary passions and to derive a healing policy from the fundamental and unchanging principles of the Constitution.

I found the States suffering from the effects of a civil war. Resistance to the General Government appeared to have exhausted itself. The United States had recovered possession of their forts and arsenals, and their armies were in the occupation of every State which had attempted to secede. Whether the territory within the limits of those States should be held as conquered territory, under military authority emanating from the President as the head of the Army was the first question that presented itself for decision.

Now military governments, established for an indefinite period, would have offered no security for the early suppression of discontent, would have divided the people into the vanquishers and the vanquished, and would have envenomed hatred rather than have restored affection. Once established, no precise limit to their continuance was conceivable. They would have occasioned an incalculable and exhausting expense. Peaceful emigration to and from that portion of the country is one of the best means that can be thought of for the restoration of harmony, and that emigration would have been prevented; for what emigrant from abroad, what industrious citizen at home, would place himself willingly under military rule? The chief persons who would have followed in the train of the Army would have been dependents on the General Government or men who expected profit from the miseries of their erring fellow-citizens. The powers of patronage and rule which would have been exercised under the President over a vast and populous and naturally wealthy region are greater than, unless under extreme necessity, I should be willing to intrust to any one man. They are such as, for myself, I could never, unless on occasions of great emergency, consent to exercise. The willful use of such powers, if continued through a period of years, would have endangered the purity of the general administration and the liberties of the States which remained loyal.

Besides, the policy of military rule over a conquered territory would have implied that the States whose inhabitants may have taken part in the rebellion had by the act of those inhabitants ceased to exist. But the true theory is that all pretended acts of secession were from the beginning null and void. The States cannot commit treason nor screen the individual citizens who may have committed treason any more than they can make valid treaties or engage in lawful commerce with any foreign power. The States attempting to secede placed themselves in a condition where their vitality was impaired, but not extinguished; their functions suspended, but not destroyed.

But if any State neglects or refuses to perform its offices there is the more need that the General Government should maintain all its authority and as soon as practicable resume the exercise of all its functions. On this principle I have acted, and have gradually and quietly, and by almost imperceptible steps, sought to restore the rightful energy of the General Government and of the States. To that end provisional governors have been appointed for the States, conventions called, governors elected, legislatures assembled, and Senators and Representatives chosen to the Congress of the United States. At the same time the courts of the United States, as far as could be done, have been reopened, so that the laws of the United States may be enforced through their agency. The blockade has been removed and the custom-houses reestablished in ports of entry, so that the revenue of the United States may be collected. The Post-Office Department renews its ceaseless activity, and the General Government is thereby enabled to communicate promptly with its officers and agents. The courts bring security to persons and property; the opening of the ports invites the restoration of industry and commerce; the post-office renews the facilities of social intercourse and of business. And is it not happy for us all that the restoration of each one of these functions of the General Government brings with it a blessing to the States over which they are extended? Is it not a sure promise of harmony and renewed attachment to the Union that after all that has happened the return of the General Government is known only as a beneficence?

I know very well that this policy is attended with some risk; that for its success it requires at least the acquiescence of the States which it concerns; that it implies an invitation to those States, by renewing their allegiance to the United States, to resume their functions as States of the Union. But it is a risk that must be taken. In the choice of difficulties it is the smallest risk; and to diminish and if possible to remove all danger, I have felt it incumbent on me to assert one other power of the General Government—the power of pardon. As no State can throw a defense over the crime of treason, the power of pardon is exclusively vested in the executive government of the United States. In exercising that power I have taken every precaution to connect it with the clearest recognition of the binding force of the laws of the United States and an unqualified acknowledgment of the great social change of condition in regard to slavery which has grown out of the war. . . .

3. VIEWS ON RECONSTRUCTION   DECEMBER 3, 1867

The continued disorganization of the Union, to which the President has so often called the attention of Congress, is yet a subject of profound and patriotic concern. We may, however, find some relief from that anxiety in the reflection that the painful political situation, although before untried by ourselves, is not new in the experience of nations. Political science, perhaps as highly perfected in our own time and country as in any other, has not yet disclosed any means by which civil wars can be absolutely prevented. An enlightened nation, however, with a wise and beneficent constitution of free government, may diminish their frequency and mitigate their severity by directing all its proceedings in accordance with its fundamental law. . . .

Candor compels me to declare that at this time there is no Union as our fathers understood the term, and as they meant it to be understood by us. The Union which they established can exist only where all the States are represented in both Houses of Congress; where one State is as free as another to regulate its internal concerns according to its own will, and where the laws of the central Government, strictly confined to matters of national jurisdiction, apply with equal force to all the people of every section. That such is not the present "state of the Union" is a melancholy fact, and we must all acknowledge that the restoration of the States to their proper legal relations with the Federal Government and with one another, according to the terms of the original compact, would be the greatest temporal blessing which God, in His kindest providence, could bestow upon this nation. It becomes our imperative duty to consider whether or not it is impossible to effect this most desirable consummation. . . .

To me the process of restoration seems perfectly plain and simple. It consists merely in a faithful application of the Constitution and laws. The execution of the laws is not now obstructed or opposed by physical force. There is no military or other necessity, real or pretended, which can prevent obedience to the Constitution, either North or South. All the rights and all the obligations of States and individuals can be protected and enforced by means perfectly consistent with the fundamental law. The courts may be everywhere open, and if open their process would be unimpeded. Crimes against the United States can be prevented or punished by the proper judicial authorities in a manner entirely practicable and legal. There is therefore no reason why the Constitution should not be obeyed, unless those who exercise its powers have determined that it shall be disregarded and violated. The mere naked will of this Government, or of some one or more of its branches, is the only obstacle that can exist to a perfect union of all the States.

On this momentous question and some of the measures growing out of it I have had the misfortune to differ from Congress, and have expressed my convictions without reserve, though with becoming deference to the opinion of the legislative department. Those convictions are not only unchanged, but strengthened by subsequent events and further reflection. The transcendent importance of the subject will be a sufficient excuse for calling your attention to some of the reasons which have so strongly influenced my own judgment. The hope that we may all finally concur in a mode of settlement consistent at once with our true interests and with our sworn duties to the Constitution is too natural and too just to be easily relinquished.

It is clear to my apprehension that the States lately in rebellion are still members of the National Union. When did they cease to be so? The "ordinances of secession" adopted by a portion (in most of them a very small portion) of their citizens were mere nullities. If we admit now that they were valid and effectual for the purpose intended by their authors we sweep from under our feet the whole ground upon which we justified the war. Were those States afterwards expelled from the Union by war? The direct contrary was averred by this Government to be its purpose, and was so understood by the all those who gave their blood and treasure to aid in its prosecution. It cannot be that a successful war, waged for the preservation of the Union, had the legal effect of dissolving it. The victory of the nation's arms was not the disgrace of her policy; the defeat of secession on the battlefield was not the triumph of its lawless principle. Nor could Congress, with or without the consent of the Executive, do anything which would have the effect, directly or indirectly, of separating the States from each other. To dissolve the Union is to repeal the Constitution which holds it together, and that is a power which does not belong to any department of this Government, or to all of them united. . . .

The acts of Congress in question are not only objectionable for their assumption of ungranted power, but many of their provisions are in conflict with the direct prohibitions of the Constitution. The Constitution commands that a republican form of government shall be guaranteed to all the States; that no person shall be deprived of life, liberty, or property without due process of law, arrested without a judicial warrant, or punished without a fair trial before an impartial jury; that the privilege of habeas corpus shall not be denied in time of peace, and that no bill of attainder shall be passed even against a single individual. Yet the system of measures established by these acts of Congress does totally subvert and destroy the form as well as the substance of republican government in the ten States to which they apply. It binds them hand and foot in absolute slavery, and subjects them to a strange and hostile power, more unlimited and more likely to be abused than any other now known among civilized men. It tramples down all those rights in which the essence of liberty consists, and which a free government is always most careful to protect. It denies the habeas corpus and the trial by jury. Personal freedom, property, and life, if assailed by the passion, the prejudice, or the rapacity of the ruler, have no security whatever. It has the effect of a bill of attainder or bill of pains and penalties, not upon a few individuals, but upon whole masses, including the millions who inhabit the subject States, and even their unborn children. These wrongs, being expressly forbidden, cannot be constitutionally inflicted upon any portion of our people, no matter how they may have come within our jurisdiction, and no matter whether they live in States, Territories, or districts. . . .

The blacks in the South are entitled to be well and humanely governed, and to have the protection of just laws for all their rights of person and property. If it were practicable at this time to give them a Government exclusively their own, under which they might manage their own affairs in their own way, it would become a grave question whether we ought to do so, or whether common humanity would not require us to save them from themselves. But under the circumstances this is only a speculative point. It is not proposed merely that they shall govern themselves, but that they shall rule the white race, make and administer State laws, elect Presidents and members of

Congress, and shape to a greater or less extent the future destiny of the whole country. Would such a trust and power be safe in such hands? . . .

The plan of putting the Southern States wholly and the General Government partially into the hands of Negroes is proposed at a time peculiarly unpropitious. The foundations of society have been broken up by civil war. Industry must be reorganized, justice reestablished, public credit maintained, and order brought out of confusion. To accomplish these ends would require all the wisdom and virtue of the great men who formed our institutions originally. I confidently believe that their descendants will be equal to the arduous task before them, but it is worse than madness to expect that Negroes will perform it for us. Certainly we ought not to ask their assistance till we despair of our own competency.

The great difference between the two races in physical, mental, and moral characteristics will prevent an amalgamation or fusion of them together in one homogeneous mass. If the inferior obtains the ascendency over the other, it will govern with reference only to its own interests—for it will recognize no common interest—and create such a tyranny as this continent has never yet witnessed. Already the Negroes are influenced by promises of confiscation and plunder. They are taught to regard as an enemy every white man who has any respect for the rights of his own race. If this continues it must become worse and worse until all order will be subverted, all industry cease, and the fertile fields of the South grow up into a wilderness. Of all the dangers which our nation has yet encountered, none are equal to those which must result from the success of the effort now making to Africanize the half of our country.

The unrestricted power of removal from office is a very great one to be trusted even to a magistrate chosen by the general suffrage of the whole people and accountable directly to them for his acts. It is undoubtedly liable to abuse, and at some periods of our history perhaps has been abused. If it be thought desirable and constitutional that it should be so limited as to make the President merely a common informer against other public agents, he should at least be permitted to act in that capacity before some open tribunal, independent of party politics, ready to investigate the merits of every case, furnished with the means of taking evidence, and bound to decide according to established rules. This would guarantee the safety of the accuser when he acts in good faith, and at the same time secure the rights of the other party. I speak, of course, with all proper respect for the present Senate, but it does not seem to me that any legislative body can be so constituted as to insure its fitness for these functions.

It is not the theory of this Government that public offices are the property of those who hold them. They are given merely as a trust for the public benefit, sometimes for a fixed period, sometimes during good behavior, but generally they are liable to be terminated at the pleasure of the appointing power, which represents the collective majesty and speaks the will of the people. The forced retention in office of a single dishonest person may work great injury to the public interests. The danger to the public service comes not from the power to remove, but from the power to appoint. Therefore it was that the framers of the Constitution left the power of removal unrestricted, while they gave the Senate a right to reject all appointments which in its opinion were not fit to be made. A little reflection on this subject will probably satisfy all who have the good of the country at heart that our best course is to take the Constitution for our guide, walk in the path marked out by the founders of the Republic, and obey the rules made sacred by the observance of our great predecessors. . . .

4. ANSWER TO IMPEACHMENT ARTICLE I   MARCH 23, 1868

. . . Edwin M. Stanton was appointed Secretary for the Department of War . . . by President Lincoln. . . .

. . . Stanton became the principal officer to one of the Executive Departments of the Government within the true intent and meaning of the second section of the second article of the Constitution. . . .

. . . Stanton continued to hold the same . . . under the appointment and commission aforesaid, at the pleasure of the President. . . .

. . . this respondent, the President of the United States, responsible for the conduct of the Secretary for the Department of War, and having the constitutional right to resort to and rely upon the person holding that office for advice concerning the great and difficult public duties enjoined on the President by the Constitution and laws of the United States, became satisfied that he could not allow the said Stanton to continue to hold the office of Secretary for the Department of War without hazard of the public interest . . . thereupon by force of the Constitution and laws of the United States which devolves on the President the power and the duty to control the conduct of the business of that Executive Department of the Government, and by reason of the constitutional duty of the President to take care that the laws be faithfully executed, this respondent did necessarily consider and did determine that the said Stanton ought no longer to hold the said office of Secretary for the Department of War. . . .

. . . having regard to the responsibility of the President for the conduct of the said Secretary, and having regard to the permanent executive authority of the office . . . it was impossible, consistently with the public interests, to allow the said Stanton to continue to hold the said office. . . .

. . . it was practically settled by the First Congress of the United States . . . that the Constitution of the United States conferred on the President, as part of the executive power and as one of the necessary means and instruments of performing the executive duty imposed on him by the Constitution . . . the power at any and all times of removing from office all executive officers for cause to be judged by the President alone. . . .

5. ALASKA AND AMERICAN VIRGIN ISLANDS ACQUISITIONS   DECEMBER 9, 1868

The acquisition of Alaska was made with the view of extending the national jurisdiction and republican principles in the American hemisphere. Believing that a further step could be taken in the same direction, I last year entered into a treaty with the King of Denmark for the purchase of the islands of St. Thomas and St. John, on the best terms then attainable, and with the consent of the people of those islands. This treaty has been entered into with Denmark, enlarging the time fixed for final ratification of the original treaty.

6. FINAL UNIVERSAL PARDON PROCLAMATION   DECEMBER 25, 1868

. . . Whereas the authority of the Federal Government having been re-established in all the States and Territories within the jurisdiction of the United States, it is believed that such prudential reservations and exceptions as at the dates of said several proclamations were deemed necessary and proper may now be wisely and justly relinquished, and that an universal amnesty and pardon for participation in said rebellion extended to all who have borne any part therein will tend to secure permanent peace, order, and prosperity throughout the land, and to renew and fully restore confidence and fraternal feeling among the whole people, and their respect for and attachment to the National Government, designed by its patriotic founders for the general good.

Now, therefore, be it known that I, Andrew Johnson, President of the United States, by virtue of the power and authority in me vested by the Constitution and in the name of the sovereign people of the United States, do hereby proclaim and declare, unconditionally and without reservation, to all and to every person who, directly or indirectly, participated in the late insurrection, or rebellion a full pardon and amnesty for the offense of treason against the United States or of adhering to their enemies during the late civil war, with restoration of all rights, privileges and immunities under the Constitution and the laws which have been made in pursuance thereof. . . .

18

Ulysses S. Grant

1. FIRST INAUGURAL ON SUFFRAGE   MARCH 4, 1869

. . . The question of suffrage is one which is likely to agitate the public so long as a portion of the citizens of the nation are excluded from its privileges in any State. It seems to me very desirable that this question should be settled now; and I entertain the hope and express the desire that it may be the ratification of the fifteenth article of amendment to the Constitution. . . .

2. RESTORATION OF UNION TO PEACEFUL AND PROPER RELATIONS   APRIL 7, 1869

While I am aware that the time in which Congress proposes now to remain in session is very brief, and that it is its desire, as far as is consistent with the public interest, to avoid entering upon the general business of legislation, there is one subject which concerns so deeply the welfare of the country that I deem it my duty to bring it before you.

I have no doubt that you will concur with me in the opinion that it is desirable to restore the States which were engaged in the rebellion to their proper relations to the Government and the country at as early a period as the people of those States shall be found willing to become peaceful and orderly communities and to adopt and maintain such constitutions and laws as will effectually secure the civil and political rights of all persons within their borders. The authority of the United States, which has been vindicated and established by its military power, must undoubtedly be asserted for the absolute protection of all its citizens in the full enjoyment of the freedom and security which is the object of a republican government; but whenever the people of a rebellious State are ready to enter in good faith upon the accomplishment of this object, in entire conformity with the constitutional authority of Congress, it is certainly desirable that all causes of irritation should be removed as promptly as possible, that a more perfect union may be established and the country be restored to peace and prosperity.

The convention of the people of Virginia which met in Richmond on Tuesday, December 3, 1867, framed a constitution for that State, which was adopted by the convention on the 17th of April, 1868, and I desire respectfully to call the attention of Congress to the propriety of providing by law for the holding of an election in that State at some time during the months of May and June next, under the direction of the military commander of that district, at which the question of the adoption of that constitution shall be submitted to the citizens of the State; and if this should seem desirable, I would recommend that a separate vote be taken upon such parts as may be thought expedient, and that at the same time and under the same authority there shall be an election for the officers provided under such constitution, and that the constitution, or such parts thereof as shall have been adopted by the people, be submitted to Congress on the first Monday of December next for its consideration, so that if the same is then approved the necessary steps will have been taken for the restoration of the State of Virginia to its proper relations to the Union. I am led to make this recommendation from the confident hope and belief that the people of that State are now ready to cooperate with the National Government in bringing it again into such relations to the Union as it ought as soon as possible to establish and maintain, and to give to all its people those equal rights under the law which were asserted in the Declaration of Independence in the words of one of the most illustrious of its sons.

I desire also to ask the consideration of Congress to the question whether there is not just ground for believing that the constitution framed by a convention of the people of Mississippi for that State, and once rejected, might not be again submitted to the people of that State in like manner, and with the probability of the same result.

Figure 18.1 Ulysses S. Grant statue, courtesy of Ian Wagreich.

3. EIGHT-HOUR DAY   MAY 19, 1869

Whereas the Act of Congress approved June 25, 1868 constituted, on and after that date, eight hours a day's work for all laborers, workmen and mechanics employed by or on behalf of the Government of the United States, and repealed all Acts and parts of Acts inconsistent therewith; Now therefore, I Ulysses S. Grant, President of the United States, do hereby direct that, from and after this date, no reduction shall be made in the wages paid by the Government by the day to such laborers workmen and mechanics, on account of such reduction of the hours of labor. . . .

4. LAST MESSAGE TO CONGRESS   DECEMBER 5, 1876

In submitting my eighth and last annual message to Congress it seems proper that I should refer to and in some degree recapitulate the events and official acts of the past eight years.

It was my fortune, or misfortune, to be called to the office of Chief Executive without any previous political training. From the age of 17 I had never even witnessed the excitement attending a presidential campaign but twice antecedent to my own candidacy, and at but one of them was I eligible as a voter.

Under such circumstances it is but reasonable to suppose that errors of judgment must have occurred. Even had they not, differences of opinion between the Executive, bound by an oath to the strict performance of his duties, and writers and debaters must have arisen. It is not necessarily evidence of blunder on the part of the Executive because there are these differences of views. Mistakes have been made, as all can see and I admit, but it seems to me oftener in the selections made of the assistants appointed to aid in carrying out the various duties of administering the Government—in nearly every case selected without a personal acquaintance with the appointee, but upon recommendations of the representatives chosen directly by the people. It is impossible, where so many trusts are to be allotted, that the right parties should be chosen in every instance. History shows that no Administration from the time of Washington to the present has been free from these mistakes. But I leave comparisons to history, claiming only that I have acted in every instance from a conscientious desire to do what was right, constitutional, within the law, and for the very best interests of the whole people. Failures have been errors of judgment, not of intent.

19

Rutherford B. Hayes

1. THE SUBJECT OF SUPREME IMPORTANCE   MARCH 5, 1877

... The permanent pacification of the country upon such principles and by such measures as will secure the complete protection of all its citizens in the free enjoyment of all their constitutional rights is now the one subject in our public affairs which all thoughtful and patriotic citizens regard as of supreme importance.

Many of the calamitous effects of the tremendous revolution which has passed over the Southern States still remain. The immeasurable benefits which will surely follow ... the hearty and generous acceptance of the legitimate results of that revolution have not yet been realized. Difficult and embarrassing questions meet us at the threshold of this subject. The people of those states are still impoverished, and the inestimable blessing of wise, honest, and peaceful local self-government is not fully enjoyed. Whatever difference of opinion may exist as to the cause of this condition of things, the fact is clear that in the progress of events the time has come when such government is the imperative necessity required by all the varied interests. . . . But it must not be forgotten that only a local government which recognizes and maintains inviolate the rights of all is a true self-government.

With respect to the two distinct races whose peculiar relations to each other have brought upon us the deplorable complications and perplexities which exist in those States, it must be a government which guards the interests of both races carefully and equally. . . .

2. HARMONIZE RACE RELATIONS   APRIL 22, 1877

The appointment of colored men to places under you for which they are qualified, will tend to secure to people of their race consideration and will diminish race prejudice. Other elements of your population are, of course, not to be overlooked. . . . endeavor to arrange your subordinate appointments so as to harmonize and meet the wishes and approval of all classes of good citizens, and at the same time to promote the efficiency of the service.

3. REFLECTIONS ON THE GREAT RAILROAD STRIKES   AUGUST 5, 1877

The strikes have been put down by force, but now for the real remedy. Can't something [be] done by education of the strikers, by judicious control of the capitalists, by wise general policy to end or diminish the evil? The R.R. strikers, as a rule are good men, sober, intelligent, and industrious.

The mischiefs are

1. Strikers prevent men willing to work from doing so.
2. They seize and hold the property of their employers.
3. The consequent excitement furnishes opportunity for the dangerous criminal classes to destroy life and property.

Now, "every man has a right if he sees fit to quarrel with his own bread and butter, but he has no right to quarrel with the bread and butter of other people."

Every man has a right to determine for himself the value of his own labor, but he has no right to determine for other men the value of their labor. . . .

Every man has a right to refuse to work if the wages don't suit him, but he has no right to prevent others from working if they are suited with the wages.

Every man has a right to refuse to work, but no man has a right to prevent others from working.

Every man has a right to decide for himself the question of wages, but no man has a right to decide that question for other men.

4. BEYOND THE BAYONET   AUGUST 5, 1877

There are some points on which good men, North and South are agreed generally. . . .

1. We agree that it is not well that political parties should be formed on sectional lines.
2. That it is not well that parties should divide on color lines.
3. That we should not divide on any line . . . which can only be settled with the bayonet.

(Pacification and Unification Program, August 26–September 25, 1877)

5. REFLECTIONS ON SPEAKING TOURS

My speeches [at the Soldiers Home in Washington City] were wholly unpremeditated—not therefore very satisfactory to myself; rather slovenly and ill constructed. I tried to impress the people with the importance of harmony between the different sections, States, classes and races, and to discourage sectionalism and race and class prejudice.

(Diary, 3:442, August 26, 1877)

For his follow-up tour of his home region of Ohio and a Southern Tour including Kentucky, Tennessee, and Virginia, the President decided to "speak of common hardships, dangers and services. . . . Instead of hostility and strife, we desire friendly feeling and peace."

On completion of the Southern Tour, and even while opposition to the Hayes Administration and the presidential pacification program developed in both political parties and in both Houses of Congress, the president recorded in his diary:

The Country is again one and united! I am very happy to be able to feel that the course taken has turned out so well.

(Diary, 3:443, September 25, 1877)

VI

BUILDING MODERN AMERICA

THE GILDED AGE OF MARK TWAIN was marked by materialism, greed, and corruption. It was also a time of energy, enterprise, and industry. The idealism and reformism that prevailed in ante-bellum America was long gone. It had been replaced by a more down-to-earth, practical, active, hands-on, and real-world approach to life. Aristotle trumped Plato in this new industrial world order in the making. In the time of Emerson, Webster, and Melville, Americans were on a mission to seek out evil in the world and destroy it. That was then. Reform was no longer foremost in the American mind. While Americans did not exactly shake hands with the devil in the Gilded Age, they were more tolerant towards things as they were. The fratricidal Civil War had used up American taste for the quest to construct a heaven on earth. They were in this respect more tolerant. This is not to say there was no interest in reform or that there were no reformers. The reformers of the time did not engage in sweeping reforms but limited their activities to such things as civil service reform. Americans wanted to build in a physical sense. The mission was to make America. They found presidents to match their new mood.

The trend was towards making things, building things with many hands and machines. Darwinian ideas had entered through the back door. Given the preoccupation with Civil War and pulling the nation back together in the immediate aftermath of the war, Americans did not rush out to buy and read *On the Origin of Species*. Americans received ideas of evolution second-hand, in the form of Social Darwinism via the English Sociologist Herbert Spencer and his American admirers. The ideas of evolution were applied by Americans to justify their social present and the accumulation of great wealth as part of the natural order of the universe.

Not everyone received these marching orders. Henry Adams, descendant of presidents, marched to the beat of a different drummer. He postulated that the best refutation of Darwinian evolution was to be found in the history of the American presidency. When America moved from Lincoln to Johnson to Grant, that movement, said Henry Adams, was decidedly not progress. In fairness to all Lincoln's nineteenth-century successors, it must be said that looking back from a distance of more than a hundred years they were men of integrity. They simply were not Lincoln. More than that, they were not afforded Lincoln's considerable war powers to do the job.

The American presidency went into eclipse. Congress was in the ascendancy. In many respects the presidency now operated in the shadow of Congress. This new relative posture could easily be overstated. The president would now and then step out of the Congressional shadow and let his presence be felt. Another consideration that lent itself to inaction was the precarious balance of the two national parties. Politics were at equilibrium. Turnout was high. Election returns were close. Any political miscalculation or departure from the norm could upset the delicate party balance. Presidents of this period in their capacity as Chief Executive needed to "take care that the laws be faithfully executed." They also needed to beware that untimely presidential actions could lead to party defeat at the polls.

The times tamed the presidential reach. This was political reality in the years following the killing of Lincoln. The American presidency functioned in keeping with public expectations at the time. Select inherent roles assumed greater prominence. Unlike the prime minister in the British system, the American president is Head of State. In this capacity he is the symbol of the nation. In a material age which focused on physical constructions, the president was called upon to preside at many dedication ceremonies.

In this Age of Steel, when the Brooklyn Bridge was completed, President Chester A. Arthur was on hand to preside over the happy celebration. Likewise when France presented the United States with the gift of "Liberty Enlightening the World," President Grover Cleveland was there to receive and dedicate the famous statue. Dedication ceremonies such as these give meaning to the life of a nation. The Great Bridge and Lady Liberty are national treasures and monuments in American history. Solemn words from the nation's president as Head of State also stand as historical markers in our history. Documents of this kind should be preserved and consulted as we turn the page of time.

This period of our presidential history begins and ends with murder most foul of our Chief Executives. Presidential bookends Garfield and McKinley felt the sting and succumbed to assassins' bullets. James Abram Garfield had all the marks of a survivor. He had survived war and poverty. No Hollywood script could compare with the actual true life rags-to-riches story of the twentieth President of the United States. Born in a log cabin, Garfield rose up by force of will and intellect. By the age of 25 he had graduated from Williams College as a student of the Classics. Cited for bravery leading Ohio Volunteers in the Civil War, he later rose in Republican political circles. While a close observer of the sordid Republican inter-party wars of the Gilded Age, Garfield managed to retain his reputation for decency. When the 1880 Republican Convention split between warring factions, Garfield emerged on the 36th ballot as a compromise candidate.

Given the disposition of the era to dwell in the muck of materialism, it is no surprise that the age-old penchant for political place and patronage would occupy center stage. Jobs and money issues remained at the core of the politics of the Gilded Age and caused President Garfield deep anxiety and exasperation. By tradition, the president made the personnel decisions, even for minor offices like postmasters and surveyors. Thousands of place-seekers advanced their cause in person, by letter and through political surrogates. The torrent of office-seekers drove Garfield to distraction. He complained that his time was "frittered away" by "a stream of callers" seeking patronage. Looking forward to a full four-year term of this he concluded that "this kind of intellectual dissipation may cripple me for the remainder of my life."

In June 1881, after just three months in the Executive Mansion, the dutiful Garfield confessed himself overwhelmed by this unceasing and often angry process. Shortly thereafter, on July 2, 1881 a deranged and disappointed office-seeker, Charles J. Guiteau, shot the President, who died in September from his wounds. In truth, President Garfield was the victim of an assassin and medical malpractice. He might well have survived the attempt on his life had it not been for the incompetence of his team of physicians and his surgeon Dr. Doctor Willard Bliss.

The spoilsman and former Customs Collector of New York, Chester A. Arthur now occupied the presidential chair vacated by the murdered President Garfield. He had gained the Vice Presidential spot through a series of political machinations. The death of Garfield stirred the pot. Years of corruption produced a political stench so strong that even professional politicians now sought reform. In a prior age President Jackson brought his military manner and outlook to

American political practice. Political winners, like victors in war, were entitled to the spoils. This spoils system took deep root in American politics. Indeed, President Arthur had partaken freely of the established system. For a generation, Arthur's life revolved around the intrigues of the GOP.

The factionalized Republicans were split three ways among reformers and two rival machines called "Half Breeds" and "Stalwarts." Each bloc of "spoilsmen" sought whatever benefits might be found through political connivance. Arthur, a quintessential New York City "Stalwart" Republican, belonged to the organization of New York Senator Roscoe Conkling. On Conkling's advice, President Grant in 1871 appointed Chester Arthur Collector of Customs for the Port of New York, where some 75 percent of the nation's custom receipts were collected. This $100,000,000 per year "business" provided the greatest patronage source in the United States. Through its arbitrary regulations, the post rewarded Arthur with the highest salary in the Federal Government.

In the struggle for the 1880 Republican Presidential nomination, Conkling agreed to throw his support to James A. Garfield of Ohio. The second slot went to Arthur. Garfield took office in March, was shot in July, and died in September. Accidental President Arthur attempted to imbue his short term with dignity, and accepted the popular call for civil service reform. With rich irony, this single action along with his presiding role at the dedication of Brooklyn Bridge uniting the twin cities of New York and Brooklyn best represents his time as President. Arthur in his capacity as Head of State had the high honor to lead fifty thousand enthusiastic celebrants across this new eighth wonder of the world. If the President dedicated the architectural masterpiece with commemorative words, no record remains.

President Arthur confronted serious problems with regard to territorial security in Arizona and on the Mexican border. Arthur had received intelligence reports from various sources which advised him that conditions had reached an "alarming state of disorder" with respect to Arizona Territory. The reports prompted him to send a message to both houses of Congress on April 26, 1882 informing the legislative branch of the extent of the problem and the need to find the means to combat the lawlessness which prevailed throughout that western province. The President was working to build the Great American West, preparing the territories for statehood and absorbing them in the framework of the nation.

The territorial governor was a prime source of news as to developments in Arizona. President Arthur notified the Congress that "violence and anarchy prevail" and that "robbery, murder, and resistance to law have become so common as to cease causing surprise." In addition, his message to Congress mentioned that the General of the Army stated in a telegram: "the civil officers, have not sufficient force to make arrests and hold the prisoners for trial or punish them when convicted."

The main cause of the threat to the peace and good order of Arizona territory stemmed from "armed bands of desperadoes" who freely roamed the western territory. Something must be done, thought the President, to bring justice to the wild and wooly West and to regain the faith and confidence of the people in their government. The lawlessness needed to be repressed and the territory brought under the protection of the law and the courts. His message advised of the request from the Arizona Governor "that provision be made by Congress to enable him to employ and maintain temporarily a volunteer militia force to aid the civil authorities." The President proposed an alternative remedy: "On the ground of economy as well as effectiveness [it is] more advisable to permit the cooperation with the civil authorities of a part of the Army as a *posse comitatus.*" The Commander-in-Chief believed that Congress should authorize amending the law to allow a military solution to prop up territorial authorities and enable them "to execute the laws."

Congress took control in yet another area affecting the building and shaping of the nation. In the early days of Arthur's administration, on May 6, 1882, the President signed the Chinese

Exclusion Act. Here the government formally expressed the opinion that "the coming of Chinese laborers to this country endangers the good order of certain localities." Chinese immigrants were thereby excluded from further participation in the great enterprise of building the nation.

Grover Cleveland, after a razor-close election in 1884, succeeded Chester A. Arthur and moved into the White House the following March. Cleveland had been a Buffalo lawyer turned politician. Prior to the presidency, Cleveland had been Mayor of Buffalo and Governor of New York State. He won the Democratic Party nomination in 1884, and in the ensuing general election gathered votes from Democrats and "mugwump" Republicans. He is the only man in the history of the American presidency to serve two non-consecutive terms. Consequently he was the 22nd and 24th President of the United States.

His first election had been marked by a brutal and dirty political campaign. The Republicans had nominated the colorful "plumed knight" from Maine, James G. Blaine. Each political camp charged corruption against the other. Cleveland had to overcome a personal smear campaign alleging sexual indiscretions. The bachelor candidate candidly confessed to an all-male electorate that he had fathered a child. In what some historians curiously like to paint as the "Victorian Age," Cleveland benefited from a compassionate and forgiving male voting public. Religion and religious prejudice also entered into play as the Republican candidate Blaine was introduced to members of the Protestant clergy by the Reverend Samuel Burchard at the elegant Fifth Avenue Hotel in New York City. Just prior to Halloween and Election Day the reverend reminded the clergy that Democrats were the party of "Rum, Romanism, and Rebellion." Cleveland won the election.

The theme of freedom, which flows throughout the history of the American presidency, became particularly manifest again during the administration of Grover Cleveland. Admiring Frenchmen in the aftermath of the American Civil War conceived the idea of making a gift of an image of freedom to America. The idea matured and took concrete shape in the creative hands of the master French sculptor, Frederic Auguste Bartholdi. The artist cast a giant copper statue of a lady which eventually was mounted on a pedestal with torch in hand. It arrived in 300 pieces. The reassembled statue found a home in New York harbor, strategically positioned near the City of Brooklyn, New York City and visible also from Staten Island and New Jersey. The site selected by Bartholdi was Bedloe's Island, now known as Liberty Island.

The gift of France was accepted by President Cleveland on October 28, 1886. New York and Brooklyn waxed ecstatic as more than a million participated in the celebration and parades. At the dedication ceremonies on Bedloe's Island, the President acknowledged the importance of the occasion: "The people of the United States accept with gratitude from their brethren of the French Republic the grand and completed work of art we here inaugurate." The majestic work of art towered above the splendid harbor in the fashion of the ancient Colossus of Rhodes. The Colossus, one of the Seven Wonders of the World, had been erected on the island of Rhodes overlooking that harbor in celebration of a military victory to honor the Greek god Helios circa 304 B.C. Lady Liberty loomed now as a modern colossus and a monument to freedom in the new world. Technically the French had christened the enormous sculpture "La Liberté éclairant le monde." The official name translates as "Liberty Enlightening the World."

The President concluded the solemn speech of dedication:

> We will not forget that Liberty has here made her home, nor shall her chosen altar be neglected. Willing votaries will constantly keep its fires and these shall gleam upon the shores of our sister Republic thence, and joined with answering rays a stream of light shall pierce the darkness of ignorance and man's oppression, until Liberty enlightens the world.

Lady Liberty stands facing east to welcome friends and strangers. Emma Lazarus referred to this "mighty woman with a torch" as "The New Colossus." The Lady lifted her lamp at the "golden door" of freedom. Building the nation required the work of many hands from many places. The result of the work was a mosaic of peoples and a nation of immigrants.

Cleveland clung to deep convictions. He believed strongly that he should not give preference nor show favor to any select group or economic class. Even so, there were times in which he found it necessary to bend at the edges. In the main, his conception of the duties of the Chief Executive were founded on the rock-hard belief that it was not the President's role to promote the economic wellbeing of one segment of the population against another. America was built on the idea of freedom of opportunity for all. Government should abstain from interfering in the marketplace and the natural order of the economy. After a veto of one bill that was designed to assist American farmers, Cleveland explained the veto in these sharp words: "Federal aid in such cases encourages the expectation of paternal care on the part of the Government and weakens the sturdiness of our national character." He firmly believed in the adage that good Americans supported their government but the government supported no one in particular.

The aim was to prevent rather than promote government activity. This political philosophy was one he practiced as Mayor of Buffalo and Governor of New York. He carried this same philosophy of government to the presidency. The primary role of any Executive was to receive and dispose of the proposals of the Legislature. It fit the expectations of the age. He was the only Democrat elected President since Buchanan in 1856. Nor would another Democrat obtain the keys to the White House until 1912 when Wilson won a plurality in a four-way division of the vote. It was a stretch of more than a half-century.

The last third of the nineteenth century was comparatively a time of political inaction. The Civil War and Reconstruction periods had made Americans weary and wary of executive action. The electorate indicated a preference for leaders who were perceived as generally weak if mostly honorable men. Politicians engaged in a deliberate politics of avoidance of vital or controversial issues. Evenly matched political parties likewise existed in a state of suspended animation or equilibrium. Any movement could upset the balance and lead to loss of power. Risk avoidance was the order of the day. The time was ripe for Grover Cleveland.

The government role was then considered limited. This suited Cleveland just fine. He regularly disapproved of Congressional initiatives. Both of his presidential terms produced a flood of vetoes. Two of every three bills reaching his desk experienced prompt rejection. By the end of his presidency, Cleveland's vetoes numbered three times more than all his predecessors combined. However politically hazardous this austere approach, Cleveland nonetheless stuck to his principles and conveyed an integrity which clearly distinguished him from the lax ethics and addiction to spoils that characterized the times in that materialistic "Gilded Age." His motto was: "Above all tell the truth."

Two important pieces of legislation in his first term which received the president's approval in 1887 were the Interstate Commerce Act and the Dawes Severalty Act. The first was designed to build and consolidate the nation's commerce and transport network. The second was a reformist and flawed attempt at assimilating Native Americans into the mainstream culture with other Americans. The well-meaning Dawes legislation had several negative consequences for the communal and cultural life of the tribes. Both acts fit the theme of building a new nation.

Few initiatives escaped the ink of the Chief Executive's veto pen. Troubled farmers sought economic assistance in their struggle to survive. In 1887, natural disasters devastated crops in the Texas Panhandle. Congress appropriated $10,000 so that desperate farmers could purchase seed grain. The President strongly objected and in his veto message to Congress, Cleveland gave thumbs down to the disaster relief legislation.

In 1888 the American electorate turned thumbs down on incumbent President Cleveland and his campaign for re-election. On exiting the Executive Mansion, First Lady Frances Folsom Cleveland gave specific instructions to the staff to preserve things as they were, for the Cleveland family would return in four years. During the interim of those four years, Benjamin Harrison would occupy the office and the Mansion. In keeping with the tenor of the age, Harrison believed in limited and frugal government. On the first day of his presidency he proclaimed: "Expenditure should always be made with economy and only upon public necessity. Wastefulness, profligacy or favoritism in public expenditures is criminal." After taking the oath, Harrison noted in his Inaugural Address that there was no constitutional imperative to do so in public. Yet it was appropriate to do so in order to consecrate the solemn moment with the participation of the people as witness. He contended that the public ceremony created a bond and constituted a mutual covenant between the people and the president.

A century after George Washington took the presidential oath at Federal Hall, Harrison presided over a vivid celebration of the centennial. Accompanied by his cabinet and members of the Supreme Court, the President traveled on April 29, 1889 by overnight train from Washington to Elizabeth, New Jersey. The next morning, Harrison began to follow the route taken by Washington on that first inaugural day. He led a procession down to the Hudson River opposite Manhattan. Groups of young women in white dresses showered the presidential party with roses and, like his illustrious predecessor of a century earlier, Harrison stopped under garlanded arches to thank the young ladies.

Festooned ships of all descriptions filled New York harbor, when the presidential party boarded the *U.S.S. Despatch*. To the bridge went the President, escorted by military dignitaries like General William Tecumseh Sherman. After two hours of review, the President landed at the Battery and began a day-long round of parades and receptions. At City Hall, he passed through an honor guard of girls armed with lilies of the valley and roses, once again being pleasantly covered with flowers. An open-air concert attracted thousands to Madison Square. Throughout the city, neighborhoods were swathed in Stars and Stripes. At day's end, President Harrison drove to the magnificent new Metropolitan Opera house, opened in 1883, to preside over a glittering Centennial banquet attended by 800 of America's best known citizens. Toasts were offered at a banquet by ex-Presidents Rutherford B. Hayes and Grover Cleveland as well as by Chief Justice of the United States Melville W. Fuller. President Harrison paid tribute to Washington and called upon all present at the 100-year historical marker to remember American "martyrs to liberty." He concluded that the Centennial ceremony provided "lessons to inspire us to consecrate ourselves anew to this love and service of our country."

Americans in this period held conflicted views on immigration and citizenship. In the main, newcomers were welcomed at the golden door to join hands in the building of the new industrial nation. Signs of ambiguity surfaced in Benjamin Harrison's Inaugural Address. "Our naturalization laws should be amended," declared Harrison. "We accept the man as a citizen without any knowledge of his fitness." The President continued: "We should not cease to be hospitable to immigration, but . . . There are men of all races . . . whose coming is necessarily a burden upon our public revenues or a threat to social order. These should be identified and excluded." The only grandson of a president to become president, Benjamin Harrison was not granted a second term by his fellow citizens.

The return of the Clevelands to the Executive Mansion in 1893 fulfilled Frances Folsom Cleveland's 1889 prophesy. The homecoming coincided with the "Panic of 1893," one of the most severe economic collapses in American history. Cleveland's restrictive view of the proper role of government limited his response. Many economic historians, while not placing the cause of the crisis on Cleveland's doorstep, nonetheless attribute the prolonged nature of the economic downturn to the President's political philosophy. He called for honesty, reductions in spending and taxes, and tariff reform.

Cleveland's fundamental beliefs generally matched the economic outlook of American presidents throughout the nineteenth century. The presidential call for frugality in government remained a refrain that Cleveland strenuously promoted from the outset of his second term. This was especially true, given the dire economic conditions. "Under our scheme of government the waste of public money is a crime against the citizen" said the nation's CEO. The times had turned tough and presidential leadership called upon both the government and the citizens to live within their means and get even tougher. Government extravagance and wasteful spending of public funds should not be tolerated. Not only is such activity a "crime against the citizen," it tends to produce "prodigality" among the people.

American leaders regarded private property as inviolable and the involvement of government in the economic and social lives of American citizens as unconstitutional. Natural disasters and bad times simply must be endured. Americans had engaged in building an industrial nation. They now faced their first industrial depression. Times had changed as industrial workers, unlike their ancestors, could not fall back on the safety net of living off the land. With the economy frozen and stocks at an all-time low, the nation witnessed convulsions of protest. The bitter strike at the Homestead, Pennsylvania, steel mill of Andrew Carnegie raged from July to November 1892, involving 7,000 troops, violent confrontations between steelworkers and scabs, plus a score of deaths. Scabs who would work for less than union wages replaced strikers, while the militia patrolled the mill. Union militancy gradually attracted both sympathy and support through a rash of secondary strikes, but compelling power remained against them.

The prevailing political and judicial response to work stoppages included both the dispatch of troops to break the strike and the use of the courts to find strikes illegal. When workers at the Pullman Palace Car Company near Chicago struck on May 11, 1894, the American Railway Union organized a sympathy strike of all railroad workers. The strikers, led by Eugene Debs, met the unswerving opposition of the owners, who brought in strike-breakers and called for troops. Caught in the middle was Illinois Governor John Peter Altgeld, who maintained contact with both sides and sought compromise without violence. The strikers acted without legal authority and were hit with an injunction. Under the terms of the injunction, Debs was ordered to end the strike.

President Cleveland argued that interstate commerce and mail delivery were impeded by the strike. Consequently, on the 8th of July, the President declared martial law and Federal troops poured into Chicago. Death and general mayhem attended the struggle. Debs was indicted and an estimated $80,000,000 in property and wages were lost in the conflagration. Debs would soon be jailed for contempt. The Commander-in-Chief acted and the army put an end to the Pullman strike.

Protesters had long demanded relief from the gold standard which restricted the money supply and favored creditors over debtors. The Populists and their allies insisted that the Federal Government purchase and distribute silver as legal currency. Congress passed the Sherman Silver Purchase Act in 1890, which compelled the procurement of 4.5 million ounces of silver each month. Treasury notes became payable either in gold or silver. As the depression deepened, Cleveland's worst nightmare appeared. Runs on the Federal gold supply shrunk the nation's holdings and only encouraged frightened investors to further runs. Hence in 1893 the President called a Special Session of Congress specifically to repeal the Sherman Silver Purchase Act. Repeal failed to end the run on the Treasury. The end of silver purchases contracted the nation's supply and alienated debtors and silver miners. This materialistic age had a down-to-earth bent and dealt with practical considerations such as currency and the tariff. The time of reckoning would arrive with the critical presidential election of 1896.

Thrift and frugality with respect to government expenditures ran side by side with the need to maintain a "sound and stable currency." The nature of the currency continued to be the main battlefield of American politics throughout Cleveland's second term and into the presidential election of 1896. For President Cleveland gold must be the national standard and coin of the realm. Gold resisted debasement and the "danger of depreciation in the purchasing power" of the wage worker. With a gold standard the nation could proceed along the path to economic recovery. Critics of Cleveland's policy would demean "the yellow brick road" and refused to have the nation, as William Jennings Bryan shouted in his speech to the Democratic Party National Convention in Chicago, crucified on a "Cross of Gold." The Democrats in Chicago omitted any mention of the *Plessey vs. Ferguson* decision, in which the Supreme Court rendered segregation constitutional just days earlier. The issue they would carry into their campaign would not be about racial segregation—black and white. The political-economic focus was on silver and gold.

As the nineteenth century approached its close, President William McKinley also performed his duty as Head of State. It was fitting that he who wore with distinction the uniform of a Major in the Civil War was called upon to dedicate a memorial to a gallant soldier and former President Ulysses S. Grant. Nor did McKinley fail other fallen soldiers when he followed Lincoln's Gettysburg example and paid tribute in Maryland at Antietam National Battlefield to those who sacrificed their lives in service to their country. Finally, President McKinley, the first wartime president since Lincoln, presided at the centennial commemoration of the death of Washington at his Mt. Vernon home in December 1899. These are moments to remember and to cherish.

The election of 1896 marked the maturation of American politics. That election had brought William McKinley to the pinnacle of American politics. McKinley won the 1896 election by a handsome margin. This critical election ended the stalemate between the national parties and shattered the politics of equilibrium that had existed for a generation. President McKinley clearly had a mandate to govern. His governance produced prosperity at home and victory in foreign policy.

America had come a long way in the hundred years since the launching of the Republic. Now, as the nation turned the corner to welcome a new century, America could look back with pride at how far it had travelled and what had been built. New life and larger meaning had been given to the founding documents and the concept of liberty, with the emancipation of the slaves and the amendments to the Constitution which helped insure basic rights to all Americans. Yet there had been backward as well as forward movement, as with Chinese exclusion, *Plessey vs. Ferguson,* and exploitation of ethnic immigrants and Native Americans. Despite claims of material and intellectual progress, the American Dream had faded for people of color and had been scarred by nativism and xenophobia for people of faith. Religious and racial prejudice were everywhere in evidence. Lady Liberty did not protect these strangers in the land from powerful un-American strains of anti-Catholicism and anti-Semitism.

Americans got busy in these years and built the physical and industrial plants. Religious and racial advance would have to await full realization. The last third of the century had been devoted to developing the material and physical well-being of a newly constructed industrial nation. The nation got organized in every particular in this Age of Steel. Rudimentary central plumbing was installed in the White House. Time zones were developed. Major league baseball came to pass with the Cincinnati Reds and the formation of the National League. Standardized accounting and railroad gauge appeared. Corporate America came to pass. Labor organized. The AHA and AMA arrived on the scene. AP and UPI, along with newspaper chains were born. Ironically, even the anarchists organized and founded their political-philosophical journal, *On Liberty*. A national market had been created via transcontinental railroads and a transportation network which connected vast reaches of the hinterland and the Great American West to a rising urban, industrial America.

The shocking and mysterious explosion that destroyed the battleship *U.S.S. Maine* in Havana harbor on February 15, 1898 unleashed eager forces of war in the United States. Theodore Roosevelt, Assistant Secretary of the Navy, urged that the time had come to drive "the Spaniard from the New World." Spain's shrinking empire in the Western Hemisphere bumped up closest to the United States in Cuba. Revolutionary uprisings in Cuba tended to be brutally suppressed by Spain which desperately clung to fading New World glory. Events in Cuba had claimed the attention of the sensationalist "Yellow Press," particularly Joseph Pulitzer's New York *World* and William Randolph Hearst's New York *Journal*. Daily headlines highlighted and columns reported lurid tales of despicable Spanish acts. This despicable depravity demanded an honorable response by the United States. Hearst dispatched the artist Frederick Remington to the scene who then informed his boss that he could not find trouble. Remington received a cable from Hearst headquarters: "You furnish the pictures. I'll furnish the War."

War hawks beat the drums for battle. Pulitzer predicted a bonanza for his paper's circulation. Secretary Roosevelt thought it would be a "splendid thing" for the Navy. An irresponsible Spanish diplomat in Washington characterized McKinley as "feebleminded." In this atmosphere the *Maine* blew up, killing 266 crewmen. While the cause of the explosion has never been conclusively proven, there has never been any doubt about the effect. Congress appropriated $50 million for the military. Roosevelt cabled Commodore George Dewey with the Pacific fleet to prepare for attack on the Philippines.

Diplomacy stood little chance. Spain attempted to preserve peace and sought any compromise short of national humiliation. Spain's offer to negotiate Cuban independence arrived too late. President McKinley decided to act. He requested on April 11, 1898 Congressional authority to wage war. The Congress concurred. The "splendid little war" commenced. Ten weeks later it ended with the United States in control of Cuba and in possession of Puerto Rico, the Philippine Islands and Guam, Hawaii, Wake Island, and American Samoa. Building America had expanded horizons exponentially beyond simply a continental reach from sea to shining sea.

A few American historians have contended that McKinley should be acknowledged as the first modern president. The case is compelling. At the time, the Republican Party had been hailed in the tradition of Lincoln as the champion and protector of minorities. In accord with that mantle, President McKinley would visit and celebrate Tuskegee Institute in Alabama. This reach over the racial divide pointed to possible better days ahead. It had not brought the nation to Nirvana. The promise of American life had by no means been realized. There continued to be strains of religious intolerance and racial and ethnic bigotry. Yet McKinley moved the nation forward. In tune with the changing times, a modern presidency emerged with the future-friendly William McKinley. Under his leadership America took a giant step towards a prosperous and stronger place among nations in the coming century. The nation was positioned on the path toward the American Century.

20

James A. Garfield

1. A HUNDRED YEARS OF NATIONAL LIFE

MARCH 4, 1881

... We stand to-day upon an eminence which overlooks a hundred years of national life—a century crowded with perils, but crowned with the triumphs of liberty and law. Before continuing the onward march let us pause on this height for a moment to strengthen our faith and renew our hope. ...

It is now three days more than a hundred years since the adoption of the first written constitution of the United States—the Articles of Confederation and Perpetual Union. The new Republic was then beset with danger on every hand. It had not conquered a place in the family of nations. The decisive battle of the war for independence, whose centennial anniversary will soon be gratefully celebrated at Yorktown, had not yet been fought. ...

We cannot overestimate the fervent love of liberty, the intelligent courage, and the sum of common sense with which our fathers made the great experiment of self-government. When they found ... that the confederacy of States was too weak to meet the necessities of a vigorous and expanding republic, they boldly set it aside and in its stead established a National Union. ...

Under this Constitution the boundaries of freedom have been enlarged, the foundations of order and peace have been strengthened, and the growth of our people in all the better elements of national life has indicated the wisdom of the founders and given new hope to their descendants. ... Under this Constitution twenty-five States have been added to the Union. ...

The jurisdiction of this Constitution now covers an area fifty times greater than that of the original thirteen States and a population twenty times greater than that of 1780. ...

And now, at the close of this first century of growth, with the inspirations of its history in their hearts, our people have lately reviewed the condition of the nation, passed judgment upon the conduct and opinions of political parties, and have registered their will concerning the future administration of the Government. ...

2. THE TORRENT OF PATRONAGE SEEKERS

JUNE 6–13, 1881

[On 6 June, after three days absence from Washington] The stream of callers which was damned up by absence became a torrent and swept away my day.

[8 June] My day in the office was very like its predecessors. Once or twice I felt like crying out in the agony of my soul against the greed for office and its consumption of my time. My services ought to be worth more to the government than to be spent thus.

[13 June] I am feeling greatly dissatisfied for my lack of opportunity for study. My day is frittered away by the personal seeking of people, when it ought to be given to the great problem[s], which concern the whole country. Four years of this kind of intellectual dissipation may cripple me for the remainder of my life. What might not a vigorous thinker do, if he could be allowed to use the opportunities of a Presidential term in vital, useful activity! Some Civil Service Reform will come by necessity after the weariness of some years of wasted Presidents have paved the way for it.

21

Chester A. Arthur

1. PRINCIPLES AND RULES OF PUBLIC SERVICE DECEMBER 4, 1882

. . . The communication that I made to Congress at its first session, in December last, contained a somewhat full statement of my sentiments in relation to the principles and rules which ought to govern appointments to public service.

Referring to the various plans which had theretofore been the subject of discussion in the National Legislature (plans which in the main were modeled upon the system which obtains in Great Britain, but which lacked certain of the prominent features whereby that system is distinguished), I felt bound to intimate my doubts whether they, or any of them, would afford adequate remedy for the evils which they aimed to correct.

I declared, nevertheless, that if the proposed measures should prove acceptable to Congress they would receive the unhesitating support of the Executive.

Since these suggestions were submitted for your consideration there has been no legislation upon the subject to which they relate, but there has meanwhile been an increase in the public interest in that subject, and the people of the country, apparently without distinction of party, have in various ways and upon frequent occasions given expression to their earnest wish for prompt and definite action. In my judgment such action should no longer be postponed.

I may add that my own sense of its pressing importance has been quickened by observation of a practical phase of the matter, to which attention has more than once been called by my predecessors.

The civil list now comprises about 100,000 persons, far the larger part of whom must, under the terms of the Constitution, be selected by the President either directly or through his own appointees.

In the early years of the administration of the Government the personal direction of appointments to the civil service may not have been an irksome task for the Executive, but now that the burden has increased fully a hundredfold it has become greater than he ought to bear, and it necessarily diverts his time and attention from the proper discharge of other duties no less delicate and responsible, and which in the very nature of things cannot be delegated to other hands.

In the judgment of not a few who have given study and reflection to this matter, the nation has outgrown the provisions which the Constitution has established for filling the minor offices in the public service.

But whatever may be thought of the wisdom or expediency of changing the fundamental law in this regard, it is certain that much relief may be afforded, not only to the President and to the heads of the Departments, but to Senators and Representatives in Congress, by discreet legislation.

They would be protected in a great measure by the bill now pending before the Senate, or by any other which should embody its important features, from the pressure of personal importunity and from the labor of examining conflicting claims and pretensions of candidates.

I trust that before the close of the present session some decisive action may be taken for the correction of the evils which inhere in the present methods of appointment, and I assure you of my hearty cooperation in any measures which are likely to conduce to that end.

As to the most appropriate term and tenure of the official life of the subordinate employees of the Government, it seems to be generally agreed that, whatever their extent or character, the one should be definite and the other stable and that neither should be regulated by zeal in the service of party or fidelity to the fortunes of an individual.

It matters little to the people at large what competent person is at the head of this department or of that bureau if they feel assured that the removal of one and the accession of another will not involve the retirement of honest and faithful subordinates whose duties are purely administrative and have no legitimate connection with the triumph of any political principles or the success of any political party or faction. It is to this latter class of officers that the Senate bill, to which I have already referred, exclusively applies.

While neither that bill nor any other prominent scheme for improving the civil service concerns the higher grade of officials, who are appointed by the President and confirmed by the Senate, I feel bound to correct a prevalent misapprehension as to the frequency with which the present Executive has displaced the incumbent of an office and appointed another in his stead.

It has been repeatedly alleged that he has in this particular signally departed from the course which has been pursued under recent Administrations of the Government. The facts are as follows:

The whole number of Executive appointments during the four years immediately preceding Mr. Garfield's accession to the Presidency was 2,696. Of this number 244, or 9 per cent, involved the removal of previous incumbents.

The ratio of removals to the whole number of appointments was much the same during each of those four years. In the first year, with 790 appointments, there were 74 removals, or 9.3 per cent; in the second, with 917 appointments, there were 85 removals, or 8.5 per cent; in the third, with 480 appointments, there were 48 removals, or 10 per cent; in the fourth, with 429 appointments, there were 37 removals, or 8.6 per cent. In the four months of President Garfield's Administration there were 390 appointments and 89 removals, or 22.7 per cent. Precisely the same number of removals (89) has taken place in the fourteen months which have since elapsed, but they constitute only 7.8 per cent of the whole number of appointments (1,118) within that period and less than 2.6 per cent of the entire list of officials (3,459), exclusive of the Army and Navy, which is filled by Presidential appointment.

I declare my approval of such legislation as may be found necessary for supplementing the existing provisions of law in relation to political assessments.

In July last I authorized a public announcement that employees of the Government should regard themselves as at liberty to exercise their pleasure in making or refusing to make political contributions, and that their action in that regard would in no manner affect their official status.

In this announcement I acted upon the view, which I had always maintained and still maintain, that a public officer should be as absolutely free as any other citizen to give or to withhold a contribution for the aid of the political party of his choice. It has, however, been urged, and doubtless not without foundation in fact, that by solicitation of official superiors and by other modes such contributions have at times been obtained from persons whose only motive for giving has been the fear of what might befall them if they refused. It goes without saying that such contributions are not voluntary, and in my judgment their collection should be prohibited by law. A bill which will effectually suppress them will receive my cordial approval. . . .

2. MESSAGE ON TERRITORIAL SECURITY AND THE MEXICAN   APRIL 26, 1882
BORDER: ARIZONA CRISIS

By recent information received from official and other sources I am advised that an alarming state of disorder continues to exist within the Territory of Arizona, and that lawlessness has already gained such head there as to require a resort to extraordinary means to repress it.

The governor of the Territory . . . reports that violence and anarchy prevail, particularly in Cochise County and along the Mexican border; that robbery, murder, and resistance to law have become so common as to cease causing surprise, and that the people are greatly intimidated and losing confidence in the protection of the law. . . .

In a telegram from the General of the Army dated at Tucson, Ariz., on the 11th instant . . . states that he hears of lawlessness and disorders which seem well attested, and that the civil officers have not sufficient force to make arrests and hold the prisoners for trial or punish them when convicted.

Much of this disorder is caused by armed bands of desperadoes . . . by whom depredations are not only committed within the Territory, but it is alleged predatory incursions are made therefrom into Mexico.

In my message to Congress at the beginning of the present session I called attention to the existence of these bands and suggested that the setting on foot within our own territory of brigandage and armed marauding expeditions against friendly nations and their citizens be made punishable as an offense against the United States. I renew this suggestion.

To effectually repress the lawlessness prevailing within the Territory a prompt execution of the process of the courts and vigorous enforcement of the laws against offenders are needed . . . the civil authority there are unable to do without the aid of other means and forces that they can now avail themselves of.

To meet the present exigencies the governor asks that provision be made by Congress to enable him to employ and maintain temporarily a volunteer militia force to aid the civil authorities, the members of which force to be invested with the same powers and authority as are conferred by the laws of the Territory upon peace officers. . . .

On the ground of economy as well as effectiveness, however, it appears to me to be more advisable to permit the cooperation with the civil authorities of a part of the Army as a *posse comitatus*. Believing that this, in addition to such use of the Army as may be made under the powers already conferred by section 5298, Revised Statutes, would be adequate to secure the accomplishment of the ends in view, I again call the attention of Congress to the expediency of so amending section 15 of the act of June 18, 1878, chapter 263, as to allow the military forces to be employed as a *posse comitatus* to assist the civil authorities within a Territory to execute the laws therein. . . .

3. CALL FOR A PAN-AMERICAN CONFERENCE   APRIL 18, 1882

I send herewith a copy of the circular invitation extended to all the independent countries of North and South America to participate in a general congress to be held in the city of Washington on the 22nd of November next for the purpose of considering and discussing the methods of preventing war between the nations of America.

In giving this invitation I was not unaware that there existed differences between several of the Republics of South America which would militate against the happy results which might otherwise be expected from such an assemblage. The differences indicated are such as exist between Chile and Peru, between Mexico and Guatemala, and between the States of Central America.

It was hoped that these differences would disappear before the time fixed for the meeting of the congress. This hope has not been realized.

Having observed that the authority of the President to convene such a congress has been questioned, I beg leave to state that the Constitution confers upon the President the power, by and with the advice and consent of the Senate, to make treaties, and that this provision confers the power to take all requisite measures to initiate them, and to this end the President may freely confer with one or several commissioners or delegates from other nations. The congress contemplated by the invitation could only effect any valuable results by its conclusions eventually taking the form of a treaty of peace between the States represented; and, besides, the invitation to the States of North and South America is merely a preliminary act, of which constitutionality or the want of it can hardly be affirmed.

It has been suggested that while the international congress would have no power to affect the rights of nationalities there represented, still Congress might be unwilling to subject the existing treaty rights of the United States on the Isthmus and elsewhere of the opinions of a congress composed largely of interested parties.

I am glad to have it in my power to refer to the Congress of the United States, as I now do, the propriety of convening the suggested international congress, that I may thus be informed of its views, which it will be my pleasure to carry out.

Inquiry having been made by some of the Republics invited whether it is intended that this international congress shall convene, it is important that Congress should at as early a day as is convenient inform me by resolution or otherwise of its opinion in the premises. My action will be in harmony with such expression.

4. CHINESE EXCLUSION ACT CLARIFICATION REQUESTED   DECEMBER 4, 1882

. . . The recent legislation restricting immigration of laborers from China has given rise to the question whether Chinese proceeding to or from another country may lawfully pass through our own.

Construing the act of May 6, 1882, in connection with the treaty of November 7, 1880, the restriction would seem to be limited to Chinese immigrants coming to the United States as laborers, and would not forbid a mere transit across our territory. I ask the attention of Congress to the subject, for such action, if any, as may be deemed advisable.

5. THE TEMPER OF THE AMERICAN PEOPLE AND ELECTIONS   DECEMBER 1, 1884

Since the close of your last session the American people, in the exercise of their highest right of suffrage, have chosen their Chief Magistrate for the four years ensuing.

When it is remembered that at no period in the country's history has the long political contest which customarily precedes the day of the national election been waged with greater fervor and intensity, it is a subject of general congratulation that after the controversy at the polls was over, and while the slight preponderance by which the issue had been determined was as yet unascertained, the public peace suffered no disturbance, but the people everywhere patiently and quietly awaited the result.

Nothing could more strikingly illustrate the temper of the American citizen, his love of order, and his loyalty to law. Nothing could more signally demonstrate the strength and wisdom of our political institutions.

Eight years have passed since a controversy concerning the result of a national election sharply called the attention of the Congress to the necessity of providing more precise and definite regulations for counting the electoral vote.

It is of the gravest importance that this question be solved before conflicting claims to the Presidency shall again distract the country, and I am persuaded that by the people at large any of the measures of relief thus far proposed would be preferred to continued inaction.

22

Grover Cleveland

1. VETOES DISASTER RELIEF **FEBRUARY 16, 1887**

I return without my approval House bill No. 10203, entitled "An act to enable the Commissioner of Agriculture to make a special distribution of seeds in the drought-stricken counties of Texas, and making an appropriation therefor."

It is represented that a long-continued and extensive drought has existed in certain portions of the State of Texas, resulting in a failure of crops and consequent distress and destitution.

Though there has been some difference in statements concerning the extent of the people's needs in the localities thus affected, there seems to be no doubt that there has existed a condition calling for relief; and I am willing to believe that, notwithstanding the aid already furnished, a donation of seed grain to the farmers located in this region, to enable them to put in new crops, would serve to avert a continuance or return of an unfortunate blight.

And yet I feel obliged to withhold my approval of the plan, as proposed by this bill, to indulge a benevolent and charitable sentiment through the appropriation of public funds for that purpose.

I can find no warrant for such an appropriation in the Constitution, and I do not believe that the power and duty of the General Government ought to be extended to the relief of individual suffering which is in no manner properly related to the public service or benefit. A prevalent tendency to disregard the limited mission of this power and duty should, I think, be steadfastly resisted, to the end that the lesson should be constantly enforced that though the people support the Government the Government should not support the people.

The friendliness and charity of our countrymen can always be relied upon to relieve their fellow-citizens in misfortune. This has been repeatedly and quite lately demonstrated. Federal aid in such cases encourages the expectation of paternal care on the part of the Government and weakens the sturdiness of our national character while it prevents the indulgence among our people of that kindly sentiment and conduct which strengthens the bonds of a common brotherhood.

It is within my personal knowledge that individual aid has to some extent already been extended to the sufferers mentioned in this bill. The failure of the proposed appropriation of $10,000 additional to meet their remaining wants will not necessarily result in continued distress if the emergency is fully made known to the people of the country.

It is here suggested that the Commissioner of Agriculture is annually directed to expend a large sum of money for the purchase, propagation, and distribution of seeds and other things of this description, two-thirds of which are, upon the request of Senators, Representatives, and Delegates in Congress, supplied to them for distribution among their constituents.

The appropriation of the current year for this purpose is $100,000, and it will probably be no less in the appropriation for the ensuing year. I understand that a large quantity of grain is furnished for such distribution, and it is supposed that this free apportionment among their neighbors is a privilege which may be waived by our Senators and Representatives.

If sufficient of them should request the Commissioner of Agriculture to send their shares of the grain thus allowed them to the suffering farmers of Texas, they might be enabled to sow their crops, the constituents for whom in theory this grain is intended could well bear the temporary deprivation, and the donors would experience the satisfaction attending deeds of charity.

Figure 22.1 Statue of Liberty, courtesy of the National Parks Service.

2. LADY LIBERTY ENLIGHTENS THE WORLD   OCTOBER 28, 1886

The people of the United States accept with gratitude from their brethren of the French Republic the grand and complete work of art we here inaugurate. This token of the affection and consideration of the people of France demonstrates the kinship of republics, and conveys to us the assurance that in our efforts to commend to mankind the excellence of a government resting upon popular will, we still have beyond the American continent a stead-fast ally. We are not here today to bow before the representation of a fierce warlike god, filled with wrath and vengeance, but we joyously contemplate instead our own deity keeping watch and ward before the open gates of America and greater than all that have been celebrated in ancient song. Instead of grasping in her hand thunderbolts of terror and death, she holds aloft the light which illumines the way to man's enfranchisement. We will not forget that Liberty has here made her home, nor shall her chosen altar be neglected. Willing votaries will constantly keep its fires and these shall gleam upon the shores of our sister Republic thence, and joined with answering rays a stream of light shall pierce the darkness of ignorance and man's oppression, until Liberty enlightens the world.

23

Benjamin Harrison

EXCERPTS FROM INAUGURAL ADDRESS, MARCH 4, 1889

1. CALL FOR A REDUCTION IN GOVERNMENT REVENUE AND EXPENDITURES

While a Treasury surplus is not the greatest evil, it is a serious evil. Our revenue should be ample to meet the ordinary annual demands upon our Treasury, with a sufficient margin for those extraordinary but scarcely less imperative demands which arise now and then. Expenditure should always be made with economy and only upon public necessity. Wastefulness, profligacy, or favoritism in public expenditures is criminal. But there is nothing in the condition of our country or of our people to suggest that anything presently necessary to the public prosperity, security, or honor should be unduly postponed.

It will be the duty of Congress wisely to forecast and estimate these extraordinary demands, and, having added them to our ordinary expenditures, to so adjust our revenue laws that no considerable annual surplus will remain. We will fortunately be able to apply to the redemption of the public debt any small and unforeseen excess of revenue. This is better than to reduce our income below our necessary expenditures, with the resulting choice between another change of our revenue laws and an increase of the public debt. It is quite possible . . . to effect the necessary reduction in our revenues without breaking down our protective tariff or seriously injuring any domestic industry.

2. THE PRESIDENTIAL OATH IS A COVENANT WITH THE PEOPLE

Fellow citizens: There is no constitutional or legal requirement that the President shall take the oath of office in the presence of the people, but there is so manifest an appropriateness in the public induction to office of the chief executive officer of the nation that from the beginning of the Government the people, to whose service the official oath consecrates the officer, have been called to witness the solemn ceremonial. The oath taken in the presence of the people becomes a mutual covenant. The officer covenants to serve the whole body of the people by a faithful execution of the laws, so that they may be the unfailing defense and security of those who respect and observe them, and that neither wealth, station, nor the power of combinations shall be able to evade their just penalties or to wrest them from a beneficent public purpose to serve the ends of cruelty or selfishness.

3. THE BURDEN OF PRESIDENTIAL APPOINTMENTS

The duty devolved by law upon the President to nominate and, by and with the advice and consent of the Senate, to appoint all public officers whose appointment is not otherwise provided for in the Constitution or by act of Congress has become very burdensome and its wise and efficient discharge full of difficulty. The civil list is so large that a personal knowledge of any large number of the applicants is impossible. The President must rely upon the representations of others, and these are often made inconsiderately and without any just sense of responsibility. I have a right, I think, to insist that those who volunteer or are invited to give advice as to appointments shall exercise consideration and fidelity. A high sense of duty and an ambition to improve the service should characterize all public officers.

There are many ways in which the convenience and comfort of those who have business with our public offices may be promoted by a thoughtful and obliging officer, and I shall expect those whom I may appoint to justify their selection by a conspicuous efficiency in the discharge of their duties. Honorable party service will certainly not be esteemed by me a disqualification for public office, but it will in no case be allowed to serve as a shield of official negligence, incompetency, or delinquency. It is entirely creditable to seek public office by proper methods and with proper motives, and all applicants will be treated with consideration; but I shall need, and the heads of Departments will need, time for inquiry and deliberation. Persistent importunity will not, therefore, be the best support of an application for office. Heads of Departments, bureaus, and all other public officers having any duty connected therewith will be expected to enforce the civil service lawfully and without evasion. Beyond this obvious duty I hope to do something more to advance the reform of the civil service. The ideal, or even my own ideal, I shall probably not attain. Retrospect will be a safer basis of judgment than promises. We shall not, however, I am sure, be able to put our civil service upon a nonpartisan basis until we have secured an incumbency that fair-minded men of the opposition will approve for impartiality and integrity. As the number of such in the civil list is increased removals from office will diminish.

4. ON NATURALIZATION

Our naturalization laws should be so amended as to make the inquiry into the character and good disposition of persons applying for citizenship more careful and searching. Our existing laws have been in their administration an unimpressive and often an unintelligible form. We accept the man as a citizen without any knowledge of his fitness, and he assumes the duties of citizenship without any knowledge as to what they are. The privileges of American citizenship are so great and its duties so grave that we may well insist upon a good knowledge of every person applying for citizenship and a good knowledge by him of our institutions. We should not cease to be hospitable to immigration, but we should cease to be careless as to the character of it. There are men of all races, even the best, whose coming is necessarily a burden upon our public revenues or a threat to social order. These should be identified and excluded.

24

Grover Cleveland

1. DECISION TO SEND TROOPS TO QUASH THE PULLMAN STRIKE   JULY 8, 1894
IN CHICAGO

On the eighth day of July, in view of the apparently near approach of a crisis which the Government had attempted to avoid, the following Executive Proclamation was issued and at once extensively published in the city of Chicago:

Whereas, by reason of unlawful obstruction, combinations and assemblages of persons, it has become impracticable, in the judgment of the President, to enforce, by the ordinary course of judicial proceedings, the laws of the United States within the State of Illinois and especially in the city of Chicago within said State; and

Whereas, for the purpose of enforcing the faithful execution of the laws of the United States and protecting its property and obstructions to the United States mails in the State and city aforesaid, the President has employed a part of the military forces of the United States:

Now, therefore, I, Grover Cleveland, President of the United States, do hereby admonish all good citizens, and all persons who may be or may come within the City and State aforesaid, against aiding, countenancing, encouraging, or taking any part in such unlawful obstructions, combinations, and assemblages; and I hereby warn all persons engaged in or in any way connected with such unlawful obstructions, combinations, and assemblages to disperse and retire peaceably to their respective abodes on or before twelve o'clock noon of the 9th day of July instant.

Those who disregard this warning and persist in taking part with a riotous mob in forcibly resisting and obstructing the execution of the laws of the United States, or interfering with the functions of the Government, or destroying or attempting to destroy the property belonging to the United States or under its protection, cannot be regarded otherwise than as public enemies.

Troops employed against such a riotous mob will act with all the moderation and forbearance consistent with the accomplishment of the desired end; but the stern necessities that confront them will not with certainty permit discrimination between guilty participants and those who are mingling with them from curiosity and without criminal intent. The only safe course, therefore, for those not actually participating, is to abide at their homes, or at least not to be found in the neighborhood of riotous assemblages.

While there will be no vacillation in the decisive treatment of the guilty, this warning is especially intended to protect and save the innocent.

2. DEFENDS THE GOLD STANDARD   JANUARY 28, 1895

In my last annual message I commended to the serious consideration of the Congress the condition of our national finances, and in connection with the subject indorsed a plan of currency legislation which at that time seemed to furnish protection against impending danger. This plan has not been approved by the Congress. In the meantime the situation has so changed and the emergency now appears so threatening that I deem it my duty to ask at the hands of the legislative branch of the Government such prompt and effective action as will restore confidence in our financial soundness and avert business disaster and universal distress among our people.

Whatever may be the merits of the plan outlined in my annual message as a remedy for ills then existing and as a safeguard against the depletion of the gold reserve then in the Treasury, I am now convinced that its reception by the Congress and our present advanced stage of financial perplexity necessitate additional or different legislation.

With natural resources unlimited in variety and productive strength and with a people whose activity and enterprise seek only a fair opportunity to achieve national success and greatness, our progress should not be checked by a false financial policy and a heedless disregard of sound monetary laws, nor should the timidity and fear which they engender stand in the way of our prosperity.

It is hardly disputed that this predicament confronts us today. Therefore no one in any degree responsible for the making and execution of our laws should fail to see a patriotic duty in honestly and sincerely attempting to relieve the situation. Manifestly this effort will not succeed unless it is made untrammeled by the prejudice of partisanship and with a steadfast determination to resist the temptation to accomplish party advantage. We may well remember that if we are threatened with financial difficulties all our people in every station of life are concerned; and surely those who suffer will not receive the promotion of party interests as an excuse for permitting our present troubles to advance to a disastrous conclusion. It is also of the utmost importance that we approach the study of the problems presented as free as possible from the tyranny of preconceived opinions, to the end that in a common danger we may be able to seek with unclouded vision a safe and reasonable protection.

The real trouble which confronts us consists in a lack of confidence, widespread and constantly increasing, in the continuing ability or disposition of the Government to pay its obligations in gold. This lack of confidence grows to some extent out of the palpable and apparent embarrassment attending the efforts of the Government under existing laws to procure gold and to a greater extent out of the impossibility of either keeping it in the Treasury or canceling obligations by its expenditure after it is obtained.

The only way left open to the Government for procuring gold is by the issue and sale of its bonds. The only bonds that can be so issued were authorized nearly twenty-five years ago and are not well calculated to meet our present needs. Among other disadvantages, they are made payable in coin instead of specifically in gold, which in existing conditions detracts largely and in an increasing ratio from their desirability as investments. It is by no means certain that bonds of this description can much longer be disposed of at a price creditable to the financial character of our Government. The most dangerous and irritating feature of the situation . . . remains to be mentioned. It is found in the means by which the Treasury is despoiled of the gold thus obtained without canceling a single Government obligation and solely for the benefit of those who find profit in shipping it abroad or whose fears induce them to hoard it at home. We have outstanding about five hundred millions of currency notes of the Government for which gold may be demanded, and, curiously enough, the law requires that when presented and, in fact, redeemed and paid in gold they shall be reissued. Thus the same notes may do duty many times in drawing gold from the Treasury; nor can the process be arrested as long as private parties, for profit or otherwise, see an advantage in repeating the operation. More than $300,000,000 in these notes have already been redeemed in gold, and notwithstanding such redemption they are all still outstanding.

Since the 17th day of January 1894, our bonded interest-bearing debt has been increased $100,000,000 for the purpose of obtaining gold to replenish our coin reserve. Two Issues were made amounting to fifty millions each, one in January and the other in November. As a result of the first issue there was something more than $58,000,000 in gold. Between that issue and the succeeding one in November, comprising a period of about ten months, nearly $103,000,000 in gold were drawn from the Treasury. This made the second issue necessary, and upon that more than fifty-eight millions in gold was again realized. Between the date of this second issue and the present time, covering a period of only about two months, more than $69,000,000 in gold have been drawn from the Treasury. These large sums of gold were expended without any cancellation of Government obligations or in any permanent way benefiting our people or improving our pecuniary situation. . . .

It will hardly do to say that a simple increase of revenue will cure our troubles. The apprehension now existing and constantly increasing as to our financial ability does not rest upon a calculation of our revenue. The time has passed when the eyes of investors abroad and our people at home were fixed upon the revenues of the Government. Changed conditions have attracted their attention to the gold of the Government. There need be no fear that we cannot pay our current expenses with such money as we have. There is now in the Treasury a comfortable surplus of more than $63,000,000, but it is not in gold, and therefore does not meet our difficulty.

I cannot see that differences of opinion concerning the extent to which silver ought to be coined or used in our currency should interfere with the counsels of those whose duty it is to rectify evils now apparent in our financial situation. They have to consider the question of national credit and the consequences that will follow from its collapse. Whatever ideas may be insisted upon as to silver or bimetallism, a proper solution of the question now pressing upon us only requires a recognition of gold as well as silver and a concession of its importance, rightfully or wrongfully acquired, as a basis of national credit, a necessity in the honorable discharge of our obligations payable in gold, and a badge of solvency. I do not understand that the real friends of silver desire a condition that might follow inaction or neglect to appreciate the meaning of the present exigency if it should result in the entire banishment of gold from our financial and currency arrangements.

Besides the Treasury notes, which certainly should be paid in gold, amounting to nearly $500,000,000, there will fall due in 1904 one hundred millions of bonds issued during the last year, for which we have received gold, and in 1907 nearly six hundred millions of 4 per cent bonds issued in 1877. Shall the payment of these obligations in gold be repudiated? If they are to be paid in such a manner as the preservation of our national honor and national solvency demands, we should not destroy or even imperil our ability to supply ourselves with gold for that purpose.

While I am not unfriendly to silver and while I desire to see it recognized to such an extent as is consistent with financial safety and the preservation of national honor and credit, I am not willing to see gold entirely banished from our currency and finances. To avert such a consequence I believe thorough and radical remedial legislation should be promptly passed. I therefore beg the Congress to give the subject immediate attention.

In my opinion the Secretary of the Treasury should be authorized to issue bonds of the Government for the purpose of procuring and maintaining a sufficient gold reserve and the redemption and cancellation of the United States legal-tender notes and the Treasury notes issued for the purchase of silver under the law of 14 July 1890. We should be relieved from the humiliating process of issuing bonds to procure gold to be immediately and repeatedly drawn out on these obligations for purposes not related to the benefit of our Government or our people. The principal and interest of these bonds should be payable on their face in gold, because they should be sold only for gold or its representative, and because there would now probably be difficulty in favorably disposing of bonds not containing this stipulation. I suggest that the bonds be issued in denominations of twenty and fifty dollars and their multiples and that they bear interest at a rate not exceeding 3 per cent per annum. I do not see why they should not be payable fifty years from their date. We of the present generation have large amounts to pay if we meet our obligations, and long bonds are most salable. The Secretary of the Treasury might well be permitted at his discretion to receive on the sale of bonds the legal-tender and Treasury notes to be retired, and of course when they are thus retired or redeemed in gold they should be canceled. . . .

As a constant means for the maintenance of a reasonable supply of gold in the Treasury, our duties on imports should be paid in gold, allowing all other dues to the Government to be paid in any other form of money.

I believe all the provisions I have suggested should be embodied in our laws if we are to enjoy a complete reinstatement of a sound financial condition. They need not interfere with any currency scheme providing for the increase of the circulating medium through the agency of national or State banks that may commend itself to the Congress, since they can easily be adjusted to such a scheme. Objection has been made to the issuance of interest-bearing obligations for the purpose of retiring the noninterest-bearing legal tender notes. In point of fact, however, these notes have burdened us with a large load of interest, and it is still accumulating. The aggregate interest on the original issue of bonds, the proceeds of which in gold constituted the reserve for the payment of these notes, amounted to $70,326,250 on 1 January 1895, and the annual charge for interest on these bonds and those issued for the same purpose during the last year will be $9,145,000, dating from 1 January 1895.

While the cancellation of these notes would not relieve us from the obligations already incurred on their account, these figures are given by way of suggesting that their existence has not been free from interest charges and that the longer they are outstanding, judging from the experience of the last year, the more expensive they will become.

In conclusion I desire to frankly confess my reluctance to issuing more bonds in present circumstances and with no better results than have lately followed that course. I cannot, however, refrain from adding to an assurance of my anxiety to cooperate with the present Congress in any reasonable measure of relief an expression of my determination to leave nothing undone which furnishes a hope for improving the situation or checking a suspicion of our disinclination or disability to meet with the strictest honor every national obligation.

3. GOVERNMENT AND THE INDIVIDUAL   MARCH 4, 1893

Closely related to the exaggerated confidence in our country's greatness which tends to a disregard of the rules of national safety, another danger confronts us not less serious. I refer to the prevalence of a popular disposition to expect from the operation of the Government especial and direct individual advantages.

The verdict of our voters which condemned the injustice of maintaining protection for protection's sake enjoins upon the people's servants the duty of exposing and destroying the brood of kindred evils which are the unwholesome progeny of paternalism. This is the bane of republican institutions and the constant peril of our government by the people.

It degrades to the purposes of wily craft the plan of rule our fathers established and bequeathed to us as an object of our love and veneration. It perverts the patriotic sentiments of our countrymen and tempts them to pitiful calculation of the sordid gain to be derived from their Government's maintenance. It undermines the self-reliance of our people and substitutes in its place dependence upon governmental favoritism. It stifles the spirit of true Americanism and stupefies every ennobling trait of American citizenship.

The lessons of paternalism ought to be unlearned and the better lesson taught that while the people should patriotically and cheerfully support their Government its functions do not include the support of the people.

4. AMERICAN ECONOMY AND THE CURRENCY   MARCH 4, 1893

I deem it fitting on this occasion to . . . briefly refer to the existence of certain conditions and tendencies among our people which seem to menace the integrity and usefulness of their Government.

While every American citizen must contemplate with the utmost pride and enthusiasm the growth and expansion of our country, the sufficiency of our institutions to stand against the rudest shocks of violence, the wonderful thrift and enterprise of our people, and the demonstrated superiority of our free government, it behooves us to constantly watch for every symptom of insidious infirmity that threatens our national vigor.

The strong man who in the confidence of sturdy health courts the sternest activities of life and rejoices in the hardihood of constant labor may still have lurking near his vitals the unheeded disease that dooms him to sudden collapse.

It cannot be doubted that our stupendous achievements as a people and our country's robust strength have given rise to heedlessness of those laws governing our national health which we can no more evade than human life can escape the laws of God and nature.

Manifestly nothing is more vital to our supremacy as a nation and to the beneficent purposes of our Government than a sound and stable currency. Its exposure to degradation should at once arouse to activity the most enlightened statesmanship, and the danger of depreciation in the purchasing power of the wages paid to toil should furnish the strongest incentive to prompt and conservative precaution.

In dealing with our present embarrassing situation as related to this subject we will be wise if we temper our confidence and faith in our national strength and resources with the frank concession that even these will not permit us to defy with impunity the inexorable laws of finance and trade. At the same time, in our efforts to adjust differences of opinion we should be free from intolerance or passion, and our judgments should be unmoved by alluring phrases and un-vexed by selfish interests.

I am confident that such an approach to the subject will result in prudent and effective remedial legislation. In the meantime, so far as the executive branch of the Government can intervene, none of the powers with which it is invested will be withheld when their exercise is deemed necessary to maintain our national credit or avert financial disaster.

5. GOVERNMENT EXTRAVAGANCE IS A CRIME AGAINST   MARCH 4, 1893
    THE CITIZEN

The lessons of paternalism ought to be unlearned and the better lesson taught that while the people should patriotically and cheerfully support their Government its functions do not include the support of the people.

The acceptance of this principle leads to a refusal of bounties and subsidies, which burden the labor and thrift of a portion of our citizens to aid ill-advised or languishing enterprises in which they have no concern. It leads also to a challenge of wild and reckless pension expenditure, which overleaps the bounds of grateful recognition of patriotic service and prostitutes to vicious uses the people's prompt and generous impulse to aid those disabled in their country's defense.

Every thoughtful American must realize the importance of checking at its beginning any tendency in public or private station to regard frugality and economy as virtues which we may safely outgrow. The toleration of this idea results in the waste of the people's money by their chosen servants and encourages prodigality and extravagance in the home life of our countrymen.

Under our scheme of government the waste of public money is a crime against the citizen, and the contempt of our people for economy and frugality in their personal affairs deplorably saps the strength and sturdiness of our national character.

It is a plain dictate of honesty and good government that public expenditures should be limited by public necessity, and that this should be measured by the rules of strict economy; and it is equally clear that frugality among the people is the best guaranty of a contented and strong support of free institutions.

One mode of the misappropriation of public funds is avoided when appointments to office, instead of being the rewards of partisan activity, are awarded to those whose efficiency promises a fair return of work for the compensation paid to them. To secure the fitness and competency of appointees to office and remove from political action the demoralizing madness for spoils, civil service reform has found a place in our public policy and laws. The benefits already gained through this instrumentality and the further usefulness it promises entitle it to the hearty support and encouragement of all who desire to see our public service well performed or who hope for the elevation of political sentiment and the purification of political methods.

25

William McKinley

1. WAR WITH THE SPANISH EMPIRE   APRIL 11, 1898

. . . it becomes my duty now to address your body with regard to the grave crisis that has arisen in the relations of the United States to Spain by reason of the warfare that for more than three years has raged in the neighboring island of Cuba.

I do so because of the intimate connection of the Cuban question with the state of our own Union and the grave relation the course which it is now incumbent upon the nation to adopt . . .

The present revolution is but the successor of other similar insurrections which have occurred in Cuba against the dominion of Spain, extending over a period of nearly half a century. . . .

Since the present revolution began, in February 1895, this country has seen the fertile domain at our threshold ravaged by fire and sword in the course of a struggle unequaled in the history of the island and rarely paralleled as to the numbers of the combatants and the bitterness of the contest by any revolution of modern times. . . .

Our people have beheld a once prosperous community reduced to comparative want, its lucrative commerce virtually paralyzed, its exceptional productiveness diminished, its fields laid waste, its mills in ruins, and its people perishing by tens of thousands from hunger and destitution. We have found ourselves constrained, in the observance of that strict neutrality which our laws enjoin, and which the law of nations commands, to police our own waters and watch our own seaports in prevention of any unlawful act in aid of the Cubans.

. . . In April 1896, the evils from which our country suffered through the Cuban war became so onerous that my predecessor made an effort to bring about a peace through the mediation of this Government in any way that might tend to an honorable adjustment of the contest between Spain and her revolted colony. . . . It failed through the refusal of the Spanish Government then in power to consider any form of mediation or, indeed, any plan of settlement which did not begin with the actual submission of the insurgents to the mother country, and then only on such terms as Spain herself might see fit to grant. The war continued unabated. . . .

The efforts of Spain were increased, both by the dispatch of fresh levies to Cuba and by the addition to the horrors of the strife of a new and inhuman phase happily unprecedented in the modern history of civilized Christian peoples. The policy of devastation and concentration . . . was thence extended to embrace all of the island to which the power of the Spanish arms was able to reach by occupation or by military operations. . . .

The raising and movement of provisions of all kinds were interdicted. The fields were laid waste, dwellings unroofed and fired, mills destroyed, and, in short, everything that could desolate the land and render it unfit for human habitation or support was commanded by one or the other of the contending parties. . . .

By the time the present administration took office a year ago, re-concentration . . . had been made effective over the better part of the four central and western provinces. . . .

. . . No practical relief was accorded to the destitute. The overburdened towns, already suffering from the general dearth, could give no aid. So-called "zones of cultivation" established within the immediate areas of effective military control about the cities and fortified camps proved illusory as a remedy for the suffering. The unfortunates, being for the most part women and children, with aged and helpless men, enfeebled by disease and hunger, could not have tilled the soil without tools, seed, or shelter for their own support or for the supply of the cities. Re-concentration, adopted avowedly as a war measure in order to cut off the resources of the insurgents, worked its predestined result. . . . it was not civilized warfare; it was extermination. The only peace it could beget was that of the wilderness and the grave.

Meanwhile the military situation in the island had undergone a noticeable change. The extraordinary activity that characterized the second year of the war, when the insurgents invaded even the . . . fields of Pinar del Rio and carried havoc and destruction up to the walls of the city of Havana itself, had relapsed into a dogged struggle. . . . The Spanish arms regained a measure of control in Pinar del Rio and parts of Havana, but, under the existing conditions of the rural country, without immediate improvement of their productive situation. . . .

In this state of affairs my Administration found itself confronted with the grave problem of its duty. . . . The assassination of the Prime Minister, Canovas, led to a change of government in Spain. The former administration, pledged to subjugation without concession, gave place to that of a more liberal party, committed long in advance to a policy of reform, involving the wider principle of home rule for Cuba and Puerto Rico.

The overtures of this Government made through its new envoy, General Woodford . . . were met by assurances that home rule, in advanced phase, would be forthwith offered to Cuba. . . . Coincidentally with these declarations, the new Government of Spain continued and completed the policy already begun by its predecessor, of testifying friendly regard for this nation by releasing American citizens held under one charge or another connected with the insurrection, so that by the end of November not a single person entitled in any way to our national protection remained in a Spanish prison.

. . . Thousands of lives have already been saved. The necessity for a change in the condition of the reconcentrados is recognized by the Spanish Government. Within a few days past the orders of General Weyler have been revoked; the reconcentrados . . . are to be permitted to return to their homes and aided to resume the self-supporting pursuits of peace. . . .

The war in Cuba is of such a nature that short of subjugation or extermination a final military victory for either side seems impracticable. The alternative lies in the physical exhaustion of the one or the other party. . . . The prospect of such a protraction and conclusion of the present strife is a contingency hardly to be contemplated with equanimity by the civilized world, and least of all by the United States, affected and injured as we are . . . by its very existence.

Realizing this, it appeared to be my duty, in a spirit of true friendliness, no less to Spain than to the Cubans who have so much to lose by the prolongation of the struggle, to seek to bring about an immediate termination of the war. To this end I submitted, on the 27th ultimo . . . through the United States minister at Madrid, propositions to the Spanish Government looking to an armistice . . . for the negotiation of peace with the good offices of the President.

In addition, I asked the immediate revocation of the order of reconcentration, so as to permit the people to return to their farms and the needy to be relieved with provisions and supplies from the United States, cooperating with the Spanish authorities, so as to afford full relief.

The reply of the Spanish cabinet was received on the night of the 31st ultimo. It offered, as the means to bring about peace in Cuba, to confide the preparation thereof to the insular parliament. . . . As the Cuban parliament does not meet until the 4th of May next, the Spanish Government would not object . . . to accept at once a suspension of hostilities if asked for by the insurgents from the general in chief, to whom it would pertain . . . to determine the duration and conditions of the armistice.

The propositions submitted by General Woodford and the reply of the Spanish Government were both in the form of brief memoranda. . . . The function of the Cuban parliament in the matter of "preparing" peace and the manner of its doing so are not expressed in the Spanish memorandum; but from General Woodford's explanatory reports of preliminary discussions preceding the final conference it is understood that the Spanish Government stands ready to give the insular congress full powers to settle the terms of peace. . . .

With this last overture in the direction of immediate peace, and its disappointing reception by Spain, the Executive is brought to the end of his effort.

. . . Thereupon I reviewed these alternatives, in the light of President Grant's measured words . . . when after seven years of sanguinary, destructive and cruel hostilities in Cuba he reached the conclusion that the recognition of the independence of Cuba was impracticable and indefensible, and that the recognition of belligerence was not warranted by the facts according to the tests of public law. I commented especially upon the latter aspect of the question, pointing out the inconveniences and positive dangers of a recognition of belligerence which, while adding to the already onerous burdens of neutrality within our own jurisdiction, could not in any way extend our influence or effective offices in the territory of hostilities.

Nothing has since occurred to change my view in this regard, and I recognize . . . that the issuance of a proclamation of neutrality . . . could . . . accomplish nothing toward the one end for which we labor—the instant pacification of Cuba and the cessation of the misery that afflicts the island. . . .

. . . There remain the alternative forms of intervention to end the war, either as an impartial neutral by imposing a rational compromise between the contestants, or as the active ally of the one party or the other.

As to the first it is not to be forgotten that during the last few months the relation of the United States has virtually been one of friendly intervention in many ways . . . all tending to the exertion of a potential influence toward an ultimate pacific result, just and honorable to all interests concerned. The spirit of all our acts hitherto has been an earnest, unselfish desire for peace and prosperity in Cuba, untarnished by differences between us and Spain, and unstained by the blood of American citizens.

The forcible intervention of the United States as a neutral to stop the war . . . is justifiable on rational grounds. It involves, however, hostile constraint upon both the parties to the contest as well to enforce a truce as to guide the eventual settlement.

. . . I have already transmitted to Congress the report of the naval court of inquiry on the destruction of the battle ship *Maine* in the harbor of Havana during the night of the 15th of February. The destruction of that noble vessel has filled the national heart with inexpressible horror. Two hundred and fifty-eight brave sailors and marines and two officers of our Navy, reposing in the fancied security of a friendly harbor, have been hurled to death, grief and want brought to their homes, and sorrow to the nation.

The naval court of inquiry, which . . . commands the unqualified confidence of the Government, was unanimous in its conclusion that the destruction of the *Maine* was caused by an exterior explosion, that of a submarine mine. It did not assume to place the responsibility. That remains to be fixed.

In any event the destruction of the *Maine* . . . is a patent and impressive proof of a state of things in Cuba that is intolerable. That condition is thus shown to be such that the Spanish Government cannot assure safety and security to a vessel of the American Navy in the harbor of Havana on a mission of peace, and rightfully there.

. . . The long trial has proved that the object for which Spain has waged the war cannot be attained. The fire of insurrection may flame or may smolder with varying seasons, but it has not been and it is plain that it cannot be extinguished by present methods. The only hope of relief and repose from a condition which can no longer be endured is the enforced pacification of Cuba. In the name of humanity, in the name of civilization, in behalf of endangered American interests . . . the war in Cuba must stop.

In view of these facts and of these considerations, I ask the Congress to authorize and empower the President to take measures to secure a full and final termination of hostilities between the Government of Spain and the people of Cuba, and to secure in the island the establishment of a stable government, capable of maintaining order and observing its international obligations, insuring peace and tranquility and the security of its citizens as well as our own, and to use the military and naval forces of the United States as may be necessary for these purposes.

. . . The issue is now with the Congress. It is a solemn responsibility. I have exhausted every effort to relieve the intolerable condition of affairs which is at our doors. Prepared to execute every obligation imposed upon me by the Constitution and the law, I await your action.

Yesterday, and since the preparation of the foregoing message, official information was received by me that the latest decree of the Queen Regent of Spain directs General Blanco, in order to prepare and facilitate peace, to proclaim a suspension of hostilities, the duration and details of which have not yet been communicated to me.

This fact with every other pertinent consideration will . . . have your just and careful attention in the solemn deliberations upon which you are about to enter. If this measure attains a successful result, then our aspirations as a Christian, peace-loving people will be realized. If it fails, it will be only another justification for our contemplated action.

2. AMERICA LOOKS OUTWARD AND EMBRACES THE PHILIPPINE ISLANDS   NOVEMBER 21, 1899

. . . When the Spanish War broke out, Dewey was at Honk Kong, and I ordered him to go to Manila and to capture or destroy the Spanish fleet, and he had to; because, if defeated, he had no place to refit on that side of the globe, and if the Dons were victorious, they would likely cross the Pacific and ravage our Oregon and California coasts. And so he had to destroy the Spanish fleet, and did it! But that was as far as I thought then.

When next I realized that the Philippines had dropped into our laps I confess I did not know what to do with them. I sought counsel from all sides Democrats as well as Republicans—but got little help. I thought first we would take only Manila; then Luzon; then other islands, perhaps, also. I walked the floor of the White House night after night until midnight; and I am not ashamed to tell you, gentlemen, that I went down on my knees and prayed Almighty God for light and guidance more than one night. And one night late it came to me this way—I don't know how it was, but it came: (1) That we could not give them back to Spain—that would be cowardly and dishonorable; (2) that we could not turn them over to France or Germany—our commercial rivals in the Orient—

that would be bad business and discreditable; (3) that we could not leave them to themselves—they were unfit for self-government—and they would soon have anarchy and misrule over there worse than Spain's was; and (4) that there was nothing left for us to do but to take them all, and to educate the Filipinos, and uplift and civilize and Christianize them, and by God's grace do the very best we could by them, as our fellow-men for whom Christ also died. And then I went to bed, and went to sleep, and slept soundly, and the next morning I sent for the chief engineer of the War Department (our map-maker), and I told him to put the Philippines on the map of the United States [pointing to a large map on the wall of his office], and there they are, and there they will stay while I am President!

3. ANTIETAM COMMEMORATION: THE END OF THE BLOODY SHIRT   MAY 30, 1900

. . . In this presence and on this memorable field, I am glad to meet the followers of Lee and Jackson and Longstreet and Johnston with the followers of Grant and McClellan and Sherman and Sheridan, greeting each other, not with arms in their hands or malice in their souls, but with affection and respect for each other in their hearts. Standing here today, one reflection only has crowded my mind—the difference between this scene and that of thirty-eight years ago. Then the men who wore the blue and the men who wore the gray greeted each other with shot and shell, and visited death upon their respective ranks. We meet, after these intervening years, as friends, with a common sentiment—that of loyalty to the government of the United States, love for our flag and our institutions—and determined men of the North and men of the South, to make any sacrifice for the honor and perpetuity of the American nation.

. . . The past can never be undone. The new day brings its shining sun to light our duty now. I am glad to preside over a nation of nearly eighty million people, more united than they have ever been since the formation of the Federal Union. I account it a great honor to participate on this occasion with the State of Maryland in its tribute to the valor and heroism and sacrifices of the Confederate and Union armies. . . . The valor of both is the common heritage of us all. The achievements of that war . . . are just as much the inheritance of those who failed as those who prevailed; and whom [who] went to war two years ago the men of the South and the men of the North vied with each other in showing their devotion to the United States. The followers of the Confederate generals fought side by side in Cuba, in Porto Rico, and in the Philippines, and together in those far-off islands are standing today fighting and dying for the flag they love, the flag that represents more than any other banner in the world the best hopes and aspirations of mankind.

4. LAST WORDS TO THE PEOPLE   SEPTEMBER 5, 1901

I am glad to be again in the city of Buffalo and exchange greetings with her people. . . . To-day I have additional satisfaction in meeting and giving welcome to the foreign representatives assembled here, whose presence and participation in this exposition have contributed in so marked a degree to its interest and success. . . . Expositions are the timekeepers of progress. They record the world's advancement. They stimulate the energy, enterprise and intellect of the people and quicken human genius. They go into the home. They broaden and brighten the daily life of the people. They open mighty storehouses of information to the student. Every exposition, great or small, has helped to some onward step. . . . Friendly rivalry follows . . . the inspiration to useful invention and to high endeavor in all departments of human activity. . . . The quest for trade is an incentive to men of business to devise, invent, improve and economize in the cost of production.

Business life . . . is ever a sharp struggle for success. It will be none the less so in the future. Without competition we would be clinging to the clumsy antiquated processes of farming and manufacture and the methods of business of long ago, and the twentieth would be no further advanced than the eighteenth century. . . .

The Pan-American exposition has done its work thoroughly, presenting in its exhibits evidences of the highest skill and illustrating the progress of the human family in the western hemisphere. This portion of the earth has no cause for humiliation for the part it has performed in the march of civilization. It has not accomplished everything from it. It has simply done its best. . . .

The wisdom and energy of all the nations are none too great for the world's work. The success of art, science, industry and invention is an international asset and a common glory.

. . . We travel greater distances in a shorter space of time and with more ease than was ever dreamed of by the fathers. Isolation is no longer possible or desirable. The same important news is read, though in different languages, the same day in all Christendom. . . .

At the beginning of the nineteenth century there was not a mile of steam railroad on the globe. Now there are enough miles to make its circuit many times. Then there was not a line of electric telegraph; now we have a vast mileage traversing all lands and seas. God and man have linked the nations together. No nation can longer be indifferent to any other. . . .

My fellow citizens, trade statistics indicate that this country is in a state of unexampled prosperity. . . . That all the people are participating in this great prosperity is seen in every American community, and shown by the enormous and unprecedented deposits in our savings banks. . . .

. . . In these times of marvelous business energy and gain we ought to be looking to the future, strengthening the weak places in our industrial and commercial system, that we may be ready for any storm or strain.

. . . Reciprocity is the natural outgrowth of our wonderful industrial development under the domestic policy now firmly established. What we produce beyond our domestic consumption must have a vent abroad. The excess must be relieved through a foreign outlet and we should sell everywhere we can, and buy wherever the buying will enlarge our sales and productions, and thereby make a greater demand for home labor.

The period of exclusiveness is past. . . . A policy of good will and friendly trade relations will prevent reprisals. Reciprocity treaties are in harmony with the spirit of the times, measures of retaliation are not. If perchance some of our tariffs are no longer needed . . . why should they not be employed to extend and promote our markets abroad? . . . We must build the Isthmian canal, which will unite the two oceans and give a straight line of water communication with the western coasts of Central and South America and Mexico. The contraction of a Pacific cable cannot be longer postponed.

. . . This exposition would have touched the heart of that American statesman whose mind was ever alert and thought ever constant for a larger commerce and a truer fraternity of the republics of the new world. His broad American spirit is felt and manifested here. He needs no identification to an assemblage of Americans anywhere, for the name of Blaine is inseparably associated with the Pan-American movement . . . and which we all hope will be firmly advanced by the Pan-American congress that assembles this autumn in the capital of Mexico. . . .

. . . let us ever remember that our interest is in concord, not conflict, and that our real eminence rests in the victories of peace, not those of war. We hope that all who are represented here may be moved to higher and nobler effort for their own and the world's good, and that out of this city may come, not only greater commerce and trade, but more essential than these, relations of mutual respect, confidence and friendship which will deepen and endure.

Our earnest prayer is that God will graciously vouchsafe prosperity, happiness and peace to all our neighbors, and like blessings to all the peoples and powers of earth.

PART TWO

THE TWENTIETH CENTURY

VII

MODERN PRESIDENCY EMERGES

AMERICA ENTERED THE TWENTIETH CENTURY with great confidence in the future. The previous century bore witness to an upward and progressive trend. Americans had grown the Republic in spectacular manner and moved the nation from sea to shining sea. They had survived a terrible threat to the Union and a horrible, fratricidal Civil War in such a fashion so as to forge a stronger nation and a better America. Americans were a nation of doers and master builders. At times what they constructed was not only strong, but also true and beautiful. The new industrial nation was economically prosperous and the country was at peace. This was a deliberate work. It took leadership and imagination. The Brooklyn Bridge was one monument and the modern presidency another. The institution of the American presidency grew strong and matured along with the nation.

It was McKinley who made America ready to welcome the twentieth century. The election of 1900 confirmed the public faith in President McKinley as he dispatched the Democratic perennial candidacy of William Jennings Bryan for a second time. As America turned the century corner, it remained in most respects an age of innocence. It had built its body and was proud of it. National serenity prevailed as the mood of the first years of the new century. Americans remained naive as to the challenges ahead. In this new century they would take to the road and the sky. Americans would teach the world to fly. They would build great things, including skyscrapers and the Panama Canal. Yet the twentieth century would prove to be the most violent and deadly century in human history. The first generation of the new century had not the least clue as to what the future had in store. Nonetheless, the nation had built a material base and industrial body to face these new challenges to come. The nation had come of age and so had the institution of the presidency. Given all the wonders and miracles that marked their parade through time, Americans breathlessly awaited the renewal of McKinley's covenant with the Constitution and his second inauguration as President of the United States.

The welcome moment arrived. McKinley rose to the Inaugural platform on March 4, 1901. The President reminded his fellow citizens four years earlier there was "great anxiety" about the economy and the currency. That anxiety no longer existed. He further stated with pride that in place of a deficit the national government had accumulated a surplus. Taxes had been reduced while depression had been replaced by prosperity. In short, the verdict of 1896 had been "vindicated." Yet he cautioned that this healthy condition that had been achieved in four years should not "lead us to reckless ventures in business or profligacy in public expenditures."

McKinley was triumphant. Little did he know that the first year of his second term would be the last year of his life. In September he went to Buffalo to promote Pan-American cooperation. While pressing the flesh with an admiring throng he extended his hand in greeting to a man with a gun. The shooter fired two shots at point blank range into the President's chest. The date was September 6th. One bullet barely penetrated. The other proved fatal. Eight days later the President was dead. The assassin, Leon Czolgosz, claimed later to be an anarchist. He killed McKinley, he said, to advance the cause of the working class.

Six months earlier, from the Inaugural stand President McKinley declared: "The national purpose is indicated through a national election. It is the constitutional method of ascertaining the public will. When once it is registered it is a law to us all, and faithful observance should follow its decrees." The purpose of the people had been trumped by a man with a revolver. An anarchist made Theodore Roosevelt President of the United States. The first President to be known by his initials, and the youngest Chief Executive ever, paid tribute to the fallen McKinley then and thereafter. In 1903 TR would go to Canton, Ohio and there in McKinley's hometown he would celebrate the memory of his predecessor. The heir of McKinley celebrated him as the "world's chief statesman." The new leader chastised the assassin as having perpetrated a monstrous crime against the nation. The murder of McKinley was so foul "as to stand unique in the black annals of crime."

Theodore Roosevelt completed McKinley's second term and was elected in his own right in 1904. Many in the Republican Party considered the Colonel a troublemaker. Indeed, he was a volatile political force. Mark Hanna, McKinley's right-hand man, warned the Republican high command against placing TR on the ticket in 1900. In order to please Senator Thomas Platt of New York State, Roosevelt was awarded the second spot. Hanna howled "that madman was a heartbeat away." When that moment came, Hanna moaned that "damned cowboy" was president.

President Roosevelt and Senator Hanna reached an accommodation in their new association. The President also found much common ground with the Speaker of the House of Representatives, Joseph Cannon. TR celebrated the two conservative bookends of his own tenure in office—McKinley and Taft. The politically astute Roosevelt was well aware that his own presidency rested on the essentially conservative majority coalition that had been mustered by McKinley. With only a few deviations in his years occupying what now officially became "The White House," President Roosevelt worked in tandem with the grand masters of the GOP. Historians have alternatively considered McKinley and Roosevelt as the first "modern" president. There is little doubt that McKinley pioneered the modern presidency. TR carried it forward and embellished it, so perhaps joint custody should be assigned to the men who brought it into the twentieth century.

Theodore Roosevelt was a bundle of energy. Even the passage of a century cannot dim the extraordinary phenomenon of his executive tenure. By the age of 40 he was a soldier and a scholar, Dakota rancher and Washington power broker, Police Commissioner of New York City, naturalist, and sportsman. He was at home in Harvard, the frontier, Africa, the Amazon and the sidewalks of New York. One cartoonist depicted Roosevelt astride a flaring horse, prominent teeth glistening, going off in all four directions at once. Another pictured him as a boy in a bathtub moving around his private navy.

TR was happy to engage in a fight or a frolic. He enjoyed sparring with anyone willing to put on the gloves. He went to war and became a Colonel and a hero. In the Spanish American War he led the Rough Rider Regiment up what he called San Juan Hill in Cuba and then rode his celebrity in 1898 to the Governor's Mansion in Albany, New York. In so doing, TR posed a threat to the conservative masters of the GOP.

TR picked William Howard Taft as heir apparent. Taft bore the imprimatur of the Rough Rider who declared: "Taft was fit to be President of the United States." Early in 1909 Theodore Roosevelt exited office and soon left the country. There seems to be a pattern of escape in TR's behavior whenever he experienced tragedy or personal loss. In 1884, both his mother and his wife died on

Figure SVII. 1 Indian Treaty Room in the Old Executive Office Building, Washington, DC, courtesy of the Library of Congress Prints and Photographs Division, Washington, DC.

the same day. The grief from that double tragedy moved TR to put his political career on hold. Leaving his daughter behind, he ran off to the "Badlands" in the Dakotas. At the end of his presidency in 1909 and the loss of power that accompanied that forfeiture, the ex-president left for an African Safari and a European Tour. Upon returning in 1910 from his overseas adventures in Europe and Africa, and despite his promise not to run for a third term, he challenged Taft for the Republican nomination in 1912. Using a boxing analogy, TR announced "his hat was in the ring." When he lost this fight, he abandoned his Republican Party home and launched his "Bull Moose" third-party effort. In doing so, Theodore Roosevelt produced the Great Republican Schism of 1912. His electoral defeat in 1912 caused him to again abandon his American homeland. This time he fled to the Amazon in Brazil to lead an expedition on the River of Doubt.

Taft possessed many talents. He had proven his executive abilities as Governor of the Philippines. Indeed, Taft is the only man in American history to have served as President of the United States and Chief Justice of the United States. Roosevelt and Taft shared a bond with McKinley and with each other. Yet they were in many ways very different men with different temperaments, outlooks, habits, and tastes. Part of the unique Roosevelt–Taft rupture related to these startling differences. In contrast to Roosevelt's bravura and casual regard for legal and constitutional procedures, stood Taft—cautious, devoted to legal procedure, and possessed of a judicial frame of mind and temperament. They had different takes on law, diplomacy, politics, war, and even sports.

Sports can provide a special window through which to examine the mental outlook of presidents. It can be said that baseball became the national pastime once Taft took up residence in the White House. Taft was the first president to attend opening day of the baseball season and throw out the ceremonial first pitch. He did so on April 14, 1910 at League Park in Washington, DC. Theodore Roosevelt demonstrated little interest in the mental magic of the sport and preferred more contact and physical contests, such as boxing and football.

Taft preferred baseball, as a thinking man's game requiring more patience and judicial forbearance. Like chess, baseball required a measured mind that anticipated and carefully calculated projected probabilities. Boxing and baseball were analogous to war and peace. Roosevelt was more bellicose and warlike. Taft was easy-going and laid back. There was poetry to the game of baseball. Historian Jacques Barzun of Columbia University once said that "He who would understand America must study baseball."

Years before Barzun, President Taft encouraged his fellow citizens to enjoy the game. The President attended fourteen major league games during his tenure of office, two of those on the same day in St. Louis. During the memorable election year 1912, in which TR and Taft were pitted against each other in that famous presidential contest, Taft's Vice President James Schoolcraft Sherman did the honors of opening the baseball season as the President was grief stricken about the sinking of the *Titanic* and the loss of his dear friend and aide Archie Butt who went down with the ship.

The political turbulence of the year 1912 favored TR's disposition. Infighting was not Taft's style. The judiciary was more to Taft's taste. The truth is that the political war of 1912 scarred both men and deeply wounded the Republican Party. The schism in the party in 1912 presented the presidency to Democrat Woodrow Wilson, who drew but 41.8% of the vote. Taft, who regretted leaving the office to a Democrat, nonetheless felt he had saved the country from Roosevelt.

In the first decades of the twentieth century American foreign policy morphed from the "gunboat diplomacy" of TR, to the "dollar diplomacy" of Taft, and finally to Woodrow Wilson and his "missionary diplomacy." The foreign policy objectives that President William Howard Taft inherited from Theodore Roosevelt stressed the conviction that America had global stakes to

Figure SVII. 2 The Executive Office Building, credit: Michael E. McInerney and Alissa Ogen, *Executive Building: An Expression of Civil Optimism*, December, 18, 2009.

promote and protect. Roosevelt had emphasized the intricacies of diplomacy and geopolitics. Taft relied on commerce and capital.

Woodrow Wilson was not the first choice of the delegates who nominated him in 1912. The favorite was Speaker of the House Champ Clark of Missouri. A majority of delegates voted for Clark, ballot after ballot. In a blatant mockery of the idea of democracy, the Democrats, in accord with long party tradition, required a two-thirds vote for the nomination. Wilson trailed by a wide margin in the delegate count. The South and its allies held a veto and were able to block the will of the majority. In many ways Wilson's nomination could be considered a fluke. Wilson literally deemed it providential. Given the Republican schism, he coasted to victory with a plurality of the vote.

Wilson has frequently been touted as a "Progressive" Democrat. This designation remains questionable. Wilson's own early writings and statements, as well as later policies and programs, give ample reason to pause. Wilson devoted the early days of his presidency to banking and finance. Ironically, this presidential focus was highly satisfying to select conservative economic interests. These interests would benefit from a more rational, sound, and stable banking system. In fact, Senator Nelson Aldrich, grandfather of Nelson A. Rockefeller, could legitimately claim a piece of paternity with the embryonic idea of the Federal Reserve System.

The booming economy of industrial America had outgrown its banking system. Its financial nucleus remained in the hands of the financial barons of the Northeast. This created political protest and set limits to growth. Objections from the West and South continued to target Wall Street as a major cause of economic distress. America's manufacturing and corporate sectors suffered similar criticism. The established world of banking constituted a small, interlocked collection of private bankers free to enforce fiscal and monetary rules designed to achieve their own self-interest. They controlled the volume of money in circulation and the rate of interest, thus determining the availability of credit. Although the nation's economy steadily expanded, the amount of money in circulation remained static. Without a central bank there was no mechanism to prevent sharp fluctuations nationally or regionally.

Wilson regarded this archaic system as unfair and harmful to American economic development, and moved vigorously toward a total reconfiguration of the banking system. From this emerged the Federal Reserve System. On December 23, 1913, the Federal Reserve System assumed its place in the center of American finance and banking.

Wilson was in reverse gear on race. He once again segregated the Federal Government. Although he had welcomed "Negro" support in the 1912 campaign by alluding vaguely to the need for improved race relations, Wilson reflected traditional Southern views on race. The president adopted the posture that segregation served the interests of both races. The NAACP strenuously objected to Wilson's policy of separating the races in Federal facilities. Yet the President persisted, as he explained in letters to interested parties. In one letter, Wilson bluntly stated: "I would say that I do approve of the segregation that is being attempted in several of the departments."

The assassination of the Austrian Crown Prince in June 1914 changed the course of history. At the time, few Americans noticed the killing. The Great War ensued. President Wilson proclaimed America's instinctive stance of neutrality. He encouraged the contentious sides to settle peacefully as he began to try to protect American lives and trade on the high seas.

On May 7, 1915, a German U-boat sunk the great English luxury liner *Lusitania* off the Irish coast, killing 1,198 passengers, including 128 Americans. The resulting furor in the United States persuaded Berlin to suspend unrestricted submarine warfare. President Wilson registered a strong protest against German submarine strikes. At the same time he was conscious that the following year was an election year. He could not afford to alienate American voters who had divided sympathies.

In the 1916 presidential election, Wilson ran on the slogan "He Kept Us Out of War." The slogan had emerged from a chant at the Democratic National Convention emanating from German-American and Irish-American delegates. It proved to be a winning slogan.

German military strategy turned again in early 1917 to unrestricted submarine warfare as the key to victory. It was a serious miscalculation. Wilson broke off diplomatic relations. The final factor in the decision to intervene came with the interception of a secret dispatch from the German Foreign Minister Arthur Zimmerman to his Embassy in Mexico City. The "Zimmerman Telegram" instructed German diplomats to approach the Mexican Government with a simple proposal. If Mexico joined Germany in the war they would recover lost lands in Texas, Arizona, and New Mexico. This threat to the borders and national security of the United States infuriated Wilson. On April 2, 1917 less than a month from his second inauguration, the President went to Congress and demanded war with Germany.

After observing the senseless slaughter for nearly three full years, Wilson involved Americans in the global carnage. It did not take long for the American people to become disenchanted with the "Great Adventure." At the mid-term election, the President appealed to the electorate to support his wartime leadership by electing a Democratic Congress. Americans took a right turn in 1918 which served as a political barometer for the presidential election of 1920. Given the fast growing disillusionment at home, the American people gave the President a Republican House and Senate. The general disorder, high cost of living, housing shortages, race riots, the red scare and intense labor strife of 1919 also contributed to the mood of discontent.

Warren G. Harding of Ohio stepped aboard the presidential stage as the Republican hopeful. In this atmosphere of despair and disillusionment with Wilson's legacy, Harding promised a return to normalcy, and the public eagerly bought into that promise. Harding and his Vice Presidential running mate Calvin Coolidge defeated the James M. Cox and Franklin D. Roosevelt Democratic ticket by an overwhelming landslide.

Early in his presidency, Harding took a strong stand against lynching. These were days when the night riders of the Ku Klux Klan were in their saddles. Harding took the very bold step of carrying his opposition to lynching to Congress and to Montgomery, Alabama. He also took dramatic action to put the War in the past. The Chief Magistrate's invoked the power to pardon, extending his reach far across the ideological divide. Harding pardoned a number of socialist activists who had been convicted and imprisoned for their vocal opposition to the Great War. Among those pardoned was the famous Socialist Party leader, Eugene Debs.

Harding had his detractors. Ultimately, he was his own most severe critic. His insecurity about his leadership abilities was frequently made manifest. The White House became his prison and he lamented that it was "a hell of a place for a man like me to be." Scandals and sordid allegations affected his historical reputation. Yet during the days of his prominence, public opinion unblushingly paired Harding with Lincoln as the two great Republicans. His popularity surely benefited when the genial Harding was contrasted with that of his predecessor the austere, cold, and cerebral Woodrow Wilson.

Harding promised to bring harmony. The man had no sharp edges. In fact he was a man who enjoyed simple pleasures and common vices such as whiskey, poker, and women. Men and women liked him. American women wanted war no more. They sought a return to practical everyday down-to-earth matters. Above all, they did not want their sons and husbands far from hearth and home. Women cast their maiden ballots in the landslide of 1920 for Harding, conservatism, and the Republican Party. Harding had hit a nerve. He won by seven million votes.

The Harding administration achieved a modest domestic and foreign policy accomplishment record during its brief tenure. At the time of his death, on August 2, 1923, President Harding knew of some of the scandals perpetrated by his political cronies. In his anxiety, Harding proclaimed that he could take care of his enemies, but his friends had wounded and "betrayed" him. In the wake of his betrayal, it is sometimes said that the President died of a broken heart. The nation mourned the loss of Harding. Then the scandals became public, and it was the people who felt betrayed.

Vice President Calvin Coolidge was now called to take the presidential oath of office. Coolidge spent most of his public career safely disguised behind an effective stereotype of his own creation. He fit the image of a native son of the Granite State, Vermont. Coolidge had come to be known in some quarters as the "great stone face." Alice Roosevelt Longworth acidly said he looked as though he had been "weaned on a pickle." Later there was a rumor that he had died, to which Dorothy Parker replied: "How can you tell?"

Coolidge's well-honed political skills tend to be overlooked. "Silent Cal" took a page from the master political bosses who, when asked why they never said anything, would reply that if they said anything they might be called upon to repeat it. Terse and private, Coolidge's demeanor did suggest the simple rectitude, shrewdness, and practicality of New England. Saying little, Coolidge moved effectively to dispose of the scandals he inherited and won another landslide victory for himself and the Republican Party in 1924.

Belying his pose of passive indifference, Coolidge sought to illuminate his presidency through the means of twice-weekly press conferences. Rules were established to suit his purpose. None of the dozen-or-so regularly attending newsmen were permitted to quote the President directly. The substance of the President's paraphrased comments to questions submitted in advance would be attributed to a "spokesman." As Head of State, Coolidge attended to the ceremonial and symbolic functions of his office. At a moment that lives in the American memory, President Coolidge presented Charles A. Lindbergh on a nationally broadcast ceremony with the first Distinguished Flying Cross medal, in honor of his successful transatlantic flight in June 1927.

His watch bore witness to a golden economic boom called the "Coolidge Prosperity." There is little doubt that Coolidge could have been re-elected. Intentionally or not, Coolidge declared "I do not choose to run." That statement opened the door for Herbert Hoover. Marking the date, the place and the occasion in the tradition of the first president, Coolidge said his farewell at George Washington University, on February 22, 1929. There he reminded the students that peace as well as prosperity prevailed. The farewell advice of Washington had not been forgotten. Forging alliances with any nation was not on the nation's foreign policy agenda but maintaining "good will" with all nations was a top priority. As Coolidge left the presidential platform and Herbert Hoover entered stage left, the legacy of Washington was ever present.

26

Theodore Roosevelt

1. THE GREATNESS OF MCKINLEY   JANUARY 27, 1903

. . . President McKinley's rise to greatness had in it nothing of the sudden, nothing of the unexpected. . . . In 1896 the issue was fairly joined, chiefly upon a question which, as a party question, was entirely new, so that the old lines of cleavage were in large part abandoned. All other issues sank in importance when compared with the vital need of keeping our financial system on the high and honorable plane imperatively demanded by our position as a great civilized power. As a champion of such a principle President McKinley received the support not only of his own party, but of hundreds of thousands of those to whom he had been politically opposed. He triumphed, and made good with scrupulous fidelity the promises upon which the campaign was won. We were at the time in a period of great industrial depression, and it was promised for and on behalf of McKinley that if he were elected our financial system should not only be preserved unharmed, but improved, and our economic system shaped in accordance with those theories which have always marked our periods of greatest prosperity. The promises were kept, and following their keeping came the prosperity which we now enjoy. All that was foretold concerning the well-being which would follow the election of McKinley has been justified by the event.

. . . He sought by every honorable means to preserve peace, to avert war. He made every effort consistent with the national honor to bring about an amicable settlement. . . .

When it became evident that these efforts were useless, that peace could not be honorably entertained, he devoted his strength to making the war as short and as decisive as possible. It is needless to tell the result in detail. Suffice it to say that rarely indeed in history has a contest so far reaching in the importance . . . been achieved with such ease. There followed a harder task . . .

President McKinley never flinched. He refused to consider the thought of abandoning our duty in our new possessions. . . . His policy was most amply vindicated. Peace has come to the islands, together with a greater measure of individual liberty and self-government than they have ever before known. All the tasks set us as a result of the war with Spain have so far been well and honorably accomplished, and as a result this nation stands higher than ever before among the nations of mankind. . . .

No other President in our history has seen high and honorable effort crowned with more conspicuous personal success. No other President entered upon his second term feeling such right to a profound and peaceful satisfaction. Then by a stroke of horror, so strange in its fantastic iniquity as to stand unique in the black annals of crime, he was struck down. The brave, strong, gentle heart was stilled forever. . . . The hideous infamy of the deed shocked the nation to its depths, for the man thus struck at was . . . the exponent of those ideals which . . . will make . . . our country a blessed refuge for all who strive to do right. . . . We did right to mourn; for the loss was ours, not his. . . .

We are gathered together . . . to recall his memory, to pay our tribute of respect to the great chief and leader who fell in the harness. . . . He won greatness by meeting and solving the issues as they arose . . . with fearless resolution when the time of crisis came. . . . He stood among the world's chief statesmen. . . . The nation solved these mighty problems aright. Therefore, he shall stand in the eyes of history not merely as the first man of his generation, but as among the greatest figures in our national life, coming second only to the men of the two great crises in which the Union was founded and preserved.

Figure 26.1 Theodore Roosevelt with dead lion, courtesy of the Library of Congress Prints and Photographs Division, Washington, DC.

2. ACQUISITION OF PANAMA CANAL ZONE   DECEMBER 7, 1903

For four hundred years . . . the canal across the Isthmus has been planned. For two score years it has been worked at. When made it is to last for the ages. It is to alter the geography of a continent and the trade routes of the world. We have shown by every treaty we have negotiated or attempted to negotiate with the peoples in control of the Isthmus and with foreign nations in reference there to our consistent good faith in observing our obligations; on the one hand to the peoples of the Isthmus, and on the other hand to the civilized world whose commercial rights we are safeguarding and guaranteeing by our action. We have done our duty to others in letter and in spirit, and we have shown the utmost forbearance in exacting our own rights.

Last spring, under the act above referred to, a treaty concluded between the representatives of the Republic of Colombia and of our Government was ratified by the Senate. This treaty was entered into at the urgent solicitation of the people of Colombia and after a body of experts appointed by our Government especially to go into the matter of the routes across the Isthmus had pronounced unanimously in favor of the Panama route. In drawing up this treaty every concession was made to the people and to the Government of Colombia. We were more than just in dealing with them. Our generosity was such as to make it a serious question whether we had not gone too far in their interest at the expense of our own; for in our scrupulous desire to pay all possible heed, not merely to the real but even to the fancied rights of our weaker neighbor, who already owed so much to our protection and forbearance, we yielded in all possible ways to her desires in drawing up the treaty. Nevertheless the Government of Colombia not merely repudiated the treaty, but repudiated it in such manner as to make it evident by the time the Colombian Congress adjourned that not the scantiest hope remained of ever getting a satisfactory treaty from them. The Government of Colombia made the treaty, and yet when the Colombian Congress was called to ratify it the vote against ratification was unanimous. It does not appear that the Government made any real effort to secure ratification.

Immediately after the adjournment of the Congress a revolution broke out in Panama. The people of Panama had long been discontented with the Republic of Colombia, and they had been kept quiet only by the prospect of the conclusion of the treaty, which was to them a matter of vital concern. When it became evident that the treaty was hopelessly lost, the people of Panama rose literally as one man. Not a shot was fired by a single man on the Isthmus in the interest of the Colombian Government. Not a life was lost in the accomplishment of the revolution. The Colombian troops stationed on the Isthmus, who had long been unpaid, made common cause with the people of Panama, and with astonishing unanimity the new Republic was started. The duty of the United States in the premises was clear . . . the United States gave notice that it would permit the landing of no expeditionary force, the arrival of which would mean chaos and destruction along the line of the railroad and of the proposed canal, and an interruption of transit as an inevitable consequence. The de facto Government of Panama was recognized in the following telegram to Mr. Ehrman:

> "The people of Panama have, by apparently unanimous movement, dissolved their political connection with the Republic of Colombia and resumed their independence. When you are satisfied that a de facto government, republican in form and without substantial opposition from its own people, has been established in the State of Panama, you will enter into relations with it as the responsible government of the territory and look to it for all due action to protect the persons and property of citizens of the United states and to keep open the isthmian transit in accordance with the obligations of existing treaties governing the relations of the United States to that Territory."

The Government of Colombia was notified of our action by the following telegram to Mr. Beaupre:

"The people of Panama having, by an apparently unanimous movement, dissolved their political connection with the Republic of Colombia and resumed their independence, and having adopted a Government of their own, republican in form, with which the Government of the United States of America has entered into relations, the President of the United States, in accordance with the ties of friendship which have so long and so happily existed between the respective nations, most earnestly commends to the Governments of Colombia and of Panama the peaceful and equitable settlement of all questions at issue between them. He holds that he is bound not merely by treaty obligations, but by the interests of civilization, to see that the peaceful traffic of the world across the Isthmus of Panama shall not longer be disturbed by a constant succession of unnecessary and wasteful civil wars. . . . The control, in the interest of the commerce and traffic of the whole civilized world, of the means of undisturbed transit across the Isthmus of Panama has become of transcendent importance to the United States."

The above recital of facts establishes beyond question: First, that the United States has for over half a century patiently and in good faith carried out its obligations under the treaty of 1846; second, that when for the first time it became possible for Colombia to do anything in requital of the services thus repeatedly rendered to it for fifty-seven years by the United States, the Colombian Government peremptorily and offensively refused thus to do its part, even though to do so would have been to its advantage and immeasurably to the advantage of the State of Panama, at that time under its jurisdiction; third, that throughout this period revolutions, riots, and factional disturbances of every kind have occurred one after the other in almost uninterrupted succession, some of them lasting for months and even for years, while the central government was unable to put them down or to make peace with the rebels; fourth, that these disturbances instead of showing any sign of abating have tended to grow more numerous and more serious in the immediate past; fifth, that the control of Colombia over the Isthmus of Panama could not be maintained without the armed intervention and assistance of the United States. In other words, the Government of Colombia, though wholly unable to maintain order on the Isthmus, has nevertheless declined to ratify a treaty the conclusion of which opened the only chance to secure its own stability and to guarantee permanent peace on, and the construction of a canal across, the Isthmus.

Under such circumstances the Government of the United States would have been guilty of folly and weakness, amounting in their sum to a crime against the Nation, had it acted otherwise than it did when the revolution of 3 November last took place in Panama. This great enterprise of building the interoceanic canal cannot be held up to gratify the whims, or out of respect to the governmental impotence, or to the even more sinister and evil political peculiarities, of people who, though they dwell afar off, yet, against the wish of the actual dwellers on the Isthmus, assert an unreal supremacy over the territory. The possession of a territory fraught with such peculiar capacities as the Isthmus in question carries with it obligations to mankind. The course of events has shown that this canal cannot be built by private enterprise, or by any other nation than our own; therefore it must be built by the United States.

Every effort has been made by the Government of the United States to persuade Colombia to follow a course which was essentially not only to our interest and to the interests of the world, but to the interests of Colombia itself. These efforts have failed; and Colombia, by her persistence in repulsing the advances that have been made, has forced us, for the sake of our own honor, and of the interest and wellbeing, not merely of our own people, but of the people of the Isthmus of Panama and the people of the civilized countries of the world, to take decisive steps to bring to an end a condition of affairs which had become intolerable. The new Republic of Panama immediately offered to negotiate a treaty with us. This treaty I herewith submit. By it our interests are better safeguarded than in the treaty with Colombia which was ratified by the Senate at its last session. It is better in its terms than the treaties offered to us by the Republics of Nicaragua and Costa Rica. At last the right to begin this great undertaking is made available. Panama has done her part. All that remains is for the American Congress to do its part, and forthwith this Republic will enter upon the execution of a project colossal in its size and of well-nigh incalculable possibilities for the good of this country and the nations of mankind.

By the provisions of the treaty the United States guarantees and will maintain the independence of the Republic of Panama. There is granted to the United States in perpetuity the use, occupation, and control of a strip ten miles wide and extending three nautical miles into the sea at either terminal, with all lands lying outside of the zone necessary for the construction of the canal or for its auxiliary works, and with the islands in the Bay of Panama. The cities of Panama and Colon are not embraced in the canal zone, but the United States assumes their sanitation and, in case of need, the maintenance of order therein; the United States enjoys within the granted limits all the rights, power, and authority which it would possess were it the sovereign of the territory to the exclusion of the exercise of sovereign rights by the Republic. All railway and canal property rights belonging to Panama and needed for the canal pass to the United States, including any property of the respective companies in the cities of Panama and Colon; the works, property, and personnel of the canal and railways are exempted from taxation as well in the cities of Panama and Colon as in the canal zone and its dependencies. Free immigration of the personnel and importation of supplies for the construction and operation of the canal are granted. Provision is made for the use of military force and the building of fortifications by the United States for the protection of the transit. In other details, particularly as to the acquisition of the interests of the New Panama Canal Company and the Panama Railway by the United States and the condemnation of private property for the uses of the canal, the stipulations of the Hay–Herran treaty are closely followed, while the compensation to be given for these enlarged grants remains the same, being ten millions of dollars payable on exchange of ratifications; and, beginning nine years from that date, an annual payment of $250,000 during the life of the convention.

3. "ROOSEVELT COROLLARY" TO THE MONROE DOCTRINE   DECEMBER 6, 1904

In treating of our foreign policy and of the attitude that this great Nation should assume in the world at large it is absolutely necessary to consider the Army and the Navy, and the Congress, through which the thought of the Nation finds its expression, should keep ever vividly in mind the fundamental fact that it is impossible to treat our foreign policy, whether this policy takes shape in the effort to secure justice for others or justice for ourselves, save as conditioned upon the attitude we are willing to take toward our Army, and especially toward our Navy. It is not merely unwise, it is contemptible, for a nation, as for an individual, to use high-sounding language to proclaim its purposes, or to take positions which are ridiculous if unsupported by potential force, and then to refuse to provide this force. If there is no intention of providing and of keeping the force necessary to back up a strong attitude, then it is far better not to assume such an attitude. . . .

Until some method is devised by which there shall be a degree of international control over offending nations, it would be a wicked thing for the most civilized powers, for those with most

sense of international obligations and with keenest and most generous appreciation of the difference between right and wrong, to disarm. If the great civilized nations of the present day should
completely disarm, the result would mean an immediate recrudescence of barbarism in one form
or another. Under any circumstances a sufficient armament would have to be kept up to serve the
purposes of international police; and until international cohesion and the sense of international
duties and rights are far more advanced than at present, a nation desirous both of securing respect
for itself and of doing good to others must have a force adequate for the work which it feels is
allotted to it as its part of the general world duty. Therefore it follows that a self-respecting, just,
and far-seeing nation should on the one hand endeavor by every means to aid in the development
of the various movements which tend to provide substitutes for war which tend to render nations
in their actions toward one another, and indeed toward their own peoples, more responsive to the
general sentiment of humane and civilized mankind; and on the other hand that it should keep
prepared, while scrupulously avoiding wrongdoing itself, to repel any wrong, and in exceptional
cases to take action which in a more advanced stage of international relations would come under
the head of the exercise of the international police. . . .

. . . In pursuance of this policy I shall shortly lay before the Senate treaties of arbitration with
all powers which are willing to enter into these treaties with us. It is not possible at this period of
the world's development to agree to arbitrate all matters, but there are many matters of possible
difference between us and other nations which can be thus arbitrated. Furthermore, at the request
of the Interparliamentary Union, an eminent body composed of practical statesmen from all
countries, I have asked the Powers to join with this Government in a second Hague conference, at
which it is hoped that the work already so happily begun at The Hague may be carried some steps
further toward completion. This carries out the desire expressed by the first Hague conference
itself.

It is not true that the United States feels any land hunger or entertains any projects as regards
the other nations of the Western Hemisphere save such as are for their welfare. All that this country
desires is to see the neighboring countries stable, orderly, and prosperous. Any country whose
people conduct themselves well can count upon our hearty friendship. If a nation shows that it
knows how to act with reasonable efficiency and decency in social and political matters, if it keeps
order and pays its obligations, it need fear no interference from the United States. Chronic wrongdoing, or an impotence which results in a general loosening of the ties of civilized society, may in
America, as elsewhere, ultimately require intervention by some civilized nation, and in the Western
Hemisphere the adherence of the United States to the Monroe Doctrine may force the United States,
however reluctantly, in flagrant cases of such wrongdoing or impotence, to the exercise of an
international police power. If every country washed by the Caribbean Sea would show the progress
in stable and just civilization which with the aid of the Platt amendment Cuba has shown since
our troops left the island, and which so many of the republics in both Americas are constantly and
brilliantly showing, all question of interference by this Nation with their affairs would be at an end.
Our interests and those of our southern neighbors are in reality identical. They have great natural
riches, and if within their borders the reign of law and justice obtains, prosperity is sure to come
to them. While they thus obey the primary laws of civilized society they may rest assured that they
will be treated by us in a spirit of cordial and helpful sympathy. We would interfere with them only
in the last resort, and then only if it became evident that their inability or unwillingness to do justice
at home and abroad had violated the rights of the United States or had invited foreign aggression
to the detriment of the entire body of American nations. It is a mere truism to say that every nation,
whether in America or anywhere else, which desires to maintain its freedom, its independence,

must ultimately realize that the right of such independence cannot be separated from the responsibility of making good use of it.

In asserting the Monroe Doctrine, in taking such steps as we have taken in regard to Cuba, Venezuela, and Panama, and in endeavoring to circumscribe the theater of war in the Far East, and to secure the open door in China, we have acted in our own interest as well as in the interest of humanity at large. There are, however, cases in which, while our own interests are not greatly involved, strong appeal is made to our sympathies. Ordinarily it is very much wiser and more useful for us to concern ourselves with striving for our own moral and material betterment here at home than to concern ourselves with trying to better the condition of things in other nations. We have plenty of sins of our own to war against, and under ordinary circumstances we can do more for the general uplifting of humanity by striving with heart and soul to put a stop to civic corruption, to brutal lawlessness and violent race prejudices here at home than by passing resolutions about wrongdoing elsewhere. Nevertheless there are occasional crimes committed on so vast a scale and of such peculiar horror as to make us doubt whether it is not our manifest duty to endeavor at least to show our disapproval of the deed and our sympathy with those who have suffered by it. The cases must be extreme in which such a course is justifiable. There must be no effort made to remove the mote from our brother's eye if we refuse to remove the beam from our own. But in extreme cases action may be justifiable and proper. What form the action shall take must depend upon the circumstances of the case; that is, upon the degree of the atrocity and upon our power to remedy it. . . .

4. CONSERVATION OF AMERICA   NOVEMBER 11, 1907

The natural resources of the territory of the United States were, at the time of settlement, richer, more varied, and more available than those of any other equal area on the surface of the earth. The development of these resources has given us, for more than a century, a rate of increase in population and wealth undreamed of by the men who founded our Government and without parallel in history. It is obvious that the prosperity which we now enjoy rests directly upon these resources. It is equally obvious that the vigor and success which we desire and foresee for this Nation in the future must have this as its ultimate material basis.

In view of these evident facts it seems to me time for the country to take account of its natural resources, and to inquire how long they are likely to last. We are prosperous now; we should not forget that it will be just as important to our descendants to be prosperous in their time as it is to us to be prosperous in our time.

Recently I expressed the opinion that there is no other question now before the Nation of equal gravity with the question of the conservation of our natural resources; and I added that it is the plain duty of those of us who, for the moment, are responsible, to make inventory of the natural resources which have been handed down to us, to forecast as well as we may the needs of the future, and so to handle the great sources of our prosperity as not to destroy in advance all hope of the prosperity of our descendants.

It is evident that the abundant natural resources on which the welfare of this Nation rests are becoming depleted and in not a few cases are already exhausted. This is true of all portions of the United States; it is especially true of the longer-settled communities of the East. The gravity of the situation must, I believe, appeal with special force to the Governors of the States because of their close relations to the people and their responsibility for the welfare of their communities. I have therefore decided, in accordance with the suggestion of the Inland Waterways Commission, to ask the Governors of the States and Territories to meet at the White House on 13, 14 and 15 May to confer with the President and with each other upon the conservation of natural resources.

It gives me great pleasure to invite you to take part in this conference. I should be glad to have you select three citizens to accompany you and to attend the conference as your assistants or advisors. I shall also invite the Senators and Representatives of the Sixtieth Congress to be present at the sessions so far as their duties will permit.

The matters to be considered at this conference are not confined to any region or group of States, but are of vital concern to the Nation as a whole and to all the people. These subjects include the use and conservation of the mineral resources, the resources of the land, and the resources of the waters, in every part of our territory.

In order to open discussion I shall invite a few recognized authorities to present brief descriptions of actual facts and conditions . . . leaving the conference to deal with each topic as it may elect. The members of the Inland Waterways Commission will be present in order to share with me the benefit of information and suggestion, and, if desired, to set forth their provisional plans and conclusions.

. . . The conservation of our natural resources is the most weighty question now before the people of the United States. If this is so, the proposed conference, which is the first of its kind, will be among the most important gatherings in our history in its effects upon the welfare of all our people.

I earnestly hope, my dear Governor, that you will find it possible to be present.

5. TAFT IS FIT TO BE PRESIDENT   JULY, 1907

In point of courage, capacity, inflexible uprightness and disinterestedness, wide acquaintance with governmental problems and identification of himself with the urgent needs of the social and governmental work of the day, it seems to me Taft stands preeminent. He does not think of himself. He never considers how an act or an utterance will affect him personally save in so far as he must consider how it will affect his power for usefulness. His great ambition when in office is to do the job in the best way that it can possibly be done, and he neither thinks as to whether he is under obligations to anyone or as to whether anyone else is under obligations to him. A number of years ago I wrote my estimate of Taft in the *Outlook*. Since then I have been President and I have been intimately associated with him in handling many great and difficult governmental problems, and my feeling as to his preeminent fitness for the Presidency has steadily grown.

27

William Howard Taft

1. DOLLAR DIPLOMACY ESPOUSED   **DECEMBER 3, 1912**

In China the policy of encouraging financial investment to enable that country to help itself has had the result of giving new life and practical application to the open-door policy. The consistent purpose of the present administration has been to encourage the use of American capital in the development of China by the promotion of those essential reforms to which China is pledged by treaties with the United States and other powers. The hypothecation to foreign bankers in connection with certain industrial enterprises, such as the Hukuang railways, of the national revenues upon which these reforms depended, led the Department of State early in the administration to demand for American citizens participation in such enterprises, in order that the United States might have equal rights and an equal voice in all questions pertaining to the disposition of the public revenues concerned. The same policy of promoting international accord among the powers having similar treaty rights as ourselves in the matters of reform, which could not be put into practical effect without the common consent of all, was likewise adopted in the case of the loan desired by China for the reform of its currency. The principle of international cooperation in matters of common interest upon which our policy had already been based in all of the above instances has admittedly been a great factor in that concert of the powers which has been so happily conspicuous during the perilous period of transition through which the great Chinese nation has been passing.

. . . In Central America the aim has been to help such countries as Nicaragua and Honduras to help themselves. They are the immediate beneficiaries. The national benefit to the United States is two-fold. First, it is obvious that the Monroe doctrine is more vital in the neighborhood of the Panama Canal and the zone of the Caribbean than anywhere else. There, too, the maintenance of that doctrine falls most heavily upon the United States. It is therefore essential that the countries within that sphere shall be removed from the jeopardy involved by heavy foreign debt and chaotic national finances and from the ever-present danger of international complications due to disorder at home. Hence the United States has been glad to encourage and support American bankers who were willing to lend a helping hand to the financial rehabilitation of such countries because this financial rehabilitation and the protection of their customhouses from being the prey of would-be dictators would remove at one stroke the menace of foreign creditors and the menace of revolutionary disorder.

The second advantage of the United States is one affecting chiefly all the southern and Gulf ports and the business and industry of the South. The Republics of Central America and the Caribbean possess great natural wealth. They need only a measure of stability and the means of

Figure 27.1 President Taft bowing to crowd, courtesy of the Library of Congress Prints and Photographs Division, Washington, DC.

financial regeneration to enter upon an era of peace and prosperity, bringing profit and happiness to themselves and at the same time creating conditions sure to lead to a flourishing interchange of trade with this country. . . .

2. THE CHIEF MAGISTRATE AND THE NATIONAL PASTIME   MAY 4, 1910

The game of baseball is a clear straight game, and it summons to its presence everybody who enjoys clean straight athletics. It furnishes amusement to the thousands and thousands. And I like it for two reasons—first, because I enjoy it myself and second, because if by the presence of the temporary chief magistrate such a healthy amusement can be encouraged—I want to encourage it.

3. THE PRESIDENT'S ANALYSIS OF THE 1912 ELECTION   NOVEMBER 10, 1912
RESULTS

I am becoming convinced . . . that the number of Republicans who voted for Wilson, in order to escape the danger of Roosevelt, reaches into the hundreds of thousands, and I must think, therefore, that Roosevelt drew a great many Democratic votes from Wilson of the labor, socialistic, discontented, ragtag and bobtail variety. Roosevelt had in addition the votes of the faddists, the radical progressives, the people with isms, the emotional clergymen and women, in states where women voted, and all the factional sore-heads in the Republican party. . . . What I got was the irreducible minimum of the Republican party that was left after Roosevelt got through with it and after Wilson drew from it the votes of those Republicans who feared Roosevelt. Roosevelt polled a much larger vote than I thought was possible.

4. THE CHIEF DIPLOMAT MODERNIZES THE APPARATUS   DECEMBER 3, 1912

The foreign relations of the United States actually and potentially affect the state of the Union to a degree not widely realized and hardly surpassed by any other factor in the welfare of the whole Nation. The position of the United States in the moral, intellectual, and material relations of the family of nations should be a matter of vital interest to every patriotic citizen. The national prosperity and power impose upon us duties which we cannot shirk if we are to be true to our ideals. The tremendous growth of the export trade of the United States has already made that trade a very real factor in the industrial and commercial prosperity of the country. With the development of our industries the foreign commerce of the United States must rapidly become a still more essential factor in its economic welfare. Whether we have a farseeing and wise diplomacy and are not recklessly plunged into unnecessary wars, and whether our foreign policies are based upon an intelligent grasp of present-day world conditions and a clear view of the potentialities of the future, or are governed by a temporary and timid expediency or by narrow views befitting an infant nation, are questions in the alternative consideration of which must convince any thoughtful citizen that no department of national polity offers greater opportunity for promoting the interests of the whole people on the one hand, or greater chance on the other of permanent national injury, than that which deals with the foreign relations of the United States.

The fundamental foreign policies of the United States should be raised high above the conflict of partisanship and wholly dissociated from differences as to domestic policy. In its foreign affairs the United States should present to the world a united front. The intellectual, financial, and industrial interests of the country and the publicist, the wage earner, the farmer, and citizen of whatever occupation must cooperate in a spirit of high patriotism to promote that national solidarity which is indispensable to national efficiency and to the attainment of national ideals.

The relations of the United States with all foreign powers remain upon a sound basis of peace, harmony, and friendship. A greater insistence upon justice to American citizens or interests wherever it may have been denied and a stronger emphasis of the need of mutuality in commercial and other relations have only served to strengthen our friendships with foreign countries by placing those friendships upon a firm foundation of realities as well as aspirations.

Before briefly reviewing the more important events of the last year in our foreign relations, which it is my duty to do as charged with their conduct and because diplomatic affairs are not of a nature to make it appropriate that the Secretary of State make a formal annual report, I desire to touch upon some of the essentials to the safe management of the foreign relations of the United States and to endeavor, also, to define clearly certain concrete policies which are the logical modern corollaries of the undisputed and traditional fundamentals of the foreign policy of the United States.

. . . At the beginning of the present administration the United States, having fully entered upon its position as a world power, with the responsibilities thrust upon it by the results of the Spanish-American War, and already engaged in laying the groundwork of a vast foreign trade upon which it should one day become more and more dependent, found itself without the machinery for giving thorough attention to, and taking effective action upon, a mass of intricate business vital to American interests in every country in the world.

The Department of State was an archaic and inadequate machine lacking most of the attributes of the foreign office of any great modern power. With an appropriation made upon my recommendation by the Congress on August 5, 1909, the Department of State was completely reorganized. There were created Divisions of Latin American Affairs and of Far Eastern, Near Eastern, and

Western European Affairs. To these divisions were called from the Foreign Service diplomatic and consular officers possessing experience and knowledge gained by actual service in different parts of the world and thus familiar with political and commercial conditions in the regions concerned. The work was highly specialized. The result is that where previously this Government from time to time would emphasize in its foreign relations one or another policy, now American interests in every quarter of the globe are being cultivated with equal assiduity. This principle of politico-geographical division possesses also the good feature of making possible rotation between the officers of the departmental, the diplomatic, and the consular branches of the Foreign Service, and thus keeps the whole diplomatic and consular establishments under the Department of State in close touch and equally inspired with the aims and policy of the Government. Through the newly created Division of Information the foreign service is kept fully informed of what transpires from day to day in the international relations of the country, and contemporary foreign comment affecting American interests is promptly brought to the attention of the department. The law offices of the department were greatly strengthened. There were added foreign trade advisers to cooperate with the diplomatic and consular bureaus and the politico-geographical divisions in the innumerable matters where commercial diplomacy or consular work calls for such special knowledge. The same officers, together with the rest of the new organization, are able at all times to give to American citizens accurate information as to conditions in foreign countries with which they have business and likewise to cooperate more effectively with the Congress and also with the other executive departments.

. . . Expert knowledge and professional training must evidently be the essence of this reorganization. Without a trained foreign service there would not be men available for the work in the reorganized Department of State. President Cleveland had taken the first step toward introducing the merit system in the Foreign Service. That had been followed by the application of the merit principle, with excellent results, to the entire consular branch. Almost nothing, however, had been done in this direction with regard to the Diplomatic Service. In this age of commercial diplomacy it was evidently of the first importance to train adequate personnel in that branch of the service. Therefore, on November 26, 1909, by an Executive order I placed the Diplomatic Service up to the grade of secretary of embassy, inclusive, upon exactly the same strict nonpartisan basis of the merit system, rigid examination for appointment and promotion only for efficiency, as had been maintained without exception in the Consular Service. . . .

In order to assure to the business and other interests of the United States a continuance of the resulting benefits of this reform, I earnestly renew my previous recommendations of legislation making it permanent along some such lines as those of the measure now pending in Congress.

. . . In connection with legislation for the amelioration of the Foreign Service, I wish to invite attention to the advisability of placing the salary appropriations upon a better basis. I believe that the best results would be obtained by a moderate scale of salaries, with adequate funds for the expense of proper representation, based in each case upon the scale and cost of living at each post, controlled by a system of accounting, and under the general direction of the Department of State.

In line with the object which I have sought of placing our foreign service on a basis of permanency, I have at various times advocated provision by Congress for the acquisition of Government-owned buildings for the residence and offices of our diplomatic officers, so as to place them more nearly on an equality with similar officers of other nations and to do away with the discrimination which otherwise must necessarily be made, in some cases, in favor of men having large private fortunes. The act of Congress which I approved on February 17, 1911, was a right step in this direction. The Secretary of State has already made the limited recommendations permitted by the act for any one year, and it is my hope that the bill introduced in the House of Representatives to carry out these recommendations will be favorably acted on by the Congress during its present session.

In some Latin-American countries the expense of government-owned legations will be less than elsewhere, and it is certainly very urgent that in such countries as some of the Republics of Central America and the Caribbean, where it is peculiarly difficult to rent suitable quarters, the representatives of the United States should be justly and adequately provided with dignified and suitable official residences. Indeed, it is high time that the dignity and power of this great Nation should be fittingly signalized by proper buildings for the occupancy of the Nation's representatives everywhere abroad.

. . . The diplomacy of the present administration has sought to respond to modern ideas of commercial intercourse. This policy has been characterized as substituting dollars for bullets. It is one that appeals alike to idealistic humanitarian sentiments, to the dictates of sound policy and strategy, and to legitimate commercial aims. It is an effort frankly directed to the increase of American trade upon the axiomatic principle that the Government of the United States shall extend all proper support to every legitimate and beneficial American enterprise abroad. How great have been the results of this diplomacy, coupled with the maximum and minimum provision of the tariff law, will be seen by some consideration of the wonderful increase in the export trade of the United States. Because modern diplomacy is commercial, there has been a disposition in some quarters to attribute to it none but materialistic aims. How strikingly erroneous is such an impression may be seen from a study of the results by which the diplomacy of the United States can be judged....

As illustrating the commercial benefits of the Nation derived from the new diplomacy and its effectiveness upon the material as well as the more ideal side, it may be remarked that through direct official efforts alone there have been obtained in the course of this administration, contracts from foreign Governments involving an expenditure of $50,000,000 in the factories of the United States. Consideration of this fact and some reflection upon the necessary effects of a scientific tariff system and a foreign service alert and equipped to cooperate with the business men of America carry the conviction that the gratifying increase in the export trade of this country is . . . due to our improved governmental methods of protecting and stimulating it. It is germane to these observations to remark that in the two years that have elapsed since the successful negotiation of our new treaty with Japan, which at the time seemed to present so many practical difficulties, our export trade to that country has increased at the rate of over $1,000,000 a month. Our exports to Japan for the year ended June 30, 1910, were $21,959,310, while for the year ended June 30, 1912, the exports were $53,478,046, a net increase in the sale of American products of nearly 150 per cent. . . .

It is not possible to make to the Congress a communication . . . to convey an adequate impression of the enormous increase in the importance and activities of those relations. If this Government is really to preserve to the American people that free opportunity in foreign markets which will soon be indispensable to our prosperity, even greater efforts must be made. Otherwise the American merchant, manufacturer, and exporter will find many a field in which American trade should logically predominate preempted through the more energetic efforts of other governments and other commercial nations.

. . . The absolute essential is the spirit of united effort and singleness of purpose. I will allude only to a very few specific examples of action which ought then to result. America cannot take its proper place in the most important fields for its commercial activity and enterprise unless we have a merchant marine. American commerce and enterprise cannot be effectively fostered in those fields unless we have good American banks in the countries referred to. We need American newspapers in those countries and proper means for public information about them. We need to assure the permanency of a trained foreign service. We need legislation enabling the members of the foreign service to be systematically brought in direct contact with the industrial, manufacturing, and exporting interests of this country in order that American business men may enter the foreign field with a clear perception of the exact conditions to be dealt with and the officers themselves may prosecute their work with a clear idea of what American industrial and manufacturing interests require.

. . . Congress should fully realize the conditions which obtain in the world as we find ourselves at the threshold of our middle age as a Nation. We have emerged full grown as a peer in the great concourse of nations. We have passed through various formative periods. We have been self-centered in the struggle to develop our domestic resources and deal with our domestic questions. The Nation is now too matured to continue in its foreign relations those temporary expedients natural to a people to whom domestic affairs are the sole concern. In the past our diplomacy has often consisted, in normal times, in a mere assertion of the right to international existence. We are now in a larger relation with broader rights of our own and obligations to others than ourselves. A number of great guiding principles were laid down early in the history of this Government. The recent task of our diplomacy has been to adjust those principles to the conditions of to-day, to develop their corollaries, to find practical applications of the old principles expanded to meet new situations. Thus are being evolved bases upon which can rest the superstructure of policies which must grow with the destined progress of this Nation. The successful conduct of our foreign relations demands a broad and a modern view. We cannot meet new questions nor build for the future if we confine ourselves to outworn dogmas of the past and to the perspective appropriate at our emergence from colonial times and conditions. The opening of the Panama Canal will mark a new era in our international life and create new and worldwide conditions which, with their vast correlations and consequences, will obtain for hundreds of years to come. We must not wait for events to overtake us unawares. With continuity of purpose we must deal with the problems of our external relations by diplomacy modern, resourceful, magnanimous, and fittingly expressive of the high ideals of a great nation.

5. OUR CAPITAL: THE CITY OF WASHINGTON AND DISTRICT   DECEMBER 3, 1912
OF COLUMBIA

The city of Washington is a beautiful city, with a population of 352,936, of whom 98,667 are colored. The annual municipal budget is about $14,000,000. The presence of the National Capital and other governmental structures constitutes the chief beauty and interest of the city. The public grounds are extensive, and the opportunities for improving the city and making it still more attractive are very great. Under a plan adopted some years ago, one half the cost of running the city is paid by taxation upon the property, real and personal, of the citizens and residents, and the other half is borne by the General Government. The city is expanding at a remarkable rate, and this can only be accounted for by the coming here from other parts of the country of well-to-do people who, having finished their business careers elsewhere, build and make this their permanent place of residence.

On the whole, the city as a municipality is very well governed. It is well lighted, the water supply is good, the streets are well paved, the police force is well disciplined, crime is not flagrant, and while it has purlieus and centers of vice, like other large cities, they are not exploited, they do not exercise any influence or control in the government of the city, and they are suppressed in as far as it has been found practicable. Municipal graft is inconsiderable. There are interior courts in the city that are noisome and centers of disease and the refuge of criminals, but Congress has begun to clean these out, and progress has been made in the case of the most notorious of these, which is known as "Willow Tree Alley." This movement should continue. The mortality for the past year was at the rate of 17.80 per 1,000 of both races; among the whites it was 14.61 per thousand, and among the blacks 26.12 per thousand. These are the lowest mortality rates ever recorded in the District.

One of the most crying needs in the government of the District is a tribunal or public authority for the purpose of supervising the corporations engaged in the operation of public utilities. Such a bill is pending in Congress and ought to pass. Washington should show itself under the direction of Congress to be a city with a model form of government, but as long as such authority over public utilities is withheld from the municipal government, it must always be defective. . . .

While the school system of Washington perhaps might be bettered in the economy of its management and the distribution of its buildings, its usefulness has nevertheless greatly increased in recent years, and it now offers excellent facilities for primary and secondary education.

From time to time there is considerable agitation in Washington in favor of granting the citizens of the city the franchise and constituting an elective government. I am strongly opposed to this change. The history of Washington discloses a number of experiments of this kind, which have always been abandoned as unsatisfactory. The truth is this is a city governed by a popular body, to wit, the Congress of the United States, selected from the people of the United States, who own Washington. The people who come here to live do so with the knowledge of the origin of the city and the restrictions, and therefore voluntarily give up the privilege of living in a municipality governed by popular vote. Washington is so unique in its origin and in its use for housing and localizing the sovereignty of the Nation that the people who live here must regard its peculiar character and must be content to subject themselves to the control of a body selected by all the people of the Nation. I agree that there are certain inconveniences growing out of the government of a city by a national legislature like Congress, and it would perhaps be possible to lessen these by the delegation by Congress to the District Commissioners of greater legislative power for the enactment of local laws than they now possess, especially those of a police character.

Every loyal American has a personal pride in the beauty of Washington and in its development and growth. There is no one with a proper appreciation of our Capital City who would favor a niggardly policy in respect to expenditures from the National Treasury to add to the attractiveness of this city, which belongs to every citizen of the entire country, and which no citizen visits without a sense of pride of ownership. We have had restored by a Commission of Fine Arts, at the instance of a committee of the Senate, the original plan of the French engineer L'Enfant for the city of Washington, and we know with great certainty the course which the improvement of Washington should take. Why should there be delay in making this improvement in so far as it involves the extension of the parking system and the construction of greatly needed public buildings? Appropriate buildings for the State Department, the Department of justice, and the Department of Commerce and Labor have been projected, plans have been approved, and nothing is wanting but the appropriations for the beginning and completion of the structures. A hall of archives is also badly needed, but nothing has been done toward its construction, although the land for it has long been bought and paid for. Plans have been made for the union of Potomac Park with the valley of Rock Creek and Rock Creek Park, and the necessity for the connection between the Soldiers'

Home and Rock Creek Park calls for no comment. I ask again why there should be delay in carrying out these plans. We have the money in the Treasury, the plans are national in their scope, and the improvement should be treated as a national project. The plan will find a hearty approval throughout the country. I am quite sure, from the information which I have, that, at comparatively small expense, from that part of the District of Columbia which was retroceded to Virginia, the portion including the Arlington estate, Fort Myer, and the palisades of the Potomac can be acquired by purchase and the jurisdiction of the State of Virginia over this land ceded to the Nation. This ought to be done.

The construction of the Lincoln Memorial and of a memorial bridge from the base of the Lincoln Monument to Arlington would be an appropriate and symbolic expression of the union of the North and the South at the Capital of the Nation. I urge upon Congress the appointment of a commission to undertake these national improvements and to submit a plan for their execution; and when the plan has been submitted and approved, and the work carried out, Washington will really become what it ought to be—the most beautiful city in the world.

28

Woodrow Wilson

1. THE FEDERAL RESERVE SYSTEM ESTABLISHED: A GIFT TO BUSINESSMEN   JUNE 23, 1913

. . . There are occasions of public duty when these things which touch us privately seem very small; when the work to be done is so pressing and so fraught with big consequence that we know that we are not at liberty to weigh against it any point of personal sacrifice. We are now in the presence of such an occasion. It is absolutely imperative that we should give the business men of this country a banking and currency system by means of which they can make use of the freedom of enterprise and of individual initiative which we are about to bestow upon them.

We are about to set them free; we must not leave them without the tools of action when they are free. We are about to set them free by removing the trammels of the protective tariff. Ever since the Civil War they have waited for this emancipation and for the free opportunities it will bring with it. It has been reserved for us to give it to them. Some fell in love, indeed, with the slothful security of their dependence upon the Government; some took advantage of the shelter of the nursery to set up a mimic mastery of their own within its walls. Now both the tonic and the discipline of liberty and maturity are to ensue. There will be some readjustments of purpose and point of view. There will follow a period of expansion and new enterprise, freshly conceived. It is for us to determine now whether it shall be rapid and facile and of easy accomplishment. This it cannot be unless the resourceful business men who are to deal with the new circumstances are to have at hand and ready for use the instrumentalities and conveniences of free enterprise which independent men need when acting on their own initiative.

It is not enough to strike the shackles from business. The duty of statesmanship is not negative merely. It is constructive also. We must show that we understand what business needs and that we know how to supply it. No man, however casual and superficial his observation of the conditions now prevailing in the country, can fail to see that one of the chief things business needs now, and will need increasingly as it gains in scope and vigor in the years immediately ahead of us, is the proper means by which readily to vitalize its credit, corporate and individual, and its originative brains. What will it profit us to be free if we are not to have the best and most accessible instrumentalities of commerce and enterprise? What will it profit us to be quit of one kind of monopoly if we are to remain in the grip of another and more effective kind? How are we to gain and keep the confidence of the business community unless we show that we know how both to aid and to protect it? What shall we say if we make fresh enterprise necessary and also make it very difficult by leaving all else except the tariff just as we found it? The tyrannies of business, big and little, lie within the field of credit. We know that. Shall we not act upon the knowledge? Do we not know how to act upon it? If a man cannot make his assets available at pleasure . . . what satisfaction is it to him to see opportunity beckoning to him on every hand, when others have the keys of credit in their pockets and treat them as all but their own private possession? It is perfectly clear that it is our duty to supply the new banking and currency system the country needs, and it will need it immediately more than it has ever needed it before.

The only question is, when shall we supply it—now, or later, after the demands shall have become reproaches that we were so dull and so slow? Shall we hasten to change the tariff laws and then be laggards about making it possible and easy for the country to take advantage of the change? There can be only one answer to that question. We must act now at whatever sacrifice to ourselves. It is a duty which the circumstances forbid us to postpone. I should be recreant to my deepest convictions of public obligation did I not press it upon you with solemn and urgent insistence.

The principles upon which we should act are also clear. The country has sought and seen its path in this matter within the last few years. . . . We must have a currency, not rigid as now, but readily, elastically responsive to sound credit, the expanding and contracting credits of everyday transactions, the normal ebb and flow of personal and corporate dealings. Our banking laws must mobilize reserves; must not permit the concentration anywhere in a few hands of the monetary resources of the country or their use for speculative purposes in such volume as to hinder or impede or stand in the way of other more legitimate, more fruitful uses. And the control of the system of banking and of issue which our new laws are to set up must be public, not private, must be vested in the Government itself, so that the banks may be the instruments, not the masters, of business and of individual enterprise and initiative.

Figure 28.1 Woodrow Wilson and his wife riding in the backseat of a carriage to his second Inauguration, March 5, 1917, courtesy of the Library of Congress Prints and Photographs Division, Washington, DC.

The committees of the Congress to which legislation of this character is referred have devoted careful and dispassionate study to the means of accomplishing these objects . . . They are ready to suggest action. I have come to you, as the head of the Government and the responsible leader of the party in power, to urge action now, while there is time to serve the country deliberately . . . in a clear air of common counsel. . . . I therefore appeal to you with confidence. I am at your service without reserve to play my part in any way you may call upon me to play it in this great enterprise of exigent reform which it will dignify and distinguish us to perform and discredit us to neglect.

2. FEDERAL SEGREGATION POLICY AND THE CHIEF EXECUTIVE   JULY 23–SEPTEMBER 8, 1913

I do not think you know what is going on down here. We are handling the force of colored people who are now in the departments in just the way in which they ought to be handled. We are trying—and by degrees succeeding—a plan of concentration which will put them all together and will not in any one bureau mix the two races. . . .

It would not be right for me to look at this matter in any other way than as the leader of a great national party. I am trying to handle these matters with the best judgment but in the spirit of the whole country, though with entire comprehension of the considerations which certainly do not need to be pointed out to me. . . .

It is true that the segregation of the colored employees in the several departments was begun upon the initiative and at the suggestion of several of the heads of departments, but as much in the interest of the negroes as for any other reason, with the approval of some of the most influential negroes I know, and with the idea that the friction, or rather the discontent and uneasiness, which had prevailed in many of the departments would thereby be removed. It is as far as possible from being a movement against the negroes. I sincerely believe it to be in their interest. And what distresses me about your letter is to find that you look at it in so different a light.

I am sorry that those who interest themselves most in the welfare of the negroes should misjudge this action on the part of the departments, for they are seriously misjudging it. My own feeling is, by putting certain bureaus and sections of the service in the charge of negroes we are rendering them more safe in their possession of office and less likely to be discriminated against. . . .

In reply to your kind letter of September fourth, I would say that I do approve of the segregation that is being attempted in several of the departments. I have not always approved of the way in which the thing was done and have tried to change that in some instances for the better, but I think if you were here on the ground you would see, as I seem to see, that it is distinctly to the advantage of the colored people themselves that they should be organized, so far as possible and convenient, in distinct bureau where they will center their work. Some of the most thoughtful colored men I have conversed with have themselves approved of this policy. I certainly would not myself have approved of it if I had not thought it to their advantage and likely to remove many of the difficulties which have surrounded the appointment and advancement of colored men and women. . . .

3. ORDER TO INVADE MEXICO   APRIL 20, 1914

Gentlemen of the Congress: It is my duty to call your attention to a situation which has arisen in our dealings with General Victoriano Huerta at Mexico City which calls for action, and to ask your advice and cooperation in acting upon it. On the ninth of April a paymaster of the *U.S.S. Dolphin* landed at the Iturbide Bridge landing at Tampico with a whaleboat and boat's crew to take off certain supplies needed by his ship, and while engaged in loading the boat was arrested by an officer and squad of men of the army of General Huerta. Neither the paymaster nor anyone of the boat's crew was armed. Two of the men were in the boat when the arrest took place and were obliged to leave it and submit to be taken into custody, notwithstanding the fact that the boat carried . . . the flag of the United States. The officer who made the arrest was proceeding up one of the streets of the town with his prisoners when met by an officer of higher authority, who ordered him to return to the landing and await orders; and within an hour and a half from the time of the arrest orders were received from the commander of the Huertista forces at Tampico for the release of the paymaster and his men. The release was followed by apologies from the commander and later by an expression of regret by General Huerta himself.

. . . Unfortunately, it was not an isolated case. A series of incidents have recently occurred which cannot but create the impression that the representatives of General Huerta were willing to go out of their way to show disregard for the dignity and rights of this government. . . .

. . . This Government can . . . in no circumstances be forced into war with the people of Mexico. Mexico is torn by civil strife. If we are to accept the tests of its own constitution, it has no government. General Huerta has set his power up in the City of Mexico. . . . Only part of the country is under his control. If armed conflict should unhappily come as a result of his attitude of personal resentment towards this government, we should be fighting only General Huerta. . . .

. . . No doubt l could do what is necessary in the circumstances to enforce respect for our government without recourse to the Congress . . . but l do not wish to act in a matter possibly of so grave consequence except in close conference and cooperation with both the Senate and House. I, therefore, come to ask your approval that l should use the armed forces of the United States in such ways and to such an extent as may be necessary to obtain from General Huerta and his adherents the fullest recognition of the rights and dignity of the United States. . . .

4. AMERICA ENTERS THE GREAT WAR   APRIL 2, 1917

. . . I have called the Congress into extraordinary session because there are serious, very serious, choices of policy to be made, and made immediately, which it was neither right nor constitutionally permissible that I should assume the responsibility of making.

On the third of February last I officially laid before you the extraordinary announcement of the Imperial German Government that on and after the first day of February it was its purpose to put aside all restraints of law or of humanity and use its submarines to sink every vessel that sought to approach either the ports of Great Britain and Ireland or the western coasts of Europe or any of the ports controlled by the enemies of Germany within the Mediterranean. That had seemed to be the object of the German submarine warfare earlier in the war, but since April of last year the Imperial Government had somewhat restrained the commanders of its undersea craft in conformity with its promise then given to us that passenger boats should not be sunk and that due warning would be given to all other vessels which its submarines might seek to destroy, when no resistance was offered or escape attempted, and care taken that their crews were given at least a fair chance to save their lives in their open boats. The precautions taken were meager and haphazard enough, as was proved in distressing instance after instance in the progress of the cruel and unmanly business, but a certain degree of restraint was observed. The new policy has swept every restriction aside. Vessels of every kind . . . have been ruthlessly sent to the bottom without warning and without thought of help or mercy for those on board, the vessels of friendly neutrals along with those of belligerents. Even hospital ships and ships carrying relief to the sorely bereaved and stricken people of Belgium, though the latter were provided with safe conduct through the proscribed areas by the German Government itself and were distinguished by unmistakable marks of identity, have been sunk with the same reckless lack of compassion or of principle.

I was for a little while unable to believe that such things would in fact be done by any government that had hitherto subscribed to the humane practices of civilized nations. International law had its origin in the attempt to set up some law which would be respected and observed upon the seas, where no nation had right of dominion and where lay the free highways of the world. By painful stage after stage has that law been built up, with meager enough results, indeed, after all was accomplished that could be accomplished, but always with a clear view, at least, of what the heart and conscience of mankind demanded. This minimum of right the German Government has swept aside under the plea of retaliation and necessity and because it had no weapons which it could use at sea except these which it is impossible to employ as it is employing them without throwing to the winds all scruples of humanity or of respect for the understandings that were supposed to underlie the intercourse of the world. I am not now thinking of the loss of property involved, immense and serious as that is, but only of the wanton and wholesale destruction of the lives of non-combatants, men, women, and children, engaged in pursuits which have always, even in the darkest periods of modern history, been deemed innocent and legitimate. Property can be paid for; the lives of peaceful and innocent people cannot be. The present German submarine warfare against commerce is a warfare against mankind.

It is a war against all nations. American ships have been sunk, American lives taken, in ways which it has stirred us very deeply to learn of, but the ships and people of other neutral and friendly nations have been sunk and overwhelmed in the waters in the same way. There has been no discrimination. The challenge is to all mankind. Each nation must decide for itself how it will meet it. The choice we make for ourselves must be made with a moderation of counsel and a temperateness of judgment befitting our character and our motives as a nation. We must put excited feeling away. Our motive will not be revenge or the victorious assertion of the physical might of the nation, but only the vindication of right, of human right, of which we are only a single champion.

When I addressed the Congress on the twenty-sixth of February last I thought that it would suffice to assert our neutral rights with arms, our right to use the seas against unlawful interference, our right to keep our people safe against unlawful violence. But armed neutrality, it now appears, is impracticable. Because submarines are in effect outlaws when used as the German submarines have been used against merchant shipping, it is impossible to defend ships against their attacks as the law of nations has assumed that merchantmen would defend themselves against privateers or cruisers, visible craft giving chase upon the open sea. It is common prudence in such circumstances, grim necessity, indeed, to endeavor to destroy them before they have shown their own intention. They must be dealt with upon sight, if dealt with at all. The German Government denies the right of neutrals to use arms at all within the areas of the sea which it has proscribed, even in the defense of rights which no modern publicist has ever before questioned their right to defend. The intimation is conveyed that the armed guards which we have placed on our merchant ships will be treated as beyond the pale of law and subject to be dealt with as pirates would be. Armed neutrality is ineffectual enough at best; in such circumstances and in the face of such pretensions it is worse than ineffectual: it is likely only to produce what it was meant to prevent; it is practically certain to draw us into the war without either the rights or the effectiveness of belligerents. There is one choice we cannot make, we are incapable of making: we will not choose the path of submission and suffer the most sacred rights of our nation and our people to be ignored or violated. The wrongs against which we now array ourselves are no common wrongs; they cut to the very roots of human life.

With a profound sense of the solemn and even tragical [*sic*] character of the step I am taking and of the grave responsibilities which it involves, but in unhesitating obedience to what I deem my constitutional duty, I advise that the Congress declare the recent course of the Imperial German Government to be in fact nothing less than war against the government and people of the United States; that it formally accept the status of belligerent which has thus been thrust upon it; and that it take immediate steps not only to put the country in a more thorough state of defense but also to exert all its power and employ all its resources to bring the Government of the German Empire to terms and end the war.

What this will involve is clear. It will involve the utmost practicable cooperation in counsel and action with the governments now at war with Germany, and, as incident to that, the extension to those governments of the most liberal financial credits, in order that our resources may so far as possible be added to theirs. It will involve the organization and mobilization of all the material resources of the country to supply the materials of war and serve the incidental needs of the nation in the most abundant and yet the most economical and efficient way possible. It will involve the immediate full equipment of the navy in all respects but particularly in supplying it with the best means of dealing with the enemy's submarines. It will involve the immediate addition to the armed forces of the United States already provided for by law in case of war at least five hundred thousand men, who should, in my opinion, be chosen upon the principle of universal liability to service, and also the authorization of subsequent additional increments of equal force so soon as they may be needed and can be handled in training. It will involve also, of course, the granting of adequate credits to the Government, sustained, I hope, so far as they can equitably be sustained by the present generation, by well conceived taxation.

I say sustained so far as may be equitable by taxation because it seems to me that it would be most unwise to base the credits which will now be necessary entirely on money borrowed. It is our duty, I most respectfully urge, to protect our people so far as we may against the very serious hardships and evils which would be likely to arise out of the inflation which would be produced by vast loans. In carrying out the measures by which these things are to be accomplished we should keep constantly in mind the wisdom of interfering as little as possible in our own preparation and in the equipment of our own military forces with the duty—for it will be a very practical duty— of supplying the nations already at war with Germany with the materials which they can obtain only from us or by our assistance. They are in the field and we should help them in every way to be effective there. . . .

While we do these things, these deeply momentous things, let us be very clear, and make very clear to all the world what our motives and our objects are. My own thought has not been driven from its habitual and normal course by the unhappy events of the last two months, and I do not believe that the thought of the nation has been altered or clouded by them. I have exactly the same things in mind now that I had in mind when I addressed the Senate on the twenty-second of January last; the same that I had in mind when I addressed the Congress on the third of February and on the twenty-sixth of February. Our object now, as then, is to vindicate the principles of peace and justice in the life of the world as against selfish and autocratic power and to set up amongst the really free and self-governed peoples of the world such a concert of purpose and of action as will henceforth ensure the observance of those principles. Neutrality is no longer feasible or desirable where the peace of the world is involved and the freedom of its peoples, and the menace to that peace and freedom lies in the existence of autocratic governments backed by organized force which is controlled wholly by their will, not by the will of their people. We have seen the last of neutrality in such circumstances. We are at the beginning of an age in which it will be insisted that the same standards of conduct and of responsibility for wrong done shall be observed among nations and their governments that are observed among the individual citizens of civilized states.

We have no quarrel with the German people. We have no feeling towards them but one of sympathy and friendship. It was not upon their impulse that their government acted in entering this war. It was not with their previous knowledge or approval. It was a war determined upon as wars used to be determined upon in the old, unhappy days when peoples were nowhere consulted by their rulers and wars were provoked and waged in the interest of dynasties or of little groups of ambitious men who were accustomed to use their fellow men as pawns and tools. Self-governed nations do not fill their neighbor states with spies or set the course of intrigue to bring about some critical posture of affairs which will give them an opportunity to strike and make conquest. Such designs can be successfully worked out only under cover. . . . Cunningly contrived plans of deception or aggression, carried, it may be, from generation to generation, can be worked out and kept from the light only within the privacy of courts or behind the carefully guarded confidences of a narrow and privileged class. They are happily impossible where public opinion commands and insists upon full information concerning all the nation's affairs.

A steadfast concert for peace can never be maintained except by a partnership of democratic nations. No autocratic government could be trusted to keep faith within it or observe its covenants. It must be a league of honor, a partnership of opinion. Intrigue would eat its vitals away; the plottings of inner circles who could plan what they would and render account to no one would be a corruption seated at its very heart. Only free peoples can hold their purpose and their honor steady to a common end and prefer the interests of mankind to any narrow interest of their own.

Does not every American feel that assurance has been added to our hope for the future peace of the world by the wonderful and heartening things that have been happening within the last few weeks in Russia? Russia was known by those who knew it best to have been always in fact democratic at heart, in all the vital habits of her thought, in all the intimate relationships of her people that spoke their natural instinct, their habitual attitude towards life. The autocracy that crowned the summit of her political structure, long as it had stood and terrible as was the reality of its power, was not in fact Russian in origin, character, or purpose; and now it has been shaken off and the great, generous Russian people have been added in all their naive majesty and might to the forces that are fighting for freedom in the world, for justice, and for peace. Here is a fit partner for a League of Honor.

One of the things that has served to convince us that the Prussian autocracy was not and could never be our friend is that from the very outset of the present war it has filled our unsuspecting communities and even our offices of government with spies and set criminal intrigues everywhere afoot against our national unity of counsel, our peace within and without, our industries and our commerce. Indeed it is now evident that its spies were here even before the war began; and it is unhappily not a matter of conjecture but a fact proved in our courts of justice that the intrigues which have more than once come perilously near to disturbing the peace and dislocating the industries of the country have been carried on at the instigation, with the support, and even under the personal direction of official agents of the Imperial Government accredited to the Government of the United States. Even in checking these things and trying to extirpate them we have sought to put the most generous interpretation possible upon them because we knew that their source lay, not in any hostile feeling or purpose of the German people towards us (who were, no doubt as ignorant of them as we ourselves were), but only in the selfish designs of a Government that did what it pleased and told its people nothing. But they have played their part in serving to convince us at last that that Government entertains no real friendship for us and means to act against our peace and security at its convenience. That it means to stir up enemies against us at our very doors the intercepted note to the German Minister at Mexico City is eloquent evidence.

We are accepting this challenge of hostile purpose because we know that in such a government, following such methods, we can never have a friend; and that in the presence of its organized power, always lying in wait to accomplish we know not what purpose, there can be no assured security for the democratic governments of the world. We are now about to accept gage of battle with this natural foe to liberty and shall, if necessary, spend the whole force of the nation to check and nullify its pretensions and its power. We are glad, now that we see the facts with no veil of false pretense about them, to fight thus for the ultimate peace of the world and for the liberation of its peoples, the German peoples included: for the rights of nations great and small and the privilege of men everywhere to choose their way of life and of obedience. The world must be made safe for democracy. Its peace must be planted upon the tested foundations of political liberty. We have no selfish ends to serve. We desire no conquest, no dominion. We seek no indemnities for ourselves, no material compensation for the sacrifices we shall freely make. We are but one of the champions of the rights of mankind. We shall be satisfied when those rights have been made as secure as the faith and the freedom of nations can make them.

Just because we fight without rancor and without selfish object, seeking nothing for ourselves but what we shall wish to share with all free peoples, we shall, I feel confident, conduct our operations as belligerents without passion and ourselves observe with proud punctilio the principles of right and of fair play we profess to be fighting for.

I have said nothing of the governments allied with the Imperial Government of Germany because they have not made war upon us or challenged us to defend our right and our honor. The Austro-Hungarian Government has, indeed, avowed its unqualified endorsement and acceptance of the reckless and lawless submarine warfare adopted now without disguise by the Imperial German Government, and it has therefore not been possible for this Government to receive Count Tamowski, the Ambassador recently accredited to this Government by the Imperial and Royal Government of Austria-Hungary; but that Government has not actually engaged in warfare against citizens of the United States on the seas, and I take the liberty, for the present at least, of postponing a discussion of our relations with the authorities at Vienna. We enter this war only where we are clearly forced into it because there are no other means of defending our rights.

It will be all the easier for us to conduct ourselves as belligerents in a high spirit of right and fairness because we act without animus, not in enmity towards a people or with the desire to bring any injury or disadvantage upon them, but only in armed opposition to an irresponsible government which has thrown aside all considerations of humanity and of right and is running amuck. We are, let me say again, the sincere friends of the German people, and shall desire nothing so much as the early re-establishment of intimate relations of mutual advantage between us—however hard it may be for them, for the time being, to believe that this is spoken from our hearts. We have borne with their present government through all these bitter months because of that friendship—exercising a patience and forbearance which would otherwise have been impossible. We shall, happily, still have an opportunity to prove that friendship in our daily attitude and actions towards the millions of men and women of German birth and native sympathy who live amongst us and share our life, and we shall be proud to prove it towards all who are in fact loyal to their neighbors and to the Government in the hour of test. They are most of them, as true and loyal Americans as if they had never known any other fealty or allegiance. They will be prompt to stand with us in rebuking and restraining the few who may be of a different mind and purpose. If there should be disloyalty, it will be dealt with with a firm hand of stern repression; but, if it lifts its head at all, it will lift it only here and there and without countenance except from a lawless and malignant few.

. . . There are, it may be, many months of fiery trial and sacrifice ahead of us. It is a fearful thing to lead this great peaceful people into war, into the most terrible and disastrous of all wars, civilization itself seeming to be in the balance. But the right is more precious than peace, and we shall fight for the things which we have always carried nearest our hearts—for democracy, for the right of those who submit to authority to have a voice in their own governments, for the rights and liberties of small nations, for a universal dominion of right by such a concert of free peoples as shall bring peace and safety to all nations and make the world itself at last free. To such a task we can dedicate our lives and our fortunes, everything that we are and everything that we have, with the pride of those who know that the day has come when America is privileged to spend her blood and her might for the principles that gave her birth and happiness and the peace which she has treasured. God helping her, she can do no other.

5. DECORATION DAY   MAY 11, 1918

Whereas, the Congress of the United States, on the second day of April last, passed the following resolution:

". . . it being a duty peculiarly incumbent in a time of war humbly and devoutly to acknowledge our dependence on Almighty God and to implore His aid and protection, the President of the United States be, and he is hereby, respectfully requested to recommend a day of public humiliation, prayer, and fasting, to be observed by the people of the United States with religious solemnity and the offering of fervent supplications to Almighty God for the safety and welfare of our cause, His blessings on our arms, and a speedy restoration of an honorable and lasting peace to the nations of the earth;"

And Whereas, it has always been the reverent habit of the people of the United States to turn in humble appeal to Almighty God for His guidance in the affairs of their common life;

Now, Therefore, I, Woodrow Wilson, President of the United States of America, do hereby proclaim Thursday, the thirtieth day of May, a day already freighted with sacred and stimulating memories, a day of public humiliation, prayer and fasting, and do exhort my fellow-citizens of all faiths and creeds to assemble on that day in their several places of worship and there, as well as in their homes, to pray Almighty God that He may forgive our sins and shortcomings as a people and purify our hearts to see and love the truth, to accept and defend all things that are just and right, and to purpose only those righteous acts and judgments which are in conformity with His will; beseeching Him that He will give victory to our armies as they fight for freedom, wisdom to those who take counsel on our behalf in these days of dark struggle and perplexity, and steadfastness to our people to make sacrifice to the utmost in support of what is just and true, bringing us at last the peace in which men's hearts can be at rest because it is founded upon mercy, justice and good will.

6. A NEW WORLD ORDER   DECEMBER 7, 1920

When I addressed myself to performing the duty laid upon the President by the Constitution to present to you an annual report on the state of the Union, I found my thought dominated by an immortal sentence of Abraham Lincoln's—"Let us have faith that right makes might, and in that faith let us dare to do our duty as we understand it"—a sentence immortal because it embodies in a form of utter simplicity and purity the essential faith of the nation, the faith in which it was conceived, and the faith in which it has grown to glory and power. With that faith and the birth of a nation founded upon it came the hope into the world that a new order would prevail throughout the affairs of mankind, an order in which reason and right would take precedence over covetousness and force; and I believe that I express the wish and purpose of every thoughtful American when I say that this sentence marks for us in the plainest manner the part we should play alike in the arrangement of our domestic affairs and in our exercise of influence upon the affairs of the world.

By this faith, and by this faith alone, can the world be lifted out of its present confusion. . . . It was this faith which prevailed over the wicked force of Germany. You will remember that the beginning of the end of the war came when the German people found themselves face to face with the conscience of the world and realized that right was everywhere arrayed against the wrong that their government was attempting to perpetrate. I think, therefore, that it is true to say that this was the faith which won the war. Certainly this is the faith with which our gallant men went into the field and out upon the seas to make sure of victory.

This is the mission upon which Democracy came into the world. Democracy is an assertion of the right of the individual to live and to be treated justly as against any attempt on the part of any combination of individuals to make laws which will overburden him or which will destroy his equality among his fellows in the matter of right or privilege; and I think we all realize that the day has come when Democracy is being put upon its final test. The Old World is just now suffering from a wanton rejection of the principle of democracy and a substitution of the principle of autocracy as asserted in the name, but without the authority and sanction, of the multitude. This is the time of all others when Democracy should prove its purity and its spiritual power to prevail. It is surely the manifest destiny of the United States to lead in the attempt to make this spirit prevail.

There are two ways in which the United States can assist to accomplish this great object. First, by offering the example within her own borders of the will and power of Democracy to make and enforce laws which are unquestionably just and which are equal in their administration—laws which secure its full right to Labor and yet at the same time safeguard the integrity of property, and particularly of that property which is devoted to the development of industry and the increase of the necessary wealth of the world. Second, by standing for right and justice as toward individual nations. The law of Democracy is for the protection of the weak, and the influence of every democracy in the world should be for the protection of the weak nation, the nation which is struggling toward its right and toward its proper recognition and privilege in the family of nations.

The United States cannot refuse this role of champion without putting the stigma of rejection upon the great and devoted men who brought its government into existence and established it in the face of almost universal opposition and intrigue, even in the face of wanton force, as, for example, against the Orders in Council of Great Britain and the arbitrary Napoleonic decrees which involved us in what we know as the War of 1812.

I urge you to consider that the display of an immediate disposition on the part of the Congress to remedy any injustices or evils that may have shown themselves in our own national life will afford the most effectual offset to the forces of chaos and tyranny which are playing so disastrous a part in the fortunes of the free peoples of more than one part of the world. The United States is of necessity the sample democracy of the world, and the triumph of Democracy depends upon its success. . . .

29

Warren G. Harding

1. ON THE RACE QUESTION   **APRIL 12, 1921**

. . . Congress ought to wipe the stain of barbaric lynching from the banners of a free and orderly, representative democracy. We face the fact that many millions of people of African descent are numbered among our population of the total population. It is unnecessary to recount the difficulties incident to this condition, nor to emphasize the fact that it is a condition which cannot be removed. There has been suggestion, however, that some of its difficulties might be ameliorated by a humane and enlightened consideration of it, a study of its many aspects, and an effort to formulate, if not a policy, at least a national attitude of mind calculated to bring about the most satisfactory possible adjustment of relations between the races, and of each race to the national life. One proposal is the creation of a commission embracing representatives of both races, to study and report on the entire subject. The proposal has real merit. I am convinced that in mutual tolerance, understanding, charity, recognition of the interdependence of the races, and the maintenance of the rights of citizenship lies the road to righteous adjustment. . . .

2. OUR ONENESS AS AMERICANS   **OCTOBER 26, 1921**

. . . The World War brought us to full recognition that the race problem is national rather than merely sectional. There are no authentic statistics, but it is common knowledge that the World War was marked by a great migration of colored people to the North and West. They were attracted by the demand for labor and the higher wages offered. . . . It has made the South realize its industrial dependence on the labor of the black man and made the North realize the difficulties of the community in which two greatly differing races are brought to live side by side. I should say that it has been responsible for a larger charity on both sides, a beginning of a better understanding; and in the light of that better understanding perhaps we shall be able to consider this problem together as a problem of all sections and of both races, in whose solution the best intelligence of both must be enlisted.

Indeed we will be wise to recognize it as wider yet . . . our race problem in the United States is only a phase of a race issue that the whole world confronts. Surely we shall gain nothing by blinking the facts. . . .

I can say to you people of the South, both white and black, that the time has passed when you are entitled to assume that this problem of races is peculiarly and particularly your problem. More and more it is becoming a problem of the North; more and more it is the problem of Africa, of South America, of the Pacific, of the South Seas, of the world. It is the problem of democracy everywhere. . . .

The one thing we must sedulously avoid is the development of group and class organizations in this country. There has been time when we heard too much about the labor vote, the business vote, the Irish vote, the Scandinavian vote, the Italian vote and so on. But the demagogues who would array class against class and group against group have fortunately found little to reward their efforts. That is because, despite the demagogues, the idea of our oneness as Americans has risen superior to every appeal to mere class or group.

3. OUR NATIONAL GOOD FORTUNE   DECEMBER 6, 1921

It is a very gratifying privilege to come to the Congress with the Republic at peace with all the nations of the world. More, it is equally gratifying to report that our country is not only free from every impending menace of war, but there are growing assurances of the permanency of the peace which we so deeply cherish.

For approximately ten years we have dwelt amid menaces of war or as participants in war's actualities, and the inevitable aftermath, with its disordered conditions, has added to the difficulties of government. . . . Our tasks would be less difficult if we had only ourselves to consider, but so much of the world was involved, the disordered conditions are so well-nigh universal, even among nations not engaged in actual warfare, that no permanent readjustments can be effected without consideration of our inescapable relationship to world affairs in finance and trade. Indeed, we should be unworthy of our best traditions if we were unmindful of social, moral, and political conditions which are not of direct concern to us, but which do appeal to the human sympathies and the very becoming interest of a people blest with our national good fortune.

It is not my purpose to bring to you a program of world restoration. In the main such a program must be worked out by the nations more directly concerned. They must themselves turn to the heroic remedies for the menacing conditions under which they are struggling, then we can help, and we mean to help. We shall do so unselfishly because there is compensation in the consciousness of assisting, selfishly because the commerce and international exchanges in trade, which marked our high tide of fortunate advancement, are possible only when the nations of all continents are restored to stable order and normal relationship.

In the main the contribution of this Republic to restored normalcy in the world must come through the initiative of the executive branch of the Government, but the best of intentions and most carefully considered purposes would fail utterly if the sanction and the cooperation of Congress were not cheerfully accorded. . . .

Encroachment upon the functions of Congress or attempted dictation of its policy are not to be thought of, much less attempted, but there is an insistent call for harmony of purpose and concord of action to speed the solution of the difficult problems confronting both the legislative and executive branches of the Government. . . .

There is vastly greater security, immensely more of the national viewpoint, much larger and prompter accomplishment where our divisions are along party lines, in the broader and loftier sense, than to divide geographically, or according to pursuits, or personal following. For a century and a third, parties have been charged with responsibility and held to strict accounting. When they fail, they are relieved of authority; and the system has brought us to a national eminence no less than a world example. . . .

4. DEBS CHRISTMAS PARDON   DECEMBER 25, 1921

The White House Statement on the Christmas Pardon of the Socialist Leader, given out on December 23, in part revealed the reasoning for the presidential action.

. . . there is no question of his guilt and that he actively and purposely obstructed the draft. In fact, he admitted it at the time of his trial, but sought to justify his action. He was by no means, however, as rabid and outspoken in his expressions as many others, and but for his prominence and the resulting far-reaching effect of his words, very probably might not have received the sentence he did. He is an old man, not strong physically. He is a man of much personal charm and impressive personality, which qualifications make him a dangerous man calculated to mislead the unthinking and affording excuse for those with criminal intent.

30

Calvin Coolidge

---

1. THE "SECRET" PRESIDENTIAL PRESS CONFERENCE   APRIL 22, 1927

I have had called to my attention lately the fact that some of the press are beginning to get a little careless about quoting the President as the result of these conferences. It seems that it is necessary to have eternal vigilance to keep that from being done, and to caution the members of the conference against that. Of course, it is a violation of the understanding to say that the spokesman said so and so, and put in quotations on that. I think, by the way, that it would be a good plan to drop that reference to these conferences. It was never authorized in any way that I could determine by the President. It has been used from time to time but it has been used so long and there has been so much reference to it that one might as well say that the President said so and so or the White House spokesman or the official spokesman said so and so.

PRESS: Mr. President, do we understand that the term spokesman is not permissible?

PRESIDENT: It has never been authorized and has been used in a way that it is perfectly apparent that when the word is used it means the President. Now, that need not have been done, but it has been done, and having been done I think it would be better to drop that. . . . What I said about quoting the President in relation to the use of the term as spokesman wasn't said for publication. It was just said for the information of the conference. That part of the conference we will consider carried on in executive session.

PRESS: Have you any formula to suggest?

PRESIDENT: I think your ingenuity will provide you with one. The only thing I am suggesting is that you observe the rule of not quoting the President.

2. HONORING AVIATOR CHARLES LINDBERGH   JUNE 11, 1927

In a national radio broadcast, following the breathtaking transatlantic air crossing of Charles A. Lindbergh, the aviator was honored by President Coolidge.

My Fellow Countrymen: It was in America that the modern art of flying a heavier-than-air machine was first developed. . . .

On a morning just three weeks ago yesterday, this wholesome, earnest, fearless, courageous product of America rose into the air from Long Island in a monoplane christened 'The Spirit of St. Louis' in honor of his home and that of his supporters. It was no haphazard adventure. After months of most careful preparation, supported by a valiant character, driven by an unconquerable will and inspired by the imagination and the spirit of his Viking ancestors, this reserve officer, set wing across the dangerous stretches of the North Atlantic. He was alone. His destination was Paris.

Figure 30.1 Harding and Coolidge with their wives at Union Station, courtesy of the Library of Congress Prints and Photographs Division, Washington, DC.

. . . as President of the United States, I bestow the distinguished flying cross, as a symbol of appreciation for what he is and what he has done, upon Col. Charles A. Lindbergh.

3. FAREWELL SPEECH AT GEORGE WASHINGTON UNIVERSITY   FEBRUARY 22, 1929

. . . Compared with some of the older nations, our holidays are few in number. Being less frequent, they are given a more formal observance. With the possible exception of the Fourth Day of July, none of them on the secular side arouses any more popular interest than the birthday of George Washington. Of course, he is honored for what he did. He was the leader in a successful struggle for independence, which gave him a justified military reputation. He was also the foremost influence in securing the adoption of our Federal Constitution, which gave us a free Republic. Naturally, he was chosen the first President. In this office he brought into practical operation the theories of our National Government, which demonstrated that he was not only a military leader, but a sound and patriotic statesman. In addition to all his public service, he was a man of affairs. He ranks as the best business man of his day. Had there been no Revolutionary War, he would undoubtedly have become the foremost colonial figure of his time.

It is because of his success in so many fields of action that his memory makes such a wide appeal. Wherever men love liberty we find veneration for the name of George Washington. Wherever there are aspirations for a free government, whether already in being or in future expectation, there is admiration for the institutions he established. Wherever purity of character and self-sacrificing public service are admired, his name is honored and revered. Almost alone of the great figures of history, he can be accepted without any qualifications or reservations. Not only is his fame world-wide, but his life is held in universal respect.

In a day when tilling the soil went mostly by the rule of thumb, we find him developing agriculture in a scientific way. While others were speculating, usually at a loss, he was investing in land and making a profit. When the political thought of his day was centered for the most part in each local colony, he had the vision to see and the understanding to comprehend the advantages of a Federal Union. Although his own State of Virginia had a college in his youth, and there were others in the North, with the possible exception of some short studies in surveying he did not attend any of the higher institutions of learning. Yet he became a well-educated man himself, and in many of his public statements, and finally in his will, he was careful to disclose his views on the importance to republican institutions, of Government-supported free schools, and opportunities for higher education.

Here again he showed distinctly that he was nationally minded, because he coupled the personal benefits of a centralized university training with the cultivation of a national spirit in the students. Since his day so many local colleges and State universities have been established that the provisions of his will have never been put into execution. Yet it is a satisfaction to have this institution at least bearing his name in the National Capital. The views which he expressed on the all-important subject of education have that ring of truth and that soundness which makes them apply with the same force to-day as they had when they were uttered.

Although he, like Lincoln, did not have opportunity to take a college degree, yet, like the Great Emancipator, the Father of his Country had the advantage of working with a citizenship which was well permeated with college men, whom he constantly sought for his advisers in positions of responsibility. It should always be remembered that unless many of their associates had secured the liberal education which comes from college training, the career of both Washington and Lincoln would have been utterly impossible. Without well-educated leaders and general diffusion of learning among the people they would have had no success.

Outside of college walls, but usually under the guidance of competent instruction, Washington was a most painstaking and thorough student. He gained the position which he held through application to hard work. By that means his mind became well trained. He knew how to think.

Not only in what Washington said do we find much wise counsel relating to education, but we find even more in the man himself. His life justifies the existence and demonstrates the necessity of institutions for giving to our youth that broad culture which comes from application to a course in the liberal arts. We need men of technical training. They are much more necessary now than they were in the Revolutionary period. We could not maintain our modern life for any length of time without them. Washington himself would be entitled to considerable rank as an engineer in his day. It is necessary for our progress to have individuals who make a life study of one subject to the exclusion of everything else. The danger to them and from them lies in their becoming lost in particulars. While they are wonderfully skilled in their own subject, they often do not comprehend its relation to other subjects.

There would be a place in the world for the soldier and sailor who could see nothing but national defense, a place for the pacifist who would never engage in war and had no comprehension of international relations, for the physicist who had little interest in spiritual ideals, and a place in every large enterprise for the experts in accounting, in production, in transportation, and in merchandising, though they might understand nothing of the broad principles of political economy. But these talents will reach their greatest usefulness only when directed and coordinated by the wisdom of a comprehending executive who may not always know but who rarely fails to understand.

It was in this field that Washington appears to have excelled. He could not have written the Declaration of Independence. Yet, as a statesman he was easily the superior of Jefferson. He could not have prepared the intricate report on manufactures. Yet, he was a far better business man than Hamilton. His words and actions were such that he inspired confidence. The country followed him because it trusted him. They were willing to take his judgment concerning subjects which they did not themselves comprehend. In him was the essence of all great leadership, a power which gives men faith. The people looked on him and believed. They believed in themselves, in their country, and in their future destiny. In that faith they conquered.

It is possible that this kind of talent is born, not made. Yet, as we study the lives of those who have possessed it, we cannot escape the conviction that it is enlarged by rigorous training. The only military experience that Lincoln ever had was a few days' service in the Black Hawk War, to which he always referred with a mixture of amusement. Yet from his early youth we find him constantly employed in the deepest of study trying to learn how to think. Mathematical accuracy was no mere figure of speech with him. His old note papers show that he was engaged in demonstrating his conclusions in accordance with the principles of geometry. When he came to be tried out in a great conflict the dispatches he sent to his armies in the field indicate that his military judgment was unsurpassed by that of any of his generals. When the great Jefferson, master writer brilliantly discoursing on the rights of man, was markedly indifferent to declaring and defending the rights of his countrymen, it was the practical Washington who was bending all his energies to make the rights of man a reality by establishing this Republic under a Federal Constitution.

In all the efforts which our institutions of learning are making to develop science they ought not to fail to put a large emphasis on the development of wisdom. We shall fail, if we put all our endowments, all our honor, and all our efforts into our technical schools and leave unsupported our schools of liberal arts. It will be found just as impossible to secure progress without them as it is to secure civilization without religion.

In addition to the great example of his life, he left a legacy of wise advice and counsel to his fellow countrymen concerning their relations to each other, to their Government, and to their God. As he was about to leave the Army at the close of the Revolutionary War in June, 1783, he issued a letter addressed to the governors of the several States in which he summed up his solicitous interest in the cultivation of good citizenship in the following paragraph:

> I now make it my earnest prayer that God would have you, and the State over which you preside, in His holy protection; that He would incline the hearts of the citizens to cultivate a spirit of subordination and obedience to government; to entertain a brotherly affection and love for one another, for their fellow citizens of the United States at large, and particularly for their brethren who have served in the field; and, finally, that He would most graciously be pleased to dispose us all to do justice, to love mercy, and to demean ourselves with that charity, humility, and pacific temper of mind, which were the characteristics of the Divine Author of our blessed religion, and without an humble imitation of Whose example in these things we can never hope to be a happy Nation.

His better-known Farewell Address contains nothing finer than this simple, direct, but all-embracing admonition. Washington was one of the first in a practical way to conceive of the United States as an independent establishment. Before him it had been a Province. After him it was a Nation. Even following the Revolution there were many people in this country who clung to the old thought that we were a European dependency. If we were not to look to England, then we must look to France. It was the clear belief of Washington that we must look to ourselves. Habits of thought live on. There are still those among us who have an inferiority complex and there are still people in Europe who regard us as a Province. He therefore warned us in his Farewell Address to beware of permanent and political alliances. The phrase entangling alliances is not from him, but from Jefferson.

In the thought of that day an alliance meant the banding together of two or more nations for offensive and defensive purpose against certain other nations either expressed or implied. It was a purely artificial creation. It had no reference to an association of practically all nations in an attempt to recognize their common interests and discharge their common obligations. While we should at all times defend our own independence, and maintain our own sovereignty, we should not forget that all nations as well as all individuals have natural and inalienable rights "of life, liberty and the pursuit of happiness," in the words of Jefferson, and, while we should fail disgracefully in our mission in the world if we did not protect those rights for ourselves, we shall also fail if we do not respect them in others.

This principle was clearly understood by our first President, and, being understood, he did not hesitate to put it into operation. When the French undertook to interfere in our affairs in such a way as to threaten the integrity of our Government, he called them to account. When our own citizens, on the other hand, were resentfully refusing to recognize the rights of English subjects, Washington was equally insistent that our Government and our citizens should faithfully discharge their legal obligations—even to our Tory enemies. The Revolutionary War inevitably left many undecided questions pending between the United States and Great Britain. There was the question of turning over to this country certain outposts. There were also certain boundary disputes which were not adjusted until well into the next century. These in turn were followed by differences concerning fisheries. Of course everyone recalls the difficulties under which we suffered as neutrals during the Napoleonic era, which resulted in the War of 1812. A like experience came to us in the World War. We have also had issues arise, sometimes of a serious and threatening nature, with many other countries. We had them during the early period of our national life and shall undoubtedly continue to have them in the future. Both foreign and domestic affairs will constantly produce new questions for consideration.

Those who feel in a considerable state of alarm, when they learn that there are subjects requiring diplomatic adjustment at the present time would probably be somewhat relieved if they would consider the history of our international relations. So long as we continue as a Nation we shall have such relations. Because there are matters which require adjustment is no reason for grave concern. There are more and more methods by which the certainty increases that they will be composed.

It is possible to say of our foreign relations at the present time that they have rarely been in a more happy condition. The uncertainties which existed south of the Rio Grande have been very relieved. The domestic disorders in Central America are being adjusted with a satisfaction that is almost universal. Even the mouths of those who would rather criticize us than have us do right have been stopped. The recent Pan-American Congress held in Washington exhibited a spirit of friendliness and good will which was most gratifying. Competent and experienced observers have assured me that our relations with South America are on the most satisfactory basis that they have been for 25 years. On the far side of the Pacific our situation is equally satisfactory. We have no important unadjusted problem with the government of any European nation, with the exception of Russia. Outside of that country all the issues that arose, even out of the World War, have been adjusted.

Of course, our citizens meet the citizens of other countries in commercial rivalry in the market places of the world. That will always continue. It is the natural and inevitable result of foreign trade. But it does not raise any issue between our Government and other governments. We believe in a policy of national defense and maintain an Army and a Navy for that purpose. Other countries have similar military establishments. We are committed to the principle of limitation of armaments. The other great powers through the public opinion of their people and the binding obligation of their treaties are more firmly committed to this principle than we are. Each Government is conscientiously seeking to extend this principle. It does not raise any issue among us.

It seems desirable to mention this subject in order that the people of the United States may have my opinion concerning it. We have recently had a national campaign in which, of course, the opposition party was expected to criticize the foreign policy of the Government and suggest that important unsettled issues were gravely interfering with the friendly attitude which we desire to cultivate abroad. In other countries there will be similar campaigns, where the parties out of power will criticize their government in a like manner. There was nothing in our election to indicate that our own country took such statements seriously, and I therefore trust they will not be taken seriously abroad.

For the same reason, our people should not take seriously the campaign utterances of those who may be seeking to supersede the governments in power in other countries. Political utterances of this nature should be carefully differentiated from statements by responsible Government authorities. I should like the people of the United States to know that at the present time there are no questions of importance awaiting settlement between our Government and any of the European Governments with which we have relations. Our Government is on the most cordial and friendly terms with all of them.

Because this is true, there should be an attitude of kindness and good will between our people and all the European people. Whenever we see statements constantly made and seriously entertained concerning the conduct and intentions of our Government likely to prejudice it at home or abroad, there comes a time when a candid presentation of the facts is required to promote a state of better understanding. Such an expression is entirely different from a constant attitude of fault-finding and hostility toward everything that is foreign. The governments are friendly. The people and the press should be friendly. The respect and confidence of European governments is especially evidenced by the unanimous request, not to say insistence, that citizens of the United States should contribute their assistance and counsel in the effort to make a final adjustment of the problem of reparations.

Of course in past negotiations we have reached conclusions with them through the necessary process of give and take, but their actions have demonstrated that their governments feel that our conduct has been such that they can trust us. After all, the great measure of our standing in the world is determined by whether other nations turn to us for assistance when they have difficulties among themselves. Our very detachment puts us in the position where we are constantly rendering a service to the world which would not otherwise be possible. While we are not associated with any particular foreign group, in the last analysis they all know that they can apply to us when they are in need of friendly offices.

This is the position which I judge Washington wished his country to occupy. While he warned us against alliances with any, he was no less urgent in counseling the maintenance of friendly relations with all. As our strength has increased, as our power to maintain our independent position has grown, the wisdom of his warning and his counsel has become more and more apparent. Some nations are so situated that it has been and is now necessary for them to seek understandings with others in order to perpetuate their own existence. Others have interests so detached and territory so scattered that they can best protect themselves by some method of regional relations. Our situation is such that we are and can remain unhampered by any such necessities. We do not seek isolation for its own sake, or in order that we may avoid responsibility, but we cherish our position of unprejudiced detachment, because through that means we can best meet our world obligations. If we became closely identified with any specific grouping of nations, however advantageous it might be to us, we could not hope to continue to perform that service.

As we study the statesmanship of Washington, as we see it demonstrated in our domestic and foreign experience, he becomes a larger and larger figure. The clearness of his intellect, the soundness of his judgment, the wisdom of his counsel, the disinterested patriotism of his actions, are constantly revealed to us with a new and compelling force.

The reverence for his memory continues to increase. The people of the United States feel that they were exalted in his victory. The people of England feel that even in the defeat of their arms abroad he carried their ideals to victory at home. Such a conquest could not be made save by an exponent of universal truth.

VIII

DEPRESSION AND WAR

HERBERT HOOVER CAME TO THE OVAL OFFICE when America was at high tide. Peace and prosperity were the order of the day. The national mood was giddy. President Hoover seemed to be the man for the moment. Despite the fact that his Democratic opponent, Al Smith, had carried the twelve largest cities of the United States, the result in 1928 constituted a coup for Hoover and an embarrassment for the Happy Warrior. In March 1929 Hoover was inaugurated amidst great joy and jubilation. That coming summer Coolidge and Hoover, along with Frank Kellogg (Coolidge's Secretary of State) gathered together to cheer the renunciation of war in accord with the ratification of the Kellogg–Briand Treaty which had been the work of the Coolidge Administration. The Treaty would turn out to be a warm, fuzzy, international kiss of peace. The American leaders held little stock in the real world value of the Treaty.

Prosperity and confidence would slip from American hands before the year 1929 was out. In the third week of October 1929, the Stock Exchange began to rumble like a volcano, emitting early warnings. On October 24th, prices collapsed. Five days later, on "Black Tuesday," the most catastrophic day in the history of the New York Stock Exchange, billions of dollars were lost in the value of stocks.

The Wall Street Crash thrust President Hoover into unprecedented circumstances. He had inherited the feverish stock speculation on Wall Street. His rise to the White House fueled the speculative fire and raised expectations even higher. The racing exuberance pointed to danger. Sixteen million shares traded on "Black Tuesday." That record volume would not happen again for forty years, until 1969, when Richard Nixon entered the White House.

The economy too was in serious straits. In November, President Hoover proposed a stimulus to get the economy moving. It didn't work. Hoover lacked Federal regulatory powers to control private banks and brokerages and their financial practices. Moreover, his bedrock philosophy of individual responsibility impeded government subsidies or relief measures. In bad times, he believed, the spirit of volunteerism would rally the citizenry to the aid of those temporarily disadvantaged. The following year, as the economy continued to slide, Hoover's party was trounced in the mid-term elections. It was becoming clear that the troubles were not short-term.

In the face of all this bad news, there was a ray of hope. Another miracle came to pass on Thirty-Fourth Street. In defiance of the economic direction, the Empire State Building was completed. Opening day was May 1, 1931. Al Smith and FDR were present for the dedication, and President Hoover turned a switch that evening at the White House and illuminated the great lantern in the sky. It was a fleeting moment of hope in a sea of depression.

As the lights were turned on at the Empire State, darkness fell in Asia. Manchuria was invaded by Japan in September 1931. President Hoover well understood that this Japanese aggression portended trouble for the world. Given the U.S. economy and the overall mood of the country, Hoover could do nothing but sit helplessly at the White House. The national mood was becoming ugly. By 1932 the Great Depression had arrived, and got worse as the year progressed. It would serve as the backdrop for the demise of Hoover and the rise of Franklin D. Roosevelt.

The industrial depression presented the United States with more than an economic crisis, although the economic picture remained thoroughly debilitating. The fact is that the Great Depression was depressing. It seared scars upon the psyche and the soul. President Hoover tried to stem the tide. He did act. Some of his actions provided some relief, but others made things worse. The simple truth is that no one knew what to do. There was a general lack of economic intelligence in the face of this great challenge. Movement in any direction contained the risk that any action could make things worse. There is something within the American dynamic which calls for movement. There is an impulse to do something, even if it is wrong. The presidential leader was expected to act. Hoover did act, but his actions were largely counterproductive, and the people held the impression that he just sat there and did nothing.

As Herbert Hoover neared Election Day of 1932 and the end of his presidency he stoutly affirmed his political principles, even in the face of economic disaster and his own political ruin. At the annual convention of the American Bar Association in Washington three weeks before his loss to Franklin Delano Roosevelt, the President warned against deviation from fixed principles. The ABA received a wake-up call from the Chief Magistrate who alerted the members of the Bar that the country faced a political and intellectual as well as an economic crisis: "our very form of government is on trial."

Employing a poker-playing analogy in a gambling age, Franklin Roosevelt promised to shuffle the cards and give the American people a New Deal. The people liked the idea of changing horses or dealers in the economic quagmire. FDR was elected handsomely in 1932. His election began the interregnum. In the timeframe between the election and Inauguration Day, America was a horse without a rider.

Things got rapidly worse during these leaderless days. Hoover had been repudiated. Roosevelt had not been constitutionally sworn in. Hoover offered to work with him in the crisis. FDR refused, as he thought that would taint him before he began. Alone in the White House, President Hoover contemplated the path America travelled that led to this ditch. His analysis revealed a five-stage process. He decided to keep this document close to his vest for the time being.

In the midst of all of this, shots were fired. An assassin took aim at the President-elect's motorcade in Miami, Florida. Giuseppe Zangara, an out-of-work bricklayer, fired six times. Several people were hit. It was February 15, 1933. The Mayor of Chicago, Anton Cermak, was fatally wounded. He died on March 6th. Theories circulated that the Mayor was the true target on orders from the Chicago underworld. In any event, FDR escaped with his life. The nation was spared the pain of dealing with the violent death of a President-elect at a peak point of economic depression. President Hoover sent a very thoughtful note to the President-elect, saying that he rejoiced that FDR escaped without injury. Five days after the shooting in Miami, President Hoover presided over the cornerstone ceremonies for the new National Archives building in Washington, DC. American history now had a home.

The Hudson River Valley aristocrat and Governor of New York, Franklin Delano Roosevelt, approached the Inauguration stand to be sworn in as the 32nd President of the United States. A familiar figure in state and national politics since 1910, the 50-year-old FDR had suffered a crippling attack of polio in 1921. Although he would never walk unaided again, few Americans realized the extent of his disability. The nation itself now suffered from an economic paralysis. Unemployment had topped thirteen million as industry functioned at less than half the capacity of just four years previously. All banks had closed and most financial transactions had ceased. Helplessness infected the American spirit. The nation and the world waited upon the new President's words.

FDR did not disappoint his listeners. He spoke candidly and boldly to the distressed nation. "This is preeminently the time to speak the truth, the whole truth, frankly and boldly. . . . This Great Nation will endure as it has endured, will revive and will prosper." Taking a page as he regularly did from this cousin Theodore Roosevelt, he confronted the fear tearing at the heart of the nation. He defiantly declared against this national trepidation or "fear itself—nameless, unreasoning, unjustified terror which paralyzes needed efforts to convert retreat into advance."

On Sunday evening, March 12, 1933, just eight days after his inauguration, President Roosevelt spoke to a national audience estimated at sixty million listeners. National radio hookups emerged in the 1920s, but had hardly been used by Roosevelt's predecessors. This first "fireside chat" identified the new president as a master of radio communication. His resonant and comforting tone of voice, use of the familiar "my friends," and manner of confidence made this mass public event somehow seem personal and intimate. All across the nation, in homes and shops and schools and taverns, the great audience listened attentively to the President's assurances. His principal theme was the banking system and the national panic produced by bank failures. The fireside chat succeeded in restoring confidence that America's banks were now safe. The next morning, as reported by newspapers from around the nation, long lines formed at re-opened banks. The American people deposited their money in banks validated by their leader.

Once the banking system had been secured, it remained to grant a measure of financial security to the cruelest victims of the Depression, the nation's aged poor. In the 1930s there were few established provisions for the countless men and women in their fifties and sixties whose working days ended abruptly with the economic collapse. This generation of Americans had gone to work at the turn of the century, when care in old age remained exclusively a family concern. Earlier generations of mostly rural Americans would conventionally retire to their children's homes, the family providing for its own. Now, in a new America where over half the population relied on wages and lived in cities, sustenance depended on a payroll check. Meager local relief resources, like space in "poorhouses," scarcely met the new conditions of mass poverty.

The first New Deal of the Roosevelt Administration was devised to save the banking and corporate structure. It was a rescue mission to save American capitalism and the system. Radical notions arose on the political left to address the social-economic calamity. One came from California and Dr. Francis E. Townsend's Old Age Revolving Pensions plan. Each month, Townsend calculated, the government would pay all citizens over the age of sixty, $200. The one provision was that they spend it immediately. The Townsend pension formula not only would provide needed relief, comfort, and security to the nation's elderly, but offered the added feature of buoying the economy by way of a collective surge of spending. The injection of massive spending into the economic bloodstream would carry with it a multiplier effect towards breathing new life into the dormant economy. The Townsend Plan attracted widespread support so that by early 1935, Dr. Townsend claimed 3.5 million adherents.

Another radical challenge emerged in the American South. The remarkable Louisiana Governor Huey P. Long ran a successful campaign for the United States Senate in 1930. Two years later he backed FDR for President believing that the promised New Deal would redistribute the nation's wealth. Once disabused of this notion, Senator Long launched his "Share Our Wealth Society." Senator Long had cultivated a national following and "Share Our Wealth" clubs sprouted all across the country. His lavish promises would, or so he claimed, restore prosperity and support all poor people by taxing the rich. The Louisiana Democrat was a force to be reckoned with on the political front. With seven or eight million supporters and national recognition, "The Kingfish" set his sights on a challenge to the New Deal and Franklin D. Roosevelt in the presidential sweepstakes of 1936. In a meeting with the President in the Oval Office, witnessed by James Farley, Long confronted Roosevelt in a head-to-head standoff. Farley felt there was something wrong the moment Long entered the room. At first he didn't quite know what it was and then he suddenly realized that Long had not removed his hat. During the course of the conversation between the rival Democrats, Long would remove his straw boater periodically only to bang it on the President's paralyzed legs to make a point. This serious threat from the Democratic Solid South and throughout the nation to President Roosevelt was put to rest by an assassin's bullet which fatally wounded Senator Long at the Louisiana Capitol in 1935.

A third threat to the Roosevelt Administration surfaced in Detroit, Michigan. There the popular radio priest, Father Charles E. Coughlin had, like Long, been a loyal supporter of FDR in his 1932 election. Once the New Deal had been unveiled in the first "hundred days" of the administration, Father Coughlin felt betrayed and blasted the President and the New Deal over the radio via the National Broadcasting Corporation. It is curious that the President, Father Coughlin, and Senator Long were all masters of the new medium. The President artfully employed it to advance the New Deal, while Coughlin and Long were passionate radio orators who lampooned the New Deal to vast listening audiences. These radio critics contended that the New Deal failed to provide effective solutions for the economic crisis and did not attempt to redistribute the wealth to the American people.

The President felt the heat. He was sandwiched. On one end he was taunted by a political right which did not appreciate his efforts to save banks, business, and the American economic and political systems. From the left he was bombarded by forces contending that his New Deal did not satisfy the needs of the hour and shorted the American people. As the 1936 election neared, the clever incumbent politician felt the pulse of the nation and pivoted to the left. There followed what historians have labeled the "Second New Deal." The centerpiece of this would be the Social Security Act. It was Roosevelt's answer to the California doctor. It also went a long way towards silencing the voices of protest from the supporters of Father Coughlin. For the most part, this legislation was the brainchild of fellow New Yorker, Senator Robert F. Wagner, Sr. The legislation proved to be immensely popular from its inception, and henceforth became the untouchable third rail of American politics.

The Social Security Act, signed by President Roosevelt on August 15, 1935, depended upon moneys raised by taxing both employers and employees to create a fund to support a number of purposes. The Social Security program included pensions for the aged, joint federal-state initiatives of unemployment insurance, and provisions for dependent poor children and for the physically handicapped. The coverage assumed responsibility for citizens over the age of 65 not otherwise provided for. Critics favoring more generous and comprehensive coverage pointed out the weakness of the Roosevelt approach. Benefits beginning in 1942 were relatively slight. Many categories of workers were not covered, and the taxes imposed were both regressive and deflationary. Critics from the opposite direction cited the traditional American reliance on personal responsibility. President Roosevelt correctly assumed that Social Security would grow in size and proceeds over time. One of the lasting achievements of the New Deal, Social Security represented a fundamental shift with respect to the welfare of American society. It would also prove to be an enormous vote getter in 1936.

The election of 1936 proved to be a complete rout of the Democrats over the Republicans and a landslide victory of major proportions for FDR. He had demolished Republican Alf Landon,

Governor of Kansas, by 523 to 8 in the Electoral College. He carried every state but two and won over 60 percent of the popular vote. His victory produced a 76 to 16 Democratic margin in the Senate, and a Democratic House by 331 to 89. In an exit poll, one voter explained his vote for Roosevelt saying that he was the only president the nation ever had who understood that "my boss was an SOB." The campaign had been a class war waged against the wealthy upper-crust. FDR had undercut his critics on the left by tacking into the wind and absorbing their issues and arguments.

Emboldened by his landslide re-election, President Roosevelt soon committed the worst political blunder of his distinguished career. With his power and prestige soaring in the wake of his historic win, FDR miscalculated. In a surprise move, he suddenly turned against the most formidable opponent of his New Deal legislation, the Supreme Court of the United States. The Court had cannibalized the New Deal, declaring central pieces as unconstitutional, inviting the wrath of the President. During his first term, nine major New Deal initiatives had been declared unconstitutional. The National Labor Board and the Social Security Act were threatened with the same fate under the high tribunal's gavel.

The President acted on February 5, 1937 by announcing his plan to "reform" the Court. Every one of the nine members of the Supreme Court had been appointed by his predecessors. Towards the end of his tenure as Chief Justice of the United States, former President Taft consulted his crystal ball and foresaw the return of the Democrats to national power. Consequently he warned his fellow Justices: "If any of you die, I'll disown you." Taft himself did die in March of 1930 enabling President Hoover to appoint his successor. For the prestigious post Hoover turned to another former Governor of New York State and Republican presidential candidate in 1916, Charles Evans Hughes.

FDR was disingenuous about his reasons for submitting his "Reorganization of the Judiciary Bill." He said he sought to ease the heavy workload of the six justices who were over 70 by appointing a new man for the court up to the total maximum membership of fifteen, in the event they decided not to retire. This radical trial balloon never left the ground. Political and popular reaction stunned the President. Even his Vice President John Nance Garner had given the proposal the thumbs down, as did many Congressional Democrats. One Democratic Senator blasted the bill by saying: "it was more power that a good man should want or a bad man should have."

Conservative politicians from both sides of the aisle, constitutional scholars, and newspapers from across the country— all were unanimous in their revulsion at tinkering with this basic American institution. The debate in Congress soon convinced the President to abandon an obviously lost cause. The defeat proved costly. Roosevelt's legislative program stalled through the second term. The Court fight demonstrated that the President could be beaten. The high tide of the New Deal had come and gone and Roosevelt would not regain his political preeminence until the glory days of World War II.

The battle over the Court had a nasty aftermath. A vindictive streak surfaced in the President's leadership style in 1938. It wasn't very pretty. President Roosevelt engaged in an attempted "political purge" of Democrats who had not backed him in his "Court Packing" scheme the previous year. The purge of the disloyal proved a second humiliation and embarrassment for the President for it was almost a total failure. Democratic targets who survived the President's vendetta in the midterm elections of 1938 were now disposed towards a developing foggy-bottom gridlock that a famous political scientist would dub the "deadlock of democracy." For all practical purposes the waning of the New Deal had begun.

On September 3, 1939, two days after Germany's invasion of Poland began World War II, President Roosevelt spoke to the American people. "This nation will remain a neutral nation," he assured Americans, "but I cannot ask that every American remain neutral in thought as well." Both friend and foe understood perfectly well that the President supported Great Britain and the other enemies of Nazi Germany. Beginning with his January 4, 1939 State of the Union message, Roosevelt had sought to warn Americans of the mounting danger to democracy itself. Through the months immediately preceding the war, he worked toward balancing power. Thus in the summer of 1939, the President won modification of the prevailing ban on American arms sales, and abrogated a longstanding trade agreement with Japan. Yet when World War II began on September 1, 1939, Germany and Japan enjoyed huge military advantages.

In the twenty-six months which remained before the Japanese attack on Pearl Harbor brought the United States officially into the war, and despite substantial political obstacles, the imaginative and resourceful Roosevelt found means just short of war to assist the beleaguered British. The President faced considerable domestic opposition. Isolationist conviction had developed from the bleakness of the Depression as well as through a popular belief that entering World War I had been a major blunder.

Furthermore, Roosevelt had decided to run for a third term, and could not afford to move too dramatically. Rash moves could pinch his political coalition. Yet through 1940 and 1941, the association of the United States with the British became evident. "Cash and carry" and "Lend-Lease" entered the American vocabulary. Secretly the plans discussed by Roosevelt and British Prime Minister Winston Churchill, and the frequently increasing contacts between their military staffs, made the United States a virtual ally of Britain. The Lend-Lease arrangement, one memorable element of Roosevelt's maneuvering through this crisis, presented the Congress with an unlikely scenario in the beguiling rhetoric of Roosevelt at his dramatic best. In March 1941, FDR had his way with the lawmakers. The Senate approved the plan, 60 to 31; and the House of Representatives, 260 to 165. That June, President Roosevelt reported on the extent and importance of American assistance in carrying on the resistance to the Axis powers.

The United States retained official neutrality in the face of what was clearly this virtual alliance with Great Britain. The Lend-Lease program had been activated and aid began to flow in abundance to Great Britain. The next obvious stage tightening the bond was for the leaders of the two nations to meet and develop a blueprint for the future. President Roosevelt and Prime Minister Churchill did meet in a secret conference at sea that summer of 1941. The Prime Minister arrived for the Atlantic meeting aboard the *HMS Prince of Wales*. President Roosevelt and his staff sailed on the *USS Augusta* where he received Churchill in Placentia Bay off the coast of Newfoundland. There in the North Atlantic the two leaders established an eight-point agreement of war aims. This compact of principles comprised their joint vision of the postwar future. Later this agreement would be famously known as the Atlantic Charter.

Throughout the summer and fall of 1941 President Roosevelt conducted, without the knowledge of either the Congress or the American people, an undeclared war in the North Atlantic. He also moved to protect American interests in the Pacific arena. On July 25, 1941, in response to the Japanese seizure of French Indochina, President Roosevelt froze all Japanese assets in the United States, halting trade and denying access to Japan of strategic materials necessary for her industrial base. While Japanese diplomats pledged to seek a peaceful resolution to the intensifying hostility between the two nations, the Japanese Imperial Government concentrated on war strategy.

Early in November the American Embassy in Tokyo reported on plans for a sneak attack on undetermined American military bases. Realizing that only American naval power stood in the way of its own great imperial design, Japan struck. On Sunday morning, December 7th, just before 8 a.m., an aircraft carrier-based armada transported Japanese planes to within striking distance, and from that location the Empire of Japan surprised the U.S. fleet assembled at Pearl Harbor on the Hawaiian island of Oahu. Nineteen ships (including six battleships) were sunk or disabled. Excepting only American aircraft carriers which had previously set sail, the Pacific Fleet had been destroyed. The Japanese sneak attack had also destroyed 150 American planes and killed 2,403 soldiers, sailors, and civilians. It was an infamous attack and awoke a sleeping giant.

The next day President Roosevelt appeared before a joint session of Congress, denounced the treachery of Imperial Japan, and asked for a declaration of war. The United States Senate approved the war motion unanimously, 82 to 0. The motion carried in the House of Representatives by a margin of 388 to 1. The sole dissident, Rep. Jeannette Rankin of Montana, the first woman ever to sit in the House, had also voted against American entry in the Great War in 1917. The vote gave the President the power to utilize his Constitutional authority as Commander-in-Chief. FDR became Dr. Win the War. The war objective became unconditional surrender by all military enemies of the United States.

31

Herbert Hoover

1. VISION OF PROSPERITY   **MARCH 4, 1929**

This occasion is not alone the administration of the most sacred oath which can be assumed by an American citizen. It is a dedication and consecration under God to the highest office in service of our people. I assume this trust in the humility of knowledge that only through the guidance of Almighty Providence can I hope to discharge its ever-increasing burdens.

It is in keeping with tradition throughout our history that I should express simply and directly the opinions which I hold concerning some of the matters of present importance.

. . . If we survey the situation of our Nation both at home and abroad, we find many satisfactions; we find some causes for concern. We have emerged from the losses of the Great War and the reconstruction following it with increased virility and strength. From this strength we have contributed to the recovery and progress of the world. What America has done has given renewed hope and courage to all who have faith in government by the people. In the large view, we have reached a higher degree of comfort and security than ever existed before in the history of the world. Through liberation from widespread poverty we have reached a higher degree of individual freedom than ever before. The devotion to and concern for our institutions are deep and sincere. We are steadily building a new race—a new civilization great in its own attainments. The influence and high purposes of our Nation are respected among the peoples of the world. We aspire to distinction in the world, but to a distinction based upon confidence in our sense of justice as well as our accomplishments within our own borders and in our own lives. For wise guidance in this great period of recovery the Nation is deeply indebted to Calvin Coolidge. . . .

The election has again confirmed the determination of the American people that regulation of private enterprise and not Government ownership or operation is the course rightly to be pursued in our relation to business. In recent years we have established a differentiation in the whole method of business regulation between the industries which produce and distribute commodities on the one hand and public utilities on the other. In the former, our laws insist upon effective competition; in the latter, because we substantially confer a monopoly by limiting competition, we must regulate their services and rates. The rigid enforcement of the laws applicable to both groups is the very base of equal opportunity and freedom from domination for all our people, and it is just as essential for the stability and prosperity of business itself as for the protection of the public at large. Such regulation should be extended by the Federal Government within the limitations of the Constitution and only when the individual States are without power to protect their citizens through their own authority. . . .

Figure 31.1 Chief Justice William H. Taft administering the oath of office to Herbert Hoover on the east portico of the U.S. Capitol, March 4, 1929, courtesy of the Library of Congress Prints and Photographs Division, Washington, DC.

Figure 31.2 Herbert Hoover, Opening Game, 1929. Courtesy of the Library of Congress Prints and Photographs Division, Washington, DC.

Ours is a land rich in resources, stimulating in its glorious beauty, filled with millions of happy homes, blessed with comfort and opportunity. In no nation are the institutions of progress more advanced. In no nation are the fruits of accomplishment more secure. In no nation is the government more worthy of respect. No country is more loved by its people. I have an abiding faith in their capacity, integrity, and high purpose. I have no fears for the future of our country. It is bright with hope. . . .

2. THE CHIEF COMMENTS ON THE CRASH   NOVEMBER 5, 1929

I thought perhaps you might like that I discuss the business situation with you just a little, but not from the point of view of publication at all—simply for your own information. I see no particular reasons for making any public statements about it, either directly or indirectly.

The question is one somewhat of analysis. We have had a period of over-speculation that has been extremely widespread, one of those waves of speculation that are more or less uncontrollable, as evidenced by the efforts of the Federal Reserve Board, and that ultimately results in a crash due to its own weight. That crash was perhaps a little expedited by the foreign situation, in that one result of this whole phenomenon has been the congestion of capital in the loan market in New York in the driving up of money rates all over the world.

The foreign central banks having determined that they would bring the crisis to an end, at least so far as their own countries were concerned, advanced money rates very rapidly in practically every European country in order to attract capital that had drifted from Europe into New York, back into their own industry and commerce. Incidentally, the effect of increasing discount rates in Europe is much greater on their business structure than it is with us. Our business structure is not so sensitive to interest rates as theirs is. So their sharp advancement of discount rates tended to affect this market, and probably expedited or even started this movement. But once the movement has taken place we have a number of phenomena that rapidly develop. The first is that the domestic banks in the interior of the United States, and corporations, withdraw their money from the call market.

There has been a very great movement out of New York into the interior of the United States, as well as some movement out of New York into foreign countries. The incidental result of that is to create a difficult situation in New York, but also to increase the available capital in the interior. In the interior there has been, in consequence, a tendency for interest rates to fall at once because of the unemployed capital brought back into interior points.

Perhaps the situation might be clearer on account of its parallel with the last very great crisis, 1907–1908. In that crash the same drain of money immediately took place into the interior. In that case there was no Federal Reserve System. There was no way to acquaint of capital movement over the country, and the interest rates ran up to 300 percent. The result was to bring about a monetary panic in the entire country.

Here, with the Federal Reserve System and the activity of the Board, and the ability with which the situation has been handled, there has been a complete isolation of the stock market phenomenon from the rest of the business phenomena in the country. The Board, in cooperation with the banks in New York, has made ample capital available for the call market in substitution of the withdrawals. This has resulted in a general fall of interest rates, not only in the interior, but also in New York, as witness the reduction of the discount rate. So that instead of having a panic rise in interest rates with monetary rise following it, we have exactly the reverse phenomenon—we have a fallen interest rate. That is the normal thing to happen when capital is withdrawn from the call market through diminution in values.

The ultimate result of it is a complete isolation of the stock market phenomenon from the general business phenomenon. In other words the financial world is functioning entirely normal and rather more easily today than it was 2 weeks ago, because interest rates are less and there is more capital available.

The effect on production is purely psychological. So far there might be said to be from such a shock some tendency on the part of people through alarm to decrease their activities but there has been no cancellation of any orders whatsoever. There has been some lessening of buying in some of the luxury contracts, but that is not a phenomenon itself.

The ultimate result of the normal course of things would be that with a large release of capital from the speculative market there will be more capital available for the bond and mortgage market. That market has been practically starved for the last 4 or 5 months. There has been practically no— or very little at least—of mortgage or bond money available, practically no bond issues of any consequence. One result has been to create considerable reserves of business. A number of States have not been able to place their bonds for construction; a number of municipalities with bond issues have been held up because of the inability to put them out at what they considered fair rates. There are a great number of business concerns that would proceed with their activities in expansion through mortgage and bond money which have had to delay. All of which comprises a very substantial reserve in the country at the present time. The normal result will be for the mortgage and bond market to spring up again and those reserves to come in with increased activities.

The sum of it is, therefore, that we have gone through a crisis in the stock market, but for the first time in history the crisis has been isolated to the stock market itself. It has not extended into either the production activities of the country or the financial fabric of the country, and for that I think we may give the major credit to the constitution of the Federal Reserve System. And that is about a summary of the whole situation as it stands at this moment.

3. HOOVER DEFENDS POLITICAL PRINCIPLES   OCTOBER 12, 1932

. . . Today, perhaps as never before, our very form of government is on trial in the eyes of millions of our citizens. Economic stresses of unparalleled magnitude have wracked our people, and in their distress some are tempted to lay the blame for their troubles upon the system of government under which they live. It is a not unnatural instinct however mistaken it may be. It can be a dangerous thing, if wise and trusted men fail to explain to the people how often in history the people's interests have been betrayed by false prophets of a millennium, promised through seductive but unworkable and disastrous theories of government. The menace is doubled by the fact that these vain allurements are today being offered to our harassed people by men of public reputation in economics and even by men in public life. No man can foretell to what lengths the pressure of public clamor may at any time be brought to bear upon those charged with the processes of government to yield to changes which you know, before they are tried, would destroy personal liberty and sweep away the security of savings and wages built up by centuries of experience. All progress and growth is a matter of change, but change must be growth within our social and governmental concepts if it should not destroy them.

You have your duty in this area to expound the history of the painful past through which rights and liberties have been won, to warn of repetitions of old and fatal experiments under new and glamorous names, to defend our system of government against reckless assaults of designing persons. It is your task to prove again what none knows better than you, that the very citadel of the rights of the poor against the oppression of rulers and against the extortions of the rapacious is the judicial system of the country, and that the impregnable apex of that system is the Supreme Court of the United States. It is impregnable because its membership in successive generations down to this moment has comprised the highest character of our land who, preserving its great traditions, have armored it with the moral support of the people, and thus, without physical power or the need of it, is able to stand equal and alone against legislative encroachment upon the people's rights or executive usurpation of them, and, more precious than either, against private injustice and the enactment of public laws in violation of the fundamental protections of the Constitution.

These deviations from steadfast constitutional limitations, which I have last named, are of paramount significance in these times of growth and change. The last 50 years have witnessed a progress in expansion of business and industry unmatched in any five centuries of previous history. The United States has been in the forefront of this progress. Inventions in transportation, communications, and factory production have multiplied the conveniences of life and have widened the fields of human intercourse immeasurably. Economic forces have spread business across State lines and have brought new strains upon our Federal system in its relationships with the State sovereignties. Laws that once were adequate to control private operations affecting the public interest proved unequal to these new conditions. Regulation and control were more than ever necessary. In the readjustment of Federal laws to State laws required by this situation, the Supreme Court has played a part of incalculable practical value. Without its prestige, without its independence, without its wisdom and power, these delicate alterations could not have been effected except at tremendous costs of injury to our people and of excessive disturbance of political equilibrium. But for the success with which this transition to large Federal regulation over interstate commerce was accomplished, the development of our great system of economic production would have been delayed, individual rights would have been trampled down, and our system of State authorities within the Union of Federal Government could scarcely have survived with all its values of local control of local issues.

We have long recognized that certain functions in our economic life are affected with public interest, which requires that their activities shall be in some measure controlled by government, either State or Federal, in protection of the citizens. In that situation we have sought to find a bridge between these controls and the maintenance of that initiative and enterprise which assures the conduct and expansion and perfection of these functions.

One of the great good fortunes of our form of government is that in the 48 States we have 48 laboratories of social and economic experimentation. But, as I have said, many of these activities—particularly those of banking and finance, of transportation, communications, and power—have expanded beyond State borders. It has become necessary during these years to develop a gradually increasing burden of Federal control. With growth and experience, these regulatory functions require constant revision. On the one hand that we may prevent wrongdoing and give justice and equality of opportunity to our people, and on the other that we should not stifle these vital functions and services through the extinction of that enterprise and initiative which must dominate a growing organism.

And here lies also one of the most delicate relations of our Republic. We must maintain on the one hand a sense of responsibility in the States. It is the local communities that can best safeguard their liberties. We must therefore impose upon the States the maximum responsibility in these regulatory powers over economic functions. It may be even necessary in the long view of the Republic that the people of some States whose governments are negligent of the interests of their own people should be inadequately protected rather than destroy the initiative and responsibility of local communities and of all States and undermine the very foundations of local government.

On the other hand, we must be courageous in providing for extension of these regulatory powers when they run beyond the capacity of the States to protect their citizens.

In the ebb and flow of economic life our people in times of prosperity and ease naturally tend to neglect the vigilance over their rights. Moreover, wrongdoing is obscured by apparent success in enterprise. Then insidious diseases and wrongdoings grow apace. But we have in the past seen that in times of distress and difficulty wrongdoing and weakness comes to the surface and our people, in their endeavors to correct these wrongs, are tempted to extremes which may destroy rather than build.

In the separation of responsibilities between the Federal and State Governments on matters outside of the economic field we have constantly to resist the well-meaning reformer who, witnessing the failure of local communities to discharge responsibilities of government, to extinguish crime, and to set up agencies of government free of corruption, to move apace with the thousand social and other advances which the country sorely needs, constantly advocates and agitates that the powers of the Federal Government be applied, that we may have a rigid uniformity of reform throughout the Nation. Yet even here it is better that we should witness some instances of failure of municipal and State governments to discharge responsibilities in protection and government of their people rather than that we should drive this Republic to a centralization which will mean the deadening of its great mainspring of progress which is the discovery and experimentation and advancement by the local community.

Diversity within unity is the essence of government and progress in our country. If we are to preserve the foundations of liberty in the community and the State, just as is true in the case of the individual, we must have room for self-creation and self-development, for it is the sum of these accomplishments which make the progress of the Nation. We must not believe that by guaranteeing the medium of perfection to all individuals, to all communities, to all municipalities and all States, through the deadening hand of centralization, we will secure progress. . . .

4. THE RENUNCIATION OF WAR   JULY 24, 1929

In April 1928, as a result of discussions between our Secretary of State of the United States and the Minister of Foreign Affairs of France, the President directed Secretary Kellogg to propose to the nations of the world that they should enter into a binding agreement as follows:

> Article 1—The high contracting parties solemnly declare in the names of their respective peoples that they condemn recourse to war for the solution of international controversies, and renounce it as an instrument of national policy in their relations with one another.

> Article 2—The high contracting parties agree that the settlement or solution of all disputes or conflicts of whatever nature or of whatever origin they may be, which may arise among them, shall never be sought except by pacific means.

That was a proposal to the conscience and idealism of civilized nations. It suggested a new step in international law, rich with meaning, pregnant with new ideas in the conduct of world relations. It represented a platform from which there is instant appeal to the public opinion of the world as to specific acts and deeds. The magnificent response of the world to these proposals is well indicated by those now signatory to its provisions. Under the terms of the treaty there have been deposited in Washington the ratifications of the 15 signatory nations—that is, Australia, Belgium, Canada,

Czechoslovakia, France, Germany, Great Britain, India, Irish Free State, Italy, Japan, New Zealand, Poland, Union of South Africa, and the United States of America. Beyond this the Treaty has today become effective also with respect to 31 other countries, the Governments of which have deposited with the Government of the United States instruments evidencing their definitive adherence to the Treaty. These countries are: Afghanistan, Albania, Austria, Bulgaria, China, Cuba, Denmark, Dominican Republic, Egypt, Estonia, Ethiopia, Finland, Guatemala, Hungary, Iceland, Latvia, Liberia, Lithuania, the Netherlands, Nicaragua, Norway, Panama, Portugal, Peru, Rumania, Russia, Kingdom of the Serbs, Croats and Slovenes, Siam, Spain, Sweden, and Turkey.

Moreover, according to information received through diplomatic channels, the instruments of definitive adherence of Greece, Honduras, Persia, Switzerland, and Venezuela have been fully completed according to their constitutional methods and are now on the way to Washington for deposit.

I congratulate this assembly, the states it represents, and indeed, the entire world upon the coming into force of this additional instrument of humane endeavor to do away with war as an instrument of national policy and to obtain by pacific means alone the settlement of international disputes. . . . We owe its expansion to the proportions of a treaty open to the entire world and destined, as I most confidently hope, shortly to include among its parties every country of the world. . . .

May I ask you who represent governments which have accepted this Treaty, now a part of their supreme law and their most sacred obligations, to convey to them the high appreciation of the Government of the United States that through their cordial collaboration an act so auspicious for the future happiness of mankind has now been consummated. I dare predict that the influence of the Treaty for the Renunciation of War will be felt in a large proportion of all future international acts. . . .

5. U.S. CHAMBER OF COMMERCE CONFERENCE   DECEMBER 5, 1929

This body represents the industries of the United States. You have been invited to create a temporary organization for the purpose of systematically spreading into industry as a whole the measures which have been taken by some of our leading industries to counteract the effect of the recent panic in the stock market. There has necessarily been some unemployment, starting with the diversion of capital from the channels of business into the speculation, and after the break by some reduction in the demand for luxuries and semi-necessities from those who met with losses. But the large effect was to create undue pessimism, fear, uncertainty, and hesitation in business. These emotions . . . if they had been allowed to run their course would, by feeding on themselves, create difficulties. The American mind is prone to revert to previous occasions when we were much less able to organize to meet such situations.

These are potential difficulties which cannot be cured with words. If we could do so, the merest description of the fundamental stability of our vast organism of production and distribution, touched with the light of the future of the United States, would cure it instantly. The cure for such storms is action; the cure for unemployment is to find jobs.

We have, fortunately, since our previous crashes established the Federal Reserve System. The first step in recovering confidence was made by the powerful effectiveness of that system, and the strong position of the banks, the result of which has been steadily diminishing interest rates, with a smooth and rapid return into the channels of business of the money previously absorbed in the speculative market. This is a reversal of our historic experience and is a magnificent tribute to the

System. Capital is becoming more abundant in all parts of the country, the bond market is growing stronger each day and already public issues held back for months have begun to appear.

The second action necessary to maintain progress was the standard set by leading employers that so far as they were concerned there would be no movement to reduce wages, and a corresponding assurance from the leaders of labor that not only would they use their utmost influence to allay labor conflict, but would also cooperate with the employers in the present situation. These assurances have been given and thereby we not only assure the consuming power of the country but we remove fear from millions of homes.

The third line of action has been to undertake through voluntary organization of industry the continuity and expansion of the construction and maintenance work of the country, so as to take up any slack in employment which arises in other directions. The extension and organization of this work are the purpose of this meeting. The greatest tool which our economic system affords for the establishment of stability is the construction and maintenance work, the improvements and betterments, and general cleanup of plants in preparation for cheaper production and the increased demand of the future. It has long been agreed by both businessmen and economists that this great field of expenditure could, by its acceleration in time of need, be made into a great balance wheel of stability. It is agreed that its temporary speeding up to absorb otherwise idle labor brings great subsequent benefits and no liabilities. A very considerable part of our wage earners are employed directly and indirectly in construction and the preparation of and transportation of its materials. In the inevitable periods when the demand for consumable goods increases and labor is fully employed, the construction and maintenance can slacken and we can actually again gain in stability. No one would advocate the production of consumable goods beyond the daily demand; that in itself only stirs up future difficulty.

I am glad to report that such a program has met with universal approval of all those in responsible positions. Our railways and utilities and many of our larger manufacturers have shown a most distinguished spirit in undertaking to maintain and even to expand their construction and betterment programs. The State, county, and municipal governments are responding in the most gratifying way to the request to cooperate with the Federal Government in every prudent expansion of public works. Much construction work had been postponed during the past few months by reason of the shortage of mortgage money due to the diversion of capital to speculative purposes, which should soon be released.

It is to make this movement systematic in all branches of the industrial world . . . that with the great backlogs which are already assured . . . and the governmental works, you will be able to build up the construction and maintenance activities for 1930 to a higher level than that of 1929. . . .

Another of the great balance wheels of stability is our foreign trade. But in stimulating our exports we should be mainly interested in development work abroad such as roads and utilities, which increase the standards of living of peoples and thus the increased demand for goods from every nation, for we gain in prosperity by a prosperous world, not by displacing others.

All of these efforts have one end—to assure employment and to remove the fear of unemployment.

The very fact that you gentlemen come together for these broad purposes represents an advance in the whole conception of the relationship of business to public welfare. You represent the business of the United States, undertaking . . . to contribute to the advancement of stability and progress in our economic life. This is a far cry from the arbitrary and dog-eat-dog attitude of the business world of some 30 or 40 years ago. And this is not dictation or interference by the Government with business. It is a request from the Government that you cooperate in prudent measures to solve a national problem. A great responsibility and a great opportunity rest upon the business and economic organization of the country. . . .

Beyond this, a great responsibility for stability and prosperity rests with the whole people. I have no desire to preach. I may, however, mention one good old word—work.

6. DEDICATION OF THE EMPIRE STATE BUILDING   MAY 1, 1931

I most cordially congratulate you and your associates upon the completion of the Empire State Building and the opening of its doors to the service of the public. This achievement justifies pride of accomplishment in everyone who has had any part in its conception and construction and it must long remain one of the outstanding glories of a great city.

7. CORNERSTONE CEREMONY: DEPARTMENT OF JUSTICE   FEBRUARY 19, 1932
    BUILDING

A chief glory of our Nation is our system of laws, made by our own freely chosen representatives and administered by judges who owe their authority to us. With us, justice rests upon the conscience and reason of the people. It can rise no higher than its source in them. That it is in the main efficient in doing justice, preserving the social order, expediting the normal processes of our daily life and restraining evildoers, is truly a glorious achievement of a democracy.

The building that will rise upon this ground will house men and women dedicated to one of the noblest pursuits of the human mind and spirit, the preservation of the majesty of the people's law, the preservation of the people's rights against evildoers and oppressors, the amelioration of those passions which inevitably arise between rival interests and claims.

The primary reason for established government is the preservation of public peace. Law is the foundation stone of organized society. Its enforcement is the primary task of a civilization. Democracy can hope to endure only to the degree that it can find the means of enforcement of its own laws, even against the most powerfully entrenched of its own citizens. Justice in a democracy . . . can act only with the most efficient, honest organization of the enforcement machinery. For this, public officers and equipment are indispensable, but equally indispensable to their success are the self-discipline and cooperation of the people.

In the design of this building we should substitute for the ancient maxim, "Let justice prevail, though the heavens fall," the more modern conception of democracy, "Justice shall prevail, because that is the people's will."

I now lay the cornerstone of the Department of Justice building and dedicate it in the name of the people of the United States.

8. ATTEMPT ON THE LIFE OF THE PRESIDENT-ELECT   FEBRUARY 15, 1933

Together with every citizen I rejoice that you have not been injured. I shall be grateful to you for news of Mayor Cermak's condition.

9. NATIONAL ARCHIVES CORNERSTONE CEREMONY   FEBRUARY 20, 1933

There is an especial significance in this ceremony, coming within 2 days of the celebration of George Washington's Birthday. The soil on which we are standing is part of the original tract acquired by

President Washington for the Nation's Capital. The building which is rising here will house the name and record of every patriot who bore arms for our country in the Revolutionary War, as well as those of all later wars. Further, there will be aggregated here the most sacred documents of our history, the originals of the Declaration of Independence and of the Constitution of the United States. Here will be preserved all the other records that bind State to State and the hearts of all our people in an indissoluble union. The romance of our history will have living habitation here in the writings of statesmen, soldiers, and all the others, both men and women, who have built the great structure of our national life. This temple of our history will appropriately be one of the most beautiful buildings in America, an expression of the American soul. It will be one of the most durable, an expression of the American character.

Devoutly the Nation will pray that it may endure forever, the repository of records of yet more glorious progress in the life of our beloved country. I now lay the cornerstone of the Archives Building and dedicate it in the name of the people of the United States.

10. STAGES OF DEPRESSION   FEBRUARY 21, 1933

. . . How much this whole situation is the result of fear of the policies of the new administration is further indicated by a short review of the five distinct periods in recent economic history.

The first period began with the financial and monetary collapse of Europe in the last half of 1931 culminating in October, bringing contraction of credit and reduction of exports, falling prices of both commodities and securities, followed by great fear and apprehension in the people which was promptly represented by hoarding, bank failures, flight of capital, withdrawal of foreign gold balances, with final interpretation in decreased employment, demoralization of agriculture and general stagnation.

The second period following the approval by Congress of our measures of reconstruction in early February 1932 was a period of sharp recovery over a period between 60 and 90 days; during this period confidence was restored, currency began to return from hoarding, gold shipments abroad were greatly lessened, bank failures practically ceased and the whole country moved upward.

The third period began in April and continued through July. This was a period of a sharp debacle which was brought about in the Democratic House by the same character of proposals we now see again, that is by the original failure of the revenue bill, the failure to reduce expenditures recommended by the Executive with consequent fear that the movement toward balancing the budget would not be successful; the passage of a group of inflationary measures including the Patman Bill, the Goldsborough Bill, etc. The passage of a series of projects which would have required greater issues of government securities than the Treasury could support including the Garner Bills for gigantic public works and unlimited loans by the Reconstruction Corporation, etc. Public confidence was destroyed; hoarding, withdrawal of foreign gold, decrease in employment, falling prices and general economic demoralization took place.

The fourth period began about the adjournment of Congress when it was assured that these destructive measures were defeated and that constructive measures would be held. This period extended from July until October and was a period of even more definite march out of the depression. Employment was increasing at the rate of half a million men a month, bank failures ceased, hoarded currency was flowing back steadily and gold was returning from abroad, car loadings, commodity and security prices and all the other proofs of emergence from the depression were visible to everyone. Fear and despair had again been replaced by hope and confidence.

The fifth period began shortly before election when the outcome became evident, and has lasted until today. I have already recited its events. The causes of this terrible retrogression and fear in this fifth period have an exact parallel in the third period of last spring. The fact that there was no disavowal of the actions of last spring by the Democratic candidates during the campaign lends added color and alarm that the same actions and proposals which are now repeated in this period positively represent the policies of the new administration—and the people are seeking to protect themselves individually but with national damage. The movement forward in recovery of our people is again defeated by precisely the same factors as last spring and again emanating from the Democratic leaders. In the interest of every man, woman and child, the President-elect has, during the past week, been urged by the saner leaders of his own party such as Senator Glass and others, by myself, and by Democratic bankers and economists whom he has called on for advice, to stop the conflagration before it becomes uncontrollable, by announcing firmly and at once that (a) the budget will be balanced even if it means increased taxation; (b) new projects will be so restricted that government bond issues will not in any way endanger stability of government finances; (c) there will be no inflation or tampering with the currency; to which some have added that as the Democratic party coming in with an overwhelming majority in both houses, there can be no excuse for abandonment of Constitutional processes.

The President-elect is the only man who has the power to give assurances which will stabilize the public mind as he alone can execute them. Those assurances should have been given before now but must be given at once if the situation is to be greatly helped. It would allay some fear and panic whereas delay will make the situation more acute.

The present administration is devoting its days and nights to put out the fires or to localize them. I have scrupulously refrained from criticism which is well merited, but have instead been giving repeated assurances to the country of our desire to cooperate and help the new administration.

What is needed, if the country is not to drift into great grief, is the immediate and emphatic restoration of confidence in the future. The resources of the country are incalculable, the available credit is ample but lenders will not lend, and men will not borrow unless they have confidence. Instead they are withdrawing their resources and their energies. The courage and enterprise of the people still exist and only await release from fears and apprehension.

The day will come when the Democratic Party will endeavor to place the responsibility for the events of this Fifth period on the Republican Party. When that day comes I hope you will invite the attention of the American people to the actual truth.

32

Franklin D. Roosevelt

1. FIRST INAUGURAL ADDRESS   **MARCH 4, 1933**

I am certain that my fellow Americans expect that on my induction into the Presidency I will address them with a candor and a decision which the present situation of our Nation impels. This is preeminently the time to speak the truth, the whole truth, frankly and boldly. Nor need we shrink from honestly facing conditions in our country today. This great Nation will endure as it has endured, will revive and will prosper. So, first of all, let me assert my firm belief that the only thing we have to fear is fear itself—nameless, unreasoning, unjustified terror which paralyzes needed efforts to convert retreat into advance. In every dark hour of our national life a leadership of frankness and vigor has met with that understanding and support of the people themselves which is essential to victory. I am convinced that you will again give that support to leadership in these critical days.

In such a spirit on my part and on yours we face our common difficulties. They concern, thank God, only material things. Values have shrunken to fantastic levels; taxes have risen; our ability to pay has fallen; government of all kinds is faced by serious curtailment of income; the means of exchange are frozen in the currents of trade; the withered leaves of industrial enterprise lie on every side; farmers find no markets for their produce; the savings of many years in thousands of families are gone.

More important, a host of unemployed citizens face the grim problem of existence and an equally great number toil with little return. Only a foolish optimist can deny the dark realities of the moment.

Yet our distress comes from no failure of substance. We are stricken by no plague of locusts. Compared with the perils which our forefathers conquered because they believed and were not afraid, we have still much to be thankful for. Nature still offers her bounty and human efforts have multiplied it. Plenty is at our doorstep, but a generous use of it languishes in the very sight of the supply. Primarily this is because rulers of the exchange of mankind's goods have failed through their own stubbornness and their own incompetence, have admitted their failure, and have abdicated. Practices of the unscrupulous money changers stand indicted in the court of public opinion, rejected by the hearts and minds of men.

True they have tried, but their efforts have been cast in the pattern of an outworn tradition. Faced by failure of credit they have proposed only the lending of more money. Stripped of the lure of profit by which to induce our people to follow their false leadership, they have resorted to exhortations, pleading tearfully for restored confidence. They know only the rules of a generation of self-seekers. They have no vision, and when there is no vision the people perish.

The money changers have fled from their high seats in the temple of our civilization. We may now restore that temple to the ancient truths. The measure of the restoration lies in the extent to which we apply social values more noble than mere monetary profit.

Happiness lies not in the mere possession of money; it lies in the joy of achievement, in the thrill of creative effort. The joy and moral stimulation of work no longer must be forgotten in the mad chase of evanescent profits. These dark days will be worth all they cost us if they teach us that our true destiny is not to be ministered unto but to minister to ourselves and to our fellow men.

Recognition of the falsity of material wealth as the standard of success goes hand in hand with the abandonment of the false belief that public office and high political position are to be valued only by the standards of pride of place and personal profit; and there must be an end to a conduct in banking and in business which too often has given to a sacred trust the likeness of callous and selfish wrongdoing. Small wonder that confidence languishes, for it thrives only on honesty, on honor, on the sacredness of obligations, on faithful protection, on unselfish performance; without them it cannot live.

Restoration calls, however, not for changes in ethics alone. This Nation asks for action, and action now.

Our greatest primary task is to put people to work. This is no unsolvable problem if we face it wisely and courageously. It can be accomplished in part by direct recruiting by the Government itself, treating the task as we would treat the emergency of a war, but at the same time, through this employment, accomplishing greatly needed projects to stimulate and reorganize the use of our natural resources.

Hand in hand with this we must frankly recognize the overbalance of population in our industrial centers and, by engaging on a national scale in a redistribution, endeavor to provide a better use of the land for those best fitted for the land. The task can be helped by definite efforts to raise the values of agricultural products and with this the power to purchase the output of our cities. It can be helped by preventing realistically the tragedy of the growing loss through foreclosure of our small homes and our farms. It can be helped by insistence that the Federal, State, and local governments act forthwith on the demand that their cost be drastically reduced. It can be helped by the unifying of relief activities which today are often scattered, uneconomical, and unequal. It can be helped by national planning for and supervision of all forms of transportation and of communications and other utilities which have a definitely public character. There are many ways in which it can be helped, but it can never be helped merely by talking about it. We must act and act quickly.

Finally, in our progress toward a resumption of work we require two safeguards against a return of the evils of the old order: there must be a strict supervision of all banking and credits and investments, so that there will be an end to speculation with other people's money; and there must be provision for an adequate but sound currency.

These are the lines of attack I shall presently urge upon a new Congress, in special session, detailed measures for their fulfillment, and I shall seek the immediate assistance of the several States.

Through this program of action we address ourselves to putting our own national house in order and making income balance outgo. Our international trade relations, though vastly important, are in point of time and necessity secondary to the establishment of a sound national economy. I favor as a practical policy the putting of first things first. I shall spare no effort to restore world trade by international economic readjustment, but the emergency at home cannot wait on that accomplishment.

The basic thought that guides these specific means of national recovery is not narrowly nationalistic. It is the insistence, as a first consideration, upon the interdependence of the various elements in all parts of the United States—a recognition of the old and permanently important manifestation of the American spirit of the pioneer. It is the way to recovery. It is the immediate way. It is the strongest assurance that the recovery will endure.

In the field of world policy I would dedicate this Nation to the policy of the good neighbor—the neighbor who resolutely respects himself and, because he does so, respects the rights of others—the neighbor who respects his obligations and respects the sanctity of his agreements in and with a world of neighbors.

If I read the temper of our people correctly, we now realize as we have never realized before our interdependence on each other; that we cannot merely take but we must give as well; that if we are to go forward, we must move as a trained and loyal army willing to sacrifice for the good of a common discipline, because without such discipline no progress is made, no leadership becomes effective. We are, I know, ready and willing to submit our lives and property to such discipline, because it makes possible a leadership which aims at a larger good. This I propose to offer, pledging that the larger purposes will bind upon us all as a sacred obligation with a unity of duty hitherto evoked only in time of armed strife.

With this pledge taken, I assume unhesitatingly the leadership of this great army of our people dedicated to a disciplined attack upon our common problems.

Action in this image and to this end is feasible under the form of government which we have inherited from our ancestors. Our Constitution is so simple and practical that it is possible always to meet extraordinary needs by changes in emphasis and arrangement without loss of essential form. That is why our constitutional system has proved itself the most superbly enduring political mechanism the modern world has produced. It has met every stress of vast expansion of territory, of foreign wars, of bitter internal strife, of world relations.

It is to be hoped that the normal balance of Executive and legislative authority may be wholly adequate to meet the unprecedented task before us. But it may be that an unprecedented demand and need for un-delayed action may call for temporary departure from that normal balance of public procedure.

I am prepared under my constitutional duty to recommend the measures that a stricken Nation in the midst of a stricken world may require. These measures, or such other measures as the Congress may build out of its experience and wisdom, I shall seek, within my constitutional authority, to bring to speedy adoption.

But in the event that the Congress shall fail to take one of these two courses, and in the event that the national emergency is still critical, I shall not evade the clear course of duty that will then confront me. I shall ask the Congress for the one remaining instrument to meet the crisis—broad Executive power to wage a war against the emergency, as great as the power that would be given to me if we were in fact invaded by a foreign foe.

For the trust reposed in me I will return the courage and the devotion that befit the time. I can do no less.

We face the arduous days that lie before us in the warm courage of national unity; with the clear consciousness of seeking old and precious moral values; with the clean satisfaction that comes from the stern performance of duty by old and young alike. We aim at the assurance of a rounded and permanent national life.

We do not distrust the future of essential democracy. The people of the United States have not failed. In their need they have registered a mandate that they want direct, vigorous action. They

Figure 32.1 FDR statue, courtesy of Ian Wagreich.

Figure 32.1 FDR statue, courtesy of Ian Wagreich.

have asked for discipline and direction under leadership. They have made me the present instrument of their wishes. In the spirit of the gift I take it.

In this dedication of a Nation we humbly ask the blessing of God. May He protect each and every one of us. May He guide me in the days to come.

2. FIRST "FIRESIDE CHAT"   MARCH 12, 1933

I want to talk for a few minutes with the people of the United States about banking—with the comparatively few who understand the mechanics of banking but more particularly with the overwhelming majority who use banks for the making of deposits and the drawing of checks. I want to tell you what has been done in the last few days, why it was done, and what the next steps are going to be. I recognize that the many proclamations from State capitols and from Washington, the legislation, the Treasury regulations, etc., couched for the most part in banking and legal terms, should be explained for the benefit of the average citizen. I owe this in particular because of the fortitude and good temper with which everybody has accepted the inconvenience and hardships of the banking holiday. I know that when you understand what we in Washington have been about I shall continue to have your cooperation as fully as I have had your sympathy and help during the past week.

First of all, let me state the simple fact that when you deposit money in a bank the bank does not put the money into a safe deposit vault. It invests your money in many different forms of credit—bonds, commercial paper, mortgages and many other kinds of loans. In other words, the bank puts your money to work to keep the wheels of industry and of agriculture turning around. A comparatively small part of the money you put into the bank is kept in currency—an amount which in normal times is wholly sufficient to cover the cash needs of the average citizen. In other words, the total amount of all the currency in the country is only a small fraction of the total deposits in all of the banks.

What, then, happened during the last few days of February and the first few days of March? Because of undermined confidence on the part of the public, there was a general rush by a large portion of our population to turn bank deposits into currency or gold, a rush so great that the soundest banks could not get enough currency to meet the demand. The reason for this was that on the spur of the moment it was, of course, impossible to sell perfectly sound assets of a bank and convert them into cash except at panic prices far below their real value.

By the afternoon of 3rd March scarcely a bank in the country was open to do business. . . .

It was then that I issued the proclamation providing for the nationwide bank holiday, and this was the first step in the Government's reconstruction of our financial and economic fabric.

The second step was the legislation promptly and patriotically passed by the Congress confirming my proclamation and broadening my powers so that it became possible in view of the requirement of time to extend the holiday and lift the ban of that holiday gradually. This law also gave authority to develop a program of rehabilitation of our banking facilities. I want to tell our citizens in every part of the Nation that the national Congress—Republicans and Democrats alike—showed by this action a devotion to public welfare and a realization of the emergency and the necessity for speed that it is difficult to match in our history.

The third stage has been the series of regulations permitting the banks to continue their functions to take care of the distribution of food and household necessities and the payment of payrolls.

This bank holiday, while resulting in many cases in great inconvenience, is affording us the opportunity to supply the currency necessary to meet the situation. No sound bank is a dollar worse off than it was when it closed its doors last Monday. Neither is any bank which may turn out not to be in a position for immediate opening. The new law allows the twelve Federal Reserve Banks to issue additional currency on good assets and thus the banks which reopen will be able to meet every legitimate call. The new currency is being sent out by the Bureau of Engraving and Printing in large volume to every part of the country. It is sound currency because it is backed by actual, good assets.

A question you will ask is this: why are all the banks not to be reopened at the same time? The answer is simple. Your Government does not intend that the history of the past few years shall be repeated. We do not want and will not have another epidemic of bank failures.

As a result, we start tomorrow, Monday, with the opening of banks in the twelve Federal Reserve Bank cities—those banks which on first examination by the Treasury have already been found to be all right. This will be followed on Tuesday by the resumption of all their functions by banks already found to be sound in cities where there are recognized clearing houses. That means about 250 cities of the United States.

On Wednesday and succeeding days banks in smaller places all through the country will resume business, subject, of course, to the Government's physical ability to complete its survey. It is necessary that the reopening of banks be extended over a period in order to permit the banks to make applications for necessary loans, to obtain currency needed to meet their requirements and to enable the Government to make common sense checkups.

Let me make it clear to you that if your bank does not open the first day you are by no means justified in believing that it will not open. A bank that opens on one of the subsequent days is in exactly the same status as the bank that opens tomorrow.

I know that many people are worrying about State banks not members of the Federal Reserve System. These banks can and will receive assistance from member banks and from the Reconstruction Finance Corporation. These State banks are following the same course as the National banks except that they get their licenses to resume business from the State authorities, and these authorities have been asked by the Secretary of the Treasury to permit their good banks to open up on the same schedule as the national banks. I am confident that the State Banking Departments will be as careful as the national Government in the policy relating to the opening of banks and will follow the same broad policy.

It is possible that when the banks resume a very few people who have not recovered from their fear may again begin withdrawals. Let me make it clear that the banks will take care of all needs—and it is my belief that hoarding during the past week has become an exceedingly unfashionable pastime. It needs no prophet to tell you that when the people find that they can get their money—that they can get it when they want it for all legitimate purposes—the phantom of fear will soon be laid. People will again be glad to have their money where it will be safely taken care of and where they can use it conveniently at any time. I can assure you that it is safer to keep your money in a reopened bank than under the mattress.

The success of our whole great national program depends, of course, upon the cooperation of the public—on its intelligent support and use of a reliable system.

Remember that the essential accomplishment of the new legislation is that it makes it possible for banks more readily to convert their assets into cash than was the case before. More liberal provision has been made for banks to borrow on these assets at the Reserve Banks and more liberal provision has also been made for issuing currency on the security of these good assets. This currency is not fiat currency. It is issued only on adequate security, and every good bank has an abundance of such security.

. . . There will be, of course, some banks unable to reopen without being reorganized. The new law allows the Government to assist in making these reorganizations quickly and effectively and even allows the Government to subscribe to at least a part of new capital which may be required.

I hope you can see from this elemental recital of what your Government is doing that there is nothing complex, or radical, in the process.

We had a bad banking situation. Some of our bankers had shown themselves either incompetent or dishonest in their handling of the people's funds. They had used the money entrusted to them in speculations and unwise loans. This was, of course, not true in the vast majority of our banks, but it was true in enough of them to shock the people for a time into a sense of insecurity and to put them into a frame of mind where they did not differentiate, but seemed to assume that the acts of a comparative few had tainted them all. It was the Government's job to straighten out this situation and do it as quickly as possible. And the job is being performed.

I do not promise you that every bank will be reopened or that individual losses will not be suffered, but there will be no losses that possibly could be avoided; and there would have been more and greater losses had we continued to drift. I can even promise you salvation for some at least of the sorely pressed banks. We shall be engaged not merely in reopening sound banks but in the creation of sound banks through reorganization.

It has been wonderful to me to catch the note of confidence from all over the country. I can never be sufficiently grateful to the people for the loyal support they have given me in their acceptance of the judgment that has dictated our course, even though all our processes may not have seemed clear to them.

After all, there is an element in the readjustment of our financial system more important than currency, more important than gold, and that is the confidence of the people. Confidence and courage are the essentials of success in carrying out our plan. You people must have faith; you must not be stampeded by rumors or guesses. Let us unite in banishing fear. We have provided the machinery to restore our financial system; it is up to you to support and make it work. . . .

3. SOCIAL SECURITY FOR AMERICA   AUGUST 14, 1933

Today a hope of many years' standing is in large part fulfilled. The civilization of the past hundred years, with its startling industrial changes, has tended more and more to make life insecure. Young people have come to wonder what would be their lot when they came to old age. The man with a job has wondered how long the job would last.

This social security measure gives at least some protection to thirty millions of our citizens who will reap direct benefits through unemployment compensation, through old-age pensions and through increased services for the protection of children and the prevention of ill health.

We can never insure one hundred percent of the population against one hundred percent of the hazards and vicissitudes of life, but we have tried to frame a law which will give some measure of protection to the average citizen and to his family against the loss of a job and against poverty-ridden old age.

This law, too, represents a cornerstone in a structure which is being built but is by no means complete. It is a structure intended to lessen the force of possible future depressions. It will act as a protection to future Administrations against the necessity of going deeply into debt to furnish relief to the needy. The law will flatten out the peaks and valleys of deflation and of inflation. It is, in short, a law that will take care of human needs and at the same time provide for the United States an economic structure of vastly greater soundness.

I congratulate all of you ladies and gentlemen, all of you in the Congress, in the executive departments and all of you who come from private life, and I thank you for your splendid efforts in behalf of this sound, needed and patriotic legislation.

If the Senate and the House of Representatives in this long and arduous session had done nothing more than pass this Bill, the session would be regarded as historic for all time.

4. REORGANIZATION OF THE JUDICIARY AND COURT   FEBRUARY 5, 1937
   PACKING PLAN

I have recently called the attention of the Congress to the clear need for a comprehensive program to reorganize the administrative machinery of the Executive Branch of our Government. I now make a similar recommendation to the Congress in regard to the Judicial Branch of the Government, in order that it also may function in accord with modern necessities.

The Constitution provides that the President "shall from time to time give to the Congress information of the State of the Union, and recommend to their consideration such measures as he shall judge necessary and expedient." No one else is given a similar mandate. It is therefore the duty of the President to advise the Congress in regard to the Judiciary whenever he deems such information or recommendation necessary.

I address you for the further reason that the Constitution vests in the Congress direct responsibility in the creation of courts and judicial offices and in the formulation of rules of practice and procedure. It is, therefore, one of the definite duties of the Congress constantly to maintain the effective functioning of the Federal Judiciary.

The Judiciary has often found itself handicapped by insufficient personnel with which to meet a growing and more complex business. It is true that the physical facilities of conducting the business of the courts have been greatly improved, in recent years, through the erection of suitable quarters, the provision of adequate libraries and the addition of subordinate court officers. But in many ways these are merely the trappings of judicial office. They play a minor part in the processes of justice. . . .

The simple fact is that today a new need for legislative action arises because the personnel of the Federal Judiciary is insufficient to meet the business before them. . . .

The attainment of speedier justice in the courts below will enlarge the task of the Supreme Court itself. And still more work would be added by the recommendation which I make later in this message for the quicker determination of constitutional questions by the highest court.

Even at the present time the Supreme Court is laboring under a heavy burden. Its difficulties in this respect were superficially lightened some years ago by authorizing the court, in its discretion, to refuse to hear appeals in many classes of cases. This discretion was so freely exercised that in the last fiscal year, although 867 petitions for review were presented to the Supreme Court, it declined to hear 717 cases. If petitions in behalf of the Government are excluded, it appears that the court permitted private litigants to prosecute appeals in only 108 cases out of 803 applications. Many of the refusals were doubtless warranted: but can it be said that full justice is achieved when a court is forced by the sheer necessity of keeping up with its business to decline, without even an explanation, to hear 87 percent of the cases presented to it by private litigants?

It seems clear, therefore, that the necessity of relieving present congestion extends to the enlargement of the capacity of all the federal courts.

A part of the problem of obtaining a sufficient number of judges to dispose of cases is the capacity of the judges themselves. This brings forward the question of aged or infirm judges—a subject of delicacy and yet one which requires frank discussion.

In the federal courts there are in all 237 life tenure permanent judgeships. Twenty-five of them are now held by judges over seventy years of age and eligible to leave the bench on full pay. Originally no pension or retirement allowance was provided by the Congress. When after eighty years of our national history the Congress made provision for pensions, it found a well-entrenched tradition among judges to cling to their posts, in many instances far beyond their years of physical or mental capacity. Their salaries were small. As with other men, responsibilities and obligations accumulated. No alternative had been open to them except to attempt to perform the duties of their offices to the very edge of the grave.

In exceptional cases, of course, judges, like other men, retain to an advanced age full mental and physical vigor. Those not so fortunate are often unable to perceive their own infirmities. . . .

With the opening of the twentieth century, and the great increase of population and commerce, and the growth of a more complex type of litigation, similar proposals were introduced in the

Congress. To meet the situation, in 1913, 1914, 1915 and 1916, the Attorneys General then in office recommended to the Congress that when a district or a circuit judge failed to retire at the age of seventy, an additional judge be appointed in order that the affairs of the court might be promptly and adequately discharged.

In 1919 a law was finally passed providing that the President "may" appoint additional district and circuit judges, but only upon a finding that the incumbent judge over seventy "is unable to discharge efficiently all the duties of his office by reason of mental or physical disability of permanent character." The discretionary and indefinite nature of this legislation has rendered it ineffective. No President should be asked to determine the ability or disability of any particular judge.

The duty of a judge involves more than presiding or listening to testimony or arguments. It is well to remember that the mass of details involved in the average of law cases today is vastly greater and more complicated than even twenty years ago. Records and briefs must be read; statutes, decisions, and extensive material of a technical, scientific, statistical and economic nature must be searched and studied; opinions must be formulated and written. The modern tasks of judges call for the use of full energies.

Modern complexities call also for a constant infusion of new blood in the courts, just as it is needed in executive functions of the Government and in private business. A lowered mental or physical vigor leads men to avoid an examination of complicated and changed conditions. Little by little, new facts become blurred through old glasses fitted, as it were, for the needs of another generation; older men, assuming that the scene is the same as it was in the past, cease to explore or inquire into the present or the future.

We have recognized this truth in the civil service of the nation and of many states by compelling retirement on pay at the age of seventy. We have recognized it in the Army and Navy by retiring officers at the age of sixty-four. A number of states have recognized it by providing in their constitutions for compulsory retirement of aged judges.

Life tenure of judges, assured by the Constitution, was designed to place the courts beyond temptations or influences which might impair their judgments: it was not intended to create a static judiciary. A constant and systematic addition of younger blood will vitalize the courts and better equip them to recognize and apply the essential concepts of justice in the light of the needs and the facts of an ever changing world. It is obvious, therefore, from both reason and experience, that some provision must be adopted, which will operate automatically to supplement the work of older judges and accelerate the work of the court.

I, therefore, earnestly recommend that the necessity of an increase in the number of judges be supplied by legislation providing for the appointment of additional judges in all federal courts, without exception, where there are incumbent judges of retirement age who do not choose to retire or to resign. If an elder judge is not in fact incapacitated, only good can come from the presence of an additional judge in the crowded state of the dockets; if the capacity of an elder judge is in fact impaired, the appointment of an additional judge is indispensable. This seems to be a truth which cannot be contradicted.

I also recommend that the Congress provide machinery for taking care of sudden or long-standing congestion in the lower courts. The Supreme Court should be given power to appoint an administrative assistant who may be called a Proctor. He would be charged with the duty of watching the calendars and the business of all the courts in the federal system. The Chief Justice thereupon should be authorized to make a temporary assignment of any circuit or district judge hereafter appointed in order that he may serve as long as needed in any circuit or district where the courts are in arrears.

I attach a carefully considered draft of a proposed bill, which, if enacted, would, I am confident, afford substantial relief. The proposed measure also contains a limit on the total number of judges who might thus be appointed and also a limit on the potential size of any one of our federal courts.

These proposals do not raise any issue of constitutional law. They do not suggest any form of compulsory retirement for incumbent judges. Indeed, those who have reached the retirement age, but desire to continue their judicial work, would be able to do so under less physical and mental strain and would be able to play a useful part in relieving the growing congestion in the business of our courts. Among them are men of eminence and great ability whose services the Government would be loath to lose. If, on the other hand, any judge eligible for retirement should feel that his court would suffer because of an increase in its membership, he may retire or resign under already existing provisions of law if he wishes so to do. In this connection let me say that the pending proposal to extend to the justices of the Supreme Court the same retirement privileges now available to other federal judges, has my entire approval.

One further matter requires immediate attention. We have witnessed the spectacle of conflicting decisions in both trial and appellate courts on the constitutionality of every form of important legislation. Such . . . differences of judicial opinion has brought the law, the courts, and, indeed, the entire administration of justice dangerously near to disrepute.

A federal statute is held legal by one judge in one district; it is simultaneously held illegal by another judge in another district. An act valid in one judicial circuit is invalid in another judicial circuit. Thus rights fully accorded to one group of citizens may be denied to others. As a practical matter this means that for periods running as long as one year or two years or three years—until final determination can be made by the Supreme Court—the law loses its most indispensable element—equality.

Moreover, during the long processes of preliminary motions, original trials, petitions for re-hearings, appeals, reversals on technical grounds requiring re-trials, motions before the Supreme Court and the final hearing by the highest tribunal—during all this time labor, industry, agriculture, commerce and the Government itself go through an unconscionable period of uncertainty and embarrassment. And it is well to remember that during these long processes the normal operations of society and government are handicapped in many cases by differing and divided opinions in the lower courts and by the lack of any clear guide for the dispatch of business. Thereby our legal system is fast losing another essential of justice—certainty.

Finally, we find the processes of government itself brought to a complete stop from time to time by injunctions issued almost automatically, sometimes even without notice to the Government, and not infrequently in clear violation of the principle of equity that injunctions should be granted only in those rare cases of manifest illegality and irreparable damage against which the ordinary course of the law offers no protection. Statutes which the Congress enacts are set aside or suspended for long periods of time, even in cases to which the Government is not a party.

In the uncertain state of the law, it is not difficult for the ingenious to devise novel reasons for attacking the validity of new legislation or its application. While these questions are laboriously brought to issue and debated through a series of courts, the Government must stand aside. It matters not that the Congress has enacted the law, that the Executive has signed it and that the administrative machinery is waiting to function. Government by injunction lays a heavy hand upon normal processes; and no important statute can take effect—against any individual or organization with the means to employ lawyers and engage in wide-flung litigation—until it has passed through the whole hierarchy of the courts. Thus the judiciary, by postponing the effective date of Acts of the Congress, is assuming an additional function and is coming more and more to constitute a scattered, loosely organized and slowly operating third house of the National Legislature.

This state of affairs has come upon the nation gradually over a period of decades. In my annual message to this Congress I expressed some views and some hopes.

Now, as an immediate step, I recommend that the Congress provide that no decision, injunction, judgment or decree on any constitutional question be promulgated by any federal court without previous and ample notice to the Attorney General and an opportunity for the United States to present evidence and be heard. This is to prevent court action on the constitutionality of Acts of the Congress in suits between private individuals, where the Government is not a party to the suit, without giving opportunity to the Government of the United States to defend the law of the land.

I also earnestly recommend that in cases in which any court of first instance determines a question of constitutionality, the Congress provide that there shall be a direct and immediate appeal to the Supreme Court, and that such cases take precedence over all other matters pending in that court. Such legislation will, I am convinced, go far to alleviate the inequality, uncertainty and delay in the disposition of vital questions of constitutionality arising under our fundamental law.

My desire is to strengthen the administration of justice and to make it a more effective servant of public need. In the American ideal of government the courts find an essential and constitutional place. In striving to fulfill that ideal, not only the judges but the Congress and the Executive as well, must do all in their power to bring the judicial organization and personnel to the high standards of usefulness which sound and efficient government and modern conditions require. . . .

5. "LEND-LEASE" PLAN   JUNE 10, 1941

. . . We have supplied, and we will supply, planes, guns, ammunition, and other defense articles in ever-increasing quantities to Britain, China, and other democracies resisting aggression.

Wars are not won by guns alone, but wars are not won without guns. We all know this full well now. Beginning with the outbreak of the war the American public began to realize that it was in our own national interest and security to help Britain, China, and other democratic Nations.

Beginning with the outbreak of the war British and French orders began to be placed. But dollars could not be immediately turned into airplanes and ships and guns and ammunition.

In those dark days when France was falling, it was clear that this Government, to carry out the will of the people, had to render aid over and above the materiel coming off the assembly line. This Government, therefore, made available all that it possibly could out of its surplus stocks of munitions.

In June of 1940, the British Government received from our surplus stocks rifles, machine guns, field artillery, ammunition, and aircraft in a value of more than 43 million dollars. This was equipment that would have taken months and months to produce and which, with the exception of the aircraft, cost about 300 million dollars to produce during the World War period. Most of this materiel would not have been usable if we had kept it much longer. This equipment arrived in Britain after the retreat from Dunkirk, where the British had lost great quantities of guns and other military supplies. No one can appraise what effect the delivery of these supplies had upon the successful British resistance in the summer and fall of 1940 when they were fighting against such terrific odds.

Since June 1940, this Government has continued to supply war materiel from its surplus stocks, in addition to the materiel produced by private manufacturers. The fifty over-age destroyers which Britain received in exchange for the defense bases were a part of the aid supplied by the Government.

By the turn of the year 1941, the British commitments in this country for defense articles had reached the limit of their future dollar resources. Their striking power required the assurance that their munitions and equipment would steadily and certainly be augmented, not curtailed.

The will of our people, as expressed through the Congress, was to meet this problem, not only by the passage of the Lend-Lease Act but by the appropriation of 7 billion dollars made on 27 March of this year to carry out this task.

In the ninety days since the Lend-Lease Act was passed, and in the seventy-four days since the funds were appropriated, we have started in motion the vast supply program which is essential to the defeat of the Axis powers.

In these seventy-four days, more than 4¼ billion dollars out of the 7 billion dollars have been allocated to the War, Navy, Agriculture, and Treasury Departments and to the Maritime Commission to procure the aid authorized. Contracts have been let for long-range bombers, ships, tanks, and the other sinews of war that will be needed for the defense of the democracies. The balance . . . is being rapidly allocated.

To be effective, the aid rendered by us must be many sided. Ships are necessary to carry the munitions and the food. We are immediately making available to Britain 2 million gross tons of cargo ships and oil tankers.

But this is not enough. Adequate shipping for every day to come must be reasonably assured. Since the Appropriation Act was passed, 550 million dollars has been allocated for the construction of new ships under the Lend-Lease Act. Contracts have been let and the new ways required to build these ships are now nearing completion. Allied ships are being repaired by us. Allied ships are being equipped by us to protect them from mines, and are being armed by us to protect them as much as possible against raiders. Naval vessels of Britain are being repaired by us so that they can return quickly to their naval tasks.

The training program of 7,000 British pilots in our schools in this country is under way. Valuable information is being communicated, and other material assistance is being rendered in a mounting benefit to the democracies.

Millions of pounds of food are being and will be sent. Iron and steel, machine tools and the other essentials to maintain and increase the production of war materials in Britain are being sent and received in larger quantities day by day.

Since September 1939, the war goods sent to Britain have risen steadily. The over-all total exports to the British Empire have greatly increased in 1941 over 1940. What is more important, the increase of those things which are necessary for fighting have increased far beyond our other exports. In the first five months of this year we have sent more than twelve times as many airplanes to Britain as we did in the first five months of 1940. For the first four months of this year the dollar value of explosives sent to the British Empire was about seventeen times as much as for the first four months of 1940. Ninety times as much in dollar value of firearms and ammunition was sent to Britain during the first four months of this year as for the first four months of 1940.

With our national resources, our productive capacity, and the genius of our people for mass production we will help Britain to outstrip the Axis powers in munitions of war, and we will see to it that these munitions get to the places where they can be effectively used to weaken and defeat the aggressors. . . .

6. WAR AGAINST JAPAN   DECEMBER 8, 1941

Yesterday, December 7, 1941—a date which will live in infamy—the United States of America was suddenly and deliberately attacked by naval and air forces of the Empire of Japan.

The United States was at peace with that Nation and, at the solicitation of Japan, was still in conversation with its Government and its Emperor looking toward the maintenance of peace in the Pacific. Indeed, one hour after Japanese air squadrons had commenced bombing in the American Island of Oahu, the Japanese Ambassador to the United States and his colleague delivered to our Secretary of State a formal reply to a recent American message. And while this reply stated that it seemed useless to continue the existing diplomatic negotiations, it contained no threat or hint of war or of armed attack.

It will be recorded that the distance of Hawaii from Japan makes it obvious that the attack was deliberately planned many days or even weeks ago. During the intervening time the Japanese Government has deliberately sought to deceive the United States by false statements and expressions of hope for continued peace.

The attack yesterday on the Hawaiian Islands has caused severe damage to American naval and military forces. I regret to tell you that very many American lives have been lost. In addition American ships have been reported torpedoed on the high seas between San Francisco and Honolulu.

Yesterday the Japanese Government also launched an attack against Malaya.

Last night Japanese forces attacked Hong Kong.

Last night Japanese forces attacked Guam.

Last night Japanese forces attacked the Philippine Islands.

Last night the Japanese attacked Wake Island.

And this morning the Japanese attacked Midway Island.

Japan has, therefore, undertaken a surprise offensive extending throughout the Pacific area. The facts of yesterday and today speak for themselves. The people of the United States have already formed their opinions and well understand the implications to the very life and safety of our Nation.

As Commander-in-Chief of the Army and Navy I have directed that all measures be taken for our defense. But always will our whole Nation remember the character of the onslaught against us.

No matter how long it may take us to overcome this premeditated invasion, the American people in their righteous might will win through to absolute victory.

I believe that I interpret the will of the Congress and of the people when I assert that we will not only defend ourselves to the uttermost but will make it very certain that this form of treachery shall never again endanger us.

Hostilities exist. There is no blinking at the fact that our people, our territory, and our interests are in grave danger.

With confidence in our armed forces—with the un-bounding determination of our people—we will gain the inevitable triumph—so help us God.

I ask that the Congress declare that since the unprovoked and dastardly attack by Japan on Sunday, 7 December 1941, a state of war has existed between the United States and the Japanese Empire.

7. ORDER OF JAPANESE INTERNMENT   FEBRUARY 19, 1942

Whereas, the successful prosecution of the war requires every possible protection against espionage and against sabotage to national defense material, national-defense premises and national defense utilities. . . .

Now therefore by virtue of the authority vested in me as President of the United States, and Commander-in-Chief of the Army and Navy, I hereby authorize and direct the Secretary of War, and the Military Commanders whom he may from time to time designate, whenever he or any designated Commander deems such action to be necessary or desirable, to prescribe military areas in such places and of such extent as he or the appropriate Military Commander may determine, from which any or all persons may be excluded, and with respect to which, the right of any persons to enter, remain in, or leave shall be subject to whatever restriction the Secretary of War or the appropriate Military Commander may impose in his discretion.

The Secretary of War is hereby authorized to provide for residents of any such area who are excluded therefrom, such transportation, food shelter, and other accommodations as may be necessary, in the judgment of the secretary of War or the said Military commander, and until other arrangements are made, to accomplish the purpose of this order. The designation of military areas in any region or locality shall supersede designations of prohibited and restricted areas by the Attorney General under the Proclamation of December 7 and 8, 1941, and shall supersede the responsibility and authority of the Attorney General under the said Proclamations in respect of such prohibited and restricted areas.

I hereby further authorize and direct the Secretary of War and the said Military Commanders to take such other steps as he or the appropriate Military Commander may deem advisable to enforce compliance with the restrictions applicable to each military area herein above authorized to be designated, including the use of Federal troops and other Federal Agencies, with authority to accept assistance of state and local agencies.

IX

WORLD LEADER: SUPERPOWER

AUGUST 6, 1945 BEGAN WITH HARRY S. TRUMAN aboard the *U.S.S. Augusta* as it neared the North American coast, south of Newfoundland. He was returning home from the Potsdam Conference meeting with the British and Soviet heads of state which had been held amid the rubble of destroyed and defeated Berlin. Only four months before, Harry Truman had first appeared on the world stage as America recoiled at the death of his legendary predecessor, Franklin Delano Roosevelt.

Truman immediately established himself as a very different kind of man, plain-spoken, sometimes bluntly aggressive. By August President Truman had already overseen the inauguration of the United Nations, announced the death of Hitler and directed the final defeat of the Nazi dream of a Third Reich which was to reign for a thousand years. Ascending to the task of Commander-in-Chief as the thirty-third President of the United States, Truman had also assumed command of the still brutal war against the Empire of Japan. The new American Chief spent three weeks in Potsdam, joining with successive Prime Ministers of the United Kingdom, Winston Churchill and Clement Attlee in vigorous negotiation with the USSR leader Joseph Stalin.

The high stakes at Potsdam included the fate of Germany and all of Eastern Europe. Yet for President Truman the crucial issue remained Japan, still powerful and recalcitrant. The main mission for the president was victory in the Pacific Theater against a Japanese military machine that would rather perish on the battlefield than endure the shame of surrender. At Potsdam, Truman sought to obtain Stalin's assistance in achieving the unconditional surrender of Japan.

During the Potsdam Conference, President Truman received astonishing news. He was informed about the results of a test of a nuclear device in the New Mexico desert. Upon receipt of the truly astounding details, he tried to imagine a "huge ball of fire . . . a lighting effect within the radius of 20 miles, equal to several suns at midday."

Given this game-changing development, Truman would face a military decision of global consequence. The President had weighed the use of atomic power against his advisors' assurance that an invasion of Japan would cost 250,000 or more American casualties. He ordered the atomic attack. Three weeks later, on August 6th at about 8 a.m., three Army Air Force B-29s appeared over Hiroshima, a city of about 340,000 people. The lead plane, the *Enola Gay* released the first atomic bomb from 31,600 feet. An intense flash of light momentarily blinded the fliers. The plane trembled in the shock, as the men saw the huge mushroom-shaped cloud of debris rise 40,000 feet into the atmosphere. Below, an eruption of suffocating heat covered the city. Four of every five buildings were blown apart, and 130,000 people perished in a flash.

The Atomic Age had begun. President Truman said he never lost any sleep over that momentous decision. It was true that from his vantage point he had given the Japanese war machine fair warning in his ultimatum issued at Potsdam on the 26th of July. That fair notice had been dismissed by the Japanese leaders. The imperial high command promptly rejected the American ultimatum.

As a consequence of the recalcitrance of their privileged military managers, American bombers appeared again on the Japanese horizon to drop the other atomic shoe over Nagasaki. Surrender would soon follow. No American lives would be spent invading the Japanese Island. Truman knew this and it gave him great comfort. The martial mood on the ship in the aftermath of the unleashing of the first atomic blast buoyed the spirits of the American Commander-in-Chief as he joined the crew and listened to the radio broadcast of a statement just issued in his name from the White House.

The use of atomic weapons brought the final stages of World War II to a sudden stop. The end came as the Japanese delegation boarded the American battleship the *U.S.S. Missouri* in Tokyo Bay to sign the peace agreement and surrender their swords to General Douglass MacArthur. The United States won the war, accepted the unconditional surrender, and emerged from the conflict as a global superpower.

As World War II wound down, the problems of reconversion and demobilization arose. The great fear was that as the war ended, depression and unemployment would return. The President and the Congress had to grapple with the changing economic circumstances. Towards this end the Congress passed and the President signed the Employment Act of 1946. The legislation declared the economy and employment to be a responsibility of the Federal Government. By virtue of the Act, the President was officially designated the manager of the economy. In order to assist him with his new assignment, the Act also established in the Executive Office a Council of Economic Advisers to gather economic information and provide advice and guidance to the President in his newly designated capacity as economic leader.

President Truman had assumed the mantle of "Leader of the Free World." In 1943, in the midst of the war, Winston Churchill told Franklin Roosevelt that the sun had set on the British Empire. Therefore, said Churchill, if freedom was to survive and flourish in the world it was the duty of the United States of America to take the lead. More than that, in the aftermath of the war Churchill visited President Truman at his home in Independence, Missouri in March 1946. From that platform, the former Prime Minister gave his famous Iron Curtain Speech. An Iron Curtain had descended across Europe, sealing off Eastern Europe's Soviet-sponsored "police governments." Indeed the USSR had engaged in a vigorous expansion program and established a network of buffer protection in Eastern European puppet satellite states. Nor was the Communist threat restricted to the European continent.

From the end of World War II in August 1945 until the fateful spring of 1947, the Soviet Union and the United States confirmed each other's worst fears. Stalin, personally paranoid but historically conscious about external threats to the borders of Russia, wanted to institute border security for the USSR. The Soviet leader was wary about American interest in spreading trade networks and democratic institutions into Eastern Europe. Such activities invaded what he considered his sphere of influence. He perceived the American concern for freedom and democracy in the world as a thin veil for an obvious imperialist plan. From Washington's perspective, the revolutionary rhetoric and military might of the USSR appeared to imperil the people and wealth of Europe.

Given this cold conflict, American testing continued. War-ravaged Europe lay prostrate between the two superpowers. All across the devastated continent the lands of both victors and vanquished teemed with the hopeless and the hungry. Even Great Britain, long a dominant world power and the principal European bulwark against Hitler, had paid too large a price in resources. The terrible winter of 1946–1947 froze the continent, hitting England hardest. In February England secretly notified Washington that it would be compelled to abandon its traditional political and economic role in southeastern Europe. This meant withdrawing from Greece, just at the moment when a royalist government struggled against a leftist uprising. The Soviets claimed that the Greek civil war remained exclusively an internal matter between Greek factions. Americans did not believe them.

The turmoil resulted in a dramatic shift in American foreign policy. President Truman proclaimed this historic adjustment in what became known as the Truman Doctrine. The longstanding American tradition had always been that the United States avoided foreign commitments in peacetime. While the Truman Doctrine pertained specifically to helping Greece and Turkey, the President's words had larger meaning. "I believe," said Truman "that it must be the policy of the United States to support free people who are resisting attempted subjugation by armed minorities or by outside pressures." In announcing this novel policy to a joint session of Congress and in order to win over the traditionally isolationist American public, Truman followed one senator's advice to "scare the hell out of the people." President Truman had a heart and he stood ready to assist struggling or needy people. He also had a brain and no one could accuse him of being a wimp. The President could talk tough and be tough. He was man enough to stand up to Stalin or any earthly power. One of his famous statements was that "if you wanted to have a friend in Washington, get a dog."

The spring of 1948 was the worst of times for Harry S. Truman, as the world's politics seemed to career toward catastrophe. Truman addressed a joint session of Congress on March 17th and called the members to action. He sought executive authority and resources, both sweet and sour, to mend the war-torn world. The Chief Executive appealed for immediate passage of the Marshall Plan and reinstatement of the draft. The measures were expensive and troubling, especially in an election year.

The President justified the request for Congressional action by citing Soviet provocation. A Moscow-inspired coup in Czechoslovakia that February created a satellite state. It served as a rude reminder of Hitler's seizure of that tormented country a decade earlier. Europe still smarted and wounded from war. Sores needed healing, particularly in partitioned Berlin, where ominous intelligence reports pertaining to Soviet designs were unsettling. In that fractured city, American and Allied occupation sectors were isolated inside the Soviet military zone. What many in the West never fully comprehended was that the entire City of Berlin was located in East Germany, consequently West Berlin was surrounded and under psychological siege by the USSR.

The Soviets controlled their zone of influence in East Germany. Beyond Berlin and Germany, the USSR expanded their influence, creating satellite states in Bulgaria, Czechoslovakia, Hungary, Poland, and Romania. Truman had not prevented Soviet occupation of these nation states and received political criticism for failure to do so. The Soviets then launched a blockade of Berlin. The blockade was designed to push the West out of Berlin. The year 1948 was a presidential election year. The President, for domestic political reasons as well as for international considerations, simply could not afford to let the Soviets prevail.

Confronted with a recalcitrant Congress under Republican control and with a very low approval rating from the American public, President Truman now faced the possibility of World War III. Western convoys needed passage through Soviet East Germany to arrive in Berlin. The Soviet order was to search all convoys. The Tri-zone allies of Britain, France and the United States resisted. The Soviets then inaugurated the blockade on June 27th, denying all access to Berlin. The people of West Berlin were threatened with starvation. An airlift of vital supplies was adopted to avoid alternates of war or submission. President Truman supported the airlift operation, which continued to May 12, 1949 at which time the Soviets backed away from the attempted blockade and allowed ground traffic to move freely to Berlin.

Britain's diminished world role in the aftermath of World War II produced the announcement that in May 1948 it would withdraw its 50,000 troops from Palestine. Zionists around the world demanded the partition of Palestine. The idea was that part would be an Arab State, and the remainder would be a Jewish state. Implacable Arab antagonists promised to "push the Jews into the sea."

As the date for British withdrawal neared, the burden shifted to the United States and the American President. Moral, political, and strategic pressures on Truman grew nearly intolerable. The President freely acknowledged the effects of the excruciating suffering of the Holocaust and the need for a Jewish homeland. Yet his Joint Chiefs and the State Department stood determinedly against recognition of the Jewish state. Postpone it they said. Kick the problem to the UN. Do not jeopardize relations with the Arab states, lose their oil, and drive them toward the Soviet Union. The debate continued to rage inside the White House until two days before the deadline. Secretary of State George C. Marshall led the opposition to recognition. President Truman respected him more than any man in Washington. The deadline arrived at 6 p.m. on May 14, 1948. Eleven minutes later, President Truman signed the recognition papers.

Truman's foreign policy initiatives received bipartisan support, which did not translate to his domestic programs. These times of complex and difficult transition or reconversion from a wartime economy to a peacetime economy produced a political nightmare for the President. Shortages of many commodities were common. Consequently prices shot skyward, causing dangerous levels of inflation. A rash of angry, sometimes violent strikes affected basic industries. The public registered their disapproval of the administration's policies at the mid-term election in 1946 as Republicans gained majorities in both Houses of Congress for the first time since Hoover lost legislative control in 1930.

Republicans eagerly awaited the 1948 election as Truman's popular approval plunged to 30 percent. The GOP nominated two progressive governors, Thomas E. Dewey of New York and Earl Warren of California. Meanwhile, the Republican 80th Congress had stymied Truman's legislative program. The Democratic Party began to fragment. Southern Democrats objected to Truman's views on Civil Rights. Left-wing Democrats protested Truman's strong stand against the Soviet Union and gathered behind former Secretary of Commerce Henry A. Wallace, who had been fired by Truman for his views on foreign policy. The left wing also deserted Truman.

With the Republicans controlling the political landscape and his own party disintegrating, Truman never flinched. He accepted nomination in Philadelphia in July with a blistering attack on Congress. He called Congress into special session and dared them to approve his social and economic programs. When they refused to adopt his plans he scolded them publicly as a "do nothing" Congress. The highlight of his underdog campaign that fall was a 30,000 mile "whistle-stop" tour aboard a special train. It worked.

China turned Communist under Chairman Mao Tse-Tung in 1949. Communist forces of North Korea crossed the UN line and invaded South Korea on June 25, 1950. President Truman responded immediately to the challenge. He mobilized the United Nations against the aggression, committing American military might as the basis for the UN action. For the first ten weeks, the battle raged near the southern end of the Korean peninsula where UN forces faced military defeat. In September the battle turned, following the landing of American and allied troops behind enemy lines at the port of Inchon, a brilliant strategic maneuver planned and executed by General Douglas MacArthur. His forces pressed vigorously to the far northern borders of China. Full victory appeared near at hand.

China entered the war on November 26th, with a massive counteroffensive, which again moved the front toward the 38th parallel, the original demarcation line. At this point, in Washington President Truman and his advisors agreed to enter negotiations with the enemy on the basis of achieving the *status quo antebellum*. Truman's thinking reflected a global strategy that placed emphasis on the defense of Europe and the *status quo* in Asia.

The White House released a carefully worded offer to negotiate with the Chinese and North Koreans. MacArthur stunned the President a few days later when he issued a statement that demeaned "Red China," America's "real enemy." The General also wrote that the great world battle between freedom and communism had begun in Asia, and stated "there is no substitute for victory." Truman made up his mind to relieve General MacArthur of his command.

Dwight David Eisenhower succeeded Truman and entered the White House on the strength of a remarkable military career in which he combined strategic wisdom and personal charisma to lead Allied forces to victory in Europe. The five-star General had been reticent to reveal his political beliefs. In fact, Truman tried to recruit him to be the Democratic nominee but Eisenhower demurred. He was elected as a Republican in 1952. He promised that he would go to Korea and that promise engendered great favor with an admiring electorate. "I like Ike" was a winning slogan.

The first Republican elected since 1928, Eisenhower pursued moderate policies. His rhetoric signaled a shift in foreign policy from the containment of communism strategy of the Truman administration to "rolling back" communist advances in the world. The shift also involved abstaining from involvement in limited wars to a new "massive retaliation" response. In practice, Eisenhower's two terms in the White House did tend to contain communism abroad and the preservation of the *status quo* in the world.

While budget constraints prevented significant expansion of most social programs, the Eisenhower Administration actually increased the scope of government in massive public works projects. The St. Lawrence Seaway Development Corporation, a joint venture government corporation with Canada that permitted ocean shipping to penetrate to the western extent of the Great Lakes, opened in 1959. Even more consequential for American society, the Federal Highway Act of 1956 authorized the construction of 42,500 miles of limited-access interstate highways, with Federal funds committed up to 90 percent of the cost.

Gradually, this interstate highway system laid down a grid of concrete, linking every section of the nation, coast to coast. Commerce expanded, automobile use for business and pleasure swelled, and economic and social dependence on the internal combustion engine became a permanent feature of the American way of life. The huge road systems cut through urban residential neighborhoods of workers and minorities, especially in New York, Philadelphia, Chicago, and Miami, precipitating "white flight" to the suburbs. The interstate highway system immediately became one of the Eisenhower Administration's most celebrated and enduring legacies.

No sooner had Eisenhower been installed in the White House than news came that Josef Stalin had died, supposedly on March 5, 1953. Stalin's passing inspired new hope for reconciliation and the end of the Cold War. At a summit meeting scheduled for July 21, 1955 in Geneva, Switzerland, President Eisenhower joined British Prime Minister Anthony Eden, French Premier Edgar Faure and the nominal leader of the Soviet Union, Premier Nikolai Bulganin. The international situation showed signs of détente. The recently concluded Austrian Peace Treaty demonstrated the willingness of the Soviets to settle that problem, allowing Austria to be transformed from an occupied state to an independent nation.

Premier Bulganin came to Geneva accompanied by the First Secretary of the Communist Party, Nikolai Khrushchev. Eisenhower had determined to use the summit as a pulpit to issue dramatic appeals for the transformation of international relations to a new era of conciliation. His opening address to the conference July 18, 1955, struck this theme. Three days later, he shocked the world with a proposal to exchange military secrets and provide facilities and open access for Russian pilots on American air bases, requesting only reciprocal arrangements for American military in the Soviet Union. The plan met quick rejection by the suspicious Soviets. The "spirit of Geneva" did provide, however, a period of ease with respect to Cold War tension.

While tensions relaxed internationally, they elevated domestically. The Supreme Court pronounced segregation unconstitutional in *Brown v. School Board of Topeka* on May 17, 1954. This reversed the *Plessey vs. Ferguson* (1896) decision which had established segregation as constitutional. Southern Democratic politicians, the most powerful bloc in Congress, issued a "Southern Manifesto" in 1956 decrying the Court's decision and vowing resistance. In this climate in August 1957, the Eisenhower Administration pushed through Congress the first Civil Rights legislation in eight decades. The South resisted. In September 1957, Governor Orville Faubus of Arkansas defied a court order and mobilized the National Guard to prevent black students from entering Central High School in Little Rock. Eisenhower addressed the nation, and moved to enforce the law ordering Federal Troops to integrate the school.

By the time President Eisenhower prepared to leave office in January 1961, journalists and other pundits had already begun to characterize his time in office as bland. More recently Eisenhower has received considerably more respect. His leadership abilities have been accorded high acclaim. Eisenhower's Farewell Address, on January 17, 1961, sought to leave with his "fellow citizens" the sense of how his wisdom and experience interpreted the nation's problems, including the dangers of the "military-industrial complex."

The torch was now "passed to a new generation of Americans." On a frigid January day in 1961, John Fitzgerald Kennedy so clearly personified a dramatic change in the course of American history and politics. On the Inaugural platform sat his two immediate predecessors, both old men. Truman and Eisenhower were grandfathers, while the new President had a three-year old son and a newborn baby. Television now enveloped America, and Kennedy used the new medium like no previous politician. His self-deprecating wit charmed voters, particularly the young. To his own generation, Kennedy created the lore of an authentic war hero. As a naval lieutenant assigned to the Pacific theater, the enemy sank his ship in World War II. It was the beginning of an active political life which now placed him at the Inaugural podium as the youngest man ever elected President of the United States. It was a memorable day and he delivered a never-to-be-forgotten oration, remarkable for its power and poetry.

President Kennedy's vibrant style was reflected in the attitude of his administration in immediately addressing domestic and foreign problems. Kennedy perceived a globe characterized by communist insurgencies directed from Moscow which provoked insurrection throughout the underdeveloped world. Events of 1961 and 1962, including the Bay of Pigs fiasco, the Kennedy–Khrushchev Summit meeting in Vienna, and the Cuban Missile Crisis confirmed the President's world view.

Kennedy had attracted an impressive collection of intellectuals and strategic thinkers to Washington. Visions of "modernization" or "nation building" circulated throughout the nation's capital. Plans were developed for all kinds of contingencies—peaceful or otherwise. Counter-insurgency strategies would use intelligence and the newly created Special Forces or Green Berets, to thwart leftist operations. "Nation building" included the creation of economic infrastructure, training of police and civil servants, and the promotion of democratic institutions. Another innovation of Kennedy and his circle was the Peace Corps. The President signed an Executive

Order, on March 1, 1961, creating the Corps, to be followed by Congressional action several months later.

At the Vienna Summit between Kennedy and Khrushchev in June 1961 the two superpower leaders took the measure of each other. The meeting followed on the Bay of Pigs fiasco in April. Kennedy tried to correct any false impression Khrushchev may have formed in advance of the Summit. In fact, Khrushchev did underestimate the American President. He viewed Kennedy as an immature, inexperienced upstart who was more at home sailing in Cape Cod than at the serious business of world leader. At Vienna, Kennedy, intent on disabusing him on this score, asked about a medal the Chairman wore on his chest. Khrushchev beamed with pride and said that was the Lenin Peace Prize. The President pointed at the medal and (to paraphrase) advised the Soviet leader that he should take care not to do anything to lose it. Afterwards, reporters inquired of President Kennedy as to how the meeting went and he replied: "It's going to be a long, cold winter." The Cold War got colder.

The Soviet Premier was emboldened in the aftermath of Vienna to aggressively move on Berlin later that summer. In the dead of night on August 13, 1961, the Berlin Wall was erected, encircling West Berlin and separating it from East Berlin. The Wall was constructed with multiple motivations. One purpose was to prevent the long-term flight of East Germans away from communism and toward freedom. This new physical barrier caught the New Frontiersmen by surprise. When they awoke the next morning to the new reality of the Wall the President's advisers were of different minds as to how the West should respond to this Soviet audacity. One set urged immediate and direct action. They wanted to physically destroy the Wall. Another faction, wishing to avoid war at all cost, advised an ostrich-like head in the sand response. JFK found both proposed responses entirely unsatisfactory. He proceeded with caution and a watchful, waiting posture. The Berlin crisis had escalated but had not yet reached a showdown. Berlin was hot but not on fire. Later, at a more propitious moment, he would give his well-considered response to communist impudence and the Wall. JFK would go to Berlin.

Meanwhile, in the fall of 1962, the geopolitical axis shifted to the Caribbean. From October 16th to 29th, 1962, a power struggle between the world's two great nuclear powers brought mankind to the moment of annihilation. Soviet missiles secretly established and deployed in Cuba fundamentally altered the world's strategic balance. It was Nikita Khrushchev's great adventure. He had placed a nuclear dagger in the heart of the Western Hemisphere in blatant defiance of the cornerstone of American diplomacy, the Monroe Doctrine. That doctrine, he said, was "dead."

North, South, and Central America were brought under the nuclear gun. From Montreal and Seattle to beyond Lima and Caracas hundreds of millions of people were now within range. President Kennedy immediately fixed as his principal objective the disarming and removal of the missiles from Cuba. For thirteen tense and frightening days the highest level of American political, diplomatic, and military minds wrestled with how to achieve this vital goal.

The Soviet missiles had been discovered on October 15th by a U-2 surveillance flight over Cuba. The next day, Kennedy convened a dozen or so advisors as the Special Executive Committee. In Committee meetings, the initial consensus emphasized a quick and overpowering military strike. Some advocated a full-scale invasion, and replacement of the Castro government. As the entire military establishment went on high alert, Kennedy ordered calling out the reserves.

On October 22nd the President addressed the nation on television, confirming the installation of missiles and demanding their removal. Rather than the military strikes advocated by most of his advisors, Kennedy pursued a different course. He announced a tactic designed to buy time for high-stakes diplomacy. Since a "blockade" was technically an act of war, he commanded that the

U.S. Navy launch a "quarantine" to prevent all suspect shipping from reaching Cuba. In the anxious days that followed, Soviet ships at sea faced a log jam obstructing any attempt to reach Cuba.

Meanwhile, the adversaries sent both threats and proposals through the United Nations to the world's diplomatic capitals. On the evening of Friday, October 26th, a secret message arrived in Washington from Chairman Khrushchev which seemed to open a window. The Soviet leader indicated a willingness to remove the missiles in return for a pledge by the United States not to invade Cuba. The next day Moscow Radio broadcast and the American State Department received a very different proposal. Missiles in Cuba would be removed only as the United States removed its missiles from Turkey. The missile crisis deepened when an American U-2 strayed over Soviet air space, while another U-2 was shot down over Cuba.

President Kennedy listened to hours of debate before gradually forming a response. At about 8 p.m. on Saturday, October 27th, he released a public letter to Khrushchev that agreed to the original proposal, the removal of the missiles in return for a no-invasion pledge.

Top secret discussions were the order of the day. In line with that secrecy a private missive was directed to the Soviet leader assuring him that in days to come the missiles in Turkey would be removed. Excomm discussions are now published and reveal the ultimate resolve of American leaders. The discussions produced a consensus that the nuclear entry of the Soviets into the Western Hemisphere would not be permitted to stand. The world superpowers met eyeball to eyeball in the Caribbean and the Soviets blinked. Their risky adventure was parried before the entire world to see. The Soviets removed their missiles and the world avoided the greatest calamity in recorded history.

The Cold War experienced a slight thaw but was far from over. In essence, the Cold War was a desperate struggle for the minds and hearts of the people of the planet. The fundamental nature of this intellectual and spiritual contest placed heavy burdens on the President of the United States. JFK carried these burdens with style and grace. Leadership in many respects pertained to timing. The President manifested an uncanny ability to time his diplomatic moves. Ironically, he had so little time left to lead the nation.

In the last summer of his life, he undertook significant initiatives in the long and dangerous Cold War conflict with the Soviet Union. At American University, on June 10th, he boldly proposed a program of disarmament, beginning with the prohibition of atmospheric nuclear testing. Two months later, acting on this initiative, the Senate ratified the first-ever arms control agreement between Washington and Moscow, a modest but notable beginning toward détente. His words to the students at American University haunt the memory of Americans as he proclaimed nearly a half century ago: "in the final analysis, our most basic common link is that we all inhabit this small planet. We all breathe the same air. We all cherish our children's future. And we are all mortal."

Two weeks after the American University speech, he found that propitious moment to go to Berlin. The President brought a message of freedom to the citizens of that embattled city. Standing before the despised Wall, he pointed at it and transformed it into a symbol of the struggle between communism and freedom. "Today in the world of freedom" he said: "the proudest boast is 'Ich bin ein Berliner.'" For decades, the East Berliners fled toward freedom to escape communist tyranny. The Wall had been erected to stop the flow toward liberty. There by the Wall he acknowledged to the world that Americans were by no means perfect, but "we did not have to build a Wall to keep our people in."

Later that year, JFK talked of another challenge to all mankind. T.S. Eliot early in the century had asked a fundamental question: "Do I dare disturb the Universe?" Kennedy went to Texas and answered the poet in the affirmative. At dedication ceremonies for the Aerospace Medical Health

Center in San Antonio, November 21, 1963, President Kennedy told an attentive audience that for three years he had talked of a "New Frontier." The term referred, he said, "to this Nation's place in history." Americans stood at the threshold of a "great new era," which summoned mankind to "test the unknown."

His mission to San Antonio was to dedicate the Aerospace Center and "to salute" those associated with the Center. It was fitting that it be located in San Antonio, a place that served as "the home of the pioneers of the air." He specifically paid tribute to Sidney Brooks, Charles Lindbergh and Claire Chennault and their early "mastery of the skies."

"And in this New Frontier of outer space" added the young President, "history is being made every day by the men and women of the Aerospace Medical Center." Space and the edges of the unknown must be explored. On the day before he died, he talked of going over to the undiscovered other side. To make his point he borrowed a story from the distinguished Irish writer, Frank O'Connor. The Irishman wrote about his boyhood in the Emerald Isle and how he and his friends would romp across country fields. They climbed many walls but when they approached one that was frightfully high and foreboding, the boys would toss their hats over the wall. Their destiny was chartered. The boys were obliged to follow their hats into the unknown. "The Nation has tossed its cap over the wall of space" said JFK, "and we have no choice but to follow it." Once the wall of outer space has been climbed, we will then know "the wonders on the other side."

There is a curious postscript that might be attached to this inspirational tale. President Kennedy did not wear a hat. It has been rumored that he made a deal with hat manufacturers that he would carry a hat rather than wear one. Still few remember seeing him carrying one and a President should not be caught with his hat in hand. American men in the fashion of their beloved President stopped wearing hats. Perhaps they all threw their hats over the wall and just forgot to go get them.

The following day in Dallas, the fateful day of November 22nd, as the presidential motorcade moved through the city, shots rang out in Dealey Plaza. The President slumped to his left and towards First Lady Jacqueline Kennedy in the back seat of his limousine. The motorcade raced four miles to Parkland hospital in a futile attempt to save his life. President Kennedy was pronounced dead at approximately 1 p.m. The assassination had succeeded. John Fitzgerald Kennedy had crossed over into the unknown.

President Kennedy left behind a nation in mourning, a grieving widow and an undelivered speech which had been prepared for delivery to the Texas Democratic State Committee in the state capital at Austin that afternoon. The Austin Address contained an assessment of his administration. Had he lived, he intended to tell Texas Democrats:

"We have won the respect of allies and adversaries alike through our determined stand on behalf of freedom around the world, from West Berlin to Southeast Asia—through our resistance to Communist intervention in the Congo and Communist missiles in Cuba— and through our initiative in obtaining the nuclear test ban treaty which can stop the pollution of our atmosphere and start us on the path to peace. In San Jose and Mexico City, in Bonn and West Berlin, in Rome and County Cork, I saw and heard and felt a new appreciation for an America on the move—an America which has shown that it cares about the needy of its own and other lands, an America which has shown that freedom is the way to the future. . . ."

JFK concluded this undelivered speech with an appeal to discard petty bickering in favor of a higher cause and a better future "determined that this land we love shall lead all mankind into new frontiers of peace and abundance."

33

Harry S. Truman

1. ATOMIC BOMB DROPPED ON HIROSHIMA AUGUST 6, 1945

A short time ago an American airplane dropped one bomb on Hiroshima and destroyed its usefulness to the enemy. That bomb has more power than 20,000 tons of T.N.T.

The Japanese began the war from the air at Pearl Harbor. They have been repaid many fold.
. . . With this bomb we have now added a new and revolutionary increase in destruction to supplement the growing power of our armed forces. In their present form these bombs are now in production and even more powerful forms are in development.

It is an atomic bomb. It is a harnessing of the basic power of the universe. The force from which the sun draws its power has been loosed against those who brought war to the Far East

We have spent more than two billion dollars on the greatest scientific gamble in history—and we have won.

But the greatest marvel is not the size of the enterprise, its secrecy, or its cost, but the achievement of scientific brains in making it work. And hardly less marvelous has been the capacity of industry to design, and of labor to operate, the machines and methods to do things never done before. Both science and industry worked under the direction of the United States Army, which achieved a unique success in an amazingly short time. It is doubtful if such another combination could be got together in the world. What has been done is the greatest achievement of organized science in history.

We are now prepared to obliterate more rapidly and completely every productive enterprise the Japanese have in any city. We shall destroy their docks, their factories, and their communications. Let there be no mistake; we shall completely destroy Japan's power to make war.

It was to spare the Japanese people from utter destruction that the ultimatum of 26 July was issued at Potsdam. Their leaders promptly rejected that ultimatum. If they do not now accept our terms they may expect a rain of ruin from the air, the like of which has never been seen on this earth. Behind this air attack will follow sea and land forces in such numbers and power as they have not yet seen and with the fighting skill of which they are already well aware.

2. EMPLOYMENT ACT OF 1946 FEBRUARY 20, 1946

I have signed today the Employment Act of 1946. In enacting this legislation the Congress and the President are responding to an overwhelming demand of the people. The legislation gives expression to a deep-seated desire for a conscious and positive attack upon the ever-recurring problems of mass unemployment and ruinous depression.

Figure 33.1 Truman Arrives to Sign NATO Treaty, April 4, 1949, courtesy of the Truman Presidential Library and Museum.

Within three years after the First World War, we experienced farm foreclosures, business failures, and mass unemployment. In fact, the history of the last several decades has been one of speculative booms alternating with deep depression. The people have found themselves defenseless in the face of economic forces beyond their control.

Democratic government has the responsibility to use all its resources to create and maintain conditions under which free competitive enterprise can operate effectively—conditions under which there is an abundance of employment opportunity for those who are able, willing, and seeking to work.

It is not the Government's duty to supplant the efforts of private enterprise to find markets or of individuals to find jobs. The people do expect the Government, however, to create and maintain conditions in which the individual businessman and the individual job seeker have a chance to succeed by their own efforts. That is the objective of the Employment Act of 1946.

The major provisions of this important legislation can be briefly summarized:

1. The Act declares that it is "the continuing policy and responsibility of the federal Government . . . to coordinate and utilize all its plans, functions, and resources for the purpose of creating and maintaining conditions under which there shall be afforded useful employment opportunities, including self-employment, for those able, willing, and seeking to work. . . ."

2. The Congress has placed on the President the duty of formulating programs designed to accomplish the purpose of the Act. In signing this Act, I accept this responsibility. . . . This task is so great that I can perform only with the full and unqualified cooperation of all who are sincerely interested in the general welfare inside and outside the Government. Making this Act work must become one of the prime objectives of all of us. . . .

3. The Act includes a significant provision that will facilitate cooperation between the Executive and the Congress in the formulation of policies and programs. . . . It establishes a joint Congressional Committee consisting of seven Members of the Senate and seven Members of the House. This committee is given an assignment of great scope and the highest importance.

4. The Act establishes in the Executive Office of the President a Council of Economic Advisers, composed of three members to be appointed by the President with consent of the Senate. This new Council will be an important addition to the facilities available for preparing economic policies and programs. . . .

5. The Employment Act of 1946 is not the end of the road, but rather the beginning. It is a commitment by the Government to the people—a commitment to take any and all measures necessary for a healthy economy, one that provides opportunities for those able, willing, and seeking to work. We shall all try to honor that commitment.

3. TRUMAN DOCTRINE   MARCH 12, 1947

. . . The United States has received from the Greek Government an urgent appeal for financial and economic assistance. Preliminary reports from the American Economic Mission now in Greece and reports from the American Ambassador in Greece corroborate the statement of the Greek Government that assistance is imperative if Greece is to survive as a free nation.

I do not believe that the American people and the Congress wish to turn a deaf ear to the appeal of the Greek Government.

. . . The very existence of the Greek state is today threatened by the terrorist activities of several thousand armed men, led by Communists, who defy the government's authority at a number of points, particularly along the northern boundaries. A Commission appointed by the United Nations Security Council is at present investigating disturbed conditions in northern Greece and alleged border violations along the frontier between Greece on the one hand and Albania, Bulgaria, and Yugoslavia on the other.

Meanwhile, the Greek Government is unable to cope with the situation. The Greek army is small and poorly equipped. It needs supplies and equipment if it is to restore authority to the government throughout Greek territory.

Greece must have assistance if it is to become a self-supporting and self-respecting democracy.

The United States must supply this assistance. We have already extended to Greece certain types of relief and economic aid but these are inadequate.

. . . The Greek Government has been operating in an atmosphere of chaos and extremism. It has made mistakes. The extension of aid by this country does not mean that the United States condones everything that the Greek Government has done or will do. . . .

Greece's neighbor, Turkey, also deserves our attention.

The future of Turkey as an independent and economically sound state is clearly no less important to the freedom-loving peoples of the world than the future of Greece. The circumstances in which Turkey finds itself today are considerably different from those of Greece. Turkey has been spared the disasters that have beset Greece. And during the war, the United States and Great Britain furnished Turkey with material aid.

Nevertheless, Turkey now needs our support.

. . . One of the primary objectives of the foreign policy of the United States is the creation of conditions in which we and other nations will be able to work out a way of life free from coercion. This was a fundamental issue in the war with Germany and Japan. Our victory was won over countries which sought to impose their will, and their way of life, upon other nations.

To ensure the peaceful development of nations, free from coercion, the United States has taken a leading part in establishing the United Nations. The United Nations is designed to make possible lasting freedom and independence for all its members. We shall not realize our objectives, however, unless we are willing to help free peoples to maintain their free institutions and their national integrity against aggressive movements that seek to impose upon them totalitarian regimes. This is no more than a frank recognition that totalitarian regimes imposed upon free peoples, by direct or indirect aggression, undermine the foundations of international peace and hence the security of the United States.

The peoples of a number of countries of the world have recently had totalitarian regimes forced upon them against their will. The Government of the United States has made frequent protests against coercion and intimidation, in violation of the Yalta agreement, in Poland, Rumania, and Bulgaria. I must also state that in a number of other countries there have been similar developments.

At the present moment in world history nearly every nation must choose between alternative ways of life. . . .

One way of life is based upon the will of the majority, and is distinguished by free institutions, representative government, free elections, and guarantees of individual liberty, freedom of speech and religion, and freedom from political oppression.

The second way of life is based upon the will of a minority forcibly imposed upon the majority. It relies upon terror and oppression, a controlled press and radio, fixed elections, and the suppression of personal freedoms.

I believe that it must be the policy of the United States to support free peoples who are resisting attempted subjugation by armed minorities or by outside pressures.

I believe that we must assist free peoples to work out their own destinies in their own way.

I believe that our help should be primarily through economic and financial aid which is essential to economic stability and orderly political processes.

. . . It is necessary only to glance at a map to realize that the survival and integrity of the Greek nation are of grave importance in a much wider situation. If Greece should fall under the control of an armed minority, the effect upon its neighbor, Turkey, would be immediate and serious. Confusion and disorder might well spread throughout the entire Middle East.

Moreover, the disappearance of Greece as an independent state would have a profound effect upon those countries in Europe whose peoples are struggling against great difficulties to maintain their freedoms and their independence while they repair the damages of war.

It would be an unspeakable tragedy if these countries, which have struggled so long against overwhelming odds, should lose that victory for which they sacrificed so much. Collapse of free institutions and loss of independence would be disastrous not only for them but for the world. Discouragement and possibly failure would quickly be the lot of neighboring peoples striving to maintain their freedom and independence.

Should we fail to aid Greece and Turkey in this fateful hour, the effect will be far reaching to the West as well as to the East.

We must take immediate and resolute action.

I therefore ask the Congress to provide authority for assistance to Greece and Turkey in the amount of $400,000,000. . . . In requesting these funds, I have taken into consideration the maximum amount of relief assistance which would be furnished to Greece out of the $350,000,000 which I recently requested that the Congress authorize for the prevention of starvation and suffering in countries devastated by the war.

In addition to funds, I ask the Congress to authorize the detail of American civilian and military personnel to Greece and Turkey, at the request of those countries, to assist in the tasks of reconstruction, and for the purpose of supervising the use of such financial and material assistance as may be furnished. . . .

Finally, I ask that the Congress provide authority which will permit the speediest and most effective use, in terms of needed commodities, supplies, and equipment, of such funds as may be authorized.

If further funds, or further authority, should be needed for the purposes indicated in this message, I shall not hesitate to bring the situation before the Congress. . . .

4. RECOGNITION OF THE STATE OF ISRAEL   MAY 14, 1948

This government has been informed that a Jewish state has been proclaimed in Palestine, and recognition has been requested by the provisional government thereof.

The United States recognizes the provisional government as the de facto authority of the new State of Israel.

5. INTEGRATING THE ARMED FORCES   JULY 26, 1948

Establishing the President's Committee on Equality of Treatment and Opportunity In the Armed Forces.

Whereas it is essential that there be maintained in the armed services of the United States the highest standards of democracy, with equality of treatment and opportunity for all those who serve in our country's defense:

Now therefore, by virtue of the authority vested in me as President of the United States, by the Constitution and the statutes of the United States, and as Commander-in-Chief of the armed services, it is hereby ordered as follows:

1. It is hereby declared to be the policy of the President that there shall be equality of treatment and opportunity for all persons in the armed services without regard to race, color, religion or national origin. . . .
2. There shall be created in the National Military Establishment an advisory committee to be known as the President's Committee on Equality of Treatment and Opportunity in the Armed Services, which shall be composed of seven members to be designated by the President.
3. The Committee is authorized on behalf of the President to examine into the rules, procedures and practices of the Armed Services in order to determine in what respect such rules, procedures and practices may be altered or improved with a view to carrying out the policy of this order. . . .
4. All executive departments and agencies of the Federal Government are authorized and directed to cooperate with the Committee in its work, and to furnish the Committee such

information or the services of such persons as the Committee may require in the performance of its duties.

5. When requested by the Committee to do so, persons in the armed services or in any of the executive departments and agencies of the Federal Government shall testify before the Committee and shall make available for use of the Committee such documents and other information as the Committee may require.

6. The Committee shall continue to exist until such time as the President shall terminate its existence by Executive order.

6. PRESIDENT FIRES GENERAL DOUGLAS MACARTHUR   APRIL 11, 1951

... I realized that I would have no other choice myself than to relieve the nation's top field commander.

If there is one basic element in our Constitution, it is civilian control of the military. Policies are to be made by the elected political officials, not by generals or admirals. Yet time and again General MacArthur had shown that he was unwilling to accept the policies of the administration. By his repeated public statements he was not only confusing our allies as to the true course of our policies but, in fact, was also setting his policy against the President's.

I have always had, and I have to this day, the greatest respect for General MacArthur, the soldier. Nothing I could do, I knew, could change his stature as one of the outstanding military figures of our time—and I had no desire to diminish his stature. I had hoped, and I had tried to convince him, that the policy he was asked to follow was right. He had disagreed. He had been openly critical. Now, at last, his actions had frustrated a political course decided upon, in conjunction with its allies, by the government he was sworn to serve. If I allowed him to defy the civil authorities in this manner, I myself would be violating my oath to uphold and defend the Constitution. ...

The reporters were handed a series of papers, the first being my announcement of General MacArthur's relief.

"With deep regret," this announcement read, "I have concluded that General of the Army Douglas MacArthur is unable to give his whole-hearted support to the policies of the United States Government and of the United Nations in matters pertaining to his official duties. In view of the specific responsibilities imposed upon me by the Constitution of the United States and the added responsibility which has been entrusted to me by the United Nations, I have decided that I must make a change of command in the Far East. I have, therefore, relieved General MacArthur of his commands and have designated Lieutenant General Matthew B. Ridgway as his successor.

"Full and vigorous debate on matters of national policy is a vital element in the constitutional system of our free democracy. It is fundamental, however, that military commanders must be governed by the policies and directives issued to them in the manner provided by our laws and Constitution. In time of crisis, the consideration is particularly compelling.

"General MacArthur's place in history as one of our greatest commanders is fully established. The Nation owes him a debt of gratitude for the distinguished and exceptional service which he has rendered his country in posts of great responsibility. For that reason I repeat my regret at the necessity for the action I feel compelled to take in his case."

The second document was the actual order of relief. It notified General MacArthur that he was relieved.

... The American people were still faced with Communist aggression in Korea; the Communist conspiracy was still threatening the West in Europe and in Asia. I went on the air on the evening of April 11 to restate the government's policy to the American people. I explained why we were in Korea and why we could not allow the Korean affair to become a general all-out war. I proclaimed our desire to arrive at a settlement along the lines of the statement that had been drafted in March and then not used. I explained why it had become necessary to relieve General MacArthur.

"The free nations," I told the radio audience, "have united their strength in an effort to prevent a third world war.

"That war can come if the Communist leaders want it to come. But this nation and its allies will not be responsible for its coming."

34

Dwight D. Eisenhower

1. INTERSTATE HIGHWAY SYSTEM   FEBRUARY 22, 1955

Our unity as a nation is sustained by free communication of thought and by easy transportation of people and goods. The ceaseless flow of information throughout the Republic is matched by individual and commercial movement over a vast system of interconnected highways. . . .

Together, the uniting forces of our communication and transportation systems are dynamic elements in the very name we bear—United States. Without them, we would be a mere alliance of many separate parts.

The nation's highway system is a gigantic enterprise, one of our largest items of capital investment. . . . Three million, three hundred and sixty-six thousand miles of road, travelled by 58 million motor vehicles, comprise it. The replacement cost of its drainage and bridge and tunnel works is incalculable. One in every seven Americans gains his livelihood and supports his family out of it. But, in large part, the network is inadequate for the nation's growing needs.

In recognition of this, the Governors in July of last year at my request began a study of both the problem and methods by which the Federal Government might assist the States in its solution. I appointed in September the President's Advisory Committee on a National Highway Program, headed by Lucius D. Clay, to work with the Governors and to propose a plan of action for submission to the Congress. . . .

First: Each year, more than thirty-six thousand people are killed and more than a million injured on the highways. To the home where the tragic aftermath of an accident on an unsafe road is a gap in the family circle, the monetary worth of preventing that death cannot be reckoned. But reliable estimates place the measurable economic cost of the highway accident toll to the nation at more than $4.3 billion a year.

Second: The physical condition of the present road net increases the cost of vehicle operation, according to many estimates, by as much as one cent per mile of vehicle travel. At the present rate of travel, this totals more than $5 billion a year. The cost is not borne by the individual vehicle operator alone. It pyramids into higher expense of doing the nation's business. Increased highway transportation costs, passed on through each step in the distribution of goods, are paid ultimately by the individual consumer.

Third: In case of an atomic attack on our key cities, the road net must permit quick evacuation of target areas, mobilization of defense forces and maintenance of every essential economic function. But the present system in critical areas would be the breeder of a deadly congestion within hours of an attack.

Fourth: Our Gross National Product, about $357 billion in 1954, is estimated to reach over $500 billion in 1965 when our population will exceed 180 million and, according to other estimates, will travel in 81 million vehicles 814 billion vehicle miles that year. Unless the present rate of highway improvement and development is increased, existing traffic jams only faintly foreshadow those of ten years hence.

To correct these deficiencies is an obligation of Government at every level. The highway system is a public enterprise. As the owner and operator, the various levels of Government have a responsibility for management that promotes the economy of the nation and properly serves the individual user. . . .

Of all these, the Interstate System must be given top priority in construction planning. But at the current rate of development, the Interstate network would not reach even a reasonable level of extent and efficiency in half a century. State highway departments cannot effectively meet the need. Adequate right-of-way to assure control of access; grade separation structures; relocation and realignment of present highways; all these, done on the necessary scale within an integrated system, exceed their collective capacity.

If we have a congested and unsafe and inadequate system, how then can we improve it so that ten years from now it will be fitted to the nation's requirements?

A realistic answer must be based on a study of all phases of highway financing, including a study of the costs of completing the several systems of highways, made by the Bureau of Public Roads in cooperation with the State highway departments and local units of government. This study, made at the direction of the 83rd Congress in the 1954 Federal-aid Highway Act, is the most comprehensive of its kind ever undertaken.

Its estimates of need show that a 10-year construction program to modernize all our roads and streets will require expenditure of $101 billion by all levels of Government.

A sound Federal highway program, I believe, can and should stand on its own feet, with highway users providing the total dollars necessary for improvement and new construction. Financing of

Figure 34.1 Ike and JFK, December 6, 1960, courtesy of Abbie Rowe/White House Photographs/John F. Kennedy Presidential Library and Museum, Boston.

interstate and Federal-aid systems should be based on the planned use of increasing revenues from present gas and diesel oil taxes, augmented in limited instances with tolls.

I am inclined to the view that it is sounder to finance this program by special bond issues, to be paid off by the above-mentioned revenues which will be collected during the useful life of the roads and pledged to this purpose, rather than by an increase in general revenue obligations. . . .

2. "OPEN SKIES" PROPOSAL   JULY 21, 1955

Disarmament is one of the most important subjects on our agenda. It is also extremely difficult. In recent years the scientists have discovered methods of making weapons many, many times more destructive of opposing armed forces—but also of homes, and industries and lives—than ever known or even imagined before. These same scientific discoveries have made much more complex the problems of limitation and control and reduction of armament.

After our victory as Allies in World War II, my country rapidly disarmed. Within a few years our armament was at a very low level. Then events occurred beyond our borders which caused us to realize that we had disarmed too much. For our own security and to safeguard peace we needed greater strength. Therefore we proceeded to rearm and to associate with others in a partnership for peace and for mutual security.

The American people are determined to maintain and if necessary increase this armed strength for as long a period as is necessary to safeguard peace and to maintain our security. But we know that a mutually dependable system for less armament on the part of all nations would be a better way to safeguard peace and to maintain our security.

It would ease the fears of war in the anxious hearts of people everywhere. It would lighten the burdens upon the backs of the people. It would make it possible for every nation, great and small, developed and less developed, to advance the standards of living of its people, to attain better food, and clothing, and shelter, more of education and larger enjoyment of life.

Therefore the United States government is prepared to enter into a sound and reliable agreement making possible the reduction of armament. I have directed that an intensive and thorough study of this subject be made within our own government. From these studies, which are continuing, a very important principle is emerging to which I referred in my opening statement on Monday.

No sound and reliable agreement can be made unless it is completely covered by an inspection and reporting system adequate to support every portion of the agreement.

The lessons of history teach us that disarmament agreements without adequate reciprocal inspection increase the dangers of war and do not brighten the prospects of peace.

Thus it is my view that the priority attention of our combined study of disarmament should be upon the subject of inspection and reporting.

Questions suggest themselves. How effective an inspection system can be designed which would be mutually and reciprocally acceptable within our countries and the other nations of the world? How would such a system operate? What could it accomplish?

Is certainty against surprise aggression attainable by inspection? Could violations be discovered promptly and effectively counteracted? We have not as yet been able to discover any scientific or other inspection method which would make certain of the elimination of nuclear weapons. . . .

As you can see from these statements, it is our impression that many past proposals of disarmament are more sweeping than can be insured by effective inspection.

. . . I should address myself for a moment principally to the Delegates from the Soviet Union, because our two great countries admittedly possess new and terrible weapons in quantities which do give rise in other parts of the world, or reciprocally, to the fears and dangers of surprise attack.

I propose, therefore, that we take a practical step, that we begin an arrangement, very quickly, as between ourselves—immediately. These steps would include:

To give to each other a complete blueprint of our military establishments, from beginning to end, from one end of our countries to the other; lay out the establishments and provide the blueprints to each other.

Next, to provide within our countries facilities for aerial photography to the other country— we to provide you the facilities within our country, ample facilities for aerial reconnaissance, where you can make all the pictures you choose and take them to your own country to study, you to provide exactly the same facilities for us and we to make these examinations, and by this step to convince the world that we are providing as between ourselves against the possibility of great surprise attack, thus lessening danger and relaxing tension. Likewise we will make more easily attainable a comprehensive and effective system of inspection and disarmament, because what I propose, I assure you, would be but a beginning.

Now from my statements I believe you will anticipate my suggestion. It is that we instruct our representatives in the Subcommittee on Disarmament in discharge of their mandate from the United Nations to give priority effort to the study of inspection and reporting. Such a study could well include a step by step testing of inspection and reporting methods.

The United States is ready to proceed in the study and testing of a reliable system of inspections and reporting, and when that system is proved, then to reduce armaments with all others to the extent that the system will provide assured results.

The successful working out of such a system would do much to develop the mutual confidence which will open wide the avenues of progress for all our peoples.

The quest for peace is the statesman's most exacting duty. Security of the nation entrusted to his care is his greatest responsibility. Practical progress to lasting peace is his fondest hope. Yet in pursuit of his hope he must not betray the trust placed in him as guardian of the people's security. A sound peace—with security, justice, wellbeing, and freedom for the people of the world—*can* be achieved, but only by patiently and thoughtfully following a hard and sure and tested road.

3. LITTLE ROCK HIGH SCHOOL INTEGRATES   SEPTEMBER 24, 1957

For a few minutes I want to speak to you about the serious situation that has arisen in Little Rock. For this talk I have come to the President's office in the White House . . . I intend to pursue this course until the orders of the Federal Court at Little Rock can be executed without unlawful interference.

In that city, under the leadership of demagogic extremists, disorderly mobs have deliberately prevented the carrying out of proper orders from a Federal Court. Local authorities have not eliminated that violent opposition and, under the law, I yesterday issued a Proclamation calling upon the mob to disperse.

This morning the mob again gathered in front of the Central High School of Little Rock, obviously for the purpose of again preventing the carrying out of the Court's order relating to the admission of Negro children to the school.

Whenever normal agencies prove inadequate to the task and it becomes necessary for the Executive Branch of the Federal Government to use its powers and authority to uphold Federal Courts, the President's responsibility is inescapable.

In accordance with that responsibility, I have today issued an Executive Order directing the use of troops under Federal authority to aid in the execution of Federal law at Little Rock, Arkansas. This became necessary when my Proclamation of yesterday was not observed, and the obstruction of justice still continues.

It is important that the reasons for my action be understood by all citizens.

As you know, the Supreme Court of the United States has decided that separate public educational facilities for the races are inherently unequal and therefore compulsory school segregation laws are unconstitutional.

Our personal opinions about the decision have no bearing on the matter of enforcement; the responsibility and authority of the Supreme Court to interpret the Constitution are clear. Local Federal Courts were instructed by the Supreme Court to issue such orders and decrees as might be necessary to achieve admission to public schools without regard to race—and with all deliberate speed.

During the past several years, many communities in our Southern States have instituted public school plans for gradual progress in the enrollment and attendance of school children of all races in order to bring themselves into compliance with the law of the land.

They thus demonstrated to the world that we are a nation in which laws, not men, are supreme.

I regret to say that this truth—the cornerstone of our liberties—was not observed in this instance.

It was my hope that this localized situation would be brought under control by city and State authorities. If the use of local police powers had been sufficient, our traditional method of leaving the problem in those hands would have been pursued. But when large gatherings of obstructionists made it impossible for the decrees of the Court to be carried out, both the law and the national interest demanded that the President take action.

Here is the sequence of events in the development of the Little Rock school case.

In May of 1955, the Little Rock School Board approved a moderate plan for the gradual desegregation of the public schools in that city. It provided that a start toward integration would be made at the present term in the high school, and that the plan would be in full operation by 1963. This plan was challenged in the courts by some who believed that the period of time as proposed was too long.

The United States Court at Little Rock, which has supervisory responsibility under the law for the plan of desegregation in the public schools, dismissed the challenge, thus approving a gradual rather than an abrupt change from the existing system. It found that the school board had acted in good faith in planning for a public school system free from racial discrimination.

Since that time, the court has on three separate occasions issued orders directing that the plan be carried out. All persons were instructed to refrain from interfering with the efforts of the school board to comply with the law.

Proper and sensible observance of the law then demanded the respectful obedience which the nation has a right to expect from all the people. This, unfortunately, has not been the case at Little Rock. Certain misguided persons, many of them imported into Little Rock by agitators, have insisted upon defying the law and have sought to bring it into disrepute. The orders of the court have thus been frustrated.

The very basis of our individual rights and freedoms is the certainty that the President and the Executive Branch of Government will support and insure the carrying out of the decisions of the Federal Courts, even, when necessary with all the means at the President's command.

Unless the President did so, anarchy would result.

There would be no security for any except that which each one of us could provide for himself.

The interest of the nation in the proper fulfillment of the law's requirements cannot yield to opposition and demonstrations by some few persons.

Mob rule cannot be allowed to override the decisions of the courts.

Let me make it very clear that Federal troops are not being used to relieve local and state authorities of their primary duty to preserve the peace and order of the community. Nor are the troops there for the purpose of taking over the responsibility of the School Board and the other responsible local officials in running Central High School. In the present case the troops are there, pursuant to law, solely for the purpose of preventing interference with the orders of the Court.

The proper use of the powers of the Executive Branch to enforce the orders of a Federal Court is limited to extraordinary and compelling circumstances. Manifestly, such an extreme situation has been created in Little Rock. This challenge must be met with such measures as will preserve to the people as a whole their lawfully protected rights in a climate permitting their free and fair exercise.

The overwhelming majority of our people in every section of the country are united in their respect for observance of the law—even in those cases where they may disagree with that law.

They deplore the call of extremists to violence.

The decision of the Supreme Court concerning school integration affects the South more seriously than it does other sections of the country. In that region I have many warm friends, some of them in the city of Little Rock. I have deemed it a great personal privilege to spend in our Southland tours of duty while in the military service and enjoyable recreational periods since that time.

So from intimate personal knowledge, I know that the overwhelming majority of the people in the South—including those of Arkansas and of Little Rock—are of good will, united in their efforts to preserve and respect the law even when they disagree with it.

They do not sympathize with mob rule. They, like the rest of the nation, have proved in two great wars their readiness to sacrifice for America.

A foundation of our American way of life is our national respect for law.

In the South, as elsewhere, citizens are keenly aware of the tremendous disservice that has been done to the people of Arkansas in the eyes of the nation, and that has been done to the nation in the eyes of the world.

At a time when we face a grave situation abroad because of the hatred that Communism bears toward a system of government based on human rights, it would be difficult to exaggerate the harm that is being done to the prestige and influence, and indeed to the safety, of our nation and the world.

Our enemies are gloating over this incident and using it everywhere to misrepresent our nation. We are portrayed as a violator of those standards of conduct which the peoples of the world united to proclaim in the Charter of the United Nations. There they affirmed "faith in fundamental human rights and in the dignity of the human person" and did so "without distinction as to race, sex, language or religion."

And so, with confidence, I call upon citizens of the State of Arkansas to assist in bringing to an immediate end all interference with the law and its processes. If resistance to the Federal Court orders ceases at once, the further presence of Federal troops will be unnecessary and the City of Little Rock will return to its normal habits of peace and order and a blot upon the fair name and high honor of our nation in the world will be removed. . . .

4. STATEHOOD FOR HAWAII   MARCH 18, 1959

It has given me great satisfaction to sign the Act providing for the admission of Hawaii into the Union.

Since my inauguration in 1953 I have consistently urged that this legislation be enacted, so the action of the Congress so early in this session is most gratifying.

Under this legislation, the citizens of Hawaii will soon decide whether their Islands shall become our fiftieth State. In so doing, they will demonstrate anew to the world the vitality of the principles of freedom and self-determination—the principles upon which this Nation was founded 172 years ago.

5. THE CHIEF EXECUTIVE ORDERS A NEW FLAG   AUGUST 21, 1959

Executive Order 10834: The Flag of the United States

Whereas the State of Hawaii has this day been admitted into the Union; and
Whereas section 2 of title 4 of the United States Code provides as follows:

> On the admission of a new State into the Union one star shall be added to the union of the flag; and such addition shall take effect on the fourth day of July then next succeeding such admission [July 4, 1960]. . . .

6. THE MILITARY INDUSTRIAL COMPLEX   JANUARY 17, 1961

. . . This evening I come to you with a message of leave-taking and farewell, and to share a few final thoughts with you, my countrymen.

Like every other citizen, I wish the new President, and all who will labor with him, Godspeed. I pray that the coming years will be blessed with peace and prosperity for all. . . .

We now stand ten years past the midpoint of a century that has witnessed four major wars among great nations. Three of these involved our own country. Despite these holocausts, America is today the strongest, the most influential and most productive nation in the world. Understandably proud of this pre-eminence, we yet realize that America's leadership and prestige depend, not merely upon our unmatched material progress, riches and military strength, but on how we use our power in the interests of world peace and human betterment. . . .

Crises there will continue to be. In meeting them, whether foreign or domestic, great or small, there is a recurring temptation to feel that some spectacular and costly action could become the miraculous solution to all current difficulties. A huge increase in newer elements of our defense; development of unrealistic programs to cure every ill in agriculture; a dramatic expansion in basic and applied research—these and many other possibilities, each possibly promising in itself, may be suggested as the only way to the road we wish to travel.

But each proposal must be weighed in the light of a broader consideration: the need to maintain balance in and among national programs—balance between the private and the public economy, balance between cost and hoped for advantage—balance between the clearly necessary and the comfortably desirable; balance between our essential requirements as a nation and the duties imposed by the nation upon the individual; balance between actions of the moment and the national welfare of the future. Good judgment seeks balance and progress; lack of it eventually finds imbalance and frustration.

The record of many decades stands as proof that our people and their government have, in the main, understood these truths and have responded to them well, in the face of stress and threat. But threats, new in kind or degree, constantly arise. I mention two only.

A vital element in keeping the peace is our military establishment. Our arms must be mighty, ready for instant action, so that no potential aggressor may be tempted to risk his own destruction.

Our military organization today bears little relation to that known by any of my predecessors in peacetime, or indeed by the fighting men of World War II or Korea.

Until the latest of our world conflicts, the United States had no armaments industry. American makers of plowshares could, with time and as required, make swords as well. But now we can no longer risk emergency improvisation of national defense; we have been compelled to create a permanent armaments industry of vast proportions. Added to this, three and a half million men and women are directly engaged in the defense establishment. We annually spend on military security more than the net income of all United States corporations.

This conjunction of an immense military establishment and a large arms industry is new in the American experience. The total influence—economic, political, even spiritual—is felt in every city, every State house, every office of the Federal government. We recognize the imperative need for this development. Yet we must not fail to comprehend its grave implications. Our toil, resources and livelihood are all involved; so is the very structure of our society.

In the councils of government, we must guard against the acquisition of unwarranted influence, whether sought or unsought, by the military-industrial complex. The potential for the disastrous rise of misplaced power exists and will persist.

We must never let the weight of this combination endanger our liberties or democratic processes. We should take nothing for granted. Only an alert and knowledgeable citizenry can compel the proper meshing of the huge industrial and military machinery of defense with our peaceful methods and goals, so that security and liberty may prosper together.

Akin to, and largely responsible for the sweeping changes in our industrial military posture, has been the technological revolution during recent decades.

In this revolution, research has become central; it also becomes more formalized, complex, and costly. A steadily increasing share is conducted for, by, or at the direction of, the Federal government.

Today, the solitary inventor, tinkering in his shop, has been overshadowed by task forces of scientists in laboratories and testing fields. In the same fashion, the free university, historically the fountainhead of free ideas and scientific discovery has experienced a revolution in the conduct of research. Partly because of the huge costs involved, a government contract becomes virtually a substitute for intellectual curiosity. For every old blackboard there are now hundreds of new electronic computers.

The prospect of domination of the nation's scholars by Federal employment, project allocations, and the power of money is ever present—and is gravely to be regarded.

Yet, in holding scientific research and discovery in respect, as we should, we must also be alert to the equal and opposite danger that public policy could itself become the captive of a scientific-technological elite.

It is the task of statesmanship to mold, to balance, and to integrate these and other forces, new and old, within the principles of our democratic system—ever aiming toward the supreme goals of our free society.

Another factor in maintaining balance involves the element of time. As we peer into society's future, we—you and I, and our government—must avoid the impulse to live only for today, plundering, for our own ease and convenience, the precious resources of tomorrow. We cannot mortgage the material assets of our grandchildren without risking the loss also of their political and spiritual heritage. We want democracy to survive for all generations to come, not to become the insolvent phantom of tomorrow.

Down the long lane of the history yet to be written America knows that this world of ours, ever growing smaller, must avoid becoming a community of dreadful fear and hate, and be, instead, a proud confederation of mutual trust and respect.

Such a confederation must be one of equals. The weakest must come to the conference table with the same confidence as do we, protected as we are by our moral, economic, and military strength. That table, though scarred by many past frustrations, cannot be abandoned for the certain agony of the battlefield.

Disarmament, with mutual honor and confidence, is a continuing imperative. Together we must learn how to compose differences, not with arms, but with intellect and decent purpose. Because this need is so sharp and apparent I confess that I lay down my official responsibilities in this field with a definite sense of disappointment. As one who has witnessed the horror and the lingering sadness of war—as one who knows that another war could utterly destroy this civilization which has been so slowly and painfully built over thousands of years—I wish I could say tonight that a lasting peace is in sight.

Happily, I can say that war has been avoided. Steady progress toward our ultimate goal has been made. But, so much remains to be done. As a private citizen, I shall never cease to do what little I can to help the world advance along that road.

So—in this my last good night to you as your President—I thank you for the many opportunities you have given me for public service in war and peace. I trust that in that service you find some things worthy; as for the rest of it, I know you will find ways to improve performance in the future.

You and I—my fellow citizens—need to be strong in our faith that all nations, under God, will reach the goal of peace with justice. May we be ever unswerving in devotion to principle, confident but humble with power, diligent in pursuit of the Nation's great goals.

To all the peoples of the world, I once more give expression to America's prayerful and continuing aspiration:

We pray that peoples of all faiths, all races, all nations, may have their great human needs satisfied; that those now denied opportunity shall come to enjoy it to the full; that all who yearn for freedom may experience its spiritual blessings; that those who have freedom will understand, also, its heavy responsibilities; that all who are insensitive to the needs of others will learn charity; that the scourges of poverty, disease and ignorance will be made to disappear from the earth, and that, in the goodness of time, all peoples will come to live together in a peace guaranteed by the binding force of mutual respect and love.

35

John F. Kennedy

1. INAUGURAL ADDRESS JANUARY 20, 1961

We observe today not a victory of party but a celebration of freedom, symbolizing an end as well as a beginning, signifying renewal as well as change. For I have sworn before you and Almighty God the same solemn oath our forebears prescribed nearly a century and three-quarters ago.

The world is very different now. For man holds in his mortal hands the power to abolish all forms of human poverty and all forms of human life. And yet the same revolutionary belief for which our forebears fought is still at issue around the globe, the belief that the rights of man come not from the generosity of the state but from the hand of God.

We dare not forget today that we are the heirs of that first revolution. Let the word go forth from this time and place, to friend and foe alike, that the torch has been passed to a new generation of Americans, born in this century, tempered by war, disciplined by a hard and bitter peace, proud of our ancient heritage, and unwilling to witness or permit the slow undoing of those human rights to which this nation has always been committed, and to which we are committed today at home and around the world.

Let every nation know, whether it wishes us well or ill, that we shall pay any price, bear any burden, meet any hardship, support any friend, oppose any foe to assure the survival and the success of liberty.

. . . To those old allies whose cultural and spiritual origins we share, we pledge the loyalty of faithful friends. United, there is little we cannot do in a host of co-operative ventures. Divided, there is little we can do, for we dare not meet a powerful challenge at odds and split asunder.

To those new states whom we welcome to the ranks of the free, we pledge our word that one form of colonial control shall not have passed away merely to be replaced by a far more iron tyranny. We shall not always expect to find them supporting our view. But we shall always hope to find them strongly supporting their own freedom, and to remember that, in the past, those who foolishly sought power by riding the back of the tiger ended up inside.

To those peoples in the huts and villages of half the globe struggling to break the bonds of mass misery, we pledge our best efforts to help them help themselves, for whatever period is required, not because the Communists may be doing it, not because we seek their votes, but because it is right. If a free society cannot help the many who are poor, it cannot save the few who are rich.

To our sister republics south of our border, we offer a special pledge: to convert our good words into good deeds, in a new alliance for progress, to assist free men and free governments in casting off the chains of poverty. But this peaceful revolution of hope cannot become the prey of hostile powers. Let all our neighbors know that we shall join with them to oppose aggression or subversion anywhere in the Americas. And let every other power know that this hemisphere intends to remain the master of its own house.

To that world assembly of sovereign states, the United Nations, our last best hope in an age where the instruments of war have far outpaced the instruments of peace, we renew our pledge of support: to prevent it from becoming merely a forum for invective, to strengthen its shield of the new and the weak, and to enlarge the area in which its writ may run.

Finally, to those nations who would make themselves our adversary, we offer not a pledge but a request: that both sides begin anew the quest for peace, before the dark powers of destruction unleashed by science engulf all humanity in planned or accidental self-destruction.

We dare not tempt them with weakness. For only when our arms are sufficient beyond doubt can we be certain beyond doubt that they will never be employed.

But neither can two great and powerful groups of nations take comfort from our present course—both sides over-burdened by the cost of modern weapons, both rightly alarmed by the steady spread of the deadly atom, yet both racing to alter that uncertain balance of terror that stays the hand of mankind's final war.

So let us begin anew, remembering on both sides that civility is not a sign of weakness, and sincerity is always subject to proof. Let us never negotiate out of fear, but let us never fear to negotiate.

Let both sides explore what problems unite us instead of belaboring those problems which divide us.

Let both sides, for the first time, formulate serious and precise proposals for the inspection and control of arms, and bring the absolute power to destroy other nations under the absolute control of all nations.

Let both sides seek to invoke the wonders of science instead of its terrors. Together let us explore the stars, conquer the deserts, eradicate disease, tap the ocean depths and encourage the arts and commerce. Let both sides unite to heed in all corners of the earth the command of Isaiah to "undo the heavy burdens . . . let the oppressed go free."

And if a beachhead of co-operation may push back the jungle of suspicion, let both sides join in creating a new endeavor, not a new balance of power, but a new world of law, where the strong are just and the weak secure and the peace preserved.

All this will not be finished in the first one hundred days. Nor will it be finished in the first one thousand days, nor in the life of this Administration, nor even perhaps in our lifetime on this planet. But let us begin.

In your hands, my fellow citizens, more than mine, will rest the final success or failure of our course. Since this country was founded, each generation of Americans has been summoned to give testimony to its national loyalty. The graves of young Americans who answered the call to service surround the globe.

Now the trumpet summons us again—not as a call to bear arms, though arms we need; not as a call to battle, though embattled we are; but a call to bear the burden of a long twilight struggle, year in and year out, "rejoicing in hope, patient in tribulation," a struggle against the common enemies of man: tyranny, poverty, disease and war itself.

Can we forge against these enemies a grand and global alliance, North and South, East and West, that can assure a more fruitful life for all mankind? Will you join in that historic effort?

In the long history of the world, only a few generations have been granted the role of defending freedom in its hour of maximum danger. I do not shrink from this responsibility; I welcome it. I do not believe that any of us would exchange places with any other people or any other generation.

Figure 35.1 JFK and Jackie Kennedy at Blair House, May 3, 1961, courtesy of Abbie Rowe/White House Photographs/John F. Kennedy Presidential Library and Museum, Boston.

The energy, the faith, the devotion which we bring to this endeavor will light our country and all who serve it, and the glow from that fire can truly light the world.

And so, my fellow Americans, ask not what your country can do for you; ask what you can do for your country.

My fellow citizens . . . ask not what America will do for you, but what together we can do for the freedom of man.

Finally . . . ask of us here the same high standards of strength and sacrifice which we ask of you. With a good conscience our only sure reward, with history the final judge of our deeds, let us go forth to lead the land we love, asking His blessing and His help, but knowing that here on earth God's work must truly be our own.

2. BIRTH OF THE PEACE CORPS   MARCH 1, 1961

I recommend to the Congress the establishment of a permanent Peace Corps—a pool of trained American men and women sent overseas by the U.S. Government or through private organizations and institutions to help foreign countries meet their urgent needs for skilled manpower.

I have today signed an Executive Order establishing a Peace Corps on a temporary pilot basis.

The temporary Peace Corps will be a source of information and experience to aid us in formulating more effective plans for a permanent organization. In addition, by starting the Peace Corps now we will be able to begin training young men and women for overseas duty this summer with the objective of placing them in overseas positions by late fall. This temporary Peace Corps is being established under existing authority in the Mutual Security Act and will be located in the Department of State. Its initial expenses will be paid from appropriations currently available for our foreign aid program.

Throughout the world the people of the newly developing nations are struggling for economic and social progress which reflects their deepest desires. Our own freedom and the future of freedom around the world, depend, in a very real sense, on their ability to build growing and independent nations where men can live in dignity, liberated from the bonds of hunger, ignorance and poverty.

One of the greatest obstacles to the achievement of this goal is the lack of trained men and women with the skill to teach the young and assist in the operation of development projects—men and women with the capacity to cope with the demands of swiftly evolving economies, and with the dedication to put that capacity to work in the villages, the mountains, the towns and the factories of dozens of struggling nations.

The vast task of economic development urgently requires skilled people to do the work of the society—to help teach in the schools, construct development projects, demonstrate modern methods of sanitation in the villages, and perform a hundred other tasks calling for training and advanced knowledge.

To meet this urgent need for skilled manpower we are proposing the establishment of a Peace Corps—an organization which will recruit and train American volunteers, sending them abroad to work with the people of other nations.

This organization will differ from existing assistance programs in that its members will supplement technical advisers by offering the specific skills needed by developing nations if they are to put technical advice to work. They will help provide the skilled manpower necessary to carry out the development projects planned by the host governments, acting at a working level and serving at great personal sacrifice. There is little doubt that the number of those who wish to serve will be far greater than our capacity to absorb them. . . .

. . . Among the specific programs to which Peace Corps members can contribute are: teaching in primary and secondary schools, especially as part of national English language teaching programs; participation in the worldwide program of malaria eradication; instruction and operation of public health and sanitation projects; aiding in village development through school construction and other programs; increasing rural agricultural productivity by assisting local farmers to use modern implements and techniques. The initial emphasis of these programs will be on teaching. Thus the Peace Corps members will be an effective means of implementing the development programs of the host countries programs which our technical assistance operations have helped to formulate.

The Peace Corps will not be limited to the young, or to college graduates. All Americans who are qualified will be welcome to join this effort. But undoubtedly the Corps will be made up primarily of young people as they complete their formal education. . . .

In all instances the men and women of the Peace Corps will go only to those countries where their services and skills are genuinely needed and desired. U.S. Operations Missions, supplemented where necessary by special Peace Corps teams, will consult with leaders in foreign countries in order to determine where Peace Corpsmen are needed, the types of job they can best fill, and the number of people who can be usefully employed. The Peace Corps will not supply personnel for marginal undertakings without a sound economic or social justification. . . .

Membership in the Peace Corps will be open to all Americans, and applications will be available shortly. Where application is made directly to the Peace Corps—the vast majority of cases—they will be carefully screened to make sure that those who are selected can contribute to Peace Corps programs, and have the personal qualities which will enable them to represent the United States abroad with honor and dignity. In those cases where application is made directly to a private group, the same basic standards will be maintained. Each new recruit will receive a training and orientation period varying from six weeks to six months. This training will include courses in the culture and language of the country to which they are being sent and specialized training designed to increase the work skills of recruits. In some cases training will be conducted by participant agencies and universities in approved training programs. . . .

Length of service in the Corps will vary depending on the kind of project and the country, generally ranging from two to three years. Peace Corps members will often serve under conditions of physical hardship, living under primitive conditions among the people of developing nations. For every Peace Corps member service will mean a great financial sacrifice. They will receive no salary. Instead they will be given an allowance which will only be sufficient to meet their basic needs and maintain health. It is essential that Peace Corpsmen and women live simply and unostentatiously among the people they have come to assist. At the conclusion of their tours, members of the Peace Corps will receive a small sum in the form of severance pay based on length of service abroad. . . . Service with the Peace Corps will not exempt volunteers from Selective Service.

The United States will assume responsibility for supplying medical services to Peace Corps members and ensuring supplies and drugs necessary to good health.

I have asked the temporary Peace Corps to begin plans and make arrangements for pilot programs. A minimum of several hundred volunteers could be selected, trained and at work abroad by the end of this calendar year. It is hoped that within a few years several thousand Peace Corps members will be working in foreign lands.

. . . The benefits of the Peace Corps will not be limited to the countries in which it serves. Our own young men and women will be enriched by the experience of living and working in foreign lands. They will have acquired new skills and experience which will aid them in their future careers and add to our own country's supply of trained personnel and teachers. They will return better able to assume the responsibilities of American citizenship and with greater understanding of our global responsibilities.

Although this is an American Peace Corps, the problem of world development is not just an American problem. Let us hope that other nations will mobilize the spirit and energies and skill of their people in some form of Peace Corps—making our own effort only one step in a major international effort to increase the welfare of all men and improve understanding among nations.

3. CUBAN MISSILE CRISIS: REPLY TO CHAIRMAN KHRUSHCHEV   OCTOBER 27, 1962

I am replying at once to your broadcast message of 28 October, even though the official text has not yet reached me, because of the great importance I attach to moving forward promptly to the settlement of the Cuban crisis. I think that you and I, with our heavy responsibilities for the maintenance of peace, were aware that developments were approaching a point where events could have become unmanageable. So I welcome this message and consider it an important contribution to peace.

The distinguished efforts of Acting Secretary General U Thant have greatly facilitated both our tasks. I consider my letter to you of 27th October and your reply of today as firm undertakings on the part of both our governments which should be promptly carried out. I hope that the necessary measures can at once be taken through the United Nations as your message says, so that the United States in turn can remove the quarantine measures now in effect. I have already made arrangements to report all these matters to the Organization of American States, whose members share a deep interest in a genuine peace in the Caribbean area.

You referred in your letter to a violation of your frontier by an American aircraft in the area of the Chukotsk Peninsula. I have learned that this plane, without arms or photographic equipment, was engaged in an air sampling mission in connection with your nuclear tests. Its course was direct from Eielson Air Force Base in Alaska to the North Pole and return. In turning south, the pilot made a serious navigational error which carried him over Soviet territory. He immediately made an emergency call on open radio for navigational assistance and was guided back to his home base by the most direct route. I regret this incident and will see to it that every precaution is taken to prevent recurrence.

Mr. Chairman, both of our countries have great unfinished tasks and I know that your people as well as those of the United States can ask for nothing better than to pursue them free from the fear of war. Modern science and technology have given us the possibility of making labor fruitful beyond anything that could have been dreamed of a few decades ago.

I agree with you that we must devote urgent attention to the problem of disarmament, as it relates to the whole world and also to critical areas. Perhaps now, as we step back from danger, we can together make real progress in this vital field. I think we should give priority to questions relating to the proliferation of nuclear weapons, on earth and in outer space, and to the great effort for a nuclear test ban. But we should also work hard to see if wider measures of disarmament can be agreed and put into operation at an early date. The United States government will be prepared to discuss these questions urgently, and in a constructive spirit, at Geneva or elsewhere.

4. CIVIL RIGHTS: ADDRESS TO NATION   JUNE 11, 1963

This afternoon, following a series of threats and defiant statements, the presence of Alabama National Guardsmen was required on the University of Alabama to carry out the final and unequivocal order of the United States District Court of the Northern District of Alabama. That order called for the admission of two clearly qualified young Alabama residents, who happened to have been born Negro.

That they were admitted peacefully on the campus is due in good measure to the conduct of the students of the University of Alabama, who met their responsibilities in a constructive way.

I hope that every American, regardless of where he lives, will stop and examine his conscience about this and other related incidents. This Nation was founded by men of many nations and backgrounds. It was founded on the principle that all men are created equal, and that the rights of every man are diminished when the rights of one man are threatened.

Today we are committed to a worldwide struggle to promote and protect the rights of all who wish to be free. And when Americans are sent to Vietnam or West Berlin, we do not ask for whites only. It ought to be possible, therefore, for American students of any color to attend any public institution they select without having to be backed up by troops.

It ought to be possible for American consumers of any color to receive equal service in places of public accommodation, such as hotels and restaurants and theaters and retail stores, without being forced to resort to demonstrations in the street, and it ought to be possible for American citizens of any color to register and to vote in a free election without interference or fear of reprisal.

It ought to be possible, in short, for every American to enjoy the privileges of being American without regard to his race or his color. In short, every American ought to have the right to be treated as he would wish to be treated, as one would wish his children to be treated. But this is not the case.

The Negro baby born in America today, regardless of the section of the Nation in which he is born, has about one-half as much chance of completing a high school as a white baby born in the same place on the same day, one-third as much chance of completing college, one-third as much chance of becoming a professional man, twice as much chance of becoming unemployed, about one-seventh as much chance of earning $10,000 a year, a life expectancy which is 7 years shorter, and the prospects of earning only half as much.

This is not a sectional issue. Difficulties over segregation and discrimination exist in every city, in every State of the Union, producing in many cities a rising tide of discontent that threatens the public safety. Nor is this a partisan issue. In a time of domestic crisis men of good will and generosity should be able to unite regardless of party or politics. This is not even a legal or legislative issue alone. It is better to settle these matters in the courts than on the streets, and new laws are needed at every level, but law alone cannot make men see right.

We are confronted primarily with a moral issue. It is as old as the scriptures and is as clear as the American Constitution.

The heart of the question is whether all Americans are to be afforded equal rights and equal opportunities, whether we are going to treat our fellow Americans as we want to be treated. If an American, because his skin is dark, cannot eat lunch in a restaurant open to the public, if he cannot send his children to the best public school available, if he cannot vote for the public officials who represent him, if, in short, he cannot enjoy the full and free life which all of us want, then who among us would be content to have the color of his skin changed and stand in his place? Who among us would then be content with the counsels of patience and delay?

One hundred years of delay have passed since President Lincoln freed the slaves, yet their heirs, their grandsons, are not fully free. They are not yet freed from the bonds of injustice. They are not yet freed from social and economic oppression. And this Nation, for all its hopes and all its boasts, will not be fully free until all its citizens are free. We preach freedom around the world, and we mean it, and we cherish our freedom here at home, but are we to say to the world, and much more importantly, to each other that this is a land of the free except for the Negroes; that we have no second-class citizens except Negroes; that we have no class or cast system, no ghettoes, no master race except with respect to Negroes?

Now the time has come for this Nation to fulfill its promise. The events in Birmingham and elsewhere have so increased the cries for equality that no city or State or legislative body can prudently choose to ignore them.

The fires of frustration and discord are burning in every city, North and South, where legal remedies are not at hand. Redress is sought in the streets, in demonstrations, parades, and protests which create tensions and threaten violence and threaten lives.

We face, therefore, a moral crisis as a country and as a people. It cannot be met by repressive police action. It cannot be left to increased demonstrations in the streets. It cannot be quieted by token moves or talk. It is a time to act in the Congress, in your State and local legislative body and, above all, in all of our daily lives.

It is not enough to pin the blame on others, to say this is a problem of one section of the country or another, or deplore the fact that we face. A great change is at hand, and our task, our obligation, is to make that revolution, that change, peaceful and constructive for all.

Those who do nothing are inviting shame as well as violence. Those who act boldly are recognizing right as well as reality.

Next week I shall ask the Congress of the United States to act, to make a commitment it has not fully made in this century to the proposition that race has no place in American life or law. The Federal judiciary has upheld that proposition in a series of forthright cases. The executive branch has adopted that proposition in the conduct of its affairs, including the employment of Federal personnel, the use of Federal facilities, and the sale of federally financed housing.

But there are other necessary measures which only the Congress can provide, and they must be provided at this session. The old code of equity law under which we live commands for every wrong a remedy. . . . Unless the Congress acts, their only remedy is in the street.

I am, therefore, asking the Congress to enact legislation giving all Americans the right to be served in facilities which are open to the public—hotels, restaurants, theaters, retail stores, and similar establishments.

This seems to me to be an elementary right. Its denial is an arbitrary indignity that no American in 1963 should have to endure, but many do.

I have recently met with scores of business leaders urging them to take voluntary action to end this discrimination and I have been encouraged by their response, and in the last 2 weeks over 75 cities have seen progress made in desegregating these kinds of facilities. But many are unwilling to act alone, and for this reason, nationwide legislation is needed if we are to move this problem from the streets to the courts.

I am also asking Congress to authorize the Federal Government to participate more fully in lawsuits designed to end segregation in public education. We have succeeded in persuading many districts to desegregate voluntarily. Dozens have admitted Negroes without violence. Today a Negro is attending a State-supported institution in every one of our 50 States, but the pace is very slow.

Too many Negro children entering segregated grade schools at the time of the Supreme Court's decision 9 years ago will enter segregated high schools this fall, having suffered a loss which can never be restored. The lack of an adequate education denies the Negro a chance to get a decent job.

The orderly implementation of the Supreme Court decision, therefore, cannot be left solely to those who may not have the economic resources to carry the legal action or who may be subject to harassment.

Other features will be also requested, including greater protection for the right to vote. But legislation, I repeat, cannot solve this problem alone. It must be solved in the homes of every American in every community across our country.

In this respect, I want to pay tribute to those citizens North and South who have been working in their communities to make life better for all. They are acting not out of a sense of legal duty but out of a sense of human decency.

Like our soldiers and sailors in all parts of the world they are meeting freedom's challenge on the firing line, and I salute them for their honor and their courage.

My fellow Americans, this is a problem which faces us all—in every city of the North as well as the South. Today there are Negroes unemployed, two or three times as many compared to whites, inadequate in education, moving into the large cities, unable to find work, young people particularly out of work without hope, denied equal rights, denied the opportunity to eat at a restaurant or lunch counter or go to a movie theater, denied the right to a decent education, denied almost today the right to attend a State university even though qualified. It seems to me that these are matters which concern us all, not merely Presidents or Congressmen or Governors, but every citizen of the United States.

This is one country. It has become one country because all of us and all the people who came here had an equal chance to develop their talents.

We cannot say to 10 percent of the population that you can't have that right; that your children can't have the chance to develop whatever talents they have; that the only way that they are going to get their rights is to go into the streets and demonstrate. I think we owe them and we owe ourselves a better country than that.

Therefore, I am asking for your help in making it easier for us to move ahead and to provide the kind of equality of treatment which we would want ourselves; to give a chance for every child to be educated to the limit of his talents.

As I have said before, not every child has an equal talent or an equal ability or an equal motivation, but they should have the equal right to develop their talent and their ability and their motivation, to make something of themselves.

We have a right to expect that the Negro community will be responsible, will uphold the law, but they have a right to expect that the law will be fair, that the Constitution will be color blind, as Justice Harlan said at the turn of the century.

This is what we are talking about and this is a matter which concerns this country and what it stands for, and in meeting it I ask the support of all our citizens. . . .

5. BERLIN WALL SPEECH   JUNE 26, 1963

I am proud to come to this city as the guest of your distinguished Mayor, who has symbolized throughout the world the fighting spirit of West Berlin. And I am proud to visit the Federal Republic with your distinguished Chancellor who for so many years has committed Germany to democracy and freedom and progress, and to come here in the company of my fellow American, General Clay, who has been in this city during its great moments of crisis and will come again if ever needed.

Two thousand years ago the proudest boast was "*civis Romanus sum.*" Today, in the world of freedom, the proudest boast is "*Ich bin ein Berliner.*"

I appreciate my interpreter translating my German!

There are many people in the world who really don't understand, or say they don't, what is the great issue between the free world and the Communist world. Let them come to Berlin. There are some who say that communism is the wave of the future. Let them come to Berlin. And there are some who say in Europe and elsewhere we can work with the Communists. Let them come to Berlin. And there are even a few who say that it is true that communism is an evil system, but it permits us to make economic progress. *Lass' sie nach Berlin kommen.* Let them come to Berlin.

Freedom has many difficulties and democracy is not perfect, but we have never had to put a wall up to keep our people in, to prevent them from leaving us. I want to say, on behalf of my countrymen, who live many miles away on the other side of the Atlantic, who are far distant from you, that they take the greatest pride that they have been able to share with you, even from a distance, the story of the last 18 years. I know of no town, no city, that has been besieged for 18 years that still lives with the vitality and the force, and the hope and the determination of the city of West Berlin. While the wall is the most obvious and vivid demonstration of the failures of the Communist system, for all the world to see, we take no satisfaction in it, for it is, as your Mayor has said, an offense not only against history but an offense against humanity, separating families, dividing husbands and wives and brothers and sisters, and dividing a people who wish to be joined together.

What is true of this city is true of Germany—real, lasting peace in Europe can never be assured as long as one German out of four is denied the elementary right of free men, and that is to make a free choice. In 18 years of peace and good faith, this generation of Germans has earned the right to be free, including the right to unite their families and their nation in lasting peace, with good will to all people. You live in a defended island of freedom, but your life is part of the main. So let me ask you, as I close, to lift your eyes beyond the dangers of today, to the hopes of tomorrow, beyond the freedom merely of this city of Berlin, or your country of Germany, to the advance of freedom everywhere, beyond the wall to the day of peace with justice, beyond yourselves and ourselves to all mankind.

Freedom is indivisible, and when one man is enslaved, all are not free. When all are free, then we can look forward to that day when this city will be joined as one and this country and this great

Continent of Europe in a peaceful and hopeful globe. When that day finally comes, as it will, the people of West Berlin can take sober satisfaction in the fact that they were in the front lines for almost two decades.

All free men, wherever they may live, are citizens of Berlin, and, therefore, as a free man, I take pride in the words "*Ich bin ein Berliner.*"

6. HATS OFF TO AEROSPACE   NOVEMBER 21, 1963

For more than 3 years I have spoken about the New Frontier. This is not a partisan term, and it is not the exclusive property of Republicans or Democrats. It refers, instead, to this Nation's place in history, to the fact that we do stand on the edge of a great new era, filled with both crisis and opportunity, an era to be characterized by achievement and by challenge. It is an era which calls for action and for the best efforts of all those who would test the unknown and the uncertain in every phase of human endeavor. It is a time for pathfinders and pioneers.

I have come to Texas today to salute an outstanding group of pioneers, the men who man the Brooks Air Force Base School of Aerospace Medicine and the Aerospace Medical Center. It is fitting that San Antonio should be the site of this center and this school as we gather to dedicate this complex of buildings. For this city has long been the home of the pioneers in the air. It was here that Sidney Brooks, whose memory we honor today, was born and raised. It was here that Charles Lindbergh and Claire Chennault, and a host of others, who, in World War I and World War II and Korea, and even today have helped demonstrate American mastery of the skies, trained at Kelly Field and Randolph Field, which form a major part of aviation history. And in the new frontier of outer space, while headlines may be made by others in other places, history is being made every day by the men and women of the Aerospace Medical Center, without whom there could be no history.

Many Americans make the mistake of assuming that space research has no values here on earth. Nothing could be further from the truth. Just as the wartime development of radar gave us the transistor, and all that it made possible, so research in space medicine holds the promise of substantial benefit for those of us who are earthbound. . . .

I give you three examples: first, medical space research may open up new understanding of man's relation to his environment. Examinations of the astronaut's physical, and mental, and emotional reactions can teach us more about the differences between normal and abnormal, about the causes and effects of disorientation, about changes in metabolism which could result in extending the life span. When you study the effects on our astronauts of exhaust gases which can contaminate their environment, and you seek ways to alter these gases so as to reduce their toxicity, you are working on problems similar to those in our great urban centers which themselves are being corrupted by gases and which must be clear.

And second, medical space research may revolutionize the technology and the techniques of modern medicine. Whatever new devices are created, for example, to monitor our astronauts, to measure their heart activity, their breathing, their brain waves, their eye motion, at great distances and under difficult conditions, will also represent a major advance in general medical instrumentation. Heart patients may even be able to wear a light monitor which will sound a warning if their activity exceeds certain limits. An instrument recently developed to record automatically the impact of acceleration upon an astronaut's eyes will also be of help to small children who are suffering miserably from eye defects, but are unable to describe their impairment. And also by the use of instruments similar to those used in Project Mercury, this Nation's private as well as public nursing services are being improved, enabling one nurse now to give more critically ill patients greater attention than they ever could in the past.

And third, medical space research may lead to new safeguards against hazards common to many environments. Specifically, our astronauts will need fundamentally new devices to protect them from the ill effects of radiation which can have a profound influence upon medicine and man's relations to our present environment.

Here at this center we have the laboratories, the talent, the resources to give new impetus to vital research in the life centers. I am not suggesting that the entire space program is justified alone by what is done in medicine. The space program stands on its own as a contribution to national strength. And last Saturday at Cape Canaveral I saw our new Saturn C-1 rocket booster, which, with its payload, when it rises in December of this year, will be, for the first time, the largest booster in the world, carrying into space the largest payload that any country in the world has ever sent into space.

I think the United States should be a leader. A country as rich and powerful as this which bears so many burdens and responsibilities, which has so many opportunities, should be second to none. And in December, while I do not regard our mastery of space as anywhere near complete, while I recognize that there are still areas where we are behind—at least in one area, the size of the booster—this year I hope the United States will be ahead. And I am for it. We have a long way to go. Many weeks and months and years of long, tedious work lie ahead. There will be setbacks and frustrations and disappointments. There will be, as there always are, pressures in this country to do less in this area as in so many others, and temptations to do something else. . . . But this research here must go on. This space effort must go on. The conquest of space must and will go ahead. That much we know. That much we can say with confidence and conviction.

Frank O'Connor, the Irish writer, tells in one of his books how, as a boy, he and his friends would make their way across the countryside, and when they came to an orchard wall that seemed too high and too doubtful to try and too difficult to permit their voyage to continue, they took off their hats and tossed them over the wall—and then they had no choice but to follow them.

Figure 35.2 JFK and his brother Robert in the West Wing colonnade outside the Oval Office, October 3, 1962, courtesy of Cecil Stoughton/White House Photographs/John F. Kennedy Presidential Library and Museum, Boston.

This Nation has tossed its cap over the wall of space, and we have no choice but to follow it. Whatever the difficulties, they will be overcome. Whatever the hazards, they must be guarded against. With the vital help of this Aerospace Medical Center, with the help of all those who labor in the space endeavor, with the help and support of all Americans, we will climb this wall with safety and with speed—and we shall then explore the wonders on the other side.

7. NEW FRONTIERS OF PEACE AND ABUNDANCE   NOVEMBER 22, 1963
(UNDELIVERED ADDRESS)

. . .The historic bonds which link Texas and the Democratic Party are no temporary union of convenience. They are deeply embedded in the history and purpose of this State and party. For the Democratic Party is not a collection of diverse interests brought together only to win elections. We are united instead by a common history and heritage—by a respect for the deeds of the past and a recognition of the needs of the future. Never satisfied with today, we have always staked our fortunes on tomorrow. That is the kind of State which Texas has always been—that is the kind of vision and vitality which Texans have always possessed—and that is the reason why Texas will always be basically Democratic.

. . . It was the policies and programs of the Democratic Party which helped bring income to your farmers, industries to your cities, employment to your workers, and the promotion and preservation of your natural resources. No one who remembers the days of 5-cent cotton and 30-cent oil will forget the ties between the success of this State and the success of our party.

Three years ago this fall I toured this State with Lyndon Johnson, Sam Rayburn, and Ralph Yarborough as your party's candidate for President. We pledged to increase America's strength against its enemies, its prestige among its friends, and the opportunities it offered to its citizens. Those pledges have been fulfilled. The words spoken in Texas have been transformed into action in Washington, and we have America moving again.

Here in Austin, I pledged in 1960 to restore world confidence in the vitality and energy of American society. That pledge has been fulfilled. We have won the respect of allies and adversaries alike through our determined stand on behalf of freedom around the world, from West Berlin to Southeast Asia—through our resistance to Communist intervention in the Congo and Communist missiles in Cuba—and through our initiative in obtaining the nuclear test ban treaty which can stop the pollution of our atmosphere and start us on the path to peace. In San José and Mexico City, in Bonn and West Berlin, in Rome and County Cork, I saw and heard and felt a new appreciation for an America on the move—an America which has shown that it cares about the needy of its own and other lands, an America which has shown that freedom is the way to the future, an America which is known to be first in the effort for peace as well as preparedness.

In Amarillo, I pledged in 1960 that the businessmen of this State and Nation—particularly the small businessman who is the backbone of our economy—would move ahead as our economy moved ahead. That pledge has been fulfilled. Business profits—having risen 43 percent in 2 years—now stand at a record high; and businessmen all over America are grateful for liberalized depreciation for the investment tax credit, and for our programs to increase their markets at home as well as abroad. We have proposed a massive tax reduction, with particular benefits for small business. We have stepped up the activities of the Small Business Administration, making available in the last 3 years almost $50 million to more than 1,000 Texas firms, and doubling their opportunity to share in Federal procurement contracts. Our party believes that what's good for the American people is good for American business, and the last 3 years have proven the validity of that proposition.

In Grand Prairie, I pledged in 1960 that this country would no longer tolerate the lowest rate of economic growth of any major industrialized nation in the world. That pledge has been and is being fulfilled. In less than 3 years our national output will shortly have risen by a record $100 billion—industrial production is up 22 percent, personal income is up 16 percent. And the *Wall Street Journal* pointed out a short time ago that the United States now leads most of Western Europe in the rate of business expansion and the margin of corporate profits. Here in Texas—where 3 years ago, at the very time I was speaking, real per capita personal income was actually declining as the industrial recession spread to this State—more than 200,000 new jobs have been created, unemployment has declined, and personal income rose last year to an all-time high. This growth must go on. . . . And that is why we need a tax cut of $11 billion, as an assurance of future growth and insurance against an early recession. . . .

In Dallas, I pledged in 1960 to step up the development of both our natural and our human resources. That pledge has been fulfilled. The policy of "no new starts" has been reversed. The Canadian River project will provide water for 11 Texas cities. The San Angelo project will irrigate some 10,000 acres. We have launched 10 new watershed projects in Texas, completed 7 others, and laid plans for 6 more. A new national park, a new wildlife preserve, and other navigation, reclamation, and natural resource projects are all under way in this State. At the same time we have sought to develop the human resources of Texas and all the Nation, granting loans to 17,500 Texas college students, making more than $17 million available to 249 school districts, and expanding or providing rural library service to 600,000 Texas readers. And if this Congress passes, as now seems likely, pending bills to build college classrooms, increase student loans, build medical schools, provide more community libraries, and assist in the creation of graduate centers, then this Congress will have done more for the cause of education than has been done by any Congress in modern history. Civilization, it was once said, is a race between education and catastrophe—and we intend to win that race for education.

. . . In San Antonio, I pledged in 1960 that a new administration would strive to secure for every American his full constitutional rights. That pledge has been and is being fulfilled. We have not yet secured the objectives desired or the legislation required. But we have, in the last 3 years, by working through voluntary leadership as well as legal action, opened more new doors to members of minority groups—doors to transportation, voting, education, employment, and places of public accommodation—than had been opened in any 3-year or 30-year period in this century. There is no noncontroversial way to fulfill our constitutional pledge to establish justice and promote domestic tranquility, but we intend to fulfill those obligations because they are right.

. . . In El Paso, I pledged in 1960 that we would give the highest and earliest priority to the reestablishment of good relations with the people of Latin America. We are working to fulfill that pledge. An area long neglected has not solved all its problems. The Communist foothold which had already been established has not yet been eliminated. But the trend of Communist expansion has been reversed. The name of Fidel Castro is no longer feared or cheered by substantial numbers in every country. And contrary to the prevailing predictions of 3 years ago, not another inch of Latin American territory has fallen prey to Communist control. . . .

. . . In the last 3 years, we have increased our annual space effort to a greater level than the combined total of all space activities undertaken in the 1950s. We have launched into earth orbit more than 4 times as many space vehicles as had been launched in the previous 3 years. We have focused our wide-ranging efforts around a landing on the moon in this decade. We have put valuable weather and communications satellites into actual operation. We will fire this December the most powerful rocket ever developed anywhere in the world. And we have made it clear to all that the United States of America has no intention of finishing second in outer space. Texas will play a major role in this effort. The Manned Spacecraft Center in Houston will be the cornerstone of our lunar landing project, with a billion dollars already allocated to that center this year. . . .

In Fort Worth, I pledged in 1960 to build a national defense which was second to none—a position I said, which is not "first, but," not "first, if," not "first, when," but first—period. That pledge has been fulfilled. In the past 3 years we have increased our defense budget by over 20 percent; increased the program for acquisition of Polaris submarines from 24 to 41; increased our Minuteman missile purchase program by more than 75 percent; doubled the number of strategic bombers and missiles on alert; doubled the number of nuclear weapons available in the strategic alert forces; increased the tactical nuclear forces deployed in Western Europe by 60 percent; added 5 combat-ready divisions and 5 tactical fighter wings to our Armed Forces; increased our strategic airlift capabilities by 75 percent; and increased our special counter-insurgency forces by 600 percent. We can truly say today, with pride in our voices and peace in our hearts, that the defensive forces of the United States are, without a doubt, the most powerful and resourceful forces anywhere in the world.

Finally, I said in Lubbock in 1960 . . . if Lyndon Johnson and I were elected, we would get this country moving again. That pledge has been fulfilled. In nearly every field of national activity, this country is moving again—and Texas is moving with it. . . . the past 3 years have seen a new burst of action and progress—in Texas and all over America. We have stepped up the fight against crime and slums and poverty in our cities, against the pollution of our streams, against unemployment in our industry, and against waste in the Federal Government. . . .

Almost everywhere we look, the story is the same. In Latin America, in Africa, in Asia, in the councils of the world and in the jungles of far-off nations, there is now renewed confidence in our country and our convictions.

For this country is moving . . . it must not stop. It cannot stop. For this is a time for courage and a time for challenge. Neither conformity nor complacency will do. Neither the fanatics nor the faint-hearted are needed. And our duty as a party is not to our party alone, but to the Nation, and . . . to all mankind. Our duty is not merely the preservation of political power but the preservation of peace and freedom.

So let us not be petty when our cause is so great. Let us not quarrel amongst ourselves when our Nation's future is at stake. Let us stand together with renewed confidence in our cause—united in our heritage of the past and our hopes for the future—and determined that this land we love shall lead all mankind into new frontiers of peace and abundance.

X

TROUBLED YEARS

THE YEARS FOLLOWING the violent death of President Kennedy were years where America lost its bearings. These were troubled years. Americans now experienced a succession of failed presidencies. Two Democrats and two Republicans ascended to the high office of president and all four were incapable of getting America back on track. The institution of the presidency and the nation itself was gravely wounded.

Lyndon Baines Johnson was the eighth Vice President to succeed to the Presidency upon death or assassination. LBJ took charge immediately. The Warren Commission in accordance with its charge investigated the assassination of President Kennedy. The Commission's finding was that a lone assassin, Lee Harvey Oswald, had slain the President. Adherents of the work of the Warren Commission contended then, and now, "case closed." Yet, from its very inception, critics questioned the Warren Commission with regard to process and result. Controversy and speculation continues even to the present day. In fact, recently released archives confirm that the Attorney General and brother of the slain president, Robert Kennedy, along with the First Lady in mourning, Jackie Kennedy, were terribly disturbed by the timing and manner of Lyndon Johnson's swearing in on Air Force One, with the dead President aboard in the next compartment. Jackie Kennedy's extensive 1964 interview with Arthur Schlesinger, Jr. indicates that she harbored deep suspicions about Lyndon Johnson. Controversy persists among historians and others about the fateful event in the history of the presidency and the nation. The release of parts of that poignant interview with Arthur Schlesinger, Jr. has placed a new foot in the door as to reaching a final historical verdict. The door remains open.

Many Americans were confused and hurt by this tragic turn of events at the helm of the ship of state. The nation was dazed. The vast majority of Americans were disposed to give the new president the benefit of their support and their prayers. For his part, Johnson promised a grieving nation that the programs and policies of President Kennedy would continue. He proclaimed his first priority was to honor the memory of the assassinated president by enacting Kennedy's ambitious initiative in civil rights.

Over his first few months in the White House, civil rights legislation remained LBJ's top priority. He did find time to go to Flushing Meadows in New York to preside over the opening ceremonies, on April 22nd, of the 1964 World's Fair. In keeping with the motto for that World's Fair, "Peace through Understanding," President Johnson spoke to the fair goers at the Singer Bowl and managed to incorporate themes pertaining to peace and civil rights. LBJ issued a "prophesy" that "peace is not only possible in our generation; I predict it is coming even earlier."

By the spring of 1964, with the legislative battle well under control, Johnson began to focus on his own popularity and historical legacy. This simply meant becoming the greatest of all presidents.

He struck out with passion and power to put his own mark on history. Towards this end Johnson plunged into a sizable package of legislation identified as the "Great Society."

The Great Society embraced an elaborate array of benefits and controls, using the force and power of the Federal Government to provide opportunity and hope to millions of Americans. The Equal Opportunity Act of 1964, trumpeted as the first salvo in a "war against poverty," created Vista, Head Start, and the Job Corps. President Kennedy had provided the idea base for these programs when he announced in his Inaugural Address: "The World is very different now. For man holds in his mortal hands the power to abolish all forms of human poverty and all forms of human life." The war on poverty had its origins in the New Frontier. The Vista and Job Corps programs were domestic spin-offs of JFK's Peace Corps. Indeed as LBJ entered the final stages of his 1964 election campaign he again promised to continue the programs and policies of his predecessor. With the ghost of John F. Kennedy at his back, Lyndon Johnson appealed to the American electorate and they responded with warm approval, giving LBJ 61 percent of the vote.

Great Society bills flooded Congress. Two new Cabinet institutions appeared—the Department of Housing and Urban Development and the Department of Transportation. The landmark Medicare entitlement was signed by Johnson in Independence, Missouri with former President Harry Truman alongside. The signing of the Education Act of 1965 took place at the one-room schoolhouse he had attended in Texas. New legislation addressed immigration, voting rights, and housing. The National Endowments, for the Arts and for the Humanities, came into being. The President loomed large. He seemed to hover over America, immersed in the issues and legislative agenda of his "Great Society." Energetic to a fault, LBJ hammered away at his vision in order to bring it into reality and America into a new age. It can be argued that he did just that on July 2nd when he signed into law the Civil Rights Act of 1964. While Johnson's landmark legislative accomplishment did not immediately end racism and barbarity, the impenetrable legislative barrier to civil rights legislation would exist no more.

LBJ's Great Society contained a double-edge sword. The President thought in grand proportions. He thoroughly believed that the Great Society could provide America with both guns and butter. In the aftermath of the Cuban Missile Crisis of 1962, the United States would continue to encounter foreign policy challenges, but they now seemed minor in comparison to that threat to the peace of the world. Although President Johnson possessed minimal knowledge and interest in international affairs he managed a series of these challenges reasonably well early on in his administration. The challenge which tragically marked his administration and which revealed his foreign policy inadequacies and leadership flaws, was the conflict in Vietnam. The war in Vietnam, remote and inconsequential when he took office, had become the inferno which would destroy his presidency and tarnish his historical legacy.

At the time of President Kennedy's assassination there were approximately 16,000 American "advisors" in Vietnam, seeking to develop political stability and military effectiveness. LBJ involved the United States in a full-blown military effort. He placed combat boots on the ground. To Johnson and nearly all of the influential members of his administration, Ho Chi Minh represented further expansion of communism on the Asian subcontinent. A communist victory, Johnson reasoned, would place Vietnam in a position of subservience to the Soviets and Chinese. The President concluded that defeating Ho would represent a defining moment in the Cold War. At the same time, military defeat for the United States would endanger the stability of the entire Pacific Rim.

By the later years of his administration, the war in Vietnam began to flow into America's streets. In colleges and universities across the United States dissenters became more vocal and active. By 1967, with 500,000 American troops in Vietnam and more on the way, the war dominated American consciousness and overwhelmed the President's domestic plans. The Great Society was finished. Even Dr. Martin Luther King announced his opposition to Johnson's war machine. Given the Civil Rights initiatives and Great Society social programs, President Johnson felt betrayed.

The White House now became a prison for the President. Public appearances risked unseemly responses. The political situation provoked an internal challenge to his leadership and a threat to his re-nomination by the Democratic Party. In November 1967, U.S. Senator Eugene McCarthy of Minnesota launched that challenge. McCarthy filed papers to compete in the New Hampshire primary and divided the party. President Johnson won a majority of the New Hampshire Democratic voters, but McCarthy managed to obtain 42 percent of the vote, exposing the incumbent as vulnerable. Four days later, Johnson's worst political nightmare materialized when Senator Robert F. Kennedy of New York joined the race.

On March 31, 1968, with his Gallop Poll favorability rating at 23 percent, Lyndon Baines Johnson announced his withdrawal from public life. Ironically, years earlier Johnson had recognized the quicksand that Vietnam represented for him, but saw no way out. White House tapes, secretly controlled by Johnson, reveal this apparently insoluble dilemma in a ruminative conversation with his erstwhile mentor, Senator Richard Russell of Georgia.

Throughout the troubled year of 1968 violence and disorder reigned. Martin Luther King was murdered in Memphis. Disorder and chaos ruled throughout the nation on American college campuses. The barbarians were at the gates of prestigious places of higher learning such as Columbia University. Race riots were the order of the day. Blood was on the floor everywhere. "Bobby" Kennedy was tragically cut down at a moment of triumph in Los Angeles.

Enter Richard Nixon, who benefited in the end from the decade's wandering in the wilderness. The saying became: "if you remember the sixties you weren't there." In the presidential election of 1960 Nixon had lost by an eyelash to Kennedy. Now the principal beneficiary of the chaos and disorder was Richard Nixon. He became the law and order candidate. Given the social and political situation, he had the edge and managed to win the presidential election. He had hinted loudly that he had a secret plan to end the Vietnam War and the domestic disorder. It was enough to get him elected.

The new president was never loved. He was not even liked. Vice President under Eisenhower, he surely knew that affection was a critical feature of American elections. The campaign buttons for Eisenhower in the previous decade read simply: "I like Ike." He was not Ike. Yet Richard Nixon was respected by the American public. The son of a grocer had once said to a Republican National Convention: "I believe in the American Dream for I have seen it come true in my own life." There was in 1968 a need for domestic order which the Nixon candidacy promised to fill. Then there was the war in Vietnam. Nixon assured the American people that his strong suit was foreign policy. He would fix problems at home and abroad. It was believable. This time he won.

It was Richard Nixon who sat in the White House on "Moon Day" in July 1969 to see JFK's promise to land a man on the moon by the end of the decade come true. July 20th of that year was a big day for mankind, as two American astronauts, Neil Armstrong and Edwin "Buzz" Aldrich planted the Stars and Stripes on the moon. President Nixon initiated the first earth-to-moon presidential conversation with space travelers. In that conversation the President celebrated the men and the success of their mission. Unknown for three decades was the fact that the President had "Plan B" on the backburner. An alternative, undelivered message had been prepared by Nixon speechwriter, William Safire. This secret speech, revealed in 1999, had been designed in the event of disaster. "Fate has ordained that the men who went to the moon to explore in peace" the unnecessary eulogy opened "will stay on the moon to rest in peace."

In a nationally broadcast speech from the Oval Office on April 30, 1970, Nixon announced that American and allied military forces had invaded Cambodia and that land and air attacks were continuing. College campuses erupted in protests. Nixon, shaken by the student protests and the public response in major cities, resolved to persevere. His risky decision on Cambodia held the promise, he felt, of breaking a stalemate that had cost the United States such an enormous price in blood, money and prestige. Nixon entered office with the boast: "I'm not going to end up like LBJ. I'm going to stop that war. Fast."

The path towards peace, Nixon labeled "Vietnamization." This concept pledged to bolster the political stability and military competence of South Vietnam while simultaneously decreasing American troop levels by hundreds of thousands. The President's attempts to enlist the Soviet Union and China as agents in persuading Ho Chi Minh to accept United States terms of "peace with honor" failed. Left with a reliance on military means, Nixon found a potential prize in Cambodia in March 1970. Cambodia abuts Vietnam, and had for years provided refuge for North Vietnamese storage and staging areas, a vital link in the "Ho Chi Minh Trail," on which supplies and troops steadily flowed south. The Cambodian invasion, taken by the President against the recommendation of most of his advisors, would actually cause more problems than it would solve.

At home, President Nixon delicately dealt with desegregation. He entered office fifteen years after the *Brown v. Board of Education* decision by the Supreme Court ruled school segregation unconstitutional, yet only 5.2 percent of Southern Black children attended desegregated schools. As the beneficiary of Southern Republican success, Nixon faced an impasse. Elected as a "law and order" candidate, he confronted a recalcitrant South, determined to defy Federal court orders mandating racial integration. His administration opted to uphold the law in a series of subtle steps and political maneuverings that followed the President's own public embrace of the Brown decision. Within two years, desegregation of Southern public education exhibited dramatic change. Blacks in segregated schools declined from 68 percent to 38 percent. This variation destroyed the barrier of school segregation and began a new stage of incremental improvement in educational opportunity and race relations.

The winds of change covered Beijing as well as Birmingham. For more than two decades following the communist victory in China in 1949, the Republican Party provided resistance to those developments in Asia. Richard Nixon first came to national political attention in the late 1940s as a California Congressman serving on the House Committee on Un-American Activities, which conducted highly publicized hearings on domestic subversion. When the Committee began to consider the celebrated Alger Hiss–Whittaker Chambers affair, Nixon rose to the forefront on the Committee. The work of the Congressional Committee involved an investigation of the role of communism at high levels in American political life. "Loyalty" became a theme of American politics and society. Through the years the mere thought of normalizing relations and diplomatic relations remained out of the question. Meanwhile, Nixon rose steadily in status and power in a stepladder to the White House.

Secretary of State Henry Kissinger, in December 1971, made two secret trips to China to meet with Chairman Mao Tse-Tung and Premier Chou en-Lai. Three months later, without prior announcement, President Nixon arrived in Beijing, stunning the nation and the world. Nixon, erstwhile scourge of "Red China," now envisioned the "opening" of China as a major event in world history.

The China mission received plaudits from left and right. It also helped the President's re-election in 1972. While Nixon won in a major rout against the Democratic nominee George McGovern that November 7th, an event of the campaign season would ultimately bring his presidency down. Five months before Election Day, seven men entered the offices of the Democratic National Committee at the Watergate complex in downtown Washington. The predawn trespassers were discovered and arrested. The men remained silent and no evidence directly linked them to the Committee to Re-elect the President or to the White House. The incident began to fade from public view.

Six months later, in March 1973, one of the accused burglars, James McCord, talked. He claimed the break-in had been ordered by Nixon's campaign chairman, John Mitchell, a former Attorney General. The Watergate crisis occupied the next eighteen months, providing political bombshells and high constitutional drama. The FBI Director admitted destroying relevant Watergate evidence in April 1973 at the urging of White House aides. Ten days later, the President's closest advisors, H. R. Haldeman, John Erlichman, and John Dean, resigned under pressure. In May, a Senate Select Committee began televised hearings. Dean testified that the President had ordered "hush money" paid to the Watergate burglars.

The most startling testimony occurred on July 16th, when White House aide Alexander Butterfield told the Senate Committee and a national television audience that a taping system automatically recorded all of the President's meetings and telephone conversations. The Senate subpoenaed this evidence. The President claimed Executive Privilege. For an entire year the nation watched the constitutional, political and personal struggle of Richard Nixon to retain his office.

The President's troubles intensified in October when Vice President Spiro Agnew resigned in the face of an income tax prosecution. As successor, Nixon appointed House Republican Leader Gerald R. Ford, a strong supporter of the President and his policies. The constitutional struggle over the tapes continued while many leading Nixon associates received indictments for obstruction of justice. In the summer of 1974, the President took two extended international tours designed to burnish his image as a world leader. Neither the Middle Eastern tour nor the ensuing summit meeting in Moscow would equal the public impact of the Supreme Court July 24th decision. The Justices unanimously ordered the White House to turn over all subpoenaed materials to Special Prosecutor Leon Jaworski.

In the immediate aftermath of the Court's order, the Judiciary Committee of the House of Representatives issued two articles of impeachment against the President. With the tapes now available for scrutiny, Nixon acknowledged on August 5th that he had committed "a serious act of omission" by failing to disclose that six days after the Watergate break-in, he had ordered the FBI to halt its investigation.

The President went before the nation on August 8th to announce his resignation. Years later, in 1997, came the publication of additional tapes long withheld from public view through legal maneuvers directed by Nixon and his partisans. They clearly indicate the President's knowledge of the elaborate cover-up and participation in obstruction of justice. Before leaving the White House for the last time as President, on August 9th, he spoke to an impromptu assemblage of family, friends, and staff. The parting leader put a softer face on the moment and spoke in gentle tones. He talked with pride of his staff and his Cabinet. He fondly remembered his days in the White House— "the best house." At this very sad moment in his life, he tried to lift the spirits of those loyal to him and his presidency and waxed nostalgic about his youth, his father and his sainted mother.

No stranger to adversity, the President told of reading the night before a passage pertaining to the death of Theodore Roosevelt's young wife years before his elevation to the Presidency. In his grief TR exclaimed: "And when my heart's dearest died, the light went from my life forever." The lesson was that TR grew as a person in the face of that adversity and eventually learned to live again. The resignation of Richard Millhouse Nixon and his exit was reminiscent of the fall of the mighty from grace, as in a Greek tragedy.

A new round of Dicta-belt tapes released in fall 2011 reveals a different Nixon from his self-portrait. The Dicta-belts show a darker more malevolent side of a man trying to dig up dirt on his enemies. On tape he gives orders to his subordinates to discover such things as whether George McGovern had a girlfriend. He gave instructions to do research on the finances of Robert McNamara, Secretary of Defense under Presidents Kennedy and Johnson from 1961 to 1968. Beyond belief, he demanded a full report as to the public and private funeral and burial expenses for President Kennedy and his brother Bobby. Of the more than seven hundred Dicta-belt tapes, we have selected precious few as documents. This new Dicta-belt evidence suggests anew that the Nixon presidency bordered on outright paranoia. In that ugly political environment the President of the United States directed venal operations against his political foes. Once again, these were troubled years.

Somehow the President engineered a graceful exit. Much was hidden from public view. As history unfolds, and more documentary evidence surfaces, we see a troubled president in troubled times. American politics appeared to have hit a new low in Foggy Bottom. It had become highly invasive and a sewer of discontent.

Gerald R. Ford took the oath of office a few minutes past noon on August 9th. It was administered by Richard Nixon's loyal friend Chief Justice of the United States, Warren Burger. The most essential principle of the Republic, the sovereignty of the people, had been skirted. For the first time in the history of the Republic a man occupied the office of President of the United States who had not been elected by the people. The professional politicians had made that decision.

In his first public appearances, Ford spoke slowly and plainly in support of honesty and traditional values. The public and the press welcomed him warmly. Unbelievably, and partly due to media mini-management, a burst of affection spontaneously arose at the news that he made his own toast for breakfast. The media manufactured this simple message that in a Republic it was primetime news that the un-elected President buttered his own toast. Still, President Ford was not a total Milquetoast. He was his own man. In the face of communist aggression on the African continent in Angola, President Ford requested that the Congress respond to the challenge with military force. The Congressional answer, popular with a weary public, was "no more Vietnams." To which the President responded: "The Congress of the United States has lost its guts." As far as President Ford was concerned the Congress had forfeited freedom in Africa.

In the main, however, Ford perceived his role and mission as a healer. The country had suffered many blows from assassination, war, and the resignation of a president. These wounds remained open, and his calling was to bring cure and closure. Throughout that painful ordeal of Vietnam, Ford remained a leading "hawk." The new president had said that he was "a Ford not a Lincoln." Yet he pursued a Lincoln-like policy devoid of "malice." To reconcile the nation, Ford adopted two courses of action. The first declared amnesty for deserters and draft evaders during the Vietnam War. The President here adopted a policy of forgiveness and reconciliation.

Perhaps the greatest problem remained the political specter of Richard Nixon, whose legal status lay between possible indictment by the Watergate Special Prosecutor and presidential pardon. When Ford had been appointed Vice President, rumors circulated as to a prearranged deal to protect Nixon from legal action. Ford's honeymoon period continued despite his controversial actions. The Gallup poll provided evidence of his good standing with the public. Gallup revealed, on September 1st, an outstanding 71 percent favorable rating. Participating in the poll were 77 percent Republican respondents and 68 percent Democrats. With the American people supporting his back, Ford chose a Sunday in September to grant his predecessor "a full, free and absolute pardon."

The pardon of Richard Nixon was one of the prominent problems Ford faced in his presidential contest against Democratic Party nominee Jimmy Carter in the bicentennial year 1976. Jimmy Carter's unlikely victory in that election produced a one-term presidency of ambiguous content. He won by running against the Washington establishment, yet appointed many of its mainstays to prominent positions, including Cyrus Vance and Zbiegniew Brzezinski to oversee American foreign policy. While Carter proudly sported his born-again Baptist faith, his unfortunate confession in *Playboy* that he frequently "committed adultery in my heart" raised questions both about that statement and the propriety of his choice of magazine. Similar contradictions seemed to mark his political and policy judgments. In staking out initiatives on inflation, energy and tax cuts, the President's original intentions were overtaken by considerations that prompted policy confusion.

In foreign affairs, Carter came to Washington vowing a fundamental change in America's role in the world. His agenda featured an emphasis on human rights as a basic criterion for international relations, nuclear disarmament and curtailed American arms sales abroad. None of the plans found much measure of success in Carter's term. Human rights have always found favor in America. Such rights remain an intrinsic diplomatic ideal and national goal. The cause of disarmament also gained additional traction in the post-Cold War world. The fundamental fact is that Carter was perceived as a weak leader at home and abroad.

Jimmy Carter did succeed in his mission to "return" the Panama Canal to Panama. It is often overlooked that Panama and the Panama Canal were both creations of the United States. President Theodore Roosevelt had seen to that by virtue of his naked power grab of the Isthmus seventy years earlier. First TR arranged for the creation of Panama. The Treaty with Panama and the construction of the canal followed from his shadow diplomacy.

In any event the notion of turning the canal over to the Panamanians was the brainchild of previous presidents, most particularly Lyndon B. Johnson. Diplomacy in that direction continued under Nixon and Ford. It was Carter who determined and executed the final disposition and terms of the transfer. Opponents of the transfer, including Ronald Reagan, considered it another example of Carter's weakness, along with toadying to the Soviets and his failure in Iran. When the Soviets broke their promise to the President and invaded Afghanistan, a flabbergasted Carter lamented that "the Russians lied to me." Carter diplomacy with regard to the Panama Canal was ratified by the Senate as the Canal Treaty passed that chamber with one vote to spare. Prior to the vote Carter explained his case in a nationally televised address from the Oval Office. The result was that the United States no longer "owned" the canal but maintained the right to "protect it."

If Carter's canal diplomacy invited criticism, the posture of United States diplomatic policy with respect to Iran gained for Carter a firestorm of protest. The Iranian crisis began when the American Embassy in Tehran was invaded and fifty-three Americans seized as hostages by Revolutionary Guards inspired by Ayatollah Khomeni. The Embassy came under siege on November 4, 1979, and the American hostages spent 444 days in captivity.

The seemingly endless Iranian hostage crisis blighted the last year of the Carter presidency and seriously impaired his chances for re-election. For a while, it looked as though this failure to protect our Embassy in Iran might redound to the President's political benefit. Carter had been running low in the polls for most of 1979. The President had managed to alienate large numbers of Democrats, including Senator Edward Kennedy, who many considered the rightful heir apparent.

Animosity between Kennedy and Carter had existed since the early 1970s. At that time Carter was Governor of Georgia and Kennedy was licking his wounds from Chappaquiddick. Senator Kennedy sought favorable press and party relations to restore his damaged reputation. When he received an invitation to visit Georgia as a guest of the Governor and the State Democratic Party, he accepted. He was not received with southern hospitality. The Senator long remembered his visit to Georgia. When the Democratic Party gathered in New York City to nominate Carter at their National Convention in 1976, Senator Kennedy was not present. He had gone fishing.

The alienation of the two Democratic Party lions not only continued but intensified during Carter's tenure in the White House. It attained critical mass in 1979–1980. President Carter visited Colorado in spring 1979 to promote solar energy. While in Denver he held an event at Rick's Café, a swinging singles place, which used solar panels. The staged affair took place on May 3rd—"Sun Day." President Carter recorded the event in his diary. He noted that Senator Hart joined his motorcade and together they traveled from the Cosmopolitan Hotel in downtown Denver to the fashionable Rick's Café in Cherry Creek. It rained. When a member of the press mentioned to Senator Kennedy the irony of it raining on Sun Day, Kennedy said "Everywhere Carter goes it rains."

The estrangement of the President and the Senator intensified that summer. In July, President Carter addressed the nation on television. It was a memorable performance often referred to as the "Malaise Speech." Carter had published a book, and campaigned in 1976, on the theme that what the nation needed was "a government as good as its people." The theme resonated with the American people in the aftermath of Watergate. The "malaise" idiom presented a certain incongruity with his campaign theme. Without actually using the word "malaise," Carter's speech suggested there was something wrong with the people.

The President may have put his finger on the climate of opinion, but his theme had shifted from the idea that there was something wrong with the government that a good people could fix to a message that found a problem in the American soul. His diagnosis was a loss of faith, not simply with the government but in the people themselves. The symptoms were everywhere evident. The people had been infected, causing a "crisis of the American spirit." In keeping with the presidential diagnosis he had isolated the cause of the sickness: "In a nation that was proud of hard work, strong families, close-knit communities and our faith in God, too many of us now tend to worship self-indulgence and consumption." As a consequence of the crisis, America experienced "paralysis, stagnation and drift."

Having identified the cause of the malady, the President moved on to a prescription for its remedy. Once we faced the problem then we could alter the national course. We needed to "stop crying" and "start praying." The starting point for solving the spiritual crisis, thought Carter, was resolving the energy crisis. Once we won the "energy war" the road would be paved to cure the inner war. America could achieve victory on the energy front and gain energy independence by the year 2000 if we exploited our natural resources and also developed solar sources. Towards this end he would propose to Congress the establishment of a solar bank so that twenty percent of the nation's energy would be solar based by the 2000 target. Full energy independence would be realized by tapping all our resources. President Carter promised to protect the environment but "when this Nation critically needs a refinery or a pipeline, we will build it."

There appears to be an internal contradiction in the President's lengthy and important speech. Despite a crisis of confidence, the President believed in a "national will." More than three decades later the energy crisis remains unresolved.

This famous "Malaise" speech, delivered on July 15, 1979, can be considered from yet another perspective. The President's popularity had plunged to extraordinarily low levels. The crisis of confidence had much to do with the public loss of confidence in him. In state after state, polls indicated that President Carter trailed behind Senator Kennedy in a possible challenge for the Democratic nomination. The day after the speech, the President launched a massacre of his own

Cabinet. He engaged in a purge of Kennedy sympathizers. The message indicated that even he had lost confidence in the effectiveness of his administration.

President Carter had been asked by a reporter from the *New York Post* about a Kennedy challenge. His not very presidential response appeared as the paper's headline the next day: "I'll Whip His Ass." When asked about the headline, Kennedy said simply that the President misspoke and intended to say "I'll Whip Inflation." Given Carter's poor job performance ratings in the polls, a draft Kennedy movement was launched. The contest for the Democratic presidential nomination had begun.

Many believed that the re-nomination of President Carter would doom the Democratic Party in the coming presidential election. Political futures were at stake. Drafting Kennedy to make the run could save the party. Teddy answered the call. Prospects were bright. In November, two simultaneous developments changed the political landscape. One game-changer was Kennedy's disastrous television interview with family friend Roger Mudd. The date was November 4, 1979 and the venue was a CBS special entitled *Teddy*. In the course of the conversation, Mudd asked Kennedy two obvious questions. The first related to the tragedy at Chappaquiddick. The second inquiry was why Kennedy wanted to be president. Surprisingly, Kennedy was unprepared to answer either question. His answers were rambling and incoherent. In a matter of moments an unintended dagger wounded the Kennedy challenge before it left the ground.

At the same time, November 4, 1979, the storming of the American Embassy in Tehran, ironically gave a lift to President Carter. In a moment of external crisis the American people tend to rally around the flag and the President. President Carter took full advantage of the crisis in the primary campaign, along with the inherent advantages of incumbency, to shore up his political fortunes. Kennedy had difficulty getting out of the gate after the Mudd interview and staggered through the early stages of the campaign. Later, as the hostage crisis continued without resolution Kennedy got his sea legs to come on strong at the primary finish. The race tightened, but it was too late. Party rules had imprisoned the delegates so that early candidate commitments could not be switched. The showdown came at Madison Square Garden in New York City where the Democrats met in National Convention. The Kennedy forces adopted the slogan "Free the Delegates." The established rules prevailed. Kennedy withdrew his challenge on August 12, 1980 and addressed the delegates. It was a speech for the ages which ended with the peroration: "For all those whose cares have been our concern, the work goes on, the cause endures, the hope still lives and the dream shall never die."

In the general election that followed, President Carter was roundly defeated by the Republican candidate, Governor Ronald Reagan of California. In that campaign, Carter had been effectively whipsawed. The economy under Carter was terrible. For the first time in American history, the economy was marked by high unemployment and double-digit inflation. A new designation for this unknown condition became "stagflation." Ted Kennedy hit Carter hard during the primary season on the lack of jobs. Reagan mostly punched home the deadly inflation theme. As Carter moved down a narrow middle road, he got hit by the traffic going both ways. The game was up. President Carter had lost and President-elect Reagan would move America to recovery and a new "Morning in America."

There is however an epilogue that has recently attached itself to that fight for the presidency that concluded these troubled times. Ted Kennedy died on August 26, 2009. The family feud between the two Democratic Party lions lived on. Jimmy Carter published *White House Diary*, on September 20, 2010 and unleashed a bitter echo of the bad blood from three decades ago. In his *Diary* and later in an interview with Leslie Stahl, Carter lashed out against his rival with regard to national health care reform. Carter claimed that the nation would have had health care reform under his administration had not Ted Kennedy spitefully blocked its passage in the Senate. Clearly their fierce feud will never die. The nation moved on to better times after these times of trouble.

36

Lyndon B. Johnson

1. THE GREAT SOCIETY

. . . The purpose of protecting the life of our Nation and preserving the liberty of our citizens is to pursue the happiness of our people. Our success in that pursuit is the test of our success as a Nation.

For a century we labored to settle and to subdue a continent. For half a century we called upon unbounded invention and untiring industry to create an order of plenty for all of our people.

The challenge of the next half century is whether we have the wisdom to use that wealth to enrich and elevate our national life, and to advance the quality of our American civilization.

Your imagination, your initiative, and your indignation will determine whether we build a society where progress is the servant of our needs, or a society where old values and new visions are buried under unbridled growth. For in your time we have the opportunity to move not only toward the rich society and the powerful society, but upward to the Great Society.

The Great Society rests on abundance and liberty for all. It demands an end to poverty and racial injustice, to which we are totally committed in our time. But that is just the beginning.

The Great Society is a place where every child can find knowledge to enrich his mind and to enlarge his talents. It is a place where leisure is a welcome chance to build and reflect, not a feared cause of boredom and restlessness. It is a place where the city of man serves not only the needs of the body and the demands of commerce but the desire for beauty and the hunger for community.

It is a place where man can renew contact with nature. It is a place which honors creation for its own sake and for what it adds to the understanding of the race. It is a place where men are more concerned with the quality of their goals than the quantity of their goods.

But most of all, the Great Society is not a safe harbor, a resting place, a final objective, a finished work. It is a challenge constantly renewed, beckoning us toward a destiny where the meaning of our lives matches the marvelous products of labor.

. . . Many of you will live to see the day, perhaps 50 years from now, when there will be 400 million Americans—four-fifths of them in urban areas. In the remainder of this century urban population will double, city land will double, and we will have to build homes, highways, and facilities equal to all those built since this country was first settled. So in the next 40 years we must rebuild the entire urban United States.

. . . The catalog of ills is long: there is the decay of the centers and the despoiling of the suburbs. There is not enough housing for our people or transportation for our traffic. Open land is vanishing and old landmarks are violated.

Worst of all, expansion is eroding the precious and time-honored values of community with neighbors, and communion with nature. The loss of these values breeds loneliness and boredom and indifference.

Our society will never be great until our cities are great. Today the frontier of imagination and innovation is inside those cities and not beyond their borders.

New experiments are already going on. It will be the task of your generation to make the American city a place where future generations will come, not only to live but to live the good life.

A second place where we begin to build the Great Society is in our countryside. We have always prided ourselves on being not only America the strong and America the free, but America the beautiful. Today that beauty is in danger. The water we drink, the food we eat, the very air that we breathe, are threatened with pollution. Our parks are overcrowded, our seashores overburdened. Green fields and dense forests are disappearing.

A few years ago we were greatly concerned about the "Ugly American." Today we must act to prevent an ugly America.

For once the battle is lost, once our natural splendor is destroyed, it can never be recaptured. And once man can no longer walk with beauty or wonder at nature his spirit will wither and his sustenance be wasted.

A third place to build the Great Society is in the classrooms of America. There your children's lives will be shaped. Our society will not be great until every young mind is set free to scan the farthest reaches of thought and imagination. We are still far from that goal.

. . . Each year more than 100,000 high school graduates, with proved ability, do not enter college because they cannot afford it. And if we cannot educate today's youth, what will we do in 1970 when elementary school enrollment will be 5 million greater than 1960? And high school enrollment will rise by 5 million. College enrollment will increase by more than 3 million.

In many places, classrooms are overcrowded and curricula are outdated. Most of our qualified teachers are underpaid, and many of our paid teachers are unqualified. So we must give every child a place to sit and a teacher to learn from. Poverty must not be a bar to learning, and learning must offer an escape from poverty.

But more classrooms and more teachers are not enough. We must seek an educational system which grows in excellence as it grows in size. This means better training for our teachers. It means preparing youth to enjoy their hours of leisure as well as their hours of labor. It means exploring new techniques of teaching, to find new ways to stimulate the love of learning and the capacity for creation.

These are three of the central issues of the Great Society. While our Government has many programs directed at those issues, I do not pretend that we have the full answer to those problems.

But I do promise this: We are going to assemble the best thought and the broadest knowledge from all over the world to find those answers for America. I intend to establish working groups to prepare a series of White House conferences and meetings—on the cities, on natural beauty, on the quality of education, and on other emerging challenges. And from these meetings and from this inspiration and from these studies we will begin to set our course toward the Great Society. . . .

. . . For better or for worse, your generation has been appointed by history to deal with those problems and to lead America toward a new age. You have the chance never before afforded to any people in any age. You can help build a society where the demands of morality, and the needs of the spirit, can be realized in the life of the Nation.

. . . There are those timid souls who say this battle cannot be won; that we are condemned to a soulless wealth. I do not agree. We have the power to shape the civilization that we want. But we need your will, your labor, your hearts, if we are to build that kind of society.

Those who came to this land sought to build more than just a new country. They sought a new world. . . . So let us from this moment begin our work so that in the future men will look back and say: It was then, after a long and weary way, that man turned the exploits of his genius to the full enrichment of his life.

2. CIVIL RIGHTS BILL OF 1964   JULY 2, 1964

. . . One hundred and eighty-eight years ago this week a small band of valiant men began a long struggle for freedom. They pledged their lives, their fortunes, and their sacred honor not only to found a nation, but to forge an ideal of freedom—not only for political independence, but for personal liberty, not only to eliminate foreign rule, but to establish the rule of justice in the affairs of men.

That struggle was a turning point in our history. Today in far corners of distant continents, the ideals of those American patriots still shape the struggles of men who hunger for freedom.

This is a proud triumph. Yet those who founded our country knew that freedom would be secure only if each generation fought to renew and enlarge its meaning. From the minutemen at Concord to the soldiers in Vietnam, each generation has been equal to that trust.

Americans of every race and color have died in battle to protect our freedom. Americans of every race and color have worked to build a nation of widening opportunities. Now our generation of Americans has been called on to continue the unending search for justice within our own borders.

We believe that all men are created equal. Yet many are denied equal treatment.

We believe that all men have certain unalienable rights. Yet many Americans do not enjoy those rights.

We believe that all men are entitled to the blessings of liberty. Yet millions are being deprived of those blessings not because of their own failures, but because of the color of their skin.

The reasons are deeply imbedded in history and tradition and the nature of man. We can understand—without rancor or hatred—how this all happened.

But it cannot continue. Our Constitution, the foundation of our Republic, forbids it. The principles of our freedom forbid it. Morality forbids it. And the law I will sign tonight forbids it.

That law is the product of months of the most careful debate and discussion. It was proposed more than one year ago by our late and beloved President John F. Kennedy. It received the bipartisan support of more than two-thirds of the Members of both the House and the Senate. An overwhelming majority of Republicans as well as Democrats voted for it.

. . . I am taking steps to implement the law under my constitutional obligation to "take care that the laws are faithfully executed."

We must not approach the observance and enforcement of this law in a vengeful spirit. Its purpose is not to punish. Its purpose is not to divide, but to end divisions—divisions which have all lasted too long. Its purpose is national, not regional.

Its purpose is to promote a more abiding commitment to freedom, a more constant pursuit of justice, and a deeper respect for human dignity.

We will achieve these goals because most Americans are law-abiding citizens who want to do what is right.

This is why the Civil Rights Act relies first on voluntary compliance, then on the efforts of local communities and States to secure the rights of citizens. It provides for the national authority to step in only when others cannot or will not do the job.

This Civil Rights Act is a challenge to all of us to go to work in our communities and our States, in our homes and in our hearts, to eliminate the last vestiges of injustice in our beloved country.

So tonight I urge every public official, every religious leader, every business and professional man, every workingman, every housewife—I urge every American—to join in this effort to bring justice and hope to all our people—and to bring peace to our land.

My fellow citizens, we have come now to a time of testing. We must not fail. . . .

3. OPENING OF THE NEW YORK WORLD'S FAIR   APRIL 22, 1964

. . . America has been transformed from an outpost of the edge of wilderness to one of the great nations of the world. The number of people who will visit your fair will be seventy times the entire population of North America when New York was born.

The last time New York had a World's Fair, we also tried to predict the future. A daring exhibit proclaimed that in the 1960s it would really be possible to cross the country in less than 24 hours, flying as high as 10,000 feet; that an astounding 38 million cars would cross our highways. There was no mention of outer space, or atomic power, or wonder drugs that could destroy disease.

These were bold prophecies back there in 1939. But, again, the reality has far outstripped the vision.

There were also other predictions that were not made at that fair. No one prophesied that half the world would be devastated by war, or that millions of helpless would be slaughtered. No one foresaw power that was capable of destroying man, or a cold war which could bring conflict to every continent. Our pride in accomplishment must not ignore the fact that our progress has had two faces.

Its final direction—abundance or annihilation—development or desolation—that is in your hands and that is in the hands of the people around the world.

This fair represents the most promising of our hopes. It gathers together, from 80 countries, the achievements of industry, the wealth of nations, the creations of man. This fair shows us what man at his most creative and constructive is capable of doing.

But unless we can achieve the theme of this fair—"peace through understanding"—unless we can use our skill and our wisdom to conquer conflict as we have conquered science—then our hopes of today—these proud achievements—will go under in the devastation of tomorrow.

I prophesy peace is not only possible in our generation, I predict that it is coming much earlier. If I am right, then at the next world's fair, people will see an America as different from today as we are different from 1939.

They will see an America in which no man must be poor.

They will see an America in which no man is handicapped by the color of his skin or the nature of his belief—and no man will be discriminated against because of the church he attends or the country of his ancestors.

They will see an America which is solving the growing problems of crowded cities, inadequate education, deteriorating national resources and decreasing national beauty.

They will see an America concerned with the quality of American life—unwilling to accept public deprivation in the midst of private satisfaction—concerned not only that people have more, but that people shall have the best.

4. WAR IN VIETNAM: CONVERSATION WITH RICHARD RUSSELL   JUNE 11, 1964

LBJ: I'm confronted. I don't believe the American people ever want me to run. If I lose it, I think that they'll say *I've* lost. I've pulled in. At the same time, I don't want to commit us to a war. And I'm in a hell of a shape.

RUSSELL: We're just like the damn cow over a fence out there in Vietnam.

LBJ: . . . I've got a study being made now by the experts . . . whether Malaysia will necessarily go and India'll go and how much it'll hurt our prestige if we just got out and let some conference fail or something. . . . A fellow like A. W. Moursund said to me last night, "Goddamn, there's not anything that'll destroy you as quick as pulling out, pulling up stakes and running. America wants, by God, prestige and power." . . . I said, "Yeah, but I don't want to kill these folks." He said, "I don't give a damn. I didn't want to kill 'em in Korea, but if you don't stand up for America, there's nothing that a fellow in Johnson City"—or Georgia or any other place—"they'll forgive you for anything, except being weak." Goldwater and all of 'em are raising hell about . . . hot pursuit and let's go in and bomb 'em. . . . You can't clean it up. That's the hell of it.

RUSSEL: . . . It'd take a half million men. They'd be bogged down in there for ten years. . . . We're right where we started, except for seventy thousand of 'em buried over there.

LBJ: Now Dick, you think, every time you can get your mind off of other things, think about some man. . . . My great weakness in this job is I just don't know these other people. The Kennedys— they know every damn fellow in the country or have got somebody that knows 'em. They're out at these universities and everyplace in the country—New York and Chicago.

. . . .

LBJ: We're just doing fine, except for this damned Vietnam thing. We're just doing wonderful. Every index. The businessmen are going wonderful. They're up 12, 14 percent investment over last year. The tax bill has just worked out wonderfully. There're only 2.6 percent of the married people unemployed. . . . And 16 percent of these youngsters, and I'll have all them employed. . . . It's kids that are dropping out of school and then they go on a roll. But I'll take care of that with my poverty, just by organizing it all. We've got the money in these various departments— Labor and HEW and Justice. . . . I'm gonna put all of them in one and put one top administrator and really get some results. Go in and clear up these damn rolls. And I'll do it with only $300 million more than was in the budget anyway last year. . . . I was down in Kentucky the other day. We've got fifty kids there teaching beauty culture—how to fix Lynda's hair. And they're all going out and get jobs $50, $60 a week in another three months. . . . That's what we ought to do instead of paying out four billion a year on relief, for nothing, where you don't have to work. To hell with this unemployment compensation. It's relief. But I've got to find a man for Vietnam.

RUSSELL: I don't know what the hell to do. I didn't ever want to get messed up down there. I do not agree with those brain trusters who say that this thing has got tremendous strategic and economic value and that we'll lose everything in Southeast Asia if we lose Vietnam. . . . But as a practical matter, we're in there and I don't know how the hell you can tell the American people you're coming out. . . . They'll think that you've just been whipped, you've been ruined, you're scared. It'd be disastrous.

LBJ: I think that I've got to say that I didn't get you in here, but we're in here by treaty and our national honor's at stake. And if this treaty's no good, none of 'em are any good. Therefore we're there. And being there, we've got to conduct ourselves like men. That's number one. Number two, in our own revolution, we wanted freedom and we naturally look with sympathy with other people who want freedom and if you'll leave 'em alone and give 'em freedom, we'll get out tomorrow. . . . Third thing, we've got to try to find some proposal some way, like Eisenhower worked out in Korea. . . .

5. A PROMISE TO CONTINUE ON THE PATH OF JFK   OCTOBER 29, 1964

. . . For 11 months and 1 week now, I have borne the torch that passed from the hands of that great and good and gallant President on that tragic November day in 1963. I have traveled more than 100,000 miles into 44 States of this land, and every mile of the way that I have walked, I have walked the path that was opened for us and the path that was pioneered for us by John Fitzgerald Kennedy.

In your great city, and in every city, I have seen millions of Americans. I have seen a proud and a prospering and a peaceful people, and I have known that that pride and that prosperity and, above all, that peace is what John Fitzgerald Kennedy left to them.

Of all that I have done in my life, nothing has given such great pride and satisfaction to me as to stand as I did in the campaign of 1960 by the side of John F. Kennedy. I am proud and I am grateful to have been a part of the campaign which proved forever that in America no man shall be denied the opportunity to serve his countrymen because of the region in which he lives or the religion which he has.

Tonight, America is a better and a stronger nation for all of us because of that campaign that we waged in '60. Philadelphia is a city of homes and families, just as all of America is a nation of homes and families, and in the life of such a city and in the life of such a nation, religion has always, and religion must always, play a part in all that we do or all that we hope to do.

I hope that the day will never come when any man, for any cause, will try to keep religion out of our national decisions on who shall lead us or the direction we shall go.

Thank God that Americans welcome into their homes and into the lives of their families the preachers and the priests and the rabbis who serve us all so faithfully and so unselfishly.

The men of the pulpit have a place in the leadership of our people and they have a place in our public affairs. We should be grateful for their concern over the well-being of this land, for that is what America is all about, and that is what brought men to these shores, and particularly to this great State of Pennsylvania.

I do not condemn our churches or our clergymen for being concerned that America meet her moral responsibilities for peace, for preserving human freedom, and human life, and for doing what a rich nation can and should do to wipe poverty from our land. I not only don't condemn them, I thank God for their courage.

As I go on tonight to carry on the works of John Kennedy and the program that he began, I want your help, I want your hand, I want your prayers, I want your support to see that we get that job well done. . . .

The people of America know that it is right that America should continue to work with compassion and courage and confidence to make life better for all of man. For so long as there has been an American nation, the American people have been devoted to the principles of prudence, to the practice of frugality and thrift, and to the purposes of conservation and renewal.

We have made this Nation strong by warring on waste. Today, at the summit of our success, we want to change the waste that we see throughout too much of our national life.

Abraham Lincoln wiped slavery from this land 100 years ago and we here in the Brotherhood City tonight pledge that we will wipe the waste of human poverty from this land in our lifetime.

We want to wipe out the waste of idle men and idle machines.

We want to wipe out the waste of decaying cities and dying towns, and I take such pride in the great work that you have done in Philadelphia and Pittsburgh in this respect.

We want to wipe out the waste of untrained youth, unemployed fathers, and uncared-for grandparents.

We know that the happiness and the health of our people is not served by government which is indifferent to the burdens that are imposed upon them. We want compassionate government. We want concerned government, but we want government that is not careless or wasteful with the taxpayers' dollar.

There are changes that we want to make and that we must make, prudent changes, responsible changes, changes I think for the better. But we never want to change the character or the conscience of our American system.

. . . Thirty-five men before me have held the office that is entrusted to me tonight. All of those men, from George Washington to John Kennedy, have worked and prayed and hoped for peace, for unity, for progress and prosperity for their people. And so long as the trust of this office is mine to uphold that will be my work, that will be my prayer, that will be my hope for all Americans.

6. VIETNAM AND THE PRESIDENCY   MARCH 31, 1968

Tonight I want to speak to you of peace in Vietnam and Southeast Asia.

No other question so preoccupies our people. No other dream so absorbs the 250 million human beings who live in that part of the world. . . .

Their attack—during the Tet holidays—failed to achieve its principal objectives.

It did not collapse the elected government of South Vietnam or shatter its army—as the Communists had hoped.

It did not produce a "general uprising" among the people of the cities as they had predicted.

The Communists were unable to maintain control of any of the more than 30 cities that they attacked. And they took very heavy casualties. . . .

But tragically. . . . Many men . . . will be lost. . . . Armies on both sides will take new casualties. And the war will go on.

There is no need for this to be so.

. . . Tonight, I renew the offer . . . to stop the bombardment of North Vietnam. We ask that talks begin promptly, that they be serious talks on the subject of peace. . . .

. . . We are reducing . . . the present level of hostilities.

And we are doing so unilaterally, and at once. . . .

We shall accelerate the re-equipment of South Vietnam's armed forces. . . . This will enable them progressively to undertake a larger share of combat operations against the Communist invaders. . . .

One thing is unmistakably clear. . . . Our deficit must be reduced. . . .

As Hanoi considers its course, it should be in no doubt about our intentions. It must not miscalculate the pressures within our democracy in this election year.

. . . Our objective in South Vietnam has never been the annihilation of the enemy. It has been to bring about a recognition in Hanoi that its objective—taking over the South by force—could not be achieved.

. . . So tonight I reaffirm the pledge that we made at Manila—that we are prepared to withdraw our forces from South Vietnam as the other side withdraws its forces to the north, stops the infiltration, and the level of violence thus subsides. . . .

One day . . . there will be peace in Southeast Asia.

It will come because the people of Southeast Asia want it. . . .

With such an Asia, our country—and the world—will be far more secure than it is tonight.

. . . For 37 years in the service of our Nation . . . I have put the unity of the people first. . . .

And in these times as in times before, it is true that a house divided against itself by the spirit of faction, of party, of region, of religion, of race, is a house that cannot stand.

There is division in the American house now. There is divisiveness among us all tonight. And holding the trust that is mine, as President of all the people, I cannot disregard the peril to the progress of the American people and the hope and the prospect of peace for all peoples.

. . . Fifty two months and 10 days ago, in a moment of tragedy and trauma, the duties of this office fell upon me. I asked then for your help and God's, that we might continue America on its course. . . .

. . . I have concluded that I should not permit the Presidency to become involved in the partisan divisions that are developing in this political year. . . .

Accordingly, I shall not seek, and I will not accept, the nomination of my party for another term as your President. . . .

37

Richard M. Nixon

1. AN EARTH-TO-MOON CONVERSATION   JULY 20, 1969

Hello Neil and Buzz, I am talking to you by telephone from the Oval Room at the White House, and this certainly has to be the most historic telephone call ever made from the White House. I just can't tell you how proud we all are of what you have done. For every American this has to be the proudest day of our lives, and for people all over the world I am sure that they, too, join with Americans in recognizing what an immense feat this is.

Because of what you have done, the heavens have become a part of man's world, and as you talk to us from the Sea of Tranquility, it inspires us to redouble our efforts to bring peace and tranquility to earth.

For one priceless moment in the whole history of man, all the people on this earth are truly one—one in their pride in what you have done and one in our prayers that you will return safely to earth.

ASTRONAUT ARMSTRONG: Thank you, Mr. President. It is a great honor and privilege for us to be here representing not only the United States, but men of peaceable nations, men with a vision for the future. It is an honor for us to be able to participate here today.

THE PRESIDENT: Thank you very much, and I look forward, all of us look forward, to seeing you on the *Hornet* on Thursday.

ASTRONAUT ARMSTRONG: Thank you. We look forward to that very much, sir.

2. MAROONED ON THE MOON (UNDELIVERED SPEECH,   JULY 20, 1969
REVEALED IN 1999)

Fate has ordained that the men who went to the moon to explore in peace will stay on the moon to rest in peace.

These brave men, Neil Armstrong and Edwin Aldrin, know that there is no hope for their recovery. But they also know that there is hope for mankind in their sacrifice.

These two men are laying down their lives in mankind's most noble goal: the search for truth and understanding.

They will be mourned by their families and friends; they will be mourned by their nation; they will be mourned by the people of the world; they will be mourned by a Mother Earth that dared send two of her sons into the unknown.

In their exploration, they stirred the people of the world to feel as one; in their sacrifice, they bind more tightly the brotherhood of man.

In ancient days, men looked at stars and saw their heroes in the constellations. In modern times, we do much the same, but our heroes are epic men of flesh and blood.

Others will follow, and surely find their way home. Man's search will not be denied. But these men were the first, and they will remain the foremost in our hearts.

For every human being who looks up at the moon in the nights to come will know that there is some corner of another world that is forever mankind.

3. SELECT DICTA-BELT TAPES   MARCH 10, 1970

On McNamara Finances

In view of the flap over Flannigan I suppose it has occurred to you to have somebody check McNamara's blind trust. Did he have Ford stock when he went into it? Did Ford stock go up after he put his stock in trust? I am sure there are Cabinet officers in that previous administration who were in the exact same situation as Flannigan. As far as Ford Stock is concerned there would be very little difficulty in finding out not only that the stock went up but that Ford received several million dollars—hundred million dollars in government contracts during the period that Ford stock went up. At least have the matter checked out.

White House Press Facilities

Memorandum to Bob Halderman: . . . I understand that in talking with some of the workmen last night . . . that it may be . . . June 1st before some of the new press facilities will be available. I hope we can get an earlier deadline and then keep them to it. There has simply been too much malingering on this job.

I also believe that from walking through the facilities that we have gone overboard in terms of the elaborate individual cubicles that have been set up. This is likely to get us some pretty tough Congressional criticism. . . .

Attack Group

Memorandum to Bob Halderman: The more I think of it, setting up the special group including Nofsinger, Buchanan, Molinoff, and Houston for the purpose . . . solely of attacking and defending—is of the highest priority. It is out of this group that can come speeches or speech materials for not only Congressmen and Senators but Cabinet members—Agnew and Morton. Could you give me a report within a week what progress you have made in this direction?

4. DESEGREGATION   MAY 25, 1971

. . . I spoke in Mobile of the fact that we have differences between regions, we have differences between races, we have differences between religions, we have differences between the generations today, and these differences have at times been very destructive. We must recognize that we will always have those differences. People of different races, different religions, from different back-grounds, and of different ages are not always going to agree.

The question is, can those differences be resolved peacefully, and second, can they be made creative rather than destructive? Must they be a drain upon us? Must they go so far that they destroy the confidence and faith of this great Nation in its destiny and its future? I do not believe that that is necessary.

... I would say this in the North if I were speaking there; I say it in the South. I know the difficult problems most of you in the Southern States have had on the school desegregation problem. I went to school in the South, and so, therefore, I am more familiar with how Southerners feel about that problem than others. Also, I went to school in the North, or the West I should say, and I have nothing but utter contempt for the double hypocritical standard of Northerners who look at the South and point the finger and say, "Why don't those Southerners do something about their race problem?"

Let's look at the facts. In the past year, 2 years, there has been a peaceful, relatively quiet, very significant revolution. Oh, it is not over, there are problems—there was one in Chattanooga, I understand, the last couple days; there will be more. But look what has happened in the South. Today 38 percent of all black children in the South go to majority white schools. Today only 28 percent of all black children in the North go to majority white schools. There has been no progress in the North in the past 2 years in that respect. There has been significant progress in the South.

How did it come about? It came about because farsighted leaders in the South, black and white, some of whom I am sure did not agree with the opinions handed down by the Supreme Court which were the law of the land, recognized as law-abiding citizens that they had the responsibility to meet that law of the land, and they had dealt with the problem—not completely, there is more yet to be done. The recent decision of the Supreme Court presents some more problems, but I am confident that over a period of time those problems will also be handled in a peaceful and orderly way for the most part.

But let's look at the deeper significance of this. As I speak today in what is called the Heart of Dixie, I realize that America at this time needs to become one country. Too long we have been divided. It has been North versus South versus West; Wall Street versus the country and the country versus the city and the rest. That does not mean we don't have differences and will not continue to have them, but those regional differences, it seems to me, must go. Presidents of the United States should come to Alabama and Mississippi and Georgia and Louisiana more than once, more often than every 50 years or every 100 years as the case might be, to some of the cities, and they should come because this is one nation, and we must speak as one nation, we must work as one nation. ...

5. "OPENING" OF CHINA   FEBRUARY 27, 1972

This magnificent banquet marks the end of our stay in the People's Republic of China. We have been here a week. This was the week that changed the world.

As we look back over this week, we think of the boundless hospitality that has been extended to all of us by our Chinese friends.

We have, today, seen the progress of modern China. We have seen the matchless wonders of ancient China. We have seen also the beauty of the countryside, the vibrancy of a great city, Shanghai. All this we enjoyed enormously.

But most important was the fact that we had the opportunity to have talks with Chairman Mao, with Prime Minister Chou En-Lai, with the Foreign Minister and other people in the government.

The joint communique which we have issued today summarizes the results of our talks. That communique will make headlines around the world tomorrow. But what we have said in that communique is not nearly as important as what we will do in the years ahead to build a bridge across 16,000 miles and 22 years of hostility which have divided us in the past.

What we have said today is that we shall build that bridge. And because the Chinese people and the American people, as the Prime Minister has said, are a great people, we can build that long bridge.

To do so requires more than the letters, the words of the communique. The letters and the words are a beginning, but the actions that follow must be in the spirit which characterized our talks.

With Chairman Mao, with the Prime Minister, and with others with whom we have met, our talks have been characterized by frankness, by honesty, by determination, and above all, by mutual respect.

Our communique indicates, as it should, some areas of difference. It also indicates some areas of agreement. To mention only one that is particularly appropriate here in Shanghai, is the fact that this great city, over the past, has on many occasions been the victim of foreign aggression and foreign occupation. And we join the Chinese people, we the American people, in our dedication to this principle: That never again shall foreign domination, foreign occupation, be visited upon this city or any part of China or any independent country in this world.

Mr. Prime Minister, our two peoples tonight hold the future of the world in our hands. As we think of that future, we are dedicated to the principle that we can build a new world, a world of peace, a world of justice, a world of independence for all nations.

If we succeed in working together where we can find common ground, if we can find the common ground on which we can both stand, where we can build the bridge between us and build a new world, generations in the years ahead will look back and thank us for this meeting that we have held in this past week. Let the great Chinese people and the great American people be worthy of the hopes and ideals of the world, for peace and justice and progress for all.

In that spirit, I ask all of you to join in a toast to the health of Chairman Mao, of Prime Minister Chou En-Lai, and to all of our Chinese friends here tonight, and our American friends, and to that friendship between our two peoples to which Chairman Chang has referred so eloquently.

6. THE RESIGNATION   AUGUST 9, 1974

I think the record should show that this is one of those spontaneous things that we always arrange whenever the President comes in to speak, and it will be so reported in the press, and we don't mind, because they have to call it as they see it.

But on our part, believe me, it is spontaneous.

You are here to say goodbye to us, and we don't have a good word for it in English—the best is au revoir. We will see you again.

I just met with the members of the White House staff, you know, those who serve here in the White House, day in and day out, and I asked them to do what I ask all of you to do to the extent that you can and, of course, are requested to do so: to serve our next President as you have served me and previous Presidents—because many of you have been here for many years—with devotion and dedication, because this office, great as it is, can only be as great as the men and women who work for and with the President.

This house, for example—I was thinking of it as we walked down this hall, and I was comparing it to some of the great houses of the world that I have been in. This isn't the biggest house. Many, and most, in even smaller countries, are much bigger. This isn't the finest house. Many in Europe, particularly, and in China, Asia, have paintings of great, great value, things that we just don't have here and, probably, will never have until we are 1,000 years old or older.

But this is the best house. It is the best house, because it has something far more important than numbers of people who serve, far more important than numbers of rooms or how big it is, far more important than numbers of magnificent pieces of art.

This house has a great heart, and that heart comes from those who serve. I was rather sorry they didn't come down. We said goodbye to them upstairs. But they are really great. And I recall after so many times I have made speeches, and some of them pretty tough, yet, I always come back, or after a hard day—and my days usually have run rather long—I would always get a lift from them, because I might be a little down but they always smiled.

And so it is with you. I look around here, and I see so many on this staff that, you know, I should have been by your offices and shaken hands, and I would love to have talked to you and found out how to run the world—everybody wants to tell the President what to do, and boy, he needs to be told many times—but I just haven't had the time. But I want you to know that each and every one of you, I know, is indispensable to this Government.

I am proud of this Cabinet. I am proud of all the members who have served in our Cabinet. I am proud of our sub-Cabinet. I am proud of our White House Staff. As I pointed out last night, sure, we have done some things wrong in this Administration, and the top man always takes the responsibility, and I have never ducked it. But I want to say one thing: We can be proud of it— 5½ years. No man or no woman came into this Administration and left it with more of this world's goods than when he came in. No man or no woman ever profited at the public expense or the public till. That tells something about you.

Mistakes, yes. But for personal gain, never. You did what you believed in. Sometimes right, sometimes wrong. And I only wish that I were a wealthy man—at the present time, I have got to find a way to pay my taxes—[*laughter*]—and if I were, I would like to recompense you for the sacrifices that all of you have made to serve in government.

But you are getting something in government—and I want you to tell this to your children, and I hope the Nation's children will hear it, too—something in government service that is far more important than money. It is a cause bigger than yourself. It is the cause of making this the greatest nation in the world, the leader of the world, because without our leadership, the world will know nothing but war, possibly starvation or worse, in the years ahead. With our leadership it will know peace, it will know plenty.

We have been generous, and we will be more generous in the future as we are able to. But most important, we must be strong here, strong in our hearts, strong in our souls, strong in our belief, and strong in our willingness to sacrifice, as you have been willing to sacrifice, in a pecuniary way, to serve in government.

There is something else I would like for you to tell your young people. You know, people often come in and say, "What will I tell my kids?" They look at government and say, sort of a rugged life, and they see the mistakes that are made. They get the impression that everybody is here for the purpose of feathering his nest. That is why I made this earlier point—not in this Administration, not one single man or woman.

And I say to them, there are many fine careers. This country needs good farmers, good businessmen, good plumbers, good carpenters.

I remember my old man. I think that they would have called him sort of a little man, common man. He didn't consider himself that way. You know what he was? He was a streetcar motorman first, and then he was a farmer, and then he had a lemon ranch. It was the poorest lemon ranch in California, I can assure you. He sold it before they found oil on it. [*laughter*] And then he was a grocer. But he was a great man, because he did his job, and every job counts up to the hilt, regardless of what happens.

Nobody will ever write a book, probably, about my mother. Well, I guess all of you would say this about your mother—my mother was a saint. And I think of her, two boys dying of tuberculosis, nursing four others in order that she could take care of my older brother for 3 years in Arizona, and seeing each of them die, and when they died, it was like one of her own.

Yes, she will have no books written about her. But she was a saint.

Now, however, we look to the future. I had a little quote in the speech last night from TR. As you know, I kind of like to read books. I am not educated, but I do read books—[*laughter*]—and the TR quote was a pretty good one.

Here is another one I found as I was reading, my last night in the White House, and this quote is about a young man. He was a young lawyer in New York. He had married a beautiful girl, and they had a lovely daughter, and then suddenly she died, and this is what he wrote. This was in his diary. He said,

> She was beautiful in face and form and lovelier still in spirit. As a flower she grew and as a fair young flower she died. Her life had been always in the sunshine. There had never come to her a single great sorrow. None ever knew her who did not love and revere her for her bright and sunny temper and her saintly unselfishness. Fair, pure and joyous as a maiden, loving, tender and happy as a young wife. When she had just become a mother, when her life seemed to be just begun and when the years seemed so bright before her, then by a strange and terrible fate death came to her. And when my heart's dearest died, the light went from my life forever.

That was TR in his twenties. He thought the light had gone from his life forever—but he went on. And he not only became President but, as an ex-President, he served his country, always in the arena, tempestuous, strong, sometimes wrong, sometimes right, but he was a man.

And as I leave, let me say, that is an example I think all of us should remember. We think sometimes when things happen that don't go the right way; we think that when you don't pass the bar exam the first time—I happened to, but I was just lucky; I mean, my writing was so poor the bar examiner said, "We have just got to let the guy through." We think that when someone dear to us dies, we think that when we lose an election, we think that when we suffer a defeat that all is ended. We think, as TR said, that the light had left his life forever.

Not true. It is only a beginning, always. The young must know it; the old must know it. It must always sustain us, because the greatness comes not when things go always good for you, but the greatness comes and you are really tested, when you take some knocks, some disappointments, when sadness comes, because only if you have been in the deepest valley can you ever know how magnificent it is to be on the highest mountain.

And so I say to you on this occasion, as we leave, we leave proud of the people who have stood by us and worked for us and served this country.

We want you to be proud of what you have done. We want you to continue to serve in government, if that is your wish. Always give your best, never get discouraged, never be petty; always remember, others may hate you, but those who hate you don't win unless you hate them, and then you destroy yourself.

And so, we leave with high hopes, in good spirit, and with deep humility, and with very much gratefulness in our hearts. I can only say to each and every one of you, we come from many faiths, we pray perhaps to different gods—but really the same God in a sense—but I want to say for each and every one of you, not only will we always remember you, not only will we always be grateful to you but always you will be in our hearts and you will be in our prayers. . . .

38

Gerald R. Ford

1. FORD PARDONS NIXON **SEPTEMBER 8, 1974**

I have come to a decision which I felt I should tell you and all of my fellow American citizens, as soon as I was certain in my own mind and in my own conscience that it is the right thing to do.

I have learned already in this office that the difficult decisions always come to this desk. I must admit that many of them do not look at all the same as the hypothetical questions that I have answered freely and perhaps too fast on previous occasions.

My customary policy is to try and get all the facts and to consider the opinions of my countrymen and to take counsel with my most valued friends. But these seldom agree, and in the end, the decision is mine. To procrastinate, to agonize, and to wait for a more favorable turn of events that may never come or more compelling external pressures that may as well be wrong as right, is itself a decision of sorts and a weak and potentially dangerous course for a President to follow.

I have promised to uphold the Constitution, to do what is right as God gives me to see the right, and to do the very best that I can for America. I have asked your help and your prayers, not only when I became President but many times since. The Constitution is the supreme law of our land and it governs our actions as citizens. Only the laws of God, which govern our consciences, are superior to it.

As we are a nation under God, so I am sworn to uphold our laws with the help of God. And I have sought such guidance and searched my own conscience with special diligence to determine the right thing for me to do with respect to my predecessor in this place, Richard Nixon, and his loyal wife and family.

Theirs is an American tragedy in which we all have played a part. It could go on and on and on, or someone must write the end to it. I have concluded that only I can do that, and if I can, I must. There are no historic or legal precedents to which I can turn in this matter, none that precisely fit the circumstances of a private citizen who has resigned the Presidency of the United States. But it is common knowledge that serious allegations and accusations hang like a sword over our former President's head, threatening his health as he tries to reshape his life, a great part of which was spent in the service of this country and by the mandate of its people.

After years of bitter controversy and divisive national debate, I have been advised, and I am compelled to conclude that many months and perhaps more years will have to pass before Richard Nixon could obtain a fair trial by jury in any jurisdiction of the United States under governing decisions of the Supreme Court.

I deeply believe in equal justice for all Americans, whatever their station or former station. The law, whether human or divine, is no respecter of persons; but the law is a respecter of reality.

The facts, as I see them, are that a former President of the United States, instead of enjoying equal treatment with any other citizen accused of violating the law, would be cruelly and excessively penalized either in preserving the presumption of his innocence or in obtaining a speedy determination of his guilt in order to repay a legal debt to society.

During this long period of delay and potential litigation, ugly passions would again be aroused. And our people would again be polarized in their opinions. And the credibility of our free institutions of government would again be challenged at home and abroad.

In the end, the courts might well hold that Richard Nixon had been denied due process, and the verdict of history would even more be inconclusive with respect to those charges arising out of the period of his Presidency, of which I am presently aware.

But it is not the ultimate fate of Richard Nixon that most concerns me, though surely it deeply troubles every decent and every compassionate person. My concern is the immediate future of this great country.

In this, I dare not depend upon my personal sympathy as a long-time friend of the former President, nor my professional judgment as a lawyer, and I do not.

As President, my primary concern must always be the greatest good of all the people of the United States whose servant I am. As a man, my first consideration is to be true to my own convictions and my own conscience.

My conscience tells me clearly and certainly that I cannot prolong the bad dreams that continue to reopen a chapter that is closed. My conscience tells me that only I, as President, have the constitutional power to firmly shut and seal this book. My conscience tells me it is my duty, not merely to proclaim domestic tranquility but to use every means that I have to insure it.

I do believe that the buck stops here, that I cannot rely upon public opinion polls to tell me what is right.

I do believe that right makes might and that if I am wrong, 10 angels swearing I was right would make no difference.

I do believe, with all my heart and mind and spirit, that I, not as President but as a humble servant of God, will receive justice without mercy if I fail to show mercy.

Finally, I feel that Richard Nixon and his loved ones have suffered enough and will continue to suffer, no matter what I do, no matter what we, as a great and good nation, can do together to make his goal of peace come true.

Now, therefore, I, Gerald R. Ford, President of the United States, pursuant to the pardon power conferred upon me by Article II, Section 2, of the Constitution, have granted and by these presents do grant a full, free, and absolute pardon unto Richard Nixon for all offenses against the United States which he, Richard Nixon, has committed or may have committed or taken part in during the period from 20 January 1969 through 9 August 1974.

In witness whereof, I have hereunto set my hand this eighth day of September, in the year of our Lord nineteen hundred and seventy-four, and of the Independence of the United States of America the one hundred and ninety-ninth.

2. WHITE HOUSE CONVERSATION ON THE WORLD   DECEMBER 12, 1975

SIDEY [*Time Magazine*]: Has the world improved over the past year?
THE PRESIDENT: I inherited a fine foundation. We had to build from there. We had to convince

our NATO allies I stood for American strength. Now the Alliance is stronger and our relations bilaterally are better than ever. . . . U.S.–Japanese relations are now the best ever. . . . There were some problems in the UN. . . .

In Southeast Asia, we have lost Indochina, but my trip in December was very helpful in convincing them that the U.S. continues to be an Asian power and we will resist expansion.

With the USSR we have a chance for a SALT II agreement. . . . But we do have serious differences: Portugal, Angola. . . .

SIDEY: Are the Soviets cheating on SALT?

THE PRESIDENT: I don't believe they are cheating. . . .

SIDEY: Is your relationship with Brezhnev good?

THE PRESIDENT: I think it is a good candid working relationship.

SIDEY: . . . do you see the outcome of U.S.–Soviet competition other than military?

THE PRESIDENT: . . . I think our country can more than hold its own in economic or other competition with our free system.

SIDEY: What are your foreign policy nightmares?

THE PRESIDENT: The danger of some miscalculation by some nuclear power. . . .

SIDEY: What if Israel should become a nuclear power to stabilize the Middle East?

THE PRESIDENT: It wouldn't be helpful.

SIDEY: Won't nuclear weapons inevitably be used? Kennedy thought so.

THE PRESIDENT: I am not pessimistic from the leaders I know: it doesn't have to happen.

SIDEY: Do you have enough power in foreign policy?

THE PRESIDENT: There are frustrations—Angola is frustrating. . . .

SIDEY: Your religion. What has all this power done to that?

THE PRESIDENT: I still pray. I think there is a higher order of things. . . .

SIDEY: How about the third century?

THE PRESIDENT: The first hundred years stabilized the government structure. The second gave us the industrial corporation. Now we have new problems. Everything is big—it tends to smother the individual. . . .

SIDEY: You are hard to parse. You are conservative in budgetary terms, yet pursue détente. How do you define yourself?

THE PRESIDENT: I grew up an isolationist, Fortress American environment. World War II showed us that the world was different. I became convinced of the role of the U.S. in the world. . . .

39

James E. Carter

1. CARTER GIVES THE CANAL TO PANAMA   FEBRUARY 1, 1978

Seventy-five years ago, our Nation signed a treaty which gave us rights to build a canal across Panama, to take the historic step of joining the Atlantic and Pacific Oceans. The results of the agreement have been of great benefit to ourselves and to other nations throughout the world who navigate the high seas.

The building of the canal was one of the greatest engineering feats of history. Although massive in concept and construction, it's relatively simple in design and has been reliable and efficient in operation. We Americans are justly and deeply proud of this great achievement.

The canal has also been a source of pride and benefit to the people of Panama—but a cause of some continuing discontent. Because we have controlled a 10-mile-wide strip of land across the heart of their country and because they considered the original terms of the agreement to be unfair, the people of Panama have been dissatisfied with the treaty. It was drafted here in our country and was not signed by any Panamanian. Our own Secretary of State who did sign the original treaty said it was "vastly advantageous to the United States and . . . not so advantageous to Panama."

In 1964, after consulting with former Presidents Truman and Eisenhower, President Johnson committed our Nation to work towards a new treaty with the Republic of Panama. And last summer, after 14 years of negotiation under two Democratic Presidents and two Republican Presidents, we reached and signed an agreement that is fair and beneficial to both countries. The United States Senate will soon be debating whether these treaties should be ratified.

Throughout the negotiations, we were determined that our national security interests would be protected; that the canal would always be open and neutral and available to ships of all nations; that in time of need or emergency our warships would have the right to go to the head of the line for priority passage through the canal; and that our military forces would have the permanent right to defend the canal if it should ever be in danger. The new treaties meet all of these requirements.

Let me outline the terms of the agreement. There are two treaties—one covering the rest of this century, and the other guaranteeing the safety, openness, and neutrality of the canal after the year 1999, when Panama will be in charge of its operation.

For the rest of this century, we will operate the canal through a nine-person board of directors. Five members will be from the United States and four will be from Panama. Within the area of the present Canal Zone, we have the right to select whatever lands and waters our military and civilian forces need to maintain, to operate, and to defend the canal.

. . . The treaties also have been overwhelmingly supported throughout Latin America, but predictably, they are opposed abroad by some who are unfriendly to the United States and who would like to see disorder in Panama and a disruption of our political, economic, and military ties with our friends in Central and South America and in the Caribbean.

I know that the treaties also have been opposed by many Americans. Much of that opposition is based on misunderstanding and misinformation. I've found that when the full terms of the agreement are known, most people are convinced that the national interests of our country will be served best by ratifying the treaties.

The first treaty says, and I quote:

> The United States of America and the Republic of Panama commit themselves to protect and defend the Panama Canal. Each Party shall act, in accordance with its constitutional processes, to meet the danger resulting from an armed attack or other actions which threaten the security of the Panama Canal or [of] ships transiting it.

What we want is the permanent right to use the canal—and we can defend this right through the treaties—through real cooperation with Panama. The citizens of Panama and their government have already shown their support of the new partnership, and a protocol to the neutrality treaty will be signed by many other nations, thereby showing their strong approval.

The new treaties will naturally change Panama from a passive and sometimes deeply resentful bystander into an active and interested partner, whose vital interests will be served by a well-operated canal. This agreement leads to cooperation and not confrontation between our country and Panama. . . .

The Canal Zone cannot be compared with United States territory. We bought Alaska from the Russians, and no one has ever doubted that we own it. We bought the Louisiana Purchases—Territories from France, and that's an integral part of the United States.

The new treaties give us what we do need—not ownership of the canal, but the right to use it and to protect it. As the Chairman of the Joint Chiefs of Staff has said, "The strategic value of the canal lies in its use."

. . . Recently, I discussed the treaties with David McCullough, author of *The Path Between the Seas*, the great history of the Panama Canal. He believes that the canal is something that we built and have looked after these many years; it is "ours" in that sense, which is very different from just ownership. . . .

"We cannot avoid meeting great issues," Roosevelt said. "All that we can determine for ourselves is whether we shall meet them well or ill."

. . . In this historic decision, he would join us in our pride for being a great and generous people, with the national strength and wisdom to do what is right for us and what is fair to others.

2. PEACE BETWEEN EGYPT AND ISRAEL   MARCH 26, 1979

During the past 30 years, Israel and Egypt have waged war. But for the past 16 months, these same two great nations have waged peace. Today we celebrate a victory. . . . Two leaders who will loom large in the history of nations, President Anwar Sadat and Prime Minister Menachem Begin, have conducted this campaign with all the courage, tenacity, brilliance and inspiration of any generals who have ever led men and machines onto the field of battle. . . .

We have won at last the first step of peace. . . . We must not minimize the obstacles which still lie ahead. Differences still separate the signatories to this treaty from one another, and also from some of their neighbors who fear what they have just done. . . .

We have no illusions—we have hopes, dreams and prayers, yes but not illusions. . . .

3. IRANIAN HOSTAGE RESCUE MISSION FAILS   APRIL 25, 1980

Late yesterday, I cancelled a carefully planned operation which was underway in Iran to position our rescue team for later withdrawal of American hostages, who have been held captive there since 4 November. Equipment failure in the rescue helicopters made it necessary to end the mission.

As our team was withdrawing . . . two of our American aircraft collided on the ground following a refueling operation in a remote desert location in Iran. Other information about this rescue mission will be made available to the American people when it is appropriate to do so.

There was no fighting; there was no combat. But to my deep regret, eight of the crewmen of the two aircraft which collided were killed, and several other Americans were hurt in the accident. Our people were immediately airlifted from Iran. Those who were injured have gotten medical treatment, and all of them are expected to recover.

No knowledge of this operation by any Iranian officials or authorities was evident to us until several hours after all Americans were withdrawn from Iran.

Our rescue team knew and I knew that the operation was certain to be difficult and it was certain to be dangerous. We were all convinced that if and when the rescue operation had been commenced that it had an excellent chance of success. They were all volunteers; they were all highly trained. I met with their leaders before they went on this operation. They knew then what hopes of mine and of all Americans they carried with them.

To the families of those who died and who were wounded, I want to express the admiration I feel for the courage of their loved ones and the sorrow that I feel personally for their sacrifice.

The mission . . . was not directed against the people of Iran. It was not undertaken with any feeling of hostility toward Iran or its people. It has caused no Iranian casualties. . . .

This rescue attempt had to await my judgment that the Iranian authorities could not or would not resolve this crisis on their own initiative. With the steady unraveling of authority in Iran and the mounting dangers that were posed to the safety of the hostages themselves and the growing realization that their early release was highly unlikely, I made a decision to commence the rescue operations plans.

. . . It was my decision to attempt the rescue operation. It was my decision to cancel it when problems developed in the placement of our rescue team for a future rescue operation. The responsibility is fully my own.

In the aftermath of the attempt, we continue to hold the Government of Iran responsible for the safety and for the early release of the American hostages. . . .

. . . as President, I also know that the Nation shares not only my disappointment that the rescue effort could not be mounted, because of mechanical difficulties, but also my determination to persevere and to bring all of our hostages home to freedom.

. . . We will seek to continue, along with other nations and with the officials of Iran, a prompt resolution of the crisis. . . .

4. CRISIS IN CONFIDENCE: THE MALAISE SPEECH   JULY 15, 1979

. . . During the past 3 years I've spoken to you on many occasions about national concerns, the energy crisis, reorganizing the Government, our Nation's economy, and issues of war and especially peace.

. . . Gradually, you've heard more and more about what the Government thinks . . . and less and less about our Nation's hopes, our dreams, and our vision of the future. . . .

I invited to Camp David people from almost every segment of our society—business and labor, teachers and preachers, Governors, mayors, and private citizens. And then I left Camp David to listen to other Americans. . . . It has been an extraordinary 10 days, and I want to share with you what I've heard. . . .

From a southern Governor: "Mr. President, you are not leading this Nation—you're just managing the Government."

. . . This kind of summarized a lot of other statements: "Mr. President, we are confronted with a moral and a spiritual crisis."

Several of our discussions were on energy, and I have a notebook full of comments and advice. I'll read just a few.

"We can't go on consuming 40 percent more energy than we produce. When we import oil we are also importing inflation plus unemployment."

"We've got to use what we have. The Middle East has only 5 percent of the world's energy, but the United States has 24 percent."

. . . all the legislation in the world can't fix what's wrong with America. So I want to speak to you first tonight about a subject even more serious than energy or inflation. I want to talk to you right now about a fundamental threat to American democracy.

. . . The threat is nearly invisible in ordinary ways. It is a crisis of confidence. It is a crisis that strikes at the very heart and soul and spirit of our national will. We can see this crisis in the growing doubt about the meaning of our own lives and in the loss of a unity of purpose for our Nation.

. . . Confidence has defined our course and has served as a link between generations. We've always believed in something called progress. We've always had a faith that the days of our children would be better than our own.

Our people are losing that faith, not only in government itself but in the ability as citizens to serve as the ultimate rulers and shapers of our democracy. . . . We always believed that we were part of a great movement of humanity itself called democracy, involved in the search for freedom and that belief has always strengthened us in our purpose. . . .

In a nation that was proud of hard work, strong families, close-knit communities, and our faith in God, too many of us now tend to worship self-indulgence and consumption. Human identity is no longer defined by what one does, but by what one owns. . . . Owning things and consuming things does not satisfy our longing for meaning. . . .

Looking for a way out of this crisis, our people have turned to the Federal Government and found it isolated from the mainstream of our Nation's life. . . . The gap between our citizens and our Government has never been so wide. . . .

One of the visitors to Camp David . . . put it this way: "We've got to stop crying and start sweating, stop talking and start walking, stop cursing and start praying. The strength we need will not come from the White House, but from every house in America."

We know the strength of America. We are strong. We can regain our unity. We can regain our confidence. We are the heirs of generations who survived threats much more powerful and awesome than those that challenge us now. . . .

We ourselves [are] . . . the same Americans who just 10 years ago put a man on the Moon. We are the generation that dedicated our society to the pursuit of human rights. . . .

We are at a turning point in our history. There are two paths to choose. One is a path . . . that leads to fragmentation and self-interest. Down that road lies a mistaken idea of freedom, the right path to grasp for ourselves some advantage over others.

. . . Energy will be the immediate test of our ability to unite this Nation. . . . On the battlefield of energy we can win for our Nation a new confidence. . . .

. . . Our excessive dependence on OPEC has already taken a tremendous toll on our economy and our people. . . . It's a cause of the increased inflation and unemployment that we now face. . . . This intolerable dependence on foreign oil threatens our economic independence and the very security of our Nation. . . .

. . . I will soon submit legislation to Congress calling for the creation of this Nation's first solar bank, which will help us achieve the crucial goal of 20 percent of our energy coming from solar power by the year 2000.

. . . We will protect our environment. But when this Nation critically needs a refinery or a pipeline, we will build it. . . .

XI

VICTORY—ASCENDANCY

RONALD REAGAN ENTERED THE WHITE HOUSE with a settled world view. Global upheavals great and small—terrorism, espionage, civil wars, arms escalation, and the threat of nuclear destruction—began he insisted, early in the century with the Russian Revolution of 1917. The momentous upheaval in Russia brought with it a fundamental instability that was the equivalent of a political tsunami for Russia and her neighbors. That political storm continued through the century under the successors of Lenin and Trotsky. From Reagan's perspective, that Bolshevik eruption left in its wake a specter that continued to haunt not only Europe but ultimately the entire free world throughout almost the entire twentieth century.

President Reagan's admirers have always insisted that this seemingly simplistic world view actually masked Reagan's political genius. This was one of the elements that made Reagan the "Great Communicator." In that role he had delivered thousands of speeches to friendly conservative audiences who shared his assurances that world affairs simply reflected the moral struggle between the forces of good and evil. In a commencement address at Notre Dame University, in the early days of his first administration, he talked to the students about their heritage of freedom and the founding fathers:

> They gave us more than a nation. They brought to all mankind for the first time the concept that man was born free, that each of us has inalienable rights, ours by the grace of God, and that government was created by us for our convenience, having only the powers that we choose to give it. This is the heritage that you're about to claim. . . .

The plain style of the President employed a simple language so that he would be better understood. His enormous political and diplomatic success remains a mystery to many analysts and particularly pundits on the left. It must be remembered that a younger Ronald Reagan was a Franklin Roosevelt New Deal Democrat and that both he and FDR possessed an enigmatic dimension in their personalities. Both were able to connect with the American people through existing technological channels. FDR did so via carefully crafted radio "fireside chats," while Reagan mesmerized the viewing audience through the camera's penetrating eye. These kinds of comparisons are sometimes tricky and can be misleading. It will also be recalled that in the famous Kennedy–Nixon debates, it was generally agreed that those who visually observed the debates on television declared Kennedy the winner. Those who listened on radio in something of fireside fashion were confident that Nixon came out on top. Evidently each of these presidents had specially developed skills. FDR and Nixon had voices that resonated on radio. Kennedy and Reagan were good looking, highly telegenic and comfortable in their skin with a visual media which had a global reach.

Reagan also employed Kennedy images and metaphors to dramatize his public messages, often succeeding in making them his own. An example is the use of the metaphor which actually originated with John Winthrop on the *Arbella* when he urged the faithful: "We must be as a city upon a hill—the eyes of all people are upon us." This was an American theme endorsed by the two presidents. There were policy similarities as well. This was true with regard to both domestic and foreign policy. President Kennedy's economic policy was founded on tax cuts. His theme was to turn the tide. Tax reduction, he maintained, would lead to a strong economy for "a rising tide lifts all boats." President Reagan agreed and proceeded with his tax-cutting policy to restore the nation to economic health. This restoration and recovery did in fact take place during Reagan's watch. His words warrant attention. In a major 1984 address relative to that recovery, President Reagan pointed to the parallel economic recovery of the 1960s:

> . . . Far from being weak, this recovery has been one of the strongest since the 1960s. More people are on the job than ever before in our history. From solid growth in housing to new frontiers in high technology, from a healthy recovery in real wages to a big improvement in productivity, and from record increases in venture capital to new highs in the stock market, America is moving forward, getting stronger, and confounding everyone who said it can't be done. . . .

It is striking that he employed the phrase "new frontiers."

Healthy economies provide a solid base to pursue successful foreign policy. This provides a key to understand the compatible approaches of Kennedy and Reagan to the wider world. Both presidents were Cold Warriors to the hilt. Both went to Berlin, centerpiece of the Cold War, and pointed at the Berlin Wall as symbol of the struggle between freedom and tyranny. Standing in firm solidarity with the citizens of Berlin, President Kennedy mounted the podium and declared that Americans and other free peoples did not claim to be perfect, but "we did not have to build a wall to keep our people in." President Reagan followed John F. Kennedy's footsteps to Berlin a quarter-century later. "We come to Berlin, we American presidents," said Reagan "because it's our duty to speak, in this place, of freedom. . . ." Standing on a platform facing the Brandenburg Gate, the President demanded that the Soviet leader, Mr. Gorbachev, open the Gate and "tear down this wall."

Neither President Reagan nor Harry Truman felt the need to either coddle the Soviets or to apologize for America's firm foreign policy posture in defense of freedom. It was not Berlin or Moscow alone which held the attention of President Reagan. He was greatly concerned about the situation in South Africa. Replying to a wire he received from his friend, the entertainer Sammy Davis, Jr., Ronald Reagan assured Sammy that "we are doing all we can about the tragic situation in South Africa. . . ." Reagan went on to explain the political, diplomatic, and economic complexities in dealing with the "great moral issue" of apartheid. It once again was an ethical contest between good and evil. He ended with a promise:

> Believe me; I see apartheid as an evil that must be eliminated. We must continue our efforts to bring this about. But we have a better chance of doing so if we maintain contact than if we pick up our marbles and walk away. You have my promise, we won't let up.

At bottom, Reagan saw the wisdom of Kennedy in building a healthy economy in connection with promoting the cause of freedom abroad. With sure economic footing they could take significant steps forward in advancing the cause of freedom in Berlin, Johannesburg and across the globe.

Victory in the ideological contest came in the latter days of the second term of the Reagan administration. The Cold War was over. The Iron Curtain was no more. The victory belonged to Reagan, but it belonged to the American presidency and the American people as well. Reagan's Vice President, George H. W. Bush, now the successor of Reagan, presided over the mop-up operations in the aftermath of the Cold War. It was during his presidency that the free people of Europe did in fact tear down that wall and remove that monstrous ideological symbol of oppression. Eastern and Central Europe could now breathe free. The Cold War struggle for the minds and hearts of mankind penetrated the Soviet Union itself, which came undone. The Russian Revolution was over. It had failed. The dissolution of the USSR was an event which brought joy to the hearts of the Russian people. Leningrad was repatriated and was once again St. Petersburg.

At one point in the long tense struggle, the Soviet Premier Nikita Khrushchev travelled to the United Nations in New York City, banged his shoe on the podium and promised: "We will bury you." He insisted that American children would live under communism. Ironically, Stalin's daughter had defected to live under freedom. So too, did Khrushchev's son. Now the end of the Cold War witnessed America and Russia join hands in a world that had to a great extent found a new birth of freedom.

In 1989, President Bush celebrated not only his own inauguration but also commemorated that April the bicentennial of the inauguration of George Washington. From Federal Hall, Bush said:

> Today we reaffirm ethics, honor, and strength in government. Two centuries ago, in his first Inaugural Address, Washington spoke of a government "exemplified by all the attributes which can win the affections of its citizens and command the respect of the world."

Later that same year President Bush arrived in Budapest, Hungary and presented a major address at the famous Karl Marx University. The leader of the free world in the great hall of that university with a veiled statue of Marx at the end of the hall, told the assembled community:

> The Soviet Union has withdrawn troops, which I also take as a step in overcoming Europe's division. And as those forces leave, let the Soviet leaders know they have everything to gain and nothing to lose or fear from peaceful change. We can—and I am determined that we will—work together to move beyond containment, beyond the Cold War.

It was a special time, place, and moment in world history.

America and the world did move beyond the Cold War. Yet a limited hot war was just around the corner. The Iraq dictator Saddam Hussein invaded neighboring Kuwait in August 1990. It was a brutal, nasty incursion into a peaceful kingdom. Among the atrocities perpetrated by the Iraq invaders was the senseless slaughter of Arabian thoroughbred horses. The barbarity of the Iraqi invasion of oil-rich Kuwait troubled the conscience of President Bush who, in accord with the Truman Doctrine, decided that such a vicious aggression would be countered by a civilized alliance of nations. He meticulously assembled plans with his military advisers for operation Desert Storm. As the time to strike approached, the President ruminated on the awesome responsibility of his office to do the right thing. He knew war. Bush was a bona fide hero in World War II. The idea of sending young American boys into action in a distant part of the world was not a happy thought. As he pondered the coming events on the eve of the New Year, he wrote an historic touching note to his children. He was concerned about the use of force and the consequent loss of life. With this momentous decision ahead, he wrote:

Every human life is precious. When the question is asked "How many lives are you willing to sacrifice"—it tears at my heart. The answer, of course, is none—none whatsoever. We have waited to give sanctions a chance, we have moved a tremendous force so as to reduce the risk to every American soldier if force must be used; but the question of loss of life still lingers and plagues the heart.

In the fashion of his predecessor, he concluded: "I look at today's crises as good vs. evil . . . yes, it is that clear." President Bush would in the end adhere to principle. As a father he cautioned: "So dear kids—batten down the hatches."

The initial responses of the United States consisted of moderate calls for diplomacy and compromise. After some reflection, President Bush decided to treat the event as an aggression on a major scale that violated the covenants of international law. On August 6, 1990 with the announcement of Operation Desert Shield, American troops were committed to the Saudi Arabian border to prevent further Iraqi advances. By November, American forces in the Gulf totaled 230,000. Through the autumn and early winter, Bush skillfully used the United Nations to create an alliance of the world's leading powers, who were attracted to U.S. leadership by a mixture of motives.

Some nations may have acted on the principle of opposing aggression. Many Arab neighbors feared Saddam Hussein's regional objectives. All parties silently acknowledged the primacy of oil. The willingness of the United States to expend major resources wherever needed brought to bear key United Nations votes producing a vast international alliance against Iraq.

With Saddam defying all demands to capitulate, the first Allied air attacks on Baghdad began on January 17, 1991. On February 23rd, with the collapse of Soviet efforts to find a compromise, the American-led alliance invaded Iraq in Operation Desert Storm. The war ended—to everyone's surprise—in about one hundred hours, with the rout of Iraqi forces. President Bush had presented the case for war in a nationally televised broadcast from the Oval Office on January 16th. As he explained his reasons for committing the nation to war, he asked the American people to listen to a marine corporal who said: "Let's free these people, so we can go home and be free again." The idea of freedom was behind Desert Storm and the Gulf War.

Victory in the Cold War opened the entire world to new economic and business opportunities for the decade of the 1990s. Joint ventures and privatization enterprises sprung up obviously in places formerly occupied by communists, but these activities were enthusiastically entered into all around the world. Trade agreements would be another important way to link disparate nations together in a global economy. In tune with the times, President William Jefferson Clinton signed into law the North American Free Trade Agreement (NAFTA) on December 8, 1993.

The NAFTA Treaty embodied concepts that committed the United States for the first time to the creation of a global marketplace for production and exchange of goods and services. The agreement was a bitter pill for some factions to swallow. The political landscape was littered with upset losers from both political parties. The new president in his very first year in office engaged in high-stakes risks in backing the agreement and won. Negotiations to create a low- or free-tariff market, including Canada, the United States, and Mexico, began during the Reagan administration and were completed by George Herbert Walker Bush, who joined Mexican president Carlos Salinas de Gortari and Canadian Prime Minister Brian Mulroney to sign the pact on December 17, 1992.

The real fight, left to Clinton, came in the Congress, where powerful forces sought to defeat the Agreement. Central to NAFTA and all other regional trading agreements is the elimination or sharp reduction of tariffs among the partners, thus making goods and services flow freely across borders, enlarging the markets of all participants to include the consumers of the participating parties. The idea of free trade had long been an article of faith for Democrats, reaching back as far as Grover

Cleveland in the nineteenth century. In that tradition Woodrow Wilson likewise endorsed the concept. The adoption of an income tax in 1913 provided elbow room for both Republicans and Democrats from the age-old tariff economic battlefield. At bottom, believers in the removal of trade barriers contended that trade expanded and spread wealth to producers, invigorated consumption, and promoted prosperity. The link to Reagan and Kennedy continued as free trade advocates were confident that from prosperity came stability and world peace.

President Clinton had his finger on the political pulse of the nation and was in tune with the global possibilities that had been opened by President Reagan which followed the fall of the Soviet Union, whose economic premises and global political influence sharply constricted the advance of capitalism. Even so, Clinton's success in passing NAFTA came only after a bruising challenge. Opposition arose from a general fear that American industries and jobs would inevitably be drawn southward. In Mexico, cheap labor and casual environmental enforcement dramatically lowered the cost of production. Goods manufactured under these conditions, opponents held, could be sold on the American market at prices that American manufacturers, paying union wages and observing environmental laws, simply could not match. This nightmare scenario dominated the position of the AFL/CIO and their Congressional supporters of the unions, primarily Democrats. This rift in the Democratic Party caused friction amidst the rank and file and between the unions and the Democratic leadership. The irony for the Congressional Democrats of this union stripe was that their leader, the President of the United States, stood against them.

During the presidential campaign of 1992, a third-party candidate, Ross Perot, who directed his thrust primarily against incumbent President Bush, still gave the Clinton campaign internal fits. He repeatedly heard a "giant sucking sound" from Mexico and other points south. American jobs were moving south. The Democratic Party candidate showed his innate political instinct and skills and spoke artfully about the need for "side agreements" on labor and the environment. This was the trade strategy he employed as President of the United States. He believed not only in NAFTA but in "the larger trading universe" beyond. Like-minded supporters carried into the Congressional debate often arcane references to the General Agreement on Tariffs and Trade (GATT), which envisioned the global market on the horizon. The President also dealt behind the scenes with members from both parties, who demanded special protection for commodities like sugar, peanuts and wheat. The deals were made. In the crucial House vote, NAFTA prevailed 234 to 230, with more Republican supporters than the President's own party. Upon signing the Agreement into law, Clinton confidently proclaimed an historic achievement.

Throughout his public life Bill Clinton demonstrated that he had mastered the art of politics. When it got too hot in the kitchen, he got out of the kitchen. In his first term as President the heat was on at the White House. He and his wife Hilary had presented themselves to the American people as a team. It was Hilary who led the fight for National Health Care. That fight was lost. When the dust settled from the mid-term election of 1994, the Bill/Hilary Clinton team lost again. The margin was huge and carried an unmistakable message. President Clinton got the message. The second half of his first term required serious adjustments. These political changes needed to be in place prior to his re-election campaign in 1996. He pivoted. In January of the election year he announced that the "era of big government is over." With this new political philosophy at his back, Bill Clinton escaped defeat in another three-way race which divided his overall opposition and the Republican rank and file. The philosophical shift paid significant dividends. He increased his percentage of the vote from 41 to 49 percent. Even so, he remained a plurality not a majority president.

As with many American presidents the second term was no picnic in the park. The President and First Lady had to shadow box with alleged improprieties from their Arkansas days, including some commercial ventures. The extended inquiry into these business matters came to be immortalized as "Whitewater." On yet another front, stories out of Arkansas began to attract the attention of the national media. For those muckraking journalists, ambulance-chasing lawyers, and historians who liked to present presidential history with a view to backstairs at the White House, Bill Clinton was a gift. It was as if the ghost of Warren G. Harding had returned to 1600 Pennsylvania Avenue. A raw media frenzy focused on every tiny trace of sexual innuendo as a tiger would pounce upon red meat.

Reports had circulated that while Governor, Bill Clinton had used state troopers to lure women to the executive mansion. Among those identified was a low-level state employee named Paula Corbin Jones. Ms. Jones decided to file suit against the President. A small network of influential lawyers, who were politically and personally opposed to Clinton, began to help Paula Jones, mostly behind the scenes. Among several others, the prominent Republican lawyer Kenneth Starr quietly provided advice to Jones's case handlers. As early as 1994 Starr, recommended by a panel of judges, was appointed as an Independent Counsel to investigate the Whitewater allegations.

Meanwhile, the Jones case endured several phases, alternately neglected and derided in the media as successive teams of lawyers came and went. In 1997 The Supreme Court unanimously ruled that the case could go forward. Ms. Jones refused an offer of $700,000 to settle and the case continued. The Whitewater investigation had failed to produce any indictments. Nor did subsequent political uproars, dubbed "Travel-gate" and "File-gate," advance beyond the media circus.

In the fall of 1997, a New York literary agent named Lucianne Goldberg reported a tale which would spin into Clinton history. The story featured Miss Goldberg's friend, a former White House employee named Linda Tripp, who had taped hours of conversations with a woman named Monica Lewinsky, who for months had carried on a clandestine sexual relationship with President Clinton at the White House. At the beginning of 1998, on January 12, these Lewinsky tapes made their way to Kenneth Starr. Five days later President Clinton testified in the Jones case and denied a sexual relationship with Ms. Lewinsky. On January 26, 1998 the President felt compelled to address the issue on national television. This moment of his presidency carved an indelible imprint on the public mind. Wagging his finger at the television audience he again denied having sex with "that woman."

For more than a year, American politics had but one subject, the Clinton–Lewinsky sex scandal. From its public revelation in January 1998 to the end of the impeachment trial on February 12, 1999, Washington throbbed with salacious gossip, while radio, television, and newspapers sent the nation the unraveling facts, rumors and allegations. Some of the newly established cable news networks adopted programming seemingly based on "all Monica, all the time." Critics and defenders of the President used all media outlets to joust. Periodically, as allegation became sensational fact, interest soared. Throughout the year Kenneth Starr deposed and brought before Grand Juries a parade of witnesses, including President Clinton. Early in September 1998 Starr informed House leaders that he had found "substantial and credible information . . . that may constitute grounds for impeachment." A month later, the President agreed to an $850,000 settlement with Ms. Paula Jones without admission of crime or apology.

Meanwhile, House Judiciary Committee Hearings quickly devolved into a partisan brawl. Impeachment charges were brought to the House floor. This precipitated an even larger political quarrel and the eventual passage, on December 19, of two articles of impeachment. The first of these articles charged that the President had perjured himself in sworn testimony. The second charged that he had obstructed justice.

The nation faced a political crisis of a type not encountered for 131 years. In 1868, Andrew Johnson, the vice president who entered the White House after the assassination of Abraham

Lincoln, had survived in office by one vote in the United States Senate trial. In January 1999, Clinton—the first elected President ever to be impeached—faced the Senate jurors in different circumstances.

The Republicans controlled the Senate with a 55 to 45 majority. Two-thirds (67 votes) were needed to convict. The case was presented by the thirteen House managers who repeatedly recounted all the lurid details of the scandal and insisted that the President's perjury and obstruction fell within the Constitutional definition of "high crimes and misdemeanors." On February 12, 1999 the Senate voted. The Democrats maintained strict party discipline and held all party members for the President. The Republicans divided, and the Clinton presidency was saved. History was repeated, for it was Republican senators who had salvaged the presidency of Andrew Johnson, in the aftermath of the Civil War. On the perjury charge the vote was in the President's favor 55 to 45, with ten Republicans breaking ranks to support President Clinton. The obstruction of justice vote also failed, 50–50, with five Republicans defecting to the President's cause.

There is no justification for his lying under oath. The entire business did smack of vindictiveness and political payback for the fate of Richard Nixon. The public and the Senate were not interested in the destruction of another presidency. While Clinton supporters were ecstatic about the failure of either article to achieve even a majority vote, the President's adamant detractors continued to vilify him. There are many lessons yet to be learned, and America would be well served by future historical exploration of the politics of personal destruction as practiced in our time. In this age, the politically correct police are constantly on punitive patrol, and personages high and low live under the vile threat of calumny or slander. People placed in special positions of the nation's trust, such as President Clinton, have for better or worse come under heavy fire in the brave new post-Cold War period. The effect, polls indicated, had produced a loss of personal respect for the President, for the office, and for politics and politicians in general. It prompts wonder as to whether this has become a template of our times as to how Americans perceive and treat our neighbor. In the decade after the Cold War the dictum of Pogo of cartoon fame seemed to address a larger truth: "We have met the enemy and they are us." Shortly after the impeachment business had been concluded in the Senate, Clinton appeared in the Rose Garden and left us some presidential words to contemplate. These five sentences contained a poignant call for American reconciliation and renewal.

America might find it in the national heart to forgive and forget the transgressions of the high and mighty. Have the occupants in the White House or in the Governors' mansions throughout the land been as considerate or forgiving to the inmates of our penal system, many of whom were falsely accused, unfairly prosecuted, and unjustly convicted? So many juveniles coming from broken homes have been convicted as adults often for crimes they never committed since they are cornered to plea bargain in order to avoid an even greater travesty of justice. The Chief Magistrates in our time from both parties could take a page from the liberal application of the constitutional "pardon power" by such Chief Magistrates as Washington and Lincoln. As America entered the new millennium a "kinder and gentler America" would remain a fleeting national desire.

40

Ronald Reagan

1. HISTORY AND THE AMERICAN HERITAGE   MAY 17, 1981

. . . This experiment in man's relation to man is a few years into its third century. . . .

. . . there are great unsolved problems. Federalism, with its built in checks and balances, has been distorted. Central government has usurped powers that properly belong to local and State governments. And in so doing, in many ways that central government has begun to fail to do the things that are truly the responsibility of a central government.

All of this has led to the misuse of power and preemption of the prerogatives of people and their social institutions. . . . Not too many years ago . . . schools were relatively free from government interference. In recent years, government has spawned regulations covering virtually every facet of our lives. The independent and church-supported colleges and universities have found themselves enmeshed in that network of regulations and the costly blizzard of paperwork that government is demanding. Thirty-four congressional committees and almost 80 subcommittees have jurisdiction over 439 separate laws affecting education at the college level alone. Almost every aspect of campus life is now regulated—hiring, firing, promotions, physical plant, construction, recordkeeping, fundraising and, to some extent, curriculum and educational programs.

. . . If ever the great independent colleges and universities . . . give way to and are replaced by tax-supported institutions, the struggle to preserve academic freedom will have been lost.

We're troubled today by economic stagnation, brought on by inflated currency and prohibitive taxes and burdensome regulations. The cost of stagnation in human terms, mostly among those least equipped to survive it, is cruel and inhuman.

... The good news is that something is being done about all this because the people of America have said, "Enough already." . . . We forgot that we were the keepers of the power, forgot to challenge the notion that the state is the principal vehicle of social change, forgot that millions of social inter-actions among free individuals and institutions can do more to foster economic and social progress than all the careful schemes of government planners.

Well, at last we're remembering, remembering that government has certain legitimate functions which it can perform very well, that it can be responsive to the people, that it can be humane and compassionate, but that when it undertakes tasks that are not its proper province, it can do none of them as well or as economically as the private sector.

For too long government has been fixing things that aren't broken and inventing miracle cures for unknown diseases.

We need you. We need your youth. We need your strength. We need your idealism to help us make right that which is wrong. . . . May I suggest, don't discard the time-tested values upon which civilization was built simply because they're old. More important, don't let today's doom criers and cynics persuade you that the best is past, that from here on it's all downhill. Each generation sees farther than the generation that preceded it because it stands on the shoulders of that generation. . . .

The people have made it plain already. They want an end to excessive government intervention in their lives and in the economy, an end to the burdensome and unnecessary regulations and a punitive tax policy that does take "from the mouth of labor the bread it has earned." They want a government that cannot only continue to send men across the vast reaches of space and bring them safely home, but that can guarantee that you and I can walk in the park of our neighborhood after dark and get safely home. And finally, they want to know that this Nation has the ability to defend itself against those who would seek to pull it down.

. . . There's a task force under the leadership of the Vice President, George Bush, that is to look at those regulations I've spoken of. They have already identified hundreds of them that can be wiped out with no harm to the quality of life. And the cancellation of just those regulations will leave billions and billions of dollars in the hands of the people for productive enterprise and research and development and the creation of jobs.

The years ahead are great ones for this country, for the cause of freedom and the spread of civilization. The West won't contain communism, it will transcend communism. It . . . will dismiss it as some bizarre chapter in human history whose last pages are even now being written.

William Faulkner, at a Nobel Prize ceremony some time back, said man "would not only [merely] endure: he will prevail" against the modern world because he will return to "the old verities and truths of the heart." And then Faulkner said of man, "He is immortal because he alone among creatures . . . has a soul, a spirit capable of compassion and sacrifice and endurance."

One can't say those words—compassion, sacrifice, and endurance—without thinking of the irony that one who so exemplifies them, Pope John Paul II, a man of peace and goodness, an inspiration to the world, would be struck by a bullet from a man towards whom he could only feel compassion and love. It was Pope John Paul II who warned in last year's encyclical on mercy and justice against certain economic theories that use the rhetoric of class struggle to justify injustice. He said, "In the name of an alleged justice the neighbor is sometimes destroyed, killed, deprived of liberty or stripped of fundamental human rights."

For the West, for America, the time has come to dare to show to the world that our civilized ideas, our traditions, our values, are not—like the ideology and war machine of totalitarian societies—just a facade of strength. It is time for the world to know our intellectual and spiritual values are rooted in the source of all strength, a belief in a Supreme Being, and a law higher than our own.

When it's written, history of our time won't dwell long on the hardships of the recent past. But history will . . . determine the fate of freedom for a thousand years—Did a nation borne of hope lose hope? Did a people forged by courage find courage wanting? Did a generation . . . forsake honor at the moment of great climactic struggle for the human spirit?

If history asks such questions, it also answers them. And the answers are to be found in the heritage left by generations of Americans before us. They stand in silent witness to what the world will soon know and history someday record: that in the [its] third century, the American Nation came of age, affirmed its leadership of free men and women serving selflessly a vision of man with God, government for people, and humanity at peace. . . .

My hope today is that in the years to come—and come it shall—when it's your time to explain to another generation the meaning of the past and thereby hold out to them their promise of the

Figure 40.1 Four presidents toast each other in the White House Blue Room, October 8, 1981, courtesy of the Ronald Reagan Presidential Library and Museum.

future, that you'll recall the truths and traditions of which we've spoken. It is these truths and traditions that define our civilization and make up our national heritage. And now, they're yours to protect and pass on.

I have one more hope for you: when you do speak to the next generation about these things, that you will always be able to speak of an America that is strong and free, to find in your hearts an unbounded pride in this much-loved country, this once and future land, this bright and hopeful nation whose generous spirit and great ideals the world still honors.

2. CHIEF DIPLOMAT DENOUNCES THE "EVIL EMPIRE"   MARCH 8, 1983

. . . There is sin and evil in the world, and we're enjoined by Scripture and the Lord Jesus to oppose it with all our might. Our nation, too, has a legacy of evil with which it must deal. The glory of this land has been its capacity for transcending the moral evils of our past. For example, the long struggle of minority citizens for equal rights, once a source of disunity and civil war is now a point of pride for all Americans. We must never go back. There is no room for racism, anti-Semitism, or other forms of ethnic and racial hatred in this country.

I know that you've been horrified, as have I, by the resurgence of some hate groups preaching bigotry and prejudice. Use the mighty voice of your pulpits and the powerful standing of your churches to denounce and isolate these hate groups in our midst. The commandment given us is clear and simple: "Thou shalt love thy neighbor as thyself."

But whatever sad episodes exist in our past, any objective observer must hold a positive view of American history, a history that has been the story of hopes fulfilled and dreams made into reality.

Especially in this century, America has kept alight the torch of freedom, but not just for ourselves but for millions of others around the world.

And this brings me to my final point today. During my first press conference as President, in answer to a direct question, I pointed out that, as good Marxist-Leninists, the Soviet leaders have openly and publicly declared that the only morality they recognize is that which will further their cause, which is world revolution. I think I should point out I was only quoting Lenin, their guiding spirit, who said in 1920 that they repudiate all morality that proceeds from supernatural ideas— that's their name for religion—or ideas that are outside class conceptions. Morality is entirely subordinate to the interests of class war. And everything is moral that is necessary for the annihilation of the old, exploiting social order and for uniting the proletariat.

Well, I think the refusal of many influential people to accept this elementary fact of Soviet doctrine illustrates an historical reluctance to see totalitarian powers for what they are. We saw this phenomenon in the 1930s. We see it too often today.

This doesn't mean we should isolate ourselves and refuse to seek an understanding with them. I intend to do everything I can to persuade them of our peaceful intent, to remind them that it was the West that refused to use its nuclear monopoly in the forties and fifties for territorial gain and which now proposes 50-percent cut in strategic ballistic missiles and the elimination of an entire class of land-based, intermediate-range nuclear missiles.

At the same time, however, they must be made to understand we will never compromise our principles and standards. We will never give away our freedom. We will never abandon our belief in God. And we will never stop searching for a genuine peace. But we can assure none of these things America stands for through the so-called nuclear freeze solutions proposed by some.

The truth is that a freeze now would be a very dangerous fraud, for that is merely the illusion of peace. The reality is that we must find peace through strength. . . .

A number of years ago, I heard a young father, a very prominent young man in the entertainment world, addressing a tremendous gathering in California. It was during the time of the Cold War, and communism and our own way of life were very much on people's minds. And he was speaking to that subject. And suddenly, though, I heard him saying, "I love my little girls more than anything." And I said to myself, "Oh, no, don't. You can't—don't say that." But I had underestimated him. He went on: "I would rather see my little girls die now still believing in God, than have them grow up under communism and one day die no longer believing in God."

There were thousands of young people in that audience. They came to their feet with shouts of joy. They had instantly recognized the profound truth in what he had said, with regard to the physical and the soul and what was truly important.

Yes, let us pray for the salvation of all of those who live in that totalitarian darkness—pray they will discover the joy of knowing God. But until they do, let us be aware that while they preach the supremacy of the state, declare its omnipotence over individual man, and predict its eventual domination of all peoples on the Earth, they are the focus of evil in the modern world.

It was C. S. Lewis who, in his unforgettable *Screwtape Letters*, wrote:

The greatest evil is not done now in those sordid "dens of crime" that Dickens loved to paint. It is not even done in concentration camps and labor camps. In those we see its final result. But it is conceived and ordered . . . in clear, carpeted, warmed, and well-lighted offices, by quiet men with white collars and cut fingernails and smooth-shaven cheeks who do not need to raise their voice.

Well, because these "quiet men" do not "raise their voices," because they sometimes speak in soothing tones of brotherhood and peace, because, like other dictators before them, they're always making "their final territorial demand," some would have us accept them at their word and accommodate ourselves to their aggressive impulses. But if history teaches anything, it teaches that simple-minded appeasement or wishful thinking about our adversaries is folly. It means the betrayal of our past, the squandering of our freedom.

So, I urge you to speak out against those who would place the United States in a position of military and moral inferiority. You know, I've always believed that old Screwtape reserved his best efforts for those of you in the church. So, in your discussions of the nuclear freeze proposals, I urge you to beware the temptation of pride—the temptation of blithely declaring yourselves above it all and label both sides equally at fault, to ignore the facts of history and the aggressive impulses of an evil empire, to simply call the arms race a giant misunderstanding and thereby remove yourself from the struggle between right and wrong and good and evil.

I ask you to resist the attempts of those who would have you withhold your support for our efforts, this administration's efforts, to keep America strong and free, while we negotiate real and verifiable reductions in the world's nuclear arsenals and one day, with God's help, their total elimination.

While America's military strength is important, let me add here that I've always maintained that the struggle now going on for the world will never be decided by bombs or rockets, by armies or military might. The real crisis we face today is a spiritual one; at root, it is a test of moral will and faith. . . .

Figure 40.2 President Reagan and Pope John Paul II at Fairbanks, Alaska, May 2, 1984, courtesy of the Ronald Regan Presidential Library and Museum.

I believe we shall rise to the challenge. I believe that communism is another sad, bizarre chapter in human history whose last pages even now are being written. I believe this because the source of our strength in the quest for human freedom is not material, but spiritual. And because it knows no limitation, it must terrify and ultimately triumph over those who would enslave their fellow man. For in the words of Isaiah: "He giveth power to the faint; and to them that have no might He increased strength. . . . But they that wait upon the Lord shall renew their strength; they shall mount up with wings as eagles; they shall run, and not be weary."

Yes, change your world. One of our Founding Fathers, Thomas Paine, said, "We have it within our power to begin the world over again." We can do it, doing together what no one church could do by itself.

3. "STAR WARS" MISSILE DEFENSE CONCEPT   MARCH 23, 1983

. . . The subject I want to discuss with you, peace and national security, is both timely and important. Timely, because I've reached a decision which offers a new hope for our children in the 21st century, a decision I'll tell you about in a few minutes. And important because there's a very big decision that you must make for yourselves. This subject involves the most basic duty that any President and any people share, the duty to protect and strengthen the peace. . . .

There was a time when we depended on coastal forts and artillery batteries, because, with the weaponry of that day, any attack would have had to come by sea. Well, this is a different world, and our defenses must be based on recognition and awareness of the weaponry possessed by other nations in the nuclear age.

We can't afford to believe that we will never be threatened. There have been two world wars in my lifetime. We didn't start them and, indeed, did everything we could to avoid being drawn into them. But we were ill-prepared for both. Had we been better prepared, peace might have been preserved.

For 20 years the Soviet Union has been accumulating enormous military might. They didn't stop when their forces exceeded all requirements of a legitimate defensive capability. And they haven't stopped now. During the past decade and a half, the Soviets have built up a massive arsenal of new strategic nuclear weapons—weapons that can strike directly at the United States. . . .

When I took office in January 1981, I was appalled by what I found: American planes that couldn't fly and American ships that couldn't sail for lack of spare parts and trained personnel and insufficient fuel and ammunition for essential training. The inevitable result of all this was poor morale in our Armed Forces, difficulty in recruiting the brightest young Americans to wear the uniform, and difficulty in convincing our most experienced military personnel to stay on.

There was a real question then about how well we could meet a crisis. And it was obvious that we had to begin a major modernization program to ensure we could deter aggression and preserve the peace in the years ahead. . . .

If the Soviet Union will join with us in our effort to achieve major arms reduction, we will have succeeded in stabilizing the nuclear balance. Nevertheless, it will still be necessary to rely on the specter of retaliation, on mutual threat. And that's a sad commentary on the human condition. Wouldn't it be better to save lives than to avenge them? Are we not capable of demonstrating our peaceful intentions by applying all our abilities and our ingenuity to achieving a truly lasting stability? I think we are. Indeed, we must.

After careful consultation with my advisers, including the Joint Chiefs of Staff, I believe there is a way. Let me share with you a vision of the future which offers hope. It is that we embark on a program to counter the awesome Soviet missile threat with measures that are defensive. Let us turn to the very strengths in technology that spawned our great industrial base and that have given us the quality of life we enjoy today.

What if free people could live secure in the knowledge that their security did not rest upon the threat of instant U.S. retaliation to deter a Soviet attack, that we could intercept and destroy strategic ballistic missiles before they reached our own soil or that of our allies?

I know this is a formidable, technical task, one that may not be accomplished before the end of this century. Yet, current technology has attained a level of sophistication where it's reasonable for us to begin this effort. It will take years, probably decades of effort on many fronts. There will be failures and setbacks, just as there will be successes and breakthroughs. And as we proceed, we must remain constant in preserving the nuclear deterrent and maintaining a solid capability for flexible response. But isn't it worth every investment necessary to free the world from the threat of nuclear war? We know it is.

In the meantime, we will continue to pursue real reductions in nuclear arms, negotiating from a position of strength that can be ensured only by modernizing our strategic forces. At the same time, we must take steps to reduce the risk of a conventional military conflict escalating to nuclear war by improving our nonnuclear capabilities.

America does possess—now—the technologies to attain very significant improvements in the effectiveness of our conventional, nonnuclear forces. Proceeding boldly with these new technologies, we can significantly reduce any incentive that the Soviet Union may have to threaten attack against the United States or its allies.

As we pursue our goal of defensive technologies, we recognize that our allies rely upon our strategic offensive power to deter attacks against them. Their vital interests and ours are inextricably linked. Their safety and ours are one. And no change in technology can or will alter that reality. We must and shall continue to honor our commitments.

I clearly recognize that defensive systems have limitations and raise certain problems and ambiguities. If paired with offensive systems, they can be viewed as fostering an aggressive policy, and no one wants that. But with these considerations firmly in mind, I call upon the scientific community in our country, those who gave us nuclear weapons, to turn their great talents now to the cause of mankind and world peace, to give us the means of rendering these nuclear weapons impotent and obsolete.

Tonight, consistent with our obligations of the ABM treaty and recognizing the need for closer consultation with our allies, I'm taking an important first step. I am directing a comprehensive and intensive effort to define a long-term research and development program to begin to achieve our ultimate goal of eliminating the threat posed by strategic nuclear missiles. This could pave the way for arms control measures to eliminate the weapons themselves. We seek neither military superiority nor political advantage. Our only purpose—one all people share—is to search for ways to reduce the danger of nuclear war.

My fellow Americans, tonight we're launching an effort which holds the promise of changing the course of human history. There will be risks, and results take time. But I believe we can do it. As we cross this threshold, I ask for your prayers and your support.

4. THE *CHALLENGER* TRAGEDY   JANUARY 28, 1986

. . . Today is a day for mourning and remembering. Nancy and I are pained to the core by the tragedy of the shuttle *Challenger*. We know we share this pain with all of the people of our country. This is truly a national loss.

Nineteen years ago, almost to the day, we lost three astronauts in a terrible accident on the ground. But we've never lost an astronaut in flight; we've never had a tragedy like this. And perhaps we've forgotten the courage it took for the crew of the shuttle. But they, the *Challenger* Seven, were aware of the dangers, but overcame them and did their jobs brilliantly. We mourn seven heroes: Michael Smith, Dick Scobee, Judith Resnik, Ronald McNair, Ellison Onizuka, Gregory Jarvis, and Christa McAuliffe. We mourn their loss as a nation together.

For the families of the seven, we cannot bear, as you do, the full impact of this tragedy. But we feel the loss, and we're thinking about you so very much. Your loved ones were daring and brave, and they had that special grace, that special spirit that says, "Give me a challenge, and I'll meet it with joy." They had a hunger to explore the universe and discover its truths. They wished to serve, and they did. They served all of us. We've grown used to wonders in this century. It's hard to dazzle us. But for 25 years the United States space program has been doing just that. We've grown used to the idea of space, and perhaps we forget that we've only just begun. We're still pioneers. They, the members of the *Challenger* crew, were pioneers.

And I want to say something to the schoolchildren of America who were watching the live coverage of the shuttle's takeoff. I know it is hard to understand, but sometimes painful things like this happen. It's all part of the process of exploration and discovery. It's all part of taking a chance and expanding man's horizons. The future doesn't belong to the fainthearted; it belongs to the brave. The *Challenger* crew was pulling us into the future, and we'll continue to follow them.

I've always had great faith in and respect for our space program, and what happened today does nothing to diminish it. We don't hide our space program. We don't keep secrets and cover things up. We do it all up front and in public. That's the way freedom is, and we wouldn't change it for a minute. We'll continue our quest in space. There will be more shuttle flights and more shuttle crews and, yes, more volunteers, more civilians, more teachers in space. Nothing ends here; our hopes and our journeys continue. I want to add that I wish I could talk to every man and woman who works for NASA or who worked on this mission and tell them: "Your dedication and professionalism have moved and impressed us for decades. And we know of your anguish. We share it."

There's a coincidence today. On this day 390 years ago, the great explorer Sir Francis Drake died aboard ship off the coast of Panama. In his lifetime the great frontiers were the oceans, and an historian later said, "He lived by the sea, died on it, and was buried in it." Well, today we can say of the *Challenger* crew: Their dedication was, like Drake's, complete.

The crew of the space shuttle *Challenger* honored us by the manner in which they lived their lives. We will never forget them, nor the last time we saw them, this morning, as they prepared for their journey and waved goodbye and "slipped the surly bonds of earth" to "touch the face of God."

5. TEAR DOWN THIS WALL   JUNE 12, 1987

. . . Twenty four years ago, President John F. Kennedy visited Berlin, speaking to the people of this city and the world at the city hall. . . .

We come to Berlin, we American presidents, because it's our duty to speak, in this place, of freedom. . . .

Our gathering today is being broadcast throughout Western Europe and North America. I understand that it is being seen and heard as well in the East. To those listening throughout Eastern Europe, I extend my warmest greetings and the good will of the American people. To those listening in East Berlin, a special word: Although I cannot be with you, I address my remarks to you just as

Figure 40.3 Ronald Reagan at the Berlin Wall, June 12, 1987 courtesy of the Ronald Reagan Presidential Library and Museum.

surely as to those standing here before me. For I join you, as I join your fellow countrymen in the West, in this firm, this unalterable belief: Es gibt nur ein Berlin. [There is only one Berlin.]

Behind me stands a wall that encircles the free sectors of this city, part of a vast system of barriers that divides the entire continent of Europe. From the Baltic, south, those barriers cut across Germany in a gash of barbed wire, concrete, dog runs, and guard towers. Farther south, there may be no visible, no obvious wall. But there remain armed guards and checkpoints all the same—still a restriction on the right to travel, still an instrument to impose upon ordinary men and women the will of a totalitarian state. Yet it is here in Berlin where the wall emerges most clearly; here, cutting across your city, where the news photo and the television screen have imprinted this brutal division of a continent upon the mind of the world. Standing before the Brandenburg Gate, every man is a German, separated from his fellow men. Every man is a Berliner, forced to look upon a scar.

President von Weizsacker has said: "The German question is open as long as the Brandenburg Gate is closed." Today I say: As long as this gate is closed, as long as this scar of a wall is permitted to stand, it is not the German question alone that remains open, but the question of freedom for all mankind. Yet I do not come here to lament. For I find in Berlin a message of hope, even in the shadow of this wall, a message of triumph.

In this season of spring in 1945, the people of Berlin emerged from their air raid shelters to find devastation. Thousands of miles away, the people of the United States reached out to help. And in 1947 Secretary of State—as you've been told—George Marshall announced the creation of what would become known as the Marshall plan. Speaking precisely 40 years ago this month, he said: "Our policy is directed not against any country or doctrine, but against hunger, poverty, desperation, and chaos."

In the Reichstag a few moments ago, I saw a display commemorating this 40th anniversary of the Marshall plan. I was struck by the sign on a burnt-out, gutted structure that was being rebuilt. I understand that Berliners of my own generation can remember seeing signs like it dotted throughout the Western sectors of the city. The sign read simply: "The Marshall plan is helping here to strengthen the free world." A strong, free world in the West, that dream became real. Japan rose from ruin to become an economic giant. Italy, France, Belgium—virtually every nation in Western Europe saw political and economic rebirth; the European Community was founded.

In West Germany and here in Berlin, there took place an economic miracle, the Wirtschaftswunder. Adenauer, Erhard, Reuter, and other leaders understood the practical importance of liberty—that just as truth can flourish only when the journalist is given freedom of speech, so prosperity can come about only when the farmer and businessman enjoy economic freedom. The German leaders reduced tariffs, expanded free trade, lowered taxes. From 1950 to 1960 alone, the standard of living in West Germany and Berlin doubled.

Where four decades ago there was rubble, today in West Berlin there is the greatest industrial output of any city in Germany—busy office blocks, fine homes and apartments, proud avenues, and the spreading lawns of parkland. Where a city's culture seemed to have been destroyed, today there are two great universities, orchestras and an opera, countless theaters, and museums. Where there was want, today there's abundance—food, clothing, automobiles—the wonderful goods of the Ku'damm. From devastation, from utter ruin, you Berliners have, in freedom, rebuilt a city that once again ranks as one of the greatest on Earth. The Soviets may have had other plans. But, my friends, there were a few things the Soviets didn't count on Berliner herz, Berliner humor, ja, und Berliner schnauze. [Berliner heart, Berliner humor, yes, and a Berliner schnauze.] [*laughter*]

In the 1950s, Khrushchev predicted: "We will bury you." But in the West today, we see a free world that has achieved a level of prosperity and well-being unprecedented in all human history. In the Communist world, we see failure, technological backwardness, declining standards of health, even want of the most basic kind—too little food. Even today, the Soviet Union still cannot feed itself. After these four decades, then, there stands before the entire world one great and inescapable conclusion: Freedom leads to prosperity. Freedom replaces the ancient hatreds among the nations with comity and peace. Freedom is the victor.

And now the Soviets themselves may, in a limited way, be coming to understand the importance of freedom. We hear much from Moscow about a new policy of reform and openness. Some political prisoners have been released. Certain foreign news broadcasts are no longer being jammed. Some economic enterprises have been permitted to operate with greater freedom from state control. Are these the beginnings of profound changes in the Soviet state? Or are they token gestures, intended to raise false hopes in the West, or to strengthen the Soviet system without changing it? We welcome change and openness; for we believe that freedom and security go together, that the advance of human liberty can only strengthen the cause of world peace.

There is one sign the Soviets can make that would be unmistakable, that would advance dramatically the cause of freedom and peace. General Secretary Gorbachev, if you seek peace, if you seek prosperity for the Soviet Union and Eastern Europe, if you seek liberalization: Come here to this gate! Mr. Gorbachev, open this gate! Mr. Gorbachev, tear down this wall!

I understand the fear of war and the pain of division that afflict this continent—and I pledge to you my country's efforts to help overcome these burdens. To be sure, we in the West must resist Soviet expansion. So we must maintain defenses of unassailable strength. Yet we seek peace; so we must strive to reduce arms on both sides. Beginning 10 years ago, the Soviets challenged the Western alliance with a grave new threat, hundreds of new and more deadly SS-20 nuclear missiles, capable of striking every capital in Europe. The Western alliance responded by committing itself to a counterdeployment unless the Soviets agreed to negotiate a better solution; namely, the elimination of such weapons on both sides. For many months, the Soviets refused to bargain in earnestness. As the alliance, in turn, prepared to go forward with its counterdeployment, there were difficult days—days of protests like those during my 1982 visit to this city—and the Soviets later walked away from the table.

But through it all, the alliance held firm. And I invite those who protested then—I invite those who protest today—to mark this fact: Because we remained strong, the Soviets came back to the table. And because we remained strong, today we have within reach the possibility, not merely of limiting the growth of arms, but of eliminating, for the first time, an entire class of nuclear weapons from the face of the Earth. As I speak, NATO ministers are meeting in Iceland to review the progress of our proposals for eliminating these weapons. At the talks in Geneva, we have also proposed deep cuts in strategic offensive weapons. And the Western allies have likewise made far-reaching proposals to reduce the danger of conventional war and to place a total ban on chemical weapons.

While we pursue these arms reductions, I pledge to you that we will maintain the capacity to deter Soviet aggression at any level at which it might occur. And in cooperation with many of our allies, the United States is pursuing the Strategic Defense Initiative—research to base deterrence not on the threat of offensive retaliation, but on defenses that truly defend; on systems, in short, that will not target populations, but shield them. By these means we seek to increase the safety of Europe and all the world. But we must remember a crucial fact: East and West do not mistrust each other because we are armed; we are armed because we mistrust each other. And our differences are not about weapons but about liberty. When President Kennedy spoke at the City Hall those 24 years ago, freedom was encircled, Berlin was under siege. And today, despite all the pressures upon this city, Berlin stands secure in its liberty. And freedom itself is transforming the globe.

In the Philippines, in South and Central America, democracy has been given a rebirth. Throughout the Pacific, free markets are working miracle after miracle of economic growth. In the industrialized nations, a technological revolution is taking place—a revolution marked by rapid, dramatic advances in computers and telecommunications.

In Europe, only one nation and those it controls refuse to join the community of freedom. Yet in this age of redoubled economic growth, of information and innovation, the Soviet Union faces a choice: It must make fundamental changes, or it will become obsolete. Today thus represents a moment of hope. We in the West stand ready to cooperate with the East to promote true openness, to break down barriers that separate people, to create a safer, freer world.

And surely there is no better place than Berlin, the meeting place of East and West, to make a start. Free people of Berlin: Today, as in the past, the United States stands for the strict observance and full implementation of all parts of the Four Power Agreement of 1971. Let us use this occasion, the 750th anniversary of this city, to usher in a new era, to seek a still fuller, richer life for the Berlin of the future. Together, let us maintain and develop the ties between the Federal Republic and the Western sectors of Berlin, which is permitted by the 1971 agreement.

And I invite Mr. Gorbachev: Let us work to bring the Eastern and Western parts of the city closer together, so that all the inhabitants of all Berlin can enjoy the benefits that come with life in one of the great cities of the world. To open Berlin still further to all Europe, East and West, let us expand the vital air access to this city, finding ways of making commercial air service to Berlin more convenient, more comfortable, and more economical. We look to the day when West Berlin can become one of the chief aviation hubs in all central Europe.

With our French and British partners, the United States is prepared to help bring international meetings to Berlin. It would be only fitting for Berlin to serve as the site of United Nations meetings, or world conferences on human rights and arms control or other issues that call for international cooperation. There is no better way to establish hope for the future than to enlighten young minds, and we would be honored to sponsor summer youth exchanges, cultural events, and other programs for young Berliners from the East. Our French and British friends, I'm certain, will do the same. And it's my hope that an authority can be found in East Berlin to sponsor visits from young people of the Western sectors.

One final proposal, one close to my heart: Sport represents a source of enjoyment and ennoblement, and you many have noted that the Republic of Korea—South Korea—has offered to permit certain events of the 1988 Olympics to take place in the North. International sports competitions of all kinds could take place in both parts of this city. And what better way to demonstrate to the world the openness of this city than to offer in some future year to hold the Olympic games here in Berlin, East and West?

In these four decades, as I have said, you Berliners have built a great city. You've done so in spite of threats—the Soviet attempts to impose the East-mark, the blockade. Today the city thrives in spite of the challenges implicit in the very presence of this wall. What keeps you here? Certainly there's a great deal to be said for your fortitude, for your defiant courage. But I believe there's something deeper, something that involves Berlin's whole look and feel and way of life—not mere sentiment. No one could live long in Berlin without being completely disabused of illusions. Something instead, that has seen the difficulties of life in Berlin but chose to accept them, that continues to build this good and proud city in contrast to a surrounding totalitarian presence that refuses to release human energies or aspirations. Something that speaks with a powerful voice of affirmation, that says yes to this city, yes to the future, yes to freedom. In a word, I would submit that what keeps you in Berlin is love—love both profound and abiding.

Perhaps this gets to the root of the matter, to the most fundamental distinction of all between East and West. The totalitarian world produces backwardness because it does such violence to the spirit, thwarting the human impulse to create, to enjoy, to worship. The totalitarian world finds even symbols of love and of worship an affront. Years ago, before the East Germans began rebuilding their churches, they erected a secular structure: the television tower at Alexander Platz. Virtually ever since, the authorities have been working to correct what they view as the tower's one major flaw, treating the glass sphere at the top with paints and chemicals of every kind. Yet even today when the Sun strikes that sphere—that sphere that towers over all Berlin—the light makes the sign of the cross. There in Berlin, like the city itself, symbols of love, symbols of worship, cannot be suppressed.

As I looked out a moment ago from the Reichstag, that embodiment of German unity, I noticed words crudely spray-painted upon the wall, perhaps by a young Berliner, "This wall will fall. Beliefs become reality." Yes, across Europe, this wall will fall. For it cannot withstand faith; it cannot withstand truth. The wall cannot withstand freedom.

And I would like, before I close, to say one word. I have read, and I have been questioned since I've been here about certain demonstrations against my coming. And I would like to say just one thing, and to those who demonstrate so. I wonder if they have ever asked themselves that if they should have the kind of government they apparently seek, no one would ever be able to do what they're doing again.

Figure 40.4 President Reagan, Soviet General Secretary Gorbachev, and Vice President (and President-elect) George H.W. Bush on Governor's Island, December 7, 1988, courtesy of the Ronald Reagan Presidential Library and Museum.

6. AMERICANS: KEEPERS OF MIRACLES   JANUARY 14, 1989

Over the years I've greatly enjoyed this opportunity to get together with you and report on the week's events here in Washington. But next week, after witnessing the inauguration of George Bush as President, Nancy and I will head back to the ranch. We go with full hearts, with best wishes for George and Barbara, and with gratitude to all of you. It's been a privilege to serve the people and the Nation we've always loved and love so much today.

It's difficult, of course, to put all the events of 8 busy, tumultuous years in perspective; in fact, that's best left to the impartial judgment of history. But as I look back over these Saturday talks, I can't help but think about how often at moments of accomplishment and triumph, as well as crisis and heartbreak, we came together in this way: a President giving his accounting to those, under our system of government, to whom he is accountable. We've shared a great deal together; for me it's been a special relationship. Believe me, Saturdays will never seem the same. I'll miss you.

But you know, somehow messages of farewell, leave-taking, and nostalgia don't quite capture my mood today. Don't get me wrong, we've had great years and done much together. The economy is booming. Long-festering social problems like drugs, crime, and a decline in our educational standards are being dealt with. And for the first time in the postwar era, the Soviet menace shows some signs of relenting. This last development is, of course, so heartening to those of us who have lived through all the brooding terrors of the postwar era. We're prayerful and hopeful—hopeful that the next generation of Americans will not have to contend as we did with the nightmares of nuclear terror and totalitarian expansionism.

You know, shortly after World War II and the struggle against Nazi Germany, Winston Churchill looked with grave concern and sadness at a world that evolved so quickly, as he put it, from "triumph and tragedy." But then as he began to detect the vigor and resolve of America against the Soviet menace and for freedom in Europe and everywhere in the world—a vigor and resolve shared equally by an American President and an American Congress of different political parties—he grew hopeful and grateful for this unselfish, bipartisan unity.

There's a story I want to tell you today about a meeting Churchill had with a group of American journalists in 1952 at a time when all the troubles of the cold war, including the hardship of morally and militarily rearming the West, were keenly felt. His friend and physician, Lord Moran, recorded Churchill's appraisal of American leadership. "What other nation in history," Churchill asked, "when it became supremely powerful, has had no thought of territorial aggrandizement, no ambition but to use its resources for the good of the world? I marvel at America's altruism, her sublime disinterestedness." "All at once I realized," Lord Moran wrote, "Winston was in tears, his eyes were red, his voice faltered. He was deeply moved."

Well, generous words, honest emotion from a great world leader; and now, more than a quarter century later, as the decade of the eighties comes to a close, there is hope that the generosity and resolve that Churchill saw in the American people is at last paying an historic dividend: the possibility of a new time in human history when all the problems that so haunted the postwar world give way to peace and expansion of freedom.

So, you can see why to me, the story of these last 8 years and this Presidency goes far beyond any personal concerns. It is a continuation really of a far larger story, a story of a people and a cause—a cause that from our earliest beginnings has defined us as a nation and given purpose to our national existence.

The hope of human freedom—the quest for it, the achievement of it—is the American saga. And I've often recalled one group of early settlers making a treacherous crossing of the Atlantic on a small ship when their leader, a minister, noted that perhaps their venture would fail and they would become a byword, a footnote to history. But perhaps, too, with God's help, they might also found a new world, a city upon a hill, a light unto the nations.

Those words and that destiny beckon to us still. Whether we seek it or not, whether we like it or not, we Americans are keepers of the miracles. We are asked to be guardians of a place to come to, a place to start again, a place to live in the dignity God meant for his children. . . .

41

George H. W. Bush

1. REMARKS AT BICENTENNIAL CELEBRATION OF GEORGE   **APRIL 30, 1989**
WASHINGTON'S INAUGURATION IN NEW YORK CITY

. . . Everyone here today can still feel the pulse of history, the charge and power of that great moment in the genesis of this nation. Here the first Congress was in session, beginning a tradition of representative government that has endured for 200 years. . . . And here our first President issued a solemn address.

. . . George Washington defined and shaped this office. It was Washington's vision, his balance of power and restraint as he watched over the Constitutional Convention in 1787, that gave the delegates enough confidence to vest powers in a Chief Executive unparalleled in any freely elected government, before or since. It was Washington's vision, his balance, his integrity that made the Presidency possible. The Constitution was, and remains, a majestic document. But it was a blueprint, an outline for democratic government, in need of a master builder to ensure its foundations were strong. Based on that document, Washington created a living, functioning government. He brought together men of genius, a team of giants, with strong and competing views. He harnessed and directed their energies. And he established a precedent for 40 Presidents to follow.

. . . For all of the turmoil and transformation of the last 200 years, there is a great constancy to this office and this Republic. So much of the vision of that first great President is reflected in the paths pursued by modern Presidents.

Today we reaffirm ethics, honor, and strength in government. Two centuries ago, in his first Inaugural Address, Washington spoke of a government "exemplified by all the attributes which can win the affections of its citizens and command the respect of the world." Today, we say that leaders are not elected to quarrel but to govern. On that spring day in 1789, Washington pledged that "no party animosities will misdirect the comprehensive and equal eye which ought to watch over this great assemblance of communities and interests."

Today, we seek a new engagement in the lives of others, believing that success is not measured by the sum of our possessions, our positions, or our professions, but by the good we do for others. Two hundred years ago today, Washington said there exists "in the economy and course of nature, an indissoluble union between virtue and happiness, between duty and advantage." And so, today we speak of values. At his inauguration, Washington said that "the foundations of our national policy will be laid in the pure and immutable principles of private morality." And over the last 200 years, we've moved from the revolution of democracy to the evolution of peace and prosperity.

But so much remains constant; so much endures: our faith in freedom—for individuals, freedom to choose, for nations, self-determination and democracy; our belief in fairness—equal standards,

Figure 41.1 George Herbert Walker Bush takes the oath of office as the 41st President of the United States, administered by Supreme Court Chief Justice Rehnquist at the US Capitol, Washington, DC, January 20, 1989, courtesy of the George H.W. Bush Presidential Library and Museum.

equal opportunity, the chance for each of us to achieve, on our own merits, to the very limit of our ambitions and potential; our enduring strength—abroad, a strength our allies can count on and our adversaries must respect, and at home, a sense of confidence, of purpose, in carrying forward our nation's work.

. . . The Presidency, then as now, in oath and in office, derives from the strength and the will of the people.

George Washington, residing at Mount Vernon, felt himself summoned by his country to serve his country—not to reign, not to rule, but to serve. It was the noblest of impulses because democracy brought a new definition of nobility. And it means that a complete life, whether in the 18th or 20th century, must involve service to others. Today, just as Washington heard the voice of his country calling him to public service, a new generation must heed that summons; more must hear that call.

And today we stand—free Americans, citizens in an experiment of freedom that has brought sustained and unprecedented progress and blessings in abundance. As we dedicate a museum of American constitutional government, let us together rededicate ourselves to the principles to which Washington gave voice 200 years ago. Let our motivation derive from the strength and character of our forefathers, from the blood of those who have died for freedom, and from the promise of the future that posterity deserves. Let us commit ourselves to the renewal of strong, united, representative government in these United States of America. God bless you, and may God forever bless this great nation of ours. . . .

2. THE LEADER OF THE FREE WORLD AT KARL MARX UNIVERSITY IN BUDAPEST   JULY 12, 1989

. . . While Hungary rediscovers its natural role in the affairs of Europe, the world again looks to you for inspiration. A popular nonfiction book in my country today is entitled *Budapest 1900*. Dr. John Lukacs lovingly describes the Budapest of memory, with its proud stock exchange and great opera, a time when Europe's first electric subway ran underneath the handsome shops of Andrassy Avenue. A city that rivaled Paris in its splendor, Vienna in its music, London in its literature—a center of learning that enlightened the world and gave America one kind of genius in Joseph Pulitzer, another in Bela Bartok. But for four decades, this great city, this great nation—so central to the continent in every respect—has been separated from Europe and the West.

And today Hungary is opening again to the West, becoming a beacon of light in European culture. And I see people in motion . . . I see a new beginning for Hungary. The very atmosphere of this city, the very atmosphere of Budapest, is electric and alive with optimism. Your people and your leaders . . . are not afraid to break with the past, to act in the spirit of truth.

And what better example of this could there be than one simple fact: Karl Marx University has dropped *Das Kapital* from its required reading list. Some historians argue that Marxism arose out of a humane impulse. But Karl Marx traced only one thread of human existence and missed the rest of the tapestry—the colorful and varied tapestry of humanity. He regarded man as hapless, unable to shape his environment or destiny. But man is not driven by impersonal economic forces; he's not simply an object acted upon by mechanical laws of history. Rather, man is imaginative and inventive. He is artistic, with an innate need to create and enjoy beauty. He is a loving member of a family and a loyal patriot to his people. Man is dynamic, determined to shape his own future.

The creative genius of the Hungarian people, long suppressed, is again flourishing in your schools, your businesses, your churches. And this is more than a fleeting season of freedom; it is Hungary returning to its normal, traditional values. It is Hungary returning home. . . .

Along your border with Austria, the ugly symbol of Europe's division and Hungary's isolation is coming down, as the barbed wire fences are rolled and stacked into bales. For the first time, the Iron Curtain has begun to part. And Hungary, your great country, is leading the way.

The Soviet Union has withdrawn troops, which I also take as a step in overcoming Europe's division. And as those forces leave, let the Soviet leaders know they have everything to gain and nothing to lose or fear from peaceful change. We can . . . work together to move beyond containment, beyond the Cold War.

. . . No, there is no mistaking the fact that we are on the threshold of a new era. And there's also no mistaking the fact that Hungary is at the threshold of great and historic change. You're writing a real constitution, and you're moving toward democratic, multiparty elections. And this is partly possible because brave men and women have formed opposition parties. . . . Hungarian leaders are going to show the ultimate political courage: the courage to submit to the choice of the people in free elections.

. . . I am here today to offer Hungary the partnership of the United States of America. Three vital spheres stand out in our partnerships: economics, the environment, and democratic and cultural exchange. The United States believes in the acceleration of productive change, not in its delay. So, this is our guiding principle: The United States will offer assistance, not to prop up the status quo but to propel reform.

. . . To make the transition to a productive economy will test your mettle as a people. The prices of some commodities may rise. Some inefficient businesses and factories will close. But the Hungarian Government is increasingly leaving the business of running the shops to the shopkeepers, the farms to the farmers. And the creative drive of the people, once unleashed, will create momentum of its own. . . .

Last Thursday at the White House, I invited leaders from business, education, labor, and other fields to come to the White House and discuss the new private sector opportunities opening up in Hungary; and their response was enthusiastic. This was especially true of Hungarian-Americans, so proud to be building a bridge. . . .

. . . I am also pleased to announce that the United States has proposed an agreement between our two countries to establish scientific and technical cooperation in the basic sciences and in specific areas, including the environment, medicine, and nuclear safety.

It is my hope that this visit will also lead to a wider exchange between East and West so our scientists, our artists, and our environmentalists can learn from one another; so that our soldiers and statesmen can discuss peace; and our students—God bless them—can discuss the future.

But to discuss anything requires a common language. The teaching of the English language is one of the most popular American exports. And as students, you know that English is the lingua franca of world business, the key to clinching deals from Hong Kong to Toronto. So, to open the global market to more Hungarians, I am pleased to announce that the Peace Corps will, for the first time, operate in a European country. And our Peace Corps instructors will come to Budapest and all 19 counties to teach English.

And in such exchanges, we want to help you in your quest for a new beginning as a democratic Hungary. So, the United States is also committing more than $6 million to cultural and educational opportunities in Eastern Europe. We will make available funds for a series of major new U.S.–Hungarian exchange programs—among Congressmen and legislative experts; among labor-business leaders; among legal experts; among community leaders, educators, and young people.

We are creating dozens of fellowships to enable Hungarians to study at American universities. And we will fund endowed chairs in American studies at your universities, and books—many thousands of them—to fill the shelves of your new international management center and the libraries of schools and universities across Hungary. And the United States will also open, within the next several years, an American House in the center of Budapest. Today the celebrated American architect Robert Stern is releasing his design for this center, which will be an open house of books, magazines, and video cassettes—an open house of ideas.

And so, in conclusion—in economic reform and democratic change, in cultural and environmental cooperation—there are great opportunities and great challenges. Hungary has a lot of work ahead, and so do the United States and Hungary, working together to build this better future—dynamic future. . . .

3. BATTEN DOWN THE HATCHES   DECEMBER 31, 1990

Dear George, Jeb, Neil, Marvin, Doro

I am writing this letter on the last day of 1990.

First, I can't begin to tell you how great it was to have you here at Camp David. I loved the games (the Marines are still smarting over their 1 and 2 record), I loved Christmas Day, marred only by the absence of Sam and Ellie. I loved the movies—some of 'em—I loved the laughs. Most of all, l loved seeing you together. We are a family blessed; and Christmas simply reinforced all that.

I hope I didn't seem moody. I tried not to.

When I came into this job I vowed that I would never wring my hands and talk about "the loneliest job in the world" or wring my hands about the pressures or the trials.

Having said that I have been concerned about what lies ahead. There is no "loneliness" though because I am backed by a first rate team of knowledgeable and committed people. No President has been more blessed in this regard. . . .

I have thought long and hard about what might have to be done.

As I write this letter at year's end, there is still some hope that Iraq's dictator will pull out of Kuwait. I vary on this. Sometimes I think he might, at others I think he simply is too unrealistic—too ignorant of what he might face. I have the peace of mind that comes from knowing that we have tried hard for peace. We have gone to the U.N.; we have formed an historic coalition; there have been diplomatic initiatives from country after country. . . . And so here we are a scant 16 days from a very important date—the date set by the U.N. for his total compliance with all UN resolutions including getting out of Kuwait—totally.

I guess what I want you to know as a father is this:

Every Human life is precious. When the question is asked "How many lives are you willing to sacrifice"—it tears at my heart. The answer, of course, is none—none whatsoever. We have waited to give sanctions a chance, we have moved a tremendous force so as to reduce the risk to every American soldier if force has to be used; but the question of loss of life still lingers and plagues the heart.

My mind goes back to history:

How many lives might have been saved if appeasement had given way to force earlier on in the late '30s or earliest '40s? How many Jews might have been spared the gas chambers, or how many Polish patriots might be alive today?

I look at today's crises as good vs. evil . . . yes, it is that clear.

I know my stance must cause you a little grief from time to time; and this hurts me; but here at year's end I just wanted you to know that I feel . . . every human life is precious . . . the little Iraqi kids' too. . . .

Principle must be adhered to—Saddam cannot profit in any way at all from his aggression and from his brutalizing the people of Kuwait.

Sometimes in life you have to act as you think best. You can't compromise, you can't give in . . . even if your critics are loud and numerous.

So, dear kids—batten down the hatches.

Senator Inouye of Hawaii told me: "Mr. President, do what you have to do. If it is quick and successful everyone can take the credit. If it is drawn out, then be prepared for some in Congress to file impeachment papers against you." . . . that's what he said, and he's 100% correct. And so I shall say a few more prayers, mainly for our kids in the Gulf, and I shall do what must be done and I shall be strengthened every day by our family love which lifts me up every single day of my life.

I am the luckiest Dad in the whole wide world. I love you. . . .

4. WAR IN THE PERSIAN GULF   JANUARY 16, 1991

Just two hours ago, allied air forces began an attack on military targets in Iraq and Kuwait. These attacks continue as I speak. Ground forces are not engaged.

This conflict started 2nd August, when the dictator of Iraq invaded a small and helpless neighbor. Kuwait—a member of the Arab League and a member of the United Nations—was crushed; its people, brutalized. Five months ago, Saddam Hussein started this cruel war against Kuwait. Tonight, the battle has been joined.

This military action, taken in accord with United Nations resolutions and with the consent of the United States Congress, follows months of constant and virtually endless diplomatic activity on the part of the United Nations, the United States, and many, many other countries. Arab leaders sought what became known as an Arab solution, only to conclude that Saddam Hussein was unwilling to leave Kuwait. Others traveled to Baghdad in a variety of efforts to restore peace and justice. Our Secretary of State, James Baker, held an historic meeting in Geneva, only to be totally rebuffed. This past weekend, in a last-ditch effort, the Secretary-General of the United Nations went to the Middle East with peace in his heart—his second such mission. And he came back from Baghdad with no progress at all in getting Saddam Hussein to withdraw from Kuwait.

Now the 28 countries with forces in the Gulf area have exhausted all reasonable efforts to reach a peaceful resolution—and have no choice but to drive Saddam from Kuwait by force. We will not fail.

As I report to you, air attacks are underway against military targets in Iraq. We are determined to knock out Saddam Hussein's nuclear bomb potential. We will also destroy his chemical weapons facilities. Much of Saddam's artillery and tanks will be destroyed. Our operations are designed to best protect the lives of all the coalition forces by targeting Saddam's vast military arsenal. Initial reports from General Schwarzkopf are that our operations are proceeding according to plan.

Our objectives are clear: Saddam Hussein's forces will leave Kuwait. The legitimate government of Kuwait will be restored to its rightful place, and Kuwait will once again be free. Iraq will eventually comply with all relevant United Nations resolutions, and then, when peace is restored, it is our hope that Iraq will live as a peaceful and co-operative member of the family of nations, thus enhancing the security and stability of the Gulf.

Some may ask: Why act now? Why not wait? The answer is clear: The world could wait no longer. Sanctions, though having some effect, showed no signs of accomplishing their objective. Sanctions were tried for well over 5 months, and we and our allies concluded that sanctions alone would not force Saddam from Kuwait.

While the world waited, Saddam Hussein systematically raped, pillaged, and plundered a tiny nation, no threat to his own. He subjected the people of Kuwait to unspeakable atrocities—and among those maimed and murdered, innocent children.

While the world waited, Saddam sought to add to the chemical weapons arsenal he now possesses, an infinitely more dangerous weapon of mass destruction—a nuclear weapon. And while the world waited, while the world talked peace and withdrawal, Saddam Hussein dug in and moved massive forces into Kuwait.

While the world waited, while Saddam stalled, more damage was being done to the fragile economics of the Third World, emerging democracies of Eastern Europe, to the entire world, including to our own economy.

The United States, together with the United Nations, exhausted every means at our disposal to bring this crisis to a peaceful end. However, Saddam clearly felt that by stalling and threatening and defying the United Nations, he could weaken the forces arrayed against him.

While the world waited, Saddam Hussein met every overture of peace with open contempt. While the world prayed for peace, Saddam prepared for war.

I had hoped that when the United States Congress, in historic debate, took its resolute action, Saddam would realize he could not prevail and would move out of Kuwait in accord with the United Nation resolutions. He did not do that. Instead, he remained intransigent, certain that time was on his side.

Saddam was warned over and over again to comply with the will of the United Nations: Leave Kuwait, or be driven out. Saddam has arrogantly rejected all warnings. Instead, he tried to make this a dispute between Iraq and the United States of America.

Well, he failed. Tonight, 28 nations—countries from 5 continents, Europe and Asia, Africa, and the Arab League—have forces in the Gulf area, standing shoulder to shoulder against Saddam Hussein. These countries had hoped the use of force could be avoided. Regrettably, we now believe that only force will make him leave.

Prior to ordering our forces into battle, I instructed our military commanders to take every necessary step to prevail as quickly as possible, and with the greatest degree of protection possible for American and allied service men and women. I've told the American people before that this will not be another Vietnam, and I repeat this here tonight. Our troops will have the best possible support in the entire world, and they will not be asked to fight with one hand tied behind their back. I'm hopeful that this fighting will not go on for long and that casualties will be held to an absolute minimum.

This is an historic moment. We have in this past year made great progress in ending the long era of conflict and cold war. We have before us the opportunity to forge for ourselves and for future generations a new world order—a world where the rule of law, not the law of the jungle, governs the conduct of nations. When we are successful—and we will be—we have a real chance at this new world order, an order in which a credible United Nations can use its peacekeeping role to fulfill the promise and vision of the U.N.'s founders.

We have no argument with the people of Iraq. Indeed, for the innocents caught in this conflict, I pray for their safety. Our goal is not the conquest of Iraq. It is the liberation of Kuwait. It is my hope that somehow the Iraqi people can, even now, convince their dictator that he must lay down his arms, leave Kuwait, and let Iraq itself rejoin the family of peace-loving nations.

Thomas Paine wrote many years ago: "These are the times that try men's souls." Those well-known words are so very true today. But even as planes of the multinational forces attack Iraq, I prefer to think of peace, not war. I am convinced not only that we will prevail but that out of the horror of combat will come the recognition that no nation can stand against a world united, no nation will be permitted to brutally assault its neighbor.

No President can easily commit our sons and daughters to war. They are the Nation's finest. Ours is an all-volunteer force, magnificently trained, highly motivated. The troops know why they're there. And listen to what they say, for they've said it better than any President or Prime Minister ever could.

Listen to Hollywood Huddleston, Marine lance corporal. He says, "Let's free these people, so we can go home and be free again." And he's right. The terrible crimes and tortures committed by Saddam's henchmen against the innocent people of Kuwait are an affront to mankind and a challenge to the freedom of all.

Listen to one of our great officers out there, Marine Lieutenant General Walter Boomer. He said: "There are things worth fighting for. A world in which brutality and lawlessness are allowed to go unchecked isn't the kind of world we're going to want to live in."

Listen to Master Sergeant J.P. Kendall of the 82nd Airborne: "We're here for more than just the price of a gallon of gas. What we're doing is going to chart the future of the world for the next 100 years. It's better to deal with this guy now than 5 years from now."

And finally, we should all sit up and listen to Jackie Jones, an Army lieutenant, when she says, "If we let him get away with this, who knows what's going to be next?"

I have called upon Hollywood and Walter and J.P. and Jackie and all their courageous comrades-in-arms to do what must be done. Tonight, America and the world are deeply grateful to them and to their families. And let me say to everyone listening or watching tonight: When the troops we've sent in finish their work, I am determined to bring them home as soon as possible.

Tonight, as our forces fight, they and their families are in our prayers. May God bless each and every one of them, and the coalition forces at our side in the Gulf, and may He continue to bless our nation, the United States of America.

42

William Jefferson Clinton

1. NORTH ATLANTIC FREE TRADE AGREEMENT   **DECEMBER 8, 1993**

. . . I believe we have made a decision now that will permit us to create an economic order in the world that will promote more growth, more equality, better preservation of the environment, and a greater possibility of world peace. We are on the verge of a global economic expansion that is sparked by the fact that the United States at this critical moment decided that we would compete, not retreat.

In a few moments, I will sign the North American free trade act into law. NAFTA will tear down trade barriers between our three nations. It will create the world's largest trade zone and create 200,000 jobs in this country by 1995 alone. The environmental and labor side agreements negotiated by our administration will make this agreement a force for social progress as well as economic growth. Already the confidence we've displayed by ratifying NAFTA has begun to bear fruit. We are now making real progress toward a worldwide trade agreement so significant that it could make the material gains of NAFTA for our country look small by comparison.

Today we have the chance to do what our parents did before us. We have the opportunity to remake the world. For this new era, our national security we now know will be determined as much by our ability to pull down foreign trade barriers as by our ability to breach distant ramparts. Once again, we are leading. And in so doing, we are rediscovering a fundamental truth about ourselves: When we lead, we build security, we build prosperity for our own people.

We've learned this lesson the hard way. Twice before in this century, we have been forced to define our role in the world. After World War I we turned inward, building walls of protectionism around our Nation. The result was a Great Depression and ultimately another horrible World War. After the Second World War, we took a different course: We reached outward. Gifted leaders of both political parties built a new order based on collective security and expanded trade. They created a foundation of stability and created in the process the conditions which led to the explosion of the great American middle class, one of the true economic miracles in the whole history of civilization. Their statecraft stands to this day: the IMF and the World Bank, GATT, and NATO.

In this very auditorium in 1949, President Harry Truman signed one of the charter documents of this golden era of American leadership, the North Atlantic Treaty that created NATO. "In this pact we hope to create a shield against aggression and the fear of aggression," Truman told his audience, "a bulwark which will permit us to get on with the real business of Government and society, the business of achieving a fuller and happier life for our citizens."

Now, the institutions built by Truman and Acheson, by Marshall and Vandenberg, have accomplished their task. The Cold War is over. The grim certitude of the contest with communism has been replaced by the exuberant uncertainty of international economic competition. And the great question of this day is how to ensure security for our people at a time when change is the only constant.

Make no mistake, the global economy with all of its promise and perils is now the central fact of life for hardworking Americans. It has enriched the lives of millions of Americans. But for too many those same winds of change have worn away at the basis of their security. For two decades, most people have worked harder for less. Seemingly secure jobs have been lost. And while America once again is the most productive nation on Earth, this productivity itself holds the seeds of further insecurity. After all, productivity means the same people can produce more or, very often, that fewer people can produce more. This is the world we face.

We cannot stop global change. We cannot repeal the international economic competition that is everywhere. We can only harness the energy to our benefit. Now we must recognize that the only way for a wealthy nation to grow richer is to export, to simply find new customers for the products and services it makes. That, my fellow Americans, is the decision the Congress made when they voted to ratify NAFTA.

I am gratified with the work that Congress has done this year, bringing the deficit down and keeping interest rates down, getting housing starts and new jobs going upward. But we know that over the long run, our ability to have our internal economic policies work for the benefit of our people requires us to have external economic policies that permit productivity to find expression not simply in higher incomes for our businesses but in more jobs and higher incomes for our people. That means more customers. There is no other way, not for the United States or for Europe or for Japan or for any other wealthy nation in the world.

That is why I am gratified that we had such a good meeting after the NAFTA vote in the House with the Asian-Pacific leaders in Washington. I am gratified that, as Vice President Gore and Chief of Staff Mack McLarty announced 2 weeks ago when they met with President Salinas, next year the nations of this hemisphere will gather in an economic summit that will plan how to extend the benefits of trade to the emerging market democracies of all the Americas.

And now I am pleased that we have the opportunity to secure the biggest breakthrough of all. Negotiators from 112 nations are seeking to conclude negotiations on a new round of the General Agreement on Tariffs and Trade; a historic worldwide trade pact, one that would spur a global economic boom, is now within our grasp. Let me be clear. We cannot, nor should we, settle for a bad GATT agreement. But we will not flag in our efforts to secure a good one in these closing days. We are prepared to make our contributions to the success of this negotiation, but we insist that other nations do their part as well. We must not squander this opportunity. I call on all the nations of the world to seize this moment and close the deal on a strong GATT agreement within the next week.

I say to everyone, even to our negotiators: Don't rest. Don't sleep. Close the deal. I told Mickey Kantor the other day that we rewarded his laborious effort on NAFTA with a vacation at the GATT talks. [*laughter*]

My fellow Americans, bit by bit all these things are creating the conditions of a sustained global expansion. As significant as they are, our goals must be more ambitious. The United States must seek nothing less than a new trading system that benefits all nations through robust commerce but that protects our middle class and gives other nations a chance to grow one, that lifts workers and the environment up without dragging people down, that seeks to ensure that our policies reflect our values.

Our agenda must, therefore, be far reaching. We are determining that dynamic trade cannot lead to environmental despoliation. We will seek new institutional arrangements to ensure that trade leaves the world cleaner than before. We will press for workers in all countries to secure rights that we now take for granted, to organize and earn a decent living. We will insist that expanded trade be fair to our businesses and to our regions. No country should use cartels, subsidies, or rules of entry to keep our products off its shelves. And we must see to it that our citizens have the personal security to confidently participate in this new era. Every worker must receive the education and training he or she needs to reap the rewards of international competition rather than to bear its burdens.

Next year, our administration will propose comprehensive legislation to transform our unemployment system into a reemployment and job retraining system for the 21st century. And above all, I say to you we must seek to reconstruct the broad-based political coalition for expanded trade. For decades, working men and women and their representatives supported policies that brought us prosperity and security. That was because we recognized that expanded trade benefited all of us but that we have an obligation to protect those workers who do bear the brunt of competition by giving them a chance to be retrained and to go on to a new and different and, ultimately, more secure and more rewarding way of work. In recent years, this social contract has been sundered. It cannot continue.

When I affix my signature to the NAFTA legislation a few moments from now, I do so with this pledge: To the men and women of our country who were afraid of these changes and found in their opposition to NAFTA an expression of that fear—what I thought was a wrong expression and what I know was a wrong expression but nonetheless represented legitimate fears—the gains from this agreement will be your gains, too.

I ask those who opposed NAFTA to work with us to guarantee that the labor and side agreements are enforced, and I call on all of us who believe in NAFTA to join with me to urge the Congress to

Figure 42.1 William Jefferson Clinton, courtesy of the Library of Congress Prints and Photographs Division Washington, DC.

create the world's best worker training and retraining system. We owe it to the business community as well as to the working men and women of this country. It means greater productivity, lower unemployment, greater worker efficiency, and higher wages and greater security for our people. We have to do that.

We seek a new and more open global trading system not for its own sake but for our own sake. Good jobs, rewarding careers, broadened horizons for the middle-class Americans can only be secured by expanding exports and global growth. For too long our step has been unsteady as the ground has shifted beneath our feet. Today, as I sign the North American Free Trade Agreement into law and call for further progress on GATT, I believe we have found our footing. And I ask all of you to be steady, to recognize that there is no turning back from the world of today and tomorrow. We must face the challenges, embrace them with confidence, deal with the problems honestly and openly, and make this world work for all of us. America is where it should be, in the lead, setting the pace, showing the confidence that all of us need to face tomorrow. We are ready to compete, and we can win.

2. THE ERA OF BIG GOVERNMENT IS OVER   JANUARY 27, 1996

. . . Earlier this week, I had the privilege of delivering the State of the Union address and discussing the challenges we face today, only five years from a new century. As I said, the state of our union is strong.

We are entering an age of possibility in which more Americans from all walks of life will have more chances to build the future of their dreams than ever before.

But we also face stiff challenges . . . we must meet and meet together if we are to preserve the American Dream for all Americans, maintain America's leadership for peace and freedom, and continue to come together around our basic values.

These are the seven challenges I set forth Tuesday night—to strengthen our families, to renew our schools and expand educational opportunity, to help every American who's willing to work for it achieve economic security, to take our streets back from crime, to protect our environment, to reinvent our government so that it serves better and costs less, and to keep America the leading force for peace and freedom throughout the world.

We will meet these challenges, not through big government. The era of big government is over. But we can't go back to a time when our citizens were just left to fend for themselves. We will meet them by going forward as one America, by working together in our communities, our schools, our churches and synagogues, our workplaces across the entire spectrum of our civic life.

As we move forward with tomorrow's challenges, we also must take care of yesterday's unfinished business. First, we must balance the budget. In the 12 years before I took office, the deficit skyrocketed and our national debt quadrupled. I came to Washington determined to act—and we did.
. . .

I've been working with Republicans and Democrats in Congress to forge a balanced budget. . . . Though significant differences remain between our two plans, Republicans and I have enough cuts in common to balance the budget in seven years and to provide a modest tax cut without devastating Medicare, Medicaid, education or the environment, and without raising taxes on working families.

So, again, last Tuesday I asked Congress to join with me to make the cuts we agree on. Let's give the American people the balanced budget they deserve, with a modest tax cut and the lower interest rates and brighter hope for the future it will bring. My door is open. Let's get back to work. . . .

And while we are balancing the budget, there is another piece of business Congress must take care of right now. Like each of us, our nation is only as good as its word. For 220 years, the government of the United States has honored its obligation and kept its word. Through the Civil War, two world wars and the depression, America has paid its bills and kept its word. When we borrow money, we promise to pay it back and we pay it back, no matter what.

Our strong economy is built on the bedrock of this commitment. The world's economy relies on the full faith and credit of the United States and . . . that enables us to keep all of our interest rates down so that we can afford to borrow and grow and live.

From time to time, to keep its word, Congress has had to pass debt ceiling legislation so the government can meet its obligations. Congress has always done this when necessary. . . .

Since November, Congress has failed to act on the debt ceiling. To prevent our nation from going into default, the Treasury Secretary, Robert Rubin, has been forced to take extraordinary actions. . . .

But our options are running out.

What could happen if the United States government failed to meet its obligations? Our unbroken record of keeping our word could end, with taxpayers bearing the costs for years to come because interest rates would go up on United States obligations. And interest rates could also go up for businesses, consumers and homeowners, many of whom have interest rates that vary according to the government's interest rates. And for tens of millions of Americans the unthinkable could happen. The social security checks they count on would not be able to be mailed out.

My fellow Americans, we are a great country. We have never, never broken our word or defaulted on our obligations in our entire 220 year history. We've never failed to pay social security for senior citizens who've earned it. . . .

We have worked hard . . . to restore confidence in the way our government does America's business. Americans are just beginning to believe again. This is no time to turn back. . . .

3. WHITE HOUSE AFFAIR DENIAL   JANUARY 26, 1998

I want to say one thing to the American people: I did not have sexual relations with that woman, Miss Lewinsky. I never told anybody to lie, not a single time. Never. These allegations are false. Now I have to get back to work for the American people.

4. POST-IMPEACHMENT PRESIDENTIAL COMMENTS ON   FEBRUARY 12, 1999
ACQUITTAL

Now that the Senate has fulfilled its constitutional responsibility, bringing this process to a conclusion, I want to say again to the American people how profoundly sorry I am for what I said and did to trigger these events and the great burden they have imposed on the Congress and the American people.

I also am humbled and very grateful for the support and the prayers I have received from millions of Americans over this past year.

Now I ask all Americans—and I hope all Americans here in Washington and throughout our land—will rededicate ourselves to the work of serving our nation and building our future together.

This can be and this must be a time of reconciliation and renewal for America. . . .

PART THREE

THE AMERICAN PRESIDENCY AND THE NEW MILLENNIUM

XII

THE NEW MILLENNIUM: GROUND ZERO

THE YEAR 2000 ARRIVED without the feared catastrophe of a worldwide computer crash (Y2K). It was an election year and the result of that election would herald a new president for the early years of the next millennium. The election was to be decided on November 7. The day came and went. It was all over except for the counting. The election of 2000 was uncomfortably close and fiercely contested but a wise nation held together as it embarked upon the new millennium. President George W. Bush reached out to embrace all Americans in his Inaugural Address: "What you do is as important as anything the government does. I ask you . . . to be citizens not spectators; citizens, not subjects."

The election had been contested primarily on domestic grounds. The fundamental issue had been the economy. Within two weeks of his Inauguration, President Bush in a radio address to the nation announced that he would send a tax relief plan to the Congress. The plan promised to provide needed relief for taxpayers and serve to stimulate the national economy. It would, he said, create jobs. The Republicans controlled both houses of Congress and enabled President Bush to win passage of the largest tax cut in American history. That was how the new president greeted the new age.

A century earlier, McKinley would meet his maker in September 1901. The murder of McKinley stunned the nation. A century later Bush would be severely tested as a consequence of the national tragedy which took place on September 11, 2001. The ground shifted. It was the Pearl Harbor of the New Millennium. An infamous sneak terror attack on centers of American civilization unfolded that late-summer morning and surprised a nation and the world. The attack targeted New York and Washington, DC but truly constituted a crime against humanity. Terrorists commandeered airline passenger jets in Boston, Washington, and Newark, converting them into deadly missiles of mass destruction. Two of these missiles were directed at the Twin Towers of the World Trade Center in lower Manhattan. The towers exploded from the impact and soon after fell to earth. Just short of three thousand lives were lost in the terrorist massacre.

President Bush was talking with children when the news was whispered in his ear. Critics cruelly lashed out at him. Some insinuated that he should immediately rush to the scene of the crime. Impulsive action of this sort would have been folly. He would go to ground zero on September 14th. Standing in the rubble with one arm draped around a firefighter and with a bullhorn in his other hand, he addressed the workers, and the people of the New York metropolis, the nation and the world. When someone in the crowd yelled that he couldn't hear, the President replied "I can hear you." Soon the whole world would hear the response of the United States. The moment was captured in an iconic photo.

The massive death and destruction of September 11, 2001 changed everything. The temper of the times suddenly shifted. America went on alert. Throughout American history Americans have responded to challenges and crises by rallying to support their president. The savage assaults on American civilization had shocked and angered the public. They were ready to endorse a wide range of actions to protect the Republic. It was an historic change in how Americans travelled, conducted banking transactions, dealt with immigration issues, and practically everything else. American flags were now universally visible. Life would go on. Yet things would never be the same.

Patriotism and Security shook hands in the aftermath of the assault. After the memorable presidential visit to ground zero in lower Manhattan with New York Firefighters and other first responders, George W. Bush addressed the American people the following day on radio. The president informed Americans that extensive meetings with National Security Council members were in process in order to develop a plan for a "comprehensive assault on terrorism."

He cautioned citizens that the contest would not be easy or short. "We are planning a broad and sustained campaign," said the President "to secure our country and eradicate the evil of terrorism."

He talked of the spirit of "patriotism and defiance" he had witnessed amidst the rescue workers at ground zero and paid tribute to the victims and the families of 9/11. He congratulated the Congress and both political parties for their patriotic display of unity. Finally, President Bush concluded with a promise to prevail over America's enemies. The Commander-in-Chief launched a "war on terrorism."

American intelligence centers determined that the strikes against the World Trade Center and the Pentagon had been planned and executed by a Middle Eastern set of terrorists called Al Qaida under the guidance of their infamous leader, Osama Bin Laden. Intelligence sources pointed to the Taliban regime in Afghanistan as having provided aid and shelter to Bin Laden and Al Qaida. Consequently the United States initiated retaliation and conducted an aerial bombing assault and put boots on the ground in support of a resistance movement to overthrow the Afghan government. The Taliban government quickly collapsed but the attempt to capture Bin Laden failed. The fugitive terror leader managed to elude his American pursuers for years to come.

The fanatical followers of Bin Laden were not quite as successful in avoiding capture and imprisonment. The Patriot Act of 2001 enabled American authorities to round up hundreds of Taliban and Al Qaida operatives and incarcerate them at the American base in Guantánamo, Cuba. There followed a serious controversy about the legality of this practice of detaining captured terrorists and holding them indefinitely without recourse to trial. It became for some a cause célèbre to shut down Guantánamo. Prior to his election in 2008 Barack Obama promised to close the prison.

In tones reminiscent of FDR's condemnation of the "bandit nations" before Pearl Harbor, President Bush invoked in his 2002 State of the Union Address the phrase "axis of evil" in speaking of the regimes hostile to American interests. A global fear was that these evil adventurers would acquire and use nuclear weapons. With this in mind President Bush methodically constructed a case for a U.S. invasion of Iraq. The President's indictment rested on three propositions: (1) harboring terrorists, (2) development of weapons of mass destruction and (3) human rights violations.

Allied forces with UN support moved on Iraq in March 2003. A military aerial campaign described as "Shock and Awe" rained explosives on the capital city of Baghdad. The Iraq regime crumbled and Saddam Hussein became a fugitive in his own country. Eventually captured and tried, he was found guilty and executed in 2006. Despite the ease with which Saddam Hussein was dispatched and his Republican Guard annihilated, the Iraq War would not officially end until December 2011. The end would come three years after Barack Obama was elected President in 2008.

Bush not only achieved re-election in 2004 but increased the margins of Republican Party control in Congress, adding three seats in the House and four seats in the Senate. In the presidential election of 2004 the President carried thirty states, picking up Iowa and New Mexico while his Democrat opponent, Senator John Kerry of Massachusetts managed only twenty. Bush won the popular vote by more than three million votes, and the electoral vote 286 to 251 or 53.2% to 46.7%. The election gained even greater validity since it produced a remarkably high voter turnout.

The election said something important about the political disposition of the American mind. There remained little room, however, for President Bush to rest too comfortably upon this electoral re-affirmation by the American people. As is common throughout the history of the American presidency, second terms almost invariably pose impediments to successful administration of the government. The long historical record shows declining approval ratings along with other cracks in terms of presidential performance in the encore term. The second term of George W. Bush proved no exception to the historic rule.

The winds of change were on the horizon in 2005, the first year of his second term. The gathering storm was real. It was named Katrina. The president's popularity dipped seriously as a consequence of this devastating hurricane and the public's perception and evaluation of the government's response to this powerful force of nature. The monster hurricane wreaked havoc all along the American coastline with the Gulf of Mexico. The focus hit home in the City of New Orleans. The damage was extraordinary and the victims were many. One seriously hurt by the storm was the President of the United States, George W. Bush.

The president carried a heavy burden altogether in charting the economy through heavy seas and presiding as Commander-in-Chief over the conduct of two foreign wars. The cumulative effect of the 2006 tide was, said the President, a "thumping" for his administration and his party. In the mid-term election of 2006 the American people returned to historic electoral patterns and the "out" party placed a check on President Bush by achieving Democrat majorities in both the House and the Senate. The result stalemated the Bush agenda. It established gridlock once again in Foggy Bottom. The economy began to slip in 2007 and 2008. The 2006 canvass and the new power base in Congress augured well for Democrat prospects in the presidential election of 2008.

The political penalty of the second term came in two installments—2006 and 2008. Of course, it was not the President who paid the price in 2008 since he was not a candidate on the ballot. The debris fell to the nominee of the Republican Party that year, Senator John McCain of Arizona. McCain, although a military hero and former POW, had thin support from the Republican base as he had few ardent friends among Republican conservatives. Considered a maverick, McCain also brought his own baggage to the 2008 canvass. After a close-fought Democratic Primary season between the former first lady and sitting New York Senator Hilary Clinton and the new upcoming U.S. Senator from Chicago, Barack Obama, the latter gained the upper hand once Ted Kennedy endorsed him. Obama won his party's nomination and easily defeated McCain in the general election. The Democratic Party now exercised full political control in Washington, DC.

The nomination and election of Barack Obama had an electrifying effect throughout the country. Many promises had been made. Hopes had risen to the sky. With the election result the machinery was in place to realize new hopes and old dreams. The new President began his tenure of office in an atmosphere of high expectations. Euphoria prevailed. Shortly into his presidency it was announced that Obama had been awarded the Nobel Prize for Peace "for his extraordinary efforts to strengthen international diplomacy and cooperation between peoples." At home and abroad there were indeed great expectations and high hopes.

Domestically there was much work to be done. Congress had his back. President Obama held the cards to pursue his program of change. The nation looked to the new president to save the situation and restore confidence. The economy was in the ditch. He was called upon to fix it. This presented political and economic opportunities. The mantra at the White House became: "a crisis is a terrible thing to waste." Obama proposed and the Democratic Congress passed a larger stimulus package than ever before in American history to resuscitate the ailing economy. The effect of the stimulus on the economy is a matter of dispute. Clearly it did not solve the problem and some argue that the unnecessary spending added to the problem of expanding deficits and bloated national debt.

The most controversial initiative of the Obama Administration was the passage of his health care bill. The bill was multifaceted and politically convoluted. Committed supporters heaped high praise on the "historic" bill which managed passage in both houses of Congress by wafer-thin margins. In order to accomplish passage the President resorted to heavy persuasion and horse-trading. A "public option" feature died on the vine. The scrapping of this option was a tremendous disappointment to many on the far left. Others considered the health care bill to constitute a takeover of the health industry by the government. Critics challenged the measure as fundamentally unconstitutional. Consequently, a serious contingent began to organize for its repeal, while state attorney generals filed court cases to secure a judicial reversal.

A new battlefield occupied center stage when disaster struck the Gulf of Mexico once again on April 20, 2010. This time it was oil rather than water. The BP *Deepwater Horizon* rig exploded that night in the waters of the Gulf. The explosion killed eleven platform workers and injured several others. The suffering people from Texas to Florida felt the pain. This was the worst environmental disaster in U.S. history. Oil spread far and wide, covering 1000 miles of shoreline. The damage was both short- and long-term.

Damage control became the watchword of the hour. The catastrophe caused political fallout and special problems for the President. Ten days after the explosion the President ordered a halt to new offshore drilling until safeguards had been put in place. BP took several steps, with at best mixed results, to contain the enormous damage caused by the Gulf explosion, while the President travelled in May to the disaster region attempting with moderate success to control the collateral political damage attached to the catastrophe.

If the Obama Administration and the Democratic Congress considered their stimulus and the health care creations political victories, it was crystal clear that the general public thought otherwise. The mid-term election results of 2010 confirmed the political miscalculations of the Democratic Party high command. The GOP had a field day, winning a majority in the House and made serious inroads in the Senate. The political map of U.S. counties blazed bright red in testimony to the depth of the Republican victory at all levels. The Gulf States heavily fortified the Republican tendencies, electing Republican Governors and U.S. Senators and a grand total of 57 Republican against only 18 Democrat House members. The Democrats had squandered in the first two years of Barack Obama's presidency the overwhelming advantages they had harvested in 2006 and 2008. Bush had labeled the 2006 GOP defeat a "thumping." President Obama acknowledged that under his command in 2010 the Democrats experienced a "shellacking."

The Presidential Election of 2012 now presented itself as a test of strength. The mid-term election of 2010 constituted a referendum on Obama's performance in the presidency. The numbers from the shellacking of 2010 demonstrated that the President now stood at the edge of the precipice. His re-election was in jeopardy. If Obama wanted to be re-elected he would have to earn it. That meant making meaningful adjustments to the Democratic strategic game plan.

Work was needed too with respect to American foreign policy in the Middle East. In June 2010 a restless Iranian people took to the streets by the thousands. It was called the "Green" movement and it stood opposed to the re-election of Ahmadinejad. This was an opportunity for American diplomacy to align with popular internal sentiment in Iran. It was a rare teaching moment. A moment missed. The Iranian security forces moved in to crush the populist democratic outburst with a ruthless vengeance.

Spring 2011 presented new possibilities for political rebirth. The President went hunting. He sent a squadron of Navy Seals and CIA operatives on a mission into the heart of Pakistan. The team located their prey, terrorist leader Osama bin Laden, in a compound north of Islamabad. President Obama announced on May 2, 2011 that the mastermind of 9/11 had been killed in a firefight with U.S. Special Forces. "The death of Bin Laden," said Obama "marks the most significant achievement to date in our nation's effort to defeat Al Qaida." It was a special victory for Obama that served him well at home and abroad. President Bush applauded his successor for a major accomplishment in the war against terror. Osama was dead. Obama was politically alive.

The winds of change were moving at full force through the Arab world. A potent political upheaval was underway. The discontent of Arab people with their leaders and oppressive regimes became manifest throughout Arab dominions. Reminiscent of earlier waves of freedom in the face of totalitarian communism in Eastern Europe, this outburst received the label of the "Arab Spring."

In May 2011 President Obama made what he labeled a major diplomatic statement on these developments. The administration missed one opportunity with respect to Iran in 2010. The President had a second opportunity to align himself and the USA with the momentum of democracy in Arab lands. It was fortuitous for Barack Obama. Here was an opportunity to parlay the elimination of bin Laden with popular democratic movements in the Arab world. In a major speech, Obama took pains to link the death of Bin Laden with the popular surge in the Arab Spring: "Bin Laden was no martyr. He was a mass murderer" said Obama, "He rejected democracy and individual rights for Muslims in favor of violent extremism. His agenda focused on what he could destroy, not what he could build." Things had changed in the Middle East: "By the time we found bin Laden, Al Qaida's agenda had come to be seen by the vast majority of the region as a dead end, and the people of the Middle East and North Africa had taken their future into their own hands."

If Obama originally hesitated to move the U.S. behind the first protests in the Middle East which erupted in Tehran he now announced that "it will be the policy of the United States to promote reform across the region and to support transitions to democracy." The Arab Spring would find American support for popular upheavals in Egypt, Tunisia, Syria, Libya, and elsewhere in the Arab world. He credited Iraq for adopting a peaceful democratic path and for placing itself in a position to play a "key role" in the region's future. On the other hand the President indicated that he and the global community were frustrated with the conflict between Arabs and Israelis. The answer, thought Obama, was for Israel to return to 1967 borders. The nation of Israel naturally winced at the new posture of the President with regard to the Middle East.

President Obama developed a strategic plan for re-election from mid-2011 to January 2012. The plan for the most part dismissed the past and the record which led to the shellacking that Democrats experienced in the mid-term election of 2010. He refused to pivot with regard to his administrative program as President Clinton had done after his 1994 mid-term election thrashing. President Clinton read the returns and acknowledged in his State of the Union the "era of big government is over." The well-executed pivot placed Clinton in position to win re-election in 1996. Rather than pivot, Obama shifted the game in his State of the Union Address, on January 24, 2012, to formulate a political blueprint for the future. He would double down on big government even as the blueprint placed the onus on the Congress for the failure to move the country forward.

There is a tradition for historians not to evaluate a sitting president. It is a reasonable and worthy tradition. The historic results are not in and not all presidential documents are available. We do not know whether Barack Obama will be re-elected. Certainly a long list of Republican aspirants signed on for the challenge of 2012, having smelled blood in the water after the mid-term results in 2010. Their intra-party warfare produced a winnowing and cannibalization of men and ideas within the Republican fold. As the 2012 Republican primary season progressed, there remained one man standing. Former Governor of Massachusetts, Mitt Romney emerged as the presumptive nominee of the GOP and the alternative to President Obama in the fall election. Internecine warfare seems to have leveled the playing field at least temporarily. It remains to be seen whether the President can regain the form if not the euphoria of 2008 or whether the 2010 returns are predictive of the near term presidential sweepstakes. The event will mark another milestone in the history of the American presidency.

43

George W. Bush

1. TAX RELIEF PLAN FEBRUARY 8, 2001

. . . This is the land of economic miracles, and we are experiencing one here in our country. Latino businesses are growing faster than the Government can count. Back in 1997 there were 1.4 million Latino-owned businesses. Since then, the number has been growing by an estimated 25 percent. No one is entirely sure of the total. Your success has left all statistics behind, and America is better off for it.

The businesses you have built prove the continuing power of the American ideal, a promise of advancement to men and women of every background. This country appreciates you. We appreciate your vision, your hard work. And I congratulate you for your success.

To succeed, Latino-owned businesses need the same things all businesses need: moderate regulation, a sensible legal system, and a growing economy. For several months, however, our economic growth has been in doubt. And now, it may be in danger.

Americans are hearing, and some feeling, the economic slowdown. Americans hear about the news—many are beginning to actually feel what it means to be in an economic slowdown. Consumer confidence has slumped. Many business leaders are worried. A warning light is flashing on the dashboard of our economy. And we just can't drive on and hope for the best. We must act without delay.

My job is to lead. A President should not wait on events. He must try to shape them. And the warning signs are clear. All of us here in Washington, the President and the Congress, are responsible to confront the danger of an economic slowdown and to blunt its effects.

Today I am sending to Congress my plan to provide relief to all income taxpayers, which I believe will help jump-start the American economy. We must give over-charged taxpayers some of their own money back. We must give low income families fairer treatment. We must give small businesses a better chance to grow and to hire. For all these reasons, I urge Congress to help me strengthen our economy by lightening the tax load, the tax burden on the American people.

Here's how my tax relief plan will work. We will simplify our tax code, reducing today's five brackets to four lower ones: 10 percent, 15 percent, 25 percent, and 33 percent. Families with children will also receive a tax credit of $1,000 per child. We will end the death tax, reduce the marriage penalty, and expand tax incentives for charitable giving.

My plan is directed toward individuals and small businesses. It offers relief for everyone who pays income taxes, and it keeps our national commitments to Social Security and debt reduction. These are the details. But it is the results that will matter most.

If we pass this tax relief plan in a timely manner, three important things will happen: First, we will return $1,600 to the typical American family with two children. Working families earning between $35,000 and $75,000 will keep anywhere from $600 to $3,000 more each year. With this tax relief, families can save or pay off debt or pay for higher energy bills. This $1,600 is good for a family. Multiplied by millions of families, it is good for our Nation's economy. It means greater demand for your goods and your services at a time when demand may be slowing. I'm committed to accelerating economic growth. Lower interest rates will certainly help, but they need to be reinforced with tax relief as well.

There is talk in Congress of bringing this relief even quicker by making it retroactive to the beginning of this year. I strongly support that idea. We need tax relief now. In fact, we need tax relief yesterday. And I will work with Congress to provide it.

Our economy faces this challenge: Investors and consumers have too little money, and the U.S. Treasury is holding too much. The Federal Government is simply pulling too much money out of the private economy, and this is a drag on our growth.

Over the past 6 years, the Federal share of our GDP has risen from 18 percent to 21 percent, about as much as our Government took during World War II. President John Kennedy faced a similar situation in the 1960s. He warned then against storing up dollars in Washington by taking away more than the Government needed to pay its necessary expenses. "High tax rates," he said, and I quote, "are no longer necessary. They are, in fact, harmful. These high tax rates do not leave enough money in private hands to keep this country's economy growing and healthy."

. . . The second effect of my plan is to substantially reduce the taxpayers that bar too many Americans from the middle class. Our new 10-percent rate, along with the child credit, will cut Federal marginal tax rates by 40 percent on many struggling taxpayers.

I've talked about this problem for over a year, and I'll talk about it until we fix it. Under current law, say a waitress is working hard to get ahead, and she . . . faces a higher marginal tax rate than a successful lawyer earning 10 times as much. That is not right, and that is not fair. The Government would take from her nearly one-half of every extra dollar she earns. Her hardest hours are taxed at the highest rates.

Today, tax codes are sending—our tax code sends this message to this woman: Stay where you are; you'll never get ahead. But that is not the message of America, as far as I'm concerned. And it must not be the message of our tax code. Our tax system must reward the dreams of a better life.

My plan dramatically reduces the marginal rate on many low income earners, rewarding overtime or a hard-won raise, encouraging Americans on their path to the middle class. Six million families, one out of every five families with children, will no longer pay Federal income taxes at all under our plan.

This country has prospered mightily over the last 20 years. But a lot of folks feel as if they've been looking at somebody else's party, that they've been looking from the outside. It's time to open the door and welcome everyone in.

. . . Every big business began as a small business. Many of the great companies of our time were founded when the maximum tax rate on small businesses was only 28 percent. Today, many small businesses are paying a tax rate as high as 40 percent. Thousands of sole proprietors, people with dreams, pay high, high rates. That's not how one encourages innovation or job creation or expansion.

My tax relief plan reduces the marginal rates that many small businesses pay. We want you to have a fighting chance in a difficult economy. We also want people to have more funds to reinvest and to grow their businesses. We want to make sure that the next generation of success stories continues far into the future. I hope all of you will help me in this task. We have minds to change, and we've got some laws to pass. Our course is set, and I believe our case is strong.

Figure 43.1 Standing upon the ashes of the worst terrorist attack on American soil, Sept. 14, 2001, President Bush pledges that the voices calling for justice from across the country will be heard. Responding to the President's words, rescue workers cheer and chant, "U.S.A, U.S.A." Photo by Eric Draper, Courtesy of the George W. Bush Presidential Library

. . . I urge the Congress to pass my tax relief plan with the swiftness these uncertain times demand. . . .

2. AT GROUND ZERO IN NEW YORK CITY   **SEPTEMBER 14, 2001**

AUDIENCE: U.S.A.! U.S.A.! U.S.A.!

THE PRESIDENT: Thank you all. I want you all to know—

AUDIENCE MEMBER: Can't hear you.

THE PRESIDENT: I can't go any louder. [*laughter*] I want you all to know that America today— America today is on bended knee in prayer for the people whose lives were lost here, for the workers who work here, for the families who mourn. This Nation stands with the good people of New York City and New Jersey and Connecticut as we mourn the loss of thousands of our citizens.

AUDIENCE MEMBER: I can't hear you.

THE PRESIDENT: I can hear you. I can hear you. The rest of the world hears you. And the people who knocked these buildings down will hear all of us soon.

AUDIENCE: U.S.A.! U.S.A.! U.S.A.!

THE PRESIDENT: The Nation sends its love and compassion to everybody who is here. Thank you for your hard work. Thank you for making the Nation proud. And may God bless America.

AUDIENCE: U.S.A.! U.S.A.! U.S.A.!

3. THE PRESIDENT'S RADIO ADDRESS: WAR ON TERROR   SEPTEMBER 15, 2001

Good morning. This weekend I am engaged in extensive sessions with members of my National Security Council, as we plan a comprehensive assault on terrorism. This will be a different kind of conflict against a different kind of enemy.

This is a conflict without battlefields or beachheads, a conflict with opponents who believe they are invisible. Yet, they are mistaken. They will be exposed, and they will discover what others in the past have learned: Those who make war against the United States have chosen their own destruction. Victory against terrorism will not take place in a single battle but in a series of decisive actions against terrorist organizations and those who harbor and support them.

We are planning a broad and sustained campaign to secure our country and eradicate the evil of terrorism. And we are determined to see this conflict through. Americans of every faith and background are committed to this goal.

Yesterday I visited the site of the destruction in New York City and saw an amazing spirit of sacrifice and patriotism and defiance. I met with rescuers who have worked past exhaustion, who cheered for our country and the great cause we have entered.

In Washington, DC, the political parties and both Houses of Congress have shown a remarkable unity, and I'm deeply grateful. A terrorist attack designed to tear us apart has instead bound us together as a nation. Over the past few days, we have learned much about American courage, the courage of firefighters and police officers who suffered so great a loss, the courage of passengers aboard United 93 who may well have fought with the hijackers and saved many lives on the ground.

Now we honor those who died, and prepare to respond to these attacks on our Nation. I will not settle for a token act. Our response must be sweeping, sustained, and effective. We have much do to and much to ask of the American people.

You will be asked for your patience, for the conflict will not be short. You will be asked for resolve, for the conflict will not be easy. You will be asked for your strength, because the course to victory may be long.

In the past week, we have seen the American people at their very best everywhere in America. Citizens have come together to pray, to give blood, to fly our country's flag. Americans are coming together to share their grief and gain strength from one another.

Great tragedy has come to us, and we are meeting it with the best that is in our country, with courage and concern for others, because this is America. This is who we are. This is what our enemies hate and have attacked. And this is why we will prevail.

4. AMERICA STRIKES BACK   OCTOBER 7, 2001

. . . On my orders, the United States military has begun strikes against Al Qaida terrorist training camps and military installations of the Taliban regime in Afghanistan. These carefully targeted actions are designed to disrupt the use of Afghanistan as a terrorist base of operations and to attack the military capability of the Taliban regime. We are joined in this operation by our staunch friend, Great Britain. Other close friends, including Canada, Australia, Germany, and France, have pledged forces as the operation unfolds. More than 40 countries in the Middle East, Africa, Europe, and across Asia have granted air transit or landing rights. Many more have shared intelligence. We are supported by the collective will of the world.

More than 2 weeks ago, I gave Taliban leaders a series of clear and specific demands: Close terrorist training camps; hand over leaders of the Al Qaida network; and return all foreign nationals, including American citizens, unjustly detained in your country. None of these demands were met. And now the Taliban will pay a price. By destroying camps and disrupting communications, we will make it more difficult for the terror network to train new recruits and coordinate their evil plans.

Initially, the terrorists may burrow deeper into caves and other entrenched hiding places. Our military action is also designed to clear the way for sustained, comprehensive, and relentless operations to drive them out and bring them to justice. At the same time, the oppressed people of Afghanistan will know the generosity of America and our allies. As we strike military targets, we'll also drop food, medicine, and supplies to the starving and suffering men and women and children of Afghanistan.

The United States of America is a friend to the Afghan people, and we are the friends of almost a billion worldwide who practice the Islamic faith. The United States of America is an enemy of those who aid terrorists and of the barbaric criminals who profane a great religion. . . .

Today we focus on Afghanistan, but the battle is broader. Every nation has a choice to make. In this conflict, there is no neutral ground. If any government sponsors the outlaws and killers of innocents, they have become outlaws and murderers, themselves. And they will take that lonely path at their own peril.

. . . A Commander-in-Chief sends America's sons and daughters into a battle in a foreign land only after the greatest care and a lot of prayer. We ask a lot of those who wear our uniform. We ask them to leave their loved ones, to travel great distances, to risk injury, even to be prepared to make the ultimate sacrifice of their lives. They are dedicated; they are honorable; they represent the best of our country. And we are grateful. . . .

Since September 11, an entire generation of young Americans has gained new understanding of the value of freedom and its cost in duty and in sacrifice.

The battle is now joined on many fronts. We will not waver; we will not tire; we will not falter; and we will not fail. Peace and freedom will prevail.

Thank you. May God continue to bless America.

5. SIGNING THE HOMELAND SECURITY ACT OF 2002   NOVEMBER 25, 2002

Today I have signed into law H.R. 5005, the "Homeland Security Act of 2002." The Act restructures and strengthens the executive branch of the Federal Government to better meet the threat to our homeland posed by terrorism. In establishing a new Department of Homeland Security, the Act for the first time creates a Federal department whose primary mission will be to help prevent, protect against, and respond to acts of terrorism on our soil.

Section 103(a) (8) of the Act provides for 12 Assistant Secretary positions without defined titles or duties in the new Department that are to be "appointed by the President, by and with the advice and consent of the Senate." Sections 201(b) (1) and 201(b) (2) of the Act provide for two Assistant Secretary positions with defined titles and duties that are to be "appointed by the President." The text and structure of the Act make clear that these two presidentially appointed Assistant Secretary positions were created in addition to the 12 unspecified Assistant Secretary positions, and the executive branch shall construe the relevant provisions accordingly. With respect to section 201(h), upon the recommendations of the Secretary of Homeland Security, the Director of Central Intelligence, the Secretary of Defense, the Assistant to the President for National Security Affairs, and other appropriate executive branch officials, I will determine which elements of the

Department of Homeland Security are concerned with the analysis of foreign intelligence information.

Section 214(a) (1)(D)(ii) provides that voluntarily shared critical infrastructure information shall not be used or disclosed by any Federal employee without the written consent of the person or entity submitting the information, except when disclosure of the information would be to the Congress or the Comptroller General. The executive branch does not construe this provision to impose any independent or affirmative requirement to share such information with the Congress or the Comptroller General and shall construe it in any event in a manner consistent with the constitutional authorities of the President to supervise the unitary executive branch and to withhold information the disclosure of which could impair foreign relations, the national security, the deliberative processes of the Executive, or the performance of the Executive's constitutional duties.

Section 231 establishes an "Office of Science and Technology" within the National Institute of Justice, and under the general authority of the Assistant Attorney General for the Office of Justice Programs. According to subsection 231(b), "The Office shall be headed by a Director, who shall be an individual appointed based on approval by the Office of Personnel Management of the executive qualifications of the individual." The executive branch will construe this provision in a manner consistent with the requirements of the Appointments Clause of Article II of the Constitution. Because the Director would exercise significant governmental authority and thus be an "officer" whose appointment must be made in conformity with the Appointments Clause, I hereby direct the Attorney General to appoint the Director.

Section 232(e) of the Act provides that the Director of the Office of Science and Technology within the Department of Justice shall have sole authority over decisions relating to publications issued by the Office. The executive branch shall construe this provision in a manner consistent with the constitutional authorities of the President to supervise the unitary executive branch.

Section 306(a) of the Act provides that research conducted by the Department shall be unclassified "to the greatest extent practicable." In addition, section 425 adds section 44901(d)(3) to title 49 of the United States Code, requiring the submission of classified reports concerning the screening of checked baggage for explosives in the aviation system to certain committees of Congress. The executive branch shall construe and carry out these provisions, as well as other provisions of the Act, including those in title II of the Act, in a manner consistent with the President's constitutional and statutory authorities to control access to and protect classified information, intelligence sources and methods, sensitive law enforcement information, and information the disclosure of which could otherwise harm the foreign relations or national security of the United States.

Section 311(h) of the Act provides for the preparation and transmittal to the Congress of reports prepared by the Homeland Security Science and Technology Advisory Committee. The executive branch shall construe this provision in a manner consistent with the constitutional authorities of the President to supervise the unitary executive branch and to recommend for the consideration of the Congress such measures as the President judges necessary and expedient.

Several sections of the Act, including section 414, 476, and 873(c), purport to require the submission of budget requests for the new Department to the Congress and to require such requests to be in a particular form. The executive branch shall construe this provision in a manner consistent with the constitutional authority of the President to recommend for the consideration of the Congress such measures as the President judges necessary and expedient.

Section 452(c) (2) of the Act prohibits various officers of the Department or the Office of Management and Budget from reviewing reports and other material prepared by the Citizenship and Immigration Services Ombudsman. The executive branch shall construe this section in a manner consistent with the President's constitutional authority to supervise the unitary executive branch.

Section 473(f) of the Act purports to require the Secretary of Homeland Security or the Attorney General to comply with requests from the General Accounting Office (GAO) for certain information in the course of GAO preparation of reports on demonstration projects relating to disciplinary action. The executive branch shall construe this provision in a manner consistent with the constitutional authorities of the President to supervise the unitary executive branch and to withhold information the disclosure of which could impair foreign relations, the national security, the deliberative processes of the Executive, or the performance of the Executive's constitutional duties. . . .

Section 1331 adds an amended section 4107(b) (1) (A) to title 5, United States Code, which requires that, in exercising authority to assign and fund academic degree training for certain Federal employees, an agency "take into consideration the need to maintain a balanced workforce in which women, members of racial and ethnic minority groups, and persons with disabilities are appropriately represented in Government service." The executive branch shall construe this provision in a manner consistent with the Equal Protection component of the Due Process Clause of the Fifth Amendment to the Constitution.

Figure 43.2 Father and son presidents in the Oval Office, courtesy of Eric Draper/George W. Bush Presidential Library and Museum.

6. MILLENNIUM CHALLENGE ACCOUNT AND CHALLENGE CORPORATION

FEBRUARY 5, 2003

. . . I am pleased to transmit a legislative proposal to establish the Millennium Challenge Account and the Millennium Challenge Corporation.

. . . This new compact for development breaks with the past by tying increased assistance to performance and creating new accountability for all nations. This proposal implements my commitment to increase current levels of core development assistance by 50 percent over the next 3 years, thus providing an annual increase of $5 billion by fiscal year 2006. To be eligible for this new assistance, countries must demonstrate commitment to three standards—ruling justly, investing in their people, and encouraging economic freedom. Given this commitment, and the link between financial accountability and development success, special attention will be given to fighting corruption.

The goal of the Millennium Challenge Account initiative is to reduce poverty by significantly increasing economic growth in recipient countries through a variety of targeted investments. The MCA will be administered by a new, small Government corporation, called the Millennium Challenge Corporation, designed to support innovative strategies and to ensure accountability for measurable results. The Corporation will be supervised by a Board of Directors chaired by the Secretary of State and composed of other Cabinet-level officials. The Corporation will be led by a Chief Executive Officer appointed by the President, by and with the advice and consent of the Senate. This proposal provides the Corporation with flexible authorities to optimize program implementation, contracting, and personnel selection while pursuing innovative strategies.

The Millennium Challenge Account initiative recognizes the need for country ownership, financial oversight, and accountability for results to ensure effective assistance. We cannot accept permanent poverty in a world of progress. The MCA will provide people in developing nations the tools they need to seize the opportunities of the global economy. I urge the prompt and favorable consideration of this legislation

7. ADDRESS TO THE NATION ON IRAQ

MARCH 17, 2003

My fellow citizens, events in Iraq have now reached the final days of decision. For more than a decade, the United States and other nations have pursued patient and honorable efforts to disarm the Iraqi regime without war. That regime pledged to reveal and destroy all its weapons of mass destruction as a condition for ending the Persian Gulf War in 1991.

Since then, the world has engaged in 12 years of diplomacy. We have passed more than a dozen resolutions in the United Nations Security Council. We have sent hundreds of weapons inspectors to oversee the disarmament of Iraq. Our good faith has not been returned.

The Iraqi regime has used diplomacy as a ploy to gain time and advantage. It has uniformly defied Security Council resolutions demanding full disarmament. Over the years, U.N. weapon inspectors have been threatened by Iraqi officials, electronically bugged, and systematically deceived. Peaceful efforts to disarm the Iraqi regime have failed again and again because we are not dealing with peaceful men.

Intelligence gathered by this and other governments leaves no doubt that the Iraq regime continues to possess and conceal some of the most lethal weapons ever devised. This regime has already used weapons of mass destruction against Iraq's neighbors and against Iraq's people.

The regime has a history of reckless aggression in the Middle East. It has a deep hatred of

America and our friends. And it has aided, trained, and harbored terrorists, including operatives of Al Qaida.

The danger is clear: Using chemical, biological or, one day, nuclear weapons obtained with the help of Iraq, the terrorists could fulfill their stated ambitions and kill thousands or hundreds of thousands of innocent people in our country or any other.

The United States and other nations did nothing to deserve or invite this threat. But we will do everything to defeat it. Instead of drifting along toward tragedy, we will set a course toward safety. Before the day of horror can come, before it is too late to act, this danger will be removed.

The United States of America has the sovereign authority to use force in assuring its own national security. That duty falls to me as Commander-in-Chief, by the oath I have sworn, by the oath I will keep.

Recognizing the threat to our country, the United States Congress voted overwhelmingly last year to support the use of force against Iraq. America tried to work with the United Nations to address this threat because we wanted to resolve the issue peacefully. We believe in the mission of the United Nations. One reason the U.N. was founded after the Second World War was to confront aggressive dictators actively and early, before they can attack the innocent and destroy the peace.

In the case of Iraq, the Security Council did act in the early 1990s. Under Resolutions 678 and 687 . . . the United States and our allies are authorized to use force in ridding Iraq of weapons of mass destruction. This is not a question of authority. It is a question of will.

Last September, I went to the U.N. General Assembly and urged the nations of the world to unite and bring an end to this danger. On November 8th, the Security Council unanimously passed Resolution 1441 finding Iraq in material breach of its obligations and vowing serious consequences if Iraq did not fully and immediately disarm.

Today, no nation can possibly claim that Iraq has disarmed, and it will not disarm so long as Saddam Hussein holds power. For the last 4½ months, the United States and our allies have worked within the Security Council to enforce that Council's longstanding demands. Yet, some permanent members of the Security Council have publicly announced they will veto any resolution that compels the disarmament of Iraq. These governments share our assessment of the danger but not our resolve to meet it.

Many nations, however, do have the resolve and fortitude to act against this threat to peace, and a broad coalition is now gathering to enforce the just demands of the world. The United Nations Security Council has not lived up to its responsibilities, so we will rise to ours.

In recent days, some governments in the Middle East have been doing their part. They have delivered public and private messages urging the dictator to leave Iraq, so that disarmament can proceed peacefully. He has thus far refused.

All the decades of deceit and cruelty have now reached an end. Saddam Hussein and his sons must leave Iraq within 48 hours. Their refusal to do so will result in military conflict, commenced at a time of our choosing. For their own safety, all foreign nationals, including journalists and inspectors, should leave Iraq immediately.

Many Iraqis can hear me tonight in a translated radio broadcast, and I have a message for them: If we must begin a military campaign, it will be directed against the lawless men who rule your country and not against you. As our coalition takes away their power, we will deliver the food and medicine you need. We will tear down the apparatus of terror, and we will help you to build a new Iraq that is prosperous and free. In a free Iraq, there will be no more wars of aggression against your neighbors, no more poison factories, no more executions of dissidents, no more torture chambers and rape rooms. The tyrant will soon be gone. The day of your liberation is near.

It is too late for Saddam Hussein to remain in power. It is not too late for the Iraqi military to act with honor and protect your country by permitting the peaceful entry of coalition forces to eliminate weapons of mass destruction. Our forces will give Iraqi military units clear instructions on actions they can take to avoid being attacked and destroyed. I urge every member of the Iraqi military and intelligence services: If war comes, do not fight for a dying regime that is not worth your own life.

And all Iraqi military and civilian personnel should listen carefully to this warning: In any conflict, your fate will depend on your actions. Do not destroy oil wells, a source of wealth that belongs to the Iraqi people. Do not obey any command to use weapons of mass destruction against anyone, including the Iraqi people. War crimes will be prosecuted. War criminals will be punished. And it will be no defense to say, "I was just following orders."

Should Saddam Hussein choose confrontation, the American people can know that every measure has been taken to avoid war and every measure will be taken to win it. Americans understand the costs of conflict because we have paid them in the past. War has no certainty, except the certainty of sacrifice. Yet, the only way to reduce the harm and duration of war is to apply the full force and might of our military, and we are prepared to do so.

If Saddam Hussein attempts to cling to power, he will remain a deadly foe until the end. In desperation, he and terrorist groups might try to conduct terrorist operations against the American people and our friends. These attacks are not inevitable. They are, however, possible. And this very fact underscores the reason we cannot live under the threat of blackmail. The terrorist threat to America and the world will be diminished the moment that Saddam Hussein is disarmed.

Our Government is on heightened watch against these dangers. Just as we are preparing to ensure victory in Iraq, we are taking further actions to protect our homeland. In recent days, American authorities have expelled from the country certain individuals with ties to Iraqi intelligence services. Among other measures, I have directed additional security of our airports and increased Coast Guard patrols of major seaports. The Department of Homeland Security is working closely with the Nation's Governors to increase armed security at critical facilities across America.

Should enemies strike our country, they would be attempting to shift our attention with panic and weaken our morale with fear. In this, they would fail. No act of theirs can alter the course or shake the resolve of this country. We are a peaceful people. Yet we're not a fragile people, and we will not be intimidated by thugs and killers. If our enemies dare to strike us, they and all who have aided them will face fearful consequences.

We are now acting because the risks of inaction would be far greater. In 1 year, or 5 years, the power of Iraq to inflict harm on all free nations would be multiplied many times over. With these capabilities, Saddam Hussein and his terrorist allies could choose the moment of deadly conflict when they are strongest. We choose to meet that threat now, where it arises, before it can appear suddenly in our skies and cities.

The cause of peace requires all free nations to recognize new and undeniable realities. In the 20th century, some chose to appease murderous dictators, whose threats were allowed to grow into genocide and global war. In this century, when evil men plot chemical, biological, and nuclear terror, a policy of appeasement could bring destruction of a kind never before seen on this Earth.

Terrorists and terror states do not reveal these threats with fair notice, in formal declarations, and responding to such enemies only after they have struck first is not self-defense; it is suicide. The security of the world requires disarming Saddam Hussein now.

As we enforce the just demands of the world, we will also honor the deepest commitments of our country. Unlike Saddam Hussein, we believe the Iraqi people are deserving and capable of human liberty. And when the dictator has departed, they can set an example to all the Middle East of a vital and peaceful and self-governing nation.

The United States, with other countries, will work to advance liberty and peace in that region. Our goal will not be achieved overnight, but it can come over time. The power and appeal of human liberty is felt in every life and every land. And the greatest power of freedom is to overcome hatred and violence and turn the creative gifts of men and women to the pursuits of peace.

That is the future we choose. Free nations have a duty to defend our people by uniting against the violent. And tonight, as we have done before, America and our allies accept that responsibility.

8. MEDICARE PRESCRIPTION DRUG . . . AND MODERNIZATION ACT OF 2003   DECEMBER 8, 2003

In a few moments I will have the honor of signing an historic act of Congress into law. I'm pleased that all of you are here to witness the greatest advance in health care coverage for America's seniors since the founding of Medicare.

With the Medicare Act of 2003, our Government is finally bringing prescription drug coverage to the seniors of America. With this law, we're giving older Americans better choices and more control over their health care, so they can receive the modern medical care they deserve. With this law, we are providing more access to comprehensive exams, disease screenings, and other preventative care, so that seniors across this land can live better and healthier lives. With this law, we are creating Health Savings Accounts. We do so . . . that all Americans can put money away for their health care tax-free.

Our Nation has the best health care system in the world, and we want our seniors to share in the benefits of that system. Our Nation has made a promise, a solemn promise to America's seniors. We have pledged to help our citizens find affordable medical care in the later years of life. . . .

. . . Medicare is a great achievement of a compassionate Government, and it is a basic trust we honor. Medicare has spared millions of seniors from needless hardship. Each generation benefits from Medicare. Each generation has a duty to strengthen Medicare, and this generation is fulfilling our duty.

First and foremost, this new law will provide Medicare coverage for prescription drugs. Medicare was enacted to provide seniors with the latest in modern medicine. In 1965, that usually meant house calls or operations or long hospital stays. Today, modern medicine includes outpatient care, disease screenings, and prescription drugs. Medicine has changed, but Medicare has not—until today.

Medicare today will pay for extended hospital stays for ulcer surgery; that's at a cost of about $28,000 per patient. Yet Medicare will not pay for the drugs that eliminate the cause of most ulcers, drugs that cost about $500 a year. It's a good thing that Medicare pays when seniors get sick. Now, you see, we're taking this a step further:

Medicare will pay for the prescription drugs so that fewer seniors will get sick in the first place. Drug coverage under Medicare will allow seniors to replace more expensive surgeries and hospitalizations with less expensive prescription medicine. And even more important, drug coverage under Medicare will save our seniors from a lot of worry. Some older Americans spend much of their Social Security checks just on their medications. Some cut down on the dosage to make a bottle of pills last longer. Elderly Americans should not have to live with those kinds of fears and hard choices. This new law will ease the burden on seniors and will give them the extra help they need.

Seniors will start seeing help quickly. During the transition to the full prescription benefit, seniors will receive a drug discount card. This Medicare-approved card will deliver savings of 10 to 25 percent off the retail price of most medicines. Low-income seniors will receive the same savings plus a $600 credit on their cards to help them pay for the medications they need.

In about 2 years, full prescription coverage under Medicare will begin. In return for a monthly premium of about $35, most seniors without any prescription drug coverage can now expect to see their current drug bills cut roughly in half. This new law will provide 95-percent coverage for out-of-pocket drug spending that exceeds $3,600 a year. For the first time, we're giving seniors peace of mind that they will not have to face unlimited expenses for their medicine.

The new law offers special help to one-third of older Americans with low incomes, such as a senior couple with low savings and an annual income of about $18,000 or less. These seniors will pay little or no premium for full drug coverage. Their deductible will be no higher than $50 per year, and their copayment on each prescription will be as little as $1. Seniors in the greatest need will have the greatest help under the modernized Medicare system.

. . . If you want to keep your Medicare the way it is, along with the new prescription benefit that is your right. If you want to improve benefits, maybe dental coverage or eyeglass coverage or managed care plans that reduce out-of-pocket costs, you'll be free to make those choices as well.

And when seniors have the ability to make choices, health care plans within Medicare will have to compete for their business by offering higher quality service. For the seniors of America, more choices and more control will mean better health care. These are the kinds of health care options we give to the Members of Congress and Federal employees. They have the ability to pick plans to—that are right for their own needs. What's good for Members of Congress is also good for seniors. Our seniors are fully capable of making health care choices, and this bill allows them to do just that.

A third purpose achieved by this legislation is smarter medicine within the Medicare system. For years, our seniors have been denied Medicare coverage—have been denied Medicare coverage for a basic physical exam. Beginning in 2005, all newly enrolled Medicare beneficiaries will be covered for a complete physical.

The Medicare system will now help seniors and their doctors diagnose health problems early, so they can treat them early and our seniors can have a better quality life. For example, starting next year, all people on Medicare will be covered for blood tests that can diagnose heart diseases. Those at high risk for diabetes will be covered for blood sugar screening tests. Modern health care is not complete without prevention, so we are expanding preventive services under Medicare.

Fourth, the new law will help all Americans pay for out-of-pocket health costs. This legislation will create health savings accounts, effective January 1, 2004, so Americans can set aside up to $4,500 every year, tax-free, to save for medical expenses. Depending on your tax bracket, that means you'll save between 10 to 35 percent on any costs covered by money in your account. Our laws encourage people to plan for retirement and to save for education. Now the law will make it easier for Americans to save for their future health care as well.

A health savings account is a good deal, and all Americans should consider it. Every year, the money not spent would stay in the account and gain interest tax-free, just like an IRA. And people will have an incentive to live more healthy lifestyles because they want to see their health savings account grow. These accounts will be good for small-business owners and employees. More businesses can focus on covering workers for major medical problems such as hospitalization for an injury or illness. And at the same time, employees and their families will use these accounts to cover doctors' visits or lab tests or other smaller costs. Some employers will contribute to employee health accounts. This will help more American families get the health care they need at the price they can afford.

The legislation I'm about to sign will set in motion a series of improvements in the care available to all America's senior citizens. And as we begin, it is important for seniors and those approaching retirement to understand their new benefits. This coming spring, seniors will receive a letter to explain the drug discount card. In June, these cards, including the $600 annual drug credit for low-income seniors, will be activated. This drug card can be used through the end of 2005. In the fall of that year, seniors will receive an information booklet giving simple guidance on changes in the program and the new choices they will have. Then in January of 2006, seniors will have their new coverage, including permanent coverage for prescription drugs.

These reforms are the act of a vibrant and compassionate Government. We show our concern for the dignity of our seniors by giving them quality health care. We show our respect for seniors by giving them more choices and more control over their decision making. We're putting individuals in charge of their health care decisions. And as we move to modernize and reform other programs of this Government, we will always trust individuals and their decisions and put personal choice at the heart of our efforts.

The challenges facing seniors on Medicare were apparent for many years, and those years passed with much debate and a lot of politics and little reform to show for it. And that changed with the 108th Congress. This year we met our challenge with focus and perseverance. We confronted problems, instead of passing them along to future administrations and future Congresses. We overcame old partisan differences. We kept our promise and found a way to get the job done.

This legislation is the achievement of Members in both political parties. And this legislation is a victory for all of America's seniors.

Now I'm honored and pleased to sign this historic piece of legislation, the Medicare Prescription Drug, Improvement, and Modernization Act of 2003.

9. ENERGY STRATEGY FOR 21ST CENTURY   AUGUST 8, 2005

. . . I'm really proud to be here with the men and women of the Sandia National Laboratory. We just had a fascinating tour of the facility. It was a little quick, but I learned a lot, and I want to thank Tom Hunter for his hospitality and his enthusiasm for the projects that go on here and his praise for the people who work here.

I thank you for coming, and it's such an honor to be here. I know full well that the work you do here keeps our military strong, it keeps our Nation competitive, and our country is really grateful for your dedication and for the fact that you lend your expertise into helping Americans.

. . . This bill will strengthen our economy, and it will improve our environment, and it's going to make this country more secure. The Energy Policy Act of 2005 is going to help every American who drives to work, every family that pays a power bill, and every small-business owner hoping to expand.

The bill is the result of years of effort. It is the result of good folks coming . . . who have made a commitment to deliver results for the American people. This bill launches an energy strategy for the 21st century, and I've really been looking forward to signing it.

. . . I want to remind you about the fact that this economy of ours has been through a lot. And that's why it was important to get this energy bill done, to help us continue to grow. We've been through a stock market decline. We went through a recession. We went through corporate scandals.

We had an attack on our homeland, and we had the demands of an ongoing war on terror. And to grow this economy, we worked together to put together an economic growth policy, an economic growth package, the cornerstone of which was to cut the taxes on the American people. And that tax relief plan is working. This economy is strong, and it's growing stronger. And what this energy bill is going to do, it's just going to help keep momentum in the right direction so people can realize their dreams.

Last week we had some good news that America added just over 200,000 jobs—new jobs—in the month of July. Since May of 2003, we've added nearly 4 million new jobs. More Americans are working today than ever before in our Nation's history. Workers are taking more of what they earn—taking home more of what they earn. Inflation is low. Mortgage rates are low. Homeownership in America is at an all-time high. In other words, this economy is moving. And what this energy bill does is it recognizes that we need more affordable and reliable sources of energy in order to make sure the economy continues to grow.

It's an economic bill, but as Pete mentioned, it's also a national security bill. For more than a decade, America has gone without a national energy policy. It's hard to believe, isn't it? We haven't had a strategy in place. We've had some ideas, but we have not had a national energy policy. And as a result, our consumers are paying more for the price of their gasoline. Electricity bills are going up. We had a massive blackout two summers ago that cost this country billions of dollars and disrupted millions of lives. And because we didn't have a national energy strategy over time, with each passing year, we are more dependent on foreign sources of oil.

. . . We need a comprehensive approach to deal with the situation we're in. In other words, we need to conserve more energy. We need to produce more energy. We need to diversify our energy supply, and we need to modernize our energy delivery. And so they worked hard and listened to a lot of good ideas, and they've taken really important steps.

Now, one of the things that I appreciate about the people on the stage here is that they were able to set aside kind of the partisan bickering that oftentimes—too many times—deadlocks Washington, DC.

. . . These Members, when they say they're going to strengthen our economy and protect our environment and help our national security, are telling it like it is. And let me tell you why. First, the bill makes an unprecedented commitment to energy conservation and efficiency. . . . The bill sets higher efficiency standards for Federal buildings and for household products. It directs the Department of Transportation to study the potential for sensible improvements in fuel-efficiency standards for cars and trucks and SUVs. It authorizes new funding for research into cutting-edge technologies that will help us do more with less energy.

The bill recognizes that America is the world's leader in technology and that we've got to use technology to be the world's leader in energy conservation. The bill includes incentives for consumers to be better conservers of energy. If you own a home, you can receive new tax credits to install energy-efficient windows and appliances. If you're in the market for a car, this bill will help you save up to $3,500 on a fuel-efficient hybrid or clean-diesel vehicle. And the way the tax credit works is that the more efficient the vehicle is, the more money you will save. Energy conservation is more than a private virtue; it's a public virtue. And with this bill I sign today, America is taking the side of consumers who make the choice to conserve.

Second, this bill will allow America to make cleaner and more productive use of our domestic energy resources, including coal and nuclear power and oil and natural gas. By using these reliable sources to supply more of our own energy, we'll reduce our reliance on energy from foreign countries, and that will help this economy grow so people can work.

Coal is America's most abundant energy resource. It accounts for more than one-half of our electricity production. The challenge is to develop ways to take advantage of our coal resources while keeping our air clean.

When I ran for President in 2000, I promised . . . to invest $2 billion over 10 years to promote clean coal technology. So far, working with the United States Congress, we've provided more than $1.3 billion for research in the innovative ways to improve today's coal plants and to help us build even cleaner coal plants in the future. And the bill I sign today authorizes new funding for clean coal technology so we can move closer to our goal of building the world's first zero emission coal-fired power plant.

Nuclear power is another of America's most important sources of electricity. Of all our Nation's energy sources, only nuclear power plants can generate massive amounts of electricity without emitting an ounce of air pollution or greenhouse gases. And thanks to the advances in science and technology, nuclear plants are far safer than ever before. Yet America has not ordered a nuclear plant since the 1970s. To coordinate the ordering of new plants, the bill I sign today continues the Nuclear Power 2010 Partnership between Government and industry. It also offers a new form of Federal risk insurance for the first six builders of new nuclear power plants. With the practical steps in this bill, America is moving closer to a vital national goal. We will start building nuclear power plants again by the end of this decade.

Meeting the needs of our growing economy also means expanding our domestic production of oil and natural gas, which are vital fuels for transportation and electricity and manufacturing. The energy bill makes practical reforms to the oil and gas permitting process to encourage new exploration in environmentally sensitive ways.

The bill authorizes research into the prospects of unlocking vast amounts of now—energy now trapped in shale and tar sands. It provides incentives for oil refineries to expand their capacity, and that's consumer-friendly. The more supply, the more reliable your gasoline will be and the more— less pressure on price.

The bill includes tax incentives to encourage new construction of natural gas pipelines. It clarifies Federal authority to site new receiving terminals for liquefied natural gas, so that consumers across this Nation can benefit from more affordable, clean-burning natural gas.

Thirdly, the bill I sign today will help diversify our energy supply by promoting alternative and renewable energy sources. The bill extends tax credits for wind, biomass, landfill gas, and other renewable electricity sources. The bill offers new incentives to promote clean, renewable geothermal energy. It creates a new tax credit for residential solar power systems. And by developing these innovative technologies, we can keep the lights running while protecting the environment and using energy produced right here at home. When you hear us talking about less dependence on foreign sources of energy, one of the ways to become less dependent is to enhance the use of renewable sources of energy.

The bill also will lead to a greater diversity of fuels for cars and trucks. The bill includes tax incentives for producers of ethanol and biodiesel. The bill includes a flexible, cost-effective renewable fuel standard that will double the amount of ethanol and biodiesel in our fuel supply over the next 7 years. Using ethanol and biodiesel will leave our air cleaner. And every time we use a home-grown fuel, particularly these, we're going to be helping our farmers and, at the same time, be less dependent on foreign sources of energy.

. . . The bill I sign today also includes strong support for hydrogen fuel technology. When hydrogen is used in a fuel cell, it can power consumer products from computers to cell phones to cars that emit pure water instead of exhaust fumes. I laid out a hydrogen fuel initiative, and I want to thank the Members of Congress for adding to the momentum of this initiative through this energy bill. The goal of the research and development for hydrogen-powered automobiles is to make it possible for today's children to take their driver's test in a pollution-free car.

Fourth, the energy bill will help ensure that consumers receive electricity over dependable modern infrastructure. The bill removes outdated obstacles to investment in electricity transmission lines in generating facilities. The bill corrects the provision of the law that made electric reliability standards optional instead of mandatory. Most of you probably consider it mandatory that the lights come on when you flip a switch. [*laughter*] Now the utility companies will have to consider it mandatory as well. [*laughter*]

To keep local disputes from causing national problems, the bill gives Federal officials the authority to select sites for new power lines. We have a modern interstate grid for our phone lines and our highways. With this bill, America can start building a modern 21st century electricity grid as well.

The bill I sign today is a critical first step. It's a first step toward a more affordable and reliable energy future for the American citizens. This bill is not going to solve our energy challenges overnight. Most of the serious problems, such as high gasoline costs or the rising dependence on foreign oil, have developed over decades. It's going to take years of focused effort to alleviate those problems. But in about 2 minutes, we're going to have a strategy that will help us do that.

And as we work to solve our energy dependence—dependency, we've got to remember that the market for energy is global, and America is not the only large consumer of hydrocarbons. As the economies of nations like India and China grow rapidly, their demand for energy is growing rapidly as well. It's in our interest to help these expanding energy users become more efficient, less dependent on hydrocarbons. You see, by helping them achieve these goals, it will take pressure off the global supply, and it will help take pressure off price for American consumers.

And so, last month, I joined with the leaders of India and China and Australia and Japan and South Korea to create a new Asia Pacific Partnership on Clean Development. This is an innovative program which is authorized by this energy bill. And through it, our goal is to spread the use of clean, efficient energy technologies throughout the Pacific Rim.

After years of debate and division, Congress passed a good bill. It's my honor to have come to the great State of New Mexico to sign it. I'm confident that one day Americans will look back on this bill as a vital step toward a more secure and more prosperous nation that is less dependent on foreign sources of energy.

10. HURRICANE KATRINA   AUGUST 31, 2005

I've just received an update from Secretary Chertoff and other Cabinet Secretaries involved on the latest developments in Louisiana, Mississippi, and Alabama. As we flew here today, I also asked the pilot to fly over the Gulf Coast region so I could see firsthand the scope and magnitude of the devastation.

The vast majority of New Orleans, Louisiana, is under water. Tens of thousands of homes and businesses are beyond repair. A lot of the Mississippi Gulf Coast has been completely destroyed. Mobile is flooded.

We are dealing with one of the worst natural disasters in our Nation's history.

And that's why I've called the Cabinet together. The people in the affected regions expect the Federal Government to work with the State government and local government with an effective response. I have directed Secretary of Homeland Security Mike Chertoff to chair a Cabinet-level task force to coordinate all our assistance from Washington. FEMA Director Mike Brown is in charge of all Federal response and recovery efforts in the field. I've instructed them to work closely with State and local officials as well as with the private sector to ensure that we're helping, not hindering, recovery efforts.

This recovery will take a long time. This recovery will take years.

Our efforts are now focused on three priorities: Our first priority is to save lives. We're assisting local officials in New Orleans in evacuating any remaining citizens from the affected area. I want to thank the State of Texas and particularly Harris County and the city of Houston and officials with the Houston Astrodome for providing shelter to those citizens who found refuge in the Superdome in Louisiana. Buses are on the way to take those people from New Orleans to Houston.

FEMA has deployed more than 50 disaster medical assistance teams from all across the country to help those in the affected areas. FEMA has deployed more than 25 urban search and rescue teams with more than 1,000 personnel to help save as many lives as possible. The United States Coast Guard is conducting search and rescue missions. They're working alongside local officials, local assets. The Coast Guard has rescued nearly 2,000 people to date.

The Department of Defense is deploying major assets to the region. These include the *USS Bataan* to conduct search and rescue missions, eight swift water rescue teams, the Iwo Jima Amphibious Readiness Group to help with disaster response equipment, and the hospital ship *USNS Comfort* to help provide medical care.

The National Guard has nearly 11,000 Guardsmen on State active duty to assist Governors and local officials with security and disaster response efforts. FEMA and the Army Corps of Engineers are working around the clock with Louisiana officials to repair the breaches in the levees so we can stop the flooding in New Orleans.

Our second priority is to sustain lives by ensuring adequate food, water, shelter, and medical supplies for survivors and dedicated citizens—dislocated citizens. FEMA is moving supplies and equipment into the hardest hit areas. The Department of Transportation has provided more than 400 trucks to move 1,000 truckloads containing 5.4 million "Meals Ready to Eat" or MREs, 13.4 million liters of water, 10,400 tarps, 3.4 million pounds of ice, 144 generators, 20 containers of pre-positioned disaster supplies, 135,000 blankets, and 11,000 cots. And we're just starting.

There are more than 78,000 people now in shelters. HHS and CDC are working with local officials to identify operating hospital facilities so we can help them, help the nurses and doctors provide necessary medical care. They're distributing medical supplies, and they're executing a public health plan to control disease and other health-related issues that might arise.

Our third priority is executing a comprehensive recovery effort. We're focusing on restoring power and lines of communication that have been knocked out during the storm. We'll be repairing major roads and bridges and other essential means of transportation as quickly as possible. There's a lot of work we're going to have to do. In my flyover, I saw a lot of destruction on major infra-structure. Repairing the infrastructure, of course, is going to be a key priority.

The Department of Energy is approving loans from the Strategic Petroleum Reserve to limit disruptions in crude supplies for refineries. A lot of crude production has been shut down because of the storm. I instructed Secretary Bodman to work with refiners, people who need crude oil, to alleviate any shortage through loans. The Environmental Protection Agency has granted a nation-wide waiver for fuel blends to make more gasoline and diesel fuel available throughout the country. This will help take some pressure off of gas price. But our citizens must understand this storm has disrupted the capacity to make gasoline and distribute gasoline.

We're also developing a comprehensive plan to immediately help displaced citizens. This will include housing and education and health care and other essential needs. I've directed the folks in my Cabinet to work with local folks, local officials, to develop a comprehensive strategy to rebuild the communities affected. And there's going to be a lot of rebuilding done. I can't tell you how devastating the sights were.

I want to thank the communities in surrounding States that have welcomed their neighbors during an hour of need. A lot of folks left the affected areas and found refuge with a relative or a friend, and I appreciate you doing that. I also want to thank the American Red Cross and the Salvation Army and the Catholic Charities and all other members of the armies of compassion. I think the folks in the affected areas are going to be overwhelmed when they realize how many Americans want to help them.

At this stage in the recovery efforts, it's important for those who want to contribute, to contribute cash. You can contribute cash to a charity of your choice, but make sure you designate that gift for hurricane relief. You can call 1-800-HELP-NOW, or you can get on the Red Cross web page, redcross.org. The Red Cross needs our help. And I urge our fellow citizens to contribute.

The folks on the Gulf Coast are going to need the help of this country for a long time. This is going to be a difficult road. The challenges that we face on the ground are unprecedented. But there's no doubt in my mind we're going to succeed. Right now the days seem awfully dark for those affected. I understand that. But I'm confident that, with time, you can get your life back in order, new communities will flourish, the great city of New Orleans will be back on its feet, and America will be a stronger place for it.

The country stands with you. We'll do all in our power to help you. May God bless you. . . .

11. USA PATRIOT IMPROVEMENT AND REAUTHORIZATION ACT OF 2005   MARCH 9, 2006

Today, I have signed into law H.R. 3199, the "USA PATRIOT Improvement and Reauthorization Act of 2005," and then S. 2271, the "USA PATRIOT Act Additional Reauthorizing Amendments Act of 2006." The bills will help us continue to fight terrorism effectively and to combat the use of the illegal drug methamphetamine that is ruining too many lives.

The executive branch shall construe the provisions of H.R. 3199 that call for furnishing information to entities outside the executive branch, such as sections 106A and 119, in a manner consistent with the President's constitutional authority to supervise the unitary executive branch and to withhold information the disclosure of which could impair foreign relations, national security, the deliberative processes of the Executive, or the performance of the Executive's constitutional duties.

The executive branch shall construe section 756(e)(2) of H.R. 3199, which calls for an executive branch official to submit to the Congress recommendations for legislative action, in a manner consistent with the President's constitutional authority to supervise the unitary executive branch and to recommend for the consideration of the Congress such measures as he judges necessary and expedient.

12. ADDRESS TO THE NATION ON THE WAR ON TERROR IN IRAQ   JANUARY 10, 2007

Good evening. Tonight in Iraq, the Armed Forces of the United States are engaged in a struggle that will determine the direction of the global war on terror and our safety here at home. The new strategy I outline tonight will change America's course in Iraq and help us succeed in the fight against terror. When I addressed you just over a year ago, nearly 12 million Iraqis had cast their ballots for a unified and democratic nation. The elections of 2005 were a stunning achievement. We thought that these elections would bring the Iraqis together and that as we trained Iraqi security forces, we could accomplish our mission with fewer American troops.

But in 2006, the opposite happened. The violence in Iraq, particularly in Baghdad, overwhelmed the political gains the Iraqis had made. Al Qaida terrorists and Sunni insurgents recognized the mortal danger that Iraq's elections posed for their cause, and they responded with outrageous acts of murder aimed at innocent Iraqis. They blew up one of the holiest shrines in Shi'a Islam, the Golden Mosque of Samarra, in a calculated effort to provoke Iraq's Shi'a population to retaliate. Their strategy worked. Radical Shi'a elements, some supported by Iran, formed death squads. And the result was a vicious cycle of sectarian violence that continues today. The situation in Iraq is unacceptable to the American people, and it is unacceptable to me. Our troops in Iraq have fought bravely. They have done everything we have asked them to do. Where mistakes have been made, the responsibility rests with me. It is clear that we need to change our strategy in Iraq. So my national security team, military commanders, and diplomats conducted a comprehensive review. We consulted Members of Congress from both parties, our allies abroad, and distinguished outside experts. We benefited from the thoughtful recommendations of the Iraq Study Group, a bipartisan panel led by former Secretary of State James Baker and former Congressman Lee Hamilton. In our discussions, we all agreed that there is no magic formula for success in Iraq. And one message came through loud and clear: Failure in Iraq would be a disaster for the United States. The consequences of failure are clear. Radical Islamic extremists would grow in strength and gain new recruits. They would be in a better position to topple moderate governments, create chaos in the region, and use oil revenues to fund their ambitions. Iran would be emboldened in its pursuit of nuclear weapons. Our enemies would have a safe haven from which to plan and launch attacks on the American people. On September the 11th, 2001, we saw what a refuge for extremists on the other side of the world could bring to the streets of our own cities. For the safety of our people, America must succeed in Iraq.

The most urgent priority for success in Iraq is security, especially in Baghdad. Eighty percent of Iraq's sectarian violence occurs within 30 miles of the capital. This violence is splitting Baghdad into sectarian enclaves and shaking the confidence of all Iraqis. Only Iraqis can end the sectarian violence and secure their people, and their Government has put forward an aggressive plan to do it.

Our past efforts to secure Baghdad failed for two principal reasons: There were not enough Iraqi and American troops to secure neighborhoods that had been cleared of terrorists and insurgents, and there were too many restrictions on the troops we did have. Our military commanders reviewed the new Iraqi plan to ensure that it addressed these mistakes. They report that it does. They also report that this plan can work.

Now let me explain the main elements of this effort. The Iraqi Government will appoint a military commander and two deputy commanders for their capital. The Iraqi Government will deploy Iraqi Army and National Police brigades across Baghdad's nine districts. When these forces are fully deployed, there will be 18 Iraqi Army and National Police brigades committed to this effort, along with local police. These Iraqi forces will operate from local police stations, conducting patrols and setting up checkpoints and going door to door to gain the trust of Baghdad residents. This is a strong commitment, but for it to succeed, our commanders say the Iraqis will need our help. So America will change our strategy to help the Iraqis carry out their campaign to put down sectarian violence and bring security to the people of Baghdad. This will require increasing American force levels. So I've committed more than 20,000 additional American troops to Iraq. The vast majority of them—five brigades—will be deployed to Baghdad. These troops will work alongside Iraqi units and be embedded in their formations. Our troops will have a well-defined mission: to help Iraqis clear and secure neighborhoods; to help them protect the local population; and to help ensure that the Iraqi forces left behind are capable of providing the security that Baghdad needs.

Many listening tonight will ask why this effort will succeed when previous operations to secure Baghdad did not. Well, here are the differences. In earlier operations, Iraqi and American forces cleared many neighborhoods of terrorists and insurgents, but when our forces moved on to other targets, the killers returned. This time, we'll have the force levels we need to hold the areas that have been cleared. In earlier operations, political and sectarian interference prevented Iraqi and American forces from going into neighborhoods that are home to those fueling the sectarian violence. This time, Iraqi and American forces will have a green light to enter those neighborhoods, and Prime Minister Maliki has pledged that political or sectarian interference will not be tolerated.

This new strategy will not yield an immediate end to suicide bombings, assassinations, or IED attacks. Our enemies in Iraq will make every effort to ensure that our television screens are filled with images of death and suffering. Yet over time, we can expect to see Iraqi troops chasing down murderers, fewer brazen acts of terror, and growing trust and cooperation from Baghdad's residents. When this happens, daily life will improve, Iraqis will gain confidence in their leaders, and the Government will have the breathing space it needs to make progress in other critical areas. Most of Iraq's Sunni and Shi'a want to live together in peace, and reducing the violence in Baghdad will help make reconciliation possible. A successful strategy for Iraq goes beyond military operations. Ordinary Iraqi citizens must see that military operations are accompanied by visible improvements in their neighborhoods and communities. So America will hold the Iraqi Government to the benchmarks it has announced.

To establish its authority, the Iraqi Government plans to take responsibility for security in all of Iraq's Provinces by November. To give every Iraqi citizen a stake in the country's economy, Iraq will pass legislation to share oil revenues among all Iraqis. To show that it is committed to delivering a better life, the Iraqi Government will spend $10 billion of its own money on reconstruction and infrastructure projects that will create new jobs. To empower local leaders, Iraqis plan to hold provincial elections later this year. . . .

America will change our approach to help the Iraqi Government as it works to meet these benchmarks. In keeping with the recommendations of the Iraq Study Group, we will increase the embedding of American advisers in Iraqi Army units and partner a coalition brigade with every Iraqi Army division. We will help the Iraqis build a larger and better equipped army, and we will accelerate the training of Iraqi forces, which remains the essential U.S. security mission in Iraq. We will give our commanders and civilians greater flexibility to spend funds for economic assistance. We will double the number of Provincial Reconstruction Teams. These teams bring together military and civilian experts to help local Iraqi communities pursue reconciliation, strengthen the moderates, and speed the transition to Iraqi self-reliance. And Secretary Rice will soon appoint a reconstruction coordinator in Baghdad to ensure better results for economic assistance being spent in Iraq.

As we make these changes, we will continue to pursue Al Qaida and foreign fighters. Al Qaida is still active in Iraq. Its home base is Anbar Province. Al Qaida has helped make Anbar the most violent area of Iraq outside the capital. A captured Al Qaida document describes the terrorists' plan to infiltrate and seize control of the Province. This would bring Al Qaida closer to its goals of taking down Iraq's democracy, building a radical Islamic empire, and launching new attacks on the United States, at home and abroad.

Our military forces in Anbar are killing and capturing Al Qaida leaders, and they are protecting the local population. Recently, local tribal leaders have begun to show their willingness to take on Al Qaida. And as a result, our commanders believe we have an opportunity to deal a serious blow to the terrorists. So I have given orders to increase American forces in Anbar Province by 4,000 troops. These troops will work with Iraqi and tribal forces to keep up the pressure on the terrorists. America's men and women in uniform took away Al Qaida's safe haven in Afghanistan, and we will not allow them to reestablish it in Iraq.

Succeeding in Iraq also requires defending its territorial integrity and stabilizing the region in the face of extremist challenges. This begins with addressing Iran and Syria. These two regimes are allowing terrorists and insurgents to use their territory to move in and out of Iraq. Iran is providing material support for attacks on American troops. We will disrupt the attacks on our forces. We'll interrupt the flow of support from Iran and Syria, and we will seek out and destroy the networks providing advanced weaponry and training to our enemies in Iraq.

We're also taking other steps to bolster the security of Iraq and protect American interests in the Middle East. I recently ordered the deployment of an additional carrier strike group to the region. We will expand intelligence sharing and deploy Patriot air defense systems to reassure our friends and allies. We will work with the Governments of Turkey and Iraq to help them resolve problems along their border. And we will work with others to prevent Iran from gaining nuclear weapons and dominating the region. We will use America's full diplomatic resources to rally support for Iraq from nations throughout the Middle East. Countries like Saudi Arabia, Egypt, Jordan, and the Gulf States need to understand that an American defeat in Iraq would create a new sanctuary for extremists and a strategic threat to their survival. These nations have a stake in a successful Iraq that is at peace with its neighbors, and they must step up their support for Iraq's unity Government. We endorse the Iraqi Government's call to finalize an international compact that will bring new economic assistance in exchange for greater economic reform. And on Friday, Secretary Rice will leave for the region to build support for Iraq and continue the urgent diplomacy required to help bring peace to the Middle East.

The challenge playing out across the broader Middle East is more than a military conflict. It is the decisive ideological struggle of our time. On one side are those who believe in freedom and moderation; on the other side are extremists who kill the innocent and have declared their intention to destroy our way of life. In the long run, the most realistic way to protect the American people is to provide a hopeful alternative to the hateful ideology of the enemy by advancing liberty across a troubled region. It is in the interests of the United States to stand with the brave men and women who are risking their lives to claim their freedom and to help them as they work to raise up just and hopeful societies across the Middle East. From Afghanistan to Lebanon to the Palestinian Territories, millions of ordinary people are sick of the violence and want a future of peace and opportunity for their children. And they are looking at Iraq. They want to know: Will America withdraw and yield the future of that country to the extremists, or will we stand with the Iraqis who have made the choice for freedom?

The changes I have outlined tonight are aimed at ensuring the survival of a young democracy that is fighting for its life in a part of the world of enormous importance to American security. Let me be clear: The terrorists and insurgents in Iraq are without conscience, and they will make the year ahead bloody and violent. Even if our new strategy works exactly as planned, deadly acts of violence will continue, and we must expect more Iraqi and American casualties. The question is whether our new strategy will bring us closer to success. I believe that it will. . . .

Now America is engaged in a new struggle that will set the course for a new century. We can and we will prevail. We go forward with trust that the Author of Liberty will guide us through these trying hours. . . .

44

Barack H. Obama

1. GUANTÁNAMO

Executive Order 13492—By the authority vested in me as President by the Constitution and the laws of the United States of America, in order to effect the appropriate disposition of individuals currently detained by the Department of Defense at the Guantánamo Bay Naval Base (Guantánamo) and promptly to close detention facilities at Guantánamo, consistent with the national security and foreign policy interests of the United States and the interests of justice. . . .

. . . *Closure of Detention Facilities at Guantánamo.* The detention facilities at Guantánamo for individuals covered by this order shall be closed as soon as practicable, and no later than 1 year from the date of this order. If any individuals covered by this order remain in detention at Guantánamo at the time of closure of those detention facilities, they shall be returned to their home country, released, transferred to a third country, or transferred to another United States detention facility in a manner consistent with law and the national security and foreign policy interests of the United States. . . .

2. STIMULUS

Today I have signed into law H.R. 1, the "American Recovery and Reinvestment Act of 2009." The Act provides a direct fiscal boost to help lift our Nation from the greatest economic crisis in our lifetimes and lay the foundation for further growth. This recovery plan will help to save or create as many as three to four million jobs by the end of 2010, the vast majority of them in the private sector. It will make the most significant investment in America's roads, bridges, mass transit, and other infrastructure since the construction of the interstate highway system. It will make investments to foster reform in education, double renewable energy while fostering efficiency in the use of our energy, and improve quality while bringing down costs in healthcare. Middle-class families will get tax cuts and the most vulnerable will get the largest increase in assistance in decades.

. . . We have inherited an economic crisis as deep and as dire as any since the Great Depression. Economists from across the spectrum have warned that failure to act quickly would lead to the disappearance of millions of more jobs and national unemployment rates that could be in the double digits. I want to thank the Congress for coming together around this hard-fought compromise. No one policy or program will solve the challenges we face right now, nor will this crisis recede in a short period of time. However, with this Act we begin the process of restoring the economy and making America a stronger and more prosperous Nation. . . .

Figure 44.1 Michelle and Barack Obama watch the 2009 Inaugural Parade from the viewing stand in front of the White House, courtesy of the Library of Congress Prints and Photographs Division, Washington, DC.

3. HEALTH CARE   MARCH 23, 2010

. . . Today, after almost a century of trying . . . health insurance reform becomes law in the United States of America.

It is fitting that Congress passed this historic legislation this week. For as we mark the turning of spring, we also mark a new season in America. In a few moments, when I sign this bill, all of the overheated rhetoric over reform will finally confront the reality of reform.

And while the Senate still has a last round of improvements to make on this historic legislation . . . the bill I'm signing will set in motion reforms that generations of Americans have fought for and marched for and hungered to see.

It will take 4 years to implement fully many of these reforms, because we need to implement them responsibly. We need to get this right. But a host of desperately needed reforms will take effect right away.

This year, we'll start offering tax credits to about 4 million small-business men and women to help them cover the cost of insurance for their employees. That happens this year.

This year, tens of thousands of uninsured Americans with preexisting conditions, the parents of children who have a preexisting condition, will finally be able to purchase the coverage they need. That happens this year.

This year, insurance companies will no longer be able to drop people's coverage when they get sick. . . .

This year, all new insurance plans will be required to offer free preventive care. And this year, young adults will be able to stay on their parents' policies until they're 26 years old. . . .

And this year, seniors who fall in the coverage gap known as the doughnut hole will start getting some help. They'll receive $250 to help pay for prescriptions. . . . And I want seniors to know . . . these reforms will not cut your guaranteed benefits. . . .

Once this reform is implemented, health insurance exchanges will be created, a competitive marketplace where uninsured people and small businesses will finally be able to purchase affordable, quality insurance. They will be able to be part of a big pool and get the same good deal that Members of Congress get. That's what's going to happen under this reform. And when this exchange is up and running millions of people will get tax breaks to help them afford coverage, which represents the largest middle-class tax cut for health care in history. . . .

This legislation will also lower costs for families and for businesses and for the Federal Government, reducing our deficit by over $1 trillion in the next two decades. It is paid for, it is fiscally responsible, and it will help lift a decades-long drag on our economy. . . .

That our generation is able to succeed in passing this reform is a testament to the persistence and the character of the American people, who championed this cause, who mobilized, who organized, who believed that people who love this country can change it. It's also a testament to the historic leadership and uncommon courage of the men and women of the United States Congress, who've taken their lumps during this difficult debate.

. . . You know, there are few tougher jobs in politics or Government than leading one of our legislative Chambers. In each Chamber, there are men and women who come from different places and face different pressures, who reach different conclusions about the same things and feel deeply concerned about different things.

And by necessity, leaders have to speak to those different concerns. It isn't always tidy; it is almost never easy. But perhaps the greatest and most difficult challenge is to cobble together out of those differences the sense of common interest and common purpose that's required to advance the dreams of all people, especially in a country as large and diverse as ours.

And we are blessed by leaders in each Chamber who not only do their jobs very well but who never lost sight of that larger mission. They didn't play for the short term; they didn't play to the polls or to politics. . . .

. . . Today I'm signing this reform bill into law on behalf of my mother, who argued with insurance companies even as she battled cancer in her final days. . . .

. . . Our presence here today is remarkable and improbable. With all the punditry, all of the lobbying, all of the game-playing that passes for governing in Washington, it's been easy at times to doubt our ability to do such a big thing, such a complicated thing, to wonder if there are limits to what we as a people can still achieve. . . .

. . . We are a nation that faces its challenges and accepts its responsibilities. We are a nation that does what is hard, what is necessary, what is right. Here in this country, we shape our own destiny. That is what we do. That is who we are. That is what makes us the United States of America.

And we have now just enshrined, as soon as I sign this bill, the core principle that everybody should have some basic security when it comes to their health care. . . .

4. SOLYNDRA, INC.   MAY 26, 2010

. . . I try to visit places like this about once a week, hear from folks as often as possible who are actually doing the extraordinary work of building up America. And I appreciated the chance to tour your plant and to see the incredible, cutting-edge solar panels that you're manufacturing, but also the process that goes into the manufacturing of these solar panels. And it is just a testament to American ingenuity and dynamism and the fact that we continue to have the best universities in the world, the best technology in the world, and most importantly, the best workers in the world. And you guys all represent that. So thank you very much for that.

And while I'm at it, I also want to give some credit to those guys in the back who have been building this facility so that we can put more people back to work and build more solar panels to send all across the country. Thank you for the great work that you guys are doing.

Now, it's fitting that this technology is being pioneered here in California. Where else, right? For generations, this part of the country has embodied the entrepreneurial spirit that has always defined America's success: People heading west.

It was here where weary but hopeful travelers came with pickaxes in search of a fortune. It was here that tinkerers and engineers turned a sleepy valley into a center of innovation and industry. It's here that companies like Solyndra are leading the way toward a brighter and more prosperous future.

5. BP OIL DISASTER   JUNE 15, 2010

. . . As we speak, our nation faces a multitude of challenges. At home, our top priority is to recover and rebuild from a recession that has touched the lives of nearly every American. Abroad, our brave men and women in uniform are taking the fight to Al Qaida wherever it exists. And tonight, I've returned from a trip to the Gulf Coast to speak with you about the battle we're waging against an oil spill that is assaulting our shores and our citizens.

On April 20th, an explosion ripped through BP *Deepwater Horizon* drilling rig, about 40 miles off the coast of Louisiana. Eleven workers lost their lives. Seventeen others were injured. And soon, nearly a mile beneath the surface of the ocean, oil began spewing into the water.

Because there has never been a leak this size at this depth, stopping it has tested the limits of human technology. That's why just after the rig sank, I assembled a team of our nation's best scientists and engineers to tackle this challenge—a team led by Dr. Steven Chu, a Nobel Prize-winning physicist and our nation's Secretary of Energy. Scientists at our national labs and experts from academia and other oil companies have also provided ideas and advice.

As a result of these efforts, we've directed BP to mobilize additional equipment and technology. And in the coming weeks and days, these efforts should capture up to 90 percent of the oil leaking out of the well. This is until the company finishes drilling a relief well later in the summer that's expected to stop the leak completely.

Already, this oil spill is the worst environmental disaster America has ever faced. And unlike an earthquake or a hurricane, it's not a single event that does its damage in a matter of minutes or days. The millions of gallons of oil that have spilled into the Gulf of Mexico are more like an epidemic, one that we will be fighting for months and even years.

But make no mistake: We will fight this spill with everything we've got, for as long as it takes. We will make BP pay for the damage. . . . And we will do whatever's necessary to help the Gulf Coast and its people recover from this tragedy.

. . . From the very beginning of this crisis, the federal government has been in charge of the largest environmental cleanup effort in our nation's history—an effort led by Admiral Thad Allen, who has almost 40 years of experience responding to disasters. We now have nearly 30,000 personnel who are working across four states to contain and clean up the oil. Thousands of ships and other vessels are responding in the Gulf. And I've authorized the deployment of over 17,000 National Guard members along the coast. These servicemen and women are ready to help stop the oil from coming ashore, they're ready to help clean the beaches, train response workers, or even help with processing claims—and I urge the governors in the affected states to activate these troops as soon as possible.

Because of our efforts, millions of gallons of oil have already been removed from the water through burning, skimming and other collection methods. . . . We've approved the construction of new barrier islands in Louisiana to try to stop the oil before it reaches the shore, and we're working with Alabama, Mississippi and Florida to implement creative approaches to their unique coastlines.

. . . We have to recognize that despite our best efforts, oil has already caused damage to our coastline and its wildlife. And sadly, no matter how effective our response is, there will be more oil and more damage before this siege is done. That's why the second thing we're focused on is the recovery and restoration of the Gulf Coast.

. . . men and women who call this region home have made their living from the water. That living is now in jeopardy. I've talked to shrimpers and fishermen who don't know how they're going to support their families this year. . . . The sadness and the anger they feel is not just about the money they've lost. It's about a wrenching anxiety that their way of life may be lost.

. . . Tomorrow, I will meet with the chairman of BP and inform him that he is to set aside whatever resources are required to compensate the workers and business owners who have been harmed as a result of his company's recklessness. And this fund will not be controlled by BP. In order to ensure that all legitimate claims are paid out in a fair and timely manner, the account must and will be administered by an independent third party.

Beyond compensating the people of the Gulf in the short term, it's also clear we need a long-term plan to restore the unique beauty and bounty of this region. The oil spill represents just the latest blow to a place that's already suffered multiple economic disasters and decades of environmental degradation that has led to disappearing wetlands and habitats. . . .

. . . The third part of our response plan is the steps we're taking to ensure that a disaster like this does not happen again. A few months ago, I approved a proposal to consider new, limited offshore drilling under the assurance that it would be absolutely safe—that the proper technology would be in place and the necessary precautions would be taken.

. . . I've established a National Commission to understand the causes of this disaster and offer recommendations on what additional safety and environmental standards we need to put in place. Already, I've issued a six-month moratorium on deepwater drilling. I know this creates difficulty for the people who work on these rigs, but for the sake of their safety, and for the sake of the entire region, we need to know the facts before we allow deepwater drilling to continue. And while I urge the Commission to complete its work as quickly as possible, I expect them to do that work thoroughly and impartially.

One place we've already begun to take action is at the agency in charge of regulating drilling and issuing permits, known as the Minerals Management Service. Over the last decade, this agency has become emblematic of a failed philosophy that views all regulation with hostility—a philosophy that says corporations should be allowed to play by their own rules and police themselves. At this agency, industry insiders were put in charge of industry oversight. Oil companies showered regulators with gifts and favors, and were essentially allowed to conduct their own safety inspections and write their own regulations.

. . . So one of the lessons we've learned from this spill is that we need better regulations, better safety standards, and better enforcement when it comes to offshore drilling. But a larger lesson is that no matter how much we improve our regulation of the industry, drilling for oil these days entails greater risk. After all, oil is a finite resource. We consume more than 20 percent of the world's oil, but have less than 2 percent of the world's oil reserves. And that's part of the reason oil companies are drilling a mile beneath the surface of the ocean—because we're running out of places to drill on land and in shallow water.

. . . For decades, we've talked and talked about the need to end America's century-long addiction to fossil fuels. And for decades, we have failed to act with the sense of urgency that this challenge requires. Time and again, the path forward has been blocked—not only by oil industry lobbyists, but also by a lack of political courage and candor.

The consequences of our inaction are now in plain sight. . . . Each day, we send nearly $1 billion of our wealth to foreign countries for their oil. And today, as we look to the Gulf, we see an entire way of life being threatened by a menacing cloud of black crude.

We cannot consign our children to this future. The tragedy unfolding on our coast is the most painful and powerful reminder yet that the time to embrace a clean energy future is now. Now is the moment for this generation to embark on a national mission to unleash America's innovation and seize control of our own destiny.

This is not some distant vision for America. The transition away from fossil fuels is going to take some time, but over the last year and a half, we've already taken unprecedented action to jumpstart the clean energy industry. As we speak, old factories are reopening to produce wind turbines, people are going back to work installing energy-efficient windows, and small businesses are making solar panels. . . .

. . . As we recover from this recession, the transition to clean energy has the potential to grow our economy and create millions of jobs. . . . When I was a candidate for this office, I laid out a set of principles that would move our country towards energy independence. Last year, the House of Representatives acted on these principles by passing a strong and comprehensive energy and climate bill—a bill that finally makes clean energy the profitable kind of energy for America's businesses.

Now, there are costs associated with this transition. And there are some who believe that we can't afford those costs right now. I say we can't afford not to change how we produce and use energy—because the long-term costs to our economy, our national security, and our environment are far greater.

So I'm happy to look at other ideas and approaches from either party—as long they seriously tackle our addiction to fossil fuels. Some have suggested raising efficiency standards in our buildings like we did in our cars and trucks. Some believe we should set standards to ensure that more of our electricity comes from wind and solar power. Others wonder why the energy industry only spends a fraction of what the high-tech industry does on research and development—and want to rapidly boost our investments in such research and development.

. . . Each year, at the beginning of shrimping season, the region's fishermen take part in a tradition that was brought to America long ago by fishing immigrants from Europe. It's called "The Blessing of the Fleet," and today it's a celebration where clergy from different religions gather to say a prayer for the safety and success of the men and women who will soon head out to sea—some for weeks at a time.

. . . For as a priest and former fisherman once said of the tradition, "The blessing is not that God has promised to remove all obstacles and dangers. The blessing is that He is with us always," a blessing that's granted "even in the midst of the storm."

. . . This nation has known hard times before and we will surely know them again. What . . . has always seen us through—is our strength, our resilience, and our unyielding faith that something better awaits us if we summon the courage to reach for it. . . .

6. MID-TERM ELECTION   NOVEMBER 3, 2010

Press Conference

JAKE TAPPER [ABC News]: I have a policy question and a personal one. The policy question is, you talked about how the immediate goal is the Bush tax cuts and making sure that they don't expire for those who earn under 200–250,000. Republicans . . . want all of the Bush tax cuts extended. Are you willing to compromise on that? Are you willing to negotiate at all, for instance, allow them to expire for everyone over $1 million? Where are you willing to budge on that?

And the second one is, President Bush, when he went through a similar thing, came out and he said, "This was a thumpin'." You talked about how it was humbling. . . . .And I'm wondering, when you call your friends, like Congressman Perriello or Governor Strickland, and you see 19 State legislatures go to the other side, governorships in swing States, the Democratic Party set back, what does it feel like?

THE PRESIDENT: It feels bad. The toughest thing over the last couple of days is seeing really terrific public servants not have the opportunity to serve anymore . . . there are just some terrific Members of Congress who took really tough votes because they thought it was the right thing, even though they knew this could cause . . . problems and even though a lot of them came from really tough swing districts or majority-Republican districts. . . .

There's also a lot of questioning on my part in terms of could I have done something differently or done something more so that those folks would still be here. It's hard. And I take responsibility for it in a lot of ways.

Shellacking Acknowledged

MATT SPETALNICK [Reuters]: How do you respond to those who say the election outcome . . . was voters saying that they see you as out of touch with their personal economic pain?

THE PRESIDENT: . . . the track record has been that when I'm out of this place, that's not an issue. When you're in this place, it is hard not to seem removed. And one of the challenges that we've got to think about is how do I meet my responsibilities here in the White House . . . but still have that opportunity to engage with the American people on a day-to-day basis and . . . give them confidence that I'm listening to them.

Those letters that I read every night, some of them just break my heart. Some of them provide me encouragement and inspiration. But nobody's filming me reading those letters. . . .

. . . I think it's important to point out as well that a couple of great communicators, Ronald Reagan and Bill Clinton, were standing at this podium 2 years into their presidency getting very similar questions because the economy wasn't working the way it needed to be and there were a whole range of factors that made people concerned that maybe the party in power wasn't listening to them.

This is something that I think every president needs to go through, because the responsibilities of this office are so enormous and so many people are depending on what we do, and in the rush of activity, sometimes we lose track of the ways that we connected with folks that got us here in the first place.

. . . I'm not recommending for every future president that they take a shellacking . . . like I did last night . . . And the relationship that I've had with the American people is one that built slowly, peaked at this incredible high, and then during the course of the last 2 years, as we've, together, gone through some very difficult times, has gotten rockier and tougher. And it's going to . . . have some more ups and downs during the course of me being in this office.

Skinning the Cat: Cap and Trade

LAURA MECKLER [*Wall Street Journal*]: You said earlier that it was clear that Congress was rejecting the idea of a cap and trade program and that you wouldn't be able to move forward with that. Looking ahead, do you feel the same way about EPA regulating carbon emissions? Would you be open to them doing essentially the same thing through an administrative action, or is that off the table as well?

And secondly, just to follow up on what you said about changing the way Washington works . . . you said you didn't do enough to change the way things were handled in this city . . . to get your health care bill passed, you needed to make some of those deals. Do you wish, in retrospect, you had not made those deals and even if it meant the collapse of the program?

THE PRESIDENT: . . . making sure that families had security and that we're on a trajectory to lower health care costs was absolutely critical for this country. But you are absolutely right that when you are navigating through a House and a Senate in this kind of pretty partisan environment that it's a ugly mess when it comes to process . . . that is something that really affected how people viewed the outcome. That is something that I regret, that we couldn't have made the process more—healthier than it ended up being. . . .

With respect to the EPA, I think the smartest thing for us to do is to see if we can get Democrats and Republicans, in a room, who are serious about energy independence and are serious about keeping our air clean and our water clean and dealing with the issue of greenhouse gases, and seeing are there ways that we can make progress in the short term and invest in technologies in the long term that start giving us the tools to reduce greenhouse gases and solve this problem.

. . . it's too early to say whether or not we can make some progress on that front. I think we can. Cap and trade was just one way of skinning the cat; it was not the only way. It was a means, not an end. . . .

7. KILLING OSAMA BIN LADEN   MAY 1, 2011

. . . Tonight I can report to the American people and to the world that the United States has conducted an operation that killed Osama bin Laden, the leader of Al Qaida and a terrorist who's responsible for the murder of thousands of innocent men, women, and children.

It was nearly 10 years ago that a bright September day was darkened by the worst attack on the American people in our history. The images of 9/11 are seared into our national memory: hijacked planes cutting through a cloudless September sky; the Twin Towers collapsing to the ground; black smoke billowing up from the Pentagon; the wreckage of Flight 93 . . . where the actions of heroic citizens saved even more heartbreak and destruction.

Figure 44.2 Former President George W. Bush and Laura Bush, along with President and Mrs. Obama, pause at the North Memorial Pool of the National September 11 Memorial in New York City, on the tenth anniversary of the 9/11 attacks. Official White House photo by Chuck Kennedy.

. . . On September 11, 2001, in our time of grief, the American people came together. We offered our neighbors a hand, and we offered the wounded our blood. We reaffirmed our ties to each other and our love of community and country. On that day, no matter where we came from, what God we prayed to, or what race or ethnicity we were, we were united as one American family.

We were also united in our resolve to protect our Nation and to bring those who committed this vicious attack to justice. We quickly learned that the 9/11 attacks were carried out by Al Qaida . . . which had openly declared war on the United States and was committed to killing innocents in our country and around the globe. And so we went to war against Al Qaida to protect our citizens, our friends, and our allies.

Over the last 10 years, thanks to the tireless and heroic work of our military and our counterterrorism professionals, we've made great strides in that effort. We've disrupted terrorist attacks and strengthened our homeland defense. In Afghanistan, we removed the Taliban Government, which had given bin Laden and Al Qaida safe haven and support. And around the globe, we worked with our friends and allies to capture or kill scores of Al Qaida terrorists, including several who were a part of the 9/11 plot.

. . . bin Laden avoided capture and escaped across the Afghan border into Pakistan. Meanwhile, Al Qaida continued to operate from along that border and operate through its affiliates across the world.

And so shortly after taking office, I directed Leon Panetta, the Director of the CIA, to make the killing or capture of bin Laden the top priority of our war against Al Qaida, even as we continued our broader efforts to disrupt, dismantle, and defeat his network.

Then, last August, after years of painstaking work by our intelligence community, I was briefed on a possible lead to bin Laden. It was far from certain, and it took many months to run this thread to ground. I met repeatedly with my national security team as we developed more information about the possibility that we had located bin Laden hiding within a compound deep inside Pakistan. And finally, last week, I determined that we had enough intelligence to take action and authorized an operation to get Osama bin Laden and bring him to justice.

Today, at my direction, the United States launched a targeted operation against that compound in Abbottabad, Pakistan. A small team of Americans carried out the operation with extraordinary courage and capability. No Americans were harmed. They took care to avoid civilian casualties. After a firefight, they killed Osama bin Laden and took custody of his body.

For over two decades, bin Laden has been Al Qaida's leader and symbol and has continued to plot attacks against our country and our friends and allies. The death of bin Laden marks the most significant achievement to date in our Nation's effort to defeat Al Qaida.

Yet his death does not mark the end of our effort. There's no doubt that Al Qaida will continue to pursue attacks against us. We must—and we will—remain vigilant at home and abroad.

As we do, we must also reaffirm that the United States is not—and never will be—at war with Islam. I've made clear, just as President Bush did . . . that our war is not against Islam. Bin Laden was not a Muslim leader; he was a mass murderer of Muslims. Indeed, Al Qaida has slaughtered scores of Muslims in many countries, including our own. So his demise should be welcomed by all who believe in peace and human dignity.

. . . As a country, we will never tolerate our security being threatened, nor stand idly by when our people have been killed. We will be relentless in defense of our citizens and our friends and allies. We will be true to the values that make us who we are. And on nights like this one, we can say to those families who have lost loved ones to Al Qaida's terror: Justice has been done.

. . . Finally, let me say to the families who lost loved ones on 9/11 that we have never forgotten your loss nor wavered in our commitment to see that we do whatever it takes to prevent another attack on our shores.

. . . Let us remember that we can do these things not just because of wealth or power, but because of who we are: one nation under God, indivisible, with liberty and justice for all. . . .

8. THE ARAB SPRING AND THE MIDDLE EAST   MAY 19, 2011

. . . The State Department is a fitting venue to mark a new chapter in American diplomacy. For 6 months, we have witnessed an extraordinary change taking place in the Middle East and North Africa . . . people have risen up to demand their basic human rights. Two leaders have stepped aside. More may follow. And though these countries may be a great distance from our shores, we know that our own future is bound to this region by the forces of economics and security, by history and by faith. Today I want to talk about this change, the forces that are driving it, and how we can respond in a way that advances our values and strengthens our security.

. . . we've done much to shift our foreign policy following a decade defined by two costly conflicts. After years of war in Iraq, we've removed 100,000 American troops and ended our combat mission there. In Afghanistan, we've broken the Taliban's momentum, and this July we will begin to bring our troops home and continue a transition to Afghan lead. And after years of war against Al Qaida and its affiliates, we have dealt Al Qaida a huge blow by killing its leader. . . . Bin Laden was no martyr. He was a mass murderer . . . He rejected democracy and individual rights for Muslims in favor of violent extremism. His agenda focused on what he could destroy, not what he could build. . . . By the time we found bin Laden, Al Qaida's agenda had come to be seen by the vast majority of the region as a dead end, and the people of the Middle East and North Africa had taken their future into their own hands.

. . . the events of the past 6 months show us that strategies of repression and strategies of diversion will not work anymore. Satellite television and the internet provide a window into the wider world, a world of astonishing progress in places like India and Indonesia and Brazil. Cell phones and social networks allow young people to connect . . . And so a new generation has emerged.

. . . The question before us is what role America will play as this story unfolds. For decades, the United States has pursued a set of core interests in the region: countering terrorism and stopping the spread of nuclear weapons, securing the free flow of commerce and safe-guarding the security of the region, standing up for Israel's security and pursuing Arab–Israeli peace.

We will continue to do these things, with the firm belief that America's interests are not hostile to people's hopes. . . . As we did in the Gulf war, we will not tolerate aggression across borders, and we will keep our commitments to friends and partners.

Yet . . . failure to speak to the broader aspirations of ordinary people will only feed the suspicion that has festered for years that the United States pursues our interests at their expense. Given that this mistrust runs both ways, as Americans have been seared by hostage-taking and violent rhetoric and terrorist attacks that have killed thousands of our citizens, a failure to change our approach threatens a deepening spiral of division between the United States and the Arab world.

. . . The status quo is not sustainable. Societies held together by fear and repression may offer the illusion of stability for a time, but they are built upon fault lines that will eventually tear asunder.

. . . The United States supports a set of universal rights. And these rights include free speech, the freedom of peaceful assembly, the freedom of religion, equality for men and women under the rule of law, and the right to choose your own leaders. . . .

. . . It will be the policy of the United States to promote reform across the region and to support transitions to democracy. That effort begins in Egypt and Tunisia. . . . Tunisia was at the vanguard of this democratic wave and Egypt is both a longstanding partner and the Arab world's largest nation. Both nations can set a strong example through free and fair elections, a vibrant civil society, accountable and effective democratic institutions, and responsible regional leadership. . . .

. . . In Libya, we saw the prospect of imminent massacre. We had a mandate for action. . . . Had we not acted . . . thousands would have been killed. . . . While Libya has faced violence . . . it's not the only place where leaders have turned to repression to remain in power. Most recently, the Syrian regime has chosen the path of murder and the mass arrests of its citizens. The United States has condemned these actions, and working with the international community, we have stepped up our sanctions on the Syrian regime. . . .

. . . So far, Syria has followed its Iranian ally, seeking assistance from Tehran in the tactics of suppression.

. . . Let's remember that the first peaceful protests in the region were in the streets of Tehran, where the Government brutalized women and men and threw innocent people into jail . . . we will continue to insist that the Iranian people deserve their universal rights. . . .

. . . If America is to be credible, we must acknowledge that at times our friends in the region have not all reacted to the demands for consistent change . . . That's true in Yemen. . . . And that's true today in Bahrain.

. . . The Iraqi people have rejected the perils of political violence in favor of a democratic process. . . . Iraq is poised to play a key role in the region if it continues its peaceful progress. . . .

. . . America must use all our influence to encourage reform in the region. . . . Our message is simple: If you take the risks that reform entails, you will have the full support of the United States. . . . Through our efforts, we must support those basic rights to speak your mind and access information. . . . In the 21st century, information is power, the truth cannot be hidden, and the legitimacy of governments will ultimately depend on active and informed citizens.

. . . What we will oppose is an attempt . . . to hold power through coercion and not consent. . . . That is the choice that must be made—not simply in the Israeli–Palestinian conflict, but across the entire region . . . a choice that will define the future of a region that served as the cradle of civilization. . . .

. . . Our commitment to Israel's security is unshakeable. . . . But precisely because of our friendship, it's important that we tell the truth: The status quo is unsustainable. . . .

. . . For decades, the conflict between Israelis and Arabs has cast a shadow over the region. . . . The international community is tired of an endless process that never produces an outcome. The dream of a Jewish and democratic state cannot be fulfilled with permanent occupation.

. . . What America and the international community can do is to state frankly what everyone knows: a lasting peace will involve two states for two peoples—Israel as a Jewish state and the homeland for the Jewish people and the state of Palestine as the homeland for the Palestinian people. . . .

. . . The United States believes that negotiations should result in two states, with permanent Palestinian borders with Israel, Jordan, and Egypt, and permanent Israeli borders with Palestine. We believe the borders of Israel and Palestine should be based on the 1967 lines with mutually agreed swaps, so that secure and recognized borders are established for both states. . . .

As for security . . . Provisions must also be robust enough to prevent a resurgence of terrorism, to stop the infiltration of weapons, and to provide effective border security. The full and phased withdrawal of Israeli military forces should be coordinated with the assumption of Palestinian security responsibility in a sovereign, non-militarized state. . . .

9. AMERICAN JOBS ACT   OCTOBER 6, 2011

. . . Next week, the Senate will vote on the "American Jobs Act." And I think by now I've made my views pretty well known. Some of you are even keeping a tally of how many times I've talked about the "American Jobs Act." And the reason I keep going around the country talking about this jobs bill is because people really need help right now. Our economy really needs a jolt right now.

. . . This jobs bill can help guard against another downturn if the situation in Europe gets any worse. It will boost economic growth; it will put people back to work.

. . . And by the way, this is not just my belief. This is what independent economists have said, not politicians, not just people in my administration. Independent experts who do this for a living have said this jobs bill will have a significant effect for our economy and for middle-class families all across America. And what these independent experts have also said is that if we don't act, the opposite will be true. There will be fewer jobs; there will be weaker growth.

So as we look towards next week, any Senator out there who's thinking about voting against this jobs bill when it comes up for a vote, needs to explain exactly why they would oppose something that we know would improve our economic situation at such an urgent time for our families and for our businesses.

Congressional Republicans say one of the most important things we can do is cut taxes. Then they should love this plan. This jobs bill would cut taxes for virtually every worker and small business in America. If you're a small-business owner that hires someone or raises wages, you would get another tax cut. If you hire a veteran, you get a tax cut. Right now there's a small business in Ohio that does high-tech manufacturing, and they've been expanding for the past 2 years. They're considering hiring more, and this tax break would encourage them to do it.

. . . Some of you were with me when we visited a bridge between Ohio and Kentucky that's been classified as functionally obsolete. . . . We've heard about bridges in both States that are falling apart, and that's true all across the country. . . .

The proposals in this bill are not just random investments to create make-work jobs, they are steps we have to take if we want to build an economy that lasts, if we want to be able to compete with other countries for jobs that restore a sense of security to middle-class families. And to do that, we've got to have the most educated workers. We have to have the best transportation and communications networks. We have to support innovative small businesses. We've got to support innovative manufacturers.

Now, what's true is we've also got to rein in our deficits and live within our means, which is why this jobs bill is fully paid for by asking millionaires and billionaires to pay their fair share. And some see this as class warfare. I see it as a simple choice: We can either keep taxes exactly as they are for millionaires and billionaires, with loopholes that lead them to have lower tax rates in some cases than plumbers and teachers, or we can put teachers and construction workers and veterans back on the job.

. . . There are too many people hurting in this country for us to do nothing and the economy is just too fragile for us to let politics get in the way of action. We've got a responsibility to the people who sent us here. So I hope every Senator thinks long and hard about what's at stake when they cast their vote next week.

BEN FELLER [Associated Press]: I'd like to ask you about two economic matters. Federal Reserve Chairman Bernanke warned Congress this week that the economic recovery is close to faltering. Do you agree?

And secondly, on your jobs bill, the American people are sick of games. . . . They want results. Wouldn't it be more productive to work with Republicans on a plan that you know could pass Congress as opposed to going around the country talking about your bill and singling out—calling out Republicans by name?

THE PRESIDENT: Well, first of all, with respect to the state of the economy, there is no doubt that growth has slowed. I think people were much more optimistic at the beginning of this year. But the combination of a Japanese tsunami, the Arab Spring, which drove up gas prices, and most prominently, Europe, I think, has gotten businesses and consumers very nervous. . . .

. . . There is no doubt that the economy is weaker now than it was at the beginning of the year. And every independent economist who has looked at this question carefully believes that for us to make sure that we are taking out an insurance policy against a possible double-dip recession, it is important for us to make sure that we are boosting consumer confidence, putting money into their pockets, cutting taxes where we can for small businesses, and that it makes sense for us to put people back to work doing the work that needs to be done. . . .

10. LIBYA: SHADOW OF TYRANNY LIFTED   OCTOBER 20, 2011

. . . Today the Government of Libya announced the death of Muammar Qadhafi. This marks the end of a long and painful chapter for the people of Libya, who now have the opportunity to determine their own destiny in a new and democratic Libya.

For four decades, the Qadhafi regime ruled the Libyan people with an iron fist. Basic human rights were denied. Innocent civilians were detained, beaten, and killed, and Libya's wealth was squandered. The enormous potential of the Libyan people was held back, and terror was used as a political weapon.

Today we can definitively say that the Qadhafi regime has come to an end. . . . And one of the world's longest serving dictators is no more.

. . . Faced with the potential of mass atrocities and a call for help from the Libyan people, the United States and our friends and allies stopped Qadhafi's forces in their tracks. A coalition that included the United States, NATO, and Arab nations persevered through the summer to protect Libyan civilians. And meanwhile, the courageous Libyan people fought for their own future and broke the back of the regime.

So this is a momentous day in the history of Libya. The dark shadow of tyranny has been lifted. . . . We look forward to the announcement of the country's liberation, the quick formation of an interim government, and a stable transition to Libya's first free and fair elections. . . .

Now, we're under no illusions. Libya will travel a long and winding road to full democracy. There will be difficult days ahead. But the United States, together with the international community, is committed to the Libyan people. You have won your revolution. And now we will be a partner as you forge a future that provides dignity, freedom, and opportunity.

. . . For us here in the United States, we are reminded today of all those Americans that we lost at the hands of Qadhafi's terror. Their families and friends are in our thoughts and in our prayers. . . .

For nearly 8 months, many Americans have provided extraordinary service in support of our efforts to protect the Libyan people and to provide them with a chance to determine their own destiny. Our skilled diplomats have helped to lead an unprecedented global response. Our brave pilots have flown in Libya's skies, our sailors have provided support off Libya's shores, and our leadership at NATO has helped guide our coalition. Without putting a single U.S. service member on the ground, we achieved our objectives, and our NATO mission will soon come to an end. . . .

11. IRAQ WAR ENDS   OCTOBER 21, 2011

. . . As a candidate for President, I pledged to bring the war in Iraq to a responsible end, for the sake of our national security and to strengthen American leadership around the world. After taking office, I announced a new strategy that would end our combat mission in Iraq and remove all of our troops by the end of 2011.

As Commander-in-Chief, ensuring the success of this strategy has been one of my highest national security priorities. Last year, I announced the end to our combat mission in Iraq. And to date, we've removed more than 100,000 troops. Iraqis have taken full responsibility for their country's security.

A few hours ago, I spoke with Iraqi Prime Minister Maliki. I reaffirmed that the United States keeps its commitments. He spoke of the determination of the Iraqi people to forge their own future. . . .

So today I can report that, as promised, the rest of our troops in Iraq will come home by the end of the year. . . .

12. KEYSTONE XL PIPELINE   JANUARY 18, 2012

Earlier today I received the Secretary of State's recommendation on the pending application for the construction of the Keystone XL Pipeline. As the State Department made clear last month, the rushed and arbitrary deadline insisted on by congressional Republicans prevented a full assessment of the pipeline's impact, especially the health and safety of the American people, as well as our environment. As a result, the Secretary of State has recommended that the application be denied. And after reviewing the State Department's report, I agree.

This announcement is not a judgment on the merits of the pipeline, but the arbitrary nature of a deadline that prevented the State Department from gathering the information necessary to approve the project and protect the American people. I'm disappointed that Republicans in Congress forced this decision, but it does not change my administration's commitment to American-made energy that creates jobs and reduces our dependence on oil. Under my administration, domestic oil and natural gas production is up, while imports of foreign oil are down. In the months ahead, we will continue to look for new ways to partner with the oil and gas industry to increase our energy security—including the potential development of an oil pipeline from Cushing, Oklahoma, to the Gulf of Mexico—even as we set higher efficiency standards for cars and trucks and invest in alternatives like biofuels and natural gas. . . .

13. A BLUEPRINT FOR THE FUTURE   JANUARY 24, 2012

. . . The state of our Union is getting stronger. And we've come too far to turn back now. As long as I'm President, I will work with anyone in this Chamber to build on this momentum. But I intend to fight obstruction with action, and I will oppose any effort to return to the very same policies that brought on this economic crisis in the first place. No, we will not go back to an economy weakened by outsourcing, bad debt, and phony financial profits. Tonight, I want to speak about how we move forward, and lay out a blueprint for an economy that's built to last—an economy built on American manufacturing, American energy, skills for American workers, and a renewal of American values.

This blueprint begins with American manufacturing. On the day I took office, our auto industry was on the verge of collapse. Some even said we should let it die. With a million jobs at stake, I refused to let that happen. In exchange for help, we demanded responsibility. We got workers and automakers to settle their differences. We got the industry to retool and restructure. Today, General Motors is back on top as the world's number one automaker. Chrysler has grown faster in the U.S. than any major car company. Ford is investing billions in U.S. plants and factories. And together, the entire industry added nearly 160,000 jobs.

We bet on American workers. We bet on American ingenuity. And tonight, the American auto industry is back. What's happening in Detroit can happen in other industries. It can happen in Cleveland, Pittsburgh and Raleigh. We can't bring every job back that's left our shores. But right now, it's getting more expensive to do business in places like China. Meanwhile, America is more productive. A few weeks ago, the CEO of Master Lock told me that it now makes business sense for him to bring jobs back home. Today, for the first time in 15 years, Master Lock's unionized plant in Milwaukee is running at full capacity. So we have a huge opportunity, at this moment, to bring manufacturing back. But we have to seize it. Tonight, my message to business leaders is simple: Ask yourselves what you can do to bring jobs back to your country, and your country will do everything we can to help you succeed.

We should start with our tax code. Right now, companies get tax breaks for moving jobs and profits overseas. Meanwhile, companies that choose to stay in America get hit with one of the highest tax rates in the world. It makes no sense, and everyone knows it.

So let's change it. First, if you're a business that wants to outsource jobs, you shouldn't get a tax deduction for doing it. That money should be used to cover moving expenses for companies like Master Lock that decide to bring jobs home.

Second, no American company should be able to avoid paying its fair share of taxes by moving jobs and profits overseas. From now on, every multinational company should have to pay a basic minimum tax, and every penny should go towards lowering taxes for companies that choose to stay here and hire here in America.

Third, if you're an American manufacturer, you should get a bigger tax cut. If you're a high-tech manufacturer, we should double the tax deduction you get for making your products here. And if you want to relocate in a community that was hit hard when a factory left town, you should get help financing a new plant, equipment, or training for new workers.

. . . It is time to stop rewarding businesses that ship jobs overseas and start rewarding companies that create jobs right here in America. Send me these tax reforms, and I will sign them right away.

We're also making it easier for American businesses to sell products all over the world. Two years ago, I set a goal of doubling U.S. exports over 5 years. With the bipartisan trade agreements we signed into law, we're on track to meet that goal—ahead of schedule. Soon, there will be millions of new customers for American goods in Panama, Colombia and South Korea. Soon, there will be new cars on the streets of Seoul imported from Detroit, Toledo and Chicago.

Figure 44.3 Five recent presidents, courtesy of Eric Draper/George W. Bush Presidential Library and Museum.

I will go anywhere in the world to open new markets for American products. . . . Over a thousand Americans are working today because we've stopped a surge in Chinese tires. But we need to do more. It's not right when another country lets our movies, music and software be pirated. It's not fair when foreign manufacturers have a leg up on ours only because they're heavily subsidized.

Tonight, I'm announcing the creation of a Trade Enforcement Unit that will be charged with investigating unfair trading practices in countries like China. There will be more inspections to prevent counterfeit or unsafe goods from crossing our borders. And this Congress should make sure that no foreign company has an advantage over American manufacturing when it comes to accessing financing or new markets like Russia. Our workers are the most productive on Earth, and if the playing field is level, I promise you—America will always win.

Index